PERSONALITY:
THEORY AND RESEARCH

PERSONALITY:
THEORY AND RESEARCH
FOURTH EDITION

Lawrence A. Pervin
Rutgers, The State University

JOHN WILEY & SONS, INC.
New York • Chichester • Brisbane • Toronto • Singapore

Cover: Painting *Schnertz* by Jawlensky from Sotheby Parke Bernet.
(Agent: Art Resource, Inc.)

Library of Congress Cataloging in Publication Data:

Pervin, Lawrence A.
　Personality: theory and research.

　Bibliography: p.
　Includes indexes.
　1. Personality.　I. Title.
BF698.P375　1984　155.2　83-21610
ISBN 0-471-88577-0

Printed in the United States of America

10　9　8　7　6　5　4　3　2　1

To Bobbie, David, and Levi

PREFACE

The revision of a textbook provides the author with an opportunity to update material and to respond to student feedback concerning earlier presentations. This edition reflects efforts in both directions. There has been an attempt to make sure that the chapters reflect current developments in the field of personality. In particular, a separate chapter has been devoted to cognitive, information-processing theory (Chapter 14), which increasingly influences the thinking and research of many psychologists. Also, the entire manuscript has been edited to clarify ambiguities and to remove needlessly technical discussions. At the same time, I have tried to retain a comprehensive and scholarly approach toward the material.

In my efforts along these lines I have been assisted by many. Students in my classes have been a constant source of stimulation and useful feedback. In terms of outside review, the comments of Professor Rhoda Lindner of California State University-Long Beach have been of invaluable assistance. I would also like to express my appreciation for the helpful reviews of the following professors: David Cohen, California State College-Bakersfield; Joel Cooper, Princeton University; K. Edward Dietiker, California State College-Bakersfield; M. Robin DiMatteo, University of California-Riverside; Phillip Finney, Southeast Missouri State University; Adrienne Gans, New York University; Bernadette Gray-Little, University of North Carolina; Laurie Heatherington, University of Scranton; Alexandra Kaplan, Wellesley College; Irving Kirsch, University of Connecticut; Randall Kleinhesselink, Washington State University; Chris Koronakos, Western Michigan University; Ramsey Liem, Boston College; Richard Moreland, University of Pittsburgh; Carol Oyster, University of Delaware; Damaris Rohsenow, S.U.N.Y.-Binghamton; and Elizabeth Swearingen, University of Delaware. In terms of editorial work, I am indebted to the efforts of Mrs. Alice Greenwald and Mr. Martin Stanford who assisted in making the text more readable while remaining faithful to the ideas presented. Carol Luitjens, my editor at Wiley, has been a constant source of support and creative ideas. Mrs. Libby Brusca, who typed much of the revision, has been someone I could always count on, something that is precious during the difficult process of revision. Finally, my family, to whom the book is dedicated, has remained a bastion of support and understanding during this as well as the earlier revision of the text.

LAWRENCE A. PERVIN

CONTENTS

---

5   A Phenomenological Theory: Carl Rogers' Person-Centered Theory of Personality   149

---

6   A Phenomenological Theory: Applications and Evaluation of Rogers' Theory   179

PERSONALITY:
THEORY AND RESEARCH

Tchelitchew, Pavel. *Head, VI.* 1950. Collection The Museum of Modern Art, New York.
Gift of Edgar Kaufmann, Jr.

THEORIZING ABOUT HUMAN BEHAVIOR

HAPTER FOCUS: How can we define personality? How can we organize what is known about personality and point to future directions for research? What do we want a theory of personality to do? How do we know when we have a good theory? These are some of the questions we address in this chapter. We thus discuss what a theory is, what a theory of personality should include, and how to tell how good a theory is. Although theories are based on facts, they are also influenced by the personalities of the psychologists who develop them. We therefore approach theories from a human as well as a scientific viewpoint. Finally, we discuss how competition among theories leads to scientific progress.

Every person is in certain respects
a. like all other people.
b. like some other people.
c. like no other person.

Adapted from Kluckhohn *and* Murray, 1953, p. 53

Probably no field of psychology has been more perplexing to its students with respect to theory than that of personality.

Sears, 1950, p. 115

This book is about personality. It explores ways of approaching psychological functioning, insights into the varied determinants of personality, and increased knowledge of how personality can be studied. In sum, it is an exploration into a greater understanding of why people behave as they do and how we may proceed toward a clearer understanding of behavior.

DEFINING PERSONALITY

Every person and event is unique. However, there is enough similarity among many people and the events of their lives to consider what they have in common. It is these patterns of human behavior that the psychologist attempts to understand.

In psychology, the field of **personality** is concerned with the total individual and with individual differences. While recognizing that all people are similar in some ways, those interested in personality are particularly concerned with the ways people differ from one another. Why do some achieve and others not? Why do some perceive things one way and others in a different way? Why do talents vary? Why do some people become mentally ill while others do not under similar conditions?

Personality theorists attempt to understand the complex relationships among the different aspects of an individual's functioning, including such aspects as learning, perception, and motivation. Personality research is not the study of perception but rather of how individuals differ in their perceptions and how these differences relate to their total functioning. The study of personality focuses not only on a particular psychological process but also on the relationships of different processes. Understanding how these processes act together to form an integrated whole often involves more than an understanding of each of them separately. People function as organized wholes, and it is in the light of such organization that we must understand them.

There are few aspects of human functioning that do not reflect and express an individual's personality. How, then, are we to define personality? To the general public it may represent a value judgment—if you like someone, it is because he or she has a "good" personality. To the scientist and student of personality, the term *personality* is used to define a field of study. A definition of personality reflects the kinds of problems to be studied and the methods to be used in studying these problems.

At present, however, there is no generally agreed-upon single definition of personality. Some personality psychologists study the biochemical and physiological aspects of how individuals function and use methods appropriate to these areas of investigation. Other personality psychologists look at individuals and observe their overt behavior. Still others define personality in terms of characteristics, such as unconscious processes, which must be inferred from behavior and cannot be observed directly. A good illustration of an inference based on behavior is the study of what is called "repression." No one can observe directly that an event was forgotten because it is painful to recall. However, one can infer that such a process is taking place, and by making this inference psychologists can help to explain why some things are remembered and others forgotten. Finally, some psychologists define personality strictly as the ways in which individuals interact with other individuals or as the roles that individuals ascribe to themselves and use to function in society. Thus, these and other possible definitions of personality range from processes internal to the organism to overt behavior in an interpersonal context.

It is clear that various definitions of personality are possible and have been used. Each leads to a concentration on different kinds of behavior and to the use of different methods of study. These definitions may be more concrete or more abstract. They may describe what goes on inside individuals, or how individuals interact with each other. They may describe what is directly observable or what must be inferred. They may define what is unique to particular individuals or what is characteristic of most, or all, individuals.

In considering definitions of personality it is important to keep two issues in mind. First, a definition reflects the kinds of behavior the psychologist will pay attention to and the kinds of methods that will be used to study this behavior. Second, there is no one right or wrong definition of personality. Definitions of personality are not necessarily true or false but are more or less useful to psychologists in assessing personality, in pursuing research, and in communicating their findings to others. Insofar as they lead to an increase in our ability to understand, predict, and influence behavior, they are more or less useful to psychology as a science.

For the present, the following is suggested as a working definition of personality: *Personality represents those characteristics of the person or of people generally that account for consistent patterns of behavior.* A number of points can be made in this context. First, personality concepts must be defined in terms that permit psychologists to agree on ways to observe and measure behavior. To study personality systematically we must be able to agree on what we are looking at and how we are to measure it. Second, personality is characterized by regularities in one individual's functioning as well as by regularities that are similar from person to person. While we are each unique in some ways, in other ways we are like some other people and in some ways we are like all other people. Personality is a concept that expresses such regularities within a person and similarities between people. Personality represents the attributes of individuals that distinguish them from other individuals and make them unique as well as the attributes of functioning that are common to all humans. Third, personality includes both the more stable, unchanging aspects of the person's functioning—sometimes called *structure*—and the more fluid, changing aspects—sometimes called *process*. Just as the system of the physical organism consists of parts of the body and various processes relating these parts to one another, so the psychological organism consists of stable parts and fluid processes that relate these parts to one another. In this sense, the personality is a system. Fourth, personality includes cognitions (thought processes), affects (emotions), as well as overt behaviors. Perhaps most of all, personality concerns the complex relationships among cognitive, affective, and overt behavioral processes in the person. Finally, it may be noted that these processes occur in relation to stimuli and situations, some created by the surrounding environment and others created by the person. What is important to recognize, however, is that people do not operate in a vacuum, but rather that they respond to and express themselves in relation to situations and circumstances.

Our working definition is based on certain assumptions about the nature of human personality:

1. *The human organism has characteristics distinct from those of other species that are particularly important for the study of personality.* Compared with members of other species, we are less dependent on biological influences and more dependent on psychosocial factors. We are less dependent than members of other species on primary sources of motivation such as hunger and thirst. Our considerable ability for conceptual thinking and language means that we can communicate and transmit learned patterns of behavior

(culture) to a degree unique among the species. This ability also means that we have a lengthened perspective of past and future, and therefore we need not be bound by immediately present stimuli. Further, it means that we can reflect upon ourselves—we can consider ourselves as objects, so to speak. We can both experience and reflect on our experience; we can be ourselves and think about being ourselves. Finally—and very important for understanding personality—the human organism has a slower rate of maturation than members of other species.

2. *Human behavior is complex.* An understanding of personality must include an appreciation of the complexity of human behavior. Often there are many reasons for an individual's behavior, which may vary from person to person, although the observable behavior may be the same. The same events may be understood differently by different individuals, and the same behavior may have many different roots in different individuals. Complexity also exists because behavior arises not only from personalities but also in relation to situations and circumstances.

3. *Behavior is not always what it appears to be.* There is no fixed relationship between a certain behavior and its causes; there may be different causes for the same behavior shown by two individuals at one time or by the same individual at different times. To understand the significance or meaning of an act for the individual, we must know something about that individual and about the situation in which the act occurred.

4. *We are not always aware of or in control of the factors determining our behavior.* This follows from the concept of the unconscious, although it is not necessary to accept all aspects of the Freudian view of the unconscious to agree with it. This simply suggests that at times people cannot explain why they act in ways contrary to their own expressed wishes. Whether these acts are significant or minor, frequent or infrequent, they occur and remain to be accounted for in some way.

These qualities of human functioning greatly complicate our efforts to measure, interpret, and predict behavior. They suggest that often we capture only glimpses of a person. Although they make the study of personality frustrating, frequent surprises and occasional insights into patterns of behavior also make it exciting.

The scientific exploration of personality, then, attempts to understand how people are alike while recognizing that individuals are unique in some ways. It attempts to discover, understand, and explain regularities in human behavior. Further, it develops theories to help order phenomena and to suggest strategies for further research. There are many theories of personality. They range from those believed by the general public and used by them in their daily living to those developed through the use of sophisticated mathematical techniques and computer technology. Each theory tends to look at different behavior or to study the same behavior in different ways. Therefore, it is hardly surprising that the field often is so perplexing to students of human behavior.

PERSONALITY THEORY AS AN ANSWER TO THE QUESTIONS OF WHAT, HOW, AND WHY

Although personality theorists may study one or another aspect of psychological functioning, a complete theory of personality must suggest answers to such questions as: How can people be consistent in their behavior and at the same time show variation over time and place? How does personality develop? How can we account for psychopathology, abnormal behavior due to psychological causes? A theory should be descriptive and explanatory when suggesting answers to these questions. It should tell what is there and suggest reasons for what is observed.

If we study individuals intensively, we want to know what they are like, how they became that way, and why they behave as they do. Thus, we want a theory to answer the questions of *what, how,* and *why*. The "what" refers to the characteristics of the person and how they are organized in relation to one another. Is the person honest, persistent, and high in need for achievement? The "how" refers to the determinants of a person's current personality. To what extent and in what ways did genetic and environmental forces interact to produce this result? The "why" refers to the reasons for the individual's behavior. Answers refer to the motivational aspects of the individual—why he or she moves at all, and why in a specific direction. If an individual seeks to make a lot of money, why was this particular path chosen? If a child does well in school, is it to please parents, to use talents, to bolster self-esteem, or to show up friends? Is a mother overprotective because she happens to be affectionate, because she seeks to give her children what she missed as a child, or because she seeks to avoid any expression of the resentment and hostility she feels for the child? Is a person depressed as a result of humiliation, because of the loss of a loved one, or because of feelings of guilt? A theory should help us understand to what extent depression is characteristic of a person, how this personality characteristic is developed, why depression is experienced in specific circumstances, and why the person behaves in a certain manner when depressed. If two people tend to be depressed, why does one go out and buy things while another withdraws into a shell? Let us consider questions such as these in more systematic detail.

Structure

Theories can be compared in terms of the concepts they use to answer the what, how, and why of personality. **Structural concepts** refer to the more stable and enduring aspects of personality. They represent the building blocks of personality theory. In this sense they are comparable to parts of the body or to concepts such as atoms and molecules in physics. Such structural concepts as *response, habit, trait,* and *type* have been popular in efforts to conceptualize what people are like. The concept of trait refers to the consistency of individual response to a variety of situations, and approximates the kind of concept the layman uses to describe people. Examples of traits are rigidity, honesty, and emotionality. The concept of type refers to the clustering of many different traits. Compared to the trait concept, that of type implies a greater degree of regularity and generality to behavior. Although people can have one or another degree of many traits, they are generally described as being a specific type. For example, individuals have been described as being introverts or extroverts—and in terms of whether they move toward, away from, or against others (Horney, 1945).

It is possible to use conceptual units other than trait or type to describe personality structure. Theories of personality differ in the kinds of units or structural concepts they use. They also differ in the way they conceptualize the organization of these units. Some theories involve a *complex* structural system, one in which many component parts are linked to one another in a variety of ways. Other theories involve a *simple* structural system, in which a few component parts have few connections to one another. The human brain is a far more complex structure than the brain of a fish because it has more parts, which can be distinguished from one another, and more linkages or interconnections among these parts. Theories of personality also differ in the extent to which they view the structural units as organized in a hierarchy; that is, in the extent to which some structural units are seen as higher in order and therefore as controlling the functioning of other units. The human nervous system is more complex than that of other species, not only because it has more different parts and more linkages among them but also because some parts, like the brain, regulate the functioning of other parts in the system. An analogy can be found in business structures. Some business organizations are more complex than others. Complex business organizations have many units, with many linkages among the units, and a ranking of people who have responsibility for making decisions. Simple business organizations have few units, few linkages among the units, and few levels in the chain of command—General Motors, say, as opposed to a mom-and-pop store. Similarly, personality theories differ in the numbers and kinds of structural units they emphasize and in the extent to which they emphasize complexity or organization within the system.

Process

Just as theories can be compared in their structures, so they can be compared in the dynamic, *motivational concepts* they use to account for behavior. These concepts refer to the **process** aspects of human behavior.

Again think of the human body. It can be considered both as an organization of parts and as processes that relate those parts one to another. Similarly, a business organization consists of units and processes through which the units function in relation to one another and to the outside world. Organizational processes could, for example, be described in terms of how much conflict exists among the parts and how that conflict is handled.

Some theories view personality processes as resulting from efforts of the individual to reduce tension. Other theories emphasize the efforts of the organism toward growth and self-fulfillment. According to the former view, physiological needs within the organism create tensions that the individual seeks to reduce by satisfying needs. Hunger or thirst creates tension that can be relieved by eating or drinking. According to the latter view, individuals seek to grow and realize their inner potentials even at the cost of increased tension.

The most widely accepted model for earlier theories of motivation was, in fact, that of tension reduction. The organism was viewed as seeking a state of rest, quiet, or balance—often called *homeostasis* or *equilibrium*. Pleasure was to be derived from satisfying needs or reducing tension. Recently, research on animals and humans has suggested that organisms often seek tension. Monkeys, for example, will work to solve puzzles independent of any reward—in fact, rewards may interfere with their performance. The exploratory and play behavior of members of many species is well known. Observations such as these led White (1959) to formulate a process in human functioning he called **competence motivation.** According to this view, a significant process in personality functioning is the motivation toward dealing competently or effectively with the environment. Individuals appear to take pleasure in increasing tension or excitement and in trying out new behaviors. As individuals mature, more of their behavior appears to be involved with developing skills merely for the sake of mastery or for dealing effectively with the environment, and less of their behavior appears to be exclusively in the service of reducing tension.

Motivation—**Personality theories emphasize different kinds of motivation (e.g., tension-reduction, self-actualization, power, etc.).**

The concept of competence motivation has served to emphasize behaviors neglected by earlier theorists, but we need not choose between the tension reduction and the competence motivation models of personality dynamics. As one leading motivational theorist (Maslow, 1954) suggests, it is likely that at times the individual is stimulated by physiological needs and seeks to reduce tension, at other times is stimulated by self-fulfilling tendencies, and at yet other times is stimulated by social needs for praise and respect. Such an integrated view is possible, but theorists have tended to use one or another model to account for the more momentary, fluid aspects of human behavior.

Growth and Development

Growth and **development** are related to the concepts of structure and process in personality theory. An interpretation of growth and development must account for changes in structure from infancy to maturity, and for the corresponding developments in process. A theory of growth must describe the process through which development occurs and must outline the reasons for various patterns of growth. Significant among the *environmental determinants of personality* are experiences individuals have as a result of membership in a particular culture. Each culture has its own institutionalized and sanctioned patterns of learned behaviors, rituals, and beliefs. The institutionalization of some behavior patterns means that most members of a culture will have certain personality characteristics in common. Even in a complex society like ours, one in which the number and rigidity of institutionalized patterns of behavior are minimal, the importance of cultural forces in shaping personality functioning is considerable. These forces influence our needs and means of satisfying them, our relationships to authority, our self-concepts, our experiences of the major forms of anxiety and conflict, and our ways of dealing with them. They affect what we think is funny and sad, how we cope with life and death, what we view as healthy and sick. In the words of C. Kluckhohn (1949), "Culture regulates our lives at every turn. From the moment we are born until we die there is, whether we are conscious of it or not, constant pressure upon us to follow certain types of behavior that other men have created for us" (p. 327).

Although certain patterns of behavior develop as a result of membership in a culture, others are developed as a result of membership in some stratified section or class of the population. Few aspects of an individual's personality can be understood without reference to the group to which that person belongs. One's social class group—whether lower class or upper class, working class or professional—is of particular importance. Social class factors help determine the status of individuals, the roles they perform, the duties they are bound by, and the privileges they enjoy. These factors influence how they see themselves and how they perceive members of other social classes, how they earn and spend money. Like cultural factors, social class factors influence the ways individuals define situations and how they respond to them. There is evidence that social class factors are related in a population to the prevalence of mental illness and to the types of mental disorders found. In a study of social class and mental illness, Hollingshead and Redlich (1958) found that while each type of mental disorder occurs in all social classes, proportions in the various classes differ. For example, upper-class patients tended to be neurotic and lower-class patients to be psychotic. Within the neurotic and psychotic categories, members of different classes tended to behave differently.

Beyond the similarities determined by environmental factors such as membership in the same culture or social class, environmental factors lead to considerable variation in the personality functioning of members of a single culture or class. Of particular significance among these is the influence of the family on personality. Although membership in a culture and a social class leads to the use of institutionalized child-rearing practices and to conformity with certain patterns of behavior, significant differences among families—and the peculiar, individualistic relationships within families—are crucial to personality development. Parents may be warm and loving or hostile and rejecting, overprotective and possessive or aware of their children's need for freedom and autonomy. Each pattern of parental behavior affects the personality development of the child.

Some theories of personality attach particular importance to early social interaction between infant and mother. The interpersonal relations theory of Sullivan (1953), for example, suggests that a significant component of personality is the *self-system* (a person's perceptions of the self), which develops out of relationships with significant figures in the environment. During infancy the developing self-system is influenced by the amount of anxiety the mother communicates, often in a subtle way, to the child. In later years, the self-system is influenced by reflected appraisals—how the individual perceives others as perceiving and responding to him or her. Of particular significance here is whether the person sees the self as good or bad as a result of perceptions of the evaluative judgments made by others.

Parents influence their children's behavior in at least three important ways:

1.   Through their own behavior they present situations that elicit certain behavior in children (e.g., frustration leads to aggression).
2.   They serve as role models for identification.
3.   They selectively reward behaviors.

Along with environmental factors, genetic factors play a major role in determining personality, particularly in relation to what is unique in the individual. Although many psychologists historically have argued the relative importance of environmental and genetic factors in shaping personality as a whole, recent theorists have recognized that the importance of these factors may vary from one personality characteristic to another. Genetic factors are generally more important in such characteristics as intelligence and temperament, less important in regard to values, ideals, and beliefs. Theorists have also begun to explore possible interactions between genetic and environmental factors. Thus, for example, the concept of *re-action range* (Gottesman, 1963) suggests that while heredity fixes a number of possible behavioral outcomes, environment ultimately determines the behavior. That is, heredity may set a range within which the further development of the characteristic is determined by the environment. However, the relationship may be even more complicated than this since genetically influenced characteristics may lead the person to act upon, and in return be influenced by, the environment in a particular way. Thus, rather than a simple cause-effect relationship we have an ongoing interaction or reciprocal process involving person and environment.

In summary, personality is determined by many interacting factors, including genetic, cultural, social class, and familial forces. Heredity sets limits on the range of development of characteristics; within this range, characteristics are determined by environmental forces. Heredity provides us talents that a culture may or may not reward and cultivate. It is possible to see the interaction of these many genetic and environmental forces in any significant aspect of personality. Theories of personality differ in the importance attributed to questions of growth and development, in the relative weight given to genetic and environmental factors, and in interpretations of the mechanisms through which personality development

Genetic Influences on Personality Development—**Personality development reflects the interaction of environmental and genetic forces. The triplets pictured here had been separated in infancy and discovered one another as young men. They found that they not only looked alike but smiled and talked in the same way.**

occurs. Ultimately, however, it is the task of any personality theory to account for the development of structures and patterns of behaving. A theory of personality should explain what is developed, how it is developed, and why it is developed.

Psychopathology and Behavior Change

In attempting to account for these varied aspects of human behavior, a complete theory of personality must include analyses of the nature of psychopathology in general and the development of various kinds of psychopathology in particular. Further, such a theory should suggest psychotherapies or means by which such forms of behavior can be modified. What is important is that there be an adequate conceptualization of behavioral change, and that part of this be relevant to an understanding of the process through which the change from psychopathology to health can be helped to take place.

Summary

This section has explored five areas a complete theory of personality must take into account and in relation to which theories of personality can be compared: structure, process, development, psychopathology, and change. These areas represent conceptual abstractions: A person is not structure or process, and what appears as structure at one moment may appear as process at another. Someone may be said to have a strong conscience (structure) that makes him or her feel guilty (process). Such conceptual abstractions, convenient devices for understanding and explaining human behavior, are found in biology as well as psychology. Similarly, development and change are neither independent of structure or process nor independent of one another. They represent an effort to find pattern and regularity in human behavior, ways in which individuals are similar and ways in which they are unique. The concepts developed by a theory represent efforts toward accounting for the organization of personality characteristics, the conditions under which personality develops, and the processes that characterize personality functioning—what we have labeled the what, how, and why of personality.

IMPORTANT ISSUES IN PERSONALITY THEORY

A theory of personality must conceptualize the varied areas of functioning that have been described. A number of theories have attempted this difficult task. Throughout the relatively brief history of personality theory, a number of issues have confronted theorists repeatedly. The ways in which they treat these issues do much to define the major characteristics of each theoretical position. Thus, in reviewing various personality theories we need to keep certain issues in mind, to see how much attention each theorist gives to these issues and how that theorist resolves each issue.

Philosophical View of the Person

A philosophical view concerning the fundamental nature of the human organism tends to underlie current personality theories. One theory emphasizes the instinctual aspect of humans, another the social; one theory stresses free will, another determinism; one theory discusses simple and mechanistic relationships, another complex and dynamic ones; one theory views the person as an organism that reasons, chooses, and decides (rational view), another views the person as an organism that is driven, compelled, irrational (animal view). A third theory views the person as automatically responding to outside stimuli (machine view), while a fourth views the person as processing information like a computer (computer view). Philosophical assumptions concerning human nature are important because they focus on specific problems and lead to particular forms of research.

Proponents of different points of view have had different life experiences and have been influenced by different historical traditions. Thus, beyond scientific evidence and fact, theories of personality are influenced by personal factors, by the spirit of the time (Zeitgeist) and by philosophical assumptions characteristic of members of a given culture (Pervin, 1984). Although based on observed data, theories selectively emphasize certain kinds of data and go beyond what is known, and therefore can be influenced by personal and cultural factors. In developing a personality theory, individuals are influenced by important events in their own lifetimes. To some extent, in developing psychological theories we talk about ourselves. This in itself is not a problem. Only when personal experiences become more important than other kinds of experience and ignore research evidence do personal determinants of a theory become a problem.

Along with these personal determinants are the influences on the theorist of the prevailing mood or spirit within the field at the time—the **Zeitgeist**. There are phases in psychology during which one topic of research is emphasized and one point of view stressed. For example, for some time personality theory emphasized the importance of drives or needs that appeared to have some physiological basis. More recent theory has tended to emphasize cognitive factors—how individuals come to organize and conceptualize their environment. Reflecting the Zeitgeist, both types of theory emphasize certain kinds of empirical observations and suggest that research follow a defined path.

Internal and External Determinants of Behavior

One critical issue that tends to express an underlying philosophical view concerns the relationship between internal and external behavior determinants. All theories of personality recognize that factors inside the organism, and events in the surrounding environment, are important in determining behavior. However, the theories differ in the level of importance given to internal and external determinants and in their interpretation of the relationship between the two (Pervin & Lewis, 1978). Consider, for example, the difference between Freud's theory that we are controlled by unknown, internal forces and Skinner's suggestion that "a person does not act upon the world, the world acts upon him" (1971, p. 211). Whereas the Freudian views the organism as active and responsible for behavior, the Skinnerian views it as a passive victim of controlling events in the environment. The Freudian view suggests that we focus our attention on what is going on *inside* the person; the Skinnerian view suggests that such efforts are foolhardy and that we would be wise to concentrate on environmental variables.

Although the Freudian and Skinnerian views may represent extremes that many psychologists avoid, most psychologists nevertheless weight their theories in the direction of internal or external factors. Periodically there is a shift in emphasis from internal to external factors or vice versa, with an occasional call for investigation of the relationship between the two. For example, in the 1940s one psychologist spoke out against the prevalent tendency to overestimate the unity of internal, and underestimate the importance of external factors in personality (Ichkeiser, 1943); in the 1970s another psychologist was asking "Where is the person in personality research?" (Carlson, 1971). Most recently debate concerning the role of internal and external forces in governing behavior has been highlighted in the *person–situation controversy.* In 1968, the social learning theorist Walter Mischel wrote a book, *Personality and Assessment,* that criticized traditional personality theories for their emphasis on stable and enduring internal structures, which leads to the perception of people's behavior as fairly unchanging over time and across situations. Instead of emphasizing broad personality characteristics that function independently of external factors, Mischel suggested that changes in environmental or external conditions modify how people behave. Such changes result in relatively situation-specific behavior: each environmental situation acts independently to affect individual behavior.

Since the publication of Mischel's book and its development of this issue, considerable attention has been given to the internal–external (or person–situation) controversy. First there was debate about whether persons or situations control behavior, then about whether persons or situations are more important, and, finally, acceptance of the view that both are important and interact with one another (Endler & Magnusson, 1976; Magnusson & Endler, 1977). Almost all researchers today suggest an emphasis on person–situation interaction, even though fundamental disagreements remain. Even when persons, situations, and interactions are all accepted as important, there are theoretical differences about *what* in the person interacts *how* and with *what* in the situation. Thus, the internal–external debate remains lively and is an issue to be kept in mind in considering various theoretical points of view.

The Unity of Behavior and the Concept of the Self

Most psychologists agree that human behavior results not only from the operation of specific parts but also from the relationships among these parts. To a certain extent this is true for a mechanical system such as an automobile; it is even more true for a living system such as the human body. Rather than being made up of isolated responses, human behavior generally expresses *pattern, organization,* and *integration.* Like a smooth-running car, the parts are operating in harmony with one another. They all seem to function together toward their common goals, instead of each part functioning independently toward different goals that may be in conflict with one another. Indeed, when behavior appears disorganized and disintegrated, we suspect that something is drastically wrong with the person. How, then, are we to formulate this pattern and organization? What is it that gives an integrative quality to behavior? The concept of the **self** has often been used in this regard, but while many personality theorists gives major attention to this concept, others choose to disregard it entirely.

Traditionally the concept of the self has been emphasized for three reasons. First, our awareness of ourselves represents an important aspect of our phenomenological or subjective experience. Second, considerable research suggests that how we feel about ourselves influences our behavior in many situations. Third, the concept of the self is used to express the organized, integrated aspects of human personality functioning. In asking whether the concept of the self is necessary, the noted theorist Gordon Allport suggested that many psychologists have tried in vain to account for the integration, organization, and unity of the human person by not making use of the concept of the self. For example, many behavioral psychologists have found it difficult to discuss the person as a whole because they deny the importance of internal factors. Other psychologists, after struggling with a fragmented conceptualization of personality, have returned to the concept of self as a way of representing the coherence, unity, and goal-directedness of human behavior (Allport, 1955).

The concept of the self has been used in a variety of ways, although some theorists have rejected it entirely because they fear it suggests control of our behavior by a strange inner being. But without a concept of self, the theorist is left with the task of developing an alternative concept or set of principles to express the integrated, systematic aspects of human functioning. On the other hand, reliance on the concept of the self leaves the theorist with the task of defining self in a way that does not make it impossible to study systematically. Thus, the various ways to account for the organized aspects of personality, and the utility of the concept of the self in this regard, remain major issues of concern for personality psychologists.

Varying States of Awareness and the Concept of the Unconscious

A fourth issue of continuing concern to most personality theorists is how to conceptualize the role of varying states of consciousness in individual functioning. Most psychologists grant that the potential for different states of consciousness exists. The effects of drugs, along with interest in Eastern religion and techniques of meditation, have served to heighten the concern of personality theorists with the whole range of altered states of consciousness. Most theorists also accept the view that we are not always attentive to or aware of factors that influence our behavior, but many are uncomfortable with Freud's theory of the unconscious. They feel that it is used to account for too much, and that it does not lend itself to empirical investigation. But how are we to account for such diverse phenomena as slips of the tongue, dreams, occasional inability to give a "rational" explanation for our behavior, and our ability under special circumstances to remember events of the past that appeared to have been forgotten? Are these related or separate phenomena? Must they be understood in terms of the working of an unconscious, or are alternative explanations possible? As we shall see, the issue here is important not only in relation to personality theory but also in relation to personality measurement. To what extent can we rely on people to give accurate reports concerning themselves? Must we use tests that will bypass the defenses to get to the unconscious? In relation to the concept of the self, are people aware of all their feelings about and perceptions of themselves? Or are some of these feelings and perceptions unconscious? If we cannot recognize some important feelings about and perceptions of ourselves, what are the implications of this fact on attempts at measurement of the self concept?

Relationships Among Cognition, Affect, and Overt Behavior

Earlier in this chapter personality was defined as including cognitions (thought processes), affects (emotions, feelings), and overt behavior. Not all psychologists agree that these are all worthy of investigation and, even where such agreement exists, there are major differences concerning relationships among them. As we shall see later in the text, radical behaviorism led to a focus on overt behavior and the rejection of investigation of internal processes such as thoughts and feelings. Then, starting in the 1950s, a cognitive revolution took place in psychology that led to the field being dominated by cognitive theories. For some time the area of affect was ignored, though in recent years there are signs of a strong developing interest in affect, both in its own right and in its implications for thought and action.

Personality psychologists differ in the relative weight or attention they give to each of these areas of functioning and in their view of the causal relations that exist among them. The first matter is of particular interest since it concerns what is investigated, how research is conducted, and how we assess personality. That is, different methods of personality investigation and assessment are involved in the study of human thoughts, feelings, and behaviors. For some time cognitive psychologists have argued that cognitions are primary in causal relationships; that is, they cause both feelings and behaviors. Other psychologists, however, have argued that affects or emotions are primary and can direct thought processes. Such psychologists also argue that affects are important in the development and channelizing of motivation. Finally, there has lately been a growing acceptance of the view that thought, feeling, and overt behavior influence each other mutually or reciprocally (Pervin, 1983, 1984).

It is interesting to think about one's own personality and consider the relevance of these phenomena. For example, how much of your personality is expressed in overt behavior? Could we know all there is to know about you from observing your overt behavior? From knowing your thoughts? From knowing your feelings? Or, does personality involve all three and, most significantly, relationships among what you are thinking, what you are feeling, and how you behave?

The Influence of the Past, Present, and Future on Behavior

A final issue that may be noted here is the importance of the past, present, and future in governing behavior. Theorists would undoubtedly agree that behavior can be influenced only by factors operating in the present. In this sense, only the present is important in understanding behavior. But the present can be influenced by experience of the remote past or of the recent past. Similarly, what one is thinking about in the present can be influenced by thoughts about the immediate future or about the distant future. People vary in the extent to which they worry about the past and the future. And personality theorists differ in their concern with and conceptualization of the past and the future as determinants of behavior in the present. At one extreme lies psychoanalytic theory, which attaches importance to early learning experiences. At the other extreme lies cognitive theory, which emphasizes the individual's plans for the future. However, the issue is not whether events that happened in the past can have lasting effects or whether anticipations about the future can have effects in the present (theorists undoubtedly would agree that both are possible and occur), but how to conceptualize the role of past experiences and future anticipations and connect their influence to what is occurring in the present.

Summary

In attempting to account for the *what, why,* and *how* of human functioning, personality theorists are confronted with many issues. Six issues of particular importance have been mentioned here: the philosophical view of the person; the relation between internal (person) and external (situation) influences in determining behavior; the concept of the self and how to account for the organized aspects of personality functioning; the role of varying states of awareness and the concept of the unconscious; the relationships among cognition, affect, and behavior; and the role of the past, present, and future in governing behavior. Of course, many other issues concern personality theorists and account for differences among them, but the purpose here has been to point to the main ones. The importance of these and other issues will become increasingly clear as we consider the positions of the various theorists in the chapters that follow.

THEORY AND THEORETICAL ISSUES

A theory of personality suggests ways of bringing together and systematizing a wide variety of findings. It also may suggest which directions in research are the most critical or potentially the most useful. Stated most simply, theories help to pull together what we know and to suggest how we may discover what is yet unknown. Stated more systematically, a **theory** consists of a set of assumptions and concepts that tie together various empirical findings and suggest new relationships among them that should obtain under certain defined conditions. Viewed in this light, theories involve systematic ordering of ideas and planned approaches to research.

This description could lead to the assumption that the place of theory in psychology is well accepted and that there is consensus about its desirability. However, just as there is disagreement about the view of the person implied in a theory, so there is disagreement concerning the positive contributions of theory and the proper time for its development in psychology. There are those who emphasize that theories sharpen research objectives, make research more organized, and help the psychologist avoid wasting time on meaningless or irrelevant variables. "My argument is that it is only with the rubble of bad theories that we should be able to build better ones, and without theory of some kind, somewhere, psychological observation and description would at best be chaotic and meaningless" (Hebb, 1951, p. 39).

In contrast, there are those who argue that theories inhibit the search for new variables in a variety of areas. Here theory is seen as masking the discovery of new ideas. Accidental discoveries are used to illustrate how science can progress without—indeed, in spite of—theory. Whereas the former view emphasizes the contributions of theory to the development of new lines of research and new techniques, the latter view emphasizes how much of theory-related research takes a wrong path and eventually is discarded (Skinner, 1950).

Those who choose to use theories suggest that facts acquire significance only in the light of theory and that theory makes research cumulative. Those who choose to operate without theory suggest that we should pay attention to gathering facts and develop theories only after we have a considerable body of knowledge upon which to base them. Although some theorists feel that concepts such as drive and need add to understanding, others do not. "In the final analysis of behavior, is it not simpler to say a man drinks because he has been deprived of water for six hours rather than to say because he is thirsty? Such statements as 'thirsty' are perfectly acceptable in common parlance but cannot be allowed in scientific analysis" (Lundin, 1961, p. 40).

Theory is not something that can be taken lightly. It can be useful or destructive, guiding or misleading, revealing or blinding. Yet is it possible to function without theory? B. F. Skinner, a leading learning theorist, believes that it is and argues for caution in the use of theory. On the other hand, others argue that with all the possible variables and phenomena to be studied, only some are chosen, and that the selectivity involved in choice must assume some theory. If selection is not made on the basis of conscious theory, it is made on the basis of unconscious forces (Miller, 1951). To the extent that this may be the case, it seems reasonable to argue in favor of conscious, well-formulated theories.

Yet, of course, all men . . . are theorists. They differ not in whether they use theory, but in the degree to which they are aware of the theory they use.

The choice before the man in the street and the research worker alike is not whether to theorize but whether to articulate his theory, to make it explicit, to get it out in the open where he can examine it.

(Gage, 1963, p. 94)

Evaluation of Theories

What criteria can be used systematically to evaluate theories of personality? The criteria for such an analysis follow from the functions of theory—the organization of existing information and the selection of fruitful areas for investigation. The corresponding criteria for evaluation of theories of personality are *comprehensiveness, parsimony* or *simplicity,* and *research relevance* (Hall & Lindzey, 1978). The first two relate to the organizing function of theory, the third to its guiding function.

A good theory is comprehensive in that it encompasses and accounts for a wide variety of data. Such a theory is directed to each of the realms of behavior discussed previously. It is important to ask how many different kinds of phenomena the theory can account for. However, we must not be merely quantitative. No theory can account for everything, so one must also ask whether the phenomena accounted for by one theory are as important or central to human behavior as the phenomena encompassed by another theory. What constitutes a phenomenon that is critical to our understanding of behavior may often be ambiguous. However, it is important to recognize that comprehensiveness includes both the number and the significance of the facts accounted for by the theory.

Along with being comprehensive, a theory should be simple and parsimonious. It should account for varied phenomena in an economical, internally consistent way. A theory that makes use of a different concept for every aspect of behavior or of concepts that contradict one another is a poor theory. These goals of simplicity and comprehensiveness in turn raise the question of the appropriate level of organization and abstraction of a personality theory. As theories become more comprehensive and more parsimonious, they tend to become more abstract. It is important that, in becoming abstract, theories remain relevant both to groups of people and to specific individuals.

As Hall and Lindzey (1978) point out, a theory is not true or false but useful or not useful. A good theory has research relevance in that it leads to many new hypotheses, which can then be confirmed empirically. It has what Hall and Lindzey call empirical translation: it specifies variables and concepts in such a way that there is agreement about their meaning and about their potential for measurement. Empirical translation means that the concepts in a theory are clear, explicit, and lead to the expansion of knowledge; they must have predictive power. In other words, a theory must contain testable hypotheses about relationships among phenomena. A theory that is not open to the "negative test," one that potentially cannot be shown to be inaccurate, is a poor theory. This would lead to argument and debate, but not to scientific progress. Whatever the life of a theory, if it has led to new insights and new research techniques it has made a valuable contribution to science. "Theories of psychology are seldom disproved; they just fade away. Of course, all present theories of personality are doomed to pass into history. They should be tolerated only in proportion to their heuristic value to research" (Jensen, 1958, p. 295).

These criteria of comprehensiveness, parsimony, and research relevance provide the basis for a comparative evaluation of theories of personality. In comparing theories, however, we should have two questions in mind: Do they address themselves to the same phenomena? Are they at the same stage of development? Two theories that deal with different kinds of behavior may each be evaluated in relation to these three criteria. Nevertheless, we need not choose between the two theories. Each can be allowed to lead to new insights, with the hope that at some point both can be integrated into a single more comprehensive theory. Finally, a new and immature theory may be unable to account for many phenomena but may lead to a few important observations and show promise of becoming more comprehensive with time. Such a theory may be unable to explain phenomena considered to be understood by another established theory but may represent a breakthrough in significant areas formerly left untouched.

Theory and the History of Scientific Progress

We have discussed ways to evaluate theories and the importance of evaluating a theory in relation both to the phenomena it attempts to explain and to its stage of development. A look at the history of developments in most fields of science will help us understand some of the relevant issues. According to Kuhn (1970), there have been three distinct **stages of scientific development**: an early developmental stage, a stage of normal science, and a period of scientific revolution. The *early developmental stage* of scientific activity is characterized by continual competition between a number of distinct schools or views of nature. Each school believes it functions according to the dictates of scientific method and observation. Indeed, what differentiates these competing views is not the degree of commitment to scientific method but rather their differing ways of viewing the world and of practicing science within it. Since at this stage of development there is no common body of data and belief, each school builds the field anew from its own foundation and chooses its own supporting observations and experiments. Fact gathering during this time has a random quality. One rarely observes a systematic accumulation of knowledge. Essentially, during the early development stage, the field is without a commonly accepted model, or **paradigm**, that defines the field of observations and the methods to be used in research.

The *stage of normal science* begins with the acceptance of such a paradigm or model and is based on clear scientific achievement. During this stage there is acceptance of and commitment to a model that defines which problems are legitimate areas of inquiry and points out the appropriate methods of research. A more rigid definition of the field occurs, research is more focused, observations more restricted, and knowledge more cumulative. Each new bit of knowledge

serves as a building block for the next. The scientists during this period are somewhat tradition-bound and are committed to the accepted model. Instead of many
competing schools in the field, there tend to be relatively few, and frequently only
one.

Since no paradigm or theory can ever explain all facts, ultimately there are
some observations during the period of normal science that do not fit the accepted models. These observations or *anomalies* create a crisis in which tradition
is shattered and, after a period of turmoil, a new paradigm is accepted. Copernicus, Newton, and Einstein were each associated with a stage of scientific revolution. In each case, a time-honored theory was rejected in favor of a new theory.
In each case also, the new theory was incompatible with the old one and offered
explanations of critical observations that could not be explained within the earlier
paradigm. However, typically, acceptance of the new paradigm occurs after a period of intense competition among competing views and a period of wide-open research. This period thus shares some characteristics with the early developmental
phase—competition among alternative views, wide-open research, debate over
fundamental issues, occasional recourse to philosophy, and additions to knowledge that are noncumulative. What differentiates this state from the early development stage is that it follows a period of articulation of a paradigm and is a response to specific observations that have presented problems for that paradigm.
Although the new paradigm may not be very well articulated and may be limited
in scope, it is accepted because it offers solution to critical issues in the field.
Rather than representing a competing paradigm or point of view, it replaces an
old one and involves a reevaluation of prior fact. Once accepted, the new paradigm is associated with a new period of normal science until new observations
arise and the stage is set for a further scientific revolution. The successive transi-
tion from one paradigm to another via revolution is the usual developmental pattern of a mature science.

The field of personality today is filled with issues that divide scientists along
sharply defined lines and that lead to alternative, competing schools of thought.
It is important to recognize that such theoretical differences exist and that they
may not be readily resolved by debate or soon resolved by experimental proof.
Kuhn suggests that the social sciences are still in the early developmental stage
and have not yet arrived at their first universally received paradigm. If this is the
case, we should not be surprised to find competing views that make a common
claim to science and emphasize different observations and modes of research.
Unfortunately, there may be nothing in the laws of science that allows us to
choose among these views. And, though they compete with one another, each
may result in significant contributions to knowledge in the field.

Theory and the Study of Personality

What then is the role of theory in the study of personality? The entire plan of this
book suggests that theory is important to our goals of understanding and explaining human behavior. It can be said that the current state of personality theory is

at a low ebb and that what is available is hardly worth considering. It is true that we have not had a good personality theory in some time; perhaps we have never had a good one. But it is on the basis of our past failures that we will have to build future successes. As a minimum, at least we now know some directions of investigation that are *not* worthy of our efforts. As Kuhn notes, history suggests that the road to a firm research consensus is extraordinarily difficult.

We can be critical of personality theory, as many rightfully have been, and we can even turn away from theory and devote ourselves to detailed research problems, as many psychologists are doing. But, in the final analysis, theory is necessary, and a good theory of personality will be developed. The choice is not between "theories or no theories", but rather in the degree to which a theory is so tightly constructed that it narrows the potential for "play in research" and the degree to which a theory is abstract. A theory can be abstract or concrete, complex or simple. It can lead to rigorous research or haphazard research, to the investigation of many problems or the investigation of a few. Freedom to explore and theories of lesser abstraction and complexity are most useful during the early stages of the development of a science. Focused, rigorous, and complex theories are more useful when observation and data are well advanced.

Theory, then, is both inevitable and useful in the study of personality. At this point, our concerns are how explicit we make theories, how good they are, and how well we use them. Theories imply views of humans but we must also appreciate that "in truth, man is at once both biological animal and social product, both master and servant of fate, both rational and irrational, both driver and driven. His behavior can be fully explained only by placing each aspect in its proper perspective. Of all the dynamic physical systems constituting the universe, man is the most complex" (Krech & Crutchfield, 1958, p. 272). Ideally, a theory of personality should involve laws that help us understand how each person is different as well as how all people are the same. In the pursuit of such laws, we must develop theories that will permit coherent organization of what is known, *and* leave room for us to move on to insights into the unknown.

MAJOR CONCEPTS AND SUMMARY

personality	self
structure	theory
process	comprehensiveness, parsimony
tension reduction model	(simplicity), research relevance
competence motivation model	stages of scientific development
Zeitgeist	paradigm
person–situation controversy	

A theory consists of a set of assumptions and concepts that tie together empirical findings and suggests new relationships that should hold true under defined conditions. Theories define areas of observation and methods of research. In doing so, they focus attention but may also restrict observation. Theories of personality are expected to answer questions concerning the structure of the organism (what), the processes of personality functioning (why), and the growth and development of these structures and processes (how). In evaluating theories we are interested in the criteria of comprehensiveness, parsimony, and research relevance.

Although it is tempting to believe that science is completely objective and free of personal bias, there is evidence that personal values and arbitrariness affect theories of personality and strategies for research: "An apparently arbitrary element, compounded of personal and historical accident, is always a formative ingredient of the beliefs espoused by a given scientific community in a given time" (Kuhn, 1970, p. 4). Such arbitrariness may be particularly evident during the early developmental stage of a science and may help us understand the conflicting positions that arise in relation to significant issues. Finally, an awareness of the history of scientific progress in other disciplines can help us understand the presence of competing theories of personality today and the potential contributions each may make to future advances.

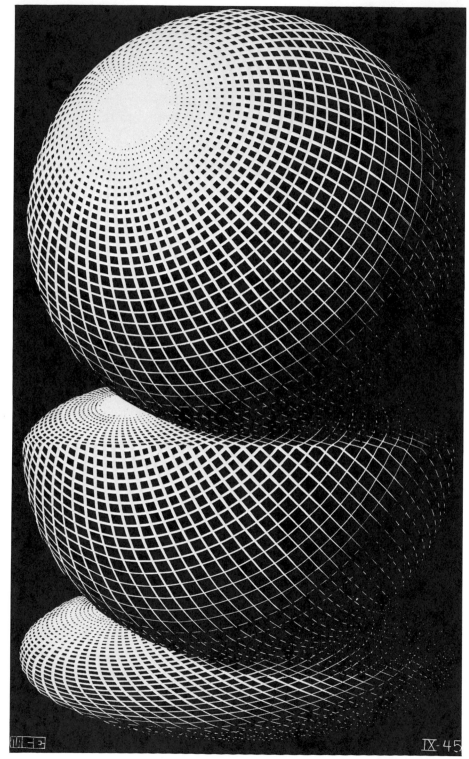

Three Spheres by Escher. © Beeldrecht, Amsterdam/VAGA, New York. Collection
Haags Gemeentemuseum-The Hague, 1983.

THE SCIENTIFIC STUDY OF PEOPLE

CHAPTER FOCUS: In this chapter we consider the process of personality research in terms of research goals and the factors that influence the process. We discuss alternative approaches as exemplified by research on the concepts of stress, helplessness, and control. And we also discuss the strengths and limitations of each approach and the commitments of various investigators to one approach or another. In conclusion, we focus on the human and social forces that influence research, from conceptualization of a problem to influences on public social policy.

The well-known virtue of the experimental method is that it brings situational variables under tight control. It thus permits rigorous tests of hypotheses and confident statements about causation. The correlational method, for its part, can study what man has not learned to control or can never hope to control. . . . The correlator's method is to observe and organize the data from Nature's experiments.

Cronbach, 1957, p. 672

Different kinds of data and differing levels of information are obtained in the laboratory and the clinic. Each is necessary, useful, and desirable.

Lazarus and Davison, 1971, p. 197

Research has to do with the systematic study of observed relationships among events. It involves the gathering of data in the search for facts or principles that can be interpreted in a broader theoretical framework. Research forms a connecting link with theory. Theory without research is mere speculation, but unending research without theory is meaningless fact-gathering.

A personality theory attempts to answer the questions of what, how, and why, to provide formulations to explain structure, dynamics, development, psychopathology, and change. A personality theory suggests that certain relationships should exist among specific phenomena. Research involves the use of data-gathering techniques to observe relevant phenomena; it attempts to determine whether the suggested relationships do in fact exist. Where there are two competing theories of personality, we look for a crucial test—a place where the two theories predict different relationships among phenomena and research can determine which relationships exist. This is not to say that our understanding of personality is never advanced by research unrelated to theory or even by "chance" findings; it suggests that the general course of an increase in our understanding is through a relationship between theory and research. This chapter will describe some systematic efforts in personality research, outline some of the issues and problems, and illustrate how personality research tends to reflect differences in theoretical assumptions and styles.

Personality researchers vary in the types of issues they investigate, how they define variables (the sources of variation they consider important for investigation), and their general styles of research. Some choose to work with global, wide-range variables such as types, need for achievement or cognitive style. Others choose to work with such more specific and focused variables as trait, habit, or learned stimulus-response bond. Some researchers use concepts that are defined in relation to a theory and are intangible—again, such as need for achievement and cognitive style. Others choose variables that are defined in relation to measurement procedures and thought to be tangible, such as anxiety defined in terms of physiological response or habit defined in terms of a learned stimulus-response bond. Some researchers study how individuals vary in their responses to the same situation while others examine how situations influence behavior in a systematic way. Some study a few individuals intensively while others feel comfortable with large numbers; some use statistical techniques whereas others avoid them completely; some "go inside the person's mind" while others stay out of "the black box;" some study behavior in the clinic, others in the laboratory; some value "flexibility" and "freedom to explore" while others value "rigor" and "sharpness of focus." This is not to say that all psychologists are of one type or the other or that there is one consistent position on all such issues, but rather that there is individual variation in the strategies psychologists use in their research. While psychological research in general, and personality research in particular, are part of science, they involve humans whose research behavior is at least partly determined by personality characteristics.

At times for logical reasons, and at times for reasons of temperament, in personality research there are relationships among type of theory, data-gathering technique, and research strategy. For example, "clinical" theories of personality tend to be associated with unstructured personality tests and frequently make use of clinical situations in which the investigator (clinician) cannot exercise control over the relevant variables. "Empirical" theories are likely to be associated with structured personality tests and with direct control or manipulation of the variables by the experimenter. It is possible, in fact, desirable, to study the same variables from different theoretical viewpoints and in relation to different sources of data. More typically, however, independent lines of pursuit develop, each expressing its own link between theory and research.

RESEARCH TACTICS AND GUIDING CONCEPTS

Humans are complex animals and research on them is a complex pursuit. While all personality researchers hold certain goals and scientific values in common, they differ in strategy concerning the best route to these goals. In some cases, the difference in research strategy or tactic is minor, the choice of one experimental procedure or test over another. In other cases, however, the difference is major and expresses a more fundamental difference in approach. In this chapter we will consider three major approaches to personality research—naturalistic observation and clinical research, personality tests and questionnaires, and laboratory research. Before doing so, however, let us consider some of the more general issues that relate to the utilization of one or another approach.

Two Disciplines of Scientific Psychology

In his 1957 presidential address to the American Psychological Association, Lee J. Cronbach described two streams of method, thought, and affiliation in psychology—the *experimental* and the *correlational*. In the experimental approach, the researcher changes conditions or manipulates variables and observes the consequences. The goal is to produce consistent variation in behavior as a result of certain treatments. It is the consequences that are uniform for all subjects that are of interest. The method has the virtues of permitting tight control over variables, rigorous tests of hypotheses, and confident statements about causation. However, it may lead to the neglect of variables that cannot be controlled by the researcher and, since the interest is in effects on the group as a whole, it may lead to the neglect of important differences among people.

What is neglected in the experimental approach becomes the focus of concern in the correlational approach. According to Cronbach, the correlational psychologist is "in love" with just those variables the experimenter chooses to ignore. Thus, the psychologist who follows the correlation tradition is interested in differences among individuals, in particular in how people may often respond differentially to the same situation or experimental condition. The goal here is to observe and organize data in terms of relationships that already exist. The virtue of the correlational method is that it allows one to study phenomena that do not lend themselves to experimental control. It also allows one to study many different aspects of people at the same time. However, the limitation of the approach is that it does not provide for rigorous tests of hypotheses or confident statements about causation in the way that may be true for the experimental approach.

There are two things of interest concerning Cronbach's description of the two disciplines in psychology. The first is that researchers typically follow one or another tradition; that is, rarely do researchers attempt to follow both courses of action in their research. Beyond this, often they are critical of the research issues and research methods followed by members of the alternative tradition. Second, in one form or another the distinction between research traditions described by Cronbach existed for some time previously, and it continues to exist today. Thus, for example, in his presidential address to the American Psychological Association Dashiell (1939) distinguished between the *experimental* attitude and the *clinical* attitude. Through careful experimentation, the researcher aims to gain control over variables. Through careful observation, the clinician tries to discover the totality of the individual. More recently, a contemporary observer of the field of personality notes again the existence of two distinct traditions—each typified by a specific subject matter, methodology, and theoretical orientation (Hogan, 1982). In the one tradition, there is an emphasis on experimental methodology, single aspects of human performance, and what is true for people generally. In the other tradition, there is an emphasis on clinical case study or questionnaire research, individual differences, and relationships among the parts.

In sum, we have evidence of a historical tendency for personality research to follow one of two traditions. In a sense, the traditions differ in attitude or viewpoint. Such a difference need not logically lead to differences in what is studied or how it is studied—subject matter and research methodology. However, these linkages have tended to occur. Thus, historically personality researchers have tended to fall on one or the other side of three basic orientations: (1) "making things happen" in research (experimental) versus "studying what has occurred" (correlational); (2) all persons versus the single individual; (3) one aspect of the person versus the total individual.

RESEARCH ON STRESS AND HELPLESSNESS

The personality theories covered in this text reflect differences in these traditions, and we shall return to this issue later in the chapter. At this point, however, it may be useful to examine the research approaches themselves. In doing so, we shall start with approaches to research that involve maximum experimental control and progress to those that involve the least control by the experimenter. Although any effort to categorize approaches to personality research will encounter some problems, three categories will be considered—experimental or laboratory research, personality tests and questionnaires (correlational), and naturalistic observation and clinical research. The effort here will be to see how data gathered from different research procedures can be consistent and lead to a greater understanding of the phenomena of interest. The topic chosen for illustration—stress and helplessness—was selected because of its intrinsic interest and its current importance in personality research.

Laboratory, Experimental Research

We have already defined the experimental tradition as involving efforts to gain control over the variables of interest, to manipulate some variables and see the consequences for other variables, to establish if–then, causal relationships. To appreciate this approach, let us consider two major research programs directed toward an understanding of the effects of stress and helplessness. The focus here will be on the use of experimental procedures in the laboratory setting, though we shall see that these efforts have been influenced by and expanded into the use of other research procedures as well.

The first example of laboratory research concerns the effects of stress. In the first part of this research two psychologists, Glass and Singer (1972), were concerned with the consequences of adaptation to stress generally and urban stress in particular. They made use of the laboratory because they felt that this was the best way to sort out the effects of different variables. Noise was used as the source of stress, rather than such urban problems as crowding, garbage, crime, and so on, because it could be clearly defined and manipulated in the laboratory. Thus their studies of the problem of urban stress came to focus largely on the consequences of adaptation to unpredictable and uncontrollable high-intensity noise. Prior naturalistic research had suggested that the effects of such stresses as noise depend on cognitive factors associated with unpredictability and uncontrollability. Glass and Singer set out to investigate the relationship between these factors and performance. Two basic questions were asked: Is adaptation to a stress such as noise achieved at such cost to the individual that behavioral aftereffects are observed? Do such consequences vary with the meanings attributed to the noise?

In a number of laboratory studies Glass and Singer manipulated the intensity, predictability, and controllability of noise and examined the effects on performance in tasks of varying complexity. Initially they found that subjects could adapt to the noise under almost all of the conditions and that, by and large, performance was disrupted only when subjects had to perform highly complex tasks under conditions of unpredictable or uncontrollable noise. However, other observations led them to believe that the negative effects of noise were more important after termination of the stress than during the process of adaptation or coping itself. Further investigations of the effects of noise on performance clearly indicated that behavioral problems occurred after the noise stopped. Noise was found to have an aftereffect on tasks such as solving puzzles and proofreading even if there was no effect when the noise itself was heard.

The authors speculated that unpredictable noise was particularly stressful because the individual experienced not only the aversiveness of the noise itself but also the anxiety of not being able to do anything to prepare for it because they did not know when it would occur. Was this true and why the aftereffect phenomenon? In some further research, the authors found that the perception of control reduced the negative aftereffects of unpredictable noise. They concluded that uncontrollable noise (stress) results in a sense of helplessness: "Consider first what an organism experiences during inescapable or unavoidable stress. Nothing he can do will affect the occurrence of the stressor, for there are no available resources that will enable him to counter it. If the aversive event is also unpredictable, there cannot even be preparation for stimulation. The individual is at the mercy of his environment, in which case we may describe his psychological state as one of helplessness" (Glass & Singer, 1972, p. 86). The authors viewed their work as fitting in with the view that it is not only the stressful event that is significant, but also the experience of lack of control or helplessness that may be associated with it. What Glass and Singer demonstrated was that the perception of control alone was enough to make a difference: the individual does not actually have to exert control!

Glass and Singer extended their research to other stresses, such as electric shock and social stress (harassment by an administrative assistant). In each case they found that the negative aftereffects of stress were a function of unpredictablility and perceived lack of control. They reasoned that the perception of control reduces the aversive impact of the stress and thereby the behavioral aftereffects. As demonstrated in their studies, belief in actual or potential control reduces feelings of helplessness and thereby the magnitude of the stress response (tension) and the adverse aftereffects. The sequence suggested runs:

unpredictable stress → increased sense of helplessness → greater magnitude of stress response (attempt to cope) → greater negative behavioral aftereffects

Addressing themselves to the questions raised initially, Glass and Singer concluded that adaptation to stress may be achieved at considerable cost to the individual resulting in negative behavioral aftereffects; that is, the cumulative effects of the responses to the stress may go beyond the effects of any single response. Furthermore, the consequences of stress appear to vary with the meanings attributed to the stress. In particular, the perception of lack of control or helplessness seems to result in negative aftereffects. The unpredictability of stress appears to be a critical variable influencing the perception of helplessness. The findings indicated that psychological factors, not simply the physical characteristics of stimuli, are the principal determinants of the adverse aftereffects of aversive stimuli.

As we shall see later, this experimental work on stress provided the foundation for important research on factors contributing to coronary heart disease. Before turning to this research however, which involves the utilization of correlational methods as well as experimental methods, let us consider another illustration of the experimental approach to personality research. This second illustration of the utility of laboratory research involves the important work of Seligman and the concept of **learned helplessness**. In the course of some early work on fear conditioning and learning, Seligman and his co-workers observed that dogs who had experienced uncontrollable shocks in one situation transferred their sense of helplessness to another situation where shock was avoidable. In the first situation, dogs were put in a situation where no response they made could affect the onset, offset, duration, or intensity of the shocks. When placed in a second, different situation where jumping over a barrier could lead to escape from shock, most of the dogs seemed to give up and accept the shock passively. They had learned in the first condition that they were helpless to influence the shocks and transferred this learning to the second condition. Note that this was true for most of the dogs (about two-thirds), but not for all—an important difference among individuals that will be returned to later.

The behavior of the dogs who had learned that they were helpless was particularly striking in contrast with that of dogs who received no shock or shock under different conditions. Given the situation where escape and avoidance were possible, the latter dogs would run frantically until they accidentally stumbled on the response that led to escape. Thereafter they would progressively learn to move to that response more quickly until, finally, they were able to avoid the shock altogether. In contrast to such "healthy" dogs, the learned helplessness dogs would similarly first run frantically, but then they would stop, lie down, and whine.

With succeeding trials the dogs would give up more and more quickly and accept the shock more passively—the classic learned helplessness response. The depth of their despair would become so great that it became extremely difficult to change the nature of their expectations. The experimenters tried to make it easier for the dogs to escape and tried to get them to come to safety by attracting them with food—to no avail. By and large, the dogs would just lie there. Even outside that situation, the behavior of the helpless dogs was different from that of the non-helpless dogs: "When an experimenter goes to the home cage and attempts to remove a nonhelpless dog, it does not comply eagerly: it barks, runs to the back of the cage, and resists handling. In contrast, helpless dogs seem to wilt; they passively sink to the bottom of the cage, occasionally even rolling over and adopting a submissive posture; they do not resist" (Seligman, 1975, p. 25).

Further research demonstrated that the same phenomena found in dogs could be produced in humans (Hiroto, 1974). In this research one group of college students heard a loud noise that they could turn off by pushing a button, a second group of students heard the same noise but could not stop it, while a third (control) group did not hear a noise. All three groups of subjects were then put in another situation where in order to escape the noise they had to move their hand from one side of the box to the other once a light signal had gone on. The members of the first and third groups quickly learned to escape the noise by moving their hands while the members of the learned helplessness group failed to escape the noise; most sat passively and accepted the painful noise. The measure of the learned helplessness effect was response latency or how long it took the subjects to move their hand once the light signal went on. In sum, manipulation of the escape versus no-escape conditions in the first phase of the experiment produced clear evidence of differences in learned helplessness in the second phase of the experiment (Figure 2.1).

Further research demonstrated that such learned helplessness could generalize beyond the initial task to a broad range of behaviors (Hiroto & Seligman, 1975). More recently, studies have demonstrated that learned helplessness can occur through observing helpless models (Brown & Inouye, 1978; DeVellis, DeVellis, & McCauley, 1978). Individuals will give up more easily if they see themselves as similar to a helpless model than if they observe a successful model or if they perceive themselves as more competent than the observed model.

Seligman's explanation of the learned helplessness phenomenon was that the animal or person learns that outcomes are not affected by its behavior. The expectation that outcomes are independent of the organism's response then has motivational, cognitive, and emotional implications: (1) Uncontrollable events undermine the organism's motivation to initiate other responses that might result in control. (2) As a result of uncontrollability of previous events, the organism has difficulty learning that its response can have an effect on other events. (3) Repeated experiences with uncontrollable events eventually lead to an emotional state similar to that identified in humans as depression.

This is the theory of helplessness, a theory that also leads to suggestions concerning prevention and cure. First, to prevent an organism from expecting events

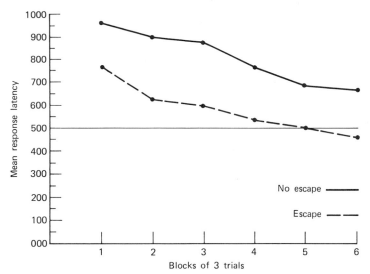

FIGURE 2.1   Learned Helplessness in Humans. As in the animal research, subjects who were first in the no-escape treatment condition took longer to respond and failed to escape more often in the test situation than did subjects who were first in the escape condition. (Hiroto, 1974)

to be independent of its behavior, one should provide it with experiences where it can exercise control. In particular, the experience of controlling trauma protects the organism from the effects caused by experiences of unescapable trauma. Here Seligman notes that the dogs in the original research who did not become helpless even when exposed to inescapable shock probably had histories of controllable trauma prior to coming to the laboratory. This hypothesis was, in fact, tested and it was found that dogs with little experience in controlling anything were particularly susceptible to helplessness. Finally, in terms of therapy, the depressed person who suffers from expectations of uncontrollability needs to be directed toward experiences that will result in recovery of the belief that responding produces reinforcement. In therapy this involves games and tasks of increasing difficulty, starting with those that ensure success (Beck, 1976).

The learned helplessness model and associated research are indeed impressive. The negative effects of experience with uncontrollable events have been produced in cats, fish, and rats as well as in dogs and humans. However, as time has gone on research with humans has suggested that additional factors beyond experience with uncontrollability appear to be important in determining the consequent effects. At least with humans, the effects of experience with uncontrollable events appear to depend on how the person interprets what has occurred. Observation of varying effects depending on modifications in the experimental design or on individual differences in people has led to a reformulated model of learned helplessness. While we have not yet covered all of the experimental research on learned helplessness, much of the research following from the reformulated model has followed correlational rather than experimental procedures. We shall review some of this research in the next section. At this point, however, we may take stock of some of the defining characteristics of experimental research as seen in the efforts of Glass and Singer and of Seligman. In these research programs, we have seen the careful manipulation and control of the relevant variables and, by and large, a focus on systematic influences that are independent of individual differences. We shall consider the strengths of the experimental approach, as well as its limitations, once we have had a chance to place it in perspective relative to the other approaches to research.

Correlational Research and Questionnaires

As noted by Cronbach, in correlational research the researcher gives up control over the variables of interest because they cannot be isolated from one another, because practical considerations preclude such an approach, or because there is an interest in individual differences. For example, if one is interested in how stress and helplessness are associated with depression and coronary heart disease in humans, it would be difficult as well as unethical to produce experimentally the phenomena of interest. However, one can take already existent illustrations of the phenomena and try to associate them or correlate them with other variables. Thus, for example, one can see if there is an association or correlation between people being depressed and reporting earlier experiences of helplessness, or between heart attacks and earlier experiences of stress.

An interesting comparison of the experimental and correlational perspectives may be made by returning briefly to the experimental research on learned helplessness in humans (Figure 2.1). Remember that it was demonstrated that human subjects who were first in the no-escape treatment condition took longer to respond to a signal light and more often failed to escape in the test situation than did subjects who were first in the escape condition. The interpretation was that in the no-escape condition the subjects learned that outcomes were not affected by their behavior. Would subjects who already differ in their beliefs concerning their ability to influence outcomes also differ in their performance in the second situation? In other words, could one find in people differences that occurred naturally and also reproduced the effects of the experimental manipulations? We can now consider another feature of Hiroto's research on learned helplessness in humans. Hiroto not only considered the effects of no-escape and escape treatment conditions on later performance, but he also considered the effects of differences in the personality characteristics known as **locus of control**.

The concept of locus of control is part of Rotter's (1966, 1982) social learning theory of personality and represents a generalized expectancy concerning the determinants of rewards and punishments in one's life. At one extreme are people who believe in their ability to control life's events; that is, internal locus of control. At the other extreme are people who believe that life's events, such as rewards and punishments, are the result of external factors such as chance, luck, or fate; that is, external locus of control. The *Internal–External Scale* (I–E Scale) has been developed to measure individual differences in perception of the extent to which rewards and punishments are generally under internal or external control. Representative items are presented in Figure 2.2. Since the beliefs of external locus of control people sounded very much like the beliefs that are part of learned helplessness, Hiroto suspected that people differing in the personality characteristic of locus of control would perform differently in the test situation. Dividing subjects up into extreme groups of internal and external locus of control on the basis of responses to the I–E Scale, Hiroto exposed members of each group to the no-escape and escape conditions and then looked at their performance in the second or test situation. As expected, he found that external locus of control subjects, regardless of their pretreatment, were slower to escape or avoid than were the internal locus of control subjects (Figure 2.3). In other words, the personality variable of externality appeared to function like the pretreatment variable of inescapability. An association was found between an already existent personality difference and performance in a test situation.

To illustrate further the correlational approach to personality research, as well as the combined use of questionnaires with experimental procedures, let us continue with the story of research on learned helplessness. Earlier we noted that the original formulation of learned helplessness could not account for the varied consequences of uncontrollability often found in human subjects. This led to a reformulated model of learned helplessness (Abramson, Seligman, & Teasdale, 1978; Abramson, Garber, & Seligman, 1980). According to this reformulation, when people find themselves helpless, they ask *why* they are helpless. People answer the question *why* in terms of *casual attributions*. Three dimensions of casual attribution are suggested as important. First, people may attribute the cause of their helplessness to themselves or to the nature of the situation. In the former case, the cause of helplessness is seen as being internal or personal; in the latter case, it is seen as being external or universal. Second, people may attribute helplessness to factors specific to the situation they are in or to more general condi-

---

1a. Many of the unhappy things in people's lives are partly due to bad luck.
1b. People's misfortunes result from the mistakes they make.
2a. One of the major reasons why we have wars is because people don't take enough interest in politics.
2b. There will always be wars, no matter how hard people try to prevent them.
3a. Sometimes I can't understand how teachers arrive at the grades they give.
3b. There is a direct connection between how hard I study and the grades I get.
4a. The average citizen can have an influence in government decisions.
4b. This world is run by the few people in power and there is not much the little guy can do about it.

FIGURE 2.2   Illustrative Items from Rotter's Internal-External Locus of Control Scale.

Mean response latencies of the 6 escape-avoidance trial blocks for internal and external control.

FIGURE 2.3 Locus of Control and Performance. The personality variable of externality appears to function like the pretreatment variable of inescapability. In view of the parallel effects created by inescapability and externality, it is likely that the same underlying process exists in each, that is, the expectancy that responding and reinforcement are independent. (Hiroto, 1974)

tions in the world around them or in themselves. Third, people may perceive the conditions of their situation to be stable and relatively permanent or to be unstable and perhaps temporary.

In sum, three dimensions of casual attribution are suggested in the reformulated model of learned helplessness: **internal (personal)–external (universal), specific–global,** and **stable–unstable**. The attribution made by the person is seen as determining a broad range of important consequences. For example, the attribution of lack of control to internal, personal factors is seen as leading to a greater loss in self-esteem than an attribution to external, universal factors. Personal helplessness, as when, for example, a student perceives continuous failure to be due to his or her own stupidity or incompetence, leads to a much greater loss of self-esteem than does universal helplessness, as when, for example, the student perceives continuous failure to be due to poor teaching. If the person attributes lack of control to general factors, there will be greater generalization of the learned helplessness response to other situations than if a more situation—specific attribution is made. And, if the person attributes lack of control to stable factors, such as lack of ability or difficulty of the curriculum, there will be greater permanence of the effects over time than if helplessness is attributed to unstable factors such as how the person felt that day or how one was lucky or unlucky.

Which attribution is made in response to helplessness will influence, then, whether expectations of future helplessness are chronic or acute, broad or narrow, and whether or not self-esteem is lowered. Of particular import is the suggestion that internal, global, and stable attributions have important implications for the development of depression.

An experimental approach to the reformulated model of learned helplessness would involve the manipulation of causal attributions and observation of the resultant motivational and emotional effects. Thus, for example, subjects could be exposed to conditions that would lead them to make internal or external attributions for failure and differences in consequent effects on self-esteem would be predicted. Although there is some support for the attributional reformulation from experimental research, most such studies have had methodological problems in producing the desired attributions or helplessness effects. To facilitate research in this area, an **Attributional Style Questionnaire** (ASQ) has been developed to measure individual differences in the use of the three specified attributional dimensions (Peterson, Semmel, von Baeyer, Abramson, Metalsky, & Seligman, 1982). In this questionnaire subjects are asked to give a cause for each of 12 hypothetical events and to then rate the cause on scales relevant to the internal–external, stable–unstable, and specific–global dimensions. An illustrative question appears in Figure 2.4. Six of the hypothetical events involve good

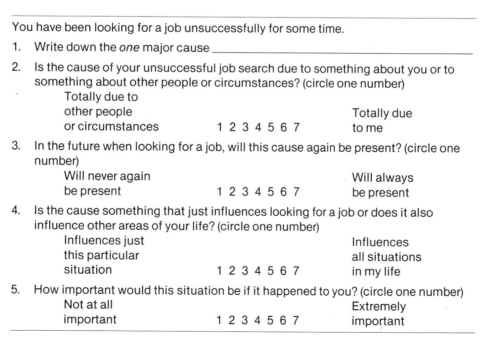

You have been looking for a job unsuccessfully for some time.

1. Write down the *one* major cause _____

2. Is the cause of your unsuccessful job search due to something about you or to something about other people or circumstances? (circle one number)

   Totally due to
   other people   Totally due
   or circumstances   1 2 3 4 5 6 7   to me

3. In the future when looking for a job, will this cause again be present? (circle one number)

   Will never again   Will always
   be present   1 2 3 4 5 6 7   be present

4. Is the cause something that just influences looking for a job or does it also influence other areas of your life? (circle one number)

   Influences just   Influences
   this particular   all situations
   situation   1 2 3 4 5 6 7   in my life

5. How important would this situation be if it happened to you? (circle one number)

   Not at all   Extremely
   important   1 2 3 4 5 6 7   important

FIGURE 2.4 Illustrative Item—The Attributional Style Questionnaire (ASQ) (Peterson, Semmel, von Baeyer, Abramson, Metalsky, & Seligman, 1982, p. 292) events (e.g., "You become very rich.") and six involve bad events (e.g., "You go out on a date and it goes badly."). In addition, some events are interpersonal while others have to do with achievement. The assumption is that people have characteristic attributional tendencies or styles and that these can be measured with a questionnaire.

According to the reformulated learned-helplessness model, attributing uncontrollable bad events to internal, stable, and global factors leads to depression. This would suggest that people scoring high on these dimensions on the ASQ should show more depression than people scoring low on these dimensions. Indeed, the authors of the ASQ report an association or correlation between a style in which internal, stable, and global attributions are made for bad events and depressive symptoms in college students, adults, and patients. Scores on the ASQ have been found to be associated with the development of depressive symptoms following poor performance by college students on a midterm examination. Finally, in a study using a similar questionnaire, it was found that depression was associated with blame directed at one's character but not with blame directed at one's behavior (Peterson, Schwartz, & Seligman, 1981). Bad events attributed to character ("I'm that kind of person.") were viewed as less controllable than events attributed to behavior ("I did something."). In addition, characterological blame was associated with more stable and global attributions than was behavior blame. However, self-blame or characterological blame could not be determined to be a cause of depression. That is, characterological self-blame was found to be associated with but not a cause of later depressive symptoms.

The final point made in relation to the above study is important both for the reformulated learned-helplessness model of depression and for an appreciation of the limits of correlational research. The above research suggests an association between internal, global, and stable attributions for bad events and depression but the research does not demonstrate that such cognitive attributions cause depression. Could they be a part of depression and caused by the same factors that lead to the depression? Indeed, a major study of people before and after they became depressed found that depression-related cognitions did not predict future depression and appeared to be more of a concomitant of depression than a cause of it. Prior to becoming depressed, the future depressives did not attribute failure to internal causes or perceive themselves as having little control over events in their lives (Lewinsohn, Steinmetz, Larson, & Franklin, 1981).

Another study addresses the same issue and also illustrates how both experimental procedures and questionnaires can be used in the same research (Danker-Brown & Baucom, 1982). In this research, college students were asked to solve problems presented as part of an intelligence test. Students in the experimental group were given false feedback that prevented them from solving any of the problems. This was the learned-helplessness condition. Students in the other group were given feedback that indicated successful solution of the problems. Following this, the subjects filled out a cognitions questionnaire designed to measure their explanations for their performance on the intelligence test. Then the subjects filled out a mood questionnaire that is sensitive to mood changes following failure and were asked to solve problems on an anagrams task.

Scores on the mood questionnaire and the anagrams task suggested that the experimental manipulation was effective in producing symptoms of helplessness among the students forced to fail the problems. Thus, the experimental (learned-helplessness) group showed significantly more depressive mood on the questionnaire and significantly less productive effort on the anagrams task than did the control group. So much for the experimental part and the effect of learned helplessness on emotion and motivation. What of the relation of the cognitive attributions to the prior conditions and the consequent emotions and motivations? Did the learned–helplessness condition lead to differing cognitions, and were these differing cognitions associated with depression and a motivational deficit? The answer to the first question appears to be affirmative. Students in the experimental and control groups responded differently to the questionnaire that asked about their views of their own intelligence and the causes for their performance on the task. However, an association could not be found between responses to this questionnaire and subsequent measures of depression and motivational deficit. In other words, in contrast with what the model would suggest, an association could not be found between the kinds of attributions made by subjects in the experimental group and the magnitude of their subsequent depression and decrease in productive performance: "Results of the current study fail to confirm a relationship between self-statements including attributions and the development of helplessness symptoms in human adults. On must question whether attributions are necessary in explaining the development of helplessness symptoms" (Danker-Brown & Baucom, 1982, p. 800). Thus, we are left with associational evidence for the model but causal linkages among events, attributions, and mood or motivation remain to be demonstrated.

And what of the research on the effects of stress? The experimental research of Glass and Singer suggests that continuous efforts at adaptation to stress may result in negative aftereffects. Does correlational research have anything to contribute to our understanding of these or related phenomena? The experimental work on stress suggests that unpredictable negative events are stressful because they lead to the experience of helplessness. Can correlational research, in particular the study of individual differences, help to clarify some of these relationships?

Following up on his earlier work, Glass became interested in the role of stress-related psychological factors in heart disease or cardiac disorders. Coronary heart disease is a major cause of death. While many factors have been found to be associated with high risk for heart disease (e.g., age, sex, hypertension, obesity, heavy cigarette smoking), understanding of the cause of these disorders remains incomplete and no combination of these risk factors predicts the majority of new cases. Clinical investigation, which we shall come to in the next section, suggests that psychological factors play a role in determining the risk of developing cardiac disorders. One aspect of the investigation of psychological factors has involved study of the role of stressful life events. Here a relationship has been found between stressful life events and risk of heart disease. Thus, such stressful life events as economic distress, job dissatisfaction, marital unhappiness, and the sudden death of a spouse all have been correlated with increased risk of heart disease. At the same time, not all people react to stress in the same way and the observation was made that there appears to be a particular personality pattern associated with increased risk for heart disease. This personality variable has come to be known as the **Type A behavior pattern**, sometimes as the Type A personality, and it has been the subject of considerable investigation.

As noted, the initial observation of a possible link between a pattern of personality characteristics and risk of heart disease was made on a clinical basis by medical cardiologists. They observed that many younger patients suffering from cardiac disorders had a particular constellation of behavioral charactersitics including competitive achievement striving, a sense of time urgency, and aggressiveness (Figure 2.5). Observation of this pattern was followed by the development of a structured interview procedure to measure individual differences in this regard. The interview developed consists of 25 questions about the person's life which are designed to elicit competitiveness, impatience, and hostility from the Type A person. For example, the person is asked about the reaction to working with a slow person or having to wait on line. In addition, a questionnaire was developed to measure individual differences in Type A characteristics--the **Jenkins Activity Survey** (JAS, Figure 2.5). The questionnaire inquires about competitive-

---

Illustrative Characteristics:

conscientious	fast thinking	expresses bravado
intense	fast acting	aggressive sexually
sets high standards	firm handshake	poor listener
desires power	vigilant	energetic movements
needs to control	self-centered	restless
competitive	easily angered	clipped speech

Illustrative Items and Responses

1. How would your wife (or closest friend) rate you?
   "Definitely hard driving and competitive."   Type A
   "Definitely relaxed and easy going."   non-Type A

2. Do you ever set deadlines or quotas for yourself at work or home?
   "Yes, once per week or more often."   Type A
   "No." "Only occasionally."   non-Type A

3. Has your spouse or some friend ever told you that you eat too fast?
   "Yes, often."   Type A
   "No."   non-Type A

FIGURE 2.5   Illustrative Type A Characteristics and Items from the Jenkins Activity Survey (JAS) (Jenkins, 1979; Zymanski, 1972; Surwit, Williams, & Shapiro, 1982) ness, the wish for quick action, living a pressured style of life, and hostility. Individuals taking the questionnaire are then scored on a continuum in terms of the extent to which they exemplify the Type A behavior pattern.

Glass and his co-workers modified the JAS for use with college students and set out to clarify the relationship between Type A characteristics and stress in the production of coronary disease (Glass, 1977; Glass & Carver, 1980). Observations of behavior in the laboratory and in the natural environment indeed indicated that individuals scoring high on the JAS show more achievement striving, a greater sense of time urgency, and more aggressiveness than do low-scoring individuals. In addition, the former display a greater effort to exercise control over the environment and to deny uncontrollability. For example, relative to individuals scoring low on the JAS, Type A individuals:

1. Attempt to solve more problems when no time limit is set.
2. Earn more academic honors.
3. Set higher academic goals.
4. Work at levels closer to the limits of their endurance.
5. Report less fatigue.
6. Report a time interval of one minute as elapsing faster.
7. Respond with greater hostility when provoked or frustrated though they are not necessarily uniformly more aggressive.
8. Respond to stress with a greater increase in motivation.
9. Show greater learned helplessness in an uncontrollable situation if the cues signifying lack of control are salient and cannot be denied.

The conclusion reached from these findings was the following: "At the crux of all of these behavioral effects, we would submit, is an attempt by the Type A to assert control over environmental demands and requirements . . . The coronary-prone behavior pattern thus might be described as a characteristic type of responding to environmental stressors that threaten the individual's sense of control. The Type A is engaged in a continual struggle for control . . ." (Glass & Carver, 1980, p. 232).

The JAS has been used by other investigators as well to measure individual differences in the Type A pattern and a number of important relationships have been established (Matthews, 1982). Many of these results fit with Glass' suggestion that Type A individuals strive to assert and maintain control over stressful aspects of their environment. For example, in one study that compared coronary patients with hospitalized (general medical and psychiatric) patients and nonhospitalized controls, it was found that both patient groups had a higher percentage reporting a significant loss during the previous year and that the coronary patients had the highest JAS scores (Theorell & Rahe, 1975). In addition, there are studies that show an association between high scores on the JAS and physiological responses consistent with those predisposing for heart disease as well as with the actual development of heart disease.

CURRENT APPLICATIONS AND IMPLICATIONS

Type A Behavior—Can It Lead To Burnout?

Recently psychologists have been interested in the phenomenon of job burnout—emotional exhaustion associated with stress on the job. Such burnout has been observed among a variety of helping professionals and associated with stressors such as excessive caseloads, lack of time, and lack of support or appreciation. While burnout has been studied in relation to job stress, there also are personality characteristics associated with the burnout syndrome. People who "burn out" emotionally on the job often are perfectionistic and try too hard to reach unrealistic goals.

The past year has witnessed the retirement of a number of successful professional coaches, many of whom show the burnout syndrome and the Type A pattern of behavior. Take, for example, the history of Dick Vermeil, the highly successful former coach of the Philadelphia Eagles professional football team. Many years ago he developed the motto: The Best Way To Kill Time Is To Work It To Death. And work he did—up to twenty hours a day. The point was to achieve a lot and fast. In the words of one person: "You couldn't even drink a glass of water slow around him." Winning was the point, but winning only increased the tension and the need for further work. There was a driven quality to it all, as if something inside him was out of con-

SOURCE: *Sports Illustrated*, March 28, 1983.

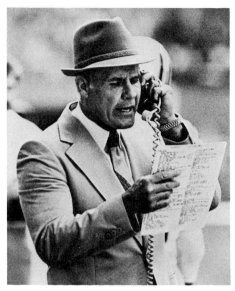

Stress—**Dallas football coach Tom Landry.**

trol as he tried to control the events around him. Assistant coaches would resign, fearful that they would end up with a heart attack. Ultimately it was too much for him as well, and the decision to get out had to be made. As a fellow coach said: "There are now more factors than ever that an NFL coach cannot control."

What advice do other successful coaches have to offer? Tom Landry, the highly successful coach of the Dallas Cowboys for the past twenty-three years says: "A long time ago I tried to judge what I could and could not control and stopped worrying about what I couldn't."

In general, the above studies are illustrative of research that can be done within the correlational tradition. The main thrust in both the attribution-learned helplessness research and the Type A research was on the establishment of patterns of relations or correlations utilizing groups differing on a particular personality characteristic. In some cases there was the utilization of an experimental procedure in a laboratory setting but even in these cases there was the use of already established differences, measured by questionnaires, to investigate the variables of interest. In other cases, of course, associations were established without any experimental manipulation of the variables at all. Although a causal relationship between internal, global, stable attributions and depression has not been established, correlational research has provided a basis for the investigation of such relationships. Similarly, although casual links between Type A behavior characteristics and heart disease have not been established, a number of potentially important relationships have been discovered. In addition, the studies discussed in this section illustrate the importance of individual differences in casual attribution and response to stress, and thereby the potential value of studying individual differences more generally.

Naturalistic Observation and Clinical Research

We have now considered the experimental and correlational approaches to research by focusing on the concepts of stress and helplessness. We have seen how in the experimental approach there is direct manipulation of the variables of interest while in the correlational approach naturally occurring differences are related to one another or exposed to the same experimental conditions. In the latter case, experimental control, and the potential for establishing clear cause–effect relationships, is relinquished in the interest of studying phenomena that cannot otherwise be investigated and/or in the interest of focusing on individual differences. Turning now to naturalistic observation and clinical research, we shall consider research in which experimental control is minimal or not existent at all. In considering naturalistic observation and clinical research, it should be noted that they are not identical and do not necessarily follow from one another. Researchers who prefer one of these methods are often critical of the other. However, the two are considered together here because both exemplify a research tradition in which there is minimal experimental control and maximum effort to study phenomena as they naturally occur.

Naturalistic observation has to do with the study of phenomena as they occur in their own environment, without any efforts to control what occurs. Biologists use naturalistic observation as a primary mode of research. Animals are studied in their natural habitats as inquiry is made into patterns of behavior characteristic of the members of the species. In psychology, the play behavior of children, patterns of mother–infant interaction, aggressive behavior in adolescents, and many other phenomena have been studied through naturalistic observation. **Clinical research** involves the intensive study of individuals in terms of verbal reports, observation of naturally occurring behavior, or the analysis of autobiographical and biographical documents (Howe, 1982; Runyan, 1981, 1982). Verbal reports of what occurred in the natural setting may be used, for example, where direct observation of behavior by the investigator is impossible. The material gathered by Freud illustrates this approach, though his observations included the behavior of patients in therapy sessions as well. Interviews of people after they have experienced a trauma (physical injury, loss of home or a loved one) would be another example. In terms of appreciating this general approach to research, we can recall that interest in the Type A behavior pattern began with clinical observations made by physicians treating patients. These clinical observations were the basis for the development of the structured interview and JAS assessment devices. It is often the case that interest in particular phenomena begins with naturalistic observation or clinical research. It is also the case that data from these approaches are used to check findings reported through the use of experimental procedures. However, before we get too far into consideration of the relationships among the research procedures, let us consider some illustrative research efforts and their findings in detail.

How have naturalistic observation and clinical research been used in relation to stress, helplessness, and control? The concept of anxiety, related to that of stress, has received considerable clinical attention. The noted psychoanalyst Rollo May, in an early review of the literature, concluded that "the special characteristics of anxiety are the feelings of uncertainty and helplessness in the face of danger" (1950, p. 191). Uncertainty, or lack of cognitive structure, and a sense of helplessness, or lack of control, are mentioned repeatedly in the clinical literature. The former often is expressed in the "fear of the unknown" and is often seen as related to a sense of powerlessness or helplessness—an unknown danger creates a situation where activity cannot be directed toward any one goal, with a resultant feeling of mental paralysis and helplessness (Kris, 1944). Among the many valuable naturalistic and clinical investigations of responses to stress have been the studies by Grinker and Spiegel (1945) of the reactions of World War II flying personnel to battle stress and the studies of Janis (1965) of reactions of individuals to loss and illness.

After World War II, two psychoanalysts (Grinker & Spiegel, 1945) reported on their experiences interviewing and treating individuals engaged in the air battle. Their book, *Men under Stress*, is a fascinating account of the stress that is common for all combatants and the varied reactions that occur among different individuals. After describing the kinds of dangers to which the airmen are exposed and their use of group morale to deal with the constant threats facing them, the authors raise the question: Of what is the airman afraid? Their description of the relationship between helplessness and anxiety runs:

Although the fear of the aircraft and of human inefficiency are a constant source of stress, the greatest fear is attached to enemy activity. The enemy has only two forms of defense against our combat aircraft: fighter planes and flak [antiaircraft guns]. The enemy's fighter aircraft are efficient and highly respected by our combat crew members. But they are not as great a

Tactics of Research—**The experimenter here is observing the child's behavior through a one-way mirror.**

source of anxiety as flak. Enemy planes are objects that can be fought against. They can be shot down or outmaneuvered. Flak is impersonal, inexorable, and as used by the Germans, deadly accurate. It is nothing that can be dealt with—*a greasy black smudge in the sky until the burst is close.*

Grinkler and Spiegel, 1945, p. 34

Grinkler and Spiegel similarly describe the response of ground forces to enemy air and mortar attack. What is so stressful is that "there is nothing in the environment which can be used to anticipate the approach of danger . . . any stimuli may actually mean the beginning of an attack. Inhibition of anxiety becomes increasingly difficult" (1945, p. 52). According to these psychoanalysts, the initial reaction to such stress is heightened tension and alertness. The person becomes mentally and physically prepared for trouble so as to counteract the threat and avoid loss of control. A variety of means can be used to deal with the threat but, in the final analysis, "mastery, or its opposite, helplessness, is the key to the ultimate emotional reaction" (p. 129). Confidence is lessened by near-misses, physical fatigue, and the loss of friends. Efforts to see the self as invulnerable (incapable of being harmed), become increasingly difficult: "Out of the ensuing helplessness is born the intense anxiety" (p. 129). Some strive to hold on to ideas of personal invulnerability ("It can't happen to me"), while others hold on to a faith in magical or supernatural powers ("God is my co-pilot").

Clinical Research—**During World War II psychiatrists and psychologists treated and studied combat men under stress, such as flying personnel subjected to enemy flak.**

Whatever the nature of the efforts, they can be viewed as attempts to deal with the threatened loss of control or experience of helplessness. With prolonged stress, the development of almost any type of neurotic and psychosomatic (psychologically induced illness) reaction is possible. These reactions are grouped under the term *operational fatigue* and generally include a mixture of anxiety, depression, and psychosomatic reaction. The depression that is so common in such cases is associated with a sense of failure ("I've let my buddies down") and wounded pride. In sum, the main component of the anxiety is the sense of helplessness in the presence of a perceived danger. Prolonged stress of this sort leads to a psychological and physical breakdown expressed in a variety of neurotic reactions that are often accompanied by fatalism and depression.

These observations of Grinkler and Spiegel are interesting, not only in relation to stress and helplessness, but in relation to our understanding of depression as well. Note that they tie depression to prolonged stress, a sense of failure, and wounded pride. Bibring (1953) emphasizes similar factors in his clinical analysis of patient reports of depression as well as other naturally occurring phenomena. Thus, for example, he describes a patient who became depressed whenever his fear of remaining weak was aroused, another patient who became depressed when confronted with a power beyond her reach, and people who became psychologically depressed during the economic depression of the 1930s and the political crises prior to the Second World War. The common theme running throughout trivial and complicated cases of depression is, Bibring suggests, helplessness, a feeling of doom, and a blow to the person's self-esteem. Similarly, two psychiatrists studying suicidal ideation that precedes suicide attempts concluded that it "is associated with a person's feeling of being unable to alter his circumstances through his own actions and also by a narrowing of his span of awareness into the future. This suggests a hopeless, helpless, and narrowed view of the personal future" (Melges & Weisz, 1971, p. 249). These reports show striking similarities to the phenomena emphasized in the learned helplessness model of depression, though again no causal relationships are being established.

Observations of patient's responses to illness also illustrate this research approach to the study of stress. Individuals about to be examined by a physician are bothered by the uncertainty as to what will be found. During the examination they wonder and worry about each step in the examination and search for clues about what is going on. Psychologist Irving Janis has been interested in how people attempt to master stress. Among his many studies has been research on the responses of patients to long-term illness. Through observation and interview of cancer victims, he has developed some hypotheses concerning the process of the response to their form of stress. The typical process involves a sense of shock and numbness upon being informed of the bad news. Preoccupation with their "doomed" status may then alternate with blaming of others and denial of the implications of the fatal illness. Where a reasonably healthy process is in action, there follows a period of grieving or "working through" of the loss and a gradual readaptation to the life that remains.

Janis has been particularly concerned with the process of "working through" and the anticipatory preparation for the difficulties that will follow some painful event. In one of his early studies he compared the postoperative responses of three groups of patients: those who had extremely high preoperative fear, those who had moderate anticipatory fear, and those who had extremely low anticipatory fear. He found that people who were extremely fearful before the operation were more likely than others to be anxiety ridden after the operation. However, people who were not afraid before the operation had more than minimal distress after the operation. These individuals were found to be more likely than others to express extreme postoperative anger and resentment. The patients who expressed the least postoperative emotional disturbance were those who had displayed a moderate degree of preoperative fear. Janis' conclusion was that the arousal of anticipatory fear prior to confronting the actual stressful situation is necessary for effective psychological coping with stress. Such anticipatory fear and the "working through" process allow for mental rehearsal and inner preparation for the dangers that follow. Such rehearsal and preparation are valuable in precluding an overwhelming sense of helplessness when the full impact of the surgery and illness must be recognized. They are useful in making plans for future action which can greatly reduce feelings of helplessness. In contrast, the person who denies the threat and at first experiences little apparent stress may later experience rage and/or gloom as actual consequences are recognized: "Thus the work of worrying is conceived as increasing the level of tolerance for subsequent threat or danger stimuli. The more thorough the work of worrying, the more reality tested the person's self-delivered reassurances are likely be be and hence, the more emotional control he will have under conditions of subsequent danger or deprivation'' (Janis, 1965, p. 238). One implication is that preparatory communications to patients about to undergo stressful experiences are extremely important in the process of "emotional inoculation" against overwhelming stress.

To summarize the work of Grinker and Spiegel and that of Janis, we may note that in both cases there is the use of firsthand observation and interview material from individuals undergoing periods of extreme stress. Also, both sets of investigations have emphasized the process through which individuals attempt to cope with threat. Finally, in both cases there has been an emphasis on the person's efforts at control and responses to a perceived sense of helplessness.

GOALS OF RESEARCH: RELIABILITY AND VALIDITY

Until now, we have considered differing research traditions and alternative research approaches. At the same time, all research efforts share certain goals in common. Earlier we noted that our goal was to make meaningful observations that could be interpreted in a theoretical framework. At this point we can be more specific about the criteria we want to apply in evaluating our data. In research, we are seeking systematic observations that can be replicated and that relate to the concept of interest to us; that is, in research, we seek reliable and valid observations.

The concept of **reliability** relates to the extent to which our observations are stable, dependable, or can be replicated. There are many different kinds of reliability and many different factors may contribute to a lack of reliability. However, an essential in all scientific research is that other investigators be able to reproduce or replicate the observations reported by one investigator. We must have stable, consistent observations to even begin to make theoretical interpretations. What are some of the factors that might contribute to unreliable observations? On the subject side, if subject performance is greatly influenced in unsystematic ways by transient factors such as attitude or mood, then unreliable observations are likely. On the experimenter side, variations in instructions to subjects as well as in measuring or interpreting responses can lead to a lack of reliability. The particular basis for a lack of reliability can vary from research tradition to research tradition and from experiment to experiment. In general, however, a continuing problem for psychologists is that periodically we find that the same data are not obtained by other investigators. Again, for scientific research to be cumulative and of significance we must have reliable observations.

In addition to reliable observations, our data must be valid. The concept of **validity** relates to the extent to which our observations indeed reflect the phenomena or variables of interest to us. What use to us is it if we have reliable observations but they do not relate to what we think they do? Suppose, for example, that we have a reliable test for locus of control or attributional style but there is no evidence that the test measures what it purports to measure. Of what use is such a measure? Suppose we taken certain behaviors to be expressive of learned helplessness, but they reflect other phenomena. Of what use is such a measure? Problems such as this may seem trivial in some areas. For example, we know that a scale is both a reliable and a valid measure of weight, and we know that a ruler is both reliable and a valid measure of height. But how do we know that not solving certain problems is a measure of learned helplessness, that responses to the ASQ are indicative of attributional style, or that responses to the JAS are valid indicators of Type A behavior patterns? Indeed, it is not unusual for different tests or measures of the same concept not to agree with one another. In fact, the structured-interview measure of Type A behavior pattern and the JAS measure of this pattern agree with one another to a substantial, but by no means a perfect, extent. Which, then, is the true or valid measure of Type A behavior pattern? If there are two different measures of temperature, how can we know which is the true or valid measure? The answer is the measure that gives us the most reliable and theoretically useful results. If there are two different measures of a personality concept, how do we know which is the true or valid measure? Here too we would consider the reliability, meaningfulness, and usefulness of the observations. In sum, validity concerns the extent to which we can be sure that we are measuring the phenomena or variables of interest to us.

The complexities of psychological research are such that certain problems may enter that affect both the reliability and the validity of the data. As a human enterprise, research in personality lends itself to influences that are part of everyday interpersonal behavior. The investigation of such influences might be called the *social psychology of research*. Let us consider here two important illustrations. First, there may be factors influencing the behavior of human subjects that are not part of the experimental design. Among such factors may be cues implicit in the experimental setting which suggest to the subject that the experimenter has a certain hypothesis and, "in the interest of science," the subject behaves in a way that will confirm it. Such effects are known as **demand characteristics** and suggest that the psychological experiment is a form of social interaction in which subjects give purpose and meaning to things (Orne, 1962; Weber & Cook, 1972). The purpose and meaning given to the research may vary from subject to subject in ways that are not part of the experimental design and thereby serve to reduce both reliability and validity.

Complementing these sources of error or bias in the subject are unintended sources of influence or error in the experimenter. Without realizing it, experimenters may either make errors in recording and analyzing data or emit cues to the subjects and thus influence their behavior in a particular way. Such unintended **experimenter expectancy effects** may lead subjects to behave in accordance with the hypothesis (Rosenthal, 1964; Rosenthal & Rubin, 1978). For example, consider the classic case of Clever Hans (Pfungst, 1911). Hans was a horse who by tapping his foot could add, subtract, multiply, and divide. A mathematical problem would be presented to the horse and, incredibly enough, he was able to come up with the answer. In attempting to discover the secret of Hans' talents, a variety of situational factors were manipulated. If Hans could not see the questioner or if the questioner did not know the answer, Hans was not able to come up with the correct answer. On the other hand, if the questioner knew the answer and was visible, Hans could tap out the answer with his foot. Apparently the questioner unknowingly signaled Hans when to start and stop tapping his hoof. The tapping would start when the questioner inclined his head forward, increased in speed when the questioner bent forward more, and stop when the questioner straightened up.

To summarize the above discussion, we can say that in research we are interested in obtaining reliable, valid, and theoretically significant information. From this discussion, it should be clear that we can make reliable observations without their being valid but we cannot make valid observations that are unreliable. We can obtain theoretically inconsequential results that can be replicated and valid, but we cannot obtain theoretically significant results that cannot be confirmed by other investigators or do not appear to relate to what they are supposed to measure. Obtaining data that are reliable, valid, and theoretically meaningful are goals of all research efforts, and we shall keep them in mind as we consider the potential strengths and limitations of each of the approaches discussed thus far.

EVALUATING ALTERNATIVE RESEARCH TACTICS

Having considered the goals of all personality research, we are in a position to evaluate the three major research strategies. We shall see that as a consequence of proceeding along different lines, each tactic may be characterized as having strengths as well as potential limitations.

Laboratory, Experimental Research

In many ways, experimental laboratory research represents the scientific ideal. Ask people for their image of a scientist and they are likely to conjure up the image of a person in a white smock in a laboratory, clipboard in hand, noting meter readings of machines or making minor adjustments to a piece of apparatus. Much of the research in physics and biology, two or our most advanced sciences, would approximate this image. What is the basis for this? The strength of the experimental approach to research is the potential for careful manipulation of the variables of interest, the gathering of objective data free from biased or subjective interpretation, and the establishment of cause–effect relationships. In the experiment that is properly designed and carried out, every step is carefully planned to limit effects to the variables of interest. Few variables are studied so that there is not the problem of disentangling complex relationships. Systematic relationships between changes in some variables and consequences for other variables are established so that the experimenter can say: "If X, then Y." Full details of the experimental procedure are reported so that the results can be replicated by investigators in other laboratories.

Psychologists who are critical of laboratory research suggest that too often such research is artificial and limited in relevance to other contexts. The suggestion is that what works in the laboratory may not work elsewhere. Furthermore, although relationships between isolated variables may be established, such relationships may not hold when the complexity of actual human behavior is considered. And, since laboratory research tends to involve relatively brief exposures to stimuli, such research may miss important processes that occur over time. Finally, for all of its objectivity, experimental research lends itself to the problems of demand characteristics and experimenter expectancy effects. These criticisms are in addition, of course, to the potential limitation due to the fact that not all phenomena can be produced in the laboratory.

Many of these criticisms have themselves been attacked by experimental psychologists. In defending laboratory experiments, the following statements are made: (1) Such research is the proper basis for testing causal hypotheses. The generality of the established relationships is then a subject for further investigation. (2) Some phenomena would never be discovered outside of the laboratory. (3) Some phenomena can be studied in the laboratory that would be difficult to study elsewhere (e.g., subjects are given permission to be aggressive in contrast with the often quite strong restraints in natural social settings). (4) There is little empirical support for the contention that subjects typically try to confirm the experimenter's hypothesis or for the significance of experimental artifacts more generally. Indeed, many subjects are more negativistic than conformistic (Berkowitz & Donnerstein, 1982).

Correlational Research and Questionnaires

As previously noted, many of the strengths and limitations of the correlational approach are the opposite of those of experimental research. On the one hand, there may be the opportunity to study a broader range of variables; on the other, there is less control over the variables. Consider the use of personality questionnaires in correlational research, an instrument that in itself raises many new questions. First, many psychologists would question whether we can accept the subjects' responses to questionnaires as accurate statements of what the subjects feel and do. We shall give greater attention to this issue in the next section on clinical research. Second, responses to self-report questionnaires are susceptible to particular biases. Research suggests that subjects often respond to qualities in the questionnaire items other than content or that they have a consistent tendency to respond in one or another way to a test—a **response style**. Two illustrative response-style problems can be considered. The first has been called *acquiescence* and involves the tendency to agree or disagree with items regardless of their content. For example, subjects may have a preference for responses such as "Like" and "Agree" (yea-sayers) or for responses such as "Dislike" and "Disagree" (nay-sayers). The second illustrative potential for bias in response to questionnaires involves the *social desirability* of the items. Instead of responding to the intended psychological meaning of a test item, a subject may respond to it as suggesting a socially acceptable or a socially desirable personality characteristic.

Those who defend the use of questionnaires suggest that such problems and sources of bias can be remedied through careful test construction and interpretation. For example, testgivers suggest that questionnaire responses need not be considered as true or accurate reflections of the subject's feelings and behaviors but only that the resulting scores relate to phenomena of interest. Also, others suggest that by careful item writing one can remove the potential effects of biases such as acquiescence and social desirability. Finally, still others suggest that the test items or scales can be included to measure whether subjects are faking or trying to present themselves in a particularly favorable or socially desirable way. Although such safeguards may be possible, few of them appear in many personality questionnaires. Furthermore, even when a personality test is presented as having reasonable evidence of reliability and validity, it not infrequently gives results that do not agree with those from another equally well-structured test that is presumed to measure the same personality concept. Thus, for example, while the structured interview and JAS measures of Type A behavior pattern both have been used with some degree of success in research, scores on the two do not necessarily show perfect agreement with one another, and results from the use of one do not always match those associated with the use of the other. In sum, although personality questionnaires are attractive because they are easy to use and can get at many aspects of personality that would otherwise be difficult to study, the problems in establishing their reliability and validity are often substantial.

Naturalistic Observation and Clinical Research

The advantage of naturalistic observation is that one examines the behavior of interest directly and does not have to extrapolate from a somewhat artificial setting to the real world. Naturalistic observation is the only feasible means for the study of some phenomena (e.g., wartime stress), but many psychologists argue that this approach has special merit even when it is possible to study the phenomena of interest in the laboratory. Through naturalistic observation, it is argued, one can observe the full complexity of personality processes and individual–environment relationships. On the other hand, certain phenomena may be very rare or difficult to study in the natural environment and, even when such study is possible, it may be very difficult to disentangle the relationships among the variables. In addition, whenever observations are not made in an objective way, there is the problem of different observers reporting different observations. Insofar as researchers make observations on a subjective basis, they accumulate data that declines considerably in reliability and validity.

Clinical research brings with it its own set of potential strengths and limitations, depending on what is being investigated and how the research is conducted. Most generally, clinical research has the advantage of in-depth study of processes going on in one or a few individuals. Such individualistic or idiographic research has two main features that stand in contrast with research on groups (Pervin, 1983). First, relationships established for a group as a whole may not reflect the way any individual behaves or the way some groups of individuals behave. The average learning curve, for example, may not reflect the way any one individual learns. Second, by considering only group data one may miss some valuable insights into processes going on in particular individuals. Some time ago Henry Murray argued for the utility of individual as well as group studies as follows: "In lay words, the subjects who gave the majority response may have done so for different reasons. Furthermore, a statistical answer leaves unexplained the uncommon (exhibited-by-the-minority) response. One can only ignore it as an unhappy exception to the rule. Averages obliterate the 'individual characters of individual organisms' and so fail to reveal the complex interaction of forces which determine each concrete event" (1938, p. viii).

Clinical research in personality need not involve the use of verbal report by subjects, though clearly it often does. In such cases, we are confronted with special problems associated with such data. Treating what people say as accurate reflections of what has actually occurred or actually going on has come under attack from two very different groups. On the one hand, psychoanalysts and dynamically oriented psychologists (Chapters 3 and 4) argue that people not only consciously lie but often distort things for unconscious reasons: "Children perceive inaccurately, are very little conscious of their inner states and retain fallacious recollections of occurrences. Many adults are hardly better" (Murray, 1938, p. 15). On the other hand, many experimental psychologists argue that people do not have access to their internal processes and respond to interviewer questions in terms of some inferences they make about what must have been going on rather than accurately reporting what in fact occurred (Nisbett & Wilson, 1977; Wilson, Hull, & Johnson, 1981). For example, despite experimenter evidence that subjects make decisions in accord with certain experimental manipulations, the subjects themselves may report having behaved in a particular way for very different reasons. In sum, the argument is that whether for defensive reasons or because of "normal" problems people have in keeping track of their internal processes, verbal self-reports are questionable sources of reliable and valid data.

Other psychologists argue that verbal reports should be accepted for what they are—data (Ericsson & Simon, 1980). The argument is made that there is no intrinsic reason to treat verbal reports as any less useful data than an overt motor response such as pressing a lever. Indeed, it is possible to analyze the verbal responses of people in as objective, systematic, and quantitative a fashion as their other behavioral responses. If verbal responses are not automatically discounted, then the twofold question becomes: "Which kinds of verbal responses are most useful and trustworthy, and how should such data be analyzed?" Here the argument is made that subjects can only report about things they are attending to or have attended to. If the experimenter asks the subject to remember or explain things that were never attended to do in the first place, the subject will either make an inference about what occurred or state a hypothesis about what occurred (White, 1980). Thus, if you later ask persons why they purchased one product over another in the supermarket when they were not attending to this decision at the time, they will give you an inference or a hypothesis rather than an account of what occurred.

Those who argue in favor of the use of verbal reports suggest that when they are elicited with care and the circumstances involved are appreciated, they can be a useful source of information. Although, the term introspection (i.e., verbal descriptions of process going on inside a person) was long discredited by experimental psychologists, there is now increased interest in the potential utility of such data: "If introspective reports are sometimes wrong or misleading, there is equally compelling evidence that in some instances they may provide information of truly impressive accuracy and reliability (Lieberman, 1979, p. 319). In accepting the potential utility of verbal reports, we may expand the universe of potential for rich and meaningful observation. At the same time, we must keep in mind the goals and requirements of reliability and validity. Thus, we must insist on evidence that the same observations and interpretations can be made by other investigators and that the data do reflect the concepts they are presumed to measure. In appreciating the merits and vast potential of verbal reports, we must also be aware of the potential for misutilization and naive interpretation. In sum, verbal reports as data should be held up to the same scrutiny as other research observations.

Summary

In assessing these alternative research goals we must recognize that we are considering potential, not necessary, strengths and limitations (Figure 2.6). When it comes down to it, each research effort must be evaluated on its own merits and for its own potential in advancing understanding rather than on some preconceived bias. It is clear that alternative research procedures can be used in conjunction with one another in any single research enterprise. In addition, data from alternative research procedures can be integrated in the pursuit of a more comprehensive theory.

At the same time, it is clear that psychologists do have preferences and biases concerning how research should be conducted. For all of the objectivity of science, research is a very human enterprise. Furthermore, different research theories of personality often are linked with different research strategies and thereby with different kinds of data. The observations that led to one theory of personality often are different from those that led to another theory. And, the phenomena of interest to one theory of personality are not as easily studied by the research procedures useful in the study of phenomena emphasized by another theory of personality. Personality psychologists make theoretical decisions concerning *what* should be studied and decide upon research strategies for *how* these phenomena should be studied. The point here is important: often the *what* and the *how* are linked with one another, as well as with some aspects of the personality of the researcher. These linkages make one or another approach temperamentally more suitable and aesthetically more appealing. We shall want to keep these inevitable ties between theory and research in mind as we consider historical theories of personality as well as those that are current today. In future chapters we shall begin with those that rest on clinical procedures, progress to those that rely heavily upon the correlational tradition, and conclude with the most current approaches that depend primarily on the experimental tradition. Before beginning

FIGURE 2.6   **SUMMARY OF POTENTIAL STRENGTHS AND LIMITATIONS OF ALTERNATIVE RESEARCH METHODS**

POTENTIAL STRENGTHS	POTENTIAL LIMITATIONS

EXPERIMENTAL RESEARCH

Not on test (handwritten)

POTENTIAL STRENGTHS	POTENTIAL LIMITATIONS
1. Manipulates specific variables.	1. Excludes phenomena that can not be studied in the laboratory.
2. Records data objectively.	2. Creates artificial setting that limits generality of findings.
3. Establishes cause–effect relationships.	3. Fosters demand characteristics & experimenter expectancy effects.

CORRELATION RESEARCH AND QUESTIONNAIRES

POTENTIAL STRENGTHS	POTENTIAL LIMITATIONS
1. Study wide range of variables.	1. Establishes relationships that are associational rather than causal.
2. Study relationships among many variables.	2. Ignores problems of reliability & validity of self-report questionnaires.
3. Study individual differences.	

NATURALISTIC OBSERVATION AND CLINICAL RESEARCH

POTENTIAL STRENGTHS	POTENTIAL LIMITATIONS
1. Avoid artificiality of laboratory.	1. Lead to unsystematic observation.
2. Study full complexity of person–environment relationships.	2. Encourage subjective interpretation of data.
3. Lead to in-depth study of individuals.	3. Entangle relationships among variables.

4. CASE History (handwritten)

this exploration, however, let us turn to consider briefly the ethics of research and the place of research in public policy.

THE ETHICS OF RESEARCH AND PUBLIC POLICY

As a human enterprise, research involves ethical questions, not in terms of the questions we address but in terms of how we address these questions and report our results. Over the past two decades a number of studies have brought into sharp focus some of the issues involved. For example, in one research effort that won a prize from the American Association for the Advancement of Science, subjects were told to teach other subjects ("learners") a list of paired associate words and to punish them with an electric shock when an error was made (Milgram, 1965). The issue investigated was obedience to authority. While actual shock was not used, the subjects believed that it was being used and often "administered" high levels despite pleas from the "learners" that it was painful. In another research effort in which a prison environment was simulated, subjects took on the roles of guards and prisoners (Zimbardo, 1971). Subject "guards" were found to be verbally and physically aggressive to subject "prisoners" who allowed themselves to be treated in a dehumanized way. Finally, we are all probably aware of one behavior modification program or another that has been used to shape the behavior of children or patients without their consent or voluntary participation.

Such programs are dramatic in the issues they raise, but the underlying question concerning ethical principles of research is fundamental. Do experimenters have the right to require participation? To deceive subjects? What are the ethical responsibilities of researchers to subjects and to psychology as a science? The former has been an issue of concern to the American Psychological Association, and it has adopted a list of relevant ethical principles (*Ethical Principles of Psychologists*, 1981). The essence of these principles is that "the psychologist carries out the investigation with respect and concern for the dignity and welfare of the people who participate." This includes evaluating the ethical acceptability of the research, determining whether subjects in the study will be at risk in any way, and establishing a clear and fair agreement with research participants concerning the obligations and responsibilities of each. While the use of concealment or deception is recognized as necessary in some cases, strict guidelines are presented. It is recognized as the responsibility of the investigator to protect participants from physical and mental discomfort, harm, and danger.

The ethical responsibility of psychologists includes the interpretation and presentation of results as well as the conduct of the research. Of late there has been serious concern in science generally with "the spreading stain of fraud" (APA *Monitor*, 1982). Some concern with this issue began with charges that Sir Cyril Burt, a once prominent British psychologist, intentionally misrepresented data in his research on the inheritance of intelligence. In other fields of science there have been reports of investigators intentionally manipulating data so as to enhance their chances of publication, grant funding, promotion, and public recognition. Recently, there was an investigation of whether psychologists working in the area of alcoholism had intentionally misrepresented their data. The issue of fraud is one that scientists do not like to recognize or talk about because it goes against the very fabric of the scientific enterprise. Although fraudulent data and falsified conclusions are very rare the profession of psychologists is beginning to face up to their existence and to take constructive steps in solving the problem.

Much more subtle than fraud, and undoubtedly of much broader significance, is the issue of the effects of personal and social bias on the ways in which issues are developed and the kinds of data that are accepted as evidence in support for one or another enterprise (Pervin, 1984, Chapter 10). In considering sex differences, for example, to what extent are research projects developed in a way that is free from bias and to what extent is evidence for or against the existence of sex differences equally likely to be accepted? To what extent do our own social and political values influence not only what is studied but how it is studied and the kinds of conclusions we are prepared to reach (Bramel & Friend, 1981). As noted, while scientists make every effort to be objective and remove all possible sources of error and bias from their research, this remains a human enterprise with the potential for personal, social, cultural, and political influence.

Finally, we may note in a related way the role of research in the formulation of public policy. While still in an early stage of development as a science, psychology does relate to fundamental human concerns and psychologists are often called on to suggest the relevance of this research for public policy. This has happened with intelligence tests and immigration policy, child development and the effects of early enrichment programs such as Head Start, and the effects of television violence on aggression in everyday life. Recently, Seligman's work has been related to societal functioning, with the suggestion that some social programs may operate to increase learned helplessness.

For example, many Scandinavian countries have served as a model for social reform and social welfare. While praising these accomplishments, one Swedish psychologist has warned that a potential side-effect of overly extensive programs in this area may be the development of a broad learned helplessness phenomenon in the population (Magnusson, 1980, pp. 73–74). In sum, among the issues that concern us as researchers and as consumers of research is that of how the results may be interpreted to direct, support, or refute various social policies.

MAJOR CONCEPTS AND SUMMARY

experimental research

laboratory research

correlational research

learned helplessness

locus of control

Internal–External Scale

causal attribution: internal (personal) –external (universal), specific– global, stable–unstable

Attributional Style Questionnaire (ASQ)

~~Type A behavior pattern~~

Jenkins Activity Survey (JAS)

naturalistic observation

clinical research

reliability

validity

~~demand characteristics~~

experimenter expectancy effects

response style

This chapter has concerned itself with how psychologists conduct research on important personality phenomena. The goal of research is to establish facts and principles that can be interpreted within a broader theoretical framework. While sharing certain goals in research and certain standards for evaluating research, psychologists differ in the problems they choose for investigation and in the methods they favor in conducting research. Particular attention has been given to the distinction between two disciplines of scientific psychology—the experimental approach emphasizes consistent variation in behavior as a result of manipulations of situational conditions, the correlational approach emphasizes individual differences in response to the same situational conditions. One emphasizes variation in treatments, the other variation in people.

Discussion of the two disciplines and the potential utility of combining both approaches was followed by a more detailed analysis of the major alternative approaches to research. Three were emphasized: laboratory experimentation, correlational research using questionnaires, naturalistic observation and clinical research. All three were considered in relation to the concepts of stress, helplessness, and control.

Laboratory research involves the manipulation of specific variables and the ability to state if-then causal relationships. The research cited suggests that animals and people who experience conditions where events (reinforcements) are not contingent on their behavior are likely to develop feelings of helplessness and expect that they will be unable to influence the outcomes of events in the future. The expectation that outcomes are independent of responding is seen as having motivational, cognitive, and emotional implications. Also cited was research that demonstrated that stress (noise) may have effects on performance, once the stress is removed, even if there are no observable effects during the period of stress itself. Furthermore, the consequences of stress are influenced by the meanings a person attributes to the stress. If a person experiences a lack of control or sense of helplessness as a result of unpredictability, there will likely be negative behavioral aftereffects.

Work on the concept of locus of control illustrated the use of personality questionnaires in correlational research. The Internal-External Scale was developed to measure generalized expectancies concerning the control of reinforcers. Internals have a generalized belief in their ability to control events whereas externals believe in chance, luck, and fate. Individual differences in this generalized expectancy or belief have been found to be related to differences in effort on tasks, differences in anxiety and maladjustment, and differences in the attribution of blame for failure. It has been demonstrated that there is a relationship between external locus of control and the phenomenon of learned helplessness, both of which probably are related to the same causal factors.

The correlational approach to personality research was further illustrated in discussion of the reformulated model of learned helplessness. This model emphasizes the consequences of various causal attributions made by people: internal (personal)-external (universal), specific-global, stable-unstable. Research involving the Attributional Style Questionnaire (ASQ) suggests that internal (personal), global, and stable attributions have important implications for the development of depression. However, experimental studies of attribution and depression have not yet established a causal relation between the two.

A final illustration of the use of questionnaires in personality research involved discussion of the Type A behavior pattern, which follows from a link between a pattern of personality characteristics (competitive achievement striving, sense of time urgency, aggressiveness) and increased risk of heart disease. Relationships have been found between high scores on the Jenkins Activity Survey (JAS), designed to measure the Type A behavior pattern, and behaviors assumed to put the person at risk for coronary heart disease. One suggestion made is that such people are involved in a continual struggle to control the environment.

Naturalistic observation involves the study of phenomena as they occur naturally without any efforts on the part of the researcher to manipulate or control what occurs. Clinical research involves the intensive study of individuals. These approaches were illustrated in relation to the study of stress under conditions of war, in relation to clinical descriptions of patients treated for depression, as well as in observational studies of patient responses to illness. Clinical observations were also noted as important in the original description of the Type A behavior pattern.

All research shares the goals of reliability and validity—of obtaining observations that can be replicated and for which there is evidence of a clear relation to the phenomena of interest. All human psychological research may suffer from certain sources of potential error or bias, expressed most clearly in the concepts of demand characteristics and experimenter expectancy effects. Beyond this, however, alternative approaches to personality research can be seen to have specific potential strengths and limitations. Experimental research can be quite objective and useful in establishing cause–effect relationships, though often it sets limits on what can be observed and studied. Correlational research involving questionnaires facilitates the study of a wider range of variables, as well as interrelationships among many variables, but does not lead to the establishment of cause–effect relationships. In addition, self-report questionnaires are subject to particular sources of error and bias. Naturalistic observation and clinical research facilitate investigation of the full complexity of human functioning in the real world, but are subject to the problems of unsystematic observation and subjective interpretation. Thus, alternative strategies to research are available that include within them the potential for particular insights as well as for particular pitfalls.

As a human enterprise, research involves ethical questions concerning the treatment of subjects and the reporting of data. The latter becomes particularly important as findings from psychological research begin to have an impact on public policy.

As we move now to consideration of specific theories of personality, we will have a chance to consider the application of these alternative research strategies and the implications that follow for the observation and conceptualization of personality.

Vigeland, Gustav. *The Family*. Granite in the Vigeland Sculpture Park, Oslo, Norway.

A PSYCHODYNAMIC THEORY: FREUD'S PSYCHOANALYTIC THEORY OF PERSONALITY

CHAPTER FOCUS: In this chapter we consider psychoanalytic theory as illustrative of a psychodynamic, clinical approach to personality. The psychodynamic emphasis is clear in the interpretation of behavior as a result of the interplay among motives, drives, needs, and conflicts. The clinical qualities are apparent in the emphasis on the individual, in the attention given to individual differences, and in attempts to assess and understand the total individual. The research consists mainly of clinical investigation.

It seems like an empty wrangle over words to argue whether mental life is to be regarded as co-extensive with consciousness or whether it may be said to stretch beyond this limit, and yet I can assure you that the acceptance of unconscious mental processes represents a decisive step toward a new orientation in the world and in science.

Freud, 1924. p. 26

The first personality theory to be considered is that of psychoanalysis. The psychoanalytic theory of Freud is reviewed because of its prominence in the culture of our society, its place in the history of psychology, and its importance as a model of a psychodynamic theory of personality. Psychoanalysis has reflected changing values in our society and has itself played a role in the changing of these values. As noted by Norman O. Brown: "It is a shattering experience for anyone seriously committed to the Western tradition of morality and rationality to take a steadfast, unflinching look at what Freud has to say. It is humiliating to be compelled to admit the grossly seamy side of so many grand ideals . . . To experience Freud is to partake a second time of the forbidden fruit" (1959, p. xi). Freud astutely observed that there had been three hurts to human self-love and self-image—the discovery by Copernicus that the earth was not the center of the universe, the discovery by Darwin that we do not exist independent of other members of the animal kingdom, and the discovery by Freud of the degree to which we are "influenced" by unknown, unconscious, and at times uncontrollable forces.

Psychoanalytic theory was derived from intensive work with individuals and, in turn, was applied to individuals. Although it involves assumptions relevant to all people, psychoanalytic theory has particular relevance to the study of individual differences as well as the total functioning of individuals. Furthermore, psychoanalysis exemplifies a psychodynamic theory in that it gives a prominent role to the complex interplay among forces in human behavior. In psychoanalytic theory, behavior is a result of struggles and compromises among motives, drives, needs, and conflicts. Behavior can express a motive directly or in a subtle, disguised way. The same behavior can satisfy different motives in different people, or a variety of motives in one person. For example, eating can satisfy a hunger need but it also can symbolically satisfy a need for love; or being a psychoanalyst can satisfy a need to help others, a wish to discover new aspects of psychological functioning, a wish to satisfy one's curiosity about the private lives of others, or some combination of these as well as other motives. Being a doctor can satisfy a need to help others as well as serve as a way of overcoming anxieties about illness and bodily harm. Thus, any behavior or goal can satisfy a variety of motives at the same time. It is this quality of behavior that forms a major aspect of a psychodynamic theory of personality. "Only when we have begun to understand the subtle interweaving of themes, the 'overdetermination' of any single act, belief, or fantasy, and the multiple functions that every dream, wish, action, and philosophy serves, do we begin to understand something of the individual" (Keniston, 1965, p. 49). Finally, behavior occurs at different levels of awareness, with individuals more or less aware of the forces behind their various behaviors. "The deeper we probe in our study of mental processes, the more we become aware of the richness and complexity of their content. Many simple formulas which seemed to us at first to meet the case turned out later to be inadequate. We are incessantly altering and improving them" (Freud, 1933, p. 121).

In this chapter we shall be analyzing and assessing a theory that is significant in its emphasis on individual differences, the entire personality, behavior as the result of an interplay among forces, personality as involving hierarchical organization, and phenomena as "simple" as the slip of the tongue and as "complex" as the development of culture. To increase the breadth and depth of our perspective, we shall turn our attention first to the life of the individual primarily responsible for psychoanalytic theory, and then to the view of the person and science implicit in his theory. Along with its usefulness for putting psychoanalytic theory into personal and historical perspective, a reading of the biography of Freud (Jones, 1953, 1955, 1957) gives one a sense of the genius and courage of the man responsible for the theory.

SIGMUND FREUD (1856–1939): A VIEW OF THE THEORIST

Sigmund Freud was born in Austria in 1856. He was the first child of his parents; although his father, 20 years older than his mother, had two sons by a previous marriage. His birth was followed by the birth and early death of one sibling and the birth of six more siblings. He is described as having been his mother's favorite and later was to say that "a man who has been the indisputable favorite of his mother keeps for life the feeling of a conqueror, that confidence of success that often induces real success" (Freud, 1900, p. 26). As a boy, he had dreams of becoming a great general or minister of state, but, being Jewish, he was concerned about anti-Semitism in these fields. This led him to consider medicine as a profession. As a medical student (1873–1881), he came under the influence of the noted physiologist Ernst Brücke. Brücke viewed humans in terms of a dynamic physiological system in which they are controlled by the physical principles of the conservation of energy. This view of physiological functioning was the foundation for Freud's dynamic view of psychological functioning (Sulloway, 1979).

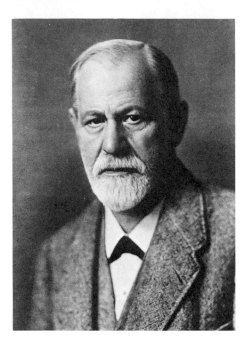

Sigmund Freud

After obtaining his medical degree, Freud did research and practiced in the field of neurology. Some of his early research involved a comparison of adult and fetal brains. He concluded that the earliest structures persist and are never buried, a view that was paralleled later by his views concerning the development of personality. Professionally, the years after medical school were filled first with theory and research, but then, for financial reasons, there was a turn toward practice. Personally, Freud experienced periodic depressions and attacks of anxiety, occasionally using cocaine to calm the agitation and dispel the depression. During these years he married and had three daughters and three sons. Throughout the later years of the nineteenth century, Freud was concerned about money. He also was subjected to incapacitating spells of migraine. In 1886 he spent a year with the French psychiatrist Jean Charcot, who was having some success in treating neurotic patients with hypnosis. While not satisfied with the effects of hypnosis, Freud was stimulated and excited by the thinking of Charcot and, essentially, changed during this time from a neurologist to a psychopathologist. Jones, the biographer of Freud, comments on Freud's development at this time. "All this work would have established Freud as a first class neurologist, a hard worker, a close thinker, but—with the exception perhaps of the book on aphasia—there was little to foretell the existence of genius" (1953, p. 220).

In 1897, the year following his father's death, Freud began his self-analysis. He continued to be bothered by periods of depression and, while intellectual pursuits helped to distract him from his pain, he looked for answers in his unconscious;

"My recovery can only come through work in the unconscious; I cannot manage with conscious efforts alone." For the rest of his life he continued self-analysis, devoting the last half hour of the working day to it. In the 1890s, he tried a variety of therapeutic techniques with his patients. First he used hypnotic suggestion as practiced by Charcot. Then he tried a concentration technique in which he pressed his hand upon the patient's head and urged the recall of memories. During these years he also collaborated with the Viennese physician Joseph Breuer, learning from him the technique of **catharsis** (a release and freeing of emotion through talking about one's problems) and collaborating with him on a book *Studies in Hysteria.* At this point, already in his forties, Freud had developed little, if any, of what was later to become known as psychoanalysis. Furthermore, his judgments of himself and of his work parallel the comment made by his biographer Jones. "I have restricted capacities or talents. None at all for the natural sciences; nothing for mathematics; nothing for anything quantitative. But what I have, of a very restricted nature, is probably very intense."

The momentum in Freud's work and thinking most clearly dates back to his self-analysis and to the beginnings, in 1896, of his use of the **free-association** method with his patients. This method of allowing all thoughts to come forth without inhibition or falsification of any kind resulted, in 1900, in what many still consider to be Freud's most significant work, *The Interpretation of Dreams.* In this book, Freud began to develop his theory of the mind and, although only 600 copies were sold in the first eight years after publication, he began to develop a following. In 1902, a Psychoanalytic Society was formed, and was joined by a number of people who went on to become outstanding psychoanalysts—Alfred Adler, Paul Federn, Otto Rank, and Sandor Ferenczi. Freud's writing and development of theory progressed, but with increased public attention, there was increased public abuse. In 1904, Freud wrote on the *Psychopathology of Everyday Life,* and in 1905 he published *Three Essays on the Theory of Sexuality.* The latter presented Freud's views on infantile sexuality and its relation to perversions and neuroses. This resulted in ridicule of Freud, who was seen as an evil and wicked man with an obscene mind. Medical institutions were boycotted for tolerating Freud's view; an early follower, Ernest Jones, was forced to resign his neurological appointment for inquiring into the sexual life of his patients.

Freud's ideas at this time were still primitive compared to the elaborate theoretical network he was to develop but he had already recognized the importance of the unconscious and of infantile sexuality, and made them the groundwork for future developments. In 1909 Freud was invited by G. Stanley Hall to give a series of lectures at Clark University in Worcester, Massachusetts. During this period, Freud was developing his theories of development and infantile fantasies, his theory of the principles of mental functioning, and his views concerning the psychoanalytic process. He had by now achieved sufficient fame and acceptance to have a waiting list of patients.

But Freud had problems, too. By 1919 he had lost all of his savings in the war. In 1920, a daughter, age 26, died. Perhaps of greatest significance was his fear for the lives of two sons who were in the war. It is out of such a historical context that Freud in 1920, at age 64, developed his theory of the death instinct—a wish to die, which is in opposition to the life instinct, or wish for survival. At this time he also developed his theory of group behavior, involving the common identification of members of a group with the leader.

Just as the war appeared to influence his thinking, so apparently did the growth of anti-Semitism during the 1930s. In 1932, for example, the Nazis in Berlin made a bonfire of his books. Shortly thereafter, Freud published his book on *Moses and Monotheism,* in which he suggested that Moses was an Egyptian noble who joined the Jews and gave them a religion. Freud attributed anti-Semitism to resentment against the strict moral code of the Jews and, in this book, appeared to say that it was not a Jew but an Egyptian who bears the onus. In this book Freud also presented some of his views concerning Christianity.

Freud died on September 26, 1939, at the age of 83. Almost to the very end, he was doing analysis daily and continuing his writing. The last 20 years of his life represent a remarkable period of personal courage and productivity. Earlier, it had taken a great deal of courage to go on with his work in spite of considerable attack from the public and his medical colleagues. During this later period, it took considerable courage to go on in spite of the loss of many of his disciples, and in spite of the brutality of the Nazis. During these later years, Freud continued to work despite extreme physical discomfort and pain, including 33 operations for cancer of the jaw. While not a wealthy man, he turned down lucrative offers that he felt would jeopardize the proper stature of his work. In 1920, he refused an offer from *Cosmopolitan* magazine to write on topics such as "The Husband's Place in the Home," saying to the magazine: "Had I taken into account the considerations that influence your edition from the beginning of my career, I am sure I should not have become known at all, either in America or Europe." In 1924 he turned down an offer of $100,000 by Samuel Goldwyn to collaborate in making films of famous love stories.

Most of what we now recognize as the major elements in Freud's theory were developed during these last 20 years. It was during these later years that Freud developed his final ideas concerning civilization, neuroses, psychoses, and perhaps most significant of all, his theory of anxiety and the mechanisms of defense. As a man he was glorified by some as being compassionate, courageous, and a genius. Others take note of his many battles and breaks with colleagues, of his eagerness to defend the "quasi-political" and "quasi-religious" character of the psychoanalytic movement, and see in him a rigid authoritarian, intolerant of the opinions of others, and eager to "be the Moses who showed the human race the promised land" (Fromm, 1959). Whatever the interpretation of Freud's personality, most, if not all, would agree that he had a passionate thirst for truth and pursued his studies with tremendous courage and integrity. Finally, most students of Freud, and psychoanalysis, would agree that factors in Freud's personal life and related historical factors (for example, the Victorian era, World War I, and anti-Semitism) played a part in the final formulation of his theory and in the development of the psychoanalytic movement.

FREUD'S VIEW OF THE PERSON AND SOCIETY

Notwithstanding Freud's statements to the contrary, it can be argued that implicit in psychoanalysis is a view of the person, a view of society, perhaps even a total Weltanschauung or philosophy of life. While Freud struggled to develop a theory based on science rather than philosophy, a theory free of biases from his personal life and the historical period of which he was a part, psychoanalytic theory reflects the themes that were current in the lay and scientific communities of late nineteenth- early twentieth-century Europe. Freud's theory was based on observations, but these were primarily observations of middle- and upper-class patients of a Victorian era, and observations by investigators trained to view phenomena in preconceived ways.

What is at the heart of the psychoanalytic view of the person is that the human is an energy system. There is the sense of a system in which energy flows, gets sidetracked, or becomes dammed-up. In all, there is a limited amount of energy, and if it gets used in one way, there is that much less energy to be used in another way. The energy that is used for cultural purposes, is withdrawn from the energy available for sexual purposes, and vice versa. If the energy is blocked from one channel of expression, it finds another, generally along the path of least resistance. Human behavior may take many forms, but basically all behavior is reducible to common forms of energy. The goal of all behavior is **pleasure**, that is, the reduction of tension or the release of energy.

Why the assumption of an energy model concerning human behavior? Whatever its scientific merits, the assumption is traceable to the excitement physical scientists were then experiencing in the field of energy dynamics. According to the nineteenth-century physicist Helmholtz's principle of the conservation of energy, matter and energy can be transformed but not destroyed. Not only physicists but members of other disciplines were studying intensively the laws of energy changes in a system. As was already noted, while in medical school Freud came under the influence of the physiologist Brücke. Brücke viewed humans as moved by forces according to the principle of the conservation of energy, a view apparently translated by Freud into the psychological realm of behavior. As Hall (1954) notes, the age of energy and dynamics provided scientists with a new conception of humans, "the view that man is an energy system and that he obeys the same physical laws which regulate the soap bubble and the movement of the planets" (pp. 12–13).

Beyond the view of the person as being an energy system, there is the view that humans, like other animals, are driven by sexual and aggressive instincts or drives. Freud's view of the importance of aggression in human behavior was based on observation, but his interpretation of these observations had the definite quality of a philosophical view. For example, in *Civilization and Its Discontents* (1930), Freud commented as follows. "The bit of truth behind all this—one so eagerly denied—is that men are not gentle, friendly creatures wishing for love, who simply defend themselves if they are attacked, but that a powerful measure of desire for aggression has to be reckoned as a part of their instinctual endowment" (p. 85). Freud goes on to comment that the instinct of aggression lies "at the bottom of all relations of affection and love between human beings—possibly with the single exception of that of a mother to her male child'' (p. 89). We have already noted that Freud published his theory of aggression and the death instinct in 1920, after the extended and bloody period of the First World War.

Along with the aggressive drive, Freud placed great emphasis on the sexual drive, and on the conflict between expression of these drives and society. The emphasis on sexual inhibition in particular, and the inhibition of the expression of instincts in general, appears to relate to the Victorian period of which Freud and his patients were a part. For Freud, the person in pursuit of pleasure was in conflict with society and civilization. People function according to the **pleasure principle**, seeking ''unbridled gratification'' of all desires. Yet, such a mode of operation runs counter to the demands of society and the external world. The energy that would otherwise be released in the pursuit of pleasure and gratification must now be restricted, inhibited, and channeled to conform to the aims of society. ''It is impossible to ignore the extent to which civilization is built up on renunciation of instinctual gratifications . . . This 'cultural privation' dominates the whole field of social relations between human beings; we know already that it is the cause of the antagonism against which all civilization has to fight . . . What he [Man] employs for cultural purposes he withdraws to a great extent from women and his sexual life'' (Freud, 1930, p. 63, p. 73). Freud believed that scientific activities, artistic endeavors, in fact the whole range of cultural productivity, are expressions of sexual and aggressive energy that is prevented from expression in a more direct way.

While such accomplishments represent one outgrowth of the conflict between the instinctual energies of the individual and society's restrictions on the possibilities for gratification, another outgrowth of this conflict is misery and neurosis. In fact, according to Freud, the price of progress in civilization is misery, the forfeiting of happiness, and a heightened sense of guilt. It is even worth the possibility of giving up civilization and returning to primitive conditions!

We can see, then, that beyond the formal conceptualization of a theory of personality, there is implicit in psychoanalysis a view of the person. According to this view humans, like other animals, are driven by instincts or drives and operate in the pursuit of pleasure. People operate as an energy system, building, storing, and releasing, in one form or another, what is basically the same energy. There are no mystical phenomena, no chance behaviors, since all behaviors are determined in the same sense that the behavior of molecules is determined. Not only is all behavior determined, but much of our behavior is determined by forces outside of awareness. ''It [psychoanalysis] has furthermore taught us that our intellect is a feeble and dependent thing, a plaything and tool of our impulses and emotions; that all of us are forced to behave cleverly or stupidly according as our attitudes and inner resistances ordain'' (Freud, quoted by Jones, 1955, p. 368). In the end, psychoanalysis sides with the instincts and seeks a reduction in the extent to which the instincts are frustrated. In sum, the person is an energy system, driven by sexual and aggressive drives and operating in the pursuit of pleasure (tension reduction), functioning in a regular, lawful way, but often unaware of the forces determining behavior, and basically in conflict with society's restrictions on the expressions of the instincts. Although the formal aspects of psychoanalytic theory went through many changes and revisions, the underlying philosophy remained implicit in each phase of Freud's development of the theory.

FREUD'S VIEW OF SCIENCE, THEORY, AND RESEARCH METHODS

It is important to note that in spite of the attention we have given to the philosophical view of the person implicit in psychoanalytic theory, Freud himself disclaimed any relationship between psychoanalysis and philosophy. Freud found the philosopher's thinking too far removed from the rigors of science and viewed psychoanalysis as a branch of psychology and a part of science.

We know that Freud was trained in the techniques of medical research, and that he was aware of issues concerning the definition of concepts and the formulation of a theory. He appreciated the beauty of science, and had a sense of the back-and-forth process between theory and research. Freud felt that the scientific task is the formulation of hypotheses which lead to observations that bring order and clarity into phenomena. He felt a need for sharp definition of concepts, but he also accepted the possibility that vague conceptions and speculative theory might be necessary during the early stages of an empirical science. Thus, Freud could insist on the importance of the instincts while calling them "mythical beings, superb in their indefiniteness." Freud argued for the utility of concepts that appear to organize empirical observations, even if it is not always possible to demonstrate the truthfulness of the concepts.

> *The true beginning of scientific activity consists rather in describing phenomena and then in proceeding to group, classify, and correlate them. Even at the stage of description it is not possible to avoid applying certain abstract ideas to the material at hand . . . They [the concepts] must at first necessarily possess some measure of uncertainty; there can be no question of any clear delimitation of their content . . . It is only after more searching investigation of the field in question that we are able to formulate with increased clarity the scientific concepts underlying it, and progressively so to modify these concepts so that they become widely applicable and at the same time consistent logically.*
>
> Freud, 1915, pp. 60–61

Although he developed an elaborate theory of personality, Freud's major contribution was in the nature of the observations he made. He was aware that theories could and would change, and he saw these observations as the ultimate contribution of psychoanalysis to the science of psychology, as they related particularly to the functioning of the unconscious. It is important to note that Freud's observations were based on the analysis of patients and, by and large, he had little use for mechanical efforts to verify psychoanalytic principles in the laboratory. When Rosenzweig (1941) wrote to Freud to tell him of his experimental studies of one psychoanalytic concept, Freud wrote back that psychoanalytic concepts were based on a wealth of reliable observations and thus were not in need of independent experimental verification. He was satisfied using the intensive clinical study of the individual case as his major research method.

In analyzing their patients, analysts work as scientists. They have expectations, but they allow the data to come forth. They record many pieces of data that do not appear to fit together and formulate principles to order and organize the data. These principles are then checked against the further observations that are made in the course of the analysis. Observations of one patient are checked against those of another patient, and observations by one analyst are checked against those by another analyst. On a broader scale, observations from work with patients are then checked against cultural documents such as folk tales, rituals, and taboos, and against observations from psychological tests administered to large groups of subjects.

It is debatable whether this approach is merely superficially related to the scientific method or is indeed a close approximation of it. It is clear that this research method allows for the accumulation of considerable data about an individual. There is probably no other method in psychology that even approximates the wealth of material gathered about a single person by the psychoanalyst. On the other hand, as Freud himself pointed out, analysts are unlike other scientists in that they do not use experiments as a significant part of their research. This gap, between the types of observations made by analysts and those made during controlled experiments, has narrowed as experimentally oriented psychologists have become interested in psychoanalysis. While Freud viewed psychoanalysis as a part of the science of psychology, most of the early research was conducted by medical professionals in a therapeutic setting. It is only within the last 20 to 30 years that psychologists have tried to apply the traditional scientific techniques of the discipline to the concepts of psychoanalysis. As we consider psychoanalytic concepts, we shall continue to see this struggle between the complex, uncontrolled observations of the clinical setting and the systematic, controlled study of phenomena in the laboratory.

PSYCHOANALYSIS: A THEORY OF PERSONALITY

Psychoanalysis is three things—a theory of personality, a method of therapy, and a technique for research. It is important to keep these different aspects in mind, since comments and criticisms appropriate to one may not be relevant to the other. For example, criticism of psychoanalysis as a therapy does not reflect on psychoanalysis as a theory, unless the theory is being tested in the course of therapy. The improvement of a patient in therapy is not critical to the theory, unless the theory makes specific predictions concerning the progress of the patient. Since therapy is such a complex process, and the nature of environmental events outside of therapy can never be predicted, the theory is rarely used to make predictions concerning the outcome of therapy. While keeping these aspects separate, however, we must also seek to see the links between them. We must seek to understand the relationships among theory, assessment, and research. At the heart of the psychoanalytic theory we shall find an emphasis on the following concepts: psychological determinism, the unconscious, behavior as goal directed and expressive of an interplay among forces (dynamics), and behavior as an outgrowth of events that occurred in the past of the individual (genetic approach).

Structure

What are the structural units used by psychoanalytic theory to account for human behavior? Included here are Freud's concepts of the unconscious, the preconscious, and the conscious, as descriptive qualities of mental life. In the early development of the theory the concept of levels of consciousness served as a focal point in psychoanalytic thinking. In fact, Freud claimed that "Psychoanalysis aims at and achieves nothing more than the discovery of the unconscious in mental life" (1924, p. 397).

Levels of Consciousness

According to the psychoanalytic theory, psychic life can be described in terms of the degree to which we are aware of phenomena: the **conscious** relates to phenomena we are aware of at any given moment, the **preconscious** to phenomena we are able to be aware of if we attend to them, and the **unconscious** to phenomena that we are unaware of, and *cannot* become aware of except under special circumstances.

Although Freud was not the first to pay attention to the importance of the unconscious, he was the first to explore in detail the qualities of unconscious life and attribute major importance to them in our daily lives. Through the analysis of dreams, slips of the tongue, neuroses, psychoses, works of art, and rituals, Freud attempted to understand the properties of the unconscious and to delineate its importance in behavior. What he found was a quality of psychic life in which nothing was impossible. The unconscious is alogical (opposites can stand for the same thing), is disregarding of time (events of different periods may coexist), and is disregarding of space (size and distance relationships are neglected so that large things fit into small things and distant places are brought together). One is reminded of William James's reference to the world of the newly born infant as a "big blooming buzzing confusion."

Within the unconscious, there is a fluidity and plasticity to phenomena that is rarely observed during our rational, waking life. It is in the dream, and in the psychic productions of psychotics, that the working of the unconscious become most apparent. Here we are exposed to the world of symbols, where many ideas may be telescoped into a single word, where a part of any object may stand for many things. It is through the process of symbolization that a penis can be represented by a snake or nose, a woman by a church, chapel, or boat, and an engulfing mother by an octopus. It is through this process that we are allowed to think of writing as a sexual act—the pen is the male organ, the paper the woman who receives, the ink (the semen) which flows out in the quick up and down movements of the pen (Groddeck, 1923). Groddeck, who, in *The Book of the It,* gives many fascinating examples of the workings of the unconscious, offers the following as an example of the functioning of the unconscious in his own life.

> *I cannot recall her [my nurse's] appearance. I know nothing more than her name, Bertha, the shining one. But I have a clear recollection of the day she went away. As a parting present she gave me a copper three-pfennig piece. A Dreier . . . Since that day I have been pursued by the number three. Words like trinity, triangle, triple alliance, convey something disreputable to me, and not merely the words but the ideas attached to them, yes, and the whole complex of ideas built up around them by the capricious brain of a child. For this reason, the Holy Ghost, as the Third Person of the Trinity, was already suspect to me in early childhood; trigonometry was a plague in my school days . . . Yes, three is a sort of fatal number for me.*

Groddeck, 1923, p. 9

The unconscious is never observed directly. What evidence then is there that supports the concept of the unconscious? Here we must first turn to the question of definition. As with many psychoanalytic concepts, alternative definitions are possible and disagreement may exist as to just what are the critical elements (Erdelyi & Goldberg, 1979). Such matters of definition are important because they influence decisions concerning whether evidence supports the validity of the concept. For example, some might consider as evidence of the unconscious our being influenced by information and processes of which we are unaware. Some might consider findings that "forgotten" memories can be recalled as evidence of the unconscious while others might insist on evidence concerning the influence of motives or drives of which the person is unaware as critical. Finally, some might insist that there must be evidence of some barrier against something becoming conscious before one can speak of unconscious functioning as opposed to preconscious functioning.

Let us consider the range of evidence that might be considered supportive of the concept of the unconscious, beginning with Freud's clinical observations. Freud realized the importance of the unconscious after observing hypnotic phenomena. As is well known, people under the effects of hypnosis can recall things they previously could not. Furthermore, they will perform things under posthypnotic suggestion without consciously "knowing" that they are behaving in accordance with that suggestion; that is, in the latter case, they will fully believe that what they are doing is voluntary and independent of any suggestion by another person. When Freud discarded the technique of hypnosis and continued with his therapeutic work, he found that often patients would become aware of memories and wishes or motives of which they previously had been unaware. Frequently, such discoveries were associated with considerable painful emotion. It is indeed a powerful clinical observation to see a patient suddenly experience tremendous anxiety, sob hysterically, or break into a rage as they recall a forgotten event or get in touch with a forbidden feeling. Thus, it was clinical observations such as these that suggested to Freud that the unconscious includes memories and wishes that not only are not currently part of our consciousness but are "deliberately buried" in our unconscious.

What of experimental evidence? A review of the relevant literature suggests that there is considerable evidence both for perception without awareness and for the role of psychodynamic factors in influencing what becomes conscious (Dixon, 1981). Let us consider the evidence for unconscious perception or **perception without awareness** wherein "the brain responds to stimuli of which the mind remains oblivious" (Dixon, 1981, p. 17). There is considerable evidence that people are influenced by factors of which they are unaware and that often they will inaccurately report the reasons for their having done something (Nisbett & Wilson, 1977). For example, we may think that we selected a new product in the grocery store because of the brand name whereas research evidence may indicate that its location and packaging design were the critical determinants. Indeed, the packaging and advertising industries are masters at emphasizing important determinants of behavior of which people may be unaware. Such evidence, however, does not directly establish that something has been perceived and influences behavior but cannot be reported. Can the person "know" something without knowing that they know it? There is considerable research evidence that this is indeed the case. Thus, for example, people can have emotional responses conditioned to sounds they cannot report hearing and may be influenced by messages going into one ear that they cannot report hearing because they are attending to messages in another ear.

Perhaps the easiest way to understand what otherwise may seem like a mystical process is to describe a piece of relevant research. This research may be seen as part of the area of subliminal stimulation or the registration of stimuli at a threshold or level that is below that required for awareness. In this research each of two groups of subjects was exposed to a picture. The two pictures used, one for each group, are presented in Figure 3.1. How similar do the two seem? Is there a significant difference? Perhaps in this case it is obvious that the one on the right contains a duck image shaped by the branches of the tree. However, in the actual research each group of subjects was shown the picture at a rapid speed so that it was barely visible. This was done through the use of a tachistoscope, an apparatus that allows the experimenter to show stimuli to subjects at very fast speeds, so they cannot be perceived, or at slow speeds. Once the picture had been shown the subjects closed their eyes and imagined a nature scene. They then drew the scene and labeled the parts. Would the two groups, those seeing the picture in Figure 3.1 on the left and those seeing the one on the right, draw different pictures? It was found that more of the subjects viewing the picture on the right had duck-related images ("duck, "water," "birds," "feathers") in their drawings; and as a group, they had significantly more such images than did subjects in the group viewing the picture on the left. Was this because of differences in what could be reported as having been perceived? The subjects did not report seeing the duck during the experiment and the majority even had trouble finding it when they were asked to look for it. The conclusion drawn was that stimuli that are not consciously perceived may still influence the imagery and thoughts of people (Eagle, Wolitzky, & Klein, 1966).

The fact that people can perceive and be influenced by stimuli of which they are unaware does not in itself suggest that there are psychodynamic or motivational forces involved. Is there evidence that such is or can be the case? Two relevant lines of research can be noted. The first has been called **perceptual defense** and involves a process by which the individual defends against the anxiety that accompanies actual recognition of a threatening stimulus. In a relevant early experiment, subjects were shown two types of words in a tachistoscope: neutral words such as apple, dance, child and emotionally toned words such as rape, whore, penis. The words were shown first at very fast speeds and then at progressively slower speeds. A record was made of the point at which the subjects were able to identify each of the words and their sweat-gland activity (a measure of tension) in response to each word. These records indicated that subjects took longer to rec-

FIGURE 3.1   The Concept of the Unconscious. (Eagle, Wolitzky, and Klein, 1966, p. 838)

ognize the emotionally toned words than the neutral words and that they showed signs of emotional response to the emotionally toned words prior to their being verbally identified (McGinnies, 1949). Despite criticism of such research (e.g., Did subjects identify the emotionally toned words earlier but were they reluctant to verbalize them to the experimenter?), there appears to be considerable evidence that people can, outside of awareness, be selectively responsive to and rejecting of specific emotional stimuli (Erdelyi & Goldberg, 1979; Tyrer, Lewis, & Lee, 1978).

A related line of research has been called **subliminal psychodynamic activation** (Silverman, 1976; 1982). In this research, there is an effort to stimulate unconscious wishes without making them conscious. In general, the experimental procedure involves using a tachistoscope to show subjects material related to wishes that are expected to be either threatening or anxiety alleviating to them and then observing whether the expected effects do occur. In the first case, the material being presented subliminally (below threshold for conscious recognition) is expected to stir up unconscious conflict and thus increase psychological disturbance. In the latter case, the material being presented subliminally is expected to diminish unconscious conflict and thus decrease psychological disturbance. For example, the content "I Am Losing Mommy" might be upsetting to some subjects whereas the content "Mommy and I Are One" might be reassuring. In a series of studies, Silverman and his colleagues have demonstrated that such subliminal psychodynamic activation effects can be produced. What is key here is that the content that is upsetting or relieving to various groups of subjects is predicted beforehand on the basis of psychoanalytic theory and that the effects only occur when the stimuli are perceived subliminally or unconsciously.

The research on perceptual defense and subliminal psychodynamic activation has been proclaimed by some as conclusive experimental evidence in support of the importance of psychodynamic, motivational factors in determining what is "deposited into" and "kept in" the unconscious (Dixon, 1981). On the other hand, the experiments have frequently been criticized on methodological grounds and at times some of the effects have been difficult to replicate or reproduce in other laboratories (Condon & Allen, 1980; Heilbrun, 1980, 1982; Oliver & Burkham, 1982). Almost all psychologists, whether psychoanalytic or otherwise, would agree at this point that unconscious processes are important in influencing what we attend to and how we feel (Glucksberg, 1982; Posner, 1981). One recent review goes so far as to suggest that "no psychological model that seeks to explain how human beings know, learn, or behave can ignore the concept of unconscious psychological processes" (Shevrin & Dickman, 1981, p. 432). What remains in need of further exploration, however, is the role of specific motivations and conflicts in keeping memories and feelings outside of awareness.

In a sense, psychology has come a long way in taking what Freud described as a decisive step towards a new orientation in the world and in science. At the same time, it should be clear that not all psychologists agree to the importance given by Freud to the unconscious.

It is hard to overestimate the importance of the concept of the unconscious to psychoanalytic theory, the moral dilemmas over responsibility that have occurred as a result of it, and the difficulties it has presented to scientists interested in rigorous, controlled investigation. Clearly, acceptance of this concept represents more than just acceptance of the principle that there are aspects of our functioning of which we are not fully aware. Far more than this, the psychoanalytic concept of the unconscious suggests that a significant portion of our behavior, perhaps the major one, is determined by unconscious forces, and that much of our psychic energy is devoted either to finding acceptable expression of unconscious ideas or to keeping them unconscious. The concept of the unconscious is deeply embedded in the rest of psychoanalytic theory. Although many new concepts were added as the theory developed, the concept of the unconscious has always remained as part of the framework for the entire theory.

Id, Ego, and Superego

In 1923 Freud developed a more formal structural model for psychoanalysis, defined by the concepts of id, ego, and superego, which refer to different aspects of people's functioning. According to the theory, the **id** represents the biological substratum of humans, the source of all drive energy. the energy for a person's functioning originally resides in the life and death, or sexual and aggressive instincts, which are part of the id. In its functioning, the id seeks the release of excitation, tension, and energy. It operates according to the **pleasure principle**—the pursuit of pleasure and the avoidance of pain. In operating this way the id seeks immediate, total release. It has qualities of a spoiled child: it wants what it wants when it wants it. The id cannot tolerate frustration and is free of inhibitions. It shows no regard for reality and can seek satisfaction through action or through imagining that it has gotten what it wants—the fantasy of gratification is as good as the actual gratification. It is without reason, logic, values, morals, or ethics. In sum, the id is demanding, impulsive, blind, irrational, asocial, selfish and, finally, pleasure loving.

In marked contrast to the id is the **superego** which represents the moral branch of our functioning, containing the ideals we strive for and the punishments (guilt) we expect when we have gone against our ethical code. This structure functions to control behavior in accordance with the rules of society, offering rewards (pride, self-love) for "good" behavior and punishments (guilt, feelings of inferiority, accidents) for "bad" behavior. The superego may function on a very primitive level, being relatively incapable of reality testing, that is, incapable of modifying its action depending on circumstances. In such cases, the person is unable to distinguish between thought and action, feeling guilty for thinking something even if it did not lead to action. Furthermore, the individual is bound by black–white, all–none judgments and by the pursuit of perfection. Excessive use of words such as good, bad, judgment, and trial are often expressive of a strict superego. But the superego can also be understanding and flexible. For example, people may be able to forgive themselves or someone else if it is clear that something was an accident or done under circumstances of severe stress. In the course of development, children learn to make such important distinctions and see things not only in all-or-none, right-or-wrong, black-or-white terms.

The third structure conceptualized in the theory is that of the **ego**. Whereas the id seeks pleasure and the superego seeks perfection, the ego seeks reality. The function of the ego is to express and satisfy the desires of the id in accordance with reality and the demands of the superego. Whereas the id operates according to the pleasure principle, the ego operates according to the **reality principle**—gratification of the instincts is delayed until an optimum time when the most pleasure can be obtained with the least pain or negative consequences. According to the reality principle, the energy of the id may be blocked, diverted, or released gradually, all in accordance with the demands of reality and the conscience. Such an operation is not in contradiction to the pleasure principle but, rather, represents a temporary suspension of it. It functions, in George Bernard Shaw's words, so as, "to be able to choose the line of greatest advantage instead of yielding in the direction of least resistance." The ego is able to separate wish from fantasy, can tolerate tension and compromise, and changes over time. Accordingly, it expresses the development of perceptual and cognitive skills, the ability to perceive more and think in more complex terms. For example, the person can begin to think in terms of the future and what is best in the long run. All of these qualities are in contrast with the unrealistic, unchanging, demanding qualities of the id.

In comparison with his investigations into the unconscious and the workings of the id, Freud did relatively little work on the functioning of the ego. He pictured the ego as a weak structure, a poor creature that owed service to three harsh mas-

"Double Scotches for me and my super-ego, and a glass of water for my id, which is driving."

Psychoanalytic Theory—**Freud emphasized the concepts of id, ego, and superego as structures of personality.** Drawing by Handelsman; © 1972 The New Yorker Magazine, Inc.

ters—the id, reality, and the superego. The "poor" ego has a hard time serving these masters and must reconcile the claims and demands of each. Of particular significance is the relation of the ego to the tyranny of the id.

> *One might compare the relation of the ego to the id with that between a rider and his horse. The horse provides the locomotive energy, and the rider has the prerogative of determining the goal and of guiding the movements of his powerful mount towards it. But all too often in the relations between the ego and the id we find a picture of the less ideal situation in which the rider is obliged to guide his horse in the direction in which it itself wants to go.*

Freud, 1933, p. 108

In sum, Freud's ego is logical, rational, tolerant of tension, the "executive" of personality, but it is a poor rider on the swift horse of the id and is subject to control by three masters.

Just before his death Freud began to give more attention to the importance of the ego in personality. This attention was then developed by his daughter, Anna Freud, and a number of analysts whose work has been categorized under the heading of ego psychology. Whereas in the earlier view the ego was viewed as existing without energy of its own and obliged to guide the id where it wanted to go, the later view emphasized the importance of the ego in conflict resolution as well as in adaptation. This view left room for the possibility that the individual may experience pleasure through the conflict-free functioning of the ego, and not only through the release of the energies of the id. According to ego psychology, the ego has a source of energy of its own and takes pleasure in mastery of the environment. This concept is related to White's (1959) concept of competence motivation. In its description of personality, this view gave increased importance to the ways in which individuals actively engage their environment and to their modes of thinking and perceiving. While these modes still could be considered as functioning in the service of the id and serving to reduce conflict, they were now viewed as having adaptive functions and importance independent of these other functions. The importance for research of such a change in view will become apparent as we discuss the dynamics (processes) of functioning in the next section.

It is important to understand the status of the concepts used by the theory. The concepts of conscious, unconscious, id, ego, superego are at a high level of abstraction and are not always defined with great precision. For example, the unconscious is at times taken to mean a structure, at times refers to forces pushing toward expression in consciousness and behavior, and at times refers to descriptive properties of psychic phenomena. Furthermore, there is some lack of clarity because the meaning of some concepts changed as the theory developed, but the exact nature of the change in meaning was never spelled out (Madison, 1961). Finally, it should be clear that these are conceptualizations of phenomena. While the language is picturesque and concrete, we must avoid regarding concepts as real things. There is no energy plant inside us with a little person controlling its power. We do not "have" an id, ego, superego but, according to the theory, there are qualities of human behavior that are usefully conceptualized in these structural terms. The structures achieve greater definition in relation to the processes implied in them, and it is to these processes that we now turn.

Process

Life and Death Instincts

We have discussed Freud's view of the person as an energy system obeying the same laws as other energy systems. Energy may be altered and transformed but essentially it is all the same energy. Within such an overall framework, the processes (dynamics) involved in psychoanalytic theory relate to the ways in which energy develops and is expressed, blocked, or transformed in some way. According to the theory, the source of all psychic energy lies in states of excitation within the body which seek expression and tension reduction. These states are called **instincts**, or **drives**, and represent constant, inescapable forces. In the earlier view, there were ego instincts, relating to tendencies toward self-preservation, and sexual instincts, relating to tendencies toward preservation of the race. In the later view, there was the **life instinct**, including both of the earlier ego and sexual instincts, and the **death instinct**, involving an aim on the part of the organism to die or return to an inorganic state. The energy of the life instinct was called **libido**. No name has come to be commonly associated with the energy of the death instinct. In fact, the death instinct remains one of the most controversial and least-accepted parts of the theory, with most analysts instead referring to the **aggressive instinct**. Both sexual and aggressive instincts are viewed as being part of the id.

In psychoanalytic theory, the instincts are characterized as aiming toward the immediate reduction of tension, toward satisfaction and pleasure. They are gratified by means of external stimuli or objects. In contrast to lower animals, the objects for humans that are capable of gratifying an instinct are many and varied. This provides for uniqueness in personality. Furthermore, in humans the instincts can be delayed and modified before they are released.

In the dynamics of functioning, what can happen to one's instincts? They can, at least temporarily, be blocked from expression or expressed without modification. More likely is some change in the quality or direction of the instinct. For example, there may be partial (aim-inhibited) satisfaction of the instincts, in which case there is partial rather than full expression of the instinct. Affection may be a partial, aim-inhibited expression of the sexual instinct, and sarcasm an expression of the aggressive instinct. It is also possible for the object of gratification of the instinct to be changed or *displaced* from the original object to another object. Thus, the love of one's mother may be displaced to the wife, kids, or dog. Each instinct may be transformed or modified, and the instincts can combine with one another. Football, for example, can gratify both sexual and aggressive instincts; in surgery there can be the fusion of love and destruction. It should already be clear how psychoanalytic theory is able to account for so much behavior on the basis of only two instincts. It is the fluid, mobile, changing qualities of the instincts and their many alternative kinds of gratification that allows for such variability in behavior. In essence, the same instinct can be gratified in a number of ways, and the same behavior can have different causes in different people or multiple gratifications for any one individual.

Virtually every process in psychoanalytic theory can be described in terms of the expenditure of energy in an object (cathexis) or in terms of a force inhibiting the expenditure of energy, that is, inhibiting gratification of an instinct (anti-cathexis). Because it involves an expenditure of energy, people who direct much of their efforts toward inhibition end up feeling tired and bored. The interplay between the expression of instincts and their inhibition, between cathexis and anticathexis, forms the foundation of the dynamic aspects of psychoanalytic theory. The key to this is the concept of **anxiety**. In psychoanalytic theory, anxiety is a painful, emotional experience, representing a threat or danger to the organism. In a state of "free-floating" anxiety, individuals are unable to relate their state of tension to an external object, in contrast to a state of fear, where the source of tension is known. Freud had two theories of anxiety. In the first theory, anxiety was viewed as a result of undischarged sexual impulses—dammed-up libido. In the later theory, anxiety represented a painful emotion that acted as a signal of impending danger to the ego. Here, anxiety, an ego function, alerts the ego to danger so that it can act.

The psychoanalytic theory of anxiety states that at some point the organism experiences a trauma, an incident of considerable harm or injury. Anxiety represents a repetition of the earlier traumatic experience, but in miniature form. Anxiety in the present, then, is related to an earlier danger. It is because the earlier trauma is not recalled that anxiety has its free-floating quality. The sources of anxiety may reside in the id, in the superego, or in reality. Where the id is the source of anxiety, the individual feels threatened with being overwhelmed by impulses. Where the superego is the source of anxiety, the individual experiences guilt and self-condemnation. It is as if the id says "I want it," the superego says "How terrible," and the ego says "I'm afraid." Basically, anxiety develops out of a conflict between the push of the id instincts and the threat of punishment by the superego.

Anxiety and the Mechanisms of Defense

Anxiety is such a painful state that we are incapable of tolerating it for very long. How is it that that we are able to deal with such a state? Why are we not anxious more of the time? The answer is that individuals develop **defense mechanisms** against anxiety. Unconsciously, we develop ways to distort reality and exclude feelings from awareness so that we do not feel anxious. What are some of the ways in which this can be done? One of the most primitive defense mechanisms is **projection**. In projection, what is internal and unacceptable is projected out and seen as external. Rather than recognize hostility in oneself, the individual sees others as being hostile. There is in this process a fluidity of boundaries, or a breakdown in the differentiation between what is self and what is other.

In a relevant experimental study, Sears (1936) investigated the degree to which subjects possessed traits such as stinginess, obstinacy, disorderliness, and bashfulness, whether the subjects had insight into their possession of the traits, and the degree to which they attributed the traits to others. He found that subjects who lacked insight into their possession of a trait tended to attribute a greater amount of the trait to others than did subjects who possessed an equal amount of the trait but had insight into this. Furthermore, subjects who lacked insight into their own possession of unacceptable traits gave more extreme ratings on the trait to others and considered the traits to be more unacceptable than did subjects who had insight.

Efforts to produce projection experimentally have been more problematic (Holmes, 1978, 1981). In a semi-experimental study Halpern (1977) tested the psychoanalytic hypothesis that defensive subjects would respond to threat by projecting feared characteristics on to disliked others. First, a measure of sexual defensiveness was obtained by scoring the number of times the subject agreed with questionnaire items such as "I never have sexual fantasies" and "I never have dreams with sexual content." Subjects were thereby divided into a high-defensive group and a low-defensive group. Members of each group were then exposed to one of two conditions. In one, subjects were exposed to pornographic photographs. Presumably such stimuli would be threatening to the high sexual defense group and provide the conditions for projection. In the other group, subjects received no stimuli of a sexual nature. Following this, all subjects were asked to rate the most unfavorable person seen in the photographs as well as themselves on a list of traits.

How might projection appear and where? The trait lustful was selected as key with the expectation that high-defensive subjects would project this trait onto the unfavorable person when they had been stimulated in the nude photograph condition. Indeed, sexually defensive subjects who viewed the nude photographs rated the unfavorable person highest on lustful whereas the nondefensive subjects who viewed the nude photographs gave this person the lowest lustful ratings. In both conditions, the high-defensive subjects rated themselves lower on the trait lustful than did the low-defensive subjects. The study is noteworthy in demonstrating that certain conditions were required for projection to occur. In addition, the study recognized that according to psychoanalytic theory people will project only those traits or motives they are seeking to defend against and will associate these characteristics with an unfavorable person; that is, *projection as a defense is only used in relation to specific characteristics, under particular conditions, and in relation to specific others.* Unfortunately, many research studies are not so careful in their definition and exploration of this mechanism of defense. As is often the case in relation to experimental investigation of psychoanalytic phenomena, alternative interpretations of the literature are possible. Thus, Sherwood (1981) concludes that there is strong research support for the existence of projection whereas Holmes (1981) concludes that such evidence does not exist. In relation to the above study, for example, Holmes questions the validity of the scale measuring sexual defensiveness and whether the subjects were indeed aroused by the nude photographs.

A second defense mechanism is that of **denial**. Here there may be either denial of reality, as in the girl who denies she lacks a penis or in the boy who in fantasy denies the lack of power, or denial of impulse, as when an irate person protests "I do not feel angry." The saying "Thou doth protest too much" gives specific reference to this defense. Denial of reality is commonly seen where people attempt to avoid recognizing the extent of a threat. The expression "Oh no!" upon hearing of the death of a close friend represents the reflex action of denial. Children have been known to deny the death of a loved animal and long afterwards to behave as if it were still alive. Denial of reality is also seen when people say, or assume, "It can't happen to me" in spite of clear evidence of impending doom. This defense was seen in Jews who were victims of the Nazis. Steiner (1966), in his book on the Nazi concentration camp Treblinka, describes how the population acted as if death did not exist, in spite of clear evidence to the contrary all around them. He notes that the extermination of a whole people was so unimaginable that the people could not accept it. They preferred to accept lies rather than to bear the terrible trauma of the truth.

Another way to deal with anxiety and threat is to isolate events in memory or to isolate emotion from the content of a memory or impulse. In **isolation**, the impulse, thought, or act is not denied access to consciousness, but it is denied the normal accompanying emotion. For example, a woman may experience the thought or fantasy of strangling her child without any associated feelings of anger. The result of using the mechanism of isolation is *intellectualization*, an emphasis on thought over emotion and feeling, and the development of logic-tight compartments. In such cases, the feelings that do exist may be split, as in the case where a male separates women into two categories, one with whom there is love but no sex and the other with whom there is sex but no love (Madonna–prostitute complex).

People who use the mechanism of isolation also often use the mechanism of **undoing**. Here, the individual magically undoes one act or wish with another act. "It is a kind of negative magic in which the individual's second act abrogates or nullifies the first, in such a manner that it is as though neither had taken place, whereas in reality both have done so" (Freud, 1936, p. 33). This mechanism is seen in compulsive acts in which the person has an unresistible impulse to perform some act (e.g., the person undoes a suicide or homicide fantasy by compulsively turning off the gas jets at home), in religious rituals, and in children's sayings such as "Don't step on the crack or you will break your mother's back."

In **reaction-formation**, the individual defends against expression of an unacceptable impulse by only recognizing and expressing its opposite. This defense is evident in socially desirable behavior that is rigid, exaggerated, and inappropriate. The person who uses reaction-formation can not admit to other feelings, as in overprotective mothers who cannot allow any conscious hostility toward their children. Reaction-formation is most clearly observable when the defense

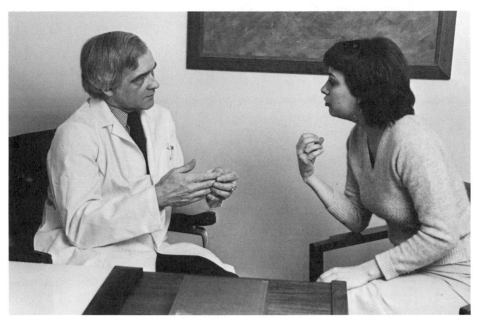

Denial—**How much information is useful to the patient?**

breaks down, as when the good, model boy shoots his parents, or when the man who "wouldn't hurt a fly" goes on a killing rampage. Of similar interest here are the occasional reports of judges who go on to commit crimes.

A mechanism often familiar to students is that of **rationalization**. Here an action is perceived, but the underlying motive is not. Behavior is reinterpreted so that it appears reasonable and acceptable. What is of particular interest about rationalization is that with this defense the individual can express the dangerous impulse, seemingly without it being frowned on by the superego. Some of the greatest atrocities of humankind have been committed in the name of the Christian God of love. The leaders of the Inquisition tortured persons who were without a "proper" attitude toward Christ. It is through the defense of rationalization that we can be hostile while expressing God's will, that we can be immoral in the pursuit of morality.

Finally, we come to the major primary defense mechanism, **repression.** In repression, a thought, idea, or wish is dismissed from consciousness. It is as if we say, "What we don't know or remember can't hurt us." Repression is viewed as playing a part in all of the other defense mechanisms and, like these other defenses, requires a constant expenditure of energy to keep that which is dangerous outside of consciousness. There has been more experimental research on repression than on any other defense mechanism and perhaps more than on any other single concept in psychoanalytic theory. An early study in this area was that by Rosenzweig (1941), in which he found that when they were personally involved with the experiment a group of Harvard undergraduates recalled a larger propor-

CURRENT APPLICATIONS AND IMPLICATIONS

Denial—Healthy Or Sick? Adaptive Or Maladaptive?

Should we avoid self-deception? Is knowing all there is to know a sign of health? Psychoanalysts generally assume that while the mechanisms of defense are useful in reducing anxiety, they also are maladaptive in turning the person away from reality. For example, consider the potentially damaging effects of denial. A person who denies threatening signs may not be in a position to respond adaptively. Thus, women who discover a lump in their breast and delay going to a doctor because of denial of the possible seriousness of the lump may seriously reduce the chances of surgical success. Or, men who deny the symptoms of a heart attack and continue to exercise or climb stairs may turn out to have made a fatal mistake.

However, there is evidence that denial and self-deception can also be constructive and adaptive. Take, for example, the person who has had a severe, incapacitating illness such as polio or cancer. Denial and self-deception can provide temporary relief from the emotional trauma and help the person to avoid being overwhelmed by anxiety, depression, or anger. Defensive processes can then facilitate optimism, and thereby allow constructive participation in rehabilitative efforts. In this case, denial as a coping process can be adaptive. It can be good for your health!

What sense can one make out of this conflicting evidence? The suggestion has been made that denial generally is maladaptive where it interferes with action that might otherwise improve the person's condition. However, denial generally is adaptive where action is impossible or irrelevant and where excessive emotion may interfere with recuperative efforts. And should the doctor tell all to the patient? Evidently this depends not only on the above, but also on the patient's personality. Some people seek out information and function best when they are fully informed. On the other hand, other people avoid information and function best when they know only what is essential. In other words, denial may or may not be adaptive depending on the circumstances involved, and information may or may not be helpful depending on the person's coping style.

SOURCES: Lazarus, 1983; S. M. Miller and C. E. Mangan, 1983.

tion of tasks that they had been able to complete than tasks they had been unable to complete. When the students did not feel threatened, they remembered more of the uncompleted tasks.

In considering the status of the concept of repression, we return in many ways to issues considered in relation to the concept of the unconscious, which is not surprising since the two are linked so closely. In a plea that we not sweep repression under the rug, Erdelyi and Goldberg (1979) have given an enlightening discussion of the problems in defining the concept and in demonstrating related phenomena in the laboratory. Consideration begins with a quote from Dostoyevsky's *Notes from Underground:*

> *Every man has reminiscences which he would not tell to everyone but only to his friends. He has other matters in his mind which he would not reveal even to his friends, but only to himself, and that in secret. But there are other things which a man is afraid to tell even to himself, and every decent man has a number of such things stored away in his mind.*

In terms of research, they suggest that there is considerable evidence that events or memories apparently hopelessly forgotten can be recovered into consciousness (Erdelyi, 1981). What is more difficult to demonstrate in the laboratory is the defensive function of repression, that is the effort to keep ideas repressed from consciousness so as to minimize psychological pain. However, rather than arguing that a lack of experimental evidence should lead us to discard the concept, they concern themselves instead with the limitations of laboratory efforts to produce the complex phenomena. In a telling discussion of the results of clinical and laboratory data, it is suggested that "the two approaches have had palpably different yields. Such differences, we believe, reflect inherent differences in the two approaches, not some peculiar inconstancy of the phenomenon itself. The genius of the clinical approach is its ability to reveal truly complex cognitive processes. . . . From the clinical standpoint, the evidence for repression is overwhelming and obvious. The weakness of the clinical approach, on the other hand, is its looseness of method . . . the strength of the laboratory-experimental approach, unlike the clinical, is its methodological vigor; its overriding weakness is its inability to deal with truly complex processes'' (Erdelyi & Goldberg, 1979, pp. 383–384).

Although these authors are critical of mainstream cognitive psychology for ignoring repression, there is evidence of growing interest in it and related phenomena. Noteworthy here is Bower's (1981) work on mood or **state-dependent memory.** Bower describes anecdotal and clinical evidence suggesting that sometimes people can recall events experienced while in a certain mood only when they are again experiencing that mood. In contrast, they will be unable to recall events experienced in a particular state if their state at attempted recall is different from or incongruent with the original state: "Memories acquired in one state are accessible mainly to that state but are 'dissociated' or *not available for recall* in an alternate state. It is as though the two states constitute different libraries into which a person places memory records, and a given memory record can be retrieved only by returning to the library, or physiological state, in which the event was first stored'' (Bower, 1981, p. 130).

In an effort to produce and study state-dependent learning in the laboratory, Bower and his colleagues used hypnosis to induce moods in their subjects. Once a mood had been induced, the subjects were given some tasks involving learning and recall. In one experiment hypnotized subjects were given a list of words to learn while happy and one to learn while sad. They then were tested for recall while in the same or opposite mood. The data clearly indicated that recall was better for the same-mood list than for the opposite-mood list. In another experiment, subjects recorded emotional events in a daily diary for a week. A week later they were hypnotized with half the subjects put in a pleasant mood and the remaining half put in an unpleasant mood. They were then asked to recall all the events they could from those recorded in their diary the week before. As expected, the subjects recalled a greater percentage of their pleasant experiences when they were in an induced pleasant mood and a greater percentage of their unpleasant experiences when they were in a congruent unpleasant mood (Figure 3.2). Finally, in another experiment, subjects were asked to recall childhood events while in either a happy mood or a sad mood. The following day, while in a neutral mood, subjects rated the recalled childhood incidents as pleasant, unpleasant, or neutral. Again, a mood–state-dependent memory effect was found—happy subjects retrieved more pleasant than unpleasant memories whereas the reverse was true for sad subjects (Figure 3.2).

What are the implications of such research for the concept of repression and the experimental study of psychoanalytic phenomena? It is clear that Bower is not studying repression directly. However, it also is clear that Bower has been impressed with and influenced by clinical descriptions of amnesia and repression. Second, while acknowledging criticism of cognitive psychologists for ignoring the role of emotion and motivation in thinking and memory, Bower argues that it is possible to study such important phenomena experimentally: "Perhaps that is as

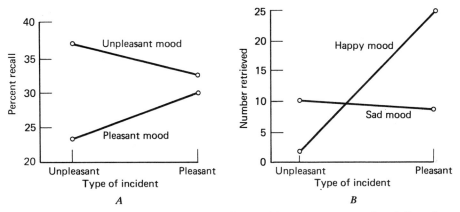

FIGURE 3.2   Mood and Memory. *A*. Percentage recall of incidents from an emotional diary depending on whether the incident was pleasant or unpleasant and whether the subject was in a pleasant or unpleasant mood during recall. *B*. Number of pleasant and unpleasant childhood incidents when the recaller was in a happy or sad mood. (Bower, 1981, p. 133)

it should be—theories developed in one field aiding our understanding of phenomena from another field. Certainly it is the goal of all basic science'' (p. 147).

Before ending this discussion of the defenses, it is important to note one further device that is used to express an impulse free of anxiety. This mechanism, of considerable social importance, is that of **sublimation.** In sublimation, the original object of gratification is replaced by a higher cultural goal, one further removed from direct expression of the instinct. Whereas the other defense mechanisms meet the instincts head on and, by and large, prevent discharge, in sublimation the instinct is turned into a new and useful channel. In contrast to the other defense mechanisms, here the ego does not have to maintain a constant energy output to prevent discharge. Freud interpreted DaVinci's Madonna as a sublimation of his longing for his mother. Becoming a surgeon, butcher, or boxer can represent sublimations, to a greater or lesser degree, of aggressive impulses. Being a psychiatrist can represent a sublimation of ''peeping tom'' tendencies. In all, as noted, Freud felt that the essence of civilization is contained in a person's ability to sublimate sexual and aggressive energies.

Growth and Development

The psychoanalytic theory of development takes into consideration the development of structures, of thinking processes, of the instincts, and in relation to all of these, the development of character (personality). There are two major aspects to the theory of development. The first is that the individual progresses through stages of development that are rooted in the biological processes of the organism. The second, the genetic approach, emphasizes the importance of early events for all later behavior. An extreme psychoanalytic position would go so far as to say that the most significant aspects of later personality have been formed by the end of the first five years of life.

The Development of Thinking Processes

The psychoanalytic theory of the development of thinking processes focuses on the change from **primary process** thinking to **secondary process** thinking. The primary process is the language of the unconscious, in which reality and fantasy are indistinguishable. The secondary process is the language of consciousness, of learning, thinking, remembering, and reality testing. Parallel to this is the development of the ego and, later, that of the superego. With the development of the ego, the individual becomes more differentiated, as a self, from the rest of the world. There is a decrease in self-preoccupation, an increase in motor ability, an increase in the use of language, and a greater ability to anticipate events and to delay gratification. The development of a healthy superego is reflected in an integrated, conflict-free set of values, an ability to accept blows to the self-esteem (to accept limitations without withdrawal into fantasy), and a sense of pride in accomplishment.

Sublimation—**In performing surgery, aggressive impulses can be turned toward useful, constructive ends.**

The Development of the Instincts

The most significant part of the psychoanalytic theory of development concerns the development of the instincts. The source of the instincts is in states of bodily tension, which tend to focus on certain regions of the body, called **erogenous zones**. According to the theory, there is a biologically determined development of, and change in, the major erogenous zones of the body. Although many erogenous zones may be active at any one time, the major source of excitation and energy tends to focus on a particular zone, with the location of that zone changing during the early developmental years. The first erogenous zone is the mouth, the second the anus and the third the genitals. The mental and emotional growth of the child are dependent on the social interactions, anxieties, and gratifications that occur in relation to these zones.

Stages of development   The first major areas of excitation, sensitivity, and energy is the mouth. It is this locus of excitation that leads to the name **oral stage**. Early oral gratification occurs in feeding, thumbsucking, and other mouth movements characteristic of infants. In adult life, traces of orality are seen in chewing gum, eating, smoking, and kissing. In the early part of the oral stage the child is passive and receptive. In the late oral stage, with the development of teeth, there can be a fusion of sexual and aggressive pleasures. In children, such a fusion of instinctual gratification is seen in the eating of animal crackers. Other evidence of such a fusion can be seen in cannibalism and in the religious communion ceremony. Five modes of functioning are possible during the oral stage, and these serve as models for dealing with later situations. These modes are taking in and swallowing, holding on, biting, spitting out, and closed mouth. In later life, we see traces of orality in various spheres. For example, academic pursuits can have oral associations within the unconscious—one is given "food for thought," asked to "incorporate" material in reading, and "regurgitate" what has been learned on exams.

In the second stage of development, the **anal stage** (ages two and three), there is excitation in the anus and in the movement of feces through the anal passageway. The expulsion of the feces is believed to bring relief from tension and pleasure in the stimulation of the mucous membranes in that region. The pleasure related to this erogenous zone involves the organism in three types of conflict. First, there is the instinctual conflict between elimination and retention. Second, there is the conflict between the instinctual pleasure in release and the ego attempts at control. And, third, there is the conflict between the wish for instinctual pleasure in evacuation and the demands of the external world for delay. This third conflict, which provides the basis for the structural conflict between id and ego, represents the first crucial conflict between the individual and society. Here the environment requires the child to violate the pleasure principle or be punished. External displeasure causes internal displeasure. The child may retaliate against such demands by intentional soiling (diarrhea); associate having bowel movements with losing something important, which leads to depression; or associate having bowel movements with giving a prize or gift to others, which may be associated with feelings of power and control.

In the **phallic stage** (ages four and five), excitation and tension come to focus in the genitals. The biological differentiation between the sexes leads to psychological differentiation. The male child develops erections, and the new excitations in this area lead to increased interest in the genitals and the realization that the female lacks the penis. This leads to the fear that he may lose his penis—**castration anxiety**. The father becomes a rival for the affections of the mother, suggestion to which is given in the song "I Want a Girl Just Like The Girl That Married Dear Old Dad." The boy's hostility toward the father is projected onto the father with the consequent fear of retaliation. This leads to what is known as the **Oedipus complex**. According to the Oedipus complex, every boy is fated to kill his father in fantasy and marry his mother. The complex can be heightened by actual seductiveness on the part of the mother. Castration anxiety can be heightened by actual threats from the father to cut off the penis. These threats occur in a surprising number of cases!

For an interesting illustration of an effort at experimental testing of the concept of the Oedipus complex, we can return to the subliminal psychodynamic activation research discussed in relation to the concept of the unconscious. In this research stimuli are presented to subjects subliminally in a tachistoscope. When certain stimuli register subliminally, they activate, it is presumed, unconscious conflicts and either intensify or alleviate these conflicts, depending on the nature of the conflict and the stimulus presented. The point of the current experiment was to manipulate the degree of oedipal conflict in males and to observe the effects on their performance in a competitive situation (Silverman, Ross, Adler, & Lustig, 1978). The stimuli chosen to intensify or alleviate oedipal conflict were *Beating Dad Is Wrong* and *Beating Dad is OK*. In addition, a number of other stimuli were presented including the neutral stimulus *People Are Walking*. These stimuli were presented tachistoscopically to male college students after they engaged in dart-throwing competition. The subjects were again tested for dart-throwing performance following exposure subliminally to each of the stimuli. As expected, the two oedipal stimuli had clear-cut effects in different directions. The *Beating Dad Is OK* stimulus was followed by significantly higher scores than those following the neutral stimulus while the *Beating Dad Is Wrong* stimulus was followed by significantly lower scores than those following the neutral stimulus (Figure 3.3).

What is interesting about his research is that while the theoretical formulation was derived from clinical material with patients, the experimental testing involved normal college males. The assumption of the experimenters was that "since most persons are vulnerable to some degree of neurotic behavior and since, according to psychoanalytic understanding, oedipal conflict often plays a central pathogenic role, we anticipated that the clinically based relationship might apply to a 'normal' college population" (p. 342). Two additional points are worthy of note since there have been difficulties in replicating this type of research. First, the results were not obtained when the stimuli were presented above threshold. The psychodynamic activation effects appear to operate at the unconscious rather than the conscious level. Second, the authors emphasize that the experimental stimuli must relate to the motivational state of the subjects and the response measured must be sensitive to changes in this motivational state. Thus, in the experiment above, subjects were first "primed" with picture and story material containing oedipal content and then the task was presented as one involving competition.

The resolution of the Oedipus complex occurs because of frustrations and disappointments by the mother, because of fear of the father, and because of the

Dart Score	Tachistoscopic Presentation of Three Stimuli		
	"Beating Dad Is Wrong"	"Beating Dad Is OK"	"People Are Walking"
Mean, Prestimulus	443.7	443.3	439.0
Mean, Poststimulus	349.0	533.3	442.3
Difference	− 94.7	+ 90.0	+ 3.3

FIGURE 3.3   Oedipal Conflict and Competitive Performance. (Partial results adapted from Silverman, Ross, Adler, & Lustig, 1978, p. 346)

possibility of partial gain through identification with the father. For the male child, the Oedipus complex is resolved through keeping the mother as a love object but gaining her through identifying with the father. In identifying with the father, the child assumes many of the same values and morals. It is in this sense that the superego has been called the heir to the resolution of the Oedipus complex.

The developmental processes during this stage are somewhat different for the female. She realizes the lack of a penis and blames the mother, the original love object. Developing **penis envy**, the female child chooses the father as the love object and imagines that the lost organ will be restored by having a child by the father. Whereas the Oedipus complex is abandoned in the boy because of castration anxiety, in the female it is started because of penis envy. As with the male, conflict during this period is in some cases accentuated by seductiveness on the part of the father toward the female child. And, as with the male, the female child resolves the conflict by keeping the father as a love object but gaining him through identification with the mother. Because the female child develops less fear than does the male child (the little girl considers her penis to be already gone), and because the boy must give up an object (mother) that is more salient than the object (father) for the girl, the female child does not resolve the oedipal issues to the same degree as does the male child. Thus, the female develops a weaker and less harsh superego, which accounts for their being kinder and softer than men.*

The development of an **identification** with the parent of the same sex is a critical issue during the phallic stage and more generally, is a critical concept in developmental psychology. In identification, individuals take on themselves the qualities of another person and integrate them into their functioning. Freud distinguished among four types of identification. In *narcissistic* (self-love) *identification,* individuals identify with qualities in those who are similar to themselves. This process leads to group membership. In *goal-oriented identification,* the individual identifies with a successful person. For example, the boy may identify with and assume the values of his father. In *object-loss identification,* the individual attempts to recover a lost object (person) through identification with it. The boy who loses a father early in life may develop an exaggerated identification with the father, or with an idealized image of him. Finally, there is *identification with the aggressor*, in which the individual identifies with a figure in authority so as to avoid punishment. This type of identification also occurs in the development of the superego and is a powerful force in socialization. It is also seen in situations of extreme threat, as in the experiences of prisoners in the Nazi concentration camps. For example, according to accounts of life in the concentration camps, some of the prisoners started to wear whatever pieces of Nazi clothing they could get and, when put in a position of authority, treated the other prisoners in a cruel, inhumane way. Sarnoff (1951) has done some research which suggests that anti-Semitism among Jews can be accounted for in terms of identification with the aggressor.

---

*Psychoanalytic theory has been criticized by feminists on a variety of grounds. Perhaps more than any other concept, the concept of penis envy is seen as expressing a chauvinistic, hostile view toward women. This issue will be addressed in Chapter 4 in the Critical Evaluation section.

The oral, anal, and phallic stages of development are **pregenital** in the sense that they occur prior to the reproductive potential of the genitals. Sexual pleasure during these stages is of an infantile kind, but it is sexual because it involves the stimulation of erogenous zones, tension reduction, and pleasure. Although Freud gave relatively little attention to developmental factors after the resolution of the Oedipus complex, he did recognize their existence. After the phallic stage, the child enters **latency**, during which there is a lessening of the sexual urge and no new libidinal developments. The meaning of the latency stage has never been clear in psychoanalytic theory. An assumption of a decrease in sexual urges and interest during the ages of six through 13 might have fit observations of Victorian children, but it does not fit observations of children in other cultures. A more plausible assumption, and one more difficult to test, is that there are no new developments during this stage in terms of the ways in which children gratify their instincts.

General lack of interest in the latency stage stems, in part, from the importance attributed to the two events that surround it. Before the latency stage there is the oedipal period, and after the latency stage there is puberty. The onset of puberty, with the reawakening of the sexual urges and oedipal feelings, marks the beginning of the **genital stage**. The significance of this period for individuals and for their functioning in society is demonstrated in the initiation rites of many primitive cultures and in the Jewish Bar Mitzvah. Dependency feelings and oedipal strivings which were not fully resolved during the pregenital stages of development now come back to rear their ugly heads. The turmoil of adolescence is partly attributable to these factors. During this stage, as in the phallic stage, the highest excitation is located in the genitals, but in contrast to the phallic stage, where the aim was forepleasure and autoeroticism, here the aim is pleasure through intercourse. It is here that the psychoanalytic concept of sexual pleasure most coincides with the commonly accepted meaning of the term. However, in the psychoanalytic view, this sexual pleasure of the genital stage represents nothing more than a later development of the sexual instinct that has been present since birth.

Erikson's psychosocial stages of development   It is probably clear that in the psychoanalytic theory of development, major attention is given to the first five years and to the development of the instincts. Ego psychologists have tried, within this framework, to give greater attention to other developments during the early years and to significant developments that take place during the latency and genital stages. Erik H. Erikson (1950), for example, one of the leading ego psychoanalysts, describes development in psychosocial terms rather than merely in sexual terms. Thus, the first stage is significant not just because of the localization of pleasure in the mouth, but because in the feeding situation a relationship of trust or mistrust is developed between the infant and the mother. Similarly, the anal stage is significant not only for the change in the nature of the major erogenous zone, but also because toilet training is a significant social situation in which the child may develop a sense of autonomy or succumb to shame and self-doubt. In the phallic stage the child must struggle with the issue of taking pleasure in, as opposed to feeling guilty about being assertive, competitive, and successful.

Erik H. Erickson

For Erikson, the latency and genital stages are periods when the individual develops a sense of industry and success, or a sense of inferiority, and perhaps most important of all, a sense of identity or a sense of role diffusion. For Erikson, the crucial task of adolescence is the establishment of a sense of ego identity, an accrued confidence that the way one views oneself has a continuity with one's past and is matched by the perceptions of others. In contrast to people who develop a sense of identity, people with role diffusion experience the feeling of not really knowing who they are, of not knowing whether what they think they are matches what others think of them, of not knowing how they have developed in this way or where they are heading in the future. During late adolescence and the college years, this struggle with a sense of identity may lead to joining a variety of groups and to considerable anguish about the choice of a career. If these issues are not resolved during this time, the individual is, in later life, filled with a sense of despair—life is too short and it is too late to start all over again.

Continuing with his description of the later stages of life and the accompanying psychological issues, Erikson suggests that some people develop a sense of intimacy, an acceptance of life's successes and disappointments, and a sense of continuity throughout the life cycle, while other people remain isolated from family and friends, appear to survive on a fixed daily routine, and focus on both past disappointments and future death. Although the ways in which people do and do not resolve these critical issues of adulthood may have their roots in childhood conflict, Erikson suggests that this is not always the case and that they have a significance of their own (Erikson, 1982). In sum, Erikson's contributions are noteworthy in three ways: (1) He has emphasized the psychosocial as well as the instinctual basis for personality development; (2) He has extended the stages of development to include the entire life cycle and has articulated the major psychological issues to be faced in these later stages; (3) He has recognized that people look to the future as well as to the past, and how they construe their future may be as significant a part of their personality as how they construe their past.

Personality types   As noted, Freud thought that the first five years of life were critical in the development of the individual. During these years, it is possible for a number of failures to occur in the development of the instincts. Such failures in the development are called **fixation**s. If individuals receive so little gratification during a stage of development that they are afraid to go to the next stage, or if they receive so much gratification that there is no motivation to move on, a fixation will occur. If a fixation occurs, the individual will try to obtain the same type of satisfaction that was appropriate for an earlier stage of development during later stages. For example, the individual partially fixated at the oral stage, may continue to seek oral gratification in eating, smoking, or drinking. A developmental phenomenon related to that fixation is **regression**. In regression, the individual seeks to return to an earlier mode of satisfaction, an earlier point of fixation. Regression will often occur under conditions of stress, so that people may only overeat, smoke, or drink during periods of frustration and anxiety. It is interesting to note in this regard that while research has not demonstrated a relationship between frustration at the oral stage and smoking, a relationship has been found between such frustration and difficulty in giving up smoking (McArthur, Waldron, & Dickinson, 1958).

The concepts of the stages of development, fixation, and regression are of tremendous importance to the psychoanalytic theory of development. One of its most fascinating aspects is the way in which personality characteristics are developed in early life and maintained thereafter. For each of the early stages of development, there is a corresponding character type that is developed because of partial fixations at that stage. The characteristics of the **oral personality**, for example, relate to processes going on during the oral stage of development which the individual maintains in later life. Oral personalities are narcissistic in that they are only interested in themselves and do not have a clear recognition of others as separate entities. Other people are seen only in terms of what they can give (feed). Oral personalities are always asking for something, either in terms of a modest, pleading request or an aggressive demand. Either way there is a persistent "sucking" quality to these people. Not being put off by facts or by reason, they "cling like leeches" on others for gratification of their needs.

The oral character may at times appear to be generous. On further inspection, however, the generosity is clearly not genuine; that is, it is based on what they want to give and not on what others want; it is forced so that the other must accept. In giving, they identify with the pleasure of receiving. Furthermore, the underlying feeling is that giving deserves a gift in return. In their work, oral characters seek security, often playing a passive, dependent role. Their pleasures are in taking things into themselves. Most of all, they fear loss, that there will not be enough to go around, and that someone will cheat them or devour them. They are like the rats of Hunt (1941) who, after an early period of food deprivation, followed by a period of consistent feeding, hoarded food to a tremendous degree when a situation of frustration and deprivation was presented to them in later life. In a study of the oral character in children, Blum and Miller (1952) found a relationship between orality (nonpurposive mouth movements) and personality traits such as extreme interest in food (consumption of ice cream and eagerness at lunchtime), social isolation, the need for approval, concern over giving and receiving, and poor tolerance of boredom. In sum, the oral character is demanding, impatient, envious, covetous, jealous, tending toward rage and depression (feeling hollow, empty) when frustrated, and generally pessimistic.

The **anal personality** stems from the anal stage of development. In contrast to gratification associated with the mouth and oral activity, which can be expressed in adulthood in a relatively unrepressed form, the gratifications of anal impulses must undergo considerable transformation. The general theme here is that the traits of the anal character are related to processes going on at the anal stage of development which have not been completely relinquished. The processes of significance are the bodily processes (accumulation and release of fecal material) and interpersonal relations (the struggle of wills over toilet training). Tying the two together, the anal person sees excretion as symbolic of enormous power. That such a view persists is shown in many everyday expressions such as the reference to the toilet as "the throne." The change from the oral to the anal character is one from "give me" to "do what I tell you," or from "I have to give you" to "I must obey you." The anal character is known by a triad of traits, called the *anal triad*. The triad is: orderliness and cleanliness, parsimony and stinginess, and obstinacy. The emphasis on cleanliness is expresssed in the saying "Cleanliness is next to godliness." The anal-compulsive personality has a need to keep everything *clean* and *in order* representing a reaction formation against an interest in things that are disorderly and unclean. The second trait of the triad, *parsimony-stinginess,* relates to the anal-compulsive's interest in holding on to things, an interest dating back to a wish to retain the powerful and important feces. Such people may even be parsimonious in their use of toilet paper. The third trait in the triad, *obstinacy,* relates to anal character's infantile defiance against parting with their stools, particularly on command by others.

Anal personalities are filled with contradictions and ambivalence. Generally, they are persevering, although at times they will put things off to the last minute. This relates to the conflict between doing things when they are supposed to, as opposed to waiting and experiencing the pleasure in delay. They are generally orderly, but in most cases there is also some trace of messiness. Thus, it is said that every compulsive housewife has a mess closet. The person who keeps an extremely neat desk generally has at least one drawer for all the waste. Often the anal character is submissive and obedient, but then there is an occassional outburst of defiance and vengeance.

Anal characters take pleasure in delay, in the building up of tension, and then pleasure in letting go. This can be seen in their eating habits where they will save the best food for last, then feeling that it is "good to the last drop." Because of their excessive concern with things that are dirty and their tendency to link their impulses with dirtiness, anal characters compulsively and rigidly strive for control over their impulses. They have a harsh conscience which makes them do the right thing at the right time. The vocabulary of such people is filled with words such as should, should not, ought, trial and judgment. The emphasis on order can lead to conservatism and an opposition to innovations, and the emphasis on power can lead to a wish to possess what others lack, an underestimation of the contributions of others, and a wish to impose one's own system on everything.

The relationships of the anal character to people and to work are suggested in the above. A central issue in interpersonal relationships is who controls whom, whether to submit or rebel. Anal characters are sensitive to external encroachments on their actual or supposed field of power. They will hold fast to their own way of doing things, expecting compliance from others. They will refuse a request or demand from others, particularly those in authority, but they will do the same things of their own free choice. The self-will and control must be perceived. Thus an anal husband may oppose expenditures of his wife, and then give, "of his own free will," in fact, more than his wife had asked for. Where they are forced to yield to the demands of another person, they will try to maintain a semblance of making a personal decision. Thus, such people may pay even the smallest amount of money by check, as if in fantasy they create their own money for every purchase.

In sum, the anal character possesses traits in adulthood that relate to pleasures dating back to the anal stage and to ways of relating interpersonally which were learned in the toilet-training situation. There is a pleasure in possessions and in having a mass of material stored up, just as earlier there was pleasure in the retention of the feces. Thus, there may be an avoidance of spending money on things that are "passing through," such as concerts and trips, and, instead, an emphasis on storing permanent things, such as records and books. There is a pleasure in storing, pleasure in evacuating, anxiety over waste, and anxiety over the loss of control of one's own impulses or domination by others. The issues are whether to hold on or to let go and whether to submit or to rebel.

Just as the oral and anal character types reflect partial fixations at the first two stages of development, so the **phallic character** represents the result of a partial fixation at the stage of the Oedipus complex. Fixation here has different implications for men and women and particular attention has been given to the results of partial fixation for males. Whereas success for the oral person means "I get," and success for the anal person means "I control," success for the phallic male means "I am a man." The phallic male must deny all possible suggestions that he has been castrated. For him success means that he is "big" in the eyes of others. He must at all times assert his masculinity and potency, an attitude reflected in the Rough Riders of Theodore Roosevelt and in the saying "Speak softly but carry a big stick." The excessive, exhibitionistic quality to the behavior of these people is expressive of the underlying anxiety and the efforts to defend against this anxiety. The female counterpart of the male phallic character is known as an hysterical personality. As a defense against Oedipal wishes, the little girl identifies to an excessive extent with her mother and femininity. She uses seductive and flirtatious behavior to maintain the interest of her father but denies their sexual intent. The pattern of behavior then is carried over into adulthood, where she may attract men with flirtatious behavior but deny sexual intent and generally appear to be somewhat naive. Hysterical women idealize life, their partners, and romantic love, often finding themselves surprised by life's uglier moments.

Whereas the phallic person generally strives to be successful, conflicts dating back to the Oedipal period may lead to feelings of guilt over success. For such a person, success means winning out over the father or mother, a breaking of an incest taboo. As with many of the derivatives of earlier fixations, the same conflict can express itself in opposite ways. The male phallic personality type may seek success on the job, many sexual conquests, and many children, all as evidence of potency, or he may be impotent in his work and sexual life because of guilt over competitive strivings with the father. While the behavior found in these two cases may appear to be opposite to one another, they tend to reflect the same issue or conflict in their dynamics. Furthermore, both sets of behaviors reflect an earlier fixation in that they are overdriven, rigid, and unresponsive to reality. Whether giving or taking, submitting or controlling, being successful or being impotent, the oral, anal, and phallic characters are unable to deal with certain types of frustrations, and rigidly adhere to modes of obtaining pleasure that were more appropriate at earlier stages of development.

The Importance of Early Experience

The genetic approach to personality evident in psychoanalytic theory emphasizes the importance of events early in life for later personality development. There are two central aspects to this emphasis. The first is the general interpretation of later personality in terms of childhood experiences. The second is the specific developmental stages that are presumed to be universal. The relevant literature is voluminous and studies can be cited in support of both points of emphasis. At the same time, the issues are quite complex and the prevailing point of view appears to change from time to time (Hobbs, 1982). At no time has a consensus been reached concerning the importance of early years for later personality development. While earlier there was growing support for such an emphasis, the prevailing current view appears, at a minimum, to be more cautious. Thus the editors of a volume on continuity and change in development conclude that "the view that emerges from this work is that humans have a capacity for change across the entire life span. It questions the traditional idea that the experience of the earlier years, which have a demonstrated contemporaneous effect, necessarily constrain the character of adolescence and adulthood. . . . Many individuals retain a greater capacity for change, and the consequences of the events of early childhood are continually transformed by later experience, making the course of human development more open than many have believed" (Brim & Kagan, 1980, p. 1).

The complexities of the issue can be illustrated with two studies. The first, conducted by a psychoanalyst (Gaensbauer, 1982), involved the study of affect development in infancy. The infant, Jenny, was first studied systematically when she was almost four months old. Prior to this time, at the age of three months, she had been physically abused three times by her father. At that time she was brought to the hospital with a broken arm and a skull fracture. She was described by hospital personnel as being a "lovable baby"—happy, cute, sociable, but also as not cuddling when held and as being "jittery" when approached by a male. Following this history of abuse she was placed in a foster home where she received adequate physical care but minimal social interaction. This was very much in contrast with her earlier experience with her natural mother who spent considerable time with her and would breast feed her "at the drop of a hat." The first systematic observation occurred almost a month after placement in the foster home. At this time her behavior was judged to be completely consistent with a diagnosis of depression—lethargic, apathetic, disinterested, collapsed posture. A systematic analysis of her facial expressions indicated five discrete affects, each meaningfully related to her unique history. Sadness was noted when she was with her natural mother. Fearfulness and anger were noted when she was approached by a male stranger but not when she was approached by a female stranger. Joy was noted as a transient affect during brief play sequences. Finally, interest–curiosity was noted when she interacted with female strangers.

After she was visited in her foster home, Jenny was placed in a different foster home where she received warm attention. Following two weeks in this environment, she was again brought to the hosptial for further evaluation, this time by her second foster mother. This time she generally appeared to be a normally responsive infant. She showed no evidence of distress and even smiled at a male stranger. After an additional month at this foster home, she was brought to the hospital *by her natural mother* for a third evaluation. Generally, she was animated and happy. However, when her mother left the room, she cried intensely. This continued following the mother's return despite repeated attempts to soothe her. Apparently separation from her natural mother continued to lead to a serious distress response. In addition, sadness and anger were frequently noted. At eight months old, Jenny was returned to her natural mother who left her husband and received counseling. At the age of twenty months, she was described as appearing to be normal and having an excellent relationship with her mother. However, there continued to be the problem of anger and distress associated with separation from her mother.

Two points are noteworthy. First, at the early age of three or four months Jenny already had a distinctive affective organization: "The capacity to express in at least rudimentary forms the emotions of joy, interest, fear, anger, and sadness, as well as the more undifferentiated emotion of distress, appears to be present by four months of age" (p. 51). Second, there appeared to be both continuities and discontinuities between Jenny's early affective experiences and her later affective reactions. "In general, she was doing well and the sunny disposition which had served her well in her early months remained with her. . . . Her anger reactions in response to separations and frustrations appeared to be the most intense, and thus seemed to have the greatest link to the past. Yet, it would be hard to say that any of her affective responses, including her temper tantrums, were outside the normal range of reactions seen in infants twenty months old. It appeared as though the influence of the traumatic period and the intensity of her emotional reactions had diminished over time'' (p. 50). The author suggested that perhaps isolated traumatic events are less important in the development of pathology than the repeated experiences of a less dramatic but more persistent nature.

The second study, conducted by a group of developmental psychologists, assessed the relationship between early attachment relationships and later psychopathology (Lewis, Feiring, McGuffog, & Jaskir, 1984). In this study, the attachment behavior of boy and girl children one year of age was observed. The observation involved a standardized procedure consisting of a period of play with the mother in an unstructured situation, followed by the departure of the mother and a period of the child being alone in the playroom, and then by the return of the mother and a second free play period. The behavior of the children was scored systematically leading them to be assigned to one of three attachment categories: avoidant, secure, or ambivalent. The avoidant and ambivalent categories were suggestive of difficulties in this area. Then at six years of age, the competence of these children was assessed through the completion by the mothers of a Child Behavior Profile. The ratings of the mothers were also checked against teacher ratings. On the basis of the Child Behavior Profile the children were classified into a normal group, an at risk group, and a clinically disturbed group.

What was the relationship between early attachment behavior and later pathology? There are two aspects of the results that are particularly noteworthy. First, the relationships were quite different for boys than for girls. For boys, attachment classification at one year of age was significantly related to later pathology. Insecurely attached boys showed more pathology at age six than did securely attached boys. On the other hand, no relationship between attachment and later pathology was observed for girls. Second, the authors noted a difference between trying to predict pathology from the early data (prospective) as opposed to trying to understand later pathology in terms of earlier attachment difficulties (retrospective). If one starts with the boys who at age six were identified as being at risk or clinically disturbed, 80 percent would be found to have been assigned to the avoidant- or ambivalent-attachment category at age one. In other words, a very strong statistical relationship. On the other hand, if one took all boys classified as insecurely attached (avoidant or ambivalent) at age one and predicted them to be at risk or clinically disturbed at age six, one would be right in only 40 percent of the cases. The reason for this is that far more of the boys were classified as insecurely attached than were later diagnosed as at risk or disturbed. Thus, the clinician viewing later pathology would have a clear basis for suggesting a strong relationship between pathology and early attachment difficulties. On the other hand, focusing on the data in terms of prediction would suggest a much more tenuous relationship and the importance of other variables as well. The early attachment relationship, at least for boys, may be critical but not an all-determining factor in later pathology. As Freud himself recognized, when we observe later pathology it is all too easy to understand how it developed. On the other hand, when we look at these phenomena prospectively we are made aware of the varied paths that development can follow.. In the words of the authors, "the findings suggest that although the child's attachment relationship plays an important role in the development of pathology, a child is neither made invulnerable by early secure attachment nor doomed to pathology by an insecure attachment."

As previously noted, the issues relevant to the importance of early experience for later personality development are complex. Perhaps we must seek a more differentiated approach to the question rather than a black- or-white answer. For example, how are we to define consistency, stability, or continuity of development (Kagan, 1980)? Do we mean that the personality of the adult is the *same* as that of the child? Or do we mean that the personality of the adult is derived from or represents some clear transformation of characteristics from childhood? The former is a much more stringent test of continuity and by that criterion one could find little supportive evidence. The latter is a more relaxed criterion and provides for more confirming evidence. But which comes closer to the heart of psychoanalytic theory? In additon, we can consider variations in the importance of early experience depending on the personality characteristic being considered and the particular experiences that occur during and following the early years. Thus, for example, the early years might be quite important for the development of what Erikson calls basic trust but less critical for other personality characteristics (Hunt, 1979). And, the role of early experience might depend on the intensity of particular experiences, their duration, and the extent to which differing experiences occurred earlier and later. Thus, for example, the effects of maternal deprivation may depend on how serious and long lasting the deprivation is as well as on the role of positive experiences both before and following deprivation (Mineka & Suomi, 1978). Finally, we may note the distinction between what may occur and what must inevitably occur. Psychoanalytic theory can be accurate in portraying the *possible* effects of early experience, particularly as seen in various forms of psychological disturbance where a pattern of relationships is established early and maintained over time, without it being the case that such effects are inevitable.

MAJOR CONCEPTS AND SUMMARY

energy system

conscious, preconscious, unconscious

id, ego, superego

pleasure principle

reality principle

life and death instincts

sexual and aggressive instincts

anxiety

mechanisms of defense

erogenous zones

oral, anal, phallic stages of development

Oedipus complex

castration anxiety

identification

fixation

regression

oral, anal, and phallic personality types

Before turning to the clinical applications of psychoanalytic theory and a final evaluation, let us take stock of the essentials of the theory of personality. The chapter began with a discussion of some of the events in Freud's life that played a role in the development of his theory and that influenced his approach toward science. Illustrative of such events were his concerns about death and destruction during the First World War, the prevailing concerns in physics and medicine with energy models, and the inhibitions concerning sexuality found in Victorian society broadly and in Freud's patients in particular. In attempting both to help his patients and to develop a lasting theory of personality, Freud developed concepts that often appeared to have explanatory value but proved to be difficult to investigate systematically in nonclinical settings. Freud was impressed with the role of *unconscious forces* in the functioning of his patients. In listening to dreams and slips of the tongue, and in trying to understand the symptoms patients brought to treatment, Freud was struck by the importance of *repressed memories and wishes* in the associations of his patients. Similarly, he was impressed with the conflicts faced by his patients between what they wished and what society or their own conscience would permit. Thus, the development of Freud's concept of *id* to represent the basic sexual and aggressive urges, the concept of the *superego* to represent the conscience or internalization of parental and societal prohibitions, and the *ego* or efforts to find gratification and pleasure in accordance with the demands of reality.

Freud attached particular importance to the role of anxiety in the functioning of his patients. Often they came in with feelings of free-floating anxiety. At the same time, he was impressed with the various devices used to ward off anxiety. Thus, the development of the theory of anxiety and the mechanisms of defense.

The wishes and fears expressed by Freud's patients appeared to relate to experiences they had during their early years. Here Freud was led to his theory of growth and development and to the concepts of *fixation* and *regression*. Experiences during the early years of life were seen as centering around various *erogenous zones*. Changes in the region of special sensitivity as well as in the region of special social contact were expressed in the concepts of the *oral, anal,* and *phallic stages of development*. The person's character or basic personality structure was seen as pretty well established by age five, after the struggles associated with the *Oedipus complex*. The theory of development provides links to many diverse aspects of psychoanalytic theory, including a link to the theory of psychopathology, to which we turn in the following chapter.

Chagall, Marc. *The Juggler of Paris*. Scala/Art Resource.

A PSYCHODYNAMIC THEORY: APPLICATIONS AND EVALUATION OF FREUD'S THEORY

CHAPTER FOCUS: In this chapter we continue to examine psychoanalytic theory as illustrative of a psychodynamic, clinical approach to personality. Attention is given to associated techniques of personality assessment, particularly projective tests such as the Rorschach Inkblot Test and the Thematic Apperception Test. We then consider Freud's attempts to understand and explain the symptoms presented by his patients and his efforts to develop a systematic method of treatment. After considering developments in psychoanalytic theory since Freud, we turn to a final critical evaluation and summary.

CLINICAL APPLICATIONS

Psychoanalysis started as and continues to be a clinical theory of personality, focusing on individual differences and the intensive study of the person. In addition, central to the theory is an emphasis on unconscious processes and the interplay among motives. A central theme in this book is that a theory of personality does not stand alone but rather is tied to and reflects ways of observing people. In addition, to the extent that the theory is associated with an approach to psychotherapy or change, the theory and approach will reflect some common basic assumptions. Let us consider, then, how basic psychoanalytic concepts get reflected in approaches to the assessment of people as well as in the understanding and treatment of psychopathology.

Assessment—Projective Techniques

While many different personality tests can be used in conjunction with psychoanalytic theory, it is *projective techniques* that are most closely linked to the theory. The term *projection* in relation to assessment techniques was first used in 1938 by Henry A. Murray, who developed the Thematic Apperception Test, but emphasis on the importance of projective techniques was first most clearly stated by L. K. Frank in 1939. Frank argued against the use of standardized tests, which he felt classified people but did not tell much about them as individuals. He argued for the use of tests that would offer insight into the private world of meanings and feelings of individuals. Such tests would allow individuals to impose their own structure and organization on stimuli and would thereby be expressive of a dynamic conception of personality. Frank suggested the use of stimuli relatively free of structure and cultural patterning:

> *A projection method for the study of personality involves the presentation of a stimulus-situation designed or chosen because it will mean to the subject, not what the experimenter has arbitrarily decided it should mean (as in most psychological experiments using standardized stimuli in order to be*

"objective"), but rather whatever it must mean to the personality who gives it, or imposes upon it, his private, idiosyncratic meaning and organization.

Frank, 1939, p. 403

In this section we consider two projective techniques, the Rorschach Inkblot Test and the Thematic Apperception Test (TAT). Both are unstructured in that they provide considerable freedom for subjects to respond in their own unique ways. Both are also disguised tests in that generally subjects are not aware of the purpose of the test or of how particular responses will be interpreted. The relation of psychoanalytic theory to projective tests can be seen as follows:

1. Psychoanalytic theory emphasizes individual differences and the complex organization of personality functioning. Personality is viewed as a process through which the individual imposes organization and structure on external stimuli in the environment. Projective techniques allow for maximum uniqueness of response, both in terms of the content and organization of the response.

2. Psychoanalytic theory emphasizes the importance of the unconscious and defense mechanisms. Projective tests involve directions and stimuli that provide few guidelines for responding and in which the purposes of the test and interpretations of responses are hidden.

3. Psychoanalytic theory emphasizes a holistic understanding of personality in terms of relationships among parts, rather than the interpretation of behavior as expressive of single parts or personality characteristics. Clinicians who use projective tests generally make holistic interpretations based on the patterning and organization of test responses rather than on interpreting a single response as reflecting a particular characteristic.

Having considered some general relationships between psychoanalytic theory and projective techniques, let us turn now to consideration of two of them in some detail.

The Rorschach Inkblot Test

The Rorschach inkblot Test was developed by Hermann Rorschach, a Swiss psychiatrist. Although inkblots had been used earlier to elicit responses from individuals, Rorschach was the first to grasp fully the potential for the use of these responses for personality assessment. Rorschach developed stimuli through putting ink on paper and folding the paper so that symmetrical but ill-defined forms were produced. These inkblots were then shown to hospitalized patients. Through a process of trial and error, those inkblots that elicited different responses from different psychiatric groups were kept, while those that did not were discarded. Rorschach experimented with thousands of inkblots and finally settled on ten.

Rorschach was well acquainted with the work of Freud, the concept of the unconscious, and a dynamic view of personality. The development of his test certainly seems to have been influenced by this view. Rorschach felt that the data from the inkblot test would have relevance for an understanding of the uncon-

Hermann Rorschach

scious and psychoanalytic theory in general, and he used psychoanalytic theory in his own interpretations of subjects' responses.

The Rorschach test consists of ten cards with inkblots on them. When showing the cards, the experimenter tries to make the subjects relaxed and comfortable while providing them with sufficient information to complete the task. Thus, the test is presented as "just one of many ways used nowadays to try to understand people" and the experimenter volunteers as little information as possible—"It is best not to know much about the procedure until you have gone through it." Subjects are asked to look at each card and tell the examiner what they see—anything that might be represented on the card. Individuals are free to select what they will see, where they will see it, and what determines their perceptions. All responses offered by the subjects are given on the test record. It also records *where* on the inkblot the subjects saw each response and *what* about the blot made it look like it did, In this way the examiners are able to determine more exactly the basis for each subject's responses.

In interpreting the Rorschach one is interested in the way in which the responses or percepts are formed, the reasons for the response, and its content. The basic assumption is that there is a correspondence between the way individuals form their perceptions and the way they generally organize and structure stimuli in their environments. Perceptions that match the structure of the inkblot suggest a good level of psychological functioning that is well oriented toward reality. On the other hand, poorly formed responses that do not fit the structure of the inkblot suggest unrealistic fantasies or bizarre behavior. The content of subject responses (whether they see mostly animate or inanimate objects, humans or animals, and content expressing affection or hostility) makes a great deal of difference in the interpretation of the subject's personality. For example, compare the interpretations we might make of two sets of responses, one where animals are seen repeatedly as fighting and a second where humans are seen as sharing and involved in cooperative efforts.

Beyond this, content may be interpreted symbolicly. An explosion may symbolize intense hostility; a pig, gluttonous tendencies; a fox, a tendency toward being crafty and aggressive; spiders, witches, and octopuses, negative images of a dominating mother; gorillas and giants, negative attitudes toward a dominating father; and an ostrich as an attempt to hide from conflicts (Schafer, 1954). General categories of content such as food and nurturant animals (cows, mother hen), hostile figures and devouring animals (beasts of prey, vultures, animals clawing), and figures of power and authority (kings, queens, generals) are interpreted in relation to symbolism. Two illustrative stimuli and responses are presented in Figure 4.1.

ILLUSTRATION NO. 1

RESPONSE
"Two bears with their paws touching one another playing pattycake or could be they are fighting and the red is the blood from the fighting."

ILLUSTRATION NO. 2

RESPONSE
"Two cannibals. Supposed to see something in this? African natives bending over a pot. Possibly cooking something–hope they're not maneaters. I shouldn't make jokes–always liking humor. (Are they male or female?) Could be male or female. More female because of breasts here. But didn't impress me at first glance as being of either sex."

FIGURE 4.1 Examples from the Rorschach Inkblot Test. The inkblot illustrations reproduced here are from the Rorschach location chart. The actual inkblot cards contain color. (Reprinted by permission of Hans Huber, Publishers.)

Rorschach Inkblot Test—The Rorschach interpreter assumes that the subject's personality is projected onto unstructured stimuli such as inkblots. Drawing by Ross; © 1974 The New Yorker Magazine, Inc.

It is important to recognize that interpretation is not made on the basis of one response alone, but in relation to the total sum of responses. However, each response is used to suggest hypotheses or possible interpretations about the individual's personality. Such hypotheses are checked against interpretations based on other responses, on the total response pattern, and on the subject's behavior while responding to the Rorschach. In relation to the latter, the examiner takes note of all unusual behavior and uses this as a source of data for further interpretation. For example, a subject who constantly asks for guidance may be interpreted as dependent. A subject who seems tense, asks questions in a subtle way, and looks at the back of the cards may be interpreted as suspicious and possibly paranoid.

The Thematic Apperception Test (TAT)

Probably the most widely used projective test is the Thematic Apperception Test (TAT) developed by Henry Murray and Christina Morgan. The test represents an extension of Murray's longstanding interest in the needs or underlying motives of individuals, fantasy behavior, and the intensive study of the individual. The TAT consists of cards with scenes on them. Most of the cards depict one or two people in some important life situation, though some of the cards are more abstract. The subject is asked to make up a story based on the scene on the card, with the story to include what is going on, the thoughts and feelings of the participants, what

Henry Murray

led up to the scene, and the outcome of what is going on. Since the scenes often are ambiguous, they leave considerable room for individuality in the content of stories made up by the subjects: "The test is based on the well-recognized fact that when a person interprets an ambiguous social situation he is apt to expose his own personality as much as the phenomenon to which he is attending" (Murray, 1938, p. 530).

Some TAT cards are shown to both male and female subjects; others are shown to members of one sex only. An illustrative card and responses given to it by two different individuals is in Figure 4.2. The card is given to female subjects and is described by Murray as: "The portrait of a young woman. A weird old woman with a shawl over her head is grimacing in the background". Common themes given in response to this card are stories of disappointment with a parent, parental pressure, and sad thoughts about the past. In addition, some women appear to see the younger woman as having a vision of her evil self or of herself in old age (Holt, 1978).

The thinking behind the TAT clearly shows its relation to the psychodynamic view. According to Murray (1938), the TAT is used to discover unconscious and inhibited tendencies. The assumption is that subjects are not aware that they are talking about themselves and that thereby the defenses can be bypassed: "If the procedure had merely exposed conscious fantasies and remembered events it would have been useful enough, but it did more than this. It gave the experimenter excellent clues for the divination of unconscious thematic formations!' (p. 534).

Sample Card
from the Thematic
Apperception Test.

ILLUSTRATION 1   This is the picture of a woman who all of her life has been a very suspicious, conniving person. She's looking in the mirror and she sees reflected behind her an image of what she will be as an old woman—still a suspicious, conniving sort of person. She can't stand the thought that that's what her life will eventually lead her to and she smashes the mirror and runs out of the house screaming and goes out of her mind and lives in an institution for the rest of her life.

ILLUSTRATION 2   This woman has always emphasized beauty in her life. As a little girl she was praised for being pretty and as a young woman was able to attract lots of men with her beauty. While secretly feeling anxious and unworthy much of the time, her outer beauty helped to disguise these feelings from the world and, sometimes, from herself. Now that she is getting on in years and her children are leaving home, she is worried about the future. She looks in the mirror and imagines herself as an old hag—the worst possible person she could become, ugly and nasty—and wonders what the future holds for her. It is a difficult and depressing time for her.

FIGURE 4.2   Illustrative TAT Card and Responses to It

TAT responses of subjects can be scored systematically according to a scheme developed by Murray or on a more impressionistic basis. It is used both in clinical work and in experimental studies of human motivation (McClelland, 1961). The TAT assumes a close relationship between the expressed fantasy (story about the TAT card) and underlying motivation as well as a relationship between such fantasy and behavior. Efforts to test these assumptions have met with mixed results. Fantasy can both be associated with the expression of motives in behavior and also serve as a substitute for the expression of motives in behavior. Thus, for example, a person with a strong motive to be aggressive with others may express this motive both in fantasy (TAT) and behavior, but the person may also express it in fantasy and block it from expression in overt behavior.

Illustrative Research Use and Evaluation   Omit

Projective techniques have been used for a great variety of research purposes, both in relation to psychoanalytic theory and apart from it. A recent study of comedians, clowns, and actors illustrates the clinical, psychodynamic approach to understanding such phenomena, including the utilization of projective tests (Fisher & Fisher, 1981). The study represented an effort to understand the origins, motivations, and personalities of those who make people laugh as opposed to those who entertain through acting. In it professional clowns, comedians, and actors were interviewed and given projective tests such as the Rorschach and TAT. Participants included such comedians as Sid Caesar, Tommy Smothers, Donald O'Connor, "Professor" Irwin Corey, and Myron Cohen. In addition, biographies and autobiographies of comedians such as Charlie Chaplin, Johnny Carson, and Dick Gregory were reviewed.

What can such research contribute to our understanding of comedians and clowns? First, in terms of early life, they were found to be funny early in life, particularly in school, despite little support from their parents for their comic endeavors. Second, a number of motivations seemed to be contributing factors to the investment in being a comedian. Among these motivations suggested by the data are the following:

1. *Power*. The ability to control an audience and "make" people laugh.

2. *Preoccupation With Good–Evil and Positive Presentation of Self*. "We would propose that a major motive of comedians in conjuring up funniness is to prove that they are not bad or repugnant. They are obsessed with defending their basic goodness" (p. 69).

3. *Concealment and Denial*. Humor is used to remove themselves from difficulty and as a screen to hide behind when feeling embarrassed or inferior.

4. *Anarchy*. Comedians belittle accepted norms, leave nothing sacred, and make everything laughable.

Let us consider illustrative Rorschach evidence for two of these motivations. First, the concern with good–bad or virtue–evil. A scoring system was devised to consider the frequency with which such themes appeared in the Rorschach records. Illustrative responses were those directly referring to good and bad (e.g., bad person, virtuous look), those referring to religious matters (e.g., church, angel, devil, heaven, purgatory), and those referring to persons often linked with good–bad (e.g., policeman, criminal, judge, sinner). The Rorschach records of 35 comedians and clowns were found to have significantly more such good–bad references than did the records of 35 actors who were not comedians. Second, the concern with concealment and denial. Many of the Rorschach responses seemed to express an attitude of denying that things are as bad or threatening as they seem. For example, consider the following responses: "Faces. Evil looking . . . The evil not very evil. A put on." "Mephisto . . . charming character." "Tiger. Loveable tiger." "Monster . . . He's nice." "Wolfman . . . He's misunderstood . . . People are afraid. If you walk up and talk to him, he's a decent thing."

Comedians and Clowns—Research using psychoanalytic theory and projective techniques suggests that comedians and clowns often are sensitive about a part of their body. Here, in a scene from *Young Frankenstein*, the bulging eyes of the comedian Marty Feldman are highlighted.

"Two devils. Funny devils. Not to be taken seriously." In analyzing the Rorschach records of comics, it was found that they contained significantly more of these "not bad" images than did the records of actors. In addition, the records of comics were found to have significantly more concealment themes (e.g., hiding, mask, disguise, magic, tricks) than did the records of actors.

One final theme noted in this study related to the tendency for comedians and clowns to be sensitive about some part of their body or their sense of self generally. Thus, for example, one can think of Jimmy Durante's jokes about his nose. This theme was of particular interest to me since just after reading this study, I came across a story about the film comic Marty Feldman following his death. In the story he was described as a short, wiry man with a prodigious nose and curly hair whose trademark was his bulging eyes. He was quoted as follows in relation to his appearance: "The sum total of the disasters of my life. If I aspired to be Robert Redford, I'd have my eyes straightened and my nose fixed and end up like every other lousy actor, with two lines on Kojak. But this way, I'm a novelty" (N.Y. *Times*, December 4, 1982). In sum, comedy is seen as a way of helping themselves deal with some sense of inferiority.

A review of this study is interesting in taking us to at least brief consideration of the strengths and limitations of such studies and projectives generally. The reviewer indicated that "as a Rorschach expert I am convinced that the projective tests, especially the Rorschach are invaluable tools for generating hypotheses. Using them to verify such hypotheses is another problem . . . It is only too easy to find what one is looking for not only in projective data but in case histories as well" (Dudek, 1982, p. 868). The Rorschach, as well as projectives generally, is a marvelous instrument for glimpsing individual fantasy and the complexity of organization of individual perception. However, the difficulties in substantiating theoretical hypotheses or in establishing the reliability and validity of the instrument itself are enormous. Those who use projective techniques emphasize that only these tests are capable of capturing the richness of personality. Ambiguous stimuli elicit individual, idiosyncratic responses. Through these responses individuals express their personalities. The Rorschach is seen as being the psychologist's "microscope" or "X ray," able to penetrate to the depths of the individual's personality. The data from other tests are looked upon as being trivial and fragmented by comparison. On the other hand, such efforts to give a multidimensional picture of the total personality create problems in empirical investigation. In part because interpretation involves so many sources or combinations of data and in part because it is hard to separate individual interpretive statements from the total description of the individual's personality, it is difficult to establish the reliability and validity of the Rorschach as well as other projective tests. Once more we are involved with the tension between the richness of psychodynamic, clinical data and the scientific requirements of systematic investigation. We have considered this tension before and it will remain with us as we now go on to consider the psychoanalytic interpretation of psychopathology and personality change.

Psychopathology

Frequently it is difficult for people to appreciate psychoanalytic theory without first appreciating the nature of the often strange and puzzling behaviors that were brought to Freud's attention. Freud spent most of his professional time working with patients with neurotic disorders. In fact, the most critical elements in his theory are based on the observations that came from working with these patients. He tested his theory through observations of these and other patients as well as evaluation of the outcome of his treatment. In the course of his work he decided that the processes of psychological functioning found in his patients were not peculiar to those with neurotic disturbances but could be found, to one degree or another, and in one form or another, in all people. Thus, while originally based on observations with patients, his theory is a general theory of personality functioning rather than only a theory of abnormal behavior.

According to Freud, all psychopathology relates to an effort to gratify instincts that have been fixated at an earlier stage of development. Thus, in psychopathology the individual still seeks sexual and aggressive gratification in infantile forms. However, because of its association with past trauma, expression of this wish may signal danger to the ego and lead to the experience of anxiety. As a result, there is a conflict situation in which the same behaviors are associated both with pleasure and pain. For example, the person may seek to be dependent on others' pleasures but fear that if this is done he or she will be vulnerable to frustration and loss (pain). Another example would be of a wish to indulge in sexual behavior that is blocked by feelings of guilt and fear of punishment or injury. A third example is the conflict between a wish to retaliate against powerful others, representing the parents, and a fear that these figures will themselves retaliate with force and destruction. In each case there is a conflict between a wish and anxiety. In such a situation the result often is that the individual "can't say no," can't be assertive, or otherwise feels blocked and unhappy.

As noted above, a critical part of the conflict is anxiety. To reduce the painful experience of anxiety, defense mechanisms, as outlined in Chapter 3, are brought into play. Thus, for example, the person may deny his or her aggressive feelings or project them onto others. In either case, the person no longer has to be afraid of the aggressive feelings. In sum, in psychopathology there is a conflict between a drive or wish (instinct) and the ego's sense (anxiety) that danger will ensue if the wish is expressed (discharged). To guard against this, and ward off anxiety, defense mechanisms are used. In structural terms, a neurosis is a result of conflict between the id and the ego. In process terms, an instinct striving for discharge triggers anxiety, leading to a defense mechanism.

In many cases the conflict between the id and ego, between instinct and defense, leads to the development of a **symptom**. A symptom, such as a tic, psychological paralysis, or compulsion, represents a disguised expression of a repressed impulse. The meaning of the symptom, the nature of the dangerous instinct, and the nature of the defense all remain unconscious. For example, a mother may be painfully obsessed with the fear that something will happen to her child. Underlying the obsession may be rage at her child and anxiety about the harm she may do to the child. The symptom of the obsession expresses both the mother's feelings that she may harm or injure the child and her defense against it in terms of excessive preoccupation with the child's welfare. To take another example, in a handwashing compulsion, in which the person feels compelled to wash his or her hands continuously, the symptom may express both the wish to be dirty or do "dirty" things and the defense against the wish in terms of excessive cleanliness. In both of these cases the person is unaware of the wish or the defense and is troubled only by the symptom. Many people do not suffer from such specific problems or symptoms but analysts suggest that all psychological problems can still be understood in these terms.

While Freud believed that all pathology centers around the Oedipus complex, frustration and trauma also can lead to regression to an earlier stage of development. The form taken in a neurosis or psychosis (severe thought disturbance) is dependent on the stage to which one regresses. The psychoses represent expressions of a regression back to the oral stage or to an early part of the anal stage (Abraham, 1924). In these forms of pathology the individual is troubled by the wish to gratify primitive instincts. Wishes to devour, or to destroy, may threaten the individual. Unconscious impulses and wishes occasionally break into consciousness; there is a return to primitive, primary process thinking. The defenses related to these earlier stages of development are projection and denial, both of which involve considerable distortion of reality. For example, the use of projection ("I do not hate others; others hate me.") leads to paranoid suspicions of the intent of others and delusions of persecution. The neuroses represent expressions of regression back to the anal stage or to the oedipal stage of development. Be-

ILLUSTRATIVE CONFLICTS		BEHAVIOR CONSEQUENCES OF DEFENSE MECHANISMS
Wish	*Anxiety*	*Defense*
I would like to have sex with that person.	Such feelings are bad and will be punished.	Denial of all sexual behavior, obsessive preoccupation with the sexual behavior of others.
I would like to strike out at all those people who make me feel inferior.	If I am hostile they will retaliate and really hurt me.	Denial of wish or fear: "I never feel angry" or "I'm never afraid of anyone or anything."
I would like to get close to people and have them feed me or take care of me.	If I do they will smother me or leave me.	Excessive independence and avoidance of getting close to people or fluctuations between approaching people and moving away from them; excessive need to take care of others.

FIGURE 4.3   Psychoanalytic Theory of Psychopathology.

cause the regression is not so far back in development, the disturbances in functioning are not so severe in the neuroses as they are in psychoses. In each case of abnormal behavior there is an unconscious conflict between a wish and a fear that dates back to an earlier period in childhood. In this sense, as adults there continue to be childlike parts of us that under some conditions, such as those of stress, may become more active and troublesome.

To summarize the psychoanalytic theory of psychopathology, there is an arrest in the development of the person that is associated with conflicts between wishes and fears. The wishes and fears that were part of a specific time period in childhood are now carried over into adolescence and adulthood. The person attempts to handle anxiety that is a painful part of this conflict by using defense mechanisms. However, if the conflict becomes too great the use of defense mechanisms can lead to neurotic symptoms or psychotic withdrawal from reality. In structural terms, neuroses reflect a conflict between id instincts and ego defense mechanisms, both of which are unconscious. In process terms, neuroses reflect the ways in which the individual attempts to use defense mechanisms to avoid anxiety and guilt (from the superego), while still allowing for some instinct gratification. Symptoms express the unconscious conflict between wish or drive and anxiety. In developmental terms, neuroses express fixations at or regressions to gratifications and modes of functioning characteristic of an earlier stage of development. The oral, anal, and phallic stages of development each have associated with them different kinds of wishes and different mechanisms of defense. Thus it is that the symptom and general form of abnormal behavior expressed by the person are tied to the stage of development at which fixation originally occurred and to the stage to which the person has regressed under stress.

Behavior Change

How does behavior change come about? Once having established a behavioral pattern, a way of thinking about and responding to situations, through what process does a change in personality take place? The psychoanalytic theory of growth suggests that there is a normal course of human personality development, one that occurs because of optimum degrees of frustration. Where there has been too little or too much frustration at a particular stage of growth, personality does not proceed normally and a fixation takes place. When this occurs, the individual repeats patterns of behavior regardless of other changes in situations. Given the development of such a neurotic pattern, how is it possible to break the cycle and to move forward? A change in significant parts of the individual's functioning can be regressive or progressive; that is, toward simpler, more rigid, and more childlike ways of functioning or toward more complex, flexible, and adult ways of functioning. Psychoanalytic theory accounts for regressive change in terms of a defensive response to anxiety or trauma. The theory of progressive change is contained in the method of psychotherapy called psychoanalysis.

In his early efforts to effect behavioral change, Freud used a method called cathartic hypnosis. The view then held was that relief from neurotic symptoms would come about through the discharge of blocked emotions. Freud did not like using hypnosis, since not all patients could be hypnotized, the results were often transient, and he did not feel that he was learning much about mental functioning. The second development in technique was that of waking suggestion. Here Freud put his hand on the patient's head and assured him that he could recall and face repressed past emotional experiences. With the increased interest in the interpretation of dreams, Freud focused on the **free association** method as basic to psychoanalysis. In free association the patient is asked to report to the analyst every thought that comes to mind, to delay reporting nothing, to withhold nothing, to bar nothing from coming to consciousness. **Dreams** are the "royal road" to the unconscious. Through the free association method the analyst and patient are able to go beyond the manifest (obvious) content of the dream to the latent content, to the hidden meaning that expresses the unconscious wish. Dreams, like symptoms, are disguises and partial wish-fulfillments. In the dream, the person can satisfy a hostile or sexual wish in a disguised, and thereby safe, way. For example, rather than dreaming of oneself killing someone, one may dream of a battle in which a particular figure is killed. In such a case the wish may remain at least somewhat obvious, but in other cases the wish may be much more disguised. Free association allows for the uncovering of the disguise. When conscious control is relaxed, the impulses, wishes, memories, and fantasies of the unconscious break through into consciousness. It is important to realize, however, that the free-association process, the stream of consciousness, is not in fact free; it is determined, as is all behavior, by the forces within the individual that are striving for expression. It is also important to recognize that ordinarily one cannot easily or immediately understand the meaning of a dream—it requires a process of uncovering or discovery.

Omit

At first, Freud thought that making the unconscious conscious was sufficient to affect change and cure. This was in keeping with the early emphasis on repressed memories as the basis for pathology. As Hendrick (1934) noted, Freud then realized that more than the recovery of memories was involved. Rather, emotional insight into the wishes and conflicts that had remained hidden was necessary.

> He [Freud] would succeed in learning the unconscious wish. He would inform the patient of it; the patient would agree and comprehend; this would effect the patient's intellectual appraisal of his problems, but not the emotional tensions themselves. Thus, early in his work, Freud learned a lesson which many who putter with his techniques have not yet assimilated; that intellectual insight cannot control the forces of the unconscious, the repression is not simply the difference between knowing and not knowing, that cure depends on far more than making conscious.
>
> Hendrick, 1934, pp. 191–192

What more than "making conscious" does progressive change depend on? The process of therapeutic change in psychoanalysis involves coming to grips with emotions and wishes that previously have been unconscious and struggling with these painful experiences within a relatively safe and benign environment. If psychopathology involves fixation at an early stage of development, then in psychoanalysis individuals become free to resume their normal psychological development. "Analytic therapy may indeed be correctly defined as a technical procedure which awakens conflicts inadequately solved during natural adolescence, and by reducing the need for repression it provides a second chance for a better solution" (Hendrick, 1934, p. 214). If psychopathology involves the damming up of the instincts and the expenditure of energy for defensive purposes, then psychoanalysis involves a redistribution of energy so that more energy is available for mature, guiltless, less rigid, and more gratifying activities. If psychopathology involves conflict and defense mechanisms, then psychoanalysis involves the reduction of conflict and the freeing of the patient from the limitations of the defensive processes. If psychopathology involves an individual dominated by the unconscious and the tyranny of the id, then psychoanalysis involves making conscious what was unconscious and putting under control of the ego what was formerly under the domination of the id or superego.

> *Our plan of cure is based upon these views. The ego has been weakened by the internal conflict; we must come to its aid. The position is like a civil war which can only be decided by the help of an ally from without. The analytical physician and the weakened ego of the patient, basing themselves upon the real external world, are to combine against the enemies, the instinctual demands of the id, and the moral demands of the superego. We form a pact with each other. The patient's sick ego promises us the most candor, promises, that is, to put at our disposal all of the material which his self-perception provides; we, on the other hand, assure him of the strictest discretion and put at his service our experience in interpreting material that has been influenced by the unconscious. Our knowledge shall compensate for his ignorance and shall give his ego once more mastery over the lost provinces of his mental life. This pact constitutes the analytic situation.*
>
> Freud, 1940, pp. 62–63

In sum, then, psychoanalysis relates to structural, process, and developmental changes. Basically, psychoanalysis is viewed as a learning process in which the individual resumes and completes the growth process that was interrupted when the neurosis began. The principle involved is the reexposure of the patient, under more favorable circumstances, to the emotional situations that could not be handled in the past. The vehicle for such reexposure is the transference relationship and the development of a transference neurosis. The term **transference** refers to the development, on the part of the patient, of attitudes toward the analyst that have as their basis attitudes held by the patient toward earlier parental figures. In the sense that transference relates to distortions of reality based on past experiences, transference occurs in everyone's daily life and in all forms of psychotherapy. In expressing transference attitudes toward the analyst, patients duplicate in therapy their interactions with people in their outer lives and their past interactions with significant figures. For example, if patients feel that the analyst's taking notes may lead to exploitation by the analyst, they are expressing attitudes they hold towards both people they meet in their daily existence and earlier figures in their lives. In free associating, oral characters may be concerned about whether they are "feeding" the analyst and whether the analyst gives them enough in return; anal characters may be concerned about who is controlling the sessions; phallic characters may be concerned about who will win in competitive struggles. Such attitudes, often part of the unconscious daily existence of the patient, come to light in the course of analysis.

While transference is a part of all relationships and of all forms of therapy, psychoanalysis is distinctive in its use of it as a dynamic force in behavior change. Many of the formal qualities of the analytic situation are structured to enhance the development of transference. The patient lying on the couch supports the development of a dependent relationship. The scheduling of frequent meetings (up to five or six times a week) strengthens the emotional importance of the analytic relationship to the patient's daily existence. Finally, the fact that patients become so tied to their analysts, while knowing so little about them as people, means that their responses are almost completely determined by their neurotic conflicts. The analyst remains a mirror or blank screen on which the individual projects wishes and anxieties.

> *Thus the technical devices of analysis which best serve for therapy also produce the best experimental situation yet devised for studying the more complex features of human nature . . . Psychoanalysis is the test tube of human*

Freud's consulting room.

experience. For one hour a day, for a limited period, a sample of human thoughts and feelings is examined under controlled conditions. A daily specimen of typical emotional reactions is taken. The endlessly involved complications of everyday life are reduced by the four walls of the treatment room; the multitude of people serving as emotional stimuli and instinctual objects are replaced by a single individual, the analyst.

Hendrick, 1934, pp. 196–197

The encouragement of transference, or providing the circumstances that allow it to develop, leads to the development of the transference neurosis. It is here that patients play out, full-blown, their old conflicts. Patients now invest the major aspects of their relationship with the analyst with the wishes and anxieties of the past. The goal is no longer to get well, but to gain from the analyst what they had to do without in childhood. Rather than seeking a way out of competitive relationships, they may only seek to castrate the analyst; rather than seek to become less dependent on others, they may seek to have the analyst gratify all of their dependency needs. The fact that these attitudes have developed within the context of the analysis allows patients and their analysts to look at and understand the instinctual and defensive components of the original infantile conflict. The fact that the patient invests considerable emotion in the situation allows for the increased understanding to be emotionally meaningful. Change occurs when insight has been gained, when patients realize, on both an intellectual and emotional level, the nature of conflicts and feel free, in terms of their new perceptions of themselves and the world, to gratify their instincts in a mature, conflict-free way.

Whereas guilt and anxiety prevented growth in the past, the analytic situation offers the individual the opportunity to deal anew with the old conflicts. Why should the response be any different at this time? Basically, change occurs in analysis because of the three therapeutic factors. First, in analysis the conflict is less intense than it was in the original situation. Second, the analyst assumes an attitude which is different from that of the parents. Finally, patients in analysis are older and more mature, that is they are able to use parts of their ego that have developed to deal with the parts of their functioning that have not. These three factors, creating as they do the opportunity for relearning, provide the basis for what Alexander and French (1946) call the "corrective emotional experience." It should be clear that developments such as these in no way suggest that psychoanalysis is an intellectual experience as opposed to an emotional experience, that insight and understanding are given by the analyst rather than gained by the patient, or that there is a denial of moral responsibility and a sanctioning of sin. Rather, psychoanalytic theory suggests that through insight into old conflicts, through an understanding of the needs for infantile gratifications and recognition of the potential for mature gratification, through an understanding of old anxieties and a recognition of their lack of relevance to current realities, patients may progress toward maximum instinctual gratification within the limits set by reality and their own moral convictions.

A CASE EXAMPLE—LITTLE HANS

Although many psychiatrists and psychologists have spent considerable times treating patients, Freud is one of the very few who have reported cases in detail. Most of Freud's cases come from early in his career. The famed Dora case, in which Freud analysed the unconscious conflicts behind a number of symptoms, was presented in 1905. The case of an obsessive neurotic, involving fears that something might happen to people, and an obsessive preoccupation with rats, was published in 1909. While these and other case presentations are useful in understanding many aspects of psychoanalytic theory, it is important to remember that they occurred prior to Freud's development of his theory of the sexual and aggressive instincts, prior to the development of the structural model, and prior to the development of the theory of anxiety and defense mechanisms.

The case of Little Hans, published in 1909, involves the analysis of a phobia in a five-year-old boy. It involves the treatment of the boy by his father and does not represent Freud's direct participation in the therapeutic process. The boy was bothered by a hysterical fear that a horse would bite him. Therefore, he refused to leave the house. The boy's father kept detailed notes on his treatment and frequently discussed his progress with Freud. Although the "patient" was not treated by Freud, the case of Little Hans is important because it illustrates the theory of infantile sexuality, the functioning of the Oedipus complex and castration anxiety, the dynamics of symptom formation, and the process of behavior change.

Our account of events in the life of Little Hans begins at age three. At this point he had a lively interest in his penis, which he called his "widdler." What was striking about Hans during this period was his pleasure in touching his own penis and his preoccupation with penises or "widdlers" in others. For example, he wanted to know if his mother had a widdler and was fascinated with the process by which cows are milked. The interest in touching his penis, however, led to threats by his mother. "If you do that, I shall send you to Dr. A. to cut off your widdler. And then what will you widdle with?" Thus, there was a direct castration threat on the part of a parent, in this case the mother. Freud pinpointed this as the beginning of Hans' castration complex.

Hans' interest in widdlers extended to noting the size of the lion's widdler at the zoo and analyzing the differences between animate and inanimate objects—dogs and horses have widdlers, tables and chairs do not. Hans was curious about many things, but Freud related his general thirst for knowledge to sexual curiosity. Hans continued to be interested in whether his mother had a widdler. "I though you (mother) were so big you'd have a widdler like a horse." When he was three-and-a-half, a sister was born, who also became a focus for his widdler concerns. "But her widdler's still quite small. When she grows up it'll get bigger all right." According to Freud, Hans could not admit what he really saw, namely, that there was no widdler there. To do so would mean that he must face his own castration anxieties. These anxieties oc-

121–125 omit

curred at a time when he was experiencing pleasure in the organ, as witnessed in his comments to his mother while she dried and powdered him after his bath.

HANS	Why don't you put your finger there.
MOTHER	Because that'd be piggish.
HANS	What's that? Piggish? Why?
HANS (*laughing*)	But it's great fun.

Thus Hans, now more than four year old, was preoccupied with his penis, experienced pleasure in it and concern about the loss of it, and began some seduction of his mother. It was at this point that his nervous disorders became apparent. The father, attributing the difficulties to sexual overexcitation due to his mother's tenderness, wrote Freud that Hans was "afraid that a horse will bite him in the street" and this fear seemed somehow to be connected with his having been frightened by seeing a large penis. As you remember, he had noticed at a very early age what large penises horses have, and at that time he inferred that, as his mother was so large, she must "have a widdler like a horse." Hans was afraid of going into the street and was depressed in the evenings. He had bad dreams and was frequently taken into his mother's bed. While walking in the street with his nurse, he became terribly frightened and sought to return home to be with his mother. The fear that horses would bite him became a fear that the horse would come into his room. He had developed a full-blown phobia, an irrational dread or fear of an object (horse). What more can we learn about this phobia? How are we to account for its development? As Freud notes, we must do more than simply call this a small boy's foolish fears.

The father attempted to deal with his son's fear of horses by offering him an interpretation. Hans was told that the fear of horses was nonsense, that the truth was that he (Hans) was fond of his mother and the fear of horses had to do with an interest in their widdlers. Upon Freud's suggestion, the father explained to Hans that women do not have widdlers. Apparently there was a period of some relief in Hans, but he continued to be bothered by an obsessive wish to look at horses, though he was then frightened by them. At this point, he had his tonsils taken out and his phobia worsened. He was afraid that a white horse would bite him. He continued to be interested in widdlers in females. At the zoo, he was afraid of all the large animals and was entertained by the smaller ones. Among the birds, he was afraid of the pelican. In spite of his father's truthful explanation, Hans sought to reassure himself. "And everyone has a widdler. And my widdler will get bigger as I get bigger, because it does grow on me." According to Freud, Hans had been making comparisons among the sizes of widdlers and was dissatisfied with his own. Big animals, reminded him of this defect and were disagreeable to him. The father's explanations heightened his castration anxiety, as expressed in the words "it does grow on me", as if it could be cut off. Thus, for this reason he resisted the information, and thus it had no therapeutic results. "Could it be that living beings really did exist which did not possess widdlers? If so, it would no longer be so incredible that they could take his own widdler away, and, as it were, make him into a woman."

Around this time, Hans reported the following dream. "In the night there was a big giraffe in the room and a crumpled one; and the big one called out because I took the crumpled one away from it. Then it stopped calling out; and then I sat down on top of the crumpled one." The father's interpretation was that he, the father, was the big giraffe, with the big penis and the mother was the crumpled giraffe, missing the genital organ. The dream was a reproduction of a morning scene in which the mother took Hans into bed with her. The father warned her against this ("The big one called out because I'd taken the crumpled one away from it") but the mother continued to encourage it. The mother encouraged and reinforced the oedipal wishes. Hans stayed with her and, in the wish fulfillment of the dream, he took possession of her ("Then the big giraffe stopped calling out; and then I sat down on top of the crumpled one").

Freud's strategy in understanding Hans' phobia was to suspend judgment and to give his impartial attention to everything there was to observe. He learned that prior to the development of the phobia, Hans had been alone with his mother at a summer place. There, two significant events occurred. First, he heard the father of one of his friends tell her that a white horse there bites and she was not to hold her finger to it. Second, while playing as if they were horses, a friend who rivaled Hans for the affection of the little girls fell down, hit his foot, and bled. In an interview with Hans, Freud learned that Hans was bothered by the blinders on horses and the black around their mouths. The phobia became extended to include a fear that horses dragging a heavy van would fall down and kick their feet. It was then discovered that the exciting cause of his phobia, the event that capitalized on a psychological readiness for the formation of a phobia, was the perception of a horse falling down. While walking outside with his mother one day, Hans had seen a horse pulling a van fall down and begin to kick his feet.

The central feature in this case of little Hans was the phobia about the horse. What is fascinating in this regard is how often associations concerning a horse came up in relation to father, mother, and Hans himself. We have already noticed Hans' interest in his mother's widdler in relation to that of a horse. To his father, he said at one point: "Daddy, don't trot away from me." Can father, who wore a mustache and eyeglasses, be the horse that Hans was afraid of, the horse that would come into his room at night and would bite him? Or, could Hans himself be the horse? Hans was known to play horse in his room, to trot about, fall down, kick about with his feet, and neigh. He repeatedly ran up to his father and bit him, just as he feared the horse would do to him. Hans was overfed. Could this relate to his concerns about large, fat horses? Finally, Hans was known to have called himself a young horse and to have a tendency to stamp his feet on the ground when angry, similar to what the horse did when it fell down. To return to the mother, could the heavily laden carts symbolize the pregnant mother and the horse falling down the birth or delivery of a child? Are such associations coincidental or can they play a significant role in our understanding of the phobia?

According to Freud, the major cause of Hans' phobia was his Oedipus conflict. Hans felt considerable affection for his mother, more than he could handle during the phallic stage of his development. While he had deep affection for the father he also considered him a rival for his mother's affections. When he and mother stayed at the summer cottage and father was away, he was able to get into bed with mother and keep her for himself. This heightened his attraction for his mother and his hostility toward his father. For Freud, "Hans was really a little Oedipus who wanted to have his father 'out of the way', to get rid of him, so that he might be alone with his handsome mother and sleep with her. This wish had originated during his summer holidays, when the alternating presence and absence of his father had drawn Hans' attention to the condition upon which depended the intimacy with his mother which he longed for." The fall and injury to his friend and rival during one of those holidays was significant in symbolizing the defeat for Hans of his rival.

When he returned home from the summer holidays. Hans' resentment toward his father increased. He tried to suppress the resentment with exaggerated affection. He arrived at an ingenious solution to the oedipal conflict. He and his mother would be parents to children and the father could be the granddaddy. Thus, as Freud notes, "the little Oedipus had found a happier solution than that prescribed by destiny. Instead of putting his father out of the way, he had granted him the same happiness that he desired himself: he made him a grandfather and let him too marry his own mother." But such a fantasy could not be a satisfactory solution, and Hans was left with considerable hostility for his father. The exciting cause of the phobia was the horse falling down. At that moment, Hans perceived a wish that his father might in the same way fall down and die. The hostility towards his father was projected onto the father and was symbolized in the horse, because he himself nourished jealous and hostile wishes against him. He feared the horse would bite him because of his wish that his father should fall down, and fears that the horse would come into his room occurred at night when he was most tempted by oedipal fantasies. In his own play as a horse and in his biting of his father, he expressed an identification with his father. The phobia expressed the wish and the anxiety, and in a secondary way, accomplished the objective of leaving Hans home to be with his mother.

In sum, both his fear that a horse would bite him and his fear that horses would fall down represented the father who was going to punish Hans for the evil wishes he was harboring against him. Hans was able to get over the phobia and, according to a later report by Freud, he appeared to be functioning well. What factors allowed for the change? First, there was the sexual enlightenment by the father. While Hans was reluctant to accept this and it at first heightened his castration anxiety, it did serve as a useful piece of reality to hold onto. Second, the analysis provided by his father and by Freud was useful in making conscious for Hans what had formerly been unconscious. Finally, the father's interest and permissive attitude toward Hans' expression of his feelings allowed for a resolution of the Oedipus conflict in favor of an identification with the father, diminishing both the wish to rival the father and the castration anxiety, and thereby decreasing the potential for symptom development.

The case of little Hans has many problems with it as a piece of scientific investigation. The interviewing was done by the father in an unsystematic way. The father himself was a close adherent of Freud's and therefore was possibly biased somewhat in his observations and interpretations. Freud himself was dependent on secondhand reports. He was aware of the limitations of the data, but he was also impressed with them. Whereas before he had based his theory on the childhood memories of adult patients, now, in the case of Little Hans, he began to observe the sexual life of children. It is hard to draw conclusions about the theory in terms of this one case. The presentation does not contain all of Freud's observations on Hans. Furthermore, it is but a single case, and it is taken from an early point (1909) in Freud's work. On the other hand, we do get an appreciation of both the wealth of information available to the analyst and, moreover, the problems inherent in evaluating and interpreting such data. We must necessarily get a feeling for Freud's ability to observe and describe phenomena and his efforts to come to terms with the complexity of human behavior. In this one case alone we have descriptions of phenomena relevant to the following: infantile sexuality, fantasies of children, functioning of the unconscious, the process of conflict development and conflict resolution, the process of symptom formation, symbolization, and the dream process. In reading such a case we cannot fail to be impressed by Freud's courageous efforts to discover the secrets of human functioning and by his willingness to pursue the job that needed to be done, in spite of limitations in his observations and in full recognition of the complexity of the phenomena he was trying to understand.

Start

RELATED POINTS OF VIEW AND RECENT DEVELOPMENTS

One interesting aspect of the history of psychoanalytic theory has been the development of schools or groups with different, often antagonistic points of view. Freud changed many aspects of psychoanalytic theory during the course of his professional career. However, he and his followers clashed on many issues. To a certain extent there was what has been described as a religious or political quality (Fromm, 1959) to psychoanalysis, with the traditional followers being considered among the faithful and those who deviated from the fundamental principles being cast outside the movement. This pattern started during Freud's lifetime and continued afterwards. A theorist such as Erikson is still highly regarded by most traditional psychoanalysts whereas the theorists to be considered below often are not. Frequently it is hard to determine the basis for the response to one or another theorist. However, as a general rule, a theorist must retain a commitment to the following concepts to be considered a part of Freudian psychoanalysis: the sexual and aggressive instincts, the unconscious, and the stages of development. As we shall see, the theories considered below questioned one or another of these concepts and thereby approached understanding humans somewhat differently.

Two Early Challenges to Freud

Among the many early analysts who broke with Freud and developed their own schools of thought were Alfred Adler and Carl G. Jung. Both were early and important followers of Freud, Adler having been president of the Vienna Psychoanalytic Society and Jung president of the International Psychoanalytic Society. Both split with Freud over what they felt was an excessive emphasis on the sexual instincts. The split with Jung was particularly painful for Freud since Jung was to be his "crown prince" and chosen successor. Other individuals also split with Freud and developed their own schools of thought. However, Adler and Jung were among the earliest and remain among the best known.

Alfred Adler (1870–1937)

For approximately a decade, Alfred Adler (1870–1937) was an active member of the Vienna psychoanalytic group. However, in 1911, when he presented his views to the other members of this group, the response was so hostile that he left it to form his own school of *Individual Psychology*. What ideas could have been considered so unacceptable to psychoanalysts? We cannot consider all of Adler's theory, but we can consider some of his early and later views to get a feeling for the important differences between them and psychoanalysis.

Perhaps most significant of all in Adler's split from Freud was his greater emphasis on social urges and conscious thoughts than on instinctual sexual urges and unconscious processes. Early in his career Adler became interested in organ inferiorities and how people compensate for them. A person with a weak organ may attempt to compensate for this weakness by special efforts to strengthen that organ or by efforts to develop other organs. For example, someone who stutters as a child may attempt to become a great speaker, or someone with a defect in vision may attempt to develop special listening sensitivities. Whereas initially Adler was interested in bodily organ weaknesses, gradually he became interested in psychological *feelings of inferiority* and *compensatory strivings* to mask or reduce these painful feelings. Thus, whereas Freudians might see Theodore Roosevelt's emphasis on toughness and carrying a "big stick" as a defense against castration anxiety, Adlerians might see him as expressing compensatory strivings against feelings of inferiority associated with boyhood weaknesses. Whereas Freudians might see an extremely aggressive woman as expressing penis envy, Adlerians might see her as expressing a masculine protest or rejection of the stereotyped

Alfred Adler

feminine role of weakness and inferiority. According to Adler, how a person attempts to cope with such feelings becomes a part of his or her *style of life*—a distinctive aspect of his or her personality functioning.

These concepts already suggest a much more social rather than biological emphasis. This social emphasis increasingly became an important part of Adler's thinking. At first Adler spoke of a *will to power* as an expression of the organism's efforts to cope with feelings of helplessness dating from infancy. This emphasis gradually shifted to an emphasis on *striving for superiority*. In its neurotic form this striving could be expressed in wishes for power and control over others; in its healthier form it expressed a "great upward drive" toward unity and perfection. In the healthy person the striving for superiority is expressed in social feeling and cooperation as well as in assertiveness and competition. From the beginning there is in people a social interest, that is an innate interest in relating to people and an innate potential for cooperation.

Adler's theory also is noteworthy for its emphasis on how people respond to feelings about the self, how people respond to goals that direct their behavior toward the future, and how the order of birth among siblings can influence their psychological development. In relation to the latter, many psychologists have noted the tendency for only sons or first born sons to achieve more than later sons in a family. For example, twenty-one of the first twenty-three American astronauts were first born or only sons. While many of Adler's ideas have found their way into the general public's thinking and are related to views later expressed by other theorists, the school of individual psychology itself has not had a major impact on personality theory and research.

✳*Birth Order*—Alfred Adler emphasized the importance of birth order in personality development. Twenty-one of the first twenty-three American astronauts were first-born or only sons.

Carl G. Jung (1875–1961)

Jung split with Freud in 1914, a few years after Adler, and developed his own school of thought, *Analytical Psychology*. Like Adler, he was distressed with what he felt was an excessive emphasis on sexuality. Instead, Jung viewed the libido as a generalized life energy. While sexuality is a part of this basic energy, the libido also includes other strivings for pleasure and creativity.

Jung accepted Freud's emphasis on the unconscious but added to it the concept of the *collective unconscious*. According to Jung, people have stored within their collective unconscious the cumulative experiences of past generations. The collective unconscious, as opposed to the personal unconscious, is shared by all humans as a result of their common ancestry. It is a part of our animal heritage, our link with millions of years of past experience: "This psychic life is the mind of our ancient ancestors, the way in which they thought and felt, the way in which they conceived of life and the world, of gods and human beings. The existence of these historical layers is presumably the source of belief in reincarnation and in memories of past lives" (Jung, 1939, p. 24).

An important part of the collective unconscious are universal images or symbols, known as *archetypes*. Archetypes, such as the Mother archetype, are seen in fairy tales, dreams, myths, and in some psychotic thoughts. Jung was struck with similar images that keep appearing, in slightly different forms, in far-distant cultures. For example, the Mother archetype might be expressed in a variety of positive or negative forms: as life-giver, as all-giving and nurturant, as the witch or threatening punisher ("Don't fool with Mother Nature"), and as the seductive female. Archetypes may be represented in our images of persons, demons, animals, natural forces, or objects. The evidence in all cases for their being a part of our collective unconscious is their universality among members of different cultures from past and current time periods.

Another important aspect of Jung's theory was his emphasis on how people struggle with opposing forces within them. For example, there is the struggle between the face or mask we present to others (*persona*) and the private or personal self. If people emphasize the persona too much there may be a loss of sense of self and a doubting about who they are. On the other hand, the persona, as expressed in social roles and customs, is a necessary part of living in society. Similarly, there is the struggle between the masculine and feminine parts of ourselves. Every male has a feminine part (*anima*) and every female has a masculine part (*animus*) to their personality. If a man rejects his feminine part he may emphasize mastery and strength to an excessive degree, appearing cold and insensitive to the feelings of others. If a woman rejects her masculine part she may be excessively absorbed

Carl Jung

in "motherhood" and unable to accomplish herself in other ways. Psychologists currently interested in stereotyped sex roles would probably applaud Jung's emphasis on these dual aspects in everyone's personality, although they might question his characterizing some as specifically masculine and others as feminine.

Another contrast in Jung's theory is that between *introversion* and *extroversion*. Everyone relates to the world primarily in one of two directions, though the other direction always remains a part of the person. In the case of introversion, the person's basic orientation is inner, toward the self. The introverted type is hesitant, reflective, and cautious. In the case of extroversion the person's basic orientation is outward, toward the outside world. The extroverted type is socially engaging, active, and venturesome. For each person there is the task of finding unity in the *self*. For Jung an important task of life is to be found in bringing into harmony or integrating the above and other opposing forces. The integration of the many opposing aspects of our personality into the self is a lifelong struggle: "Personality as a complete realization of the fullness of our being is an unattainable ideal. But unattainability is no counter argument against an ideal, for ideals are only signposts, never goals" (Jung, 1939, p. 287). The struggle described here can become a particularly important aspect of life once people have passed the age of forty and defined themselves to the outside world in a variety of ways.

As with Adler, we have been able to consider only some of the highlights of Jung's theory. Jung is considered by many to be one of the great creative thinkers of the century and his theory has influenced the thinking of people in many fields outside of psychology. While periodically there are signs of the development of a strong interest in Jung inside of psychology, his views have yet to have a significant impact on the field.

The Cultural and Interpersonal Emphasis

With the later shift in psychodynamic thinking from Europe to the United States, one finds theorists emphasizing social rather than biological forces in behavior. Collectively, these theorists are called neo-Freudians, recognizing both their theoretical debt to Freud and their development of new theoretical positions. Some of these theorists, such as Karen Horney, emigrated to the United States prior to the Second World War. Other theorists, notably Harry Stack Sullivan, were born and trained in this country.

Karen Horney (1885–1952)

Karen Horney was trained as a traditional analyst in Germany and came to the United States in 1932. Shortly thereafter she split with traditional psychoanalytic thought and developed her own theoretical orientation and psychoanalytic training program. In contrast to Adler and Jung, she felt that her views were built on the tremendous contributions of Freud, and not replacements of them. Perhaps the major difference between her and Freud centers on the queston of universal

Karen Horney

biological influences as opposed to cultural influences; "When we realize the great import of cultural conditions on neuroses, the biological and physiological conditions, which are considered by Freud to be their root, recede into the background" (1937, p. viii). She was led to this emphasis by three major considerations. First, Freud's statements concerning women made Horney think about cultural influences: "Their influence on our ideas of what constitutes masculinity or femininity was obvious, and it became just as obvious to me that Freud had arrived at certain conclusions because he failed to take them into account" (1945, p. 11). Second, she was associated with another psychoanalyst, Erich Fromm, who increased her awareness of the importance of social and cultural influences. Third, Horney's observations of differences in personality structure between patients seen in Europe and the United States confirmed the importance of cultural influences. Beyond this, these observations led her to conclude that interpersonal relationships are at the core of all healthy and disturbed personality functioning.

Horney's emphasis in neurotic functioning is on how individuals attempt to cope with *basic anxiety*—the feeling a child has of being isolated and helpless in a potentially hostile world. According to her theory of neurosis, in the neurotic person there is conflict among three ways of responding to this basic anxiety. These three patterns, or *neurotic trends*, are known as moving toward, moving against, and moving away. All three are characterized by rigidity and the lack of fulfillment of individual potential, the essence of any neurosis. In *moving toward* the person attempts to deal with anxiety by an excessive interest in being accepted, needed, and approved of. Such a person accepts a dependent role in relation to others and, except for the unlimited desire for affection, become unselfish, unde-manding, and self-sacrificing. In *moving against*, the person assumes that every-one is hostile and that life is a struggle against all. All functioning is directed toward denying a need for others and toward appearing tough. In *moving away*, the third component of the conflict, the person shrinks away from others into neurotic detachment. Such people often look at themselves and others with emo-tional detachment, a way of not getting emotionally involved with others. While each neurotic person shows one or another trend as a special aspect of their per-sonality, the problem is really that there is conflict among the three trends in the effort to deal with basic anxiety.

Before leaving Horney, her views concerning women should be considered. These views date back to her early work within traditional psychoanalytic thought and are reflected in a series of papers in *Feminine Psychology* (1973). As has been noted, from the start Horney had trouble accepting Freud's views of women. She felt that the concept of penis envy might be the result of a male bias in psychoanalysts that treat neurotic women in a particular social context: "Un-fortunately, little or nothing is known of physically healthy women, or of women under different cultural conditions" (1973, p. 216). She suggested that women are not biologically disposed toward masochistic attitudes of being weak, dependent, submissive, and self-sacrificing. Instead, these attitudes indicated the powerful influence of social forces.

Neurotic Trends—Karen Horney emphasized the neurotic trends of moving toward, mov-ing against, and moving away (as illustrated in the following three photographs) as at-tempts to cope with basic anxiety. In more moderate forms such trends exist in most people.

In sum, both in her views of women and in her general theoretical orientation Horney rejected Freud's biological emphasis in favor of a social, interpersonal one. Partly as a result of this difference she held a much more optimistic view concerning the person's capacity for change and self-fulfillment.

Harry Stack Sullivan (1892–1949)

Of the theorists considered in this section, Sullivan is the only one born and trained in the United States, the only one who never had direct contact with Freud, and the one who most emphasized the role of social, interpersonal forces in human development. In fact, his theory has been known as the *Interpersonal Theory of Psychiatry* (1953) and his followers consider themselves part of the Sullivan school of interpersonal relations.

Sullivan placed great importance on the early relationship between the infant and the mother in the development of anxiety and in the development of a sense of self. Anxiety may be communicated by the mother in her earliest interaction with the infant. Thus, from the start, anxiety is interpersonal in character. The *self*, a critical concept in Sullivan's thinking, similarly is social in origin. The self develops out of feelings experienced while in contact with others and from *reflected appraisals* or perceptions on the part of the child, as to how it is valued or appraised by others. Important parts of the self, particularly in relation to the experience of anxiety as opposed to security, are the *good-me* associated with pleasurable experiences, the *bad-me* associated with pain and threats to security, and the *not-me* or part of the self that is rejected because it is associated with intolerable anxiety.

Sullivan's emphasis on social influences is seen throughout his views on the development of the person. These views are somewhat similar to Erikson's in their emphasis on interpersonal influences, and in their emphasis on important stages beyond the Oedipus complex. Particularly noteworthy here is Sullivan's emphasis on the *juvenile era* and *preadolescence*. During the juvenile stage, roughly the grammar school years, the child's experiences with friends and teachers begin to rival the influence of parents. Social acceptance becomes important and the

Harry Stack Sullivan

Peers—Harry Stack Sullivan emphasized the importance of peers and a close friend of the same sex during preadolescence.

child's "reputation" with others becomes an important source of self-esteem or anxiety. During preadolescence a relationship to a close friend of the same sex, or chum, becomes particularly important. This relationship of close friendship, of love, forms the basis for the development of a love relationship with a person of the opposite sex during adolescence. Today, many child psychologists suggest that early relationships with peers may equal in importance the early relationships with the mother (Lewis, 1975).

As with the other theorists in this section, we have been able to consider only a few of the major concepts of Sullivan's interpersonal theory. Sullivan's work is noteworthy in its social emphasis, in its emphasis on the development of the self, and in the outstanding contributions that he made to the treatment of schizophrenic patients.

Recent Developments within Traditional Psychoanalytic Theory   *Omit*

Turning to developments within traditional psychoanalytic theory, we can consider progress associated with clinical investigations and progress associated with systematic research efforts. From its inception with Freud and continuing on to date, developments within psychoanalytic theory generally have been based on clinical investigation, that is, analysis of individual cases. One important development has been the extension of psychoanalytic investigation to age groups and forms of psychopathology rarely treated by Freud and his followers. As noted, Little Hans was treated by his father. Most psychoanalytic material on childhood and adolescence was based on memories reported by adult parents. The situation changed considerably with the efforts of individuals such as Anna Freud and Melanie Klein who used psychoanalytic concepts in the treatment of children, so that now a major part of the psychotherapy conducted with children and adolescents in Great Britain and the United States is based on psychoanalytic theory. Modifications are made in the treatment procedure according to the age group being treated (e.g., with children, play therapy is used as a substitute for dream analysis as a route to the unconscious), but the essential theoretical concepts remain the same.

In addition to the expansion of their clinical efforts to treatment of children, psychoanalysts increasingly have been concerned with different types of patient problems than those faced, in the main, by Freud. In the words of one analyst, today's patients come from a different social and cultural context than did Freud's patients and bring with them different problems. Rather than presenting themselves with "typical neuroses," they seek help with depressions, with feeling of emptiness, and with lives "lacking zest and joy" (Wolf, 1977). Such changes in the major problems coming to the attention of analysts have led to new theoretical advances, not from a dissatisfaction with Freudian theory per se but from the need to understand and solve different clinical problems.

Clinical concern with problems of self-definition and excessive vulnerability to blows to one's sense of self-esteem have led psychologists to become increasingly interested in how, during the earliest years, a person develops a sense of self (Kohut, 1977). Thus, many recent theoretical efforts, while not rejecting Freud's views concerning the roles of sex and aggression, have become more concerned with how the person attempts to protect the integrity of the sense of self from threats that arise from within the person and from the surrounding interpersonal environment. To a certain extent, this recent focus on the self represents an extension of the earlier emphasis by other analysts on ego functioning (e.g., Hartmann, Kris, Lowenstein, Rapaport, Schafer). However, there is a difference. The earlier emphasis in psychoanalytic ego psychology focused on the undefensive, conflict-free aspects of ego functioning. Such functioning is expressed in artistic, creative productions as opposed disturbed neurotic or psychotic functioning. In contrast, more recently there has been concern with disturbance in the development of ego functioning and the sense of self, and with the implications of such disturbances for the development of psychopathology.

One of the problems with such clinical analyses of the self has been that they are difficult to translate into concepts and procedures that can be used in systematic, empirical investigations. Indeed, some analysts feel that such observations from "depth psychology" are part of a theoretical framework different than personality psychology in general (Kohut, 1971). Other analysts and psychologists, however, have attempted to study psychoanalytic phenomena and principles in the laboratory. Recent reviews of the experimental testing of Freudian concepts come to a variety of conclusions, ranging from the conclusions that many concepts have been certified and generally the theory has fared well (Fisher & Cleveland, 1977; Kline, 1981) to the conclusion that there is no evidence at all for psychoanalytic theory (Eysenck & Wilson, 1973).

One problem in the experimental testing of psychoanalytic concepts has been the difficulty in producing the phenomena of interest in the laboratory. Perhaps some advances are being made. For example, we have considered earlier the work on subliminal psychodynamic activation as well as some evidence of interest on the part of experimental cognitive psychologists in phenomena such as repression. Along with these efforts are those of other psychologists who are attempting to translate Freud's clinical observations into concepts that are free of metaphor and more open to systematic observation (Klein, 1976; Schafer, 1976; 1978). Instead of concepts such as drive, libido, instinct, and force there would be greater emphasis on behavior, including all private psychological activity that can be made public (dreams, fantasies, fears, etc.).

In sum, recent developments have taken two somewhat divergent trends. On the one hand, there is a concern with new kinds of clinical phenomena and a disregard of the potential for systematic, empirical investigation. On the other hand, there is an effort to produce in the laboratory the phenomena emphasized by Freud and to translate Freudian concepts into a language that can better stand the test of scientific criticism. The clinical and laboratory investigators discussed here share a commitment to the basic principles of Freudian psychoanalytic theory.

Start 137- 144

A CRITICAL EVALUATION

In evaluating psychoanalysis as a theory of personality, we need to keep in mind three points. First, we need to be clear about whether we are considering an early or a later view in the development of the theory. Although the thrust of psychoanalysis, in terms of its emphasis on unconscious forces and on the importance of early events, has remained consistent throughout, major developments in the theory did take place between the publication of *The Interpretation of Dreams* in 1900 and Freud's death in 1939. In considering Freud's view of anxiety, for example, we must be clear that the first theory viewed anxiety as the result of repression and dammed up libido, whereas the second theory viewed anxiety as a signal of impending danger to the ego, which leads to repression. Second, in evaluating psychoanalysis we need to be clear about whether we are considering a part of the theory or the theory as a whole. Where consideration is given to a part of the theory, is that part basic to the entire structure or is the rest independent of it? For example, the latency period as a stage of development is not critical to the theory, but the genetic approach is; the theory of dreams as preservers of sleep is not critical to the theory, but the importance of the unconscious is. Finally, in considering psychoanalysis as a theory, we must keep it distinct from psychoanalysis as a method of therapy. The issue of therapeutic success with psychoanalysis has not been dealt with here because it is not critical to an understanding of the theory or an evaluation of it. If psychoanalytic theory did in fact lead to specific predictions concerning therapy, predictions which could be tested in a systematic way, then the results of therapy would be related to the validity of the theory. However, predictions of this nature are rarely made and, therefore, psychoanalysis as a theory of personality must be evaluated on grounds other than those of therapeutic effectiveness.

Major Contributions

How good a theory of personality is psychoanalysis? Clearly, Freud made major contributions to psychology and greatly influenced the developmental approach. Psychoanalysis has led to the use of new techniques, such as those of free association and dream interpretation, and has been a significant force in the development and use of special tests in the assessment of personality. There are two outstanding contributions. First, psychoanalysis made a major contribution to the discovery and investigation of phenomena. Whether ultimately these observations remain part of psychoanalytic theory or are integrated into another theory, the importance of the discovery of these phenomena remains. As we go beyond some of the superficialities of human behavior, we are impressed with the observations made by Freud. These become particularly apparent in clinical work with patients. It is striking for the therapist to observe the paranoid patient's fear that the therapist is out to make a homosexual attack upon him. It is striking to observe the chemist with obsessive-compulsive qualities describe how he first became interested in chemistry because of the "smells, stinks, and explosions" he could make. It is striking to observe the patient fantasy in the transference that the therapist is dependent on the patient's money for his groceries. And it is striking to observe how learning blocks in students may be related to fears that the teacher or other students will "castrate" them, to fears that being intelligent will mean that they are sissies, or to unconscious fear that intellectual curiosity will give rise to their sexual curiosity, just as the word "to know," in the Bible, means knowing someone sexually. Whether we choose to interpret these phenomena as characteristic of all human functioning, as Freud did, or merely as idiosyncratic to neurotics, we are forced to take account of these observations as data concerning human behavior. The importance of Freud's emphasis on certain essentials in human functioning was well expressed by the eminent anthropologist Clyde Kluckhohn.

> When I began serious field work among the Navaho and Pueblo Indians, my position on psychoanalysis was a mixed one. I had been analyzed and was thoroughly convinced that Freudian psychology was the only dynamic depth psychology of much importance . . . On the other hand, I tended to believe that psychoanalysis was strongly culture-bound . . . But the facts

uncovered in my own field work and that of my collaborators have forced me to the conclusion that Freud and other psychoanalysts have depicted with astonishing correctness many central themes in motivational life which are universal. The styles of expression of these themes and much of the manifest content are culturally determined, but the underlying psychologic drama transcends cultural difference.

This should not be too surprising—except to an anthropologist over-indoctrinated with the theory of culture relativism—for many of the inescapable givens of human life are also universal.

Kluckhohn and Morgan, 1951, p. 120.

The first major contribution by Freud, then, was the richness of his observations and the attention he paid to all details of human behavior. The second was the attention he gave to the complexity of human behavior at the same time that he developed an extremely encompassing theory. Psychoanalytic theory emphasizes that seemingly similar behavior can have very different antecedents and that very similar motives can lead to quite different behavior. Generosity can express genuine affection or an effort to deal with feelings of hostility, and the lawyer and the criminal whom he defends or prosecutes may, in some cases, be closer to one another psychologically than most of us care to realize. Out of this recognition of complexity comes a theory that accounts for almost all aspects of human behavior. No other theory of personality comes close to psychoanalytic theory in accounting for such a broad range of behavior. Few others give comparable attention to the functioning of the individual as a whole.

Many, perhaps most, of our theories of personality deal not with personality as a whole, but rather with some selected aspect or process. Freudian theory kept the whole personality more in view . . . Freud produced this general theory not out of a combination of existing elements, but largely by new creative insights. His theory therefore has a scope, a unity, and a coherence which is unmatched in psychology.

Inkeles, 1963, p. 333

Limitations of the Theory

In making these contributions, Freud stands as a genius and an investigator of tremendous courage. What then of the limitations of psychoanalysis as a theory? Comments have been made already in relation to parts of the theory but what about the theory as a whole? Two major criticisms are worthy of note. The first involves the psychoanalytic view of the person, while the second involves the scientific status of psychoanalysis as a theory. In essence, these two criticisms suggest that serious questions can be raised about the energy model used by psychoanalysis to account for behavior and the ways in which its concepts are defined.

We already have observed that Freud was influenced by the discoveries of Helmholtz concerning the conservation of matter and the views of Brücke concerning the person as an energy system. Basic to the psychoanalytic model is the view that all behavior can be understood in terms of exchanges and transformations of energy, with the goal of the organism being tension reduction. The pleasure principle, the principle fundamental to all behavioral functioning, states that the organism seeks pleasure in the form of tension reduction. Yet, there is considerable evidence which suggest that the organism does not always seek tension reduction, in fact, it often seeks stimulation. Sensory deprivation studies indicate that the organism cannot maintain a prolonged state of rest, free from stimulation and sensory bombardment by the external world. Animals appear to find stimulation of some parts of the brain pleasurable (Olds, 1958) and will work to be able to explore novel environments (Butler, 1954). White (1959), in his review of the relevant literature, notes that there are many behaviors that do not seem to fit the models of physiological drive and tension reduction. These range from the "curiosity of the cat" to the play of children. These behaviors do not appear to be related to any physiological drive, they do not appear to satisfy the organism in the sense that food satisfies a hungry organism, and they do not appear to reduce tension. There is, then, evidence that a tension-reduction model alone is inadequate to account for all aspects of human functioning.

Another problem with Freud's energy model is that it tends to shade differences and make too many things equivalent. There is a simplistic quality to the theory which suggests that everything is a result of the sexual and aggressive instincts. For example, a man's love for a woman is viewed by Freud as an aim-inhibited instinct, as a repetition of the incestuous feelings for the mother. For Freud, the sucking of the infant at the breast of the mother is the model for every love relation. Such a view, however, fails to give adequate attention to differences between a child's love and that of an adult, between the love for a mate and the love for a friend, between the love for a person and the love for one's work. It does seem likely that all of these loves have something in common, that in any one individual they share at least some earlier roots and at least some common principles of functioning. On the other hand, to consider all of them partial gratifications of the same instinct hardly seems to do justice to the considerable differences among them.

Thus, the principles concerning the transformations of energy appear to contain both assets and limitations. They provide an appreciation of the possible relationships and similarities among phenomena that might otherwise appear to be isolated and distinct. On the other hand, they tend to reduce too many phenomena to the same thing and thereby to neglect the importance of major differences among them.

In many ways it is this noting of similarities and shadings of differences that gives appeal to the clinician and creates difficulties for the experimenter. In many ways it is the looseness and ambiguity of its concepts that allows psychoanalytic theory to account for so much human behavior. But these factors raise questions concerning the status of psychoanalysis as a scientific theory. The terms of psychoanalysis are ambiguous. There are many metaphors and analogies that can, but need not, be taken literally. Examples would be latency, death instinct, Oedipus complex, and castration anxiety. Does castration anxiety refer to the fear of loss of the penis, or does it refer to the child's fear of injury to his body at a time that his body-image is of increased importance to his self-esteem? The language of the theory is so vague that investigators often are hard pressed to agree on precise meanings of the terms. How are we to define libido? Furthermore, the same word, such as repression, was used for different concepts at different times, often without a clear definition of the nature of the change of the concept.

Even where the constructs are well defined, often they are *too removed from observable and measurable behavior* to be of much empirical use. Concepts such as id, ego, and superego have considerable descriptive power, but it is often hard to translate them into relevant behavioral observations. Robert Sears, who for some time has worked on problems in child development, in general, and the process of identification, in particular, commented on this problem as follows. "We became acutely aware of the difference between the purely descriptive statement of a psychodynamic process and a testable theory of behavioral development. Psychoanalytic theory contained suggestions for the latter, but it did not specify the conditions under which greater or lesser degrees of any particular behavioral product of identification would occur" (Sears, Rau, & Alpert, 1965, p. 241). Here Sears is emphasizing the difference between a descriptive statement involving the use of a concept, and an explicit statement as to how the concept translates itself into quantitative relationships among phenomena. Within psychoanalytic theory, the relationships among phenomena are not always made explicit, and quantitative estimates of relationships are never made.

What we have, then, is a theory that is at times confusing and often difficult to test. This problem is complicated further by the way in which psychoanalysts can account for almost any outcome, even opposite outcomes. If one behavior appears, it is an expression of the instinct; if the opposite appears, it is an expression of a defense; if another form of behavior appears, it is a compromise between the instinct and the defense. For example, take Freud's comment on the interpretation of a slip of the tongue. "When a person who commits a slip gives an explanation which fits your views then you declare him to be the final authority on the subject. He says so himself! But if what he says does not suit your book, then you suddenly assert that what he says does not count, one need not believe it. Certainly that is so" (Freud, 1920, p. 46). It does not seem unlikely that such developments take place; that is, that depending on minor shifts in forces, major differences in overt behavior can appear. The problem with the theory is not that it leaves room for such complexity, but that it fails to state which behavior will occur, given a specific set of circumstances. In not providing such statements, psychoanalytic theory does not leave itself open to disproof or the negative test.

Other criticisms are relevant to psychoanalytic theory and the way in which it is defended. Psychoanalysts use observations influenced by the theory to support the theory, without giving adequate consideration to the factors relevant to the social psychology of the experimenter. Committed observers may bias the responses of their subjects and bias their own perceptions of the data. It is also true that analysts often respond to criticism of the theory by suggesting that the critics are being defensive in not recognizing phenomena such as infantile sexuality, that they do not understand the theory. To the extent that some psychoanalysts advance such arguments in a routine way, they perpetuate some of the early developments of psychoanalysis as a religious movement, rather than as a scientific theory.

In noting these criticisms of the status of psychoanalysis as a scientific theory, it is important to recognize that Freud was aware of most of these objections. He was not a naive scientist. His position, rather, was that the beginning of scientific activity consists of the description of phenomena, and that at the early stages some imprecision is inevitable. Also, Freud was acutely aware of the difficulties in making use of psychoanalytic insights for predictive purposes. He noted that the analyst was on safe ground in tracing the development of behavior from its final stage backwards, but that if he proceeded in the reverse way, an inevitable sequence of events no longer seemed to be apparent. His conclusion was that psychoanalysis does a better job at analysis than at synthesis, at explaining than at predicting. Freud did not believe that a science consists of nothing but conclusively proved propositions but, rather, insisted that the scientist be content with approximations to certainty.

In carrying on his work with that scientific credo, Freud encountered a number of limitations. For the most part, his direct analytic observations were limited to upper- and middle-class patients who presented symptoms relevant to the issues dominant in the culture at the time. It seems likely, therefore, that he exaggerated the importance of Victorian issues such as sex, morality, and guilt relative to other human concerns. Because of his training and the scientific spirit of his time, Freud appears to have relied, to an excessive degree, on a physiological energy model to account for psychological phenomena. Finally, it is unfortunate that, at the time of the development of his theory, Freud did not have the benefit of a discipline in psychology which supported his efforts to develop a scientific theory. Unfortunately, Freud was excessively dependent on a medical, therapeutic environment when he was committed to developing a system with broader relevance.

It is interesting to note that Freud's aim was to be both scientific and humanistic, "to bring concepts and order to human concerns and human concerns into the scientific community" (Havens, 1973, p. 2). We have already noted the arguments raised by scientific critics. Psychoanalysis also has been criticized by humanists as being overly intellectual, excessively abstract, and simplistic. Proponents of the existential point of view in psychology and psychiatry have been particularly critical of psychoanalysis along these lines. As has often been the case in the past, some of the harshest and most cogent criticism comes from individuals who themselves are analysts. Thus R.D. Laing (1967), a British analyst, has been critical of the extent to which psychoanalytic concepts may hide and distort human experience and critical of the tendency to label the patient "sick" as opposed to looking at "sickness" in the patient's family or in the broader society. And Thomas Szasz, also an analyst, has argued against the "myth of mental illness'' created by the model of abnormal behavior associated with psychoanalysis. Szasz (1961) notes that Freud served a tremendous humanitarian function in demonstrating that mentally ''sick'' people do not always ''will'' their pathological behavior and therefore should not be subject to moral outrage. At the same time, Szasz argues that the view of such people as ''sick'' has led to negative value judgments about them. Furthermore, it has led to serious curtailment of their rights and civil liberties. The criticism of Szasz is not so much against psychoanalytic theory itself as against the medical model of psychopathology that has come to be associated with it and the current social context of that model.

Another aspect of psychoanalytic theory related to the current social context is the criticism it has received from feminists. This has been both because of Freud's views concerning women and because of the influence of these views on female patients and the broader society (Williams, 1976). While Freud often is misinterpreted, he did see certain traits such as receptivity, dependence on others, sensitivity, vanity, and submissiveness as part of the feminine orientation. These characteristics were seen as part of women because of biological influences and because of psychological reactions to their awareness of the lack of a penis—Freud's concept of penis envy. The concept of penis envy symbolizes for many women a ''biology is destiny'' view on the part of Freud and an inadequate appreciation of cultural factors. Among others, the analyst Karen Horney questioned many of Freud's views concerning women and feminine sexuality, and, as noted earlier, proposed instead a view of feminine development that emphasized cultural influences. It is an interesting aspect of psychoanalysis that while it has come under attack by feminists, perhaps more than any other theory, it has almost always had major female figures within its ranks (e.g., Anna Freud, Helene Deutsch, Greta Bibring, Margaret Mahler, Clara Thompson, Frieda Fromm-Reichman).

Summary Evaluation

How, then, are we to summarize our evaluation of Freud and psychoanalytic theory? As an observer of human behavior, and as a person with a creative imagination, Freud was indeed a genius with few, if any, equals. The theory he developed certainly has the virtue of being comprehensive. There is no other personality theory that approximates psychoanalysis in the range of behavior considered and interpretations offered. Given such scope, the theory is economical. The structural and process concepts used by the theory are relatively few in number. Furthermore, the theory has suggested many areas for investigation and has led to a considerable amount of research. While relevant to the theory, however, much of this research does not offer an explicit test of a theory-derived hypothesis, and little of it has been used to extend and develop the theory. The major problem with psychoanalytic theory is the way in which the concepts are formulated; that is, ambiguity in the concepts and in the suggested relationships among concepts has made it very difficult to test the theory. The phenomena observed by Freud will have to be incorporated into any further theory of personality. The question for

FIGURE 4.4   **SUMMARY OF STRENGTHS AND LIMITATIONS OF PSYCHOANALYTIC THEORY**

STRENGTHS	LIMITATIONS
1. Provides for the discovery and investigation of many interesting phenomena.	1. Fails to define all its concepts clearly and distinctly.
2. Develops techniques for research and therapy (free association, dream interpretation, transference analysis).	2. Makes empirical testing difficult, at times impossible.
3. Recognizes the complexity of human behavior.	3. Endorses the questionable view of the person as an energy system.
4. Encompasses a broad range of phenomena.	4. Tolerates resistance by parts of the profession to empirical research and change in the theory.

psychoanalytic theory is whether it can be developed to provide for specific tests, or whether it will be replaced in the future by another theory that is equally comprehensive and economical but more open to systematic empirical investigation.

MAJOR CONCEPTS AND SUMMARY

[Review concepts from Chapter 3]   symptom
projective techniques *idea*   free association
Rorschach Inkblot Test *what it is*   dream interpretation
Thematic Apperception Test (TAT)   transference

In this chapter and the previous one we have considered psychoanalytic theory as illustrative of a psychodynamic, clinical approach to personality. The psychodynamic emphasis is clear in the interpretation of behavior as a result of the interplay among forces, in the emphasis on anxiety and defense mechanisms, and in the interpretation of symptoms as compromises between instinct and defense. The clinical qualities of psychoanalysis are apparent in the emphasis on the individual, the attention given to individual differences, and the attempt to assess and understand the total individual. The psychoanalytic approach is highly interpretive, making use of many constructs that are not open to direct observation to account for a wide range of individual and group behavior.

Projective techniques, such as the Rorschach Inkblot Test and Thematic Apperception Test (TAT), emphasize disguise and maximum freedom of response and illustrate the relationship between psychoanalytic theory and personality assessment. These assessment devices are widely used in clinical work with patients as well as in systematic research. The latter was illustrated in the study of comedians, clowns, and actors.

In terms of emphasis on the stability of personality, it is not surprising that psychoanalytic theory places great importance on structural concepts. The main structural concepts are those of id, ego, and superego, which roughly represent drives (instincts), an orientation toward reality, and morals (values), respectively. Psychic life is also described in terms of the extent to which thoughts and memories are available to awareness—ranging from unconscious (unavailable to awareness), preconscious (available to awareness), and conscious (part of awareness).

Psychoanalytic theory also places great emphasis on the processes (dynamics) of psychological functioning. Basically, the organism seeks expression or discharge of the life (libido) and death instincts or sexual and aggressive instincts. Because of its associaton with a past trauma, expression of an instinct may signal danger to the ego and lead to the experience of anxiety. The individual then faces a conflict situation in which he seeks to gratify the instinct but also fears doing so. Often the result is the use of mechanisms of defense (i.e., projection, denial, isolation, undoing, reaction-formation, rationalization, repression) which attempt to give some expression to the instinct in a way that does not produce anxiety. The use of mechanisms of defense always involves some distortion of reality. Only in sublimation is the individual able to express an impulse free of anxiety and without distortion of reality. In such a case id, ego, and superego are acting in unison and with freedom from conflict.

The psychoanalytic theory of development places great emphasis on stages of development (i.e., oral, anal, phallic, latency, genital) that are rooted in the biological processes of the organism. Experiences during the first five years of life are viewed as critical for the determination of later, adult personality characteristics. This is particularly true where frustration has led to fixation at a pregenital stage of development or where, because of later frustration, the individual regresses back to an earlier mode of functioning. Oral, anal, and phallic character types illustrate how adult personality characteristics may be understood in terms of partial fixations at early stages of development.

The above concepts lay the groundwork for an understanding of psychopathology. While all pathology is believed to center in the Oedipus complex, representing fixations at the phallic stage of development, frustration and trauma can lead to regression to an earlier stage of development. Thus, the exact form taken in a neurosis or a psychosis is dependent upon the stage to which the individual regresses. In psychopathology there is a struggle between striving of the id instincts for discharge and the efforts of the ego to prevent discharge and defend against anxiety. Behavior change in the direction of growth occurs when individuals are exposed to conditions that allow them to gratify their instincts in new, more mature ways which lead neither to guilt nor to external threat. In psychoanalysis, the free association method is used to facilitate the process of becoming aware of unconscious wishes and conflicts. The transference situation is used as an opportunity for insight and growth.

Finally, an evaluation of psychoanalytic theory must recognize the richness of observations, the range of behavior covered in a reasonably economical way, and the fertile areas for research suggested by the theory. At the same time the theory suffers from a number of scientific limitations (e.g., terms are ambiguous, constructs are often far removed from observable and measurable behavior, relationships among phenomena are not always made explicit). It also has come under attack from humanists for being too far removed from the actual experiences of individuals and from that which in uniquely human, and from feminists as well as others for being too involved with biological influences to a prejudicial disregard of cultural ones.

Picasso, Pablo. *Girl Before a Mirror.* 1932. Collection, The Museum of Modern Art, New York. Gift of Mrs. Simon Guggenheim.

A PHENOMENOLOGICAL THEORY: CARL ROGERS' PERSON-CENTERED THEORY OF PERSONALITY

CHAPTER FOCUS: In this chapter we consider Rogerian theory as illustrative of a phenomenological, clinical approach to personality. The clinical emphasis is apparent in the attention given to individual differences and the efforts to understand and assess the total individual. The phenomenological approach is apparent in the emphasis on the phenomenal world of the individual—how the person perceives and experiences the self and the world. Assessment and research follow in their emphasis on verbal self-report and concepts such as self and experience. The theory is a part of the humanistic, human potential movement that emphasizes self-actualization and the fulfillment of an individual's growth potential.

To me such a highly personal "view from within" is not only the best source of learning, it also points the way, perhaps, toward a new and more human science . . .

Rogers, 1972, p. 3

I see the actualizing tendency in the human organism as being basic to motivation . . . So I reaffirm, even more strongly than when I first advanced the notion, my belief that there is one central source of energy in the human organism; that it is a trustworthy function of the whole organism rather than of some portion of it; and that it is perhaps best conceptualized as a tendency toward fulfillment, toward actualization, not only toward maintenance but also toward the enhancement of the organism.

Rogers, 1977, p. 237, pp. 242–243

In the previous chapter we discussed the psychoanalytic theory of Freud. Psychoanalytic theory was considered in light of its emphasis on individual differences, the total individual, the importance of the unconscious, and human behavior as a function of the interplay among various forces—a dynamic model.

In this second chapter on a specific theoretical position, the focus is on the phenomenological theory of Carl Rogers. Originally, the theory was not one of personality. Rather it was a theory of psychotherapy and the process of behavior change. However, a theory of personality has been an outgrowth of the theory of therapy. The position of Rogers is presented because it typifies an approach to personality that stresses why people can and should be understood in terms of how they view themselves and the world around them—the **phenomenological approach.** Rogers' theory also is presented because it gives attention to the concept of the *self* and experiences related to the self, and because it illustrates a conscious, focused effort to combine clinical intuition with objective research. In his emphasis on human experience and the importance of being a fully functioning human being, Carl Rogers has had a tremendous impact on the training of counselors, of teachers, and of managers at the executive level in business. His view of the person is frankly stated, in opposition to the one presented by Freud, and is clearly related to his views of therapy and his selection of problems for research. Finally, this view and the total spirit of the theory and the theorist have resulted in the association of Rogers with a significant part of the human potential movement.

Although the American emphasis on objective and quantitative research has influenced Rogers, the theory is derived from intensive work with individuals and, in turn, is applied to individuals. Throughout his career, Rogers has spent time in the treatment of individuals and generally has begun his research efforts by examining clinical material. Like psychoanalytic theory, Rogers' theory involves assumptions relevant to all people, but the theory has particular relevance to the study of individual differences and the total functioning of individuals. For example, Rogers is interested in therapy as a unique experience for each individual. However, although it is unique, the therapy involves a predictable *process* for all individuals. Unlike the psychoanalytic emphasis on the unconscious, the theory of Rogers places emphasis on that which is conscious. For Rogers, the phenomenological world of individuals, the world as it is experienced by them, primarily in conscious terms, contains the data necessary to understand and to predict behavior. Although the private world of the individual can be known only to the individual himself, the psychologist can, by providing a supportive atmosphere, approximate an understanding of the private world of the individual.

In summary, this chapter and the next will analyze and evaluate a theory that is significant in its emphasis on individual differences, the entire personality, and behavior as a function of the private, unique way in which individuals experience their worlds. In particular, the concern is with the importance of the concept of the *self* in personality theory, with the ways in which individuals experience themselves and others, and with the conditions under which individuals are capable of becoming fully functioning people.

CARL R. ROGERS (1902–   ): A VIEW OF THE THEORIST

"I speak as a person, from a context of personal experience and personal learning." Thus does Rogers introduce his chapter "This Is Me" in his 1961 book *On Becoming A Person*. The chapter is a personal, very moving account by Rogers of the development of his professional thinking and personal philosophy. Rogers states what he does and how he feels about it.

> *This book is about the suffering and the hope, the anxiety and the satisfaction, with which each therapist's counseling room is filled. It is about the uniqueness of the relationship each therapist forms with each client, and equally about the common elements which we discover in all these relation-*

ships. This book is about the highly personal experiences of each one of us. It is about a client in my office who sits there by the corner of the desk, struggling to be himself, yet deathly afraid of being himself—striving to see his experience as it is, wanting to be that experience, and yet deeply fearful of the prospect. This book is about me, as I sit there with that client, facing him, participating in that struggle as deeply and sensitively as I am able. It is about me as I try to perceive his experience, and the meaning and the feeling and the taste and the flavor that it has for him. It is about me as I bemoan my very human fallibility in understanding that client, and the occasional failures to see life as it appears to him, failures which fall like heavy objects across the intricate, delicate web of growth which is taking place. It is about me as I rejoice at the privilege of being a midwife to a new personality—as I stand by with awe at the emergence of a self, a person, as I see a birth process in which I have had an important and facilitating part. It is about both the client and me as we regard with wonder the potent and orderly forces which are evident in this whole experience, forces which seem deeply rooted in the universe as a whole. The book is, I believe, about life, as life vividly reveals itself in the therapeutic process—with its blind power and its tremendous capacity for destruction, but with its overbalancing thrust toward growth, if the opportunity for growth is provided.

Rogers, 1961 (a), pp. 4–5

Carl R. Rogers was born on January 8, 1902, in Oak Park, Illinois. He was reared in a strict and uncompromising religious and ethical atmosphere. His parents had the welfare of the children constantly in mind and inculcated in them a worship of hard work. In behavioral terms, the religious and ethical concerns led to ''no alcoholic beverages, no dancing, cards or theatre, very little social life, and much work.'' From his description of his early life, we see two main trends which are reflected in his later work. The first is the concern with moral and ethical matters already described. The second is the respect for the methods of science, particularly where things need to be accomplished. The latter appears to have developed out of exposure to his father's efforts to operate their farm on a scientific basis and Rogers' own reading of books on scientific agriculture.

Rogers started his college education at the University of Wisconsin in the field of agriculture, but after two years he changed his professional goals and decided to enter the ministry. During a trip to the Orient, in 1922, he had a chance to observe commitments to other religious doctrines and to observe the bitter mutual hates of French and German people, who otherwise seemed to be likable individuals. Experiences like these influenced his decision to go to a liberal theological seminary, the Union Theological Seminary in New York. Although he was concerned about questions regarding the meaning of life for individuals, Rogers had doubts about specific religious doctrines. Therefore, he chose to leave the seminary, to work in the field of child guidance, and to think of himself as a clinical psychologist.

Carl R. Rogers

Rogers obtained his graduate training at Teachers College, Columbia University, receiving his Ph.D. in 1931. He describes his course and clinical experience as leading to a "soaking up" of both the dynamic views of Freud and the "rigorous, scientific, coldly objective, statistical" views then prevalent at Teachers College. Again, there were the pulls in different directions, the development of two somewhat divergent trends. In his later life Rogers attempted to bring these divergent trends into harmony with one another. Indeed, these years represent an effort to integrate the religious with the scientific, the intuitive with the objective, and the clinical with the statistical. Throughout his career, Rogers has tried continually to apply the objective methods of science to what is most basically human.

> *Therapy is the experience in which I can let myself go subjectively. Research is the experience in which I can stand off and try to view this rich subjective experience with objectivity, applying all the elegant methods of science to determine whether I have been deceiving myself. The conviction grows in me that we shall discover laws of personality and behavior which are as significant for human progress or human relationship as the law of gravity or the laws of thermodynamics.*

> Rogers, 1961 (a), p. 14

In 1968 Rogers and his more humanistically oriented colleagues formed the Center for the Studies of the Person. The development of the Center expressed a number of shifts in emphasis in the work of Rogers—from work within a formal academic structure to work with a collection of individuals who share a perspective, from work with "disturbed" individuals to work with "normal" individuals, from individual therapy to intensive group workshops, and from conventional empirical research to the phenomenological study of people: "We are deeply interested in persons but are rather 'turned-off' by the older methods of studying them as 'objects' for research" (Rogers, 1972 b, p. 67). From this perspective Rogers feels that most of psychology is sterile and generally feels alienated from the field. Yet, the field continues to value his contributions—he was president of the American Psychological Association in 1946–1947, was one of the first three psychologists to receive the Distinguished Scientific Contribution Award (1956) from the profession, and in 1972 was the recipient of the Distinguished Professional Contribution Award. In his address in receiving this award, Rogers looked back on his 46 years as a psychologist and noted his contributions to counseling ,psychotherapy research, the empirical study of emotional phenomena, the philosophy of science, and the encounter group movement. He accounted for his widespread influence in the following way: "I expressed an idea whose time had come, as though a pebble was dropped in water and spread ripples. The idea was that the individual has vast resources within himself for altering his life and these resources can be mobilized given the proper climate" (Rogers, 1973).

With Rogers, the theory, the man, and the life are interwoven. In his chapter on "This Is Me," Rogers lists fourteen principles that he has learned from thousands of hours of therapy and research. Because the man, his life, and his theory are so interwoven, the principles themselves contain much of the theory. Here are some illustrations:

1. *In my relationships with persons I have found that it does not help, in the long run, to act as though I were something that I am not.*

2. *I find I am more effective when I can listen acceptantly to myself, and can be myself.*

3. *I have found it of enormous value when I can permit myself to understand another person . . .*

4. *I have found it highly rewarding when I can accept another person.*

5. *Experience is, for me, the highest authority . . . it is to experience that I must return again and again, to discover a closer approximation to truth as it is in the process of becoming in me . . .*

6. *The facts are friendly . . . painful reorganizations are what is known as learning . . .*

7. *. . .what is most personal and unique in each one of us is probably the very element which would, if it were shared or expressed, speak most deeply to others.*

8. *It has been my experience that persons have a basically positive direction . . . I have come to feel that the more fully the individual is understood and accepted, the more he tends to drop the false fronts with*

> *which he has been meeting life, and the more he tends to move in a direction which is forward.*
>
> 9. *Life, at its best, is a flowing, changing process in which nothing is fixed.*

Rogers, 1961 (a), pp. 16–27

These, then, are the personal experiences and learnings that Rogers has gathered in his role as an individual and as a theorist. Having started with the development of a therapeutic technique, he moved to an emphasis on the full humanization of the therapist–client relationship. Maintaining and expanding on his commitment to the full realization or actualization of the human potential, Rogers has emphasized the wider applicability of his theory to virtually all aspects of human existence. What began in the arena of therapy and helping relationships now has been broadened to the arenas of education, business administration, interracial relations, and even international affairs (Holdstock & Rogers, 1977). Whereas previously Rogers referred to his theory as client-centered theory, more recently he has changed the name to person-centered theory. This change in name gives expression to his emphasis on the broader relevance of the theory of personality.

As of this writing, Rogers at the age of eighty remains active and committed to emerging persons—those who desire authenticity and freedom from facades, who have an aversion to hypocrisy and deceit, who are caring and desire to live in balance with nature as opposed to being involved with material things, and who trust their inner experience and distrust external authority: "'Power to the emerging person and the revolution he carries with him'" (quoted in Kirschenbaum, 1979, p. 405).

ROGERS' VIEW OF THE PERSON

Implicit in Rogers' learnings and explicit in his writings, is his view of the person. For Rogers, the core of our nature is essentially positive. This direction of our movement basically is toward self-actualization, maturity, and socialization. It is Rogers' contention that religion, particularly the Christian religion, has taught us to believe that we are basically sinful. Furthermore, Rogers contends that Freud and his followers have presented us with a picture of the person with an id and an unconscious that would, if permitted expression, manifest itself in incest, murder, and other crimes. According to this view, we are at heart irrational, unsocialized, and destructive of self and others. For Rogers, we may at times function in this way, but at such times we are neurotic and not functioning as fully developed human beings. When we are functioning freely, we are free to experience and to fulfill our basic nature as positive and social animals, ones that can be trusted and basically are constructive.

Aware that others may seek to draw parallels between the behaviors of other animals and the behavior of humans, Rogers draws his own parallels. For example, he observes that, although lions are often seen as "ravening beasts," actually they have many desirable qualities—they kill only when hungry and not for the sake of being destructive, they grow from helplessness and dependence to independence, and they move from being self-centered in infancy to being cooperative and protective in adulthood.

For Rogers the lion is, in some basic sense, a constructive and trustworthy member of the species *felis leo*. Aware that others may call him a naive optimist, Rogers is quick to point out that his conclusions are based on more than twenty-five years of experience in psychotherapy:

> *I do not have a Pollyana view of human nature. I am quite aware that out of defensiveness and inner fear individuals can and do behave in ways which are incredibly cruel, horribly destructive, immature, regressive, antisocial, hurtful. Yet one of the most refreshing and invigorating parts of my experience is to work with such individuals and to discover the strongly positive directional tendencies which exist in them, as in all of us, at the deepest levels.*

> Rogers, 1961 (a), p. 27

Here is a profound respect for people, a respect that is reflected in Rogers' theory of personality and his person-centered approach to psychotherapy. Although it may appear to be a somewhat extreme position, the tone and spirit of the Rogerian position is similar to that of others. A number of theories, such as those of Goldstein, Angyal, and Maslow, emphasize the continuous striving of the organism to realize its inherent potential. These theories do not assume that there are inherent destructive drives in the organism but instead posit a natural growth toward a healthy, self-realizing, self-actualizing personality. These assumptions are part of Rogers, part of his life, and part of his theory. It will be important to keep these assumptions in mind as we attempt to understand and to assess the theory.

ROGERS' VIEW OF SCIENCE, THEORY, AND RESEARCH METHODS

Although Rogers' theory and specific research tools have changed, he has remained a phenomenologist. According to the phenomenological position of Rogers (1951), the individual perceives the world in a unique way. These perceptions make up the individual's **phenomenal field.** Individuals react to the environment as they perceive it. This environment may or may not correspond with an experimenter's definition of the environment. The phenomenal field of the individual includes both conscious and unconscious perceptions, those of which the individual is aware and those of which he is not aware. But the most important determinants of behavior, particularly in healthy people, are the ones that are conscious or capable of becoming conscious. Although the phenomenal field is essentially a world that is private to individuals, we can (particularly with clinical material) attempt to perceive the world as it appears to individuals, to see behavior through their eyes and with the psychological meaning it has for them:

We are admitted freely into the backstage of the person's living, where we can observe from within some of the dramas of internal changes which are often far more compelling and moving than the drama which is presented on the stage viewed by the public. Only a novelist or a poet could do justice to the deep struggle which we are permitted to observe from within the client's own world of reality.

Rogers, 1947, p. 104

In a later paper on the subject, Rogers (1964) reiterated his commitment to phenomenology as a basis for the science of the person and as the method to be used in the development of a theory of subjective phenomena. Here Rogers distinguishes among several kinds of knowledge: subjective, objective, and interpersonal. In *subjective knowledge*, we know something from our own internal frame of reference. In *objective knowledge*, what we know has been checked against the observations of others. In interpersonal knowing, we attempt to put ourselves in someone else's shoes and to understand the phenomenal field of that person— that is, we empathize. This is called *phenomenological knowledge*. According to Rogers, it represents a legitimate and necessary part of the science of psychology. Rogers argues for the use of all three kinds of knowledge, since there is "no royal road to scientific attitude" and "no such thing as a 'scientific methodology' which will see us safely through" (Rogers, 1964, p. 117). Research in psychology must involve a persistent, disciplined effort to understand the phenomena of subjective experience. In following the path of science, these efforts need not start in the laboratory or at the calculating machine, and they should not take the advanced stages of theoretical physics as the most helpful model of science.

As has been observed, Rogers believes that clinical material, obtained during psychotherapy offers a valuable source of phenomenological data. In attempting to understand human behavior, Rogers always starts with clinical observations. He attempts to listen to recorded therapeutic interviews, as naively as possible, with as few preconceptions as possible, and to develop some hypotheses concerning the events he has observed. He attempts to steep himself in the events of the human drama, to soak up clues concerning the mystery of behavior, and then to use these observations to formulate hypotheses that can be tested in a rigorous way. Rogers believes that it is legitimate to start free of concerns for objectivity and rigor, and then to move forward to the process of empirical investigation. As previously stated, Rogers views therapy as a subjective, "letting go" experience and research as an objective effort with its own kind of elegance. He is as committed to one as a source for hypotheses as he is to the other as a tool for their confirmation.

In developing this process of a constant interplay between subjective phenomena and objective research, Rogers has made an effort to develop a theory containing explicit hypotheses and explicit statements about links among the hypotheses. Rogers has tried to define his concepts and, in most cases, to develop measures for them. Since he believes in starting with inferences that stay close to what he has observed and working toward greater elaboration and refinement, he has started with a simple theoretical model and has gradually developed a fairly complex system. In line with his belief in the possibility of change in people, he is committed to the constant refinement and elaboration of personality theory. For Rogers, both people and theories are always in a state of becoming.

Throughout his career, then, Rogers has attempted to bridge the gap between the subjective and the objective, just as in his youth he felt a need to bridge the gap between religion and science. Within this context, Rogers has been concerned with the development of psychology as a science and with the preservation of people as individuals who are not simply the pawns of science. On a number of occasions, Rogers has debated with others the questions of free will and determinism, subjective choice, and the control of human behavior. The most famous of these debates was with B. F. Skinner (Rogers, 1956), a behaviorist and learning theorist whose views will be discussed later in this book. In this debate, Rogers suggested that he and Skinner agree that people always have endeavored to understand, predict, influence, and control human behavior. Furthermore, both agree that the behavioral sciences are making progress in understanding behavior and in developing the capacity to predict and control. Both are committed to a science of human behavior. However, Rogers expresses particular concern about the following: Who will be controlled? Who will control? What type of control? Toward what end or purpose? Although Rogers argues that psychotherapy is a scientific endeavor involving efforts toward prediction, influence, and control, he stresses that the goals also involve the client becoming more self-directing, less rigid, less subject to outside influence and control, and more capable of making subjective value choices. Therapy is a lawful (determined) process in which individuals achieve greater freedom to will.

THE PERSONALITY THEORY OF CARL ROGERS

As we have stated previously, Rogers' main focus has been on the process of psychotherapy. His theory of personality is an outgrowth of his theory of therapy. Also, both the theory and the focus of the related research have changed over time, from the beginnings of a Rogerian point of view in 1942 until the extension of his efforts to the treatment of schizophrenics in 1967, and continuing through the most recent extension of his efforts to schools, industry, and the relationships between races and cultures (Rogers, 1977; 1980). Throughout, however, there is a concern with how people perceive their worlds, in particular the self, and a concern with the process of change. In contrast to the psychoanalytic emphasis on drives, instincts, the unconscious, tension reduction, and early character development, the phenomenological approach emphasizes perceptions, feelings, subjective self-report, self-actualization, and the process of change. One should keep these differences in mind as the concepts and research efforts that are part of the Rogerian theory of personality are examined.

Structure

The Self

The key structural concept in the Rogerian theory of personality is that of the **self**. According to Rogers, the individual perceives external objects and experiences and attaches meanings to them. The total system of perceptions and meanings make up the individual's phenomenal field. The particular perceptions and meanings that appear to be related to us, to ourselves, make up that part of the phenomenal field known as the self. The self is an organized pattern of perceptions that includes those parts of the phenomenal field seen by the individual as "self," "me," or "I" (Rogers, 1959). A related structural concept is that of **ideal self**. The ideal self is the self-concept the individual would most like to possess. It includes the perceptions and meanings that potentially are relevant to the self and that are valued highly by the individual.

There are two interesting points in relation to the Rogerian concept of self. First, Rogers views the perception of self as following the general laws of perception. Thus, the concept of self fits within what has traditionally been a basic part of psychology. Second, the self-concept is a series of interrelated parts. The self-concept represents an organized and consistent pattern of related perceptions. Although the self is changing, it always retains a patterned, coherent, integrated, and organized quality to it. The self is not made up of thousands of conditioned

Self-recognition—Whereas almost all other species are indifferent to their images in a mirror, or react to them as another animal, humans begin to be fascinated with their self-reflection at an early age.

responses, each having occurred independently of the others, but instead it is a patterned whole that changes with the addition of new elements and yet always retains its patterned quality. Third, the self is not a little person inside of us. The self does not "do" anything. The individual does not have a self that controls behavior. Rather there is a body of experience symbolized by the self. Finally, the pattern of experiences and perceptions known as the self is, in general, available to awareness, that is, it can be made conscious. Although individuals do have experiences of which they are unaware, the self-concept is primarily conscious. Rogers believes that such a definition of the self is accurate and a necessary one for research. A definition of the self that included unconscious material, according to Rogers, could not be studied objectively. In summary, the self is an organized body of perceptions that generally is available to awareness and follows the general rules of perception.

Measures of the Self-Concept

Rogers maintains that he did not begin his work with the concept of the self. In fact, in his first work he thought that it was a vague, scientifically meaningless term. However, as he listened to clients expressing their problems and attitudes, he found that they tended to talk in terms of the self. The concept of self finally appeared in his 1947 description of personality.

In that paper, he reported the statements made by a client, Miss Vib, who came for nine interviews. At the outset of counseling, her conscious perception of herself was reflected in statements of this kind: "I haven't been acting like myself; it doesn't seem like me; I'm a different person from what I used to be in the past." "I don't have any emotional response to situations; I'm worried about myself." "I don't understand myself; I haven't known what was happening to me." By the ninth interview, 38 days later, the perception of self had been deeply altered: "I'm taking more interest in myself." "I do have some individuality, some interests." "I can look at myself a little better." "I realize I'm just one person, with so much ability, but I'm not worried abut it; I can accept the fact that I'm not always right." Statements like these convinced Rogers, and have continued to convince him, that the self is an important element in human experience and that the goal of individuals is to become their real selves. An illustration of the way in which the self concept may be discussed in a counseling session is given in Figure 5.1 This interview segment is of particular interest because it illustrates how the person, often a college student, attempts to choose a career which, among other things, fits with some image they have of themselves and the kind of person they would like to be.

Although impressed with the self-statements of clients, and by Raimy's (1948) elaborate consideration of the utility and importance of the concept, Rogers experienced the need for an objective definition of the concept, a way to measure it, and a research tool. Rogers began his research by recording therapy interview sessions and then categorizing all words that referred to the self. After the early research with recorded interviews, he made use of the **Q-sort** developed by Stephenson (1953). The *Q-sort* technique has been used frequently to measure the

CURRENT APPLICATIONS AND IMPLICATIONS

Is the Sense of Self Uniquely Human?

Most dog owners have at some time experimented with placing a mirror in front of their dog. Is there self recognition? Animal research suggests that species lower than primates do not recognize themselves in mirrors. Chimpanzees are able to do so, provided they have had some exposure to mirrors. Given such experience, chimps will use the mirror to examine and groom themselves (self-directed behavior) rather than ignore the image or react to it as if it is another member of the species (e.g., fish showing aggressive displays toward a mirror image).

Research on the development of self-directed mirror behavior in infants suggests that the development of self recognition is a continuous process, starting as early as four months of age. At this point infants show some response to relationships between self-movements and changes in mirror images. And what of recognition of specific features of the self? If an infant looks at itself in the mirror, has rouge placed on its nose, and then looks in the mirror again, will the infant respond to the rouge mark in a way expressive of self recognition? Such specific feature recognition, in terms of self-directed mirror behavior, appears to begin at about the age of one year.

The recognition of self, whether expressed through self-directed mirror behavior or otherwise, can be related to the development of consciousness and mind. Clearly it is a matter of considerable psychological significance. Not only does it mean that we can be aware of ourselves and have feelings about ourselves, but also that we can have knowledge of and empathy for the feelings of others. It would indeed be ironic if the very processes that allow us to feel worst about ourselves also provided us with the opportunity to feel most empathic with others.

Mirror, mirror on the wall, is that me after all? This appears to be a question that only members of a few species can address. In humans some maturation is required but self recognition begins to develop fairly early and remains a significant part of life thereafter.

SOURCES: M. Lewis and J. Brooks-Gunn, 1979; G.G. Gallup, in press.

self-concept. In this approach the experimenter gives the subject a pile of cards, each containing a statement concerning some personality characteristic. One card might say "Makes friends easily," another might say "Has trouble expressing anger," and so on for each of the cards. Subjects are asked to read these statements (generally about a hundred) and then sort the cards according to which state-

S: That's why I'm in engineering college. I have an opportunity to—well, just to experiment with myself and see actually what talents I do have in that direction. They're not so bad, but I lack some—some of the very fundamental things that a good engineer should have: that is, being calm, sticking right to it, and forgetting about things that have come up. A good engineer is not emotional, that's about one of the worst things he could—No person who is emotional is a good engineer.

C: So that in some respects you've gone into engineering because you felt it would be awfully good discipline for you, is that right? Make you stop being emotional?

S: That's right.

C: It was that, perhaps, rather than being interested in engineering.

S: Well, it was mingled with a certain genuine interest. There was some that's true. But it was largely due to that, exactly what I said, to a considerable extent.

C: You don't suppose that part of your trouble is that now you're wondering whether you want to be your real self. Could that be part of it?

S: Uh, what's that?

C: Well, I just wondered. You're trying so hard to be some other fellow aren't you?

S: Yeah, because I'm not satisfied with myself.

C: You feel that the self that you are isn't worth being.

S: Yeah, that's right, and unless you can change my mind about that, then I'll continue thinking along the same line.

C: (*Laughing.*) Why, that almost sounds as though you were wishing that somebody would change your mind about it.

S: (*Very soberly.*) Yeah. Because I don't know how I can solve it the other way.

C: In other words, you're finding it a pretty rough proposition to try to be a calm, unemotional engineer when really you're something quite different.

S: Right. Yeah, that is a very tough position. I find it impossible, and I hate the idea that it's impossible.

C: And you have it partly because you feel there's nothing worthwhile about this real self of yours.

S: Yes.

C: What are some of the things your real self would like to do?

S: Oh, let's see. Well—uh, I told you I was interested in mathematics. That's one thing. Also, I was interested in anthropology. At the same time, I was interested in music and in—well, now, I used to like novels, but I don't care for them anymore, but—I would like—I think I have a gift for writing, too, and I'm ashamed of those gifts.

FIGURE 5.1   Interview Emphasizing Discussion of the Self Concept in Relation to Occupational Choice (S = student; C = Counselor). (Rogers, 1942)

ments they feel are most descriptive of them and which are least descriptive. The subjects are asked to arrange the cards into a certain distribution of which one end represents "Most characteristic of me" and the other "Least characteristic of me." Subjects are told how many piles of cards are to be used and how many cards are to go into each pile. For example, with 100 cards the subject might be asked to sort the cards into eleven piles as follows: 2-4-8-11-16-18-16-11-8-4-

2. The distribution is a normal one and expresses the subjects' comparative estimates of how descriptive each characteristic is.

In sum, the Q-sort involves a task in which the subject sorts a number of statements, in this case abut the self, into categories ranging from most characteristic to least characteristic. In addition, the identical items can be sorted into the same number of categories in terms of their ideal self—"most like my ideal self" to "least like my ideal self." This provides for a quantitative measure of the difference or discrepancy between self and ideal self. As we shall see (Chapter 6), such concepts and measures are important in relation to psychopathology and therapeutic change. The Q-sort leads to data that represent a systematic expression of subjects' perceptions of parts of their phenomenal fields. However, it does not represent a completely phenomenological report, since subjects must use statements provided by the experimenter, instead of their own, and must sort the statements into prescribed piles, representing a normal distribution, rather than according to a distribution that makes the most sense to them.

Other efforts to obtain subjective reports about the self have made use of the adjective checklist, in which subjects check adjectives that they feel are applicable to them, and the *semantic differential* (Osgood, Suci, & Tannenbaum, 1957). Developed as a measure of attitudes and the meanings of concepts, rather than as a specific test of personality, the semantic differential has potential as a useful technique for personality assessment. In filling out the semantic differential, the individual rates a concept on a number of seven-point scales defined by polar adjectives such as good–bad, strong–weak, active–passive. Thus, a subject would rate a concept such as "My Self" or "My Ideal Self" on each of the polar adjective scales. A rating on any one scale would indicate whether the subject felt one of the adjectives was very descriptive of the concept or somewhat descriptive, or whether neither adjective was applicable to the concept. The ratings are made in terms of the meaning of the concept for the individual.

Like the Q-sort, the semantic differential is a structured technique in that the subject must rate certain concepts and use the polar adjective scales provided by the experimenter. This structure provides for the gathering of data suitable for statistical analysis but, also like the Q-sort, the semantic differential does not preclude flexibility in decision as to the concepts and scales to be used. There is no single standardized semantic differential. A variety of scales can be used in relation to concepts such as father, mother, and doctor to determine the meanings of phenomena for the individual. Certainly the meanings an individual attaches to phenomena about him, including his self-concept, are basic to personality.

One example of the way in which the semantic differential can be used to assess personality is its application to a case of multiple personality. In the 1950s two psychiatrists, Corbett Thigpen and Harvey Cleckley, made famous the case of "The Three Faces of Eve." This was the case of a woman who possessed three personalities, each of which predominated for a period of time, with frequent shifts back and forth. The three personalities were called Eve White, Eve Black, and Jane. As part of a research endeavor, the psychiatrists were able to have each of the three personalities rate a variety of concepts on the semantic differential.

The ratings were then analyzed both quantitatively and qualitatively by two psychologists (C. Osgood & Z. Luria) who did not know the subject. The analysis by the psychologists included both descriptive comments and interpretations of the personalities that went beyond the objective data. For example, Eve White was described as being in contact with social reality but under great emotional stress, Eve Black as out of contact with social reality but quite self-assured, and Jane as superficially very healthy but quite restricted and undiversified. A more detailed, though still incomplete description of the three personalities based on the semantic differential ratings is presented in Figure 5.2. The analysis on the basis of these ratings turned out to fit quite well with the descriptions offered by the two psychiatrists (Osgood & Luria, 1954).

The Q-sort, adjective checklist, and semantic differential all approach the Rogerian ideal of phenomenological self-report; they provide data that are statistically reliable and theoretically relevant. It can be argued that there are many self-concepts rather than a single self-concept, that these tests do not get at unconscious factors, and that the tests are subject to defensive distortion. Rogers feels, however, that these tests provide useful measures for the concepts of self and ideal self (as he has defined them) and that they have been a necessary part of a productive research effort. We shall not discuss the status of the concept of self and its measurement until the critique and evaluation section of the next chapter. In the meantime, we explore its relationship to other parts of the theory and its place in the related research.

Process

Self-Actualization

Freud viewed the essential components of personality as relatively fixed and stable, and he developed an elaborate theory of the structure of personality. Rogers' view of personality emphasizes change, and he has used few concepts of structure in his theory. Freud considered the person as an energy system. Thus, he developed a theory of dynamics to account for how this energy is discharged, transformed, or "dammed up." Rogers thinks of the person as forward moving. Therefore, he has tended to deemphasize the tension-reducing aspects of behavior, in favor of an emphasis on **self-actualization**. Whereas Freud placed great emphasis on drives, for Rogers there is no motivation in the sense of drives per se. Instead, the basic tendency is toward self-actualization: "The organism has one basic tendency and striving—to actualize, maintain, and enhance the experiencing organism" (Rogers, 1951, p. 487). "It should be noted that this basic actualizing tendency is the only motive which is postulated in this theoretical system" (Rogers, 1959, p. 196).

Rogers has chosen to postulate a single motivation to life and to stay close to that idea rather than to be tied to abstract conceptualizations of many motives. But the conceptualization of a self-actualizing tendency is highly abstract and as yet has not been measured objectively. In a poetic passage, Rogers (1963) de-

EVE WHITE   Perceives the world in an essentially normal fashion, is well socialized, but has an unsatisfactory attitude toward herself. The chief evidence of disturbance in the personality is the fact that ME (the self-concept) is considered a little bad, a little passive, and definitely weak.

EVE BLACK   Eve Black has achieved a violent kind of adjustment in which she perceives herself as literally perfect, but, to accomplish this break, her way of perceiving the world becomes completely disoriented from the norm. If Eve Black perceives herself as good, then she also has to accept HATRED and FRAUD as positive values.

JANE   Jane displays the most "healthy" meaning pattern, in which she accepts the usual evaluations of concepts by her society yet still maintains a satisfactory evaluation of herself. The self concept, ME, while not strong (but not weak, either) is nearer the good and active directions of the semantic space.

FIGURE 5.2   Brief Personality Descriptions, Based on Semantic Differential Ratings, in a Case of Multiple Personality. (Osgood & Luria, 1954)

scribes life as an active process, comparing it to the trunk of a tree on the shore of the ocean as it remains erect, tough, resilient, maintaining and enhancing itself in the growth process: "Here in this palm-like seaweed was the tenacity of life, the forward thrust of life, the ability to push into an incredibly hostile environment and not only to hold its own, but to adapt, develop, become itself" (Rogers, 1963, p. 2).

The concept of actualization involves the tendency on the part of the organism to grow from a simple structure to a complex one, to move from dependence toward independence, from fixity and rigidity to a process of change and freedom of expression. The concept involves tendencies on the part of the organism toward need reduction or tension reduction, but emphasizes the pleasures and satisfactions that are derived from activities that enhance the organism. The concept of actualization emphasizes the creative activities of the organism emphasized by the ego psychologists in psychoanalytic theory and described by White in his concept of competence motivation: "Even when its primary needs are satisfied and its homeostatic choices are done, an organism is alive, active, and up to something" (1959, p. 315).

Self-Consistency and Congruence

The concept of an organism moving toward actualization has not been the subject of empirical investigation. Much more critical to the process aspects of the theory and to research, has been Rogers' emphasis on **self-consistency** and **congruence** between self and experience. According to Rogers, the organism functions so as to maintain consistency (an absence of conflict) among self-perceptions and congruence between perceptions of the self and experiences: "Most of the ways of behaving which are adopted by the organism are those which are consistent with

Self-actualization—Rogers emphasizes the basic tendency of the organism toward self-actualization.

the concept of the self'' (Rogers, 1951, p. 507). The concept of self-consistency was developed by Lecky (1945). According to Lecky, the organism does not seek to gain pleasure and to avoid pain but, instead, seeks to maintain its own self-structure. The individual develops a value system, the center of which is the individual's valuation of the self. Individuals organize their values and functions so as to preserve the self-system. For Lecky, people can be true only to themselves. Individuals will behave in a way that is consistent with their self-concept, even if this behavior is otherwise unrewarding to them. Thus, if you define yourself as a poor speller you will try to behave in a manner consistent with this self-perception.

Does the individual ever experience inconsistencies in the self, a lack of congruence between self and experience? If so, how does the the individual function in order to maintain consistency and congruence? According to Rogers, we experience a state of **incongruence** when there is a discrepancy between the perceived self and actual experience. For example, if you view yourself as a person without hate and you experience hate, you are in a state of incongruence. The state of incongruence is one of tension and internal confusion. When it exists, and the individual is unaware of it, he is potentially vulnerable to anxiety. Anxiety is the result of a discrepancy between experience and the perception of the self. For the most part, we are aware of our experiences and allow them into consciousness.

However, we also are capable of making experiences unavailable to awareness. Here Rogers makes reference to the process called **subception** (McCleary & Lazarus, 1949). The individual can experience a stimulus without bringing it into awareness. The individual can discriminate an experience as threatening, as being in conflict with the self-concept, and not allow it to become conscious. In the interest of maintaining congruence between self and experience, the individual denies certain experiences to awareness. The price for this is anxiety—the "subception" of the organism that the discrepant experience may enter awareness and force a change in the self-concept. Again, the person whose self-concept is that they never hate anyone will experience anxiety whenever hateful feelings are experienced to any degree at all.

The organism seeks to maintain the self-concept. Its response to a state of incongruence—to the threat presented by recognition of experiences that are in conflict with the self—is that of **defense**. An experience is dimly perceived as incongruent with the self-structure, and the organism reacts defensively so as to deny awareness of the experience. Two defensive processes are described—**distortion** of the meaning of experience and **denial** of the existence of the experience. Denial serves to preserve the self-structure from threat by denying it conscious expression. Distortion, a more common phenomenon, allows the experience into awareness but in a form that makes it consistent with the self: "Thus, if the concept of

"Hi, there, the me nobody knows!"

Incongruence—A discrepancy between the perceived self and actual experience is experienced as a state of incongruence. Drawing by H. Martin; © 1971 The New Yorker Magazine, Inc.

self includes the characteristic 'I am a poor student', the experience of receiving a high grade can be easily distorted to make it congruent with the self by perceiving in it such meanings as, 'That professor is a fool;' 'It was just luck' '' (Rogers, 1956, p. 205). What is striking about this last example is the emphasis it places on self-consistency. What is otherwise likely to be a positive experience, receiving a high grade, now becomes a source of anxiety and a stimulus for defensive processes to be set in operation. Events do not have meanings in and of themselves. Meaning is given to events by individuals with past experiences and concerns about the maintenance of a self-system.

Research on self-consistency and congruence.   Rogers is not clear as to whether he has in mind actual experiences, such as emotions, or perceptions of these experiences. That is, does a person respond defensively to the experience of hostility per se or to the dim perception of the self as a hostile person that is in conflict with other perceptions of the self? In any case, the related research has tended to focus on perceptions. An early study in this area was performed by Chodorkoff (1954). In a study of self-perception, perceptual defense, and adjustment, Chodorkoff found that subjects were slower to perceive words that were personally threatening than they were to perceive neutral words. This tendency was particularly characteristic of defensive, poorly adjusted individuals. The poorly adjusted individual, in particular, attempts to deny awareness to threatening stimuli.

Additional research by Cartwright (1956) involved the study of self-consistency as a factor affecting immediate recall. Following Rogers' theory, Cartwright hypothesized that individuals would show better recall for stimuli that are consistent with the self than for stimuli that are inconsistent. He hypothesized further that this tendency would be greater for maladjusted subjects than for adjusted subjects. In general, subjects were able to recall adjectives they felt were descriptive of themselves better than they were able to recall adjectives they felt were most unlike themselves. Also, there was considerable distortion in recall, for the latter, inconsistent adjectives. For example, a subject who viewed himself as hopeful mis-recalled the word "hopeless" as being "hopeful", and a subject who viewed himself as friendly mis-recalled the word "hostile" as being "hospitable." As predicted, poorly adjusted subjects (those applying for therapy and those for whom psychotherapy had been judged to be unsuccessful), showed a greater difference in recall than did adjusted subjects (those who did not plan on treatment and those for whom psychotherapy had been judged to be successful). This difference in recall scores was due particularly to the poorer recall of the maladjusted subjects for inconsistent stimuli. In a related study, an effort was made to determine the ability of subjects to recall adjectives used by others to describe them (Suinn, Osborne, & Winfree, 1962). Accuracy of recall was best for adjectives used by others that were consistent with the self-concept of subjects and was poorest for adjectives used by others that were inconsistent with the self-concept. In sum, the degree of accuracy of recall of self-related stimuli appears to be a function of the degree to which the stimuli are consistent with the self-concept.

The two studies just discussed relate to perception and recall. What of overt behavior? Aronson and Mettee (1968) considered this question and found results that were consistent with Rogers' view that the individual behaves in ways that are congruent with the concept of the self. In a study of dishonest behavior, they reasoned that if people are tempted to cheat they will be more likely to do so if their self-esteem is low than if it is high; that is, whereas cheating is not inconsistent with generally low self-esteem, it is inconsistent with generally high self-esteem. The data gathered indeed suggested that whether or not an individual cheats is influenced by the nature of the self-concept. People who have a high opinion of themselves are likely to behave in ways they can respect while people with a low opinion of themselves are likely to act in ways that are consistent with that self-image.

More recently there has been considerable additional research supporting the view that the self-concept influences behavior in varied ways (Markus, 1977; Markus, Crane, Bernstein, & Siladi, 1982). Much of this research, however, has been part of a different theoretical context and therefore we will wait to consider it in relation to current cognitive, information-processing views of personality (Chapter 14).

The Need for Positive Regard

We have, then, a number of studies supporting the view that the individual attempts to behave in accordance with the self-concept and that experiences inconsistent with the self-concept are often ignored or denied awareness. In the earlier writing of Rogers, no mention was made of the reasons for the development of a rift between experience and self and, therefore, the need for defense. In 1959 Rogers presented the concept of the **need for positive regard.** The need for positive regard includes attitudes such as warmth, liking, respect, sympathy, and acceptance and is seen in the infant's need for love and affection. If the parents give the child unconditional positive regard, if the child feels "prized" by his parents, there will be no need to deny experiences. However, if the parents make positive regard conditional, the child will be forced to disregard its own experiencing process whenever it conflicts with the self-concept. For example, if the child feels that it will only receive love (positive regard) for always being loving, it will deny all feeling of hate and struggle to preserve a picture of the self as loving. In this case the feeling of hate not only is incongruent with the self-concept but also threatens the child with loss of positive regard. Thus it is that the imposition of conditions of worth on the child lead to the denial of experiences, the rift between organism and self. The origins of inaccuracies in the self-concept, the origins of conflict between the individual's experience and the self-concept, lie in the individual's attempts to retain love.

To summarize, Rogers does not feel a need to use the concepts of motives and drives to account for the activity and goal-directedness of the organism. For him, the person is basically active and self-actualizing. As part of the self-actualizing

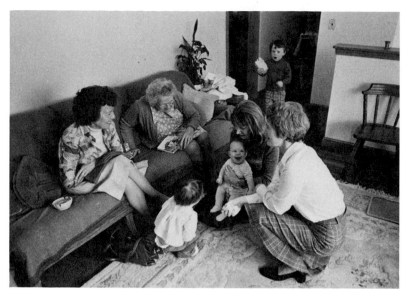

Positive Regard—Healthy personality development is fostered through the communication of unconditional positive regard to the child.

process, we seek to maintain a congruence between self and experience. However, because of past experiences with conditional positive regard, we may deny or distort experiences that threaten the self-system. The result is a state of incongruence, in which we experience anxiety and rigidly hold on to a fixed way of perceiving and experiencing.

Before we leave this section on process, we should raise some questions that are given detailed consideration in the critique and evaluation section of the next chapter. In his conceptualization of the process of awareness and denial to awareness, to what extent does Rogers depart from the Freudian notion of the unconscious? In his description of the development of anxiety and the processes of defensive denial and distortion, to what extent does Rogers depart from the Freudian concepts of anxiety and the mechanisms of defense? Clearly, there are differences in the two points of view. We shall keep these differences in mind as we study the rest of the theoretical network.

Growth and Development

The concept of growth includes the possible courses of development and the factors accounting for one or another type of development. Rogers has not really developed a theory of growth and development and has done no research in the area in terms of long-term studies or studies of parent–child interaction. Basically, Rogers believes that growth forces exist in all individuals. The natural growth process of the organism involves greater complexity, expansion, increasing autonomy, greater socialization—in sum, self-actualization. The self becomes a separate part of the phenomenal field and becomes increasingly complex. The self develops as a total whole, so that each element is part and parcel of the total self-concept. As the self emerges, the individual develops a need for positive regard. If the need for positive regard by others becomes more important than being in touch with one's own feelings, the individual will screen various experiences out of awareness and will be left in a state of incongruence.

Self-Actualization and Healthy Psychological Development

Essentially, then, the major developmental concern for Rogers is whether the child is free to grow within a state of congruence, to be self-actualizing, or whether the child will become defensive and operate out of state of incongruence. A healthy psychological development of the self takes place in a climate in which the child can experience fully, can accept itself, and can be accepted by its parents, even if they disapprove of particular pieces of behavior. This is a point that is emphasized by most child psychiatrists and psychologists. It is the difference between a parent saying to a child "I don't like what you are doing" and their saying to the child "I don't like you." In saying "I don't like what you are doing," the parent is accepting the child while not approving of the behavior.

> *Because the budding structure of the self is not threatened by loss of love, because feelings are accepted by his parent, the child in this instance does not need to deny to awareness the satisfactions which he is experiencing, nor does he need to distort his experience of the parental reaction and regard it as his own. He retains, instead, a secure self which can serve to guide his behavior by freely admitting to awareness . . . all the relevant evidence of his experience in terms of its organismic satisfaction, both immediate and longer range. His is thus developing a sound structural self in which there is neither denial nor distortion of experience.*
>
> Rogers, 1951, p. 503

In contrast to this climate is one in which the parents tell the child, verbally or in more subtle ways, that they feel that its behavior is bad and that it is bad. The child then feels that recognition of certain feelings would be inconsistent with the picture of itself as loved or lovable, leading to denial and distortion of these feelings.

Research on Parent–Child Relationships and the Development of Self-Esteem

Rogers refers to the studies by Baldwin (1945) of parent–child relationships for support of his views. These studies suggest that acceptant, democratic parental attitudes facilitate the most growth. Whereas children of parents with these attitudes showed an accelerated intellectual development, originality, emotional security, and control, the children of rejecting, authoritarian parents were unstable, rebellious, aggressive, and quarrelsome. Helper (1958) found a relationship between parental evaluations and acceptance of their children and the self-evaluations of the children. What is most critical is the children's perceptions of their parents' appraisals. If they feel that these appraisals are positive, they will find pleasure in their bodies and in their selves. If they feel that these appraisals are negative, they will develop negative appraisals of their bodies and insecurity (Jourard & Remy, 1955). Apparently, the kinds of appraisals that the parents make of their children reflect, to a considerable degree, their own degree of self-acceptance. Mothers who are self-accepting also tend to be accepting of their children (Medinnus & Curtis, 1963).

An extensive study of the origins of **self-esteem** gives further support to the importance of the dimensions suggested by Rogers. Coopersmith (1967) conducted a study of self-esteem, which he defined as the evaluation an individual makes and customarily maintains with regard to the self. Self-esteem, then is a personal judgment of worthiness. It is a general personality characteristic, not a momentary attitude or an attitude specific to individual situations. Self-esteem was measured by a 50-item Self Esteem Inventory, with most of the items coming from scales previously used by Rogers. Children in the public schools of central Connecticut filled out the inventory, and their scores were used to define groups of high, medium, and low self-esteem. When compared to children low in self-esteem, those high in self-esteem were found to be more assertive, independent, and creative. The high self-esteem subjects were also less likely to accept social definitions of reality unless they were in accord with their own observations, were more flexible and imaginative, and were capable of more original solutions to problems. In other words, the subjective estimates of self-esteem had a variety of behaviors attached to them.

Having found this behavioral support of the self-esteem measure, Coopersmith studied the origins of self-esteem. He obtained data on the children's perceptions of their parents, ratings from staff members who interviewed the mothers, and responses from the mothers to a questionnaire relating to child-rearing attitudes and practices. The results indicated that external indicators of prestige such as wealth, amount of education, and job title, did not have as overwhelming and as significant an effect on self-esteem as is often assumed. Instead, the conditions in the home and the immediate interpersonal environment had the major effect on judgments of self-worth. Apparently children are influenced in their self-judgments through a process of **reflected appraisal** in which they take the opinions of them expressed by others who are important to them and then use these opinions in their own self-judgments.

What kinds of parental attitudes and behaviors appeared to be important in the formation of self-esteem? Three areas of parent–child interaction seemed to be particularly important. The first area concerned the degree of acceptance, interest, affection, and warmth expressed toward the child. The data revealed that the mothers of children with high self-esteem were more loving and had closer relationships with their children than did mothers with low self-esteem. The interest on the part of the mother appeared to be interpreted by children as an indication of their significance, that they were worthy of the concern, attention, and time of those who were important. The second critical area of parent–child interaction related to permissiveness and punishment. The data relevant to this area of parent-child interaction revealed the following:

> *The conditions that exist within the families of children with high self-esteem are notable for the demands the parents make and the firmness and care with which they enforce these demands. Reward is the preferred mode of affecting behavior, but where punishment is required it is geared to managing undesired responses rather than to harsh treatment or loss of love . . . The total amount of punishment administered in these families is no less than in others, but it is different in its expression and is perceived as justifiable by our high self-esteem subjects.*

Coopersmith, 1967, p. 19

In contrast to this pattern, the parents of children low in self-esteem gave little guidance and relatively harsh and disrespectful treatment. The parents did not establish and enforce guidelines for their children, were apt to use punishment rather than reward, and tended to lay stress on force and loss of love.

Finally, differences were found in parent–child interactions in relation to democratic practices. Parents of children with high self-esteem established an extensive set of rules and were zealous in enforcing them, but treatment within the defined limits was noncoercive and recognized the rights and opinions of the child. Parents of children low in self-esteem set few and poorly defined limits and were autocratic, dictatorial, rejecting, and uncompromising in their methods of control. Coopersmith summarized his findings as follows: "The most general statement about the origins of self-esteem can be given in terms of three conditions: total or nearly total acceptance of the children by their parents, clearly defined and enforced limits, and the respect and latitude for individual actions that exist within the defined limits" (Coopersmith, 1967, p. 236) (Fig. 5.3). Coopersmith further suggested that it is the perception of the parents by the child and not necessarily the specific actions they express that is important, and that the total climate in the family influenced the child's perception of the parents and their motives.

Rogers' views on the parent characteristics and practices that influence the child's development of self-esteem have influenced the thinking of researchers and child-care experts. While not always referring to Rogers, in many cases their emphasis on respect for the child and protection of the child's self-esteem speaks to the influence of Rogers and other members of the human potential movement. His emphasis on the condition that promote self-actualization and the conditions that block it receives further attention in the next chapter when we consider the clinical applications of the theory.

1. *Parent–Child Relationships*: **Acceptance**. Mothers of children with high self-esteem are more loving and have closer relationships with their children than do mothers of children with less self-esteem.

   Illustrative Item (p. 177): "Children should not annoy their parents with their unimportant problems." (Source. Mother's Questionnaire)

Percentage of Mothers of Children with Low, Medium, and High Self-Esteem Expressing Agreement with Illustrative Item

Subjective Self-Esteem (%)

Reply	Low	Medium	High
Disagree	26.5	68.7	54.8
Agree	73.5	31.3	45.2

2. *Parent–Child Relationships*: **Permissiveness and Punishment**. The conditions that exist within the families of children with high self-esteem are notable for the demands the parents make and the firmness and care with which they enforce those demands. In the familial conditions of children with low self-esteem, there is a lack of parental guidance and relatively harsh and disrespectful treatment.

   Illustrative Item (p. 177): Care and consistency with which rules are enforced (Source. Mother's Interview)

Percentage of Families Demonstrating Consistent versus Little Rule Enforcement for Children Low, Medium, and High in Self-Esteem

Subjective Self-Esteem (%)

Degree of Enforcement	Low	Medium	High
Relatively careful and consistent enforcement	60.0	58.8	87.9
Moderate or little enforcement of rules	40.0	41.2	12.1

3. *Parent-Child Relationships*: **Democratic Practices**. In the families of high self-esteem children, there is a clear setting of limits, but within these limits parental treatment is noncoercive and recognizes the rights and opinions of the child. For the low self-esteem children, there are few and poorly defined limits and harsh and autocratic methods of control.

Illustrative Item (p. 214): Procedure generally employed to obtain child's cooperation or compliance. (Source. Mother's Interview)

Percentage of Families Stressing Democratic versus Autocratic Methods of
Control for Children Low, Medium, and High in Self-Esteem

Subjective Self-Esteem (%)

Procedure	Low	Medium	High
Stress discussion and reasoning	40.0	52.9	78.8
Stress force, autocratic means	60.0	47.1	21.2

CONCLUSION   The most general statement about the origins of self-esteem can be
given in terms of three conditions: total or nearly total acceptance of the children by
their parents, clearly defined and enforced limits, and the respect and latitude for individual action that exist within the defined limits.

FIGURE 5.3   Origins of Self-Esteem. (Coopersmith, 1967)

MAJOR CONCEPTS AND SUMMARY

phenomenological self

ideal self

Q-sort

self-actualization

self-consistency

congruence

incongruence

subception

defense: distortion and
   denial

need for positive regard

self-esteem

Before turning to the clinical applications of Rogers' theory of personality, let us
take stock of the theorist and the basic theory of personality. In this chapter we
have begun to see how Rogers attempted in his own life and in his theory to combine the religious and the scientific, the philosophical and the pragmatic. The emphasis by Rogers is on what is "good" and self-actualizing in people. Humans are
unique among the species. Basic to this uniqueness is the awareness of a sense of
self and movement toward self-actualization.

The ways in which we experience events, in particular ourselves, is central in Rogers' theory. The sense of self represents an organized pattern or set of experiences and perceptions. In our daily functioning we seek to preserve the sense of self and, beyond this, to move toward self-actualization, a process of continuing growth and development. It is this emphasis on self-actualization as the central motivation that links Rogers with the human potential movement.

Self-actualization involves continuous openness to experience and the ability to integrate experiences into an expanded, more differentiated sense of self. Self-actualizing, "fully-functioning" people are trusting of themselves, as well as others, open to their own experiences as well as those of others, spontaneous and flexible, free to be creative, and able to respond to others in a genuine, nondefensive way. We are most able to self-actualize when we have a sense of self and self-worth that is not easily threatened. During the early years it is up to the parents to provide the basic acceptance and respect for the child that facilitates the development of such a sense of self. If such conditions are not provided, if the child experiences itself as conditionally accepted or rejected, then there is not room for growth and self-actualization. Under such conditions the child, out of a fear of loss of love, must reject experiences that are incongruent with the desired sense of self and that therefore arouse anxiety.

The concept of self was emphasized by Rogers following his observation that clients tend to talk about their problems in terms of the self. Although impressed with self-statements of clients in therapy interviews, Rogers attempted to obtain more objective measures of the concept as well as ones that could be used in research. Illustrative measures of the self-concept include the Q-sort and the semantic differential, both of which provide the potential for comparison of the self and ideal self concepts.

We have here the basic elements of the theory. However, many of these concepts become most meaningful in relation to Rogers' discussions of the problems of his clients and the process of psychotherapy. During most of the development of the theory, Rogers' main commitment has been to psychotherapy and the process of affecting change—to understanding the conditions that provide for therapeutic change and self-actualization. The personality theory is really an outgrowth of these clinical and research efforts. Therefore, it is not be surprising to find considerable elaboration of the basic concepts when viewed (Chapter 6) within the context of psychopathology and change.

Casorati, Felice. *The Foreigner*. Florence Modern Art Gallery, Scala/Art Resource.

A PHENOMENOLOGICAL THEORY: APPLICATIONS AND EVALUATION OF ROGERS' THEORY

CHAPTER FOCUS: Rogers' theory of personality has followed from his work with clients. His major emphasis has been on how individuals are led to deny and distort experience and on the conditions that provide the basis for all growth and therapeutic change. Also considered in this chapter are other significant figures in the human potential movement (K. Goldstein, A. H. Maslow), existentialism, and an overall evaluation of Rogers' theory of personality.

I wanted only to try to live in accord with the promptings which came from my true self. Why was that so very difficult?

Hesse, 1965, p. 80

It also means that if the counselor is congruent or transparent, so that his words are in line with his feelings rather than the two being discrepant—if the counselor likes the client, unconditionally, and if the counselor understands the essential feelings of the client as they seem to the client—then there is a strong probability that this will be an effective helping relationship.

Rogers, 1961, p. 103

CLIENT   *That's why I want to go, 'cause I don't care what happens.*
THERAPIST   *M-hm, m-hm. That's why you want to go, because you really don't care about yourself. You just don't care what happens. And I guess I'd just like to say—I care about you. And I care what happens. (Silence of 30 seconds) (Jim bursts into tears and unintelligible sobs)*
THERAPIST   *(Tenderly) Somehow that just makes all the feelings pour out.*

Rogers, 1967, p. 409

CLINICAL APPLICATIONS

In this section on clinical applications we will consider Rogers' views on psychotherapy and personality change. These views are an important part of the theory; in fact, the major part of Rogers' professional life has involved these clinical applications. The person-centered approach developed first in counseling and psychotherapy, where it has been known as **client-centered therapy**, "meaning that a person seeking help was not treated as a dependent patient but rather as a responsible client" (Rogers, 1977, p. 5). Rather than focusing on an illness model of abnormal behavior and a medical model of a doctor treating a patient, Rogers has

Client-Centered Therapy—Rogers emphasizes the importance of the therapeutic atmosphere in producing positive personality change.

emphasized the individual's drive toward health, the conditions that may interfere with such growth, and the therapeutic conditions that help to remove obstacles to self-actualization.

Psychopathology

The essential elements of the Rogerian view of psychopathology have been given in the last chapter in the sections on process and growth and development. For Rogers, the healthy person does or can assimilate experiences into the self-structure. In the healthy person, there is a congruence between self and experience, an openness to experience, a lack of defensiveness. In contrast to this, the neurotic person's self-concept has become structured in ways which do not fit organismic experience. The psychologically maladjusted individual must deny to awareness significant sensory and emotional experiences. Experiences that are incongruent with the self-structure are *subceived* as threatening and are either denied or distorted. The result is a rigid, defensive maintenance of the self against experiences that threaten the wholeness of the self and frustrate the need for positive self-regard. Rogers sees no utility in diagnosing different psychopathological illnesses, viewing such diagnoses as meaningless tools. Psychotic behaviors are viewed as behaviors that are inconsistent with the self but which have broken through the defensive processes. "Thus the person who has kept sexual impulses rigidly under control, denying them as an aspect of self, may now make open sexual overtures to those with whom he is in contact. Many of the so-called irrational behaviors of psychosis are of this order" (Rogers, 1959, p. 230).

Although Rogers does not differentiate among forms of pathology, he does differentiate among types of **defensive behaviors**. The defensive behaviors described are similar to those described by Freud. For example, in *rationalization* the person distorts behavior in such a way as to make it consistent with the self. For example, if you view yourself as a person who does not make mistakes, you are likely to attribute a mistake to some other factor. Another example of defensive behavior is *fantasy*. A man who defensively believes himself to be an adequate person may fantasize that he is a prince, that all women adore him, he may deny any experiences that would be inconsistent with this image. A third example of defense behavior is *projection*. Here the individual expresses a need, but it is expressed in a form such that the need is denied to awareness and the behavior is viewed as consistent with the self. People whose self-concept involves no "bad" sexual thoughts may feel that others are making them have these thoughts. The descriptions of these defensive behaviors are quite similar to the ones given by Freud. For Rogers, however, the important aspect of these behaviors is their handling of an incongruence between self and experience by denial in awareness or distortion of perception: "It should be noted that perceptions are excluded because they are contradictory, not because they are derogatory" (Rogers, 1951, p. 506). Furthermore, the classification of the defenses is not as critical to Rogerian theory as it is to Freudian theory.

Although in his 1951 presentation of the theory Rogers interpreted psychological pathology in terms of disturbed relationships between self and experience, most of the related research has been on the relationship between the self and ideal-self concepts. Throughout the Rogers and Dymond book, *Psychotherapy and Personality Change* (1954), the discrepancy between self and ideal-self ratings is referred to as a measure of adjustment, and it has frequently been used as such in later research. The use of this measure would appear to date back to the observation by Raimy (1948) that, as successful personality reorganization occurs in psychotherapy, there is a shift from self-disapproval to self-approval statements. The discrepancy between self and ideal-self statements is then assumed to be a legitimate measure of self-esteem and healthy personality organization. Unfortunately, the self–ideal-self discrepancy does not appear to be a measure of the discrepancy between experience and self. Yet, it is this incongruence between self and experience that Rogers describes as being basic to psychopathology.

Later in his career, Rogers, along with Gendlin (1962), gave more specific attention to the experiencing process and to the measurement of this process. According to Rogers (1958, 1961a, 1967), maladjusted people are likely to be unaware of feelings that they exhibit and that are obvious to an observer. They are unaware of self-contradictory statements and seek to avoid expressions that would be revealing to themselves. Close relationships are perceived as dangerous, and involvement with others is avoided. In contrast, healthy people are likely to experience and express feelings, to take responsibility for ownership of these feelings, and to "risk" themselves in relationships with others. Rogers (Walker, Rablen & Rogers, 1960) has developed a scale to measure how individuals relate to their feelings and how they experience feelings. The scale relates to statements made by individuals, generally clients in a therapeutic interview, which are then rated by judges according to prescribed rules. For example, according to the scale maladjusted people would express disownership of feelings or a vagueness about their feelings. Statements representative of these states would be "The symptom was—it was—just being depressed" and "I am experiencing something vague and puzzling which I do not understand." In contrast to this mode of experience, healthy people accept their feelings ("I am depressed.") and are clearer about them. The scale represents an attempt to gather data, in a systematic way, on the individual's mode of relating to the self and to others. Although still not a measure of the discrepancy between self and experience, the scale does begin to give attention to the way individuals relate to their feelings, a variable that Rogers has long felt to be critical to psychopathology.

Change

Although a theory of personality has developed out of Rogers' experiences in client-centered therapy, his central focus has been on the therapeutic process itself. Rogers' main concern is with the manner in which personality change comes about. He has committed himself to a continuous subjective and objective involvement with the process of change. The titles of his books reflect this orientation and emphasis: *Clinical Treatment of the Problem Child* (1939), *Counseling and Psychotherapy* (1942), *Client-Centered Therapy* (1951), *Psychotherapy and Personality Change* (with R. F. Dymond, 1954), *The Therapeutic Relationship and Its Impact* (in collaboration with others, 1967). In summary, for Rogers, change and growth in therapy represent a special instance of growth and development that can occur in any human being. It is this process, the process of becoming, that is of greatest concern to him.

The History of Client-Centered Therapy

Seeman (1965), in his review of the development of client-centered therapy, observed that the theory and techniques of therapy have been just as much a part of a process of change as has therapy itself. Seeman described three phases in the history of client-centered therapy. In the first phase, Rogers placed great emphasis on the therapist's use of the technique of reflection of feeling. "As material is given by the client, it is the therapist's function to help him recognize and clarify the emotions which he feels" (Rogers, 1940, p. 162). According to this view, there is to be a minimum of therapist activity and guidance of what the client says—the nondirective view. In particular, the therapist was not to offer interpretations about unexpressed attitudes or about the unconscious. The task of the therapist was to recognize and clarify the client's expressed feelings. Research at this point tended to focus on the therapist's behavior. For example, a study by Gump (1944) compared nondirective methods of treatment with psychoanalytic methods.

Gump found that psychoanalytic methods involved a greater proportion of interpretation, whereas nondirective methods emphasized more reflection of feelings. In both methods, however, the client did more than 70 percent of the talking.

Rogers believed that a misconception about his goals was developing. Some counselors who thought that they were being nondirective were merely being passive and seemingly uninterested. Also, the emphasis on "technique" led to over intellectualizing by some counselors. Rogers began to realize that the same statement on the part of the counselor could be given in a way that expresses indifference and critical judgment or empathy and understanding. In the second phase, therefore, Rogers changed his focus from an emphasis on the counselors being nondirective to an emphasis on their being *client centered*. The emphasis changed from one on technique to one on attitude. The counselor was to have an attitude of interest in the phenomenal world of the client. "This formulation would state that it is the counselor's function to assume, in so far as he is able, the internal frame of reference of the client, to perceive the world as the client sees it, to perceive the client himself as he is seen by himself . . . and to communicate something of an empathetic understanding to the client" (Rogers, 1951, p. 29). Counselors were to be involved with an active experiencing of their clients' feelings. They were, in an empathic way, to get under the skin of their clients, to understand clients as the clients seem to themselves.

In this second phase, attention was given to process elements in therapy. Emphasis was placed on the client's increased awareness of previously denied attitudes, on the client's increased ability to evaluate phenomena and on reorganization of the self-concept. His 1954 book contained a variety of studies on changes in the self-concept during therapy. During this period, the Q-sort was used extensively in research. For example, Butler and Haigh (1954) used the Q-sort to compare the self–ideal-self correlations of adult clients at the University of Chicago Counseling Center with a matched group of adults who were not candidates for treatment. They found that the nonclient group had a much closer relationship or correlation between their self and ideal-self Q-sort ratings than was true for the client group. The adults there for counseling were then divided into two groups, one that waited sixty days for treatment to begin and one that completed six or more counseling interviews. Both groups again completed the Q-sort for self and ideal-self concepts—one after the period of counseling and the other after a sixty-day waiting period. The counseling group showed a clear improvement in the self–ideal-self correlation whereas this was not true for the waiting group at all. Indeed, the waiting group showed no change in this relationship over the sixty-day waiting group. Thus, the improvement in the self–ideal-self correlation for the counseling group could not be attributed to time alone. Finally, the group that received counseling and the original matched group (not candidates for therapy) again completed the self and ideal-self Q-sorts at a follow-up time. The counseling group maintained its gains in improved self–ideal-self correlation though this relationship remained below that for the matched, noncounseling group. In sum, the Q-sort data indicated that client-centered counseling results in an increase in congruence between self and ideal-self concepts and that such gains can be maintained over time.

In the third phase of client-centered therapy, there has been an increased emphasis on the therapeutic atmosphere. Rogerian therapists are not detached but involved. They express feelings and are involved in a relationship with their clients. There is an increased emphasis on experiencing rather than verbal self-exploration. Increasingly, there is the sense of a counselor and a client involved in a relationship. There is an emphasis in research on the therapeutic climate and the process of personality change.

Although client-centered therapy has been changing, it has retained from its inception certain distinguishing characteristics (Rogers, 1946, 1977). First, there is the belief in the capacity of the client. Because the basic strivings of the organism are toward growth, actualization, and congruence, the therapist need not control or manipulate the therapeutic process. Second, there is an emphasis on the importance of the therapeutic relationship. What is important is that the therapist attempt to understand the client and to communicate this understanding. In contrast to the psychoanalytic search for hidden meanings and insights into the unconscious, the Rogerian therapist believes that personality is revealed in what clients say about themselves. Diagnoses are not important since they say little about peoples' view of themselves and do not help to create the necessary therapeutic relationship. Third, there is the belief that client-centered therapy involves a predictable process. Growth occurs as the therapist establishes a helping relationship and is able to help free the strong drive of the individual to become mature, independent, and productive. "Given certain conditions, the individual has the capacity to reorganize his field of perception, including the way he perceives himself, and that a concomitant, or a resultant, of this perceptual reorganization is an appropriate alteration of behavior" (Rogers, 1947, p. 361). Finally, with his research emphasis, Rogers has tried to maintain ties among theory, therapy, and research. The client-centered theory of therapy is an if–then theory. The theory states that if certain *conditions* exist, then a *process* will occur that will lead to personality and behavioral change.

Therapeutic Conditions Necessary for Change

It is Rogers' belief that the critical variable in therapy is that of the therapeutic climate (Rogers, 1966). If therapists can provide three conditions in their relationships with their clients, in a way that is phenomenologically meaningful to the clients, then therapeutic change will occur. The three conditions hypothesized by Rogers to be critical to therapeutic movement are **congruence** or genuineness, **unconditional positive regard**, and **empathic understanding**. Genuine therapists are themselves. They do not give a façade but rather are open and transparent. Therefore, clients feel that they can be trusted. Congruent or genuine therapists feel free to be what they are, to experience events in the therapeutic encounter as they occur. They can be with their clients on a person-to-person basis and be themselves. In a genuine relationship, therapists are free to share feelings with their patients, even when negative feelings toward the client are involved: "Even with such negative attitudes, which seem so potentially damaging but which all therapists have from time to time, I am suggesting that it is preferable for the therapist to be real than to put on a false posture of interest, concern, and liking that the client is likely to sense as false" (Rogers, 1966, p. 188).

The second condition essential for therapeutic movement is that of unconditional positive regard. This means that the therapist communicates a deep and genuine caring for the client as a person; the client is prized in a total, unconditional way. The unconditional positive regard provided by the therapist provides a nonthreatening context in which clients can explore their inner selves.

Finally, the third condition of empathic understanding involves the ability of the therapist to perceive experiences and feelings and their meaning to the client during the moment-to-moment encounter of psychotherapy. It is not a diagnostic formulation of the client's experiences, or a rote reflection of what the client says, but instead a "being with" the client while being oneself. It is active listening and understanding of the feelings and personal meanings as they are experienced by the client.

A number of research studies have influenced Rogers' thinking regarding the importance of the therapeutic climate. Others have been influenced by his formulation. Essentially, Rogers is talking about factors that go beyond all forms of psychotherapy, factors that are independent of the theoretical orientation of the therapist, unless that orientation prevents the development of a helping relationship. In one important study, Fiedler (1950) had judges listen to the recorded interviews of experts and nonexperts of the psychoanalytic, nondirective (Rogerian), and Adlerian schools. The judges then sorted a number of descriptive items according to the extent to which they were characteristic of the interview. Fiedler found that, compared to nonexperts, experts were more successful in creating an "ideal" therapeutic relationship. Independent of orientation, experts were similar to one another in their ability to understand, to communicate with, and to maintain rapport with the client. In a related study, Heine (1950) investigated the relation between the theoretical orientation of therapists and therapeutic progress as viewed by clients. Clients sorted a number of statements to describe the changes they felt had occurred while in treatment and a number of statements to describe the therapeutic factors that they felt were responsible for the changes. Heine found that, according to their own reports, patients from psychoanalytic, nondirective, and Adlerian schools did not differ in the kinds of changes they reported had occurred. Furthermore, the clients who reported the greatest changes described similar factors as being responsible for these changes. A later study by Halkides (1958) found that the existence of the attitudes of genuineness, positive regard, and empathy in the therapist were related to therapeutic success.

Briefly, as persons are accepted and prized, they tend to develop a more caring attitude toward themselves. As persons are empathically heard, it becomes possible for them to listen more accurately to the flow of inner expe-

riencings. But as a person understands and prizes self, the self becomes more congruent with the experiencings. The person thus becomes more real, more genuine. These tendencies, the reciprocal of the therapist's attitudes, enable the person to be a more effective growth-enhancer for himself or herself. There is a greater freedom to be the true, whole person.

Rogers, 1980, pp. 116–117

Outcomes of Client-Centered Therapy

What, then, are the changes brought about by client-centered therapy? A significant number of research studies have been completed on the outcomes of client-centered therapy. The following is illustrative of the kinds of changes that have been studied and documented by both clinical illustration and empirical evidence:

1. *Change in ability to evaluate phenomena.* In the course of therapy, there is a shift away from using the values of others toward asserting one's own evaluations (Ruskin, 1949).
2. *Change in defensiveness and manner of experiencing.* In the course of therapy, clients become less defensive, more flexible, more consciously aware of material previously unavailable to awareness, more differentiating in their perceptions, and more open to experiencing themselves (Haigh, 1949: Kessler, 1949; Rogers, 1951; Rogers, 1953; Vargas, 1954).
3. *Change in self-concept.* In the course of therapy, clients develop a clearer, more positive and more congruent self (Butler & Haigh, 1954; Raimy, 1948; Rogers, 1951, pp. 136–141; Sheerer, 1949; Stock, 1949).
4. *Change in views of others and mode of relating to others.* In the course of therapy, clients not only develop a greater sense of their own worth but also change their evaluation of others in a positive direction. Clients also learn to accept positive feelings from others and to express their own positive feelings (Rogers, 1953; Sheerer, 1949; Stock, 1949).
5. *Change in maturity and organization of personality.* In the course of therapy, clients show an increase in the maturity of reported behavior, show greater tolerance for frustration and quicker recovery to a frustrating situation, and show personality changes on broader measures of personality than the Q-sort (Dymond, 1954; Haimowitz, 1948; Hoffman, 1949; Honietz, 1950; Muench, 1947; Thetford, 1952; Vargas, 1954).

Many findings support the specific views presented by Rogers within the client-centered framework. In a more philosophical vein, they involve what Rogers calls being one's organism, being one's experience. Rogers summarizes his views as follows: ''In therapy the individual has actually become a human organism, with all the richness which that implies. He is realistically able to control himself, and he is incorrigibly socialized in his desires. There is no beast in man. There is only man in man, and this we have been able to release'' (Rogers, 1953, p. 67).

Notice that most of the above studies were reported between the late 1940s and the mid–1950s. More recently, Rogers (1967) completed a major study of the therapeutic relationship and its impact on hospitalized schizophrenic patients. Instruments were developed to measure therapist empathy, congruence (genuineness), and unconditional positive regard. The relationship was evaluated by judges who listened to recorded passages from the therapy interviews, by the patients, and by the therapists. Scales were used to measure the process aspect of therapy, in terms of the seven areas and seven stages of the continuum discussed previously (Figure 6.1). The outcome was evaluated according to a variety of criteria—scores on tests, ratings by therapists, and changes in hospitalization status. The study is a difficult one to report and to evaluate because many variables were used and relationships held for some variables but not for others. However, some of the relevant conclusions follow:

There is a continuum that applies to all personality change and development. There are seven areas (strands) in the change process. In each area there are seven stages. At one end of the stage continuum there is fixity, rigidity, and stagnation; at the other end of the stage continuum there is changingness, flow, and process.

STRAND 1   Relationship to Feelings and Personal Meanings
Low Stage: Feelings are unrecognized or unexpressed.
High Stage: Feelings are experienced freely in the immediate moment.

STRAND 2   Manner of Experiencing
Low Stage: Individual is remote from experiencing.
High Stage: Experience is an accepted inner event.

STRAND 3   Degree of Incongruence
Low Stage: Individual is unaware of contradictory self-statements.
High Stage: Individual is able to recognize temporary moments of incongruence.

STRAND 4   Communication of Self
Low Stage: Individual avoids revealing himself.
High Stage: Individual experiences his self and is able to communicate his self-awareness.

STRAND 5   Manner in which Experience is Construed
Low Stage: Individual has rigid views which he accepts as fact.
High Stage: Personal views are recognized to be ways of construing a moment of experiencing and are open to change.

STRAND 6   Relationship to Problems
Low Stage: Problems not recognized or perceived to be external to self, and individual is closed to change.
High Stage: Individual lives his problem and seeks to cope with it.

STRAND 7   Manner of Relating
Low Stage: Close relationships avoided as dangerous.
High Stage: Individual risks being himself in the process of relating to others.

FIGURE 6.1   The Process of Personality Change. (Rogers, 1961)

1. It is possible to develop scales to measure therapy conditions and dimensions of the process of client experiencing.

2. There is evidence that positive conditions and a patient's feeling of involvement are related to positive personality change.

3. Therapist relationship factors appear to be more crucial for schizophrenics than for neurotics. Compared to neurotics, schizophrenics are less interested in self-exploration and more concerned with the issue of trust.

4. There was evidence that competent and conscientious therapists who have been unable to establish high levels of empathy, genuineness, and unconditional positive regard in their relationship may actually worsen the condition of their schizophrenic patients.

5. The establishment of a therapeutic climate is not dependent on therapist or patient factors alone, but is a complex function of the dynamic interaction between the capacities, attitudes, and motives of patient and therapist.

This study of the therapeutic relationship continues the Rogerian tradition of research on human behavior without a movement toward a fragmented study of isolated components of behavior. It continues the Rogerian tradition of the systematic observation of complex phenomena:

> *In this combining of . . . clinical intuition with hard-headed empiricism, we believe that we are groping toward a new philosophy of the behavioral sciences—one which will be freed of the rigid confines of a strict behaviorism, but which will also be free of the irresponsibility of dogmatic speculation.*

> Rogers, 1967, p. 545

A CASE EXAMPLE—MRS. OAK

One of Rogers' outstanding contributions to the field of psychotherapy has been his leadership in opening it up as an area for investigation. He has made available a verbatim transcript of therapy (Rogers, 1942), films of client-centered therapy sessions and a file of recorded therapy sessions that can be used for research purposes. In his 1954 volume on psychotherapy and personality change, Rogers presented an extensive analysis of a single case, the case of Mrs. Oak. As Rogers observes, it is the individual case that makes a total research investigation come to life, which brings diverse facts together in the interrelated way in which they exist in life. The case of Mrs. Oak is presented here to illustrate the Rogerian approach to an understanding of personality.

Mrs. Oak was a housewife in her late thirties when she came to the University of Chicago Counseling Center for treatment. At that time, she was having great difficulty in her relationship with her husband and her adolescent daughter. Mrs. Oak blamed herself for the daughter's psychosomatic illness. Mrs. Oak was described by her therapist as a sensitive person who was eager to be honest with herself and deal with her problems. She had little formal education but was intelligent and had read widely. Mrs. Oak was interviewed forty times over a period of five-and-one-half months, at which point she terminated treatment. A battery of tests was given to her at the beginning of treatment, at the end of treatment, and seven months after the end of treatment.

In the early interviews, Mrs. Oak spent much of her time talking about specific problems with her daughter and her husband. Gradually, there was a shift from these reality problems to descriptions of feelings:

> *And secondly, the realization that last time I was here I experienced a-an emotion I had never felt before—which surprised me and sort of shocked me a bit. And yet I thought, I think it has a sort of a . . . the only word I can find to describe it, the only verbalization is a kind of cleansing. I-I really felt terribly sorry for something, a kind of grief.*

> p. 311

At first the therapist thought Mrs. Oak was a shy, almost nondescript person and was neutral toward her. He quickly sensed, however, that she was a sensitive and interesting person. His respect for her grew, and he describes himself experiencing a sense of respect for, and awe of, her capacity to struggle ahead through turmoil and pain. He did not try to direct or guide her. Instead, he found satisfaction in trying to understand her, in trying to appreciate her world, in expressing the acceptance he felt toward her.

MRS. OAK   And yet the-the fact that I—I really like this I don't know, call it a poignant feeling. I mean . . . I felt things that I've never felt before. I like that, too. Uh-Uh . . . maybe that's the way to do it. I-I just don't know today.

THERAPIST   (M-hm.) Don't feel at all sure, but you know that you somehow have a real, a real fondness for this poem that is yourself. Whether it's the way to go about this or not, you don't know.

> p. 314

Given this supportive therapeutic climate, Mrs. Oak began to become aware of feelings she had previously denied to awareness. In the twenty-fourth interview, she became aware of conflicts with her daughter that related to her own adolescent development. She felt a sense of shock at becoming aware of her own competitiveness. In a later interview, she became aware of the deep sense of hurt inside of her.

MRS. OAK   And then of course, I've come to . . . to see and to feel that over this . . ., see, I've covered it up. (*Weeps.*) But . . . and . . . I've covered it up with so much bitterness, which in turn I had to cover up. (*Weeps.*) That's what I want to get rid of! I almost don't care if I hurt.

THERAPIST   (*Gently.*) You feel that here at the basis of it, as you experienced it, is a feeling of real tears for yourself. But that you can't show, mustn't show, so that's been covered by bitterness that you don't like, that you'd like to be rid of. You almost feel you'd rather absorb the hurt than to . . . than to feel bitterness. (*Pause.*) And what you seem to be saying quite strongly is, "I do hurt, and I've tried to cover it up."

MRS. OAK   I didn't know it.

THERAPIST   M-hm. Like a new discovery really.

MRS. OAK   (*Speaking at the same time.*) I never really did know. But it's . . . you know, it's almost a physical thing. It's . . . sort of as though I-I-I were looking within myself at all kinds of . . . nerve endings and-and bits of-of . . . things that have been sort of mashed. (*weeping*)

p. 326

At first, this increased awareness led to a sense of disorganization. Mrs. Oak began to feel more troubled and neurotic, as if she was going to pieces. She said she felt as though she were a piece of structure or a piece of architecture that had parts removed from it. In struggling with these feelings, Mrs. Oak began to recognize the dynamics of anxiety that had operated in her and to discover how, in an attempt to cope with anxiety, she had deserted her self. She described her previous inability to recognize and "sort of simply embrace" fear. She described her feeling that the problem for her and for many others is that they get away from self.

Intermittently, Mrs. Oak expressed her feelings toward the therapist. At first she felt resentful that the therapist was not being very helpful and that the therapist would not take responsibility for the sessions. During the course of therapy, she at times felt very strongly that the therapist didn't "add a damn thing." But, also, in the course of therapy, she developed a sense of relationship with the therapist and how this relationship compared with the descriptions her friends had given of the relationship in psychoanalysis. She concluded that her relationship with the therapist was different, was something she would never be casual about—was the basis of therapy.

> *I'm convinced, and again I may sound textbookish, that therapy is only as deep as this combination, this relationship, as the need in the client is as deep as the need, and as deep as the willingness for the relationship to grow on the part of the therapist.*

p. 399

Progress did not occur in all areas. By the end of therapy, Mrs. Oak still had sexual conflicts. However, significant gains had been made in a number of areas. She began to feel free to be herself, to listen to herself, and to make independent evaluations. Mrs. Oak began to stop rejecting the feminine role and, more generally, began to become accepting of herself as a worthwhile human being. She decided that she could not continue in her marriage, and she arrived at a mutually agreeable divorce with her husband. Finally, she obtained and held a challenging job.

The positive results described above are matched by the test results on Mrs. Oak. The psychological test responses at the beginning of therapy emphasized the neurotic aspects of her functioning. Mrs. Oak was described as a dependent, passive individual. According to the first report, she was lonely, unhappy, and without affectional ties to anyone. Interpersonal ties, where they existed, were based on a sense of duty or a sense of rebellion. Daydreams were used to escape from her conflicts and feelings of being an ugly duckling. The results of the second psychological test noted a sense of hope, although considerable self-doubt, despair, and dependency remained. A greater sense of openness to trying new things was also observed. The third psychological test reported a marked change. Mrs. Oak was described as a person with self-directed goals, who felt free to make independent value judgments and who experienced little personal threat from others. In contrast to the earlier dependency and resignation, the third test emphasized the sense of interest in and possibility of independent accomplishment. The area of sex, however, continued to be filled with conflict and with views of sex as dirty or sordid.

The positive changes observed on the psychological test were matched by changes in her sortings on the Q-sort. Although the self ratings had little resemblance to the ideal-self ratings at the beginning of therapy, the similarity became far greater by the end of therapy and continued to become increasingly similar through the follow-up period.

In sum, the test data indicated that both Mrs. Oak and others who knew her felt that she had become more mature and more accepting of herself and other people. The data suggested that therapy had contributed to a positive and relatively stable change in behavior and personality organization.

RECENT DEVELOPMENTS

Rogers' Shift in Emphasis: From Individuals to Groups and Society

Over the years, Rogers has emphasized consistently the phenomenological approach, the importance of the self, and the change process. Whereas earlier there was a clear effort to combine clinical sensitivity with scientific rigor, in recent years Rogers appeared to move increasingly toward sole reliance on personal, phenomenological types of studies: "To my way of thinking, this personal, phenomenological type of study—especially when one reads all of the responses—is far more valuable than the traditional 'hard-headed' empirical approach. This kind of study, often scorned by psychologists as being 'merely self-reports,' actually gives the deepest insight into what the experience has meant" (Rogers, 1970,

p. 133). Apparently Rogers feels that the yield of orthodox scientific studies is minute compared to the insights obtained from clinical work. At this point, Rogers defines knowledge as something that is subjectively convincing and intuitively understood. Rogers' emphasis on experience, particularly private experience, and his disappointments with graduate education in psychology have led to a certain disillusionment with current definitions of science: "I'm not really a scientist. Most of my research has been to confirm what I already felt to be true . . . Generally I never learned anything from research" (Rogers, in Bergin & Strupp, 1972, p. 314). What Rogers is searching for is a new view of the person and a more human science of the individual.

Another shift for Rogers, at least in emphasis, has been from the one-to-one therapy relationship to an interest in groups. In his book *On Encounter Groups* (Rogers, 1970), Rogers states that changes occur more rapidly and clearly in small, intensive groups. Of particular interest to Rogers has been the marital partnership group and alternatives to marriage (Rogers, 1972a). This interest is focused on the extent to which there is openness, honesty, sharing, and movement toward awareness of inner feelings in the relationship. The interest is in the here and now, in the experiencing of one's own organism, and in the growth process. Rogers' interests as a scientist, as a therapist, and as a group leaders come together in his efforts to get closer to what individuals are experiencing and in his efforts to help the individuals themselves to do so. Finally, Rogers (1977) has extended his person-centered approach to administration, minority groups, interracial, intercultural, and international relationships. Rogers expresses a revolutionary spirit in his belief that the person-centered approach may yet produce a change in the concepts, values, and procedures of our culture: "it is the *evidence* of the *effectiveness* of a person-centered approach that may turn a very small and quiet revolution into a far more significant change in the way humankind perceives the possible. I am much too close to the situation to know whether this will be a minor a major event, but I believe it represents a radical change" (p. 286).

RELATED POINTS OF VIEW

It was noted in the previous chapter that the tone and spirit of the Rogerian position are apparent in other theories of personality, particularly in the emphasis on the continuous striving of the organism to realize its inherent potential. Together with similar emphases by others, Rogers' position is part of the human potential movement which has been called the "third force" in psychology, offering an alternative to psychoanalysis and to behaviorism.

The Human Potential Movement

According to Riesman (1950), with rapid industrialization the prevailing American personality structure changed from an emphasis on behavior in accordance with tradition to behavior in accordance with individual initiative and an internal set of goals (e.g., accumulation of money, possessions, and power). With the development of bureaucratized, large cities and a consumer orientation, there was a further change in personality structure toward conformity and an anxious concern with being popular and well liked. In recent years, however, this emphasis on conformity and adjustment has changed to an emphasis on fulfillment. Along with Rogers, a number of personality theorists speak to this concern with fulfillment and with being human in the face of large institutions and the demands of society. While there are theoretical differences among them, many humanist theories of personality are joined together in the human potential movement. These theories respond to current concerns (e.g., anxiety, boredom, and lack of meaning) with an emphasis on self-actualization, fulfillment of potential, and openness to experience. Two major figures in this tradition are Kurt Goldstein and Abraham H. Maslow.

Kurt Goldstein

Kurt Goldstein came to the United States in 1935, at age 57, after achieving considerable status as a neurologist and psychiatrist in Germany. During World War I he had extensive experience working with brain-injured soldiers and this work formed the foundation for his later views. He was impressed with the separation of functions that often occurs in brain-injured patients in contrast with the smooth, coordinated brain functioning of normal individuals. What he observed as differences in brain functioning and disturbances due to brain injury he extended to other aspects of personality functioning. Thus, for example, the healthy human organism is characterized by flexible functioning while the disturbed human organism is characterized by rigid functioning. The healthy orga-

Kurt Goldstein

nism is characterized by planned and organized functioning while the disturbed organism is characterized by mechanical functioning. The healthy organism can, delay and anticipate the future while the disturbed organism is bound by the past and the immediacy of the present. Yet, at the same time, Goldstein was impressed with the tremendous adaptive powers of his brain-injured patients, the same powers that he felt were basic to all human functioning.

Like Freud, Goldstein (1939) had an energy view of the organism. However, his views concerning the movement and direction of energy flow differed considerably from Freud: "Freud fails to do justice to the positive aspect of life. He fails to recognize that the basic phenomenon of life is an incessant process of coming to terms with the environment; he only sees escape and craving for release. He only knows the lust of release, not the pleasure of tension" (1939, p. 333). Rather then seeking tension reduction, the main motive for the person is self-actualization. All aspects of human functioning are basically expressions of this one motive—to actualize the self. It can be expressed in such simple ways as eating or in such lofty ways as our highest creative productions, but in the final analysis it is this motive that guides our behavior. Each person has inner potentials that are there to be fulfilled in the growth process. It is the recognition of this that ties Goldstein to others in the human potential movement.

The threats to self-actualization come from disturbances inside the person's bodily functioning and from some forms of interaction with the environment. For example, disease, anxiety, or excessive controls from the environment may interfere with healthy functioning and with full expression of the self-actualization drive. However, the motive remains and the growth process can be continued once these internal and environmental disturbances have been eliminated. Thus, the task of the organism always is that of regulating its internal functioning and relating to the environment in such a way that the self-actualization process can be supported.

Goldstein's work with brain-injured patients was of considerable importance for workers in that area. In addition, his views on the general nature of human functioning have had a significant influence on humanist thinkers in the field of psychology.

Abraham H. Maslow

Maslow (1968, 1971) perhaps has been the major theorist in the human potential movement. It was he who described this psychology as the "third force" in American psychology. He criticized the other forces, psychoanalysis and behaviorism, for their pessimistic, negative, and limited conception of humans. He proposed, instead, that people are basically good or neutral rather than evil, that there is in everyone an impulse towards growth or the fulfillment of potentials, and that psychopathology is the result of twisting and frustration of the essential nature of the human organism. Society often causes such twisting and frustration, and there is a problem when we assume that the result is the essential nature of the organism. Rather, we should recognize what could occur were these obsta-

Abraham H. Maslow

cles to be removed. Here we see one of the reasons for the popularity of the human potential movement on the part of those who feel excessively restricted and inhibited by their environment. Maslow both speaks to these concerns and offers encouragement for the belief that things can be better if people are free to express themselves and be themselves.

In addition to this overall spirit, Maslow's views have been important in two ways. First, he has suggested a view of human motivation that distinguishes between such biological needs as hunger, sleep, and thirst and such psychological needs as self-esteem, affection, and belongingness. While we cannot survive as a biological organism without food and water, we cannot develop fully as a psychological organism without satisfaction of our other needs as well. Far too often, Maslow suggests, psychologists have been concerned with our biological needs and have developed views of motivation which suggest that people respond only to deficiency and only seek tension reduction. While accepting that such motivation exists, Maslow calls for us to recognize as well motivation that is not based on deficiency and that often involves an increase in tension—motivation that is expressed when people are being creative and fulfilling their potential.

A second major contribution by Maslow (1954) was his intensive study of healthy, self-fulfilling, self-actualizing individuals. These were figures from the past as well as some who were living at the time. From this research Maslow concluded that actualizing people have the following characteristics: they accept themselves and others for what they are; they can be concerned with themselves but also are free to recognize the needs and desires of others; they are capable of responding to the uniqueness of people and situations rather than responding in

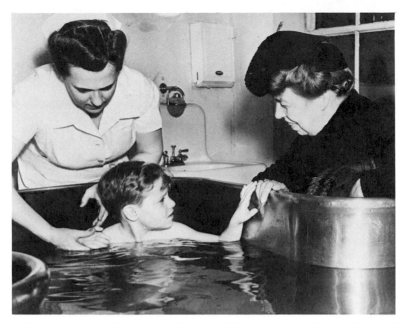

Self-Actualizing Individuals—Abraham Maslow suggested that Eleanor Roosevelt illustrated the self-actualizing person. Here she is speaking to a victim of infantile paralysis during her annual visit to the Children's Hospital.

mechanical or stereotyped ways; they can form profoundly intimate relationships with at least a few special people; they can be spontaneous and creative; and they can resist conformity and assert themselves while responding to the demands of reality. Who are such people? Illustrative figures are Lincoln, Thoreau, Einstein, and Eleanor Roosevelt. Clearly these are very special individuals and few people have all or even most of these characteristics to any substantial degree. What is suggested, however, is that all of us have it within our potential to move increasingly in the direction of these qualities.

At times the views of Maslow and other leaders of the human potential movement sound almost religious and messianic. At the same time, they do speak to the concerns of many people and do serve as a corrective influence on other views that would represent the human organism as passive, fragmented, and completely governed by tension-reducing motives from within or rewards from the environment.

Existentialism

Although new to this edition, the approach known as existentialism is not new to psychology. On the other hand, one could hardly say that it has an established or a secure place in mainstream academic psychology. Current personality texts generally contain at least some, and at times a major, reference to existentialism, yet one rarely encounters it in the personality research journals. Existentialism is an approach that many people are deeply moved by, yet there is no single representative figure, nor is there agreement about basic theoretical concepts. One may note here Rogers' reference to Rollo May, a psychologist who has been important in bringing existentialism into prominence in this country: "My friend Rollo May told me the story that I once questioned the existence of tragedy by saying that Romeo and Juliet might have been all right with a little counseling. I probably did say that. I'm more optimistic than Rollo May. He is an existentialist—so am I, but my philosophy has more room for hope" (quoted in Kirschenbaum, 1979, p. 350). There are religious existentialists, atheistic existentialists, and antireligion existentialists. There are those who emphasize hope and optimism, as well as those who emphasize despair and nothingness. There are those who emphasize the philosophical roots of existentialism and those who emphasize the phenomena of clinical cases.

Granted all this diversity, what is there that establishes a common ground among those who would define themselves as existentialists? What is there about this approach that captivates some and leads others to reject it totally? Perhaps the most defining element of existentialism is the concern with *existence*—the person in the human condition. The existentialist is concerned with phenomena that are inherent in the nature of being alive, human, existing. What constitutes the essence of existence varies for different existentialists. However, all agree that certain concerns are fundamental to the very nature of our being and cannot be ignored, dismissed, explained away, or trivialized. Perhaps most of all, for the existentialist, person and experience are to be taken seriously (Pervin, 1960).

Another major aspect of the existential view is that of the significance of the individual. The existentialist sees the person as singular, unique, irreplaceable. For the philosopher Kierkegaard, the only existential problem is to exist as an individual. A number of additional emphases are related to this valuing of the individual. First, there is an emphasis on freedom. Freedom, consciousness, and self-reflection are what distinguish humans from other animals. Second, freedom involves reponsibility. Each person is responsible for choices, for action, for being authentic or for acting in "bad faith." Ultimately, each person is responsible for their own existence. Third, there is the existential concern with death, for it is here as nowhere else that the individual is alone and completely irreplaceable. Finally, there is an emphasis on phenomenology and an understanding of the unique experience of each person. Events are looked at in terms of their meaning for the individual rather than in terms of some standardized definition or the confirmation of some hypothesis. Thus, there is an interest in how any intrinsically human phenomenon can be experienced and given meaning—time, space, life, death, the self or whatever.

We can perhaps better appreciate this approach by considering a few illustrations. For one, we can consider Rogers' (1980) discussion of loneliness. What is it that makes for the existential experience of loneliness? Rogers suggests a number of contributing factors: the impersonality of our culture, its transient quality and anomie, the fear of a close relationship. However, what most defines loneliness is the effort to share something very personal with someone and to find that it is not received or is rejected: "A person is most lonely when he has dropped something of his outer shell or façade—the face with which he has been meeting the world— and feels sure that no one can understand, accept, or care for the part of his inner self that lies revealed" (quoted in Kirschenbaum, 1979, p. 351). On the other hand, there may also be the feeling of being understood (Van Kaam, 1966). Here the person has the sense that another individual can empathize with them in an understanding, accepting way. The feeling of being understood is associated with safety and relief from existential loneliness.

Another illustration involves the search for meaning in human existence (Frankl, 1955, 1958). The existential psychiatrist Viktor Frankl struggled to find meaning while in a concentration camp during the Second World War. He suggests that the will-to-meaning is the most human phenomenon of all since other animals never worry about the meaning of their existence. Existential frustration and existential neurosis involve frustration and lack of fulfillment of the will-to-meaning. Such a "neurosis" does not involve the instincts or biological drives but rather is spiritually rooted in the person's escape from freedom and responsibility. In such cases the person blames destiny, childhood, the environment, or fate for what is. The treatment for such a condition, *logotherapy*, involves helping patients to become what they are capable of being, helping them to realize and accept the challenges of the opportunities that are open to them.

Finally, we can consider Laing's (1959) brilliant effort to give an account, in existential terms, of some forms of madness. Laing describes existential phenomenology as attempting to characterize the nature of a person's experience—of the world and of the self. *The Divided Self* represents a phenomenological account of the experience of schizoid individuals for whom there is a disruption or split in the relation with the world and the self. There is what Laing calls a *basic ontological insecurity* or lack of a firm sense of one's own self or identity. While everyone may experience some similar feelings, for certain people ontological insecurity is particularly intense and pervasive—going to the very core of their felt existence.

What are the characteristics of basic ontological insecurity and how do people attempt to cope with such feelings? Schizoid individuals experience a fundamental depersonalization such that they may experience themselves as automata, robots, machinery, or animals. The threat in interacting with others is engulfment or the loss of a sense of self. As one patient yelled at her husband in the midst of an argument: "For you this is an argument, you may win or lose, but for me it is my survival as a person that is at stake." While rejection is an ever-present threat, even more threatening is feeling dead or like stone. As one patient said: "Even feeling guilt is better than no feelings at all." Relations with others are seen as constant threats to the sense of self, and the more intimate the relation the greater the experienced threat to the sense of identity. However, the defense of isolation from others or the defensive depersonalization of others is associated with terrible loneliness and alienation. There is a sense of a false self being presented to others and the fear of others presenting a false self to them. This is not just a sense of everyone wearing a mask or playing a role at times, but rather a fundamental sense that the self may lack substance. At the same time, there may be a fear of the power and omnipotence of oneself and others.

A final noteworthy aspect of Laing's description of the schizoid experience is his concern that personality theory may itself be depersonalizing rather than self-validating: "We shall be concerned with people who experience themselves as atuomata, as robots, as bits of machinery, or even as animals. Such persons are rightly regarded as crazy. Yet why do we not regard a theory that seeks to trans-mute persons into automata as equally crazy?" (p. 23).

These represent but brief vignettes of representative existential concerns. Can they help us understand why existentialism is such a powerful force among some and so dismissed by others? For many people, existentialism speaks in a pro-found, humane way to issues that are of concern to them. Others are impressed with the importance of understanding the world of meaning and experience—ei-ther as independent of scientific pursuits or as integral to them. Such psycholo-gists often experience a freedom from the confining concerns of prediction and control and a freedom to explore the depths of human phenomena. On the other hand, other psychologists are critical of existentialism on philosophical, scien-tific, and pragmatic grounds. In particular, there is criticism of an approach that abandons hope of predicting behavior in a lawful way and that has yet to estab-lish its utility as a therapeutic effort. In writing about existentialism in 1960, I suggested that "existentialism may have much to offer and psychology considera-ble to gain" (Pervin, 1960, p. 309). Such a statement would perhaps be equally appropriate today.

CRITICAL EVALUATION

Except for occasional comments and questions, little has been done in this and the last chapter to assess the strengths and weaknesses of Rogers' theory of per-sonality. Until now, the theory has been presented along with supportive re-search. It is time, however, to take a more critical look at the theory. The phe-nomenological approach and various parts of the theory will be returned to in order to examine questions that can be raised and to discuss research that contra-dicts the theory. Three questions, each related to the other, form the basis for this evaluation: (1) To what extent does Rogers' philosophical view of the person lead to omissions or to minimal consideration of critical causes of behavior? (2) To what extent does Rogers pay a price for defining (for research purposes) the self in terms of conscious perceptions? (3) In the elaboration of his theory, in general, and in his views of the nature of anxiety and defense, in particular, to what extent does Rogers represent a departure from Freud?

Phenomenology

The phenomenological approach has been part of a significant effort by many psychologists to come to terms with human experience as it occurs. The phenome-nological approach seeks to consider life as it is experienced by the person, without neglecting that which is most human, without splitting it into unrelated parts, and without reducing it to physiological principles. Two questions may be raised in relation to this approach: What are the limitations of a phenomenological approach to psychology? To what extent does the Rogerian counselor in fact take a phenomenological approach?

There are two potential major limitations to the phenomenological approach in psychology. First, it may exclude from investigation certain critical variables, and, second, it may lead to unscientific speculation. These dangers are not unique to the phenomenological approach, but they are relevant to it. As Smith (1950) has argued, a psychology of experience or consciousness has distinct explanatory limits. Smith points to the sometimes unacceptable strivings that warp our behavior (e.g., aggressive drives) and to the defensive techniques of adjustment of which we are unaware (e.g., repression). Furthermore, Smith argues that, in the development of a scientific psychology, the psychologist must use concepts that are abstractions and must go beyond the phenomenal field of the individual. As MacLeod (1964), himself a phenomenologist, observes, to build a science of psychology, one must go beyond the phenomenal world by developing concepts that can be related to objective measures. The study of the phenomenal self is a legitimate part of psychology as long as it is studied empirically, with a boundless curiosity that is tempered by discipline and not with irresponsible speculation.

On both of these points, Rogers appears to take a reasonable position. He does not believe that the phenomenological approach is the only approach for psychology (Rogers, 1964). He does believe in the empirical investigation of the phenomenal field, in general, and of the phenomenal self, in particular. However, although Rogers acknowledges the importance of experiences of which we are unaware and often refers to the effects of defensive efforts on the part of the individual, he does little to take these effects into consideration in his research. The definition of the self, in terms of that which is conscious, appears to be more a result of Rogers' philosophical view of the person and of Rogers' desire to be able to define the concept in a way that it can be measured, than a result of a commitment to the position that there are only conscious attitudes and experiences relevant to the self. Although Rogerians, as we shall learn, often refer to the effects of defensive sortings on the self Q-sort, little is done to investigate these effects systematically and to build them into the entire research effort.

To return to our second queston, to what extent is the theory based on unbiased phenomenological investigation? In a sense, the question was well put by MacLeod (1964, p. 138) in responding to a presentation by Rogers: "On what basis are you so convinced that you have understood your client better than Mr. Freud has understood his patient?" Rogers' response was that the client-centered therapist brings fewer biases and preconceptions to therapy because of a lighter "baggage of preconceptions." The client-centered therapist is more likely to arrive at an understanding of the phenomenal world of an individual than is the Freudian analyst. In an early paper, Rogers (1947) stated that if one read the transcripts of a client-centered therapist, one would find it impossible to form an estimate of the therapist's views about personality dynamics. But we do not know that this is actually the case. Furthermore, that statement was made at a time when the theory was not very developed and therapists were being nondirective. With the development of the theory and the increased emphasis on client-centered but active involvement by the therapist, is this still true? We know that minor behaviors on the part of the interviewer, including expressions such as m-hm, may exert a profound effect on the verbalizations and behavior of the person being interviewed (Greenspoon, 1962). As one reads the transcripts of the therapy sessions, the comments of the counselor do not appear to be random or inconsequential as far as content is concerned. Counselors appear to be particularly responsive about the self and about feelings, and appear to formulate some of their statements in theory-related terms:

THERAPIST OF MRS. OAK *I'd like to see if I can capture a little of what that means to you. It is as if you've gotten very deeply acquainted with yourself on a kind of a brick-to-brick experiencing basis, and in that sense you have become more self-ish, and the notions of really . . . in the discovering of what is the core of you as separate from all the other aspects, you come across the realization, which is a very deep and pretty thrilling realization, that the core of the self is not only without hate but is really something more resembling a saint, something really very pure, is the word I would use.*

Rogers, 1954, p. 239

This point (of influence of the interviewer on the client) is quite critical, since so much of Rogers' data comes from clinical interviews.

In summary, the phenomenological approach has distinct merits and potential dangers associated with it. Rogers has recognized that it is not the only approach to psychology and that it must be associated with empirical investigation. However, he has not given adequate consideration to the role of unconscious forces in behavior or to the relationship between these forces and the conscious phenomenal field. Furthermore, we are still unclear about the extent to which the behavior of the client in client-centered therapy is, in fact, free of the biases and preconceptions of the counselor.

The Concept of Self

The concept of self is an important area for psychological investigation. A number of questions are relevant to the status of the concept and to its measurement. The concept of self, as developed by Rogers, assumes a constancy over time and across situations; that is, the way people view themselves at one point in time and in one situation is related to their views of themselves at other points in time and in other situations. Furthermore, the Rogerian concept of self assumes a total whole instead of a composite of unrelated parts. Is there any evidence to support these assumptions? The studies of Rogers have suggested that ratings of the self, of the ideal-self, and of the discrepancy between self and ideal-self remain fairly stable for nontherapy groups. As predicted, those ratings change during the course of successful therapy. Other studies support the view that the self-concept is fairly stable over time. Engel (1959) studied the stability of the concept in adolescents over a two-year period. Coopersmith studied the stability of self-esteem in grade school children during a three-year period and concluded that individuals arrive at a fairly stable appraisal of their worth by middle childhood: "Although the idea of self is open to change and alteration, it appears to be relatively resistant to such changes. Once established, it apparently provides a sense of personal continuity over space and time, and is defended against alteration, diminution, and insult" (1967, p. 21). Coopersmith also interpreted his data as suggesting that there is stability of the appraisal of the self across situations, and that appraisals of worth in specific situations are made within the context of an overall, general appraisal. A study by Akeret (1959), however, suggests that individuals may not have a unified view of themselves but, rather, may value themselves in some areas and not others. Stability of the self-concept may itself be a source of individual differences. Thus, a variety of studies indicate that some people show far greater change in their self-concept than do others.

Although there is evidence to support the view that the self-concept has some stability and can be measured reliably, it presents many assessment hazards. One problem with the tests used is that we do not know whether they contain a representative sample of items relevant to the self. For example, the items used by Butler and Haigh were taken from verbal statements of clients in client-centered therapy. Is that sample of items biased in favor of client-centered therapy (Crowne & Stephens, 1961)? A second assessment problem involves the questions raised with respect to the phenomenological approach. It concerns the extent to which subjects are capable of giving and are willing to give honest self-reports. To what extent do subjects report what they perceive to be socially desirable? To what extent are self-evaluative responses influenced by defensive behavior (Crowne & Stephens, 1961)? One study in this area suggests that social desirability is a powerful influence on self-ratings (Milgram & Helper, 1961). Another study suggests a relationship between being defensive and rating oneself favorably (Pervin & Lilly, 1967). We know that subjects will give different ratings in a personal setting than in an impersonal setting (Abernethy, 1954) and will give different responses according to whether they are subjects for research or candidates for employment (David & Pildner, 1958). It has also been found that subjects give conscious self-characterizations that are neither very favorable nor very unfavorable (Huntley, 1940). As Wylie (1974) observes in her review of the literature on the concept of self, assessment problems like these leave many questions unsettled.

The concept of self has a long history in psychology, receiving major attention during some periods and virtually disappearing from the literature during other periods (Pervin, 1984). Because of the difficulties in conceptualization and measurement, some psychologists have concluded that the relevant research has led us toward bankruptcy. Still, despite the many conceptual and methodological problems, the concept of self remains one of considerable importance to the layperson and to the field of psychology. Rogers, more than any other theorist, has given it the attention it deserves in theory, research, and clinical work. Today one reads about self-monitoring (Chapter 2), self-efficacy (Chapter 13), and self-schema (Chapter 14). However, this research occurs outside of the Rogerian framework. As we shall see, this research focuses on situation-specific and cognitive aspects of the self rather than on how the self as a whole is organized and experienced.

Conflict, Anxiety, and Defense

In his formulation of the dynamics of behavior, Rogers gives particular attention to the self-actualization process and to the efforts on the part of the organism to maintain a stable, consistent, congruent picture of the self. Little attention has been given here to the actualization concept. It is an important concept to Rogers, but one that has not been measured and that has not played a role in research. On the other hand, critical attention has been given to Rogers' concepts of congruence, anxiety, and defense, and we have already compared these process concepts with the Freudian model of anxiety and defense.

We can recall that, according to the theory, the individual may prevent awareness (through denial or distortion) of experiences that are "subceived" as threatening to the current structure of the self. Anxiety is the response of the organism to the subception that an experience incongruent with the self-structure may enter awareness, thus, forcing a change in the self-concept. The incongruence between self and experience remains as a constant source of tension and threat. The constant need to use defensive processes results in a restriction of awareness and freedom to respond.

We have, then, a model in which the essential ingredients are conflict (incongruence), anxiety, and defense. Both the Freudian and Rogerian theories involve conflict, anxiety, and defense. In both theories the defenses are used to reduce anxiety. However, the sources of anxiety and, therefore, the processes through which anxiety is reduced, are different in the two theories. For Freud, the conflict leading to anxiety is generally between the drives and some other part of the personality—the ego or the superego as mediated by the ego. For Freud, the defenses are used to deal with the threatening nature of the instincts. The result may be formation of symptoms—symptoms representing partial expressions of the instinct and partial drive reduction. Rogers rejects the assumption that the defenses involve forbidden or socially taboo impulses such as those that Freud describes as coming from the id. Instead, he emphasizes perceptual consistency. Experiences that are incongruent or inconsistent with the self-concept are rejected, whatever their social character. As observed previously, according to Rogers, favorable aspects of the self may be rejected because they are inconsistent or discrepant with the self-concept. Whereas Freud placed an emphasis on instincts and drive reduction, Rogers emphasizes experiences and their perceptual inconsistency with the self-concept. The ultimate goal for Freud was the proper channeling of the drives. The ultimate goal for Rogers is a state of congruence between organism and self. The description given by Rogers of possible modes of defense is similar to Freud's and was undoubtedly influenced by psychoanalytic theory. Generally, however, Rogers gives much less attention to differences in types of defense and does not try to relate the type of defense used to other personality variables, as is the case in psychoanalytic theory.

The above distinctions seem fairly clear, until Rogers attempts to account for the development of a rift between organismic experience and self and introduces the concept of the need for positive regard. According to Rogers, if parents make positive regard conditional, their children will not accept certain values or experiences as their own. In other words, children keep out of awareness experiences which, if they were to accept them, might result in the loss of love. According to Rogers, the basic estrangement in humans is between self and experience and this estrangement has come about because humans falsify their values for the sake of preserving the positive regard of others (Rogers, 1959, p. 226). This statement complicates Rogers' position, since it suggests that the individual disregards experiences that formerly were associated with pain (loss of love). This view is not unlike that of Freud's concerning trauma and the development of anxiety. In essence, one can again see a conflict model, in which experiences that were, in the past, associated with pain later become sources of anxiety and defense.

In both the theoretical formulations of Freud and Rogers, the concepts of conflict, anxiety, and defense play a major role in the dynamics of behavior. Both view well-adjusted people as less concerned with these processes and neurotic people as more concerned with them. For Freud, the process aspects of behavior involve the interplay among drives and the efforts on the part of the defenses to reduce anxiety and to achieve drive-reduction. For Rogers, the process aspects of behavior involve the efforts of the individual toward actualization and toward self-consistency. Although at times Rogers appears to emphasize the pain associated with the loss of positive regard, his major emphasis appears to be on the maintenance of congruence, which includes disregarding positive characteristics that are inconsistent with a negative self-concept and accepting negative characteristics that are consistent with this self-concept.

Growth and Development

Clearly, Rogers has given little elaboration to a theory of growth and development. Little, if any, attention is given to the cultural, social class, and genetic causes of personality. Minor attention is given to familial causes, but this is not related to any research effort. One finding that is relevant to the theory can be noted. A study by Katz and Zigler (1967) hypothesized that self–ideal-self discrepancy is a function of developmental level. In a study of children in fifth, eighth, and eleventh grades, self–ideal-self discrepancy was found to be related to age and intelligence. A greater discrepancy in older and brighter children was accounted for by both decreased self-evaluations and increased ideal-self images. As children grow older they accept many parental and societal ideals. They then also are capable of honestly considering themselves in relation to these ideals. They may begin to recognize and accept without distortion that they are not as bright, or athletic, or popular as they would like to be. In some areas they may even have to revise their glorified picture of themselves. This suggests that with maturity individuals show a greater capacity for guilt and for a clearer picture of strengths and limitations. This suggests the type of developmental research that could be done within a Rogerian framework. Although the study does not refute any Rogerian principle of growth and development, it does raise the question of the appropriateness of using self–ideal-self discrepancy as a measure of psychopathology since such a discrepancy in some areas may reflect a mature holding of ideals and acceptance of where one stands in relation to these ideals.

Psychopathology and Change

In an earlier study of self–ideal-self discrepancy and social competence, Zigler (Achenbach & Zigler, 1963) found that highly competent subjects showed a greater self–ideal-self discrepancy than did subjects low in social competence. The Rogerian theory of psychopathology relates to a lack of congruence between experience and self, and the self–ideal-self measure is not critical to the theory. On the other hand, self–ideal-self discrepancies have been used consistently by Rogerians as a measure of adjustment. Thus, the above finding points to some of the problems that emerge in the use of this measure. A variety of studies have found a relationship between the size of the self–ideal-self discrepancy and characteristics such as psychopathology, self-depreciation, anxiety, and insecurity. For example, Turner and Vanderlippe (1958) found that the college student who is high in self–ideal-self congruence, in contrast to the student low in such congruence, participated in more extracurricular activities, had a higher scholastic average, was more popular with fellow students, and received higher adjustment ratings on personality tests. On the other hand, other studies (e.g., Pervin & Lilly, 1967) have found a relationship between high self–ideal-self congruence and defensiveness. For example, Havener and Izard (1962) found a relationship between high congruence and unrealistically high self-esteem in paranoid schizophrenics. These subjects appear to be defending against a complete loss of positive self-regard. It appears that the self–ideal-self relationship is far too complex to be an altogether satisfactory measure of adjustment (Vernon, 1963; Wylie, 1974).

The problems associated with using differences between self and ideal-self ratings as a measure of adjustment have been recognized by Rogers and many of his followers. The problem is important both in and of itself and also in relation to evaluating the results of therapy. There is considerable evidence to suggest that different methods of therapy may lead to different kinds of change (Garfield & Begin, 1978). Some changes may be measured by particular personality tests but not by others. For example, a psychological test developed in relation to Rogerian theory may relate well to Q-sort measures of change and to the results of client-centered therapy but not to tests developed in relation to psychoanalytic theory or to the results of psychoanalysis (Grummon & John, 1954; Vargas, 1954). The reverse might be true for tests developed in relation to psychoanalytic theory. The closer the relationship between the test and the theory, the greater the likelihood of the test being sensitive to changes produced by the therapy associated with that theory. Rogers undoubtedly would agree that there are various viewpoints from which to consider the person. Thus, it could be argued that "no single test score, no one rater's rating can be considered adequately representative of the diversity of measured changes accompanying psychotherapy" (Cartwright, Kirtner, & Fiske, 1963, p. 175).

Notice that a conclusion similar to this one was reached during the course of a discussion of a case by Rogers and psychoanalysts (Rogers, 1967). Rogers, Rogerian therapists, and psychoanalysts were concerned with the positive movement that occurred in a case presented for discussion. Rogers reports that, at one extreme, the analysts could see little or no progress in therapy, whereas, at the other extreme, the client-centered therapists tended to see great and consistent movement in therapy. Apparently, psychoanalysts emphasize structure, character, and fixity in human behavior. In their view they go from the twigs of a tree to the trunk of the tree, from the superficial to the core of personality. In contrast to this view, the Rogerian emphasizes process and change in human behavior. For the Rogerian, one need not go beyond what is immediately observable to encounter that which is basic to the person.

Summary Evaluation

How, then, may the theory of Rogers be evaluated? It is reasonably comprehensive, although many areas of neglect remain. The theory really says little about the course of growth and development or about the specific factors that determine one or another pattern. In a similar vein, although Rogers refuses to accept diagnostic categories, he does little to recognize the tremendous variation in symptomatology in patients or to relate this variation to previous conditions. Furthermore, one finds strikingly little mention of sex and aggression or of feelings such as guilt and depression. Yet, much of our lives seem to be concerned with these feelings. On the other hand, Rogers has attempted to develop a comprehensive theory and has given considerable attention to the process of change. Within the area that he does cover in the theory and, in particular, within the theory of the process of change, his theory is quite economical. Out of all the complexities of psychotherapy Rogers has attempted to define the few necessary and sufficient conditions for positive personality change. Furthermore, he has attempted to develop the theory in a logically consistent manner and with explicit definitions for most variables.

Much of this theory expresses a philosophical, perhaps religious, view of the person. Assumptions most related to this view, such as the drive toward actuali-

FIGURE 6.2   **SUMMARY OF STRENGTHS AND**
              LIMITATIONS OF ROGERS' THEORY &
              PHENOMENOLOGY

STRENGTHS	LIMITATIONS
1. Focuses on important aspects of human existence.	1. May exclude certain phenomena (unconscious processes, defenses, etc.) from research and clinical concern.
2. Attempts to recognize the holistic, integrated aspects of personality.	2. Lacks objective measures of behavior beyond self-report.
3. Tries to integrate humanism and empiricism.	3. Ignores the impossibility of being totally phenomeno-logical—that is, of making observations that are totally free of bias and preconception.
4. Aims at systematic inquiry into the necessary and sufficient conditions for therapeutic change.	

zation, have remained assumptions and have not provided the basis for research. Also, the system is still without a measure of self-experience congruence. However, it is clear that the theory has provided extremely fertile ground for research. Rogers has always kept clinical work, theory, and research in close touch with one another. Most of his work reflects a reluctance to sacrifice the rigors of science for the intuitive aspects of clinical work, and all of his work reflects an unwillingness to sacrifice the rich complexities of behavior for the empirical demands of science. As is properly the case, the development of his system has been the result of a constant interplay among gross observations, theoretical formulations, and systematic research efforts.

This chapter on Rogers is concluded by stating three major contributions. Extending beyond the discipline of psychology, Rogers has developed a point of view and an approach toward counseling that has influenced teachers, members of the clergy, and people in business. Within psychology, Rogers has opened up the area of psychotherapy for research. By recording interviews, by making interviews and transcripts available to others, by developing clinically relevant measures of personality, and by demonstrating the potential value of research in the area, Rogers has led the way in the legitimization of research on psychotherapy.

Although not all of the research is supportive of client-centered therapy (Fiske & Goodman, 1965), the studies done in relation to client-centered therapy remain among the few that provide well-documented support for the effectiveness of treatment. Finally, more than any other personality theorist, Rogers has focused both theoretical and empirical attention on the nature of the self. The study of the self has always been a part of psychology, but it has, at times, been in danger of being dismissed as "mere philosophy." As MacLeod (1964) notes, you may not find many papers on the self at meetings of experimental psychologists, but clinicians find the problem staring them in the face. More than any other personality theorist, Rogers has attempted to be objective about what is otherwise left to the artists:

> *Slowly the thinker went on his way and asked himself: What is it that you wanted to learn from teachings and teachers, and although they taught you much, what was it they could not teach you? And he thought: It was the Self, the character and nature of which I wished to learn. I wanted to rid myself of the Self, to conquer it, but I could not conquer it, I could only deceive it, could only fly from it, could only hide from it. Truly, nothing in the world has occupied my thoughts as much as the Self, this riddle, that I live, that I am one and am separate and different from everybody else, that I am Siddartha; and about nothing in the world do I know less than about myself, about Siddartha.*

H. Hesse, 1951, p. 40

MAJOR CONCEPTS AND SUMMARY

[Review concepts from chapter 5]	unconditional positive regard
self–experience discrepancy	emphatic understanding
defensive behaviors	human potential movement
client-centered therapy	existentialism
congruence (genuineness)	

In this chapter and the last the phenomenological theory of personality of Carl R. Rogers has been discussed. The theory is concerned with individual differences and the entire personality of the individual. The emphasis is on the phenomenal world of individuals—how individuals perceive and experience themselves and the world about them.

The main structural concepts in the theory are the self, representing an organized pattern of perceptions relating to "me," or "I," and the ideal-self, representing the self-concept the individual would like to possess. Although structural concepts are important in terms of representing particular parts of the phenomenal field and in representing stability in an individual's functioning over time, the main focus of the theory is on process and change. The basic tendency in the individual is toward self-actualization—toward maintaining, enhancing, and actualizing the experiencing organism. Beyond this the individual is oriented toward self-consistency, interpreted as a congruence between self and experience. A state of incongruence is created when the individual perceives or subceives experiences that are contradictory with his self-image. Such experiences have been associated in the past with the loss of positive regard. The subception of such experiences is associated with tension or anxiety and leads to the use of defensive devices to remove the incongruence and reduce the anxiety. The basic defensive processes are distortion and denial, leading to a distorted representation of experience or to an unawareness of experience. This sequence of threat due to incongruence between self and experience and the consequent use of defenses forms the basis for psychopathology. There is research evidence to support the view that individuals attempt to behave in accordance with the self-concept and that experiences inconsistent with the self-concept are often ignored or denied into awareness.

Rogers has not really developed a theory of growth and development. Basically growth is seen as involving increased differentiation, expansion, and autonomy. The critical theoretical and practical questions are the circumstances that maximize the opportunity for growth. According to Rogers, it is critical that parents give their children feelings of self-worth. Presumably the conditions for growth that parents must provide for their children are the same ones that therapists must provide for their clients—congruence (genuineness), unconditional positive regard, and empathic understanding.

Rogers' view of the person and his approach to research are quite different from those of Freud. Rogers' theory emphasizes constructive forces in contrast to the psychoanalytic emphasis on that which is "innately destructive." Also, in contrast to the psychoanalytic emphasis on hidden meanings, Rogers emphasizes the usefulness of self-reports and direct sources of information. In contrast with Freud's emphasis on the past, Rogers prefers to deal with what is present or anticipated. These differences in points of view obviously translate themselves into differences in theory and research. Instead of the use of free-association and dream analysis there is the use of verbal self-report and Q-sorts. Instead of an emphasis on studies of the unconscious, there is an emphasis on studies of the conditions that promote positive change (i.e., change toward self-actualization and openness to experience) and studies of the characteristics of the self.

Evaluation of Rogers' theory has brought out certain problems and limitations. (1) There has been inadequate attention given to unconscious forces, particularly given the fact that the theory recognizes the existence of such phenomena. (2) There are problems with the definitions and assessment devices for some concepts. For example, it is not clear how one studies in a systematic way the drive toward self-actualization and there are serious questions about the extent to which the self–ideal-self discrepancy can be considered to be an accurate measure of psychopathology. (3) There is evidence that even in the Rogerian, client-cen-

tered therapy situation, the therapist is a source of considerable bias and differentially rewards certain client behaviors (Truax, 1966.

Nevertheless, Rogers, while aware of these problems, has gone on to make a
number of very significant contributions. (1) He has developed an approach to
counseling that has had a significant impact upon the field. (2) He has opened up
the entire area of psychotherapy for systematic research. (3) He has focused both
theoretical and empirical attention on the nature of the self. (4) In his emphasis
on self-actualization and openness to experience, he has provided one source of
leadership for the human potential movement and has spoken to the concerns of
many individuals in our society.

Klee, Paul. *Seneccio*. 1922. Kernstmuseum, Art Resource.

A COGNITIVE THEORY OF PERSONALITY: GEORGE A. KELLY AND HIS PERSONAL CONSTRUCT THEORY OF PERSONALITY

CHAPTER FOCUS: In this chapter we discuss Kelly's personal construct theory as illustrative of a clinical, cognitive theory of personality. What distinguishes this theory is its emphasis on how the individual perceives, interprets, and conceptualizes events and the environment. The person is viewed as a scientist who develops a theory (construct system) to predict events. A new test, the Rep test, is presented as one means of assessing construct systems and thereby of understanding an individual's personality.

To a large degree—though not entirely—the blueprint of human progress has been given the label of "science." Let us, then, instead of occupying ourselves with man-the-biological-organism or man-the-lucky-guy, have a look at man-the-scientist.

Kelly, 1955, p. 4

Man looks at his world through transparent patterns or templets which he creates and then attempts to fit over the realities of which the world is composed . . . Let us give the name constructs to these patterns that are tried on for size. They are ways of construing the world.

Kelly, 1955, pp. 8–9

In the preceding four chapters, two clinical theories of personality have been discussed—the psychodynamic theory of Freud, and the phenomenological theory of Rogers. Both theories derived from clinical contacts with patients; both emphasize individual differences; both view individuals as having some consistency across situations and over time; and both view the person as a total system. Freud and Rogers attempted to understand, predict, influence, and conceptualize behavior without fragmenting people into unrelated parts. Although sharing these characteristics in common, the two theories were presented as illustrative of different approaches to theory and research.

In this chapter, we study a third theory, one that also is expressive of the clinical approach toward understanding personality. The **personal construct theory** of George Kelly, like the theories of Freud and Rogers, was developed mostly out of considerable contact with clients in therapy. Like the theories of Freud and Rogers, Kelly's personal construct theory emphasizes the whole person. It emphasizes individual differences and the stability of behavior over time and across situations. As Kelly observes, the first consideration of personal construct theory is the individual person, rather than any part of the person, any group of persons, or any particular process in a person's behavior. The personal construct clinician cannot fragment the client and reduce the client's problem to a single issue. Instead, the clinician must view the client from a number of perspectives at one and the same time.

Although sharing these characteristics with other clinical theories, Kelly's theory is vastly different from the theories of Freud and Rogers. It is an extremely imaginative effort to interpret behavior in *cognitive* terms; that is, it emphasizes the ways in which we perceive events, the way we interpret and transform these events in relation to already existing structures, and the ways that we behave in relation to these interpretations and transformations. For Kelly a **construct** is a way of perceiving or interpreting events. For example, good–bad is a construct frequently used by people as they consider events. An individual's personal construct system is made up of the constructs, or ways of interpreting events, that are available and the relationships among these constructs. There is a strong emphasis on cognition in the theory, but Kelly insisted that his theory was not merely a theory of cognition. Kelly's theory dares to reconstrue—that is, reinterpret—the field of psychology, and he challenged others to reconstrue it with him. But, for this part of the story, let the theorist speak for himself.

TO WHOM IT MAY CONCERN

It is only fair to warn the reader about what may be in store for him. In the first place, he is likely to find missing most of the familiar landmarks of psychology books. For example, the term learning, so honorably embedded in most psychological texts, scarcely appears at all. That is wholly intentional; we are for throwing it overboard altogether. There is no ego, no emotion, no motivation, no reinforcement, no drive, no unconscious, no need. There are some brand-new psychological definitions, words like foci of convenience, preemption, propositionality, fixed-role therapy, and the credulous approach . . . Unfortunately, all this will make for periods of strange, and perhaps uncomfortable, reading. Yet, inevitably, a different approach calls for a different lexicon; and, under its influences many old terms are unhitched from their familiar meanings.

To whom are we speaking? In general, we think the reader who takes us seriously will be an adventuresome soul who is not one bit afraid of thinking unorthodox thoughts about people, who dares peer out at the world through the eyes of strangers, who has not invested beyond his means in either ideas or vocabulary, and who is looking for an ad interim, rather than an ultimate, set of psychological insights.

Kelly, 1955, pp. x–xi

GEORGE A. KELLY (1905–1966): A VIEW OF THE THEORIST

Less has been written about the life of Kelly than of Freud and Rogers, but we do know something of his background, and the nature of the man comes through in his writing. He appears to be someone who would enjoy reading his books—an adventuresome soul who is unafraid to think unorthodox thoughts about people and who dares to explore the world of the unknown with the tools of tentative hypotheses. In his review of Kelly's theory, Sechrest (1963) observes that Kelly's philosophical and theoretical positions stem, in part, from the diversity of his experience. Kelly grew up in Kansas and obtained his undergraduate education there at Friends University and at Park College in Missouri. He pursued graduate studies at the University of Kansas, the University of Minnesota, and the University of Edinburgh. He received his Ph.D. from the State University of Iowa in 1931. He developed a traveling clinic in Kansas, was an aviation psychologist during World War II, and was a professor of psychology at Ohio State University and at Brandeis University.

Kelly's early clinical experience was in the public schools of Kansas. While there, he found that teachers referred pupils to his traveling psychological clinic with complaints that appeared to say something about the teachers themselves. Instead of verifying a teacher's complaint, Kelly decided to try to understand it as an expression of the teacher's construction or interpretation of events. For example, if a teacher complained that a student was lazy, Kelly would not look at the pupil to see if the teacher was correct in the diagnosis. Rather he would try to understand the behaviors of the child and the way the teacher perceived these behaviors—that is, the teacher's construction of them—which led to the complaint of laziness. This was a significant reformulation of the problem. In practical terms, it led to an analysis of the teachers as well as the pupils, and to a wider range of solutions to the problems. Furthermore, it led Kelly to the view that there is no

George A. Kelly

objective, absolute truth, and that phenomena are meaningful only in relation to the ways in which they are construed or interpreted by the individual.

George Kelly, then, was a person who refused to accept things as black or white, right or wrong. He was a person who liked to test new experiences; a person who dismissed truth in any absolute sense and, therefore, felt free to reconstrue or reinterpret phenomena; a person who challenged the concept of "objective" reality and felt free to play in the world of "make-believe;" a person who perceived events as occurring to individuals and, therefore, was interested in the interpretations of these events by individuals; a person who viewed his own theory as only a tentative formulation and who, consequently was free to challenge views that others accepted as fact; a person who experienced the frustration and challenge, the threat and joy, of exploring the unknown.

KELLY'S VIEW OF THE PERSON

Theories of personality have implicit in them philosophical assumptions about human nature. Often, they can be uncovered only as we study why a theorist explores one phenomenon instead of another, and as we observe that different theorists go beyond the data in different ways—ways that are meaningful in relation to their own life experiences. In general, Kelly is straightforward, and his view of the person is explicit. In fact, he begins his presentation of the psychology of personal constructs with a section on his perspectives of the person. Kelly's assumption about human nature is that every person is a scientist. The scientist attempts to predict and control phenomena. Kelly believes that psychologists, operating as scientists, try to predict and control behavior, but that they do not assume that their subjects operate on a similar basis. Kelly describes this situation as follows:

> It is as though the psychologist were saying to himself, "I, being a psychologist, and therefore a scientist, am performing this experiment in order to improve the prediction and control of certain human phenomena; but my subject, being merely a human organism, is obviously propelled by inexorable drives welling up within him, or else he is in gluttonous pursuit of sustenance and shelter."

Kelly, 1955, p. 5

Kelly regards himself as having theories, testing hypotheses, and weighing experimental evidence and he considers this an appropriate view of people. Not every person is a scientist in the sense of limiting attention to some specific area and of using agreed-on techniques to collect and to evaluate data. However, these are matters of detail, whereas the principles of operation are the same. All people experience events, perceive similarities and differences among these events, formulate concepts or constructs to order phenomena and, on the basis of these constructs, seek to anticipate events. All people are similar in that they use constructs and follow the same psychological processes in the use of these constructs. In this respect, all people are scientists. However, individuals are unique in their use of particular constructs. Differences between individuals in the constructs that they use correspond to the differences among scientists in their theoretical points of view.

The view of the person as a scientist has a number of further consequences for Kelly. First, it leads to the view that we are essentially oriented toward the future. "Anticipation is not merely carried on for its own sake; it is carried on so that future reality may be better represented. It is the future which tantalizes man, not the past. Always he reaches out to the future through the window of the present" (Kelly, 1955, p. 49). Second, it suggests that we have the capacity to "represent" the environment, rather than merely to "respond" to it. Just as scientists can develop alternative theoretical formulations concerning phenomena, so individuals can interpret and reinterpret, construe and reconstrue, their environments. Life is a representation, or construction, of reality, and this allows us to make and remake ourselves. Some people are capable of viewing life in many different ways while others cling rigidly to a set interpretation. Those with a greater number of possible interpretations have a greater opportunity for selection and are likely to be more able to differentiate among different situations and different people. However, everyone can only perceive events within the limits of the categories (constructs) that are available to him or her. In Kelly's terms, we are free to construe events but are bound by our constructions. Thus, it is that we come to a new understanding of the issue of free will and determinism. According to Kelly, we are both free *and* determined. "This personal construct system provides him [Man] with both freedom of decision and limitations of action—freedom, because it permits him to deal with the meaning of events rather than forces him to be helplessly pushed about by them, and limitation, because he can never make choices outside the world of alternatives he has erected for himself" (Kelly, 1958a, p. 58). Having "enslaved" ourselves with these constructions, we are able to win freedom again and again by reconstruing the environment and life. Thus, we are not victims of past history or of present circumstances—unless we choose to construe ourselves in that way.

KELLY'S VIEW OF SCIENCE, THEORY, AND RESEARCH METHODS

Much of Kelly's thinking, including his view of science, is based on the philosophical position of **constructive alternativism.** According to this position, there is no objective reality or absolute truth to discover. Instead, there are efforts to construe events—to interpret phenomena in order to make sense of them. There are always alternative constructions available from which to choose. This is true for the scientist as it is for people who behave as scientists. In Kelly's view the scientific enterprise is not the discovery of truth or, as Freud might have suggested, the uncovering of things in the mind previously hidden. Rather, the scientific enterprise is the effort to develop construct systems that are useful in anticipating events.

Kelly was concerned about the tendency toward dogma in psychology. He thought psychologists believed that constructs of inner states and traits actually existed rather than understanding them as "things" in a theoretician's head. If someone is described as an introvert, we tend to check to see whether he *is* an introvert, rather than checking the person who is responsible for the statement. Kelly's position against "truth" and dogma is of considerable significance. It leads, for instance, to the freedom to view "make-believe" as an essential feature of science (Kelly, 1964). Kelly criticized those who view science as a way of avoiding subjective, or personal, statement and, hence, for getting down to the hard facts of reality. For Kelly, subjective thinking is an essential step in the scientific process. Subjective thinking allows one to establish the "invitational mood" in which one is free to invite many alternative interpretations of phenomena, and to entertain propositions that, initially, may seem absurd. The invitational mood is a necessary part of the exploration of the world, for the professional scientist as well as for the patient in therapy. It is the mood established by the creative novelist. But where the novelist publishes his make-believe and may even be unconcerned with the evidence supporting his constructions, the professional scientist tends to minimize the world of make-believe and to focus on objective evidence. Kelly concluded his comparison of the novelist and the scientist:

> *But neither of these differences between the novelist and the scientist is very fundamental. Both men employ nonetheless typically human tactics. The fact that the scientist is ashamed to admit his phantasy probably accomplished little more than to make it appear that he fits a popular notion of the way scientists think. And the fact that a novelist does not continue his project to the point of collecting data in support of his portrayals and generalizations suggests only that he hopes that the experiences of man will, in the end, prove him right without anyone's resorting to formal proof.*
>
> *But the brilliant scientist and the brilliant writer are pretty likely to end up saying the same thing—given, of course, a lot of time to converge upon each other. The poor scientist and the poor writer, moreover, fail in much the same way—neither of them is able to transcend the obvious. Both fail in their make-believe.*

Kelly, 1964, p. 140

According to Kelly, it is the freedom to make believe and to establish the invitational mood that allows for the development of hypotheses. A hypothesis should not be asserted as a fact, but instead should be accepted as a conclusion that allows the scientist to pursue its implications *as if* it were true. Kelly viewed a theory as a tentative expression of what has been observed and of what is expected. A theory has a **range of convenience**, indicating the boundaries of phenomena the theory can cover, and a **focus of convenience**, indicating the points within the boundaries where the theory works best. For example, Freud's theory had a broad range of convenience, providing interpretations for almost all aspects of personality, but its focus of convenience was the unconscious and abnormal behavior. Rogers' theory has a narrower range of convenience and its focus of convenience is more on the concept of the self and the process of change. Kelly points out that different theories have different ranges of convenience and different foci of convenience. Regardless of these differences, however, there are common grounds for determining whether one has a good theory.

> *A good psychological theory has an appropriate focus and range of convenience . . . It should be fertile in producing new ideas, in generating hypotheses, in provoking experimentation, in encouraging inventions. The hypotheses which are deduced from it should be brittle enough to be testable, though the theory itself may be cast in more resilient terms. The more frequently its hypotheses turn out to be valid, the more valuable the theory.*
>
> Kelly, 1955, p. 44

For Kelly, theories were modifiable and ultimately expendable. A theory is modified or discarded when it stops leading to new predictions or leads to incorrect predictions. Among scientists, as well as among people in general, how long one holds on to a theory in the face of contradictory information, is partly a matter of taste and style.

Kelly's view of science is not unique, but it is important in terms of its clarity of expression and its points of emphasis. It does have a number of important ramifications. First, since there are no "facts", and since different theories have different ranges of convenience, we need not argue about whether facts are "psychological" or "physiological." There are psychological *and* physiological constructions of the same or different phenomena. Second, Kelly's approach involved criticism of an extreme emphasis on measurement. Kelly believed that such an extreme approach means that no theoretical statement can be made unless each concept refers to something tangible, that is, something that can be measured. Kelly felt that such an approach can lead to viewing concepts as "things" rather than as representations, and to making a psychologist into a technician rather than a scientist. On the other hand, Kelly's view of science did include the need for theories to lead to research. Third, Kelly's view of science leaves room for the clinical as opposed to the experimental method, which he considered useful because it speaks the language of hypothesis, because it leads to the emergence of new variables, and because it focuses on important questions. "When one ponders the fact that mankind has probably spent more time trying to answer poorly posed questions than figuring out sensible issues, one wonders if this feature of the clinical method should not be more widely advocated in all human enterprise" (Kelly, 1955, p. 193). Here we have a fourth significant aspect of Kelly's view of science—it should focus on important issues. In Kelly's belief, many psychologists are afraid of doing anything that might not be recognized as science, and they have given up struggling with important aspects of human behavior. His

1. There is no objective reality and there are no "facts." Different theories have different constructions of phenomena. These theories also have different ranges of convenience and different foci of convenience.
2. Theories should lead to research. However, an extreme emphasis on measurement can be limiting and lead to viewing concepts as "things" rather than as representations.
3. The clinical method is useful because it leads to new ideas and focuses attention on important questions.
4. A good theory of personality should help us to solve the problems of people and society.
5. Theories are designed to be modified and abandoned.

FIGURE 7.1   Some Components of Kelly's View of Science.

suggestion was that they stop trying to be scientific and that they get on with the job of understanding people. Kelly believed that a good scientific theory should encourage the invention of new approaches to the solution of the problems of people and society.

Finally, Kelly took a firm stand against dogma, and he argued for the language of hypothesis. It was his contention that many scholars waste time trying to disprove their colleagues' claims in order to make room for their own explanations. It is as if to be "right" one has to prove the other "wrong." In Kelly's opinion, this is a terrible waste of time. Instead, he suggested that psychologists think in less concrete terms, that they invite the formulation of new hypotheses, that they not feel the need to destroy the constructions of others on events. All theories are only part of the world of make-believe, and all are destined to be modified and abandoned. It is a tribute to Kelly's sense of perspective, sense of humor, and lack of defensiveness concerning his own work that he could describe one of his own theoretical papers as involving "half-truths" only, and that he could view his theory as contributing to its own downfall. It is this theory—the theory of personal constructs—that we now discuss.

THE PERSONALITY THEORY OF GEORGE A. KELLY

Structure

The scientist develops concepts to describe and interpret the events that are of interest to him. Kelly's key structural concept for the person as a scientist is that of the **construct**. A construct is a way of **construing**, or interpreting, the world. It is a concept that the individual uses to categorize events and to chart a course of behavior. According to Kelly, a person anticipates events by observing which events tend to follow which other events, that is, by observing patterns and regularities. A person experiences events, interprets them, and places a structure and a meaning on them. In experiencing events, individuals notice that some events share characteristics that distinguish them from other events. Individuals distinguish similarities and contrasts among events. They observe that some people are tall and some short, that some are men and some are women, that some things are hard and some are soft. It is this construing of a similarity and a contrast that leads to the formation of a construct. Without constructs, life would be chaotic. Since no two events are exactly the same, we make certain abstractions by construing events as being similar to each other and different from other events, thereby developing a construct and imposing some order and regularity on the world.

It is important to note that Kelly viewed all constructs as composed of opposite pairs. At least three elements are necessary to form a construct: two of the elements of the construct must be perceived as similar to each other, and the third element must be perceived as different from these two. The way in which two elements are construed to be similar forms the **similarity pole** of the construct; the way in which they are contrasted with the third element forms the **contrast pole** of the construct. For example, observing two people helping someone and a third hurting someone could lead to the construct kind–cruel, with kind forming the similarity pole and cruel the contrast pole. Kelly stressed the importance of recognizing that a construct is composed of a similarity–contrast comparison. This suggests that we do not understand the nature of a construct when it uses only the similarity pole or the contrast pole. We do not know what the construct *respect* means to a person until we know what events the person includes under this construct and what events are viewed as being opposed to it. Interestingly, whatever constructs one applies to others are potentially applicable to the self. "One cannot call another person a bastard without making bastardy a dimension of his own life also" (Kelly, 1955, p. 133).

A construct is not dimensional in the sense of having many points between the similarity and contrast poles. Subtleties or refinements in construction of events are made through the use of other constructs, these being constructs of quantity and quality. For example, the construct *black–white* in combination with a quantity construct leads to the four-scale value of black, slightly black, slightly white, and white (Sechrest, 1963).

A construct is similar to a theory in that it has a range of convenience and a focus of convenience. A construct's range of convenience comprises all of those events for which the user would find application of the construct useful. A construct's focus of convenience comprises the particular events for which application of the construct would be maximally useful. Constructs can themselves be categorized in a variety of ways. For example, there are **core constructs** that are basic to a person's functioning, and there are **peripheral constructs** that can be altered without serious modification of the core structure.

It is fascinating as well as enlightening to think of the constructs people use. Often they are part of the person's everyday language, though the individual might be surprised to learn that these are only constructs and that alternative ways of viewing the world are possible. Think, for example, of the constructs that are part of your own construct system. What are the terms or characteristics you use to describe people? Does each term include an opposite one to form a similarity–contrast pair, or is one end of the construct missing in some cases? Can you think of constructs that people you know use to say something about themselves as individuals? What constructs are shared by members of one social class or culture and not shared by members of a different social class or culture? It is interesting to consider whether such differences in construct systems are often part of the problem in communications between groups. In fact, consider a specific application of this point: Can you think of constructs that people use and that often result in problems in interpersonal relationships? For example, a frequent problem in marital relationships is one in which both partners emphasize the core construct guilty–innocent. Typically, each then argues that he or she is the "innocent" party and their partner is "to blame" for the difficulties. Both may initially see the counselor as a judge who will render a verdict rather than as someone who may help them to view things in another light or revise their constructs. Another example would be of a friend who once said to me: "Isn't there a winner and a loser in every relationship?" That person was obviously unaware that "winner–loser" is a possible, but not a necessary, construct. Thus, while seemingly abstract, constructs can be seen as readily relating, in fact, to basic aspects of our daily lives.

Do not assume from this discussion that constructs are verbal or that they are always verbally available to a person. Although Kelly emphasized the cognitive aspects of human functioning—the ones that Freudians would call the conscious—he did take into consideration phenomena described by Freudians as being unconscious. The conscious–unconscious construct is not used by Kelly. However, Kelly did use the verbal–preverbal construct to deal with some of the elements that are otherwise interpreted as conscious or unconscious. A **verbal construct** can be expressed in words, whereas a **preverbal construct** is one that is used even though the person has no words to express it. A preverbal construct is learned before the person developed the use of language. Sometimes, one end of a construct is not available for verbalization—it is characterized as being **submerged**. If a person insists that people do only good things, one assumes that the other end of the construct has been submerged since the person must have been aware of contrasting behaviors to have formed the "good" end of the construct. Thus, constructs may not be available for verbalization, and the individual may not be able to report all of the elements that are in the construct; but this does not mean that the individual has "an unconscious." It has not been easy to develop ways of studying constructs that are not available for verbalization and generally this has been an area of empirical neglect. One recent effort involves sorting materials such as picture cards, textures, and patterns rather than people. However, the dearth of relevant studies in the area is all the more surprising given the acknowledged clinical significance of preverbal and submerged constructs (Neimeyer, 1981).

The constructs used by a person in interpreting and in anticipating events are organized as part of a system. The constructs within a system are organized into groups to minimize incompatabilities and inconsistencies. There is a hierarchical arrangement of constructs within a system. A **superordinate construct** includes

CURRENT APPLICATIONS AND IMPLICATIONS

Having Words for What You See, Taste, and Smell

"Why are we so inarticulate about these things?" said a student in referring to tastes, odors, and touch sensations. What would the implications be if we had a greater vocabulary for experience, that is, if we had more constructs for such phenomena? Can having more taste constructs develop one's sense of taste? More odor constructs one's sense of smell? Is the secret to becoming a wine connoisseur the development of one's construct system?

Utility of Constructs—Having a relevant construct may facilitate sensitivity to tastes and odors.

SOURCE: *Psychology Today*, July, 1981.

At one time it was thought that language determines how we perceive and organize the world. Such a view seems, in the light of today's evidence, too extreme. We are capable of sensing and recognizing many things for which we do not have a name or concept. However, having a concept or construct may facilitate experiencing and recalling some phenomena. For example, research on odor identification suggests that having the right words to describe an odor facilitates recognition of the odor: "People can improve their ability to identify odors through practice. More specifically, they can improve it through various cognitive interventions in which words are used to endow odors with perceptual or olfactory identity." A name for a smell helps to transform it from vague to clear. Not just any word will do, since some words seem to capture better the sensory experience than others do. The important fact, however, is that cognition does play an important role in virtually all aspects of sensory experience.

In sum, expanding one's sensory construct system alone may not provide for increased sensitivity to sensory experience but, together with practice, it can go a long way toward doing so. Want to become a wine connoisseur? Practice, but also expand your construct system.

other constructs within its context, and a **subordinate construct** is one that is included in the context of another (superordinate) construct. For example, the constructs bright–dumb and attractive–unattractive might both be subordinate to the superordinate construct good–bad. It is important to recognize that the constructs within the person's construct system are interrelated to at least some extent. A person's behavior generally expresses the construct system rather than a single construct, and a change in one aspect of the construct system generally leads to changes in other parts of the system. In addition, some constructs in the system can be in conflict with other constructs and thus produce strain and difficulties for a person in making choices (Landfield, 1982).

In terms of the above, people can be seen to differ both in the content of their constructs and in the organization of their construct systems. Individuals differ in the kinds of constructs they use, in the number of constructs available to them, in the complexity of organization of their construct systems, and in how open they are to changes in these construct systems.

To summarize, according to Kelly's theory of personal constructs, an individual's personality is his or her construct system. A person uses constructs to interpret the world and to anticipate events. The constructs used by a person define his or her world. Two people are similar to the extent that they have similar construct systems. Most important, if you want to understand a person you must know something about the constructs that person uses, the events subsumed under these constructs, the way in which these constructs tend to function, and the way in which they are organized in relation to one another to form a system.

The Role Construct Repertory Test (Rep Test)

Knowing other people, then, is knowing how they construe the world. How does one gain this knowledge of a person's constructs? Kelly's answer is direct—ask them to tell you what their constructs are. "If you don't know what is going on in a person's mind, ask him; he may tell you" (1958b, p. 330). Instead of using tests that had been developed by others in relation to different theoretical systems, Kelly developed his own assessment technique—the **Role Construct Repertory Test** (Rep test). As an assessment technique the Rep test is probably more closely related to a theory of personality than is any other comprehensive personality test. The Rep test was developed out of Kelly's construct theory and was designed to be used as a way of eliciting personal constructs.

Basically the Rep test consists of two procedures—the development of a list of persons based on a *Role Title List* and the development of constructs based on the comparison of triads of persons. In the first procedure, the subject is given a Role Title List or list of roles (figures) believed to be of importance to all people. Illustrative role titles would be: mother, father, a teacher you liked, a neighbor you find hard to understand. Generally, twenty to thirty roles are presented and subjects are asked to name a person they have known who fits each role. Following this the examiner picks three specific figures from the list and asks the subject to indicate the way in which two are alike and different from the third. The way in which two of the figures are seen as alike is called the *similarity pole* of the construct while the way in which the third is different is called the *contrast pole* of the construct. For example, a subject might be asked to consider the persons named for Mother, Father, and Liked Teacher. In considering the three, the subject might decide that the people associated with the titles Father and Liked Teacher are similar in being outgoing and different from Mother, who is shy. Thus, the construct outgoing–shy has been formed. The subject is asked to consider other groups of three persons (triads), usually twenty to thirty of them. With each presentation of a triad, the subject generates a construct. The construct given may be the same as a previous one or a new construct.

One can see how the Rep test follows from Kelly's theory since it elicits people's constructs, or ways of perceiving the world, based on their consideration of the way in which two things are similar and different from the third. It is particularly attractive since subjects are completely free to express how they construe the world. At the same time, however, it makes a number of important assumptions. First, it is assumed that the list of roles presented to the subjects is representative of the important figures in their lives. Second, it is assumed that the constructs that are verbalized by the subject are, indeed, the ones used to construe the world. In turn, this assumes that the subjects can verbalize their constructs and that they feel free to report them in the testing situation. Finally, it is assumed that the words the subjects use in naming their constructs are adequate to give the examiner an understanding of how they have organized their past events and how they anticipate the future.

In a clinical interpretation of the Rep test, the examiner considers the number of different constructs, the manner in which various figures are related to the constructs and to one another, and the relationships of the constructs to one another. An illustration of the type of record that is produced on a form of the test used in group testing is given in Figure 7.2. The subject, Mildred Beal, took the test as part of a classroom exercise. Since she had also applied for psychological counseling, there was an opportunity to check the interpretation of the test results against the information that was obtained independently during the course of therapy. The interpretation of the test results focused on the limited number of dimensions Mildred used to construe people and on her limited versatility in relating to people. Superficially, many constructs suggest some intellectual striving. However, on closer examination we find that there are really very few dimensions. One important dichotomy is between unhappy striving (hypersensitive, socially maladjusted, feelings of inferiority) and pleasant, comfortable quiescence (easygoing, relaxing, socially better than adequate). A second dominant dichotomy is in the construct friendly and understanding versus hypercritical.

The analysis of the constructs led the examiner to the following hypotheses: (1) the subject can be expected to show little versatility in handling the figures in her interpersonal world. (2) The subject can be expected to vacillate between unhappy agitation and easy self-indulgence. (3) She may be expected to intellectualize, to state insights glibly but not to retain them. (4) The therapist will initially be viewed as either friendly and understanding or hypercritical. These hypotheses tended to be confirmed by the therapist's reports. Mildred was viewed as being quite inflexible in dealing with people. The therapist observed that she perceived all social situations as forms of social pressure, in which she would win praise and social approval or be criticized and rejected. Although generally presenting herself as cheerful, she could at times become quite sad. She showed a need to be dependent on the therapist and to have him take the initiative in the interviews. On the other hand, she tended to resist all suggestions that he made. An important part of her interaction was an attempt to keep things on a superficially friendly, relaxed level, and to avoid criticism.

As has been indicated, one can describe people not only in terms of the content of their constructs but also in terms of the structure of the construct system. Both the Rep test and modifications of it have again proved to be useful in this regard. An early effort to look at structural aspects of the construct system was Bieri's (1955) study of cognitive complexity. Bieri designated the degree to which a construct system is broken down (levels in the hierarchy) or differentiated as reflecting the system's **cognitive complexity–simplicity**. A cognitively complex system contains many constructs and provides for considerable differentiation in perception of phenomena. A cognitively simple system contains few constructs and provides for poor differentiation in perception of phenomena. A cognitively complex person sees people in a differentiated way—as having a variety of qualities, whereas a cognitively simple person sees people in an undifferentiated way—even to the extent of using only one construct (for example, good–bad) in construing others. Using a modified Rep test, Bieri compared cognitively complex and cognitively simple subjects in relation to their accuracy in predicting the behavior of others and in relation to their ability to discriminate between themselves and others. As predicted, it was found that cognitively complex subjects were more accurate in predicting the behavior of others than were cognitively simple subjects. Furthermore, cognitively complex subjects were more able to recognize differences between themselves and others. Presumably the greater number of constructs available to complex subjects allows for both greater accuracy and greater potential for recognition of differences.

Bieri went on to construe cognitive complexity–simplicity as a dimension of personality, defining it as an information-processing variable: "Cognitive complexity may be defined as the capacity to construe social behavior in a multidimensional way" (Bieri, Atkins, Briar, Leaman, Miller, & Tripoldi, 1966). In one study of the way in which individuals process information, it was found that subjects high in complexity differed from subjects low in complexity in the way that they handled inconsistent information about a person. Subjects high in complexity tended to try to make use of the inconsistent information in forming an impression, whereas subjects low in complexity tended to form a consistent impression of the person and to reject all information inconsistent with that impression (Mayo & Crockett, 1964). Later research has also indicated that more complex individuals are more empathic, or better able to take the role of others, than are individuals who are cognitively simple (Adams-Webber, 1979, 1982; Crockett, 1982).

Thus, the Rep test can be used to determine the content and structure of an individual's construct system as well as to compare the effects of different construct system structures. The Rep test has the advantages of arising from a theory and

RAW PROTOCOL

Sort No.	Similar Figures	Similarity Construct	Dissimilar Figure	Contrasting Construct
1	Boss Successful person	Are related to me	Sought person	Unrelated
2	Rejecting person Pitied person	Very unhappy persons	Intelligent person	Contented
3	Father Liked teacher	Are very quiet and easygoing persons	Pitied person	Nervous hypertensive
4	Mother Sister	Look alike Are both hypercritical of people in general	Boyfriend	Friendliness
5	Ex-flame Pitied person	Feel inferior	Boyfriend	Self-confident
6	Brother Intelligent person	Socially better than adequate	Disliked teacher	Unpleasant
7	Mother Boss	Hypertensive	Father	Easygoing
8	Sister Rejecting person	Hypercritical	Brother	Understanding
9	Rejecting person Ex-flame	Feelings of inferiority	Disliked teacher	Assured of innate worth
10	Liked teacher Sought person	Pleasing personalities	Successful person	High-powered nervous
11	Mother Ex-flame	Socially maladjusted	Boyfriend	Easygoing self-confident
12	Father Boyfriend	Relaxing	Ex-flame	Uncomfortable to be with
13	Disliked teacher Boss	Emotionally unpredictable	Brother	Even temperament
14	Sister Rejecting person	Look somewhat alike	Liked teacher	Look unalike
15	Intelligent person Successful person	Dynamic personalities	Sought person	Weak personality

SOURCE: G. A. Kelly, The Psychology of Personal Constructs; New York; Norton, 1955, pp. 242–243.

FIGURE 7.2   Role Construct Repertory Test: Raw Protocol of Mildred Beal. (Kelly, 1955)

DESCRIPTIONS OF FIGURES
(Note: Constructs which were used as bases of similarity are italicized)

	Figure	Constructs Used to Describe Figure
1	Mother	*Looks like sister* *Hypercritical of people in general* *Hypertensive* *Socially maladjusted*
2	Father	*Quiet* Easygoing *Relaxing* Easygoing
3	Brother	*Socially better than adequate* Even temperament Understanding
4	Sister	*Looks like mother* *Hypercritical of people in general* *Hypercritical* *Looks like rejecting person*
5	Boyfriend	*Relaxing* Easygoing Self-confident Self-confident Friendliness
6	Liked teacher	*Quiet* *Easygoing* *Pleasing personality* Looks unlike sister and rejecting person
7	Disliked teacher	*Emotionally unpredictable* Assured of innate worth Unpleasant
8	Boss	*Related to me* *Hypertensive* *Emotionally unpredictable*
9	Rejecting person	*Very unhappy* *Hypercritical* *Looks like sister* *Feelings of inferiority*
10	Ex-flame	*Feels very inferior* *Feelings of inferiority* *Socially maladjusted* Uncomfortable to be with
11	Sought person	*Pleasing personality* Weak personality Not related to me
12	Pitied person	*Very unhappy* *Feels very inferior* Nervous Hypertensive
13	Intelligent person	*Socially better than adequate* *Dynamic personality* Contented
14	Successful person	*Related to me* *Dynamic personality* High-powered Nervous

of allowing subjects to generate their own constructs, instead of forcing subjects to use dimensions provided by the tester. In his review of the relevant literature, Bonarius (1965) gives a generally positive appraisal of this assessment technique. Two summary statements are worthy of attention.

> *The research over the past decade shows that the Rep Test, if used in a standard manner, is a safe instrument providing consistent information. That is to say, the figures and constructs elicited are indeed representative of the persons who make up an individual's social world, and of the constructs he applies to them.*

Bonarius, 1965, p. 17

> *The constructs an individual employs in social interaction are quite stable and relatively independent of the particular persons who make up his social environment. Further, not only can an individual be identified by his personal constructs, but a knowledge of his personal constructs may lead to a different, if not a better, understanding of this individual than descriptions of him by others. Finally, the research has shown convincingly that the individual prefers to express himself and to describe others by using his own personal constructs rather than provided dimensions, such as the usual Q-sort statements . . .*

Bonarius, 1965, p. 26

In sum, Kelly posits that the structure of personality consists of the construct system of the individual. An individual is what he construes himself and others to be, and the Rep Test is a device to ascertain the nature of these constructions.

Process

In his process view of human behavior, Kelly took a radical departure from traditional theories of motivation. As we have mentioned already, the psychology of personal constructs does not interpret behavior in terms of motivation, drives, and needs. For personal construct theory, the term "motivation" is redundant. The term motivation assumes that the person is inert and needs something to get started. But, if we assume that the person is basically active, the controversy as to what prods an inert organism into action becomes a dead issue. "Instead, the organism is delivered fresh into the psychological world alive and struggling" (Kelly, 1955, p. 37). Kelly contrasted other theories of motivation with his own position in the following way:

> *Motivational theories can be divided into two types, push theories and pull theories. Under push theories we find such terms as drive, motive, or even stimulus. Pull theories use such constructs as purpose, value, or need. In terms of a well-known metaphor, these are the pitchfork theories on the one*

hand and the carrot theories on the other. But our theory is neither of these. Since we prefer to look to the nature of the animal himself, ours is probably best called a jackass theory.

Kelly, 1958(a), p. 50

The concept of motive traditionally has been used to explain why humans are active and why their activity takes a specific direction. Since Kelly did not feel the need for the concept of motive to account for a person's activity, how did he account for the direction of activity of this very much alive and struggling organism? Kelly's position is simply stated in his fundamental postulate: A person's processes are psychologically channelized by the ways in which he anticipates events. Kelly offers this postulate as a given and does not question its truth. The postulate implies that we seek prediction, that we anticipate events, that we reach out to the future through the window of the present. In experiencing events, the individual observes similarities and contrasts, thereby developing constructs. On the basis of these constructs, the individual, like a true scientist, anticipates the future. As we see the same events repeated over and over, we modify our constructs so that they will lead to more accurate predictions. Constructs are tested in terms of their predictive efficiency. But what accounts for the direction of behavior? Again, like the scientist, people choose that course of behavior which they believe offers the greatest opportunity for anticipating future events. Scientists try to develop better theories, theories that lead to the efficient prediction of events, and individuals try to develop better construct systems. Thus, according to Kelly, a person chooses that alternative which promises the greatest further development of the construct system.

In making a choice of a particular construct, the individual, in a sense, makes a "bet" by anticipating a particular event or set of events. If there are inconsistencies in the construct system, the bets will not add up—they will cancel each other out. If the system is consistent, a prediction is made that can be tested. If the anticipated event does occur, the prediction has been upheld and the construct validated, at least, for the time being. If the anticipated event does not occur, the construct has been invalidated. In the latter case, the individual must develop a new construct or must loosen or expand the old construct to include the prediction of the event that took place. Maher (1966) gives the example of the child who uses the construct of reassuring–punitive in relation to his mother. The child may find that his mother is at times punitive when he had expected her to be reassuring. The child may abandon the reassuring–punitive construct for a just–unjust construct and may interpret his mother's punishment as just.

In essence, then, individuals make a prediction and consider further change in their construct systems on the basis of whether they have led to accurate prediction. Notice that individuals do not seek reinforcement or the avoidance of pain; instead, they seek validation and expansion of their construct system. If a person expects something unpleasant and that event occurs, he experiences validation regardless of the fact that it was a negative, unpleasant event that occurred. In observing individuals in a shock experiment, Pervin (1964) concluded that individuals seek to confirm their predictive strategies and will prefer the pain of an electric shock to no shock if the absence of shock would disconfirm their predictive system. One should understand that Kelly is not suggesting that the individual seeks certainty, such as would be found in the repetitive ticking of a clock. The boredom people feel with repeated events and the fatalism that comes as a result of the inevitable are usually avoided wherever possible. Rather, the individual seeks to anticipate events and to increase the range of convenience or boundaries of his construct system. Finally, this point leads to a distinction between the views of Kelly and the views of Rogers. According to Kelly, individuals do not seek consistency for consistency's sake or even self-consistency. Instead, individuals seek to anticipate events, and it is a consistent system that allows them to do this.

Thus far, Kelly's system appears to be reasonably simple and straightforward. The process view becomes more complicated with the introduction of the concepts of anxiety, fear, and threat. Kelly defined **anxiety** in the following way: Anxiety is the recognition that the events with which one is confronted lie outside the range of convenience of one's construct system. One is anxious when one is without constructs, when one has "lost his structural grip on events," when one is "caught with his constructs down." In contrast to anxiety, one experiences **fear** when a new construct appears to be about to enter the construct system. Of even greater significance is the experience of **threat**. Threat is defined as the awareness of imminent comprehensive change in one's core structure. A person feels threatened when a major shake-up in the construct system is about to occur. One feels threatened by death if it is perceived as imminent and if it involves a drastic change in one's core constructs. Death is not threatening when it does not seem imminent or when it is not construed as being fundamental to the meaning of one's life.

The experiences of anxiety and threat are critical for the functioning of the organism. People protect themselves from anxiety in various ways. Confronted by events that they cannot construe, that is, that lie outside the range of convenience, individuals may broaden a construct and permit it to apply to a greater variety of events, or they may narrow their constructs and focus on minute details. Anxiety is not the result of invalidated constructs but, rather, is the result of not having constructs to deal with a situation. On the other hand, threat is the result of a number of invalidated constructs and the resultant questioning that occurs about whether one has any constructs at all. Threat, in particular, has a wide range of ramifications. Whenever people undertake some new activity, they expose themselves to confusion and threat. Confusion may lead to something new, but it may also eventuate in a threat to the individual. Individuals experience threat when they realize that their construct system is about to be drastically affected by what has been discovered. "This is the moment of threat. It is the threshold between confusion and certainty, between anxiety and boredom. It is precisely at this moment when we are most tempted to turn back" (Kelly, 1964, p. 141). The response to threat may be to give up the adventure—to regress to old constructs in order to avoid panic. Threat occurs as we venture into human understanding and when we stand on the brink of a profound change in ourselves.

What makes the concepts of anxiety, fear, and threat so significant is that they suggest a new dimension to Kelly's view of human functioning. The dynamics of functioning can now be seen to involve the interplay between the individual's wish to expand the construct system and the desire to avoid the threat of disruption of that system: "If one wished to state negatively Kelly's position on the psychology of personal constructs, as they relate to motivation, one might say that human behavior is directed away from ultimate anxiety" (Kelly, 1955, p. 894). Thus, we have here a model of anxiety and defense. In response to anxiety, individuals may *submerge* one end of a construct in order to keep perceiving events in a familiar, comfortable way, or they may *suspend* elements that do not fit so well into a construct. Submergence and suspension are responses to anxiety. They are viewed as being similar to the psychoanalytic concept of repression. Thus, in the face of anxiety, individuals may act in ways that will make their constructs or parts of their constructs unavailable for verbalization. In the face of threat, individuals have a choice between constricted certainty and broadened understanding. Individuals always seek to maintain and to enhance their predictive systems. However, in the face of anxiety and threat, individuals may rigidly adhere to a constricted system, instead of venturing out into the risky realm of expansion of their construct systems.

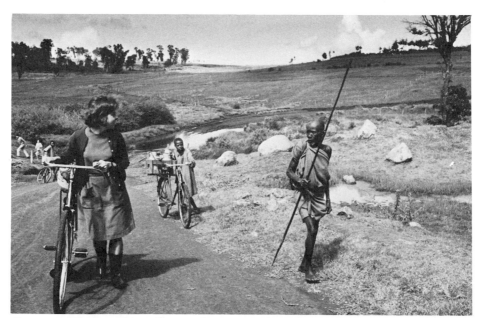

Construct Change—Peace Corps volunteers, such as the one illustrated here, had to be prepared to develop new constructs as they were exposed to new values, attitudes, and behaviors in different cultures.

To summarize, Kelly assumes an active organism, and he does not posit any motivational forces. For Kelly, the person behaves as a scientist in construing events, in making predictions, and in seeking expansion of the construct system. Sometimes, not unlike the scientist, we are made so anxious by the unknowns and so threatened by the unfamiliar that we seek to hold on to absolute truths and become dogmatic. On the other hand, when we are behaving as good scientists, we are able to adopt the invitational mood and to expose our construct systems to the diversity of events that make up life.

Growth and Development

Kelly was never very explicit about the origins of construct systems. He stated that constructs are derived from observing repeated patterns of events. But he did little to elaborate on the kinds of events that lead to differences like the ones between simple and complex construct systems. Kelly's comments relating to growth and development are limited to an emphasis on the development of preverbal constructs in infancy and the interpretation of culture as involving a process of learned expectations. People belong to the same cultural group in that they share certain ways of construing events and have the same kinds of expectations regarding certain kinds of behavior.

Developmental research associated with personal construct theory generally has emphasized two kinds of change. First, there has been exploration of increases in complexity of the construct system associated with age (Crockett, 1982; Hayden, 1982). Second, there has been exploration of qualitative changes in the nature of the constructs formed and in the ability of children to be more empathic or aware of the construct systems of others (Adams-Webber, 1982; Morrison & Cometa, 1982; Sigel, 1981). In terms of construct system complexity, there is evidence that as children develop they increase the number of constructs available to them, make finer differentiations, and also show more hierarchical organization or integration. For example, Signell (1966) found that between the ages of nine and sixteen children tend to become more abstract in their thinking, tend to have a greater number of ways of interpreting the environment available to them, and tend to be more flexible in their interpretations of events. Honess (1979) had children ages eight through thirteen describe a peer they liked and a peer they disliked. He then took the constructs generated and asked each child to indicate whether a new child they met who had one characteristic would be expected to have each of the other characteristics. In other words, each characteristic was paired with other characteristics to see the kinds of linages that would be drawn by the child. In addition, the characteristics were categorized in terms of appearance (e.g., pretty), ability (e.g., good at chess), and personality trait (e.g., happy) to see whether the constructs were organized in a hierarchy and whether connections were made across categories. Honess found that as children grow older they show an increase in construct system differentiation as well as in system organization and integration.

Development of the Construct System—The opportunity to be exposed to many stimuli facilitates development of the construct system. Aware of this, some parents try to develop what *Newsweek* magazine called "superbabies."

Two studies have been reported that are relevant to the question of the determinants of complex cognitive structures. In one study, the subjects' level of cognitive complexity was found to be related to the variety of cultural backgrounds to which they had been exposed in childhood (Sechrest & Jackson, 1961). In another study, parents of cognitively complex children were found to be more likely to grant autonomy and less likely to be authoritarian than were parents of children low in cognitive complexity (Cross, 1966). Presumably, the opportunity to examine many different events and to have many different experiences is conducive to the development of a complex structure. One would also expect to find that children who experience longstanding and severe threat from authoritarian parents would develop constricted and inflexible construct systems.

Returning to the question of qualitative change, research indicates that as children develop they become less egocentric; that is, as children develop they become less prone to view everything in terms of themselves and are more able to take the perspective of the other. Younger children (age eight) tend to describe others in the same way that they describe themselves and in terms of concrete, self-relevant activities relative to older children (age thirteen) (Honess, 1979, 1980). For example, younger children frequently describe someone in terms dependent on themselves ("We play together." "We go to the park together."), whereas older children either use descriptions independent of themselves ("He is kind.") or use self-relevant constructs that suggest more of an exchange relationship ("She is nice to me." "We like one another."). Development involves an increase in the ability to take distance on people and events, to see things as not necessarily being related to the self, and to appreciate the construct systems of others as well as one's own (Sigel, 1981).

The question of factors determining the content of constructs and the complexity of construct systems is of critical importance. In particular, it is relevant to the field of education, since a part of education appears to be the development of complex, flexible, and adaptive construct systems. Unfortunately, Kelly himself made few statements in this area, and research is only now beginning to elaborate on this part of the theory.

MAJOR CONCEPTS AND SUMMARY

construct

construct system

range of convenience

focus of convenience

similarity and contrast poles

core and peripheral constructs

verbal and preverbal constructs

submerged part of a construct

superordinate and subordinate constructs

Role Construct Repertory Test (Rep test)

cognitive complexity–simplicity

anxiety, fear, and threat

In this chapter we have reviewed parts of the life of an unusual theorist and the basic essentials of his theory of personality. George A. Kelly developed a theory out of a diversity of clinical experiences. His theory of personality avoids many of the standard terms found in the field of psychology and invites the reader to dare to interpret the human organism in a new light—as a scientist who seeks to construe the world in a way that will permit increasingly better prediction of events. The emphasis on the invitational mood is an important part of setting the stage for perceiving phenomena in a different way. The emphasis on the person as a scientist is an important part of his approach—our personality is our theory or construct system as well as the ways in which we act and feel in accordance with our construct system.

For Kelly the essential aspect of personality is the construct—the person's way of looking at, interpreting, or construing events. Constructs are developed as a result of noticing similarities and differences in events as we live our daily lives. The Rep test was developed by Kelly to assess the construct system of a person. Following the logic of personal construct theory, in the Rep test the person is asked to consider triads of persons and to indicate how two are alike and different from the third. This leads to the definition of a similarity pole and a contrast pole. Through the use of the Rep test the psychologist can attempt an analysis of the structure of the person's construct system in terms of core and peripheral constructs, superordinate and subordinate constructs, and the overall level of complexity or simplicity.

Just as the scientist seeks to predict events, so the human organism seeks to anticipate events. The function of the construct system is the anticipation of events—a task that is always before us and that we are always seeking to master. So critical is this to our functioning that we experience anxiety when our constructs do not appear to fit the events we are observing, and experience threat when our construct system itself seems endangered. Under such circumstances one or more parts of the construct system may become submerged, new experiences may be rejected, and the individual may defensively adhere to viewing events in preconceived ways.

As a result of experience we develop a construct system with a variety of kinds of constructs, involving distinct content for each individual, and an organization that reaches varying degrees of complexity or simplicity. Some constructs are learned prior to the development of language (preverbal constructs), but for most people the vast majority of the constructs in their construct system can be expressed in words. Under supportive circumstances the child and the adult feel free to expand their construct systems to include new phenomena and to organize what has been learned in new ways. In other words, increased complexity and integration are aspects of a healthy, developing construct system. Just as scientists attempt to develop theories that will include more phenomena and predict more events, so healthy development involves increasing the range of convenience and focus of convenience of the construct system. On the other hand, if new experiences are not provided or if the person feels too threatened to construe life in a different way, then the construct system may remain fixed, rigid, and unchanged.

In sum, in Kelly's theory we act and move because we are alive, not because of urges from within or pushes from without. As the scientists we are, we seek to expand our construct systems so as to better anticipate events. The only exceptions are when we are feeling so anxious or threatened that exploration and the invitational mood are impossible. A major part of Kelly's efforts were directed toward understanding people in terms of their own construct systems and toward facilitating their developing more useful ways of construing events. In the next chapter we shall learn about his efforts to develop methods to help people to change their constructions of themselves and events around them.

Picasso, Pablo. *The Actor*. The Metropolitan Museum of Art. Gift of Thelma Chrysler
Fox. 1952.

A COGNITIVE THEORY OF PERSONALITY: APPLICATIONS AND EVALUATION OF KELLY'S THEORY

CHAPTER FOCUS: In this chapter we consider the clinical applications of Kelly's personal construct theory. Kelly felt that any significant theory of personality has to suggest ways to help people. He saw the area of psychotherapy not only as a major source of interest and concern but also as a major aspect or "focus of convenience" of personal construct theory.

From the standpoint of the psychology of personal constructs, we may define a disorder as any personal construction which is used repeatedly in spite of consistent invalidation.

Kelly, 1955, p. 831

Yet we see it as the ultimate objective of the clinical psychology enterprise . . . the psychological reconstruction of life. We even considered using the term reconstruction instead of therapy. If it had not been such a mouth-filling word we might have gone ahead with the idea. Perhaps later we may.

Kelly, 1955, p. 187

CLINICAL APPLICATIONS

Psychopathology

According to Kelly, psychopathology is a disordered response to anxiety. As in the theories discussed previously, the concepts of anxiety, fear, and threat play a major role in Kelly's theory of psychopathology. However, it must be kept in mind that these concepts, although retained, have been redefined in terms relevant to personal construct theory.

For Kelly, psychopathology is defined in terms of disordered functioning of a construct system. A poor scientist is one who retains a theory and makes the same predictions despite repeated research failures. Similarly, abnormal behavior involves efforts to retain the content and structure of the construct system despite repeated incorrect predictions or invalidations. "From the standpoint of the psychology of personal constructs we may define a disorder as any personal construction which is used repeatedly in spite of consistent invalidation" (Kelly, 1955, p. 831). At the root of this rigid adherence to a construct system are anxiety, fear, and threat. Kelly stated that one could construe human behavior as being directed away from ultimate anxiety. Psychological disorders are disorders involving anxiety and faulty efforts to reestablish the sense of being able to anticipate events:

There is a sense in which all disorders of communication are disorders involving anxiety. A "neurotic" person casts about frantically for new ways of construing the events of his world. Sometimes he works on "little" events, sometimes on "big" events, but he is always fighting off anxiety. A "psychotic" person appears to have found some temporary solution for his anxiety. But it is a precarious solution, at best, and must be sustained in the face of evidence which, for most of us, would be invalidating.

Kelly, 1955, pp. 895–896

What are some of the faulty ways in which people try to hold on to their construct systems? These efforts involve problems in the ways in which constructs are applied to new events, problems in the ways in which constructs are used to make predictions, and problems in the ways in which the overall system is organized. Let us consider an illustration of each. An example of the pathological application of constructs is that of making constructs excessively **permeable** or excessively **impermeable**. An excessively permeable construct allows almost any new content into it whereas an excessively impermeable construct admits no new elements into its context. Excessive permeability can lead to the use of just a few constructs that are very broad and the lack of recognition of important differences among people and events. Too much becomes lumped together, as in stereotypes. Excessive impermeability can lead to pigeonholing each new experience, as if everything is distinctive, and to rejecting events that cannot be pigeonholed. This pattern of response is found in people who are described as being very compulsive.

An illustration of the pathological use of constructs to make predictions is excessive **tightening** and excessive **loosening**. In excessive tightening the person makes the same kinds of predictions regardless of the circumstances. In excessive loosening, the person makes excessively varied predictions with the same construct. In neither case can prediction be very accurate since both involve ignoring circumstances that might call for shifts in the construct system—in the first case through always predicting the same and in the second case through random, chaotic predictions. Tightening may be seen in the compulsive person who rigidly expects life to be the same regardless of changes in circumstances, while loosening can be seen in the psychotic person whose construct system is so chaotic that it cannot be used to communicate with others: "They [schizophrenic clients] are not caught short of constructs. But what constructs!" (Kelly, 1955, p. 497).

Personal construct researchers have investigated the extent to which schizophrenics do indeed construe people in unstable and loose ways. For example, in one study subjects were asked to rank eight photographs on six characteristics: kind, stupid, selfish, sincere, mean, and honest. They were then asked to make the ratings a second time without relying on their memory for the previous ratings. Two questions were of particular interest. First, to what extent would people see the concepts as being related? An intensity score was derived as a measure of the extent to which the subject's eight rank orderings were related to one another. A low intensity score suggested that the subject was treating these six characteristics as if they had no relation to one another. Second, to what extent would people maintain their rankings from the first series to the second series? Because the photographs remained the same and there had been no intervening experience, this correlation essentially constituted a measure of the test–retest reliability or consistency of the person's ratings. Here a consistency score was used; a low consistency score indicated that the person applied the concepts in very different ways on the two trials.

A number of patient groups and a normal group of subjects were tested in the above ways; and the average intensity scores and consistency scores were then calculated for the members of each group. The hypothesis being tested was that thought-disordered schizophrenics would have particularly low intensity and consistency scores, indicative of loose and unstable construing. Indeed, this was found to be the case (Figure 8.1). Relative both to other patient groups as well as to the normal group, the thought-disordered schizophrenic group showed significantly lower intensity and consistency scores (Bannister & Fransella, 1966). In sum, such patients can be characterized both in terms of the types of constructs formed as well as in terms of how these constructs are employed.

Finally, we come to disordered efforts to maintain the overall organization of the construct system, as illustrated in **constriction** and **dilation**. Constriction involves a narrowing of the construct system to minimize incompatibilities. The range and focus of convenience of the construct system becomes quite small. Constriction tends to be found in people who are depressed and who limit their interests, narrowing their attention to a smaller and smaller area. In contrast to this, in dilation the person attempts to broaden the construct system and to reorganize it at a more comprehensive level. Extreme dilation is observed in the behavior of the manic person who jumps from topic to topic and who makes sweeping generalizations with few ideas. It is as if everything can now be included in the construct system of this person.

These faulty devices to prevent anxiety and avoid the threat of change in the construct system illustrate Kelly's efforts to interpret pathological behavior within the framework of person construct theory. Another illustration of his interpretation of psychopathology is the case of suicide. According to the psychoanalytic view, every suicide is a potential homicide. Because of anxiety or guilt, the hostility that would otherwise be directed toward some other person be-

Group Means (Averages) of Intensity and Consistency Test Scores
for Six Groups of Subjects

	Mean Intensity	Mean Consistency
Thought-Disordered Schizophrenics	728	.18
Normals	1253	.80
Nonthought-Disordered Schizophrenics	1183	.73
Depressives	1115	.75
Neurotics	1383	.74
Organics	933	.73

FIGURE 8.1   Personal Construct Theory and Psychopathology. (Bannister & Fransella, 1966)

comes directed instead toward the self. Not so, according to the psychology of personal constructs. Kelly (1961) interpreted suicide as an act to validate one's life or as an act of abandonment. In the latter case, suicide occurs because of fatalism or because of total anxiety—because the course of events is so obvious that there is no point in waiting around for the outcome (fatalism), or because everything is so unpredictable that the only definite thing to do is to abandon the scene altogether. As noted, we often must choose between immediate certainty and wider understanding. In suicide, the choice is for the former and represents ultimate constriction. ''For the man of constricted outlook whose world begins to crumble, death may appear to provide the only immediate certainty which he can lay his hands on'' (Kelly, 1955, p. 64).

While Kelly did not emphasize the concept of hostility in relation to suicide, he did recognize its importance in human functioning. Again, however, the concept is redefined in terms relevant to personal construct theory. Kelly made an important distinction between aggression and hostility, one that often is absent in other theories. According to Kelly, **aggression** involves the active expansion of the person's construct system. This active expansion of the construct system does not interfere with the functioning of other people. In contrast to this, **hostility** occurs when one tries to make others behave in an expected way. For example, it would be hostile for a person to intimidate someone because they expected them to behave in a submissive way. According to this view, the hostile person does not intend to do harm. Rather, injury is an accidental outcome of the effort to protect one's construct system by attempting to make people behave in expected ways. Here, too, the emphasis is on protection of the construct system. The opposite of hostility is curiosity and respect for the freedom of movement of others.

To summarize Kelly's view of psychophathology, we return to the analogy of the scientist. Scientists attempt to predict events through the use of theories. Scientists develop poor theories when they fear venturing out into the unknown, when they fear testing out hypotheses and making bets, when they rigidly adhere to their theory in the face of contradictory evidence, when they can account only for trivia, and when they try to say that they are accounting for things that, in fact, are outside the range of convenience of their theories. When scientists construe in these ways, we say they are bad scientists. When people construe in these ways, we refer to them as sick people. When people know how to stay loose and also tighten up, we call them creative and reward them for their efforts. When people stay too loose or too ''up tight,'' we say they are ill and consider hospitalization. It all depends on their constructs—and on how others construe the constructs.

Change

The process of positive change is discussed by Kelly in terms of the development of better construct systems. If sickness represents the continued use of constructs in the face of consistent invalidation, psychotherapy is the process whereby clients are assisted in improving their predictions. In psychotherapy, clients are trained to be better scientists. Psychotherapy is a process of reconstruing—a process of reconstruction of the construct system. This means that some constructs need to be replaced, some new ones need to be added; some need to be tightened while others are loosened; and some need to be made more permeable while others are made less permeable. Whatever the details of the process, *psychotherapy is the psychological reconstruction of life.*

According to Kelly's theory, three conditions exist that are favorable to the formation of new constructs. First, and perhaps most important, there must be an *atmosphere of experimentation.* This means that, for example, in therapy "one does not 'play for keeps.' Constructs, in the true scientific tradition, are seen as 'being tried on for size' " (Kelly, 1955, p. 163). In psychotherapy, one creates the invitational mood and accepts the language of hypothesis. Psychotherapy is a form of experimentation. In therapy, constructs (hypotheses) are developed, experiments are performed, and hypotheses are revised on the basis of empirical evidence. By being permissive and responsive, by providing the client with the tools of experimentation, and by encouraging the client to make hypotheses, the therapist assists in the development of the client as a scientist.

The second key condition for change is the *provision of new elements.* Conditions favorable to change include new elements that are relatively unbound by old constructs. The therapy room is a "protected environment" in which new elements can be recognized and confronted. Therapists themselves represent a new element in relation to which their clients can start to develop new constructs. It is here that the question of *transference* emerges, and the therapist must ask: "In what role is the client now casting me?" Clients may attempt to transfer a construct from their repertory that was applicable in the past and to use it in relation to their therapists. They may construe the therapist as a parent, as an absolver of guilt, as an authority figure, as a prestige figure, or as a stooge. Whatever the content of the transference, the therapist tries to provide fresh, new elements in an atmosphere of make-believe and experimentation.

Along with this, therapists provide the third condition for change—they make *validating data available.* We are told that knowledge of results facilitates learning. We know that, given a supportive atmosphere and the permeable aspects of the construct system, invalidation does lead to change (Bieri, 1953; Poch, 1952). The therapist provides new elements in a situation in which the client will at first attempt to use old constructs. It is the therapist's task to share his own perceptions of and reactions to the client, against which the client can check his own hypotheses: "By providing validating data in the form of responses to a wide variety of constructions on the part of the client, some of them quite loose, fanciful, or naughty, the clinician gives the client an opportunity to validate constructs, an opportunity which is not normally available to him" (Kelly, 1955, p. 165).

We know that there are individual differences in resistance to change (Bonarius, 1965; Diggory, 1966), and that rigidity is related to psychopathology (Pervin, 1960). However, given an atmosphere of experimentation, given new elements, and given validating data, people do change. Conversely, the conditions unfavorable for change include threat, preoccupation with old material, and the lack of a "laboratory" in which to experiment. It is within the context of the former conditions of change that Kelly developed a specific therapeutic technique—**fixed-role therapy**. Fixed-role therapy assumes that, psychologically, people are what they represent themselves to be and that people are what they do. Fixed-role therapy encourages clients to *represent themselves in new ways*, to *behave in new ways*, to construe themselves in new ways and thereby, to *become new people.*

In fixed-role therapy, the clients are presented with a new personality sketch that they are asked to act out. On the basis of some understanding of the client, a group of psychologists get together to write a description of a new person. The task for the clients is to behave "as-if" they were that person. The personality sketch written for each client involves the development of a new personality. Many characteristics are presented in the sketch that are in sharp contrast with the person's actual functioning. In the light of construct theory, Kelly suggested that it might be easier for people to play up what they believe to be the opposite of the way they generally behave than to behave just a little bit differently. Design of the sketch involves setting in motion processes that will have effects throughout the construct system. Fixed-role therapy does not aim at the readjustment of minor parts. Instead, it aims at the reconstruction of a personality. If offers a new role, a new personality for the client in which new hypotheses can be tested out; it offers the client the opportunity to test out new ways of construing events under the full protection of "make-believe."

Just how does the process of fixed-role therapy work? After a personality sketch is drawn up, it is presented to the client. The client decides whether the sketch sounds like someone he would like to know and whether he would feel comfortable with such a person. This is done to make sure that the new personality will not be excessively threatening to the client. In the next phase of fixed-role therapy, the therapist invites the client to act as if he were that person. For a period of about two weeks, the client is asked to forget who he is and to be this other person. If the new person is called Tom Jones, then the client is told the following: "For two weeks, try to forget who you are or that you ever were. You are Tom Jones! You act like him! You think like him. You talk to your friends the way you think he would talk. You do the things you think he would do! You even have his interests and you enjoy the things he would enjoy!" The client may resist, he may feel that this is play-acting and that it is hypocritical, but he is encouraged, in an accepting manner, to try out and see how it goes. The client is not told that this is what he should eventually be, but he is asked to try it out. He is asked to temporarily give up being himself so that he can discover himself.

During the following weeks, the client eats, sleeps, and feels the role. Periodically, he meets with the therapist to discuss problems in acting the role. There may be some rehearsing of the personality sketch in the therapy session so that the therapist and client will have a chance to examine the functioning of the new construct system when it is actually in use. The therapist must himself be prepared to act as if he were various persons and to accept the invitational mood. He must at every moment "play in strong support of an actor—the client—who is continually fumbling his lines and contaminating his role" (Kelly, 1955, p. 399).

Fixed-Role Therapy—In Kelly's fixed-role therapy clients are encouraged to behave and represent themselves in new ways. Drawing by Lippman; © 1972 The New Yorker Magazine, Inc.

The purpose of this entire procedure is to reestablish the spirit of exploration, to establish the construction of life as a creative process. Kelly was wary of the emphasis on being oneself—how could one be anything else? He viewed remaining what one is as dull, uninteresting, and unadventuresome. Instead he suggested that people should feel free to make-believe, to play and, thereby, to become:

> *What I am saying is that it is not so much what man is that counts as it is what he ventures to make of himself. To make the leap he must do more than disclose himself; he must risk a certain amount of confusion. Then, as soon as he does catch a glimpse of a different kind of life, he needs to find some way of overcoming the paralyzing moment of threat, for this is the instant when he wonders what he really is—whether he is what he just was or is what he is about to be.*

Kelly, 1964, p. 147

Fixed-role therapy was not the only therapeutic technique discussed by Kelly. However, it is one that is particularly associated with personal construct theory, and it does exemplify some of the principles of the personal construct theory of change. The goal of therapeutic change is the individual's reconstruction of himself and others. The individual drops some constructs, creates new ones, does some tightening and loosening, and develops a construct system that leads to more accurate predictions. The therapist encourages the client to make believe, to experiment, to spell out alternatives, and to reconstrue the past in the light of new constructs. The process of therapy is very complex. Different clients must be treated differently, and the resistance to change must be overcome. However, positive change is possible in a situation where a good director assists in the playing of the human drama or a good teacher assists in the development of a creative scientist.

Research in the area of psychotherapy has focused on factors in the construct system and factors in the therapeutic relationship that affect change. As one might expect, there is evidence that superordinate constructs are harder to change than subordinate constructs, presumably because they involve more threat of potential disruption of the construct system. It also appears that constructs must undergo some loosening before change can occur. A critical factor in the loosening process is the recognition of new elements. In this regard it is interesting to note that Landfield (1971) has found that a certain amount of similarity in therapist-client construct systems is necessary to facilitate communication but, at the same time, a certain amount of structural difference appears to facilitate the change process. The psychotherapeutic process, then, can be understood as the therapist–client relationship in which there occur experiences that facilitate the reconstruction of the client's construct system.

Personal construct therapists have attempted to explore the potential utility of Kelly's theory in varied ways and in different settings (Landfield & Leitner, 1980). In some cases, this has involved substantial changes in procedure. In one approach, imagery is used to recall past events, leading to a reconstruction of these events (Morrison & Cometa, 1982). For example, a patient construed her father only in negative terms. However, with the use of imagery techniques, the patient was able to recall and imagine scenes in which the father had acted in positive ways, leading to the addition of new constructs or the increased permeability of some constructs. Despite these and related efforts, however, much of Kelly's theory of therapy, what changes and how change occurs, remains unexplored (Epting, 1981).

A CASE EXAMPLE—RONALD BARRETT

From the phenomenological point of view, and from that of personal construct theory, the client is always right. Although clinicians may choose to construe events differently, they should never ignore the constructions of their clients. Hence, Kelly was led to say: "If you do not know what is wrong with a person, ask him: he may tell you." An approach that is construed as useful in understanding the clients is to have them write a character sketch of themselves. One client who did this was Ronald Barrett, a university student who came to a counseling service with generalized complaints regarding academic, vocational, and social adjustments.

In his self-descriptive character sketch, Ronald Barrett began by indicating that he gives others the impression that he is quiet and calm, and that he dislikes drawing unfavorable attention to himself. Aside from this quiet behavior in public, however, he reported that he was likely to flare up easily. Little anger was shown to others, but he readily became frustrated and worked up about his own errors or those of others. He thought much of his behavior was an effort to impress others and to show that he was considerate and sincere. He considered morals and ethics as guides to behavior, and guilt the result of not being sufficiently kind. Ronald described himself as striving toward being logical, accurate, and aware of minor technicalities. Finally, he described himself as relatively inflexible and as attaching too much importance to kissing a girl.

In his discussion of the sketch, Kelly observed that a conventional approach to it would emphasize its compulsive aspects. However, beyond this view, Kelly suggested an approach in which the effort is made to see the world through the client's own eyes. In his analysis of Ronald's account, Kelly emphasized the need to look at the order in which the material is presented, the way in which it is organized, the terms (inconsiderate, sincerity, conscientiousness, morals, ethics, guilt, kindhearted) that are used, the themes that are repeated, and the similarities and contrasts that are made. In approaching the material in these ways, Kelly made reference to the following:

1. Ronald's vehement assertion that he ought to have the appearance of a quiet and calm personality suggests that he is sensitive to the public. The effort to retain a public mask seems critical.

2. The contrast between external calm and the feeling of sitting on a lid of explosive behavior seems significant. He appears to get upset by behaviors in others which he sees in himself and rejects—the loss of intellectual controls.

3. He reports inconsistencies in his behavior and appears to be aware of breakdowns in his construct system.

4. Sincerity is a key construct and is linked with consideration and kindheartedness. By implication, the characteristics of insincerity, inconsideration, and unkindheartedness are also critical in his construing of events. He appears to vacillate between these poles and to find neither totally satisfactory.

5. He appears to use criticism and correction as an intellectual process through which he can avoid flare-ups. His stress on technicalities is a way of leading a righteous life.

6. Ronald appears to think in terms of "nothing but," preemptive constructs and to think in stereotyped ways. He is concrete in his formulations of events and is not terribly imaginative.

At the time of Ronald's self-description, he had completed a number of therapy sessions. They, however, were not part of a fixed-role therapy program. Such a program was undertaken, and it began with the writing of a fixed-role sketch by a panel of clinicians. The central theme of the sketch was the effort to seek answers in the subtle feelings of others rather than in dispute with them. The sketch, given the name of Kenneth Norton, emphasized attention to feelings. Here is the sketch of "Kenneth Norton" that was presented to Ronald Barrett.

Kenneth Norton

Kenneth Norton is the kind of man who, after a few minutes of conversation, somehow makes you feel that he must have known you intimately for a long time. This comes about, not by any particular questions that he asks, but by the understanding way in which he listens. It is as if he had a knack of seeing the world through your eyes. The things which you have come to see as being important he, too, soon seems to sense as similarly important. Thus he catches not only your words but the punctuations of feeling with which they are formed and the little accents of meaning with which they are chosen.

Kenneth Norton's complete absorption in the thoughts of the people with whom he holds conversations appears to leave no place for any feelings of self-consciousness regarding himself. If indeed he has such feelings at all, they obviously run a poor second to his eagerness to see the world through other people's eyes. Nor does this mean that he is ashamed of himself, rather it means that he is too much involved with the fascinating worlds of other people with whom he is surrounded to give more than a passing thought to soul-searching criticisms of himself. Some people might, of course, consider this itself to be a kind of fault. Be that as it may, this is the kind of fellow Kenneth Norton is, and this behavior represents the Norton brand of sincerity.

Girls he finds attractive for many reasons, not the least of which is the exciting opportunity they provide for his understanding the feminine point of view. Unlike some men, he does not "throw the ladies a line" but, so skillful a listener is he, soon he has them throwing him one—and he is thoroughly enjoying it.

With his own parents and in his own home he is somewhat more expressive of his own ideas and feelings. Thus his parents are given an opportunity to share and supplement his new enthusiasms and accomplishments.

Kelly, 1955, pp. 374–375

At first, Ronald had trouble in understanding the role he was to play and found that he was not too successful in his role-playing. In the midst of this discouragement, however, he met a former classmate at a movie and found that the role worked better with her than with anyone else. In fact, after a while she was paying him several compliments and indicated that he had changed (presumably for the better) since he had gone away to college. Some role-playing was tried in the therapy sessions. At times, Ronald would lapse back into dominating the conversation. At other times, however, he was able to draw out the therapist, who was now acting the role of various people in Ronald's life. When Ronald performed as Kenneth Norton, the therapist rewarded him with compliments.

Although the early presentations of himself as Kenneth Norton were without spontaneity or warmth, Ronald began to feel more comfortable in the role. He reported to the therapist that he felt less insecure in social situations, that he had fewer quarrels with others, and that he seemed to be more productive in his work efforts. When a difficult situation was described in the session, the therapist asked Ronald how Kenneth Norton would have handled it and then proceeded to engage Ronald in a role-playing rehearsal of the situation. Here, Ronald behaved with greater warmth and spontaneity, and the therapist congratulated him in an effort to reinforce the new behavior. In general, the therapist tried to reinforce whatever new behavior Ronald exhibited.

The therapy of Ronald Barrett was necessarily incomplete, since after only a few sessions it was time for him to leave school. We are, unfortunately, without data on the exact kinds of changes that did occur and how long they lasted. For example, it would have been interesting to have obtained Ronald's responses to the Rep test before treatment, at the end of treatment, and at some later point in time. This, of course, is the procedure Rogers used in some of his research. In any case, we do have a picture of how a Kellyian might construe an individual and how he might seek to engage a client in a creative process of change.

RELATED POINTS OF VIEW AND RECENT DEVELOPMENTS

Virtually all personality theorists today attempt to conceptualize cognitive variables, regardless of whether they interpret these variables as only part of the organism or as virtually all of the organism. Kelly's theory was presented at a relatively early stage in the development of this now vigorous trend in the study of personality. In the chapter on theory, it was pointed out that theories are influenced by the Zeitgeist or spirit of the times. It is clear that cognition is part of the current Zeitgeist (Chapter 14), although we do not know whether the work of Kelly was merely a forerunner of what was yet to come or itself had an impact on the development. In either case, it is clear that Kelly's theory places great emphasis on the constructions individuals place upon the world, and research associated with the theory has developed within this general orientation.

Although Kelly's theory attracted considerable attention when it was presented in 1955, in the following decade relatively little research was conducted that was tied specifically to the theory. Since then, however, there have been efforts to explore the many leads suggested by personal construct theory. A major focus in this research effort has been the Rep test and the structure of construct systems. There have been studies of the reliability of the Rep test and the evidence to date suggests that the responses of individuals to the role-title list and constructs used are reasonably stable over time (Landfield, 1971). Beyond this the Rep test has been used to study a variety of individuals with psychological problems, the construct systems of married couples, and people with varied interpersonal relationships (Duck, 1982). Modifications of the Rep test have been used to study the structural complexity of construct systems, the perception of situations, and, as noted, the use of nonverbal constructs. Indeed, so much research has been conducted on the Rep test that Landfield, a major proponent of personal construct theory, has asked: " 'Would we become experimentally paralyzed within Personal Construct Psychology if we accepted a five-year moratorium in the use of the conventional Rep Grids?' " (quoted in Bonarius, Holland, & Rosenberg, 1981, p. 3).

Almost every aspect of Kelly's theory has received at least some research attention (Mancuso & Adams-Webber, 1982). Particularly noteworthy has been the area of investigation of the organization of the construct system and changes in this organization associated with development (Crockett, 1982). The developmental principles emphasized suggest a number of similarities in the developmental theories of both Kelly and Piaget: (1) an emphasis on progression from a global, undifferentiated system to a differentiated, integrated system; (2) increasing use of more abstract structures so as to be able to handle more information more economically; (3) development in response to efforts to accommodate new elements into the cognitive system; (4) development of the cognitive system as a system, as opposed to a simple addition of new parts or elements. At the same time, it is clear that there are differences between the two approaches. For example, Piaget's theory is based on considerable observation of children and is much more advanced than the growth and development views associated with personal construct theory.

Despite the wide variety of research studies and the increasing number of proponents of personal construct theory, certain problems remain. It is to these problems that we now turn as part of our overall critical evaluation of the theory.

CRITICAL EVALUATION

Kelly's theory has been presented as a cognitive theory of personality. While discussing it in these terms, it should be recognized that others have construed the theory in different terms and that Kelly himself refused to attach any labels to it. Kelly noted that his theory had been described as humanistic, phenomenological, psychodynamic, existential, and even behavioristic as well as cognitive. Kelly rejected the term cognitive principally because he felt that it was too restrictive and suggested an artificial division between cognition (thinking) and affect (feeling).

He rejected phenomenology as being concerned only with subjective reality, and behaviorism as only concerned with objective reality, whereas personal construct theory is concerned with both. If he had to pick a label, Kelly probably would have described himself as a humanist. For Kelly, humanists emphasize what is possible rather than what is inevitable, are interested in the entire person, in novelty, and in the emancipation of the mind.

Despite these statements, Kelly's theory can be viewed as primarily a cognitive theory in its emphasis on the ways individuals receive and process information about the world and in its use of the Rep test as a way of determining a person's concepts. As such, Kelly's personal construct theory is certainly in the direction of taking (insofar as one can) a cognitive view of behavior. The structural model, with its emphasis on constructs and the construct system, represents a significant contribution to personality theory. The interpretation of behavior in terms of the individual's construing of events is a useful one in theory and in practice. This interpretation allows one to take into consideration the unique aspects of the behavior of individuals and, also, the lawfulness or regularity of much of this behavior. To the extent that Kelly's emphasis on cognitive structures has influenced the current research efforts in cognitive style, the theory has made a significant contribution to research. The Rep test, which has the beauty of being derived from the theory, represents an important assessment device. Although it has been criticized by some as so flexible as to be unmanageable (Vernon, 1963), it is also recognized by others as an extremely imaginative technique, quite amenable to quantification (Kleinmutz, 1967; Mischel, 1968). A remaining, unresolved problem for the Rep test, as well as for the theory as a whole, is that it requires the individual to use words even though it is recognized that preverbal or submerged constructs may exist.

The process view of Kelly has a number of interesting facets to it. It clearly represents a departure from the drive-reduction or tension-reduction views of Freud and other theorists. In the suggestion that the individual dislikes both the monotony of the ticking of a clock and the threat of the completely unknown, personal construct theory is similar to other views which suggest that the individual experiences small degrees of variety as pleasurable and large degrees of variety or no variety at all as unpleasurable. However, the process view leaves open a number of issues. The basis for action of an individual is not really clear. For example, how does the individual know which construct will be the best predictor? How does one know which end of the construct (similarity or contrast) to use? Also, what determines the individual's response to invalidation (Sechrest, 1963)? Finally, in relation to the process view, what determines whether individuals will choose, in the face of threat, to risk change in their system or to retreat into the conservative strategies of the old system? One would guess that this choice would be dependent on the external conditions under which a prediction needed to be made, how critical the constructs involved were to the construct system, and the past experiences of the individual with the language of hypothesis. Considerations such as these are involved in Kelly's conceptualization of the process of therapy and construct change, but they are not made as explicit as would be desirable for research purposes.

In his review of Kelly's theory, Bruner (1956) referred to it as the single greatest contribution of the decade between 1945 and 1955 to the theory of personality functioning. There is clearly much to the theory that is new and worthwhile. However, there are some areas of psychology that appear to be more within the range of convenience of the psychology of personal constructs than are other areas. For example, until recently the theory has had little to say about growth and development. The theory offers an interesting analysis of anxiety, but it has almost nothing to say about the important emotion of depression. In fact, for all of its worthwhile emphasis on cognition, the theory offers a limited view of the person. Although Kelly denied the charge, the theory is noticeably lacking in emphasis on human feelings and emotions. In his review, Bruner stated that people may not be the pigs that reinforcement theory makes of them, but he wondered also whether people are only the scientists that Kelly suggests. Bruner commented further as follows: "I rather suspect that when some people get angry or inspired or in love, they couldn't care less about their systems as a whole! One gets the impression that the author is, in his personality theory, overreacting against a generation of irrationalism" (Bruner, 1956, p. 356). Despite efforts to come to grips with the area of human emotions (McCoy, 1981), many interpretations within the context of personal construct theory seem strained and, on the whole, human emotions remain an area outside of its range of convenience.

Two additional relevant issues are worthy of consideration. First, while there has been considerable investigation of construct systems, there remains little evidence that measures of these systems are related to overt behavior (Crockett, 1982; Duck, 1982). The theory would certainly suggest that this is the case, but evidence is needed. Second, significant problems remain with Kelly's theory of motivation. As noted, Kelly failed to be specific about the basis for many decisions people make in relation to the functioning of their construct systems. Beyond this, one finds elements of more traditional views of motivation entering into discussion by personal construct theorists. For example, the suggestion is made that people do not like boredom or surprise (Mancuso & Adams-Webber, 1982). However, as noted, emphases on intermediate degrees of novelty or stimulation have typically been associated with pleasure, reinforcement, or hedonic theories of motivation. One may also note how such an emphasis on emotion or pleasure enters into clinical discussion. For example, Landfield (1982) suggests that a person chooses that end of a construct that is positively valued. Furthermore, in his discussion of a case he suggests that the patient stopped having an affair for basically emotional rather than purely cognitive reasons: "After all, she did like her husband better than her lover" (p. 203).

A final note in the evaluation of Kelly's theory concerns its current status as a basis for active research. Clearly there has been activity and growing interest as expressed in the development of an international newsletter, the holding of yearly international meetings devoted to personal construct theory, and the publication of books reporting noteworthy research efforts. However, two recent reviews of these efforts question whether substantial progress is being made as opposed to development being held back by reverence, insularity, and orthodoxy. Thus, Rosenberg suggests that "there is a serious question concerning whether a continuation along the same lines will sustain the aliveness of the theory" (1980, p. 899) and Schneider criticized the papers he reviewed because they "communicated little sense of excitement about major new possibilities or developments. There is almost no criticism of Kelly's original ideas, which tend to be treated as revealed truths" (1982, p. 712). As noted some time ago by a follower of Kelly, without new ideas no theory of personality can survive (Sechrest, 1977).

In sum, personal construct theory has both strengths and limitations. On the positive side, there is the following: (1) The theory makes a significant contribution by bringing to the forefront of personality the importance of cognition and construct systems. (2) It is an approach to personality that attempts to capture both the uniqueness of the individual and the lawfulness of people generally. (3) It has developed a new, interesting, and theoretically relevant assessment technique, the Rep test. On the negative side, there is the following: (1) The theory shows relative neglect of certain important areas such as emotion and motivation. (2) Despite Kelly's view that theories are there to be reformulated and abandoned, no one since 1955 has formulated any significant new theoretical developments in personal construct theory.

With this presentation of Kelly's theory, we have completed our consideration of three personality theories formulated largely on the basis of clinical data. It may be useful now to take stock of the three theories. Following the spirit of personal construct theory, we consider a pair of theories together and finally all three to see the points of comparison and constructs that seem relevant.

Kelly and Freud

Although Kelly was extremely critical of psychoanalytic theory, he appreciated the many important observations and clinical contributions that were made by Freud. The criticisms of Freud are mainly in three areas—Freud's view of the person, the considerable dogmatism in psychoanalytic thinking, and the weaknesses of psychoanalysis as a scientific theory. Kelly was critical of Freud's view of the person-the-biological-organism, and substituted instead the view of person-the-scientist. Kelly was critical of Freud's metaphors and his emphasis on unconscious drives and instincts.

Kelly placed great reliance on understanding the individual's construction of events and on the tentativeness with which theories are put forward. Both of these reflect an open-minded attitude. Against this background, Kelly was critical of Freud's emphasis on understanding what clients mean by examining what they *do not* say. For Kelly, this approach makes psychoanalysis needlessly dogmatic and close-minded. Furthermore, Kelly viewed the followers of Freud as unnecessarily opposed to change.

FIGURE 8.2   **SUMMARY OF STRENGTHS AND LIMITATIONS OF PERSONAL CONSTRUCT THEORY**

STRENGTHS	LIMITATIONS
1. Places emphasis on cognitive processes as a central aspect of personality.	1. Has not led to research that *extends* the theory.
2. Presents a model of personality that provides both for the lawfulness of general personality functioning and the uniqueness of individual construct systems.	2. Leaves out or makes minimal contributions to our understanding of some significant aspects of personality (growth & development, emotions).
3. Includes a theory-related technique for personality assessment and research (Rep Test).	3. Is not as yet connected with more general research and theory in cognitive psychology.

The third area of major criticism of psychoanalysis was its standing as a scientific enterprise. Kelly observed that Freud's observations of the unconscious were difficult to explore scientifically. As far as Kelly was concerned, the psychoanalytic movement had shunned scientific methodology in favor of impressionist observation. Hypotheses were so elastic that they could not be invalidated. They were what Kelly called "rubber hypotheses"—they could be stretched to fit any kind of evidence. For Kelly, this was psychoanalysis' most vulnerable point.

Although Kelly was critical of psychoanalysis, he also believed that the psychoanalytic system of dynamics permitted the clinician to determine that something was going on inside the client. According to Kelly, Freud made many astute observations, and his adventurousness helped to open up the field of psychotherapy for exploration. What is particularly striking in reading Kelly is the number of times that he seems to be describing phenomena that were also described by Freud, even though he may interpret them in a different way. For example, Kelly placed great emphasis on the closeness of opposites, a view quite evident in Freud's thinking. In fact, in dreams, ideas were frequently represented by their opposites. Both Freud and Kelly were sensitive to the fact that the way people view others may also be expressive of views they hold about themselves; both were aware that one is threatened only by something that seems plausible and that one "protests too much" about things one does not want to acknowledge to be true; both viewed people as at times functioning in relation to principles they are unaware of, although in one case the concept of the unconscious was emphasized, while in the other the emphasis was on preverbal constructs; both noted that at times an individual may feel uncomfortable with praise, although in one case the concept of guilt was stressed, and in the other the emphasis was on the strangeness of new praise and the complex internal reorganization it could imply; both placed emphasis on the concept of transference in therapy; both believed that clients should not get to know their therapists too well and that therapists should avoid social contacts with their clients; both felt that diagnoses could be useful in treatment; both felt that patients are resistant to change; both felt that free associations and dreams could be useful in understanding the person's functioning; and, both believed that there was a relationship between the thinking found in some forms of pathology and that found in creative people. In Freud's case, an emphasis on primary process thinking was found in both psychopathology and creativity; for Kelly, there was an emphasis on the process of construct loosening. In addition, Freud, too, saw people as scientists: "Scientific thought is, in its essence, no different from the normal process of thinking, which we all, believers and unbelievers, alike, make use of when we are going about our business in everyday life" (Freud, 1933, p. 232). It is not surprising that the theories of Freud and Kelly share a number of observations, since the foci of convenience of the two theories are somewhat similar.

Kelly and Rogers

There also are a number of similarities in the works of Kelly and Rogers. Both view the person as more active than reactive; both theories emphasize the phenomenological approach, although Kelly believed that personal construct psychology was not just phenomenology. In both, there is an emphasis on consistency, although for Rogers this is on self-consistency, per se, and for Kelly it is so that predictions can add up rather than cancel each other out. Both stress the total system functioning of the organism.

Probably, their common emphasis on the phenomenological approach and their common avoidance of a drive model of human functioning leads to the appearance of considerable similarity between Kelly and Rogers. At one point, Kelly asked a question that would be quite characteristic of Rogers: "Is the therapist ever more familiar with the client's construct system than the client is himself?" His answer was clear. "We think not" (Kelly, 1955, p. 1020). Despite these similarities, however, there are major differences between the two theories. Kelly places considerably less emphasis on the self than does Rogers. Also, although Kelly agreed with Rogers that the present is what counts most, he refused to take a completely ahistorical approach toward behavior. Kelly was interested in the past because individuals' perceptions of their past give clues to their construct system and because a reconstruing of the past can be an important element in treatment. In general, Kelly was interested in a whole range of clinical phenomena (e.g., transference, dreams, diagnosis, the importance of preverbal constructs), which brought him closer to Freud than to Rogers in this regard.

Kelly viewed Rogers' position as more of a statement of philosophical convictions about the nature of the person than a true psychological theory. Kelly was critical of the Rogerian principle of growth and contrasted it with personal construct theory. Whereas the former emphasized an unfolding of inner potential, the latter emphasized the continuous development of a changing and ever-expanding construct system. Whereas Rogers emphasized the importance of being and becoming, Kelly emphasized the importance of make-believe and doing. The difference has important ramifications for treatment, a point that was made explicit by Kelly:

> *The nondirectionist, because of his faith in the emerging being, asks the client to pay attention to himself as he reacts with his everyday world. Somewhere the mature self is waiting to be realized. The nondirective therapist is hesitant to say what the self is, so he prefers to hold a mirror before the client in which can be seen the reflections of those vague stirrings of life which are called feelings. The personal-construct psychologist, because he sees life proceeding by means of a series of hypotheses, and validating experiences, may hold the same mirror, but he sees that mirror, and the image of validating experience which it reflects, as setting up the succession of targets toward which the growth is directed. The personal-construct psychologist is probably more inclined to urge the client to experiment with life and to seek his answers in the succession of events which life unveils than to seek them within himself . . . He urges the client to see himself in terms of an ever emerging life role rather than in terms of a self which approaches a state of maturity.*
>
> Kelly, 1955, pp. 401–402

Kelly greatly emphasized the verbal fluency and acting skill of the therapist. He opposed the view that the therapist must be known as a real person and was critical of phenomenologically oriented therapists who became involved in "lovely personal relationships." The differences between Kelly and Rogers as people are important and translate themselves into views concerning therapy. Rogers (1956), in his review of Kelly's work, expressed the belief that Kelly had found an approach congenial to his personality. However, he was critical of what he thought was Kelly's interpretation of therapy as an intellectual process. Rogers was influenced by Kelly and uses the concepts of construct complexity and construct flexibility in his analysis of changes in therapy. However, Rogers was critical of the excessive amount of activity and control assumed in fixed-role therapy. For Rogers, therapy is much more a process of feeling than of thinking, and it is important that therapists be capable of being congruent and not that they be skillful in manipulating the situation. "An overwhelming impression is that, for Kelly, therapy is seen as almost entirely an intellectual function, a view which should be comforting to many psychologists. He is continually thinking about the client, and about his own procedures, in ways so complex, that there seems no time or room for entering into an emotional relationship with the client'' (Rogers, 1956, p. 358).

Kelly, Freud, and Rogers

In their study of suicide, Farberow and Schneidman (1961) obtained the ratings by Kelly of a patient, along with the ratings by a Freudian, a Rogerian, and members of other schools of thought. In general, Kelly's ratings of the case, and presumably therefore his interpretation of it, were much more similar to those made by the Rogerian than to those made by the Freudian. In commenting on this study, Kelly (1963) noted that the theories could perhaps be understood in terms of their likenesses and differences. In his own analysis of the ratings, Kelly differentiated the theories according to the attention given to interpersonal relations, with construct psychology giving the most attention, psychoanalytic theory the least, and Rogerian theory something in between. Another dimension of importance was the attention given to aggression and hostility. Here, the psychoanalytic ratings indicated a considerable degree of emphasis, whereas the ratings by Kelly and the Rogerian suggested much less emphasis. A third dimension related to the attention given to the affective dimension of behavior. Here, the psychoanalytic and Rogerian ratings were quite high, while Kelly's indicated much less attention to this area.

Although it is not the only approach toward a comparative analysis of theories, the approach emphasized by Kelly does have merit. Thus, because three elements are the necessary number for the formation of a similarity–contrast construct, we can now use the three theories before us—those of Freud, Rogers, and Kelly—in developing comparative constructs like the ones mentioned in the preceding paragraph. As we examine other theories in successive chapters, we can seek to develop some new constructs, to drop some old ones, to make some more permeable, and to call others so unique that no further elements can be added.

With the completion of this chapter on Kelly, we bring to a close the analysis of three clinical theories of personality. Regardless of their differences, the three theorists have in common the use of clinical material as the original source of data for their hypotheses. The three theories are different, but then each theorist grew out of a different background, was himself a different personality in interacting with his patients, and had a somewhat different patient (subject) population. It may be that, although each theory differs one from the other, the theories are not mutually exclusive—an issue that will be important for us to consider as further theories are assessed; that is, all personality theories may possibly express the same things but in different terms; or it may be that they have different foci of convenience.

These three clinical theories also share an emphasis on individual differences, an emphasis on qualities within the individual that result in relatively stable behavioral characteristics across situations and over time, and an emphasis on the functioning of all parts of the individual within the context of a total system. Later chapters examine other approaches that have quite different views of the person and science, that use different techniques of assessment, and that focus on different problems in research.

MAJOR CONCEPTS AND SUMMARY

[Review concepts from Chapter 7]   aggression

permeable–impermeable constructs   hostility

tightening–loosening of constructs   fixed-role therapy

constriction–dilation

In this chapter and in the preceding one, we have discussed the personal construct theory of George A. Kelly. The theory is distinguished by its clinical approach, its emphasis on the whole person, the use of the Rep test for assessment purposes, and its emphasis on cognition—how the individual perceives, interprets, and conceptualizes events and the environment. This emphasis is further expressed in the view of people as scientists with their own theories (construct systems) and efforts to anticipate events.

The major structural concept for Kelly is that of a construct. A construct is an interpretation placed on the world by the individual. Constructs can be described in terms of their content and in terms of their characteristic mode of functioning. An individual can be described in terms of the constructs used and in terms of the structural aspects of the construct system (e.g., a complex versus a simple construct system). The emphasis on the system aspects or interrelationships among constructs again points to the holistic properties of the theory, which emphasize the entire person. The Rep test and its modifications represent the principal means for determining how individuals construe their worlds and thereby for describing the personalities of individuals.

In accounting for the activity of people, Kelly assumes that the person is active; he rejects concepts such as motives, drives, and needs. He accounts for behavior in terms of the fundamental postulate—an individual chooses that alternative which offers the greater possibility for expansion and definition of the system. As scientists choose to pursue research along lines that show promise of developing their theories, people choose to act in ways that will facilitate the expansion and development of the construct system. Anxiety, fear, and threat are experienced when individuals find themselves without constructs applicable to a situation or when they face the possibility of change in their construct systems. At the extremes of functioning, we can choose between confusion and certainty, between anxiety and boredom. Individuals can defend against anxiety and threat by processes such as loosening (making variable, unstable predictions) and tightening (making unvarying predictions). Essentially, the dynamics of functioning involve the interplay between the wish to elaborate the construct system and the desire to avoid the threat of disruption of the construct system.

Under favorable circumstances, the developing individual responds to new elements in the environment with the development of new constructs, more abstract constructs, and a more hierarchical construct system. There is a resemblance here to some of the views of Piaget. For growth and expansion of the construct system to occur, there must be the presence of new elements, relative consistency in the environment so that prediction is possible, and sufficient looseness in the construct system so that new predictions can be attempted. Pathological developments occur when anxiety leads to rigid construct system functioning or to chaotic system functioning in the face of repeated invalidations. This may involve making constructs excessively permeable or impermeable to new information, excessive loosening or tightening in making predictions, or excessive construction or dilation of the overall construct system. This may also involve efforts to extort evidence in support of the construct system from others (hostility).

The psychotherapeutic process of change involves the reconstruction of an individual's construct system so that it leads to more accurate predictions. For this to occur conditions are necessary which are similar to those that facilitate growth: an atmosphere of experimentation, the provision of new elements, and the availability of validating data. Fixed-role therapy was developed as one means of encouraging clients to experience new elements and to experiment with new opportunities for obtaining validating data. The aim is the reconstruction of the construct system, that is, of the entire personality and not a minor readjustment of parts of the person. Improvement occurs because behavior change leads to cognitive change and not because of behavior change itself.

Personal construct theory represents a remarkable effort to interpret a broad range of behavior within a cognitive framework. It has led to the development of a significant assessment device (Rep test) which is more closely linked to a specific theory than almost any other assessment device. In its emphasis on cognitive processes, it is part of the current Zeitgeist and, after a period of slow development in research activity, it recently has been associated with a number of serious research efforts. At the same time, the theory has some major weaknesses. It is difficult to test some parts of the theory and it is only with difficulty that emotions such as love, anger, guilt and depression are incorporated into its range of convenience. Finally, despite Kelly's emphasis on the invitational mood and on the need for constant elaboration and change in a theory or construct system, there have been no new fundamental developments in the theory since its publication in 1955.

Picasso, Pablo. *Acrobats at the Beach*. Pushkin Museum, Moscow/Art Resource.

TRAIT APPROACHES TO PERSONALITY: ALLPORT, EYSENCK, AND CATTELL

CHAPTER FOCUS: In this chapter we review theories that are significant in their efforts to identify the basic dimensions of personality. The basic conceptual unit is the trait, that is, a broad disposition to behave in a particular way. Two of the three trait theorists, Eysenck and Cattell, use a particular statistical procedure, factor analysis, to determine the basic traits that make up the human personality. The trait approach has been popular in American psychology and comes close to the layman's approach to describing someone's personality. Recently it has come under attack from psychologists who suggest that people's behavior varies much more from situation to situation than is suggested by trait theory.

Yet something must account for the recurrences and stabilities in personal behavior . . . we do find that personality is relatively stable over time and in different situational fields. . . . The scientific evidence for the existence of a trait always comes from demonstrating by some acceptable method the consistency in a person's behavior.

Allport, 1961, pp. 312, 343

There is a middle ground between treating all humans as if they were exactly alike, and treating them as if they were all entirely different from each other. This intermediate position is the adoption of some type of typological approach, the delineation of certain important dimensions of personality along which individuals can be ranged (extraversion–introversion would be an example of such a dimension).

Eysenck, 1982, p. 3

The scientific study of personality seeks to understand personality as one would the mechanism of a watch, the chemistry of the life processes in a mammal, or the spectrum of a remote star. That is to say, it aims at objective insights; at the capacity to predict and control what will happen next; and at the establishment of scientific laws of a perfectly general nature. . . . A trait may be defined as that which defines what a person will do when faced with a defined situation.

Cattell, 1979, pp. 1, 14

In the preceding chapters attention was given to one major representative of each theoretical point of view. In this chapter on trait theory attention is given to the views of three theorists. Whereas in earlier chapters it was easy to determine the major figure representative of that school of thought, this is not nearly as easy with trait theory. For some time Gordon W. Allport championed trait theory, but he did relatively little empirical research to further its development. Hans J. Eysenck and Raymond B. Cattell both have made important theoretical and research contributions, Eysenck's influence being greater in Great Britain and Cattell's greater in the United States.

Let us put aside the question of who is the leading theorist or representative of trait theory and consider, instead, the essentials of the point of view itself. As has been indicated, it is an approach to personality that has been an influential part of personality theory and research. At the same time, it is an approach that has come under attack by proponents of the social learning theory point of view (Chapter 13). The basic assumption of the trait point of view is that people possess broad predispositions to respond in particular ways. Such predispositions are called **traits**. In other words, people may be described in terms of the likelihood of their behaving in a particular way—for example, the likelihood of their being outgoing and friendly or their being dominant and assertive. People having a strong tendency to behave in these ways may be described as being high on these traits, for example, high on the traits of "extroversion" and "dominance," whereas people with a lesser tendency to behave in these ways would be described as low on these traits. While various trait theorists differ as to how to determine the traits that make up the human personality, they all agree that traits are the fundamental building blocks of the human personality.

Beyond this, trait theorists agree that human behavior and personality can be organized into a hierarchy. By this they mean that the parts of our personality and behavior have an organized quality such that there are links among the parts and that some are more influential or key than others. An illustration of this hierarchical point of view comes from the work of Eysenck. Eysenck suggests that as its simplest level behavior can be considered in terms of specific responses. However, some of these responses generally are linked to one another forming more general habits. Again, we generally find that groups of habits tend to occur together to form what are called traits. For example, people who prefer meeting people to reading also generally enjoy themselves at a lively party, suggesting that these two habits can be grouped together under the trait of sociability. Or, to take another example, people who act without stopping to think things over also tend to shout back at others, suggesting that these two habits can be grouped together under the trait of impulsiveness. Finally, at an even higher level of organization, various traits may tend to be linked together to form what Eysenck calls types. How we find such traits and determine the hierarchical organization of personality will be discussed shortly. What is important to recognize here is the conceptualization of personality as organized at various levels. A representation of Eysenck's view of such organization is given in Figure 9.1.

In sum, trait theories suggest that people have broad predispositions to respond in certain ways and that there is a hierarchical organization to personality. In considering the trait theories of Allport, Eysenck, and Cattell we will see that while differences emerge, these two themes remain constant.

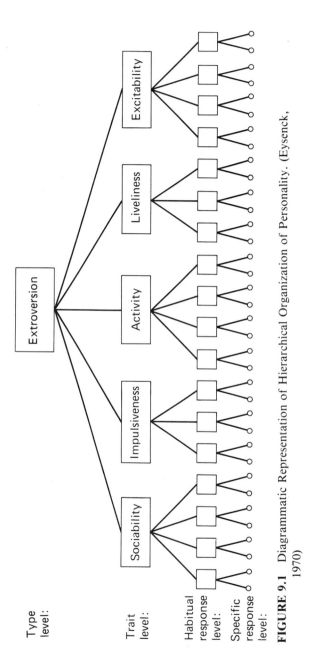

FIGURE 9.1 Diagrammatic Representation of Hierarchical Organization of Personality. (Eysenck, 1970)

THE TRAIT THEORY OF GORDON W. ALLPORT (1897–1967)

Gordon W. Allport probably will be remembered more for the issues he raised and the principles he emphasized than for a particular theoretical perspective. Throughout his long and influential career, he emphasized the human, healthy, and organized aspects of our behavior. This is in contrast with other views that emphasized the animalistic, neurotic, tension-reducing, and mechanistic aspects of behavior. In this regard, he was critical of aspects of psychoanalysis and was fond of telling the following story. At the age of 22, while traveling through Europe, Allport decided that it would be interesting to visit Freud. When he entered Freud's office, he was met with expectant silence as Freud waited to learn of Allport's mission. Finding himself unprepared for silence, Allport decided to start an informal conversation with the description of a 4-year-old boy with a dirt phobia, whom he had met on the train. After he completed his description of the boy and his compulsive mother Freud asked, "And was that little boy you?" Allport describes his response as follows:

> Flabbergasted and feeling a bit guilty, I contrived to change the subject. While Freud's misunderstanding of my motivation was amusing, it also started a deep train of thought. I realized that he was accustomed to neurotic defenses and that my manifest motivation (a sort of rude curiosity and youthful ambition) escaped him. For therapeutic progress he would have to cut through my defenses, but it so happened that therapeutic progress was not here an issue. This experience taught me that depth psychology, for all its merits, may plunge too deep, and that psychologists would do well to give full recognition to manifest motives before probing the unconscious.
>
> Allport, 1967, p. 8[1]

Allport's first publication, written with his older brother Floyd, centered on traits as an important aspect of personality theory—*Personality Traits: Their Classification and Measurement* (Allport & Allport, 1921). Allport believed that traits are the basic units of personality. According to him, traits actually exist and are based in the nervous system. They represent generalized personality dispositions that account for regularities in the functioning of a person across situations and over time. Regularity in functioning is achieved through perceiving many stimuli as equivalent and many personal acts of behavior as equivalent expressions of the same trait. Traits can be defined by three properties—frequency, intensity, and range of situations. For example, a very submissive person would *frequently* be *very* submissive over a *wide range of situations*.

Allport made a distinction among **cardinal traits**, **central traits**, and **secondary dispositions**. A cardinal trait expresses a disposition that is so pervasive and out-

---

[1]A particularly amusing aspect of this is that Allport was indeed a person who was neat, meticulous, orderly, and punctual—possessing many of the characteristics associated by Freud with the compulsive personality. Freud may not have been as far off in his question as Allport suggested.

Gordon W. Allport

standing in a person's life that virtually every act is traceable to its influence. For example, we speak of the Machiavellian person named after Niccolò Machiavelli's portrayal of the successful Renaissance ruler, of the sadistic person named after the Marquis de Sade, and also of the authoritarian personality who sees virtually everything in black-white, stereotyped ways. Generally people have few, if any, such cardinal traits. Central traits (e.g., honesty, kindness, assertiveness) express dispositions that cover a more limited range of situations than is true for cardinal traits. Secondary traits represent dispositions that are the least conspicuous, generalized, and consistent. They can be the same personality characteristics that are central traits for other people. In other words, people possess traits of varying degrees of significance and generality. It is the central traits that we usually think of in describing someone's personality.

It is important to recognize that Allport did not say that a trait expresses itself in all situations independent of the characteristics of the situation. While consistency in behavior is necessary evidence for a trait, instances of "inconsistency" do not mean that the trait does not exist. Indeed, Allport recognized the importance of the situation and the variation of behavior across situations. A trait expresses what a person generally does over many situations, not what will be done in any one situation: "We are forced to the conclusion that while the situation may modify behavior greatly, it can do so only within the limits of the potential provided by the personality. At the same time, we are forced to concede that traits of personality must not be regarded as fixed and stable, operating mechanically to the same degree on all occasions. Rather we should think of traits as *ranges of possible behavior*, to be activated at varying points within the range according to the demands of the situation" (Allport, 1961, pp. 180–181). Thus, the trait concept was necessary to explain the consistency found in behavior; recognition of the importance of the situation was necessary to explain the inconsistency or variability of behavior.

In 1924 Allport gave the first course on personality ever taught in the United States and in 1937 published a book on personality (*Personality: A Psychological Interpretation*), which for twenty-five years was a basic text in the field. In this book and in its later revision, *Pattern and Growth in Personality* (1961), Allport emphasized the importance of self-images, complex integrative functions, the mature aspects of personality, and the process of growth and becoming. Allport is known not only for his emphasis on traits but also for his emphasis on the concept of **functional autonomy**. The concept of functional autonomy suggests that while the motives of an adult may have their roots in the tension-reducing motives of the child, the adult grows out of them and becomes independent of these earlier tension-reducing efforts. What originally began as an effort to reduce hunger or anxiety can become a source of pleasure and motivation in its own right. Finally, Allport is known for his emphasis on the uniqueness of the individual. This emphasis took at least two forms. In one, Allport emphasized the utility of in-depth studies of individuals for the purpose of learning more about people generally. Such **idiographic research** involved comparing a person's values with one another, rather than against some absolute norm, and utilizing materials personally expressive of the individual. For example, Allport published 172 letters from a woman which provided the basis for clinical characterization of her personality as well as for quantitative analysis. In the second form, Allport's emphasis on the uniqueness of the individual led him to suggest that there are unique traits and unique aspects of personality functioning that cannot be captured by science. The former emphasis on idiographic research was important and currently there is a return to an interest in such endeavors (Pervin, 1983). The latter emphasis, however, was interpreted to mean that a science of personality was not possible and resulted in considerable controversy that did not help to advance the field.

Comment on Allport

Allport's interests ranged broadly across social psychology as well as personality. He raised many critical issues and discussed the trait concept with such balance and wisdom that he can still be read with profit today. Thus, for example, Allport (1961) suggested that behavior generally expresses the action of many traits, that conflicting dispositions can exist within the person, and that traits are expressed in part by the person's *selection of* situations as opposed to their *response to* situations. Although Allport emphasized the concept of trait and tried to clarify its relation to the situation, he did little research to establish the existence and utility of specific trait concepts. Similarly, although he believed that many traits were hereditary, he did not conduct research to substantiate this. To consider illustrations of such conceptual and research efforts we must turn to the works of the two remaining trait theorists—Hans J. Eysenck and Raymond B. Cattell.

THE TRAIT-TYPE, FACTOR-ANALYTIC THEORY OF
HANS J. EYSENCK (1916–   )

Hans J. Eysenck was born in Germany in 1916 and later fled to England to escape Nazi persecution. His work has been influenced by methodological advances in the statistical technique of factor analysis (Charles Spearman), by the thinking of European typologists such as Jung and Kretschmer, by the research on heredity of Sir Cyril Burt, by the experimental work on classical conditioning by the Russian physiologist Pavlov, and by the American learning theory of Clark Hull. While his work has included the sampling of both normal and pathological populations, most of it has been done at the Institute of Psychiatry, Maudsley Hospital, England.

Eysenck is strict in his standards for scientific pursuits, placing great emphasis on conceptual clarity and measurement. For this reason he consistently has been one of the harshest critics of psychoanalytic theory. While supporting trait theory, he has emphasized the need to develop adequate measures of traits, the need to develop a theory that relates performance in different areas in a conceptually meaningful way, and the importance of establishing the biological foundations for the existence of each trait. "I feel that the major, most fundamental dimensions of personality are likely to be those on which variation has had evolutionary significance, and that this evolutionary history is likely to manifest itself in strong genetic determination of individual differences along these dimensions" (Eysenck, 1977, pp. 407–408). Efforts such as these are emphasized by Eysenck as being important to avoid a meaningless circularity of explanation whereby a trait is used to explain behavior that serves as the basis for the concept of the trait in the first place. For example, Jack talks to others because he is high on the trait of

Hans J. Eysenck

sociability but we know that he is high on this trait because we observe that he spends lots of time talking to others.

The basis for Eysenck's emphasis on measurement and the development of a classification of traits is the statistical technique of **factor analysis**. Factor analysis is a technique in which one starts with a large number of test items that are administered to a large number of persons. The question to be answered is: "To which items do groups of people respond in the same way?" Through a number of statistical procedures, clusters or factors are derived, the items within any single factor being highly related to one another and being slightly related, or not at all related, to items in the other factors. According to trait theory, there are natural, unitary structures in personality, and the logic of factor analysis allows us to detect them. If things (variables, test responses) move together, that is, if they appear and disappear together, then one can infer that they have some common feature behind them, that they belong to the same unity of personality functioning. Factor analysis assumes that behaviors that function with one another are related. It is a statistical device for determining which behaviors are related to one another and thereby for determining the unities or natural elements in personality.

The process described leads to factors, in this case called traits, which are named in terms of the characteristic that seems common to the items or behaviors that have been found to be related to one another. Through some further statistical procedures Eysenck determines the basic dimensions that underlie the factors or traits that have been found. These basic dimensions are called **types**. Thus, for example the traits of sociability, impulsiveness, activity, liveliness, and excitability can be grouped together under the type concept of extroversion (Figure 9.1). Though the term "type" is used, it is important to recognize that in fact it is a dimension with a low end and a high end that is being considered, such that people may fall along various points between the two extremes.

In his earlier research Eysenck found two basic dimensions to personality which he labeled as **Introversion–Extroversion** and **Neuroticism** (stable–unstable). The relationship of these two basic dimensions of personality to the four major temperamental types distinguished by the Greek physicians Hippocrates and Galen and to a wider range of personality characteristics is presented in Figure 9.2. Since the earlier emphasis on these two dimensions, Eysenck has added a third dimension, which he calls **Psychoticism**. People high on this dimension tend to be solitary, insensitive, uncaring about others, and opposed to accepted social custom.

A further appreciation of Eysenck's theoretical system can be gained from a more detailed consideration of one of these three dimensions, that of introversion–extroversion. According to Eysenck, the typical extrovert is sociable, likes parties, has many friends, craves excitement, acts on the spur of the moment, and is impulsive. As can be seen, there appear to be two aspects to this dimension, sociability and impulsiveness, which can be separated out to a certain extent but which have been found to be related sufficiently to be linked under the same concept of extroversion. In contrast to these characteristics, the introverted person

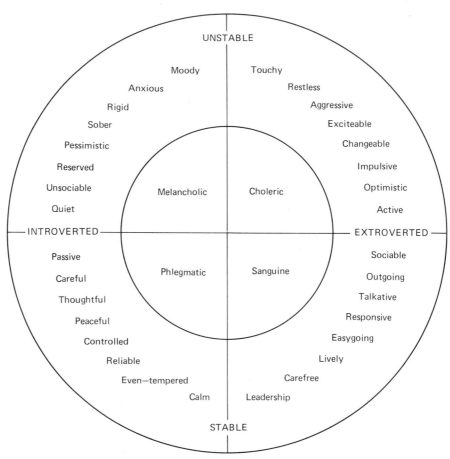

✱FIGURE 9.2   The Relationship of Two Dimensions of Personality Derived from Factor Analysis to Four Greek Temperamental Types. (Eysenck, 1975)

tends to be quiet, introspective, reserved, reflective, distrustful of impulsive decisions, and to prefer a well-ordered life to one filled with chance and risk.

Eysenck has developed two questionnaires to measure people along the dimension of introversion–extroversion—the Maudsley Personality Inventory and the Eysenck Personality Inventory. The typical extrovert will answer yes to questions such as the following: Do other people think of you as very lively? Would you be unhappy if you could not see lots of people most of the time? Do you often long for excitement? In contrast, the typical introvert will answer *yes* to these questions: Generally, do you prefer reading to meeting people? Are you mostly quiet when you are with people? Do you stop and think things over before doing anything? Other illustrative items from the Maudsley and Eysenck Personality Inventories are presented in Figure 9.3. These include items relevant to Neuroticism and a Lie scale to detect individuals faking responses to look good, as well as

Introversion–Extroversion—**Hans Eysenck suggests that a basic dimension of personality involves whether people tend to be unsociable, quiet, and passive (introverts) or sociable, outgoing, and active (extroverts).**

Intro:- more salivation
Extro.- less salivation

items relevant to Extroversion–Introversion. While the content and direction of scored responses may be obvious in some cases, in other cases this is not true. In addition to such questionnaires, other, more objective, measures have been devised. For example, there is some suggestion that the "lemondrop test" may be used to distinguish between introverts and extroverts. In this test a standard amount of lemon juice is placed on the subject's tongue. Introverts and extroverts differ in the amount of saliva produced when this is done.

What is the theoretical underpinning of this dimension? Eysenck suggests that individual variations in introversion–extroversion reflect differences in neurophysiological functioning. Basically introverts are more easily aroused by events and more easily learn social prohibitions than extroverts. As a result, introverts are more restrained and inhibited. There also is some evidence that introverts are more influenced by punishments in learning whereas extroverts are more influenced by rewards. It is hypothesized that individual differences along this dimension have both hereditary and environmental origins. Indeed, several studies of identical and fraternal twins suggest that heredity plays a major part in accounting for differences between individuals in their scores on this dimension (Shields, 1976).

Previously it was stated that Eysenck felt that an adequate trait theory should be based on careful measurement of empirically determined differences in behavior between individuals high and low on a dimension and a theory of the basis for these differences and their development. Eysenck's use of factor analysis and his theory of the nature and origin of differences in extroversion–introversion repre-

		Yes	No
1.	Do you usually take the initiative in making new friends?	___	___
2.	Do ideas run through your head so that you cannot sleep?	___	___
3.	Are you inclined to keep in the background on social occasions?	___	___
4.	Do you sometimes laugh at a dirty joke?	___	___
5.	Are you inclined to be moody?	___	___
6.	Do you very much like good food?	___	___
7.	When you get annoyed do you need someone friendly to talk to about it?	___	___
8.	As a child did you always do as you were told immediately and without grumbling?	___	___
9.	Do you usually keep "yourself to yourself" except with very close friends?	___	___
10.	Do you often make up your mind too late?	___	___

NOTE: The above items would be scored in the following way:
Extroversion—1 Yes, 3 No, 6 Yes, 9 No; *Neuroticism*—2 Yes, 5 Yes, 7 Yes, 10 Yes; *Lie Scale*—4 No, 8 Yes.

FIGURE 9.3   Illustrative Items for Extroversion, Neuroticism, and Lie Scale from the Maudsley Personality Inventory and Eysenck Personality Inventory.

sent efforts in this direction. Are there other significant and theoretically meaningful differences in behavior associated with varying scores on the extroversion-introversion dimension? A recent review of the dimension presents us with an impressive array of findings. For example, introverts are more sensitive to pain than are extroverts, they become fatigued and bored more easily than do extroverts, excitement interferes with their performance while it enhances performance for extroverts, and they tend to be more careful but less fast than extroverts (Wilson, 1978). The following are some additional differences that have been found:

1. Introverts do better in school than extroverts, particularly in more advanced subjects. Also, students withdrawing from college for academic reasons tend to be extroverts whereas those who withdraw for psychiatric reasons tend to be introverts.

2. Extroverts prefer vocations involving interactions with other people whereas introverts tend to prefer more solitary vocations. Extroverts seek diversion from job routine while introverts have a lesser need for novelty.

3. Extroverts enjoy explicit sexual and aggressive humor whereas introverts prefer more intellectual forms of humor such as puns and subtle jokes.

4. Extroverts are more active sexually, in terms of frequency and different partners, than introverts are.

5. Extroverts are more suggestible than introverts.

The last finding is interesting in relation to a study of an overbreathing epidemic in England (Moss & McEvedy, 1966). An initial report by some girls of fainting and dizziness was followed by an outbreak of similar complaints, with 85 girls needing to be taken to the hospital by ambulance—"they were going down like ninepins." A comparison of the girls who were affected with those who were not demonstrated, as expected, that the affected girls were higher in both neuroticism and extroversion. In other words, those individuals with a predisposing personality proved most susceptible to influence by suggestions of a real epidemic.

Finally, the results of a recent research investigation of study habits among introverts and extroverts may be of particular interest to college students. The research examined whether such personality differences are associated with differing preferences for where to study and how to study, as would be predicted by Eysenck's theory. In accord with Eysenck's theory of individual differences, the following was found: (1) Extroverts more often chose to study in library locations that provided external stimulation than did introverts. (2) Extroverts took more study breaks than did introverts. (3) Extroverts reported a preference for a higher level of noise and for more socializing opportunities while studying than did introverts (Campbell & Hawley, 1982). An important implication of such research is that different environmental designs for libraries and residence units might best fit the needs of introverts and extroverts.

In sum, the introversion–extroversion dimension represents an important organization of individual differences in behavioral functioning that is rooted in inherited differences in biological functioning. These differences can be discovered through the use of factor analysis and measured through the use of questionnaires as well as in laboratory procedures. Let us now pick up on the other two dimensions and at least briefly consider how the theory is extended into other realms, though generally less is known about the psychoticism dimension than is known for the neuroticism dimension. According to Eysenck, people high on neuroticism tend to be emotionally labile and frequently complain of worry and anxiety as well as of bodily aches (e.g., headaches, stomach difficulties, dizzy spells, etc.). Here too an inherited biological difference in nervous system functioning is suggested as the basis for individual differences on this dimension. In this case, the underlying principle is that individuals high on neuroticism respond quickly to stress and show a slower decrease in the stress response once the danger has disappeared than is true for more stable (low neuroticism) individuals. Although less is known about the basis for the psychoticism dimension, here too a genetic association is suggested, in particular one linked with maleness. In general, then, genetic factors play a major role in determining personality and social behavior. Indeed, according to Eysenck "genetic factors contribute something like two-thirds of the variance in major personality dimensions" (1982, p. 28).

Eysenck's theory of personality is closely linked to his theory of abnormal psychology and behavior change. The kind of symptoms or psychological difficulties one is likely to develop are related to basic personality characteristics and principles of nervous system functioning. For example, according to Eysenck a person develops neurotic symptoms because of the joint action of a biological system and of experiences that contribute to the learning of strong emotional reactions to fear-producing stimuli. Thus, the vast majority of neurotic patients tend to have high neuroticism and low extroversion scores (Eysenck, 1982, p. 25). In contrast, criminals and antisocial persons tend to have high neuroticism, high extroversion, and high psychoticism scores. Such individuals show a weak learning of societal norms.

Despite the strong genetic component in the development and maintenance of such disorders, Eysenck claims that one need not be pessimistic concerning the potential for treatment: "The fact that genetic factors play a large part in the initiation and maintenance of neurotic disorders and also of criminal activities, is very unwelcome to many people who believe that such a state of affairs must lead to therapeutic nihilism. If heredity is so important, they say, then clearly behavior modification of any kind must be impossible. This is a completely erroneous interpretation of the facts. What is genetically determined are predispositions for a person to act and behave in a certain manner, when put in certain situations" (1982, p. 29). Accordingly, it is possible for a person to avoid certain potentially traumatic situations, to unlearn certain learned fear responses, or to learn (acquire) certain codes of social conduct. Thus, while emphasizing the importance of genetic factors, Eysenck has been a major proponent of behavior therapy or the systematic treatment of abnormal behavior according to the principles of learning theory. We will not extend Eysenck's discussion of behavior therapy here since the basic principles will be covered in the chapter on learning foundations of personality (Chapter 11). However, we may conclude our discussion here by noting that Eysenck has been a frequent, outspoken critic of psychoanalytic theory and therapy. In particular, his criticism has emphasized the following points: (1) Psychoanalysis is not a scientific theory since it is not falsifiable. (2) Neurotic and psychotic disorders constitute separate dimensions rather than points on a continuum of regression. (3) Abnormal behavior represents learned maladaptive responses rather than disguised expressions of underlying, unconscious conflicts. (4) All therapy involves the application, intended or otherwise, of learning principles. In particular, therapy with neurotic behaviors involves the unlearning or extinction of learned responses (Eysenck, 1979). According to Eysenck, psychoanalysis is not generally an effective method of treatment and succeeds only to the extent that the principles of behavior therapy are unwittingly or accidentally brought into play by the analyst.

Comment on Eysenck

Befitting a trait theorist, Eysenck's scientific record has been consistent in a number of ways. Noteworthy among the positive aspects of this record we may include the following: (1) Eysenck has been a prolific contributor to diverse areas. In addition to his continuing focus on individual differences and principles of behavior change he has contributed to the study of criminology, education, aesthetics, genetics, psychopathology, and political ideology. (2) Eysenck has consistently emphasized the value of both correlation and experimental research. Referring to Cronbach's discussion of the two disciplines of scientific psychology (Chapter 2), Eysenck suggests that he has "always looked upon these two disciplines not as in any sense rivals, but as complementary to each other, and indeed each one essential for the success of the other" (1982, p. 4). (3) Eysenck has tied his personality variables to methods of measurement, a theory of nervous system functioning and learning, and an associated theory of psychopathology and behavior change. Significant here is the fact that the theory goes beyond description and can be tested. (4) Historically, Eysenck has been prepared to swim against the tide and argue in favor of unpopular views: "I have usually been against the establishment and in favor of the rebels. Readers who wish to interpret this in terms of some inherited oppositional tendency, some acquired Freudian hatred of father substitutes, or in any other way are of course welcome. I prefer to think that on these issues the majority were wrong, and I was right. But then of course I would think that; only the future will tell" (1982, p. 298).

Given these noteworthy contributions one might wonder, as was done by one recent reviewer of Eysenck's work, why Eysenck has not been "universally celebrated by psychologists everywhere" (Loehlin, 1982, p. 623). Prominent among the reasons for this is Eysenck's tendency to dismiss the contributions of others and exaggerate the empirical support for his own point of view (Buss, 1982, Loehlin, 1982). Most psychologists familiar with Eysenck's work feel that it is significant but that frequently he ignores contradictory findings and overstates the strength of positive results. In relation to this, two additional points can be made. First, alternative models have been proposed that are viewed as better fitting the findings to date. In one such model, it is suggested that individual differences on the dimensions of impulsivity and anxiety are critical (Gray, 1981). Here there is acceptance of the data emphasized by Eysenck and of the import of tying personality variables to biological functions, but different personality dimensions are emphasized. Second, many psychologists feel that it is impossible to account for so much in terms of individual differences with but two or three dimensions. As we shall see in the next section, the trait theorist Cattell suggests that we consider more traits and stay at the trait rather than the type level of personality description. Finally, there are psychologists who oppose the entire trait point of view, an issue that we will address in some detail at the end of this chapter.

THE TRAIT, FACTOR-ANALYTIC APPROACH OF RAYMOND B. CATTELL (1905–   )

Raymond B. Cattell was born in 1905 in Devonshire, England. He obtained a B.Sc. degree in chemistry from the University of London in 1924. Cattell then turned to psychology and obtained a Ph.D. degree at the same university in 1929. During these years he was a research assistant under Charles Spearman, a psychologist who pursued the view that all mental tests measure, to some extent, one basic intellectual ability. Before coming to the United States in 1937, Cattell did a number of studies in personality and acquired clinical experience while directing a child guidance clinic. Since coming to the United States he has held positions at Columbia, Harvard, Clark, and Duke Universities. For twenty years he was Research Professor of Psychology and Director of the Laboratory of Personality Assessment at the University of Illinois. During his professional career, he has written more than 200 articles and 15 books.

Although relatively little is known of the experiences that shaped Cattell's life and work, a number of influences seem apparent. First, Cattell's interest in the use of factor-analytic methods in personality research and his attempt to develop a hierarchical theory of personality organization can be related to his associations with two of the same British psychologists who influenced Eysenck, Spearman and Burt. Second, Cattell's views on motivation were influenced by another British psychologist, William McDougall.

His years spent jointly in personality research and clinical experience were a third influence on Cattell. These years sensitized him to the assets and limitations of clinical and experimental research. Finally, Cattell's earlier experience in chemistry influenced much of his later thinking in psychology. In chemistry, the development of the periodic table by Mendeleef in 1869 led to renewed experimental activity. Just as Mendeleef developed a classification of the elements in chemistry, much of Cattell's work can be viewed as an attempt to develop a classification (taxonomy) of variables for experimental research in personality.

Raymond B. Cattell

Cattell's writing conveys the sense of a person totally committed to a science of personality in general and to the factor-analytic approach in particular. In his book on *The Scientific Analysis of Personality*, Cattell (1965) opens with the following remarks:

> *Personalities react differently even to the study of personality. To the scientifically minded it is the supreme scientific challenge, promising formulae of fantastic and intriguing complexity. To others the notion that we will measure and predict in the field of human personality is a sacrilege and a threat. Yet in an age when we are investigating everything, how can we shut our eyes to the possibilities of scientifically studying personality?*

> Cattell, 1965a, p. 11

For Cattell, the understanding of personality is basic to the understanding of the more restricted and specialized disciplines in psychology, such as perception and learning. And, for Cattell, it is the factor-analytic model that will lead to the understanding of personality.

In reading Cattell there is, at times, the sense of his being unfair in underestimating the contributions of others and in overestimating the conclusiveness of his own findings. However, there is also the wonderful sense of a person who feels that he is on the path of progress and at the brink of discovery.

Cattell's View of Science, Theory, and Research Methods

An understanding of Cattell's view of science, theory, and research is critical for an understanding of his theory. Cattell ties his research method to his theory of personality more closely than perhaps any other personality theorist. For all of his exuberance, Cattell in no way minimizes the difficulties of understanding personality. Research in psychology is difficult because of the intangible and fluid quality of behavior, because of the problem of separating psychology as a science from the daily preoccupation of all humankind, and because of the unique situation in science of scientists studying themselves (Cattell, 1966b). In the face of the complexities of human behavior, Cattell argues that we must have methodological self-awareness instead of unsystematic investigation or compulsive methodology. Furthermore, he contends that we must have a close relationship between research methods and theory. Theory must be based on measurement, but measurement must be meaningful.

Cattell distinguishes among three methods in the study of personality: **bivariate, multivariate**, and **clinical.** The typical *bivariate* experiment, which follows the classical experimental design of the physical sciences, contains two variables, an independent variable that is manipulated by the experimenter and a dependent variable that is measured to observe the effects of the experimental manipulations. In contrast to the bivariate method, the *multivariate* method studies the interrelationships among many variables at once. Furthermore, in the multivariate experiment the investigator does not manipulate the variables. Instead, in multivariate research the experimenter allows life to make the experiments and then uses statistical methods to extract meaningful dimensions and causal connections. The method of factor analysis is illustrative of the multivariate method. Both the bivariate method and the multivariate method express a concern for scientific rigor. The difference between them is that, in the bivariate method, experimenters limit their attention to a few variables that they can manipulate in some way whereas, in the multivariate methods, experimenters consider many variables as they exist in a natural situation. The multivariate investigator can manipulate variables, but generally there is no need to do so.

Cattell is quite critical of the bivariate method. Many of his criticisms are similar to those discussed in Chapter 2 in relation to laboratory research. Thus, he argues that attention to the relationship between two variables represents a simplistic and piecemeal approach to personality. Human behavior is complex and expresses the interactions among many variables. Having understood the relationship between two variables, one is left with the problem of understanding how these relate to the many other variables that are important in determining behavior. Second, the fact that bivariate experimenters attempt to manipulate the independent variable means that they must neglect many matters that are of real importance in psychology. Since the more important emotional situations cannot be manipulated and therefore cannot be used in controlled experiments in humans, the bivariate researcher has been forced to attend to trivia, to look for answers in the behavior of rats, or to look for answers in physiology.

In contrast to the bivariate method, the *clinical* method has the virtues of studying important behaviors as they occur and looking for lawfulness in the functioning of the total organism. Thus, in scientific aims and in philosophical assumptions the clinical method and multivariate method are close to one another and separate from the bivariate method. Both the clinician and the multivariate researcher are interested in global events; both are interested in complex patterns of behavior as they occur in life; both allow life itself to be the source of experimental manipulation; and, both are interested in an understanding of the total personality instead of in isolated processes or fragmented pieces of knowledge. The difference between the clinician and the multivariate researcher is that while the former uses intuition to assess variables and memory to keep track of events, the latter uses experimental procedures and statistical analyses (Cattell, 1962). Thus, according to Cattell, "the clinician has his heart in the right place, but perhaps we may say that he remains a little fuzzy in the head" (1959c, p. 45). In the light of these similarities and differences, Cattell concludes that the clinical method is the multivariate method but without the latter's concern for scientific rigor. In sum, Cattell thinks the multivariate method has the desirable qualities of the bivariate and clinical methods (Figure 9.4). The statistical method Cattell associates with multivariate research is *factor analysis*, previously described in relation to the theory of Hans Eysenck. The major difference between the two theorists is that Cattell prefers to work at the trait level whereas Eysenck further factors his data to work at the type level (Figure 9.1).

The terms *measurement* and *taxonomy* are keys to understanding Cattell's efforts. We can make significant progress in research only when we have developed tools for description and measurement. Theory cannot be independent of measurement, and measurement must be related to meaningful conceptual units. Psychology is without its periodic table of the elements, but multivariate research and factor analysis *can provide* the tools for defining the basic structural elements of personality.

Bivariate	Clinical	Multivariate
Scientific rigor, controlled experiments	Intuition & professional Experience.	Scientific rigor, objective and quantitative analysis
Attention to few variables	Consideration of many variables	Consideration of many variables
Neglect of important phenomena	Study of important phenomena	Study of important phenomena
Simplistic, piecemeal	Interest in global events and complex patterns of behavior (total personality)	Interest in global events and complex patterns of behavior (total personality)

FIGURE 9.4   Cattell's Description of Bivariate, Clinical, and Multivariate Research Methods.

Cattell's Theory of Personality

Some background factors relating to Cattell's theory of personality now have been examined. The observation has been made that Cattell views behavior as complex and is committed to a multivariate, factor-analytic approach toward description and measurement. It is time now to look at the theory as it stands over thirty years of research.

Structure

Given Cattell's emphasis on taxonomy, one expects him to give considerable attention to the structure of personality. Indeed, in Kelly's terms, we may expect to find the structural aspects of personality to be the focus of convenience of Cattell's theory of personality.

Surface traits and source traits.   The basic structural element for Cattell is the **trait**, which was defined earlier as a predisposition. The concept of trait assumes some pattern and regularity to behavior over time and across situations. Some traits may be common to all people, others unique to an individual; some determined by heredity, others by the environment; some relate to motives (dynamic traits), and others to ability and to temperament. An important distinction among traits is that between **surface traits** and **source traits**. Surface traits are expressive of behaviors that on a superficial level may appear to go together but in fact do not always move up and down (vary) together and do not necessarily have a common cause. A source trait, on the other hand, expresses an association among behaviors that do vary together to form a unitary, independent dimension of personality. Whereas surface traits can be discovered through subjective methods such as asking people which personality characteristics they think go together, the refined statistical procedures of factor analysis are necessary for the discovery of source traits. These source traits represent the building blocks of personality.

Sources of data: L-data, Q-data, OT-data.   How do we discover source traits that cover a variety of responses across many situations? Where do we find our building blocks? According to Cattell, there are three sources of data: life record data **(L-data)**, questionnaire data **(Q-data)**, and objective test data **(OT-data)**. L-data relates to behavior in actual, everyday-life situations such as school grades or ratings of an individual on traits such as sociability, emotional stability, or conscientiousness. Q-data depends on introspection by the subject. Subject responses to questionnaires can be considered as accurate representations of the person or pieces of behavior that do not necessarily represent accurate appraisals of the subject himself; that is, if the subject says he is conscientious, we can either consider him to be so or just treat his response as a piece of behavior elicited by a question. Because of self-deception and faking, Cattell suggests the latter approach to Q-data.

The third source of data used to get at personality structure, OT-data, is, for Cattell, the most desirable. Cattell considers an objective test to be a behavioral miniature situation in which subjects are unaware of the relationship between their response and the personality characteristic being measured.

According to Cattell, if multivariate, factor-analytic research is indeed able to determine the basic structures of personality, then the same factors or traits should be obtained from L-data, Q-data, and OT-data. This is an important, logical, and challenging commitment. Research along these lines began with L-data. The goal of the original research was to obtain data on all aspects of human behavior, what Cattell called the **personality sphere**. It seemed most possible to gather a huge mass of data covering the personality sphere through L-data sources rather than through Q-data or OT-data sources. The strategy was to find source traits in L-data and then to determine if questionnaires and objective tests could be developed to reflect and test the same traits (Cattell, 1959b).

The original L-data research began with the assumption that the behaviors that cover the total personality sphere have their verbal symbols in language; that is, if we take all of the words used by individuals to describe behavior, we will have covered the personality sphere. A series of related analyses and experiments, including factor analysis, led to a total of fifteen L-data factors that appeared to account for most of the behaviors represented in the personality sphere.

The second part of Cattell's research strategy in collecting data on the personality sphere was to determine whether comparable factors could be found in Q-data. The main result of work with Q-data is the **Sixteen Personality Factor (16 P.F.) Inventory**. In the construction of the 16 P.F., Cattell used the personality dimensions found in ratings (L-data) as a source of hypotheses for test items. Thousands of questionnaire items were written and administered to large groups of normal people. Tests were run to see which items went together. Factor analyses were completed, leading to the development of the 16 P.F. Inventory. Of the sixteen factors or source traits measured by this questionnaire, twelve show considerable similarity with factors from L-data and four appear to be unique to Q-data. Illustrative L-data ratings for one trait and corresponding illustrative questionnaire items are presented in Figure 9.5. Cattell did not label his personality factors (traits) in standard terms to avoid misinterpretation of them. However, to convey some feeling for the kinds of trait dimensions that are found, we can consider the following terms as descriptive and illustrative: reserved–outgoing, relaxed–tense, submissive–dominant, concrete thinking–abstract thinking, practical–imaginative, and conservative–liberal. As can be seen, they cover a wide variety of aspects of personality functioning. In addition, some seem to be related to Eysenck's type dimensions while others appear to be more independent of them.

Cattell is committed to the use of questionnaires, in particular, factor analytically derived questionnaires such as the 16 P.F. On the other hand, Cattell also has expressed concern about the problems of motivated distortion and self-deception in relation to questionnaire responses. Also, he feels that the questionnaire is of particularly questionable utility with mental patients. Because of problems with L-data and Q-data, and because the original research strategy itself called for investigations with objective test (OT) data, Cattell's efforts have been concerned more recently with personality structure as derived from OT-data. It is the

---

SOURCE TRAIT C. EGO STRENGTH-VERSUS-EMOTIONALITY
AND NEUROTICISM, IN L- AND Q-DATA

Behavior ratings by observer on these elements:

Ego Strength		*Emotionality/Neuroticism*
Mature	vs	Unable to tolerate frustration
Steady, persistent	vs	Changeable
Emotionally calm	vs	Impulsively emotional
Realistic about problems	vs	Evasive, avoids necessary decisions
Absence of neurotic fatigue	vs	Neurotically fatigued (with no real effort)

Questionnaire responses on these items*:

Do you find it difficult to take no for an answer even when what you want to do is obviously impossible?
(a) yes   (b) *no*

If you had your life to live over again, would you
(a) *want it to be essentially the same?*   (b) Plan it very differently?

Do you often have really disturbing dreams?
(a) yes   (b) *no*

Do your moods sometimes make you seem unreasonable even to yourself?
(a) yes   (b) *no*

Do you feel tired when you've done nothing to justify it?
(a) *rarely*   (b) often

Can you change old habits, without relapse, when you decide to?
(a) *yes*   (b) no

---

*Answer in italic type indicates high ego strength.

FIGURE 9.5   Correspondence Between Data from Two Different Test Domains: L-Data Ratings and Q-Data Responses. (Cattell, 1965)

source traits as expressed in objective tests that are the "real coin" for personality research.

The results from L-data and Q-data researches were important in guiding the development of miniature test situations; that is, the effort was to develop objective tests, as defined by Cattell, that would measure the source traits already discovered. Thus, for example, tendencies to be assertive might be expressed in behaviors such as long exploratory distance on a finger maze test, fast tempo in arm-shoulder movement, and fast speed of letter comparisons. More than 500 tests were constructed to cover the hypothesized personality dimensions. These tests included speed tasks in which the subject had to cancel out letters, a test of motor-perceptual rigidity in which the subject had to write numbers of familiar words backwards, and a test in which two dreams were reported. The result of administering these tests to large groups of subjects and repeated factoring of data from different research situations has been the establishment of twenty-one OT-data source traits.

CURRENT APPLICATIONS AND IMPLICATIONS

"The Right Stuff"—Characteristics of Successful Business Executives

Some time ago Tom Wolfe wrote a book about the United States' first team of astronauts. At the time an all male group, these were men who felt that they had the right stuff—the manly courage it took to make it as a test pilot and astronaut. Others had the necessary skill, but if they didn't have the right stuff they just didn't make it.

Most demanding occupations have their own kind of right stuff—the personality characteristics or traits that, in addition to skill, make for success. For example, what makes for a top business executive? According to some recent research, the difference between those senior executives who make it to chief executive officer and those who do not often is subtle. Members of both groups show considerable talent and have remarkable strengths as well as a few significant weaknesses. While no one trait discriminates between the two groups, those who fall short of their ultimate goal frequently are found to have the following characteristics: insensitivity to others, untrustworthy, cold-aloof-arrogant, overly ambitious, moody, volatile under pressure, defensive. In contrast, the successful executives are most characterized by the traits of integrity and understanding others.

Actually, there is a long history of efforts to define the abilities and personal qualities of leaders. At one point, researchers began to give up on the hope of finding general leadership qualities. Leadership was seen as entirely situational in origin, with different skills and personal qualities being required in different situations. However, a recent review of the literature suggests that sounding the death bell of a trait approach to leadership probably was premature. Certain general qualities such as courage, fortitude, and conviction do stand out. In addition, the following traits seem to be generally characteristic of leaders: energetic, decisive, adaptive,

"The Right Stuff"—Success in different occupations requires possessing certain traits. Sally Ride is America's first female astronaut to be a member of the crew aboard the space shuttle.

assertive, sociable, achieving, and tolerant of stress.

Trait researchers, particularly those in industrial psychology, continue to try and define those personality characteristics that are essential for success in various fields. A variety of personality tests, including the 16 PF, are then used in many important aspects of personnel selection.

SOURCES: *Psychology Today*, February, 1983; B.M. Bass, 1981.

As mentioned before, the source traits or factors found in L-data and Q-data could, for the most part, be matched to one another. Also observed was the fact that Cattell's theory assumes that source traits are inherent structures in personality and that it should be possible to measure the same traits by ratings, questionnaires, or objective tests. How, then, do the OT-data factors match up with those derived from L-data and Q-data? Several relationships have been found between L-data and Q-data factors on the one hand, and OT-data factors on the other. However, no simple "point-to-point" relationship has been found.

The issue of the matching of factors in the three kinds of observation—ratings, questionnaires, and objective tests, is highly complex. It will be returned to in the critique and evaluation section. For now, what has been said in this section can be summarized by stating the following: (1) Cattell set out to define the structure of personality in three areas of observation, called L-data, Q-data, and OT-data. (2) He started his research in L-data, constructed a personality sphere of word symbols for behavioral characteristics, and through the factor analysis of ratings came up with fifteen source traits. (3) Guided in his research on Q-data by the L-data findings, Cattell developed the 16 P.F. Inventory, which contains twelve traits that match traits found in the L-data research and four traits that appear to be unique to questionnaire methods. (4) By using these results to guide his research in the development of objective tests, Cattell found twenty-one source traits in OT-data that appear to have a complex relationship to the traits previously found in the other data.

The source traits found in the three types of observation do not complete Cattell's formulation of the structure of personality. However, the traits presented in this section do describe the general nature of the structure of personality as formulated by Cattell. In other words, here we have the foundation for psychology's table of the elements—its classification scheme. But what is the evidence for the existence of these traits? Cattell (1979) cites the following: 1. The results of factor analyses of different kinds of data. 2. Similar results across cultures. 3. Similar results across age groups. 4. Utility in the prediction of behavior in the natural environment. 5. Evidence of significant genetic contributions to many traits.

Process

While Cattell has been concerned with the consistency of behavior and the structure of personality, he has also been concerned with process and motivation. As with traits, his efforts to determine the motivational sources of behavior continue to involve an emphasis on taxonomy and factor analysis. In his research on motivational processes, Cattell set out to determine the kinds of motives that exist and the components of a single motive. Although the motivational components of Cattell's theory are based on systematic research and the use of factor analysis, much of this explanation of the *why* of human behavior remains theoretical speculation.

According to Cattell, the basic source of human motivation lies in **ergs** or innate tendencies to react to goals in a specific way. These reflect the forces of innate biological drives. The socialization process may influence the overt expression of an erg, but the innate qualities of an erg can be observed in the emotional qualities and biological goals that are associated with it and that remain constant across cultures. Illustrative ergs are mating (sex), security–fear, and self-assertion. In contrast to Freud, Cattell does not indicate the presence of a destructiveness erg. Another group of motives, called **sentiments**, reflect environmentally determined patterns of behavior. Sentiments have their source in social institutions such as the family or school. Examples of sentiments would be the religious sentiment (''I want to worship God.''), the career sentiment (''I want to learn skills required for a job.''), and the self-sentiment (''I want never to damage my self-respect.''). Linked to sentiments and then to ergs are attitudes. An **attitude** represents a strength of interest in following out a particular course of action. An attitude may be expressed in terms of the following generalization (Cattell, 1965a, p. 176).

In these circumstances,	I	want so much	to do this	with that
stimulus situation	organism	interest of a certain intensity	specific goal and course of action	object concerned

According to Cattell, attitudes are invested with energy so as to satisfy sentiments, which themselves must be invested with energy in order to satisfy the basic ergs or biological goals ''For example, a person may study accountancy in order that he may keep his job in a big business, in order that he may earn money, in order that he may marry and have a family, and so on'' (Cattell, 1965a, p. 185). Illustrative attitudes associated with the sex and security–fear ergs are presented in Figure 9.6.

Clearly Cattell does not view the person as a static entity or as behaving the same way in all situations. How a person behaves at any one time depends on the traits and motivational variables (ergs, sentiments, attitudes) relevant to the situation. In addition, two other concepts are of particular importance in relation to accounting for variability in behavior—states and roles. The concept of **state** relates to emotional and mood changes that are partly determined by the provocative power of specific situations. Illustrative states are anxiety, depression, fatigue, arousal, and curiosity. Whereas traits describe *general* action patterns,

---

Sex Erg Attitudes

I want to love a person I find attractive.
I want to satisfy my sexual needs.
I want to dress to impress the opposite sex.
I like a novel with love interest and a ravishing heroine.

Security-Fear Erg Attitudes

I want more protection from nuclear weapons.
I want to reduce accidents and diseases.
I want to take out more insurance against illness.
I want never to be an insane patient in a mental hospital.

FIGURE 9.6   Attitudes Expressive of Sex and Fear Ergs.

Cattell emphasizes that the *exact* description of an individual at a given moment requires measurement of both traits and states: "Every practicing psychologist—indeed every intelligent observer of human nature and human history—realizes that the state of a person at a given moment determines his or her behavior as much as do his or her traits" (1979, p. 169). In other words, behavior in a particular situation cannot be predicted from traits alone without regard for whether the person is angry, tired, fearful, and so on.

The second important transient influence relates to the concept of **role**. According to Cattell, certain behaviors are more tied up with environmental situations than with the general run of personality factors. Thus, customs and mores may modify the influence of personality traits so that "everyone may shout lustily at a football match, less lustily at dinner, and not at all in church" (1979, p. 250). In addition, the concept of role gives expression to the fact that the very same stimulus is perceived in a different way by an individual according to his role in the situation. For example, a teacher may respond differently to a child's behavior in the classroom than when no longer in the role of teacher.

In sum, although Cattell believes that personality factors lead to a certain degree of stability to behavior across situations, he also believes that a person's mood (state) and the way he is presenting himself in a given situation (role) will influence his behavior: "How vigorously Smith attacks his meal depends not only on how hungry he happens to be, but also on his temperament and whether he is having dinner with his employer or is eating alone at home" (Nesselroade & Delhees, 1966, p. 583). Cattell's theory suggests that behavior expresses the individual's traits that operate in a situation, the ergs and sentiments associated with attitudes relevant to a situation, and the state and role components that may vary from time to time or situation to situation. As factor analysis has been used to develop a taxonomy of personality traits and states, what is needed now is a mapping of the environment leading to a taxonomy of situations (Cattell, 1979, p. 273).

Growth and Development

Cattell has been concerned with two major issues relevant to the growth and development of personality—the determinants of personality and the pattern of development of the structural traits. Like most personality theorists, Cattell emphasizes the importance of both heredity and learning—of nature and nurture—in the development of personality. However, he is virtually unique among major personality theorists in that he has tried to determine the specific environment and hereditary contributions to each trait.

Cattell has developed a method, the **Multiple Abstract Variance Analysis (MAVA) Method** to determine how much influence heredity and environment have in the development of different traits (Cattell, 1965b). This method involves administering a number of personality tests to the members of a large number of families. The data are then analyzed in relation to four kinds of influences: within-family environmental differences, between-family environmental differences, within-family hereditary differences, and between-family hereditary differences. Through the use of a number of equations, the researcher is able to determine the genetic and environmental influences on the development of a trait. The importance of these two influences has been found to vary with the trait. For example, it is estimated that heredity accounts for 80 to 90 percent of the variation found in scores on a measure of the intelligence ability trait. The genetic influence on neuroticism also has been found to be considerable, although it is only about half that found in intelligence. On the other hand, how emotionally sensitive one is and how carefree as opposed to cautious one is appear to be determined mainly by environmental influences. One estimate has been made that overall personality is about two-thirds determined by environment and one-third by heredity (Hundleby, Pawlik, & Cattell, 1965).

Cattell emphasizes the interaction between hereditary and environmental influences in personality development. The type of genetic endowment that individuals bring into the world will influence the responses of others to them, will influence the ways in which they learn, and will set limits on the modifiability of their personalities by environmental forces. This latter aspect of the interaction between nature and nurture is of particular importance. It is expressed in Cattell's principle of *coercion to the biosocial mean*. This suggests that society typically exerts pressure on genetically different individuals to conform to a social mean. For example, the naturally more dominant person is encouraged by society to be less dominant, and the naturally submissive person is encouraged to show more self-assertion.

The process of personality development is further complicated by maturation. Maturation may delay the full-blown appearance of genetic influences in traits. Furthermore, maturation may influence the kind of learning that occurs in relation to traits at any given time in the development of the organism. For example, learning to walk cannot occur until a certain degree of physical development has occurred. In general, it is Cattell's belief that the early years are of particular importance to personality formation. In fact, he concludes that much of the basic formation of personality occurs before the age of seven years. In relation to this complex developmental process, Cattell has conducted research on *age trends* in the formation of personality traits. This research on age trends is part of an effort to discover the personality traits that will characterize children, adolescents, and adults at every stage of their development. Age-trends research also involves the study over time of the development of each trait. Much of the age-trends research suggests that the same underlying factors can be found, both in number and in kind, in subjects from age four through adulthood (Coan, 1966). On the other hand, a study of nursery school children indicated that only about one-third of the traits found in adults are found in children (Damarin & Cattell, 1968).

As with his structure and process conceptions of personality, Cattell attempts to give full attention to the complexity of growth and development. Traits are not due to heredity or environment, but to a complex interaction of both in relation to maturational factors; what is learned becomes incorporated into the developing personality structure, and this structure influences the course of future learning. Some of this complexity is expressed in Cattell's definition of personality learning as a "multi-dimensional change in response to a multi-dimensional situation" (Cattell, 1965a, p. 282). In other words, the individual responds to complex situations in ways that simultaneously affect many different parts of the personality. Experiences, especially early experiences, represent more than one-to-one associations between a stimulus and a response. Instead, experiences relate to the development of individual traits and to the overall organization of personality traits.

Clinical Applications of Cattell's Theory

Development in general is viewed in terms of the interaction between heredity and environment. In accord with this view, the cause of psychopathology is considered both in terms of inherited influences that predispose the individual to experience conflict and environmental influences that produce personal trauma. Cattell's conception of the development of psychopathology is based on a conflict model. According to the model, a drive is stimulated and then blocked. The individual attempts to break the barrier but fails and is forced to give up the goal. This leads to a state of conflict and anxiety that results in neurotic symptoms. A state of conflict exists when satisfaction of one drive is accompanied by frustration of another. Cattell has been able to develop a formula for computing the degree to which an individual's attitudes serve to satisfy some ergs (or sentiments) at the cost of satisfying other ergs (or sentiments). In one research effort, the resulting index of conflict was found to distinguish between mental patients and non-patients, to relate to estimates made by psychiatrists of the amount of conflict in each patient, and to relate to the 16 P.F. scale of ego weakness (Williams, 1959).

Basic to Cattell's approach to psychopathology is his effort to find concrete differences between normal people and members of various patient groups (Cattell & Rickels, 1964; Cattell & Tatro, 1966; Rickels & Cattell, 1965). In an important study of neuroticism and anxiety, it was found that neurotics differ from normals on several factors. Furthermore, it was found that anxiety is only one of many factors contributing to neurosis, that is, anxiety is a part, but not all, of neurosis (Cattell & Scheier, 1961). Some factors appear to be important for all forms of neurosis, although other personality factors are important only to some forms of neurosis. Thus, for example, high scores on anxiety and neuroticism and low scores on ego strength appear to characterize all neurotics, while a low score on surgency, indicative of restraint and reticence, is characteristic only of depressives. Psychotics have been found to differ from normals in personality source traits, but in ways different from that of neurotics. Psychotics share with neurotics low scores on ego strength but do not deviate on anxiety in the striking way neurotics do (Cattell & Tatro, 1966).

These are some of the results from Cattell's research into psychopathology. The major aspects of this approach are the effort to define factors experimentally for the general population and, then, the effort to define various types of psychopathology in terms of their unique patterns of scores on these factors. In this sense it is similar to Eysenck's efforts. However, in Eysenck's case there is an underlying theory of learning that enters into his explanation for the development of pathological behavior. Although Cattell has been working on a theory of learning (Cattell, 1980), no comparable explanation is available. Another difference is that whereas Eysenck views psychopathology in terms of specific behaviors, Cattell views pathology in terms of patterns of traits—a more holistic view. Similarly, whereas Eysenck emphasizes changes in specific behaviors in the course of behavior therapy, Cattell emphasizes changes in the overall pattern of personality organization. Finally, while Eysenck has specifically been involved with the application of behavior therapy to abnormal behavior, Cattell has not been associated with any particular form of psychotherapy. In sum, an emphasis on traits and the utilization of factor analysis can lead to both similarities and differences among theorists.

Comment on Cattell

One cannot help but be impressed with the scope of Cattell's efforts. His research has touched on almost every one of the dimensions we have outlined as relevant to personality theory—structure, process, growth and development, psychopathology, and change. Cattell has been a major force in the development of new factor-analytic techniques and in the development of new techniques for determining the genetic contribution to personality. His work covers almost all age ranges and the use of a wide variety of measurement techniques. Furthermore, he has endeavored to put his work in a cross-cultural perspective. There have been studies on levels of neuroticism in different countries and a cross-cultural comparison of patterns of extroversion and anxiety (Cattell & Warburton, 1961). Also, an effort has been made to develop a culture-free intelligence test that uses materials unfamiliar to all subjects.

How, then, is this massive effort to be evaluated? Cattell can be praised for his breadth of interests, the range of questions he has attacked, and the progress he has made in systematizing his findings. However, his work has been criticized because of problems associated with the use of factor analysis, because of the questionable validity of the tests used, and because the data collected often appear to be superficial in comparison with the wide-ranging interpretations of the findings. Indeed, a curious mixture of rigorous methodology and theoretical speculation is found in Cattell. Also, as was true for Eysenck, overstatement often is characteristic of Cattell. Unfortunately, in being so committed to his point of view he is at times unduly accepting of his own efforts and disparaging of the works of others. For example, the gains of the clinical and bivariate approaches are minimized, and the ones of the multivariate approach are overstated.

In any case, it is strange that a man who has produced so much and who is so convinced of his being on the right path should be so ignored by many psychologists. Some reviews of Cattell's work have commented on this tendency of psychologists to respect Cattell but also to ignore him, and for psychologists to be unaware of the scope and sophistication of Cattell's conceptions. This is in part because of the complexity of the methods he uses and in part because of the difficulty psychologists have in interpreting his factors. However, we can rely on Cattell to continue with his efforts in spite of his being ignored by others. Cattell knows that in the past people have been resistant to the use of new scientific techniques and have been slow to act on discoveries. "Captain Lancaster discovered the cause and cure for scurvy at sea in 1605, but sailors died of scurvy for 200 years more before naval surgeons acted on the discovery. In our time, thirteen years elapsed between Fleming's discovery of penicillin and its availability for use in clinical medicine" (Cattell, 1962, p. 265). We can rely on Cattell to pursue his work because he has an aesthetic appreciation of the complexity of human behavior and because he feels that the future of the field is with him.

OVERALL EVALUATION OF TRAIT THEORY

We have now considered three approaches to a trait conceptualization of personality. It is clear that major differences exist among trait theorists. At the same time, it is the common emphasis on characteristic patterns of behaving that provides a unifying base. Previously we have considered the contributions of each theorist. Here we shall consider some issues relevant to trait theory generally. Specifically, we shall consider the evidence supporting the existence of traits, the utility of factor analysis in personality research, the evidence concerning genetic determinants of personality and, finally, the utility of the trait concept itself.

The Evidence: Trait Theory and Situationist Criticism

Over the past decade trait theory has come in for considerable criticism because of the emphasis it gives to the hierarchical organization of stable and enduring properties of the person. In particular, critics of trait theory argue that behavior is much more variable from situation to situation than trait theorists suggest (Mischel, 1968). Furthermore, the critics claim that trait theory has proven to be ineffective in predicting behavior. Instead of an emphasis on broad predispositions in the *person* to respond in a certain way, many of these critics emphasize the importance of *situations*, or rewards in the environment, in the control of human behavior. Thus, for some time debate raged over whether regularities in behavior could be accounted for by aspects of the person, such as traits, or by aspects of the situation—the person–situation controversy.

Criticism of the trait conception of personality has focused on two points. First, critics of trait theory suggest that there is a lack of evidence of cross-situational consistency to behavior (Mischel, 1968; Mischel & Peake, 1982). An incredible amount of recent personality research has centered on the question of whether people are or are not consistent over time and, more significantly, across situations. Second, critics of trait theory suggest that traits reflect systematic distortions in the ways we perceive events and biases based on our conceptions of personality characteristics that we assume go together. In other words, rather than representing *actual* behavioral co-occurrences, traits represent labels for what we *believe* goes with what (Shweder, 1982). In a sense, the suggestion here is that traits represent constructs or stereotypes rather than actual regularities in behavior. This is particularly possible, it is claimed, where the existence of traits is based on Q-data in which subjects may respond in terms of their systematic distortions of which behaviors they think go with which behaviors. Although the question of the extent of consistency in individual behavioral functioning is an old issue that concerned psychologists in the 1930s, it has lately retaken center stage in personality research.

In the renewal of investigations on the consistency question, the situationist, antitrait point of view at first predominated; of late, proponents of trait theory have rallied to the defense. Their arguments have taken varied forms, which have focused on the following topics and claims:

1. *Quality of Research*. Most studies fail to find evidence of consistency and stability because they are poorly conducted. When relevant research is properly conducted, supportive evidence is found (Block 1977; Olweus, 1981).

2. *Adequacy of Sample*. One cannot consider single acts or measures of behavior on single occasions as evidence for or against the existence of a trait. Too much error is involved in the measurement of single acts on single occasions. With an adequate sampling of many behaviors over many occasions, one increases reliability of observation and finds evidence of consistency (Epstein, 1982, 1983).

3. *Phenotype–Genotype*. Many behaviors that appear to be different (phenotype) may in fact have the same underlying basis (genotype). Thus, what antitrait theorists take to be indicative of lack of consistency may at another level, in fact, be expressive of consistency (Loevinger & Knoll, 1983).

4. *Some People More Than Others*. Some people are more consistent than others. Therefore, one will only find evidence of consistency if one studies people who are consistent on that trait (Bem & Allen, 1974).

5. *Some Situations More Than Others.* People will be more consistent in some situations than in others. One consideration here is that people will be more consistent in situations that are low in constraint or weak in pressure to conform (Monson, Hesley, & Chernick, 1982). This point is particularly interesting since the phenomena that impress the clinician concerning evidence of consistency generally show up in those situations that are less structured and more ambiguous or anxiety arousing. Another consideration here is that people may behave similarly in situations perceived by them to be similar (Champagne & Pervin, 1983; Lord, 1982).

6. *Real World versus Laboratory.* The evidence in support of consistency is better when self-report data and observations in the natural environment are used as opposed to laboratory test data (Block, 1977). Why should this be so? One reason is that laboratory situations tend to be high in situational constraint and thereby minimize individual differences in response. Another reason is that the laboratory situation removes from the individual the possibility of selecting and creating situations. In other words, in the real world people behave consistently in part because they select and shape the very situations that influence their behavior (Allport, 1961; Snyder, 1981; Wachtel, 1973).

Obviously these arguments in support of trait theory are in addition to the factor analytic and genetic evidence presented by Eysenck and Cattell in support of the existence of traits. Beyond this, it is clear that often situationist criticism presents a distorted picture of trait theory, as if it is suggested that the person or trait alone accounts for behavior—the situation has nothing to do with behavior. It is clear, however, that trait theorists recognize the importance of situations. Traits represent predispositions to respond in specific ways which become manifest when behavior is considered over a wide range of situations. Perhaps the trait position in this regard is best summarized by Eysenck as follows:

Altogether I feel the debate is an unreal one. You cannot contrast persons and situations in any meaningful sense, or ask which is more important, because clearly you will always have person-in-situations, and the relative importance of personality and situational factors depends on the nature of the situation, the selection of people, and in particular the selection of traits measured. No physicist would put such a silly question as: Which is more important in melting a substance—the situation (heat of the flame) or the nature of the substance!

Eysenck [personal communication], August 7, 1978

The person–situation debate and argument concerning evidence for and against the consistency of behavior go on. The fact of the matter is that most personality psychologists agree that there is evidence for both consistency or stability and for inconsistency or variability. They disagree about how much of each and, perhaps more significantly, the utility of a trait concept in accounting for regularities that do exist. Thus, to a certain extent, we are left with differing views as to how much variability in behavior one considers damaging to a trait concept (or, conversely, how much stability is supportive) and how much faith one has that further gains can be made through exploration of trait concepts. At this time, neither trait nor situationist theories do a terribly good job of predicting wide ranges of individual behaviors over varied situations, or of helping us to understand *both* stability and change in personality functioning (Funder & Ozer, 1983; Pervin, 1983).

The Method: Factor Analysis

Central to much of trait theory is the utilization of factor analysis. The utility of this procedure is not, however, something about which there is agreement among psychologists. A number of specific questions come into play. For example, how do we know how many factors or traits exist? Factor analysis is an objective, mathematical procedure. However, there are variations in some details that leave room for investigator judgment. Thus, although both Eysenck and Cattell use factor analysis to gain insight into the structure of personality, the factor-analytic procedure used by Eysenck results in the identification of few factors; that used by Cattell results in the identification of many.

Another issue: Are the same factors being identified in different studies? The answer should be yes if we are really discovering the basic structure of personality. It must be yes if we are to consider the results reliable and replicable. Although Cattell argues that his factors have been identified in numerous studies, others report that they have not been able to replicate them. In reviewing the evidence, one psychologist asks whether these personality factors are "sensitive plants" that can be bred under certain conditions or are "hardy perennials" and concludes that they are the former (Howarth, 1972).

A third issue concerns some questionable assumptions of factor analysis. For example, factor analysis considers the joint rise and decline of behaviors. But suppose that two behaviors are related in a complex fashion such that they sometimes move in the same direction and sometimes in the opposite direction. In this case, the factor-analytic procedure will not discern the relationship between the variables. The general point that can be made is that factor analysis considers simple, linear relationships while personality functioning may often involve more complex relationships among variables.

Given these and other questions, we may ask whether we can rely on factor analysis to discover the basic dimensions or underlying structure of personality. It is clear that Cattell remains convinced that factor analysis is an adequate, in fact, necessary tool for the job. Eysenck, though supportive of its utilization as an investigative tool, recognizes the subjective aspects involved and is critical of the value and importance attached to it by Cattell (1982, p. 263). Others have even more serious reservations. Allport, while committed to trait theory, expressed the feeling that the factors identified through this procedure "resemble sausage meat that has failed to pass the pure food and health inspection'' (1958, p. 251). Another psychologist suggests that there is ''less there than meets the eye'' (Lykken, 1971) while a third suggests that ''factor analysis is as appropriate for the unraveling of a dynamic system as complex as man as a centrifuge might be, though the latter rotation would also yield some real and independent components of man's basic stuff'' (Tomkins, 1962, p. 287). In sum, the factor-analytic procedure has its problems; and researchers in the field are far from agreeing on its place in personality research.

Genetic Determinants

Both Eysenck and Cattell place considerable emphasis on the inherited, biological component of individual traits and traits generally. Although one can be a trait theorist without emphasizing genetic determinants, most major trait theorists subscribe to such a point of view. The issue here is complex and goes far beyond trait theory. That is, the extent to which and the way in which personality characteristics are influenced by genetic factors raise issues that transcend trait theory. Research in this area has become quite sophisticated while remaining controversial. Historically, the waxing and waning of interest in and emphasis on genetic factors have often provided focal points for political controversy (Pervin, 1984, Chapter 2).

In general, evidence does appear to be accumulating to suggest that many important personality characteristics do have a genetic component to them. Recently, the interesting suggestion was made that some personality traits may be determined by the interaction of a number of genetic influences rather than by a single or additive genetic influence (Lykken, 1982). Under such circumstances, the trait will only appear where the necessary interactions have occurred and will not necessarily run in families in any consistent way. In other words, just as the contributions to behavior can be configural rather than additive, so this may be true for the influence of genes on personality trait formation.

Before leaving this issue, it is important to keep in mind that because a trait is genetically influenced does not mean that it is genetically determined or fixed. What is determined by genes is how the organism initially responds to the environment and not the trait or personality characteristic itself. In addition, as Eysenck emphasized, because a personality characteristic is inherited does not mean that it cannot be altered through chemical or psychological means.

The Trait Concept

Until now we have considered the evidence concerning consistency and factor analysis as a method of discovery. But what of the essence of the trait concept itself? Is this the best concept for us to bank on and, if not, why not?

To a certain extent, this is a hard issue to address since different trait theorists include different things in the trait concept. Some emphasize consistency more

FIGURE 9.7 **SUMMARY OF STRENGTHS AND
LIMITATIONS OF TRAIT THEORY**

STRENGTHS	LIMITATIONS
1. Investigates relationships among many variables or characteristics.	1. Neglects systematic inquiry into the relation of situations to traits and behaviors.
2. Emphasizes different kinds of research and data: laboratory, naturalistic observation, questionnaire.	2. Relies excessively at times on factor analysis and questionnaires.
3. Develops personality questionnaires.	3. Uses static concepts to the neglect of dynamic processes.

than do others. Some tie traits to observable behaviors while others, such as Eysenck, emphasize underlying regularities and thereby seek to avoid the circularity of some trait concepts (i.e., the trait being defined in terms of observed behaviors and then used to explain the very same behaviors). However, what is essential to trait theory is the emphasis on observed consistency in *behavior*, and it is with this that some personality psychologists most wish to take issue. The argument here would be that while personality structure exists, and there is consistency, trait concepts place too much emphasis on overt behavior and present a too static picture of human functioning (Pervin, 1983). Such arguments, for example, would be made by proponents of psychoanalytic theory or by proponents of other dynamic points of view. In other words, the issue here is not consistency and person versus situation, but rather that of the best way of conceptualizing the structure and consistency that do exist.

Some time ago, the personality psychologist Henry Murray explained his rejection of the trait concept in the following way: "According to my prejudice, trait psychology is over-concerned with recurrences, with consistency, with what is clearly manifested (the surface of personality), with what is conscious, ordered, and rational" (1938, p. 715). Murray's preference was for the concept of need. "Need" may be a momentary process, one that may be present within the organism without becoming manifest directly or overtly in behavior. Theories based on "needs" and "drives" have lost popularity in psychology. These concepts may or may not yet prove to be useful. Murray's criticism would appear, however, to still have merit. In other words, the problem with the trait concept may not be that it exaggerates the consistency of personality but rather that it fails to do justice to the complex interplay among the determinants of behavior. To their credit Allport, Eysenck, and Cattell have attempted to recognize and do justice to this complexity. Whether the trait concept itself is adequate to the task remains to be seen.

MAJOR CONCEPTS AND SUMMARY

Allport

cardinal traits, central traits, secondary dispositions

functional autonomy

idiographic research

Eysenck

factor analysis

types

introversion–extroversion, neuroticism, psychoticism

Cattell

bivariate, multivariate, clinical methods

factor analysis

surface traits and source traits

L-data, Q-data, OT-data

Sixteen Personality Factor Inventory (16 P.F.)

attitude

ergs and sentiments

state

role

MAVA method

trait anxiety and state anxiety

In this chapter we have explored three theories of personality that emphasize the concept of trait, or a predisposition to respond to situations in a particular way. In addition, there is the view of personality structure as hierarchically organized (e.g., habits, traits, types). One of the early proponents of trait theory was Gordon W. Allport. He viewed traits as the basic units of personality, characterized by the properties of frequency, intensity, and range of situations. He also distinguished among cardinal traits, central traits, and secondary dispositions. Allport suggested that most people can be described in terms of traits that represent ranges of possible behaviors or aggregate descriptions of their behavior over a wide range of situations.

Whereas Allport conducted little research on traits and the structure of personality, the personality theorist Hans J. Eysenck has been quite active in this regard. While finding utility in the concept of trait, and in the even more abstract concept of type, Eysenck holds to four criteria for the utility of any such personality concept: (1) It must find support in factor-analytic studies; (2) One must be able to demonstrate a biological-genetic basis for the predictions based on the theory; (3) The concept must be related to theory and to specific predictions based on the theory; (4) The concept must be related to important social events and groups. With such criteria in mind and through the factor analysis of a wide variety of data on many different subject populations, Eysenck has been led to emphasize three basic dimensions of personality: Extroversion–Introversion, Neuroticism, and Psychoticism. Major attention was given to the extroversion–introversion dimension. The biological-genetic basis for associated individual differences and the relationship of such individual differences to functioning in a wide variety of areas was discussed in relation to Eysenck's criteria for an adequate concept of personality.

The trait theory of Raymond B. Cattell has been given extended discussion. Cattell's goal is the identification of the basic dimensions of personality and the development of a set of instruments to measure these dimensions—taxonomy (classification) and measurement. Multivariate research and factor analysis are viewed as providing the tools for defining the basic structural elements of personality. These basic structural elements are called traits and represent broad dispositional tendencies. Of particular interest are source traits which represent associations among behaviors that vary (increase and decrease) together. The argument has been made that, with some few exceptions, the same source traits can be found from the analysis of life record data (L-data), questionnaire data (Q-data), and objective test data (OT-data). The Sixteen Personality Factor Inventory has been developed to measure personality using questionnaire data. However, there is a preference for the use of objective test data. Using a variety of tests and subject populations, work goes on to discover the exact number of traits necessary to describe personality and to define the nature of these traits.

Dynamic traits, relating to the why and how of behavior, are of particular interest in relation to the process aspects of behavior. The basic conceptual unit in this area is that of attitude, representing a strength of interest in following a particular course of action. Some attitudes are tied to biological drives and are called ergs. Other attitudes are related to the socialization process and are called sentiments. Predicting behavior means that one must take into consideration both the various traits of the individual and such situational, transient variables as states (mood) and role. Behavior, then, is a function of both personality and situational determinants.

Cattell is interested in maturational factors and in the relative influence of heredity and environment in determining traits. In relation to maturation, Cattell has studied the development of traits by age at every stage of development. This research suggests that the same underlying factors can be found, both in number and in kind, in subjects from age four through adulthood. The relative influence of heredity and environment in relation to each trait is defined by the method called Multiple Abstract Variance Analysis (MAVA).

Cattell's research in the area of psychopathology has involved the analysis of factors on which normal and patient populations differ; that is, psychopathology is defined by differences observed between groups on the same factor tests. High scores on some factors are common to all forms of psychopathology (e.g., high anxiety and neuroticism scores for all neurotics) while some are specific to each form of pathology. Psychotherapy, where effective, involves a change in the pattern of traits as opposed to the change of specific behaviors.

There are strengths and limitations to the contributions of each of the trait theorists as well as to trait theory as a whole. While unified by an emphasis on individual differences and the concept of trait, there is diversity among trait theorists. Allport rejects factor analysis as a major tool in research whereas both Eysenck and Cattell make major use of it. Eysenck emphasizes the type level of analysis whereas both Allport and Cattell prefer to stay at the trait level, with Allport even questioning whether this level of analysis gives adequate attention to the uniqueness of the individual. The appeal of trait theory generally is that it focuses attention on individual differences and personality as a central part of psychological investigation. However, trait theory has come under attack for what is seen as a neglect of concern with situation variables and an excessive emphasis on consistency—the person–situation controversy. In addition, critics of trait theory emphasize the limitations of factor analysis as a method for discovering the structure of personality and the limitations of what is essentially a static conceptualization.

In many ways trait theory serves as a useful bridge between the more clinical theories covered earlier and the learning, behavioral theories yet to be covered. In part, this is because Cattell emphasizes the strengths, as well as the limitations, of both clinical and bivariate research, the latter being typical of learning or behavioral research. In addition, Eysenck emphasizes the importance of many traditional learning principles in the development of personality as well as in the application of behavior therapy. Thus, while some of the theorists yet to be covered are among the harshest critics of trait theory, they would agree with at least some points of emphasis.

Before turning to these contrasting approaches, we shall study an individual case from the standpoint of the four theoretical approaches already covered—psychoanalytic, Rogerian-phenomenological, personal construct, and trait. This will offer the opportunity to compare the approaches in terms of data gathered on the same person, thereby highlighting the contributions and distinctiveness of each.

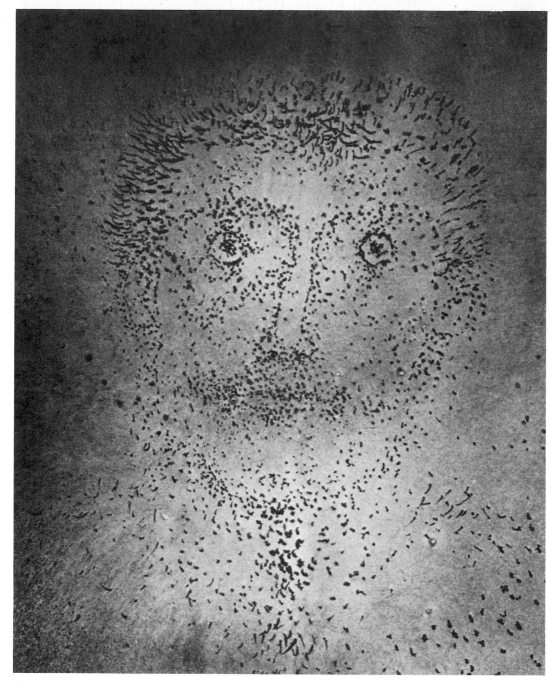

Klee, Paul. *Portrait of M.A.L.* 1924. Art Resource.

THEORY AND ASSESSMENT IN THE STUDY OF THE INDIVIDUAL: THE CASE OF JIM HERSH

Jim Hersh

Rorschach: Card 5

16 P. F.—Partial Profile

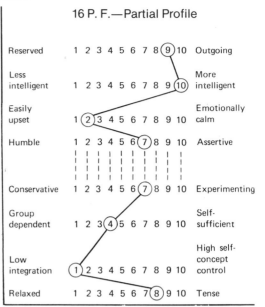

Reserved	1	2	3	4	5	6	7	8	(9)	10	Outgoing
Less intelligent	1	2	3	4	5	6	7	8	9	(10)	More intelligent
Easily upset	1	(2)	3	4	5	6	7	8	9	10	Emotionally calm
Humble	1	2	3	4	5	6	(7)	8	9	10	Assertive
Conservative	1	2	3	4	5	6	(7)	8	9	10	Experimenting
Group dependent	1	2	3	(4)	5	6	7	8	9	10	Self-sufficient
Low integration	(1)	2	3	4	5	6	7	8	9	10	High self-concept control
Relaxed	1	2	3	4	5	6	7	(8)	9	10	Tense

"Sort of brings to mind a dancing girl, sort of a stripper. Could almost be a ballet dancer on toes. Gypsy Rose Lee. Type that comes out with a magnificent gown. Sort of bowlegged. Body hidden by stuff to be discarded. A stripper (Stripper?) Nobody wears this unless it is to be taken off subsequently. Arms outstretched."

C hapter focus: In this chapter, we study the personality of an individual from the perspective of the preceding theories and methods of personality assessment.

A variety of approaches to personality have now been examined: Freud's psychoanalytic theory, Rogers' self-concept theory, Kelly's construct theory and Allport's, Eysenck's, and Cattell's trait approach. Each has been studied as an outgrowth of certain kinds of theorists as well as in relation to the data available to them. In particular, it has been emphasized that each theory tends to be associated with a different technique of *assessment* and with a different emphasis in research. *Beginning with different assumptions and styles of investigation, the theorists were led to use different tools to unravel the secrets of personality functioning. These different tools in turn led to the different observations that served as the basis for the theories examined here.*

In Chapter 1 it was suggested that theories of personality can be compared in terms of such criteria as comprehensiveness, parsimony or economy, logical consistency, and productivity in research. In this chapter we deal with another question: Are the observations obtained similar when assessment techniques associated with the different theories are applied to the same individual? Recall here the story of the wise blind men and the elephant. Each wise man examined a part of the elephant and assumed that he knew what it was. None knew that it was an elephant and each came to a different conclusion on the basis of his observations. One felt the tail and thought it was a snake, another a leg and thought it was a tree, another a trunk and thought it was a hose, and another a body and thought it was a wall. The study of one individual through the use of different techniques of assessment may provide us with a useful analogy: Do the theories refer to different parts of the same person, each representing an incomplete picture of the whole and each describing some of the same qualities in different terms, or do the theories refer to different people? When applied to an individual, are the theories talking about different parts of the individual, about the same parts but in different terms, or are they basically in conflict with one another?

THE CASE OF JIM HERSH

Jim Hersh was a student at Harvard when he agreed to serve as a subject for a project involving the intensive study of college students. He participated in the project mainly because of his interest in psychology. He also hoped that the tests given to him would give him a better understanding of himself. His autobiography reveals some of the essentials of his life. Jim was born in New York City after the end of the Second World War, the first child in a Jewish family, and received considerable attention and affection. Jim's father is a college graduate who owns an automobile sales business; his mother is a housewife who also does volunteer reading for the blind. He has a four-year-younger sister and two brothers, one five years younger and one seven years younger. The main themes in his autobiography concerned his inability to become involved with women in a satisfying way, his need for success and his relative failure since high school, and his uncertainty about whether to go on to graduate school in business administration or in clinical psychology.

Rorschach and TAT: Psychoanalytic Theory

The Rorschach Inkblot Test and Thematic Apperception Test, both projective, were administered to Jim by a professional clinical psychologist. On the Rorschach, which was first, Jim gave relatively few responses—22 in all. This is surprising in the light of other evidence of his intelligence and creative potential. It may be of interest here to follow along his responses to the first two cards and to consider the hypotheses formulated by the psychologist, who also is a practicing psychoanalyst.

CARD 1

JIM:	The first thing that comes to mind is a butterfly.
COMMENT:	Initially cautious and acts conventionally in a novel situation.
JIM:	This reminds me of a frog. Not a whole frog, like a frog's eyes. Really just reminds me of a frog.

COMMENT:	He becomes more circumspect, almost picky, and yet tends to overgeneralize while feeling inadequate about it.
JIM:	Could be a bat. More spooky than the butterfly because there is no color. Dark and ominous.
COMMENT:	Phobic, worried, depressed, and pessimistic.

CARD 2

JIM:	Could be two headless people with their arms touching. Looks like they are wearing heavy dresses. Could be one touching her hand against a mirror. If they're women, their figures are not good. Look heavy.
COMMENT:	Alert to people. Concern or confusion about sexual role. Anal-compulsive features. Disparaging of women and hostile to them—headless and figures not good. Narcissism expressed in mirror image.
JIM:	This looks like two faces facing each other. Masks, profiles—more masks than faces—not full, more of a façade, like one with a smile and one with a frown.
COMMENT:	He presents a façade, can smile or frown, but doesn't feel genuine. Despite façade of poise, feels tense with people. Repeated several times that he was not imaginative. Is he worried about his productivity and importance?

A number of interesting responses occurred on other cards. On the third card he perceived women trying to lift weights. Here again was a suggestion of conflict about his sexual role and about a passive as opposed to an active orientation. On the following card he commented that "somehow they all have an Alfred Hitchcock look of spooky animals," again suggesting a possible phobic quality to his behavior and a tendency to project dangers into the environment. His occasional references to symmetry and details suggested the use of compulsive defenses and intellectualization while experiencing threat. Disturbed and conflicted references to women come up in a number of places. At the beginning of this chapter we quoted his response to Card 5, involving a stripper. On Card 7, he perceived two women from mythology who would be good if they were mythological but bad if they were fat. On the next-to-last card he perceived "some sort of a Count, Count Dracula. Eyes, ears, cape. Ready to grab, suck blood. Ready to go out and strangle some woman." The reference to sucking blood suggested tendencies toward oral sadism, something which also appeared in another percept of vampires that suck blood. Jim followed the percept of Count Dracula with one of pink cotton candy. The tester interpreted this response as suggesting a yearning for nurturance and contact behind the oral sadism; that is, the subject uses his oral aggressive tendencies (e.g., sarcasm, verbal attacks) to defend against more passive oral wishes (e.g., to be fed, taken care of, and to be dependent).

The examiner concluded that the Rorschach suggested a neurotic structure in which intellectualization, compulsivity, and hysterical operations (irrational fears, preoccupation with his body) are used to defend against anxiety. However, it was suggested that Jim continues to feel anxious and uncomfortable with others, particularly authority figures. The report from the Rorschach concluded as follows. "He is conflicted about his sexual role. While he yearns for nurturance and contact from the motherly female, he feels very guilty about the cravings and his intense hostility toward women. He assumes a passive orientation, a continual role playing and, behind a facade of tact, he continues his rage, sorrow, and ambition."

What kinds of stories did Jim tell on the Thematic Apperception Test? Most striking about these stories was the sadness and hostility involved in all interpersonal relationships. In one story a boy is dominated by his mother, in another an insensitive gangster is capable of gross inhumanity, and in a third a husband is upset to learn that his wife is not a virgin. In particular, the relationships between men and women constantly involve one putting down the other. Consider this story.

> *Looks like two older people. The woman is sincere, sensitive, and dependent on the man. There is something about the man's expression that bespeaks of insensitivity—the way he looks at her, as if he conquered her. There is not the same compassion and security in her presence that she feels in his. In the end, the woman gets very hurt and is left to fend for herself. Normally I would think that they were married but in this case I don't because two older people who are married would be happy with one another.*

In this story we have a man being sadistic to a woman. We also see the use of the defensive mechanism of denial in Jim's suggestion that these two people cannot be married since older married people are always happy with one another. In the story that came after the one above again there is the theme of hostile mistreatment of a woman. In this story there is a more open expression of the sexual theme along with evidence of some sexual-role confusion.

> *This picture brings up a gross thought. I think of Candy. The same guy who took advantage of Candy. He's praying over her. Not the last rites, but he has convinced her that he is some powerful person and she's looking for him to bestow his good graces upon her. His knee is on the bed, he's unsuccessful, she's naive. He goes to bed with her for mystical purposes. [Blushes] She goes on being naive and continues to be susceptible to that kind of thing. She has a very, very sweet compassionate look. Could it possibly be that this is supposed to be a guy wearing a tie? I'll stick with the former.*

The psychologist interpreting these stories observed that Jim appeared to be immature, naive, and characterized by a gross denial of all that is unpleasant or dirty, the latter for him including both sexuality and marital strife. The report continued: "He is vacillating between expressing sadistic urges and experiencing a sense of victimization. Probably he combines both, often in indirect expressions of hostility while feeling unjustly treated or accused. He is confused about what meaningful relationships two people can have. He is ambivalently idealistic and pessimistic about his own chances for a stable relationship. Since he sees sex as dirty and as a mode for using or being used by his partner, he fears involvement. At the same time he craves attention, needs to be recognized, and is often preoccupied with sexual urges.''

Between the Rorschach and the Thematic Apperception Test a number of important themes come out. One theme involves a general lack of warmth in interpersonal relationships, in particular a disparaging and at times sadistic orientation toward women. In relation to women, there is conflict between sexual preoccupation and the feeling that sex is dirty and involves hostility. The second theme involves experiencing tension and anxiety behind a façade of poise. A third theme involves conflict and confusion about his sexual identity. Although there is evidence of intelligence and creative potential, there also is evidence of rigidity and inhibition in relation to the unstructured nature of the projective tests. Compulsive defenses, intellectualization, and denial are only partially successful in helping him deal with his anxieties.

What can be said about the data from the projective tests, particularly since these tests relate to psychoanalytic theory? The unstructured quality of these tests led to many personal responses that relate to unique aspects of Jim's personality. Furthermore, the unstructured quality of these tests allows for the development of a rich and varied response pattern that allows for some understanding of many different aspects of Jim's personality. Finally, the disguised quality of the tests allows us to penetrate the façade of his personality (in psychoanalytic terms his defenses) to be able to view his underlying needs, motives, or drives. We have a test that allows for considerable uniqueness of response and a theory of personality that is clinical in its emphasis on the individual. We have a test that disguises its true purpose and a theory of personality that is dynamic in its emphasis on behavior as a result of the interplay among forces, drives, conflicts, and layers of personality.

The picture of Jim given in the Rorschach and Thematic Apperception tests is quite different from that presented in the autobiography. In his autobiography Jim indicated that he received unlimited affection from his parents and was quite popular and successful through high school. He described himself as having a good relationship with his father. He described his mother as having ''great feeling for other people—she is a totally 'loving' woman.'' At the same time, we know that Jim feels he is troubled. In his autobiography he wrote that people had a high estimate of him because they could use only superficial criteria and that inwardly he was troubled. We thus have support for the interpretation in the Rorschach that he hides his tension and anxiety behind a façade of poise. There also is evidence in his autobiography of a conflicted relationship with women.

My relationships with women were somewhat better in high school than they are now, but they weren't really satisfying then either. I was operating in a small subculture then, and I was very respected by everyone, so that probably made me more popular than I would have been otherwise. I have never had a really long-term, intimate relationship with a girl and I think those are the only kind that are meaningful. I had a number of superficial relationships, but there was always a barrier set up against my really becoming involved, and that barrier has been reinforced and made stronger over the last four years. Once a girl starts liking me a great deal I start liking her less—this has obvious implications about my lack of feelings of self-worth. It's a vicious and self-defeating circle: I like a girl only until she starts to like me. Thus in high school I was much sought after, but I managed to remain safely uninvolved.

Jim did not like the Rorschach. He felt that he had to see something and that whatever he perceived would be interpreted as evidence that he was neurotic. He suggested that he didn't feel defensive about his troubles since he was willing to accept having them but he didn't want them overstated. When he read over some of the comments made by the psychologist, he observed that he himself believed that there was a sexual problem and that this would be the major issue if he went into therapy. Jim said that he had fears about ejaculating too quickly, his potency, and his ability to satisfy the female. It is interesting that the fear of losing control, or premature ejaculation, occurs in an individual who uses compulsive defenses and who strives to be in complete control of most situations.

What can be said about the relationship between the projective data and psychoanalytic theory? Clearly some of the importance of the data from the Rorschach and the TAT lies in the theoretical interpretations given to the responses, in particular the use of psychoanalytic symbolism. However, aside from this, it is difficult to determine how other theories of personality could make as much use of the data as psychoanalytic theory can. As we shall see, the data from the projectives are of a qualitatively different sort than those found in the other tests. It is only on the Rorschach that we obtain content such as "a stripper," "women trying to lift weights," "Count Dracula . . . ready to grab, suck blood. Ready to go out and strangle some woman," and "pink cotton candy." And only on the TAT are there repeated references to themes of sadness and hostility in interpersonal relationships. It is the content of the responses and the way in which the tests are handled that allows for the psychodynamic interpretations.

Obviously, Jim is not a Count Dracula and there is little overtly to suggest that he is a sadist. But the content of the projectives allows for the interpretation that an important part of his personality functioning involves a defense against sadistic urges. Obviously Jim does not still drink out of a milk bottle, but the references to sucking blood and to cotton candy, together with the rest of his responses, allow for the interpretation that he is partially fixated at the oral stage. It is interesting to observe in relation to this that Jim has an ulcer, which involves the digestive tract, and that he must drink milk to manage this condition.

Perhaps the point here is that if you let people's imaginations wander, you will be led to the world of the irrational. Freud not only allowed this but, indeed, encouraged it. He encouraged his patients to dream, to fantasize, to associate freely. He studied his subjects intensively and was exposed to the world of the individual and to the world of drives, conflicts, guilt, sex, and aggression. Encouraged to do so, Freud's patients reported feelings and memories that they were previously unaware of. Similarly, in Jim's Rorschach and TAT we have content and themes that seem out of character with the rest of his responses to other personality tests. Having access to these feelings and memories, Freud was able to draw certain relationships between them and the problems that first brought his patients to treatment. In Jim's case we can guess in the same way that it is his sexual confusion and latent hostility that make him feel anxious or insecure and that prevent him from becoming involved with women. Finding himself making discoveries in the world of the irrational and basing his theory on observations with patients, Freud was led to overemphasize the importance of the unconscious and to overemphasize the pathological in individuals. Similarly, Jim's performance on the projectives gives little indication of the skills, talents, and resources he has used to make some significant achievements.

Semantic Differential: Phenomenological Theory

How do these observations compare with those obtained from other assessment techniques? Jim filled out the semantic differential, rating the concepts self, ideal-self, father, and mother on 104 scales. Typical scales were authoritarian-democratic, conservative–liberal, affectionate–reserved, warm–cold, and strong–weak. Each of the four concepts was rated on the same scales so that comparisons could be made of the meaning of these concepts for Jim. The test is clearly different from the Rorschach in being undisguised rather than disguised. The semantic differential test does not immediately follow from Rogerian theory. However, we can interpret data from the test in relation to Rogerian theory, since there is a phenomenological quality to the data and we are assessing the individual's perception of his self and his ideal self.

First, we look at the ways in which Jim perceives his self. Jim perceives himself as intelligent, friendly, sincere, kind, and basically good. The ratings suggest that he sees himself as a wise person who is humane and interested in people. At the same time, other ratings suggest that he does not feel free to be expressive and uninhibited. Thus he rates himself as reserved, introverted, inhibited, tense, moral, and conforming. There is a curious mixture of perceptions of being involved, deep, sensitive, and kind while also being competitive, selfish, and disapproving. There is also the interesting combination of perceiving himself as being good and masculine while at the same time he perceives himself to be weak and insecure. One gets the impression of an individual who would like to believe that he is basically good and capable of genuine interpersonal relationships at the same time that he is bothered by serious inhibitions and high standards for himself and others.

This impression comes into sharper focus when we consider the self ratings in relation to those for the ideal self. In general, Jim did not see an extremely large gap between his self and his ideal self. However, large gaps did occur on a number of important scales. In an arbitrary way, we can define a gap of three or more positions on a seven-point scale as considerable and important. Thus, for example, Jim rated his self as 2 on the weak–strong scale and his ideal self as 7 on the same scale—a difference of five positions. In other words, Jim would like to be much stronger than he feels he is. Assessing his ratings on the other scales in a similar way, we find that Jim would like to be more of each of the following than he currently perceives himself to be: warm, active, equalitarian, flexible, lustful, approving, industrious, relaxed, friendly, and bold. Basically two themes appear. One has to do with *warmth*. Jim is not as warm, relaxed, and friendly as he would like to be. The other theme has to do with *strength*. Jim is not as strong, active, and industrious as he would like to be.

Jim's ratings of his mother and father give some indication of where he sees them in relation to himself in general and these qualities in particular. First, if we compare the way Jim perceives his self with his perception of his mother and father, clearly he perceives himself to be much more like his father than his mother. Also, he perceives his father to be closer to his ideal self than his mother, although he perceives himself to be closer to his ideal self than either his mother or his father. However, in the critical areas of warmth and strength, the parents tend to be closer to the ideal self than Jim is. Thus, his mother is perceived to be more warm, approving, relaxed, and friendly than Jim and his father is perceived to be stronger, more industrious, and more active than Jim. The mother is perceived as having an interesting combination of personality characteristics. On one hand, she is perceived as affectionate, friendly, spontaneous, sensitive, and good. On the other she is perceived as authoritarian, superficial, selfish, unintelligent, intolerant, and uncreative.

With the autobiography and the semantic differential we begin to get another picture of Jim. We learn of his popularity and success through high school and of his good relationship with his father. We find support for the suggestions from the projective tests of anxiety and difficulties with women. Indeed, we learn of Jim's fears of ejaculating too quickly and not being able to satisfy the female. However, we also find an individual who believes himself to be basically good and is interested in doing humane things. We become aware of an individual who has a view of his self and a view of his ideal self, and of an individual who is frustrated because of the feelings that leave a gap between the two.

Given the opportunity to talk about himself and what he would like to be, Jim talks about his desire to be warmer, more relaxed, and stronger. We feel no need here to disguise our purposes, for we are interested in Jim's perceptions, meanings, and experiences as he reports them. We are interested in what is real for Jim—in how he interprets phenomena within his own frame of reference. We want to know all about Jim, but all about Jim as he perceives himself and the world about him.

When using the data from the semantic differential, we are not tempted to focus on drives, and we do not need to come to grips with the world of the irrational. In Rogers' terms, we see an individual who is struggling to move toward self-actualization, from dependence toward independence, from fixity and rigidity to freedom and spontaneity. We find an individual who has a gap between his intellectual and emotional estimates of himself. In Rogers' terms, we observe an individual who is without self-consistency, who lacks a sense of congruence between self and experience.

Rep Test: Personal Construct Theory

Jim took the group form of Kelly's Role Construct Repertory Test (Rep test) on an occasion separate from the other tests. Here we have a test that is structured in terms of the roles that are given to the subject and in terms of the task of formulating a similarity–contrast construct. However, the subject is given total freedom in the content of the construct formed. As we noted in Chapter 7, the Rep test is derived quite logically from Kelly's theory of personal constructs. Two major themes appear in these constructs. The first theme has to do with that of the *quality of interpersonal relationships.* Basically this involves whether people are warm and giving or cold and narcissistic. This theme is expressed in constructs such as Gives Love–Is Self-oriented, Sensitive–Insensitive, and Communicates With Others as People–Is Uninterested in Others. A second major theme concerns *security* and is expressed in constructs such as Hung up–Healthy, Unsure–Self-confident, and Satisfied With Life–Unhappy. The frequency with which constructs relevant to these two themes appear suggests that Jim has a relatively constricted view of the world; that is, much of Jim's understanding of events is in terms of the Warm–Cold and Secure–Insecure dimensions. Although not evident in the data, there may be a relationship between the two dimensions. The Warm–Cold theme has a dependency quality, and it may be that he feels more secure when he is receiving love from others. Notice here that Jim did rate himself as slightly dependent on the semantic differential and on the Rorschach gave responses that suggested passivity and oral dependency.

How do the constructs given relate to specific people? On the sorts that involved himself, Jim used constructs expressing insecurity. Thus, Jim views himself as being like his sister (so hung up that their psychological health is questionable) in contrast to his brother, who is basically healthy and stable. In two other sorts, he sees himself as lacking self-confidence and lacking genuine social poise. These ways of construing himself are in contrast with the constructs used in relation to the father. The father is construed as being introverted and retiring, but he also is construed as being self-sufficient, open-minded, outstanding, and successful.

The constructs used in relation to the mother are interesting and again suggest conflict. On one hand, the mother is construed to be outgoing, gregarious, and giving of great love, while on the other she is construed to be mundane, predictable, close-minded, and conservative. The close-minded, conservative construct is particularly interesting since, in that sort, mother is paired with the person with whom he, Jim, feels most uncomfortable. Thus mother and the person with whom he feels most uncomfortable are contrasted with father, who is construed

The constructs formed by Jim are:

CONSTRUCT	CONTRAST
Self-satisfied	Self-doubting
Uninterested in communicating with students as people	Interested in communicating with students as people
Nice	Obnoxious
Sensitive to cues from other people	Insensitive to cues
Outgoing–gregarious	Introverted–retiring
Introspective–hung up	Self-satisfied
Intellectually dynamic	Mundane and predictable
Outstanding, successful	Mediocre
Obnoxious	Very likeable
Satisfied with life	Unhappy

CONSTRUCT	CONTRAST
Shy, unsure of self	Self-confident
Worldly, open-minded	Parochial, close-minded
Open, simple to understand	Complex, hard to get to know
Capable of giving great love	Somewhat self-oriented
Self-sufficient	Needs other people
Concerned with others	Oblivious to all but his own interests
So hung up that psychological health is questionable	Basically healthy and stable
Willing to hurt people in order to be "objective"	Unwilling to hurt people if he can help it
Close-minded, conservative	Open-minded, liberal
Lacking in self-confidence	Self-confident
Sensitive	Insensitive, self-centered
Lacking social poise	Secure and socially poised
Bright, articulate	Average intelligence

FIGURE 10.1   Rep Test Data

to be open-minded and liberal. The combination of sorts for all persons suggests that Jim's ideal person is someone who is warm, sensitive, secure, intelligent, open-minded, and successful. The women in his life—mother, sister, girlfriend, and previous girlfriend are construed as having some of these characteristics but also as missing others.

The Rep test gives us valuable data about how Jim construes his environment. With it we continue the phenomenological approach discussed in relation to Rogers, and again find that Jim's world tends to be perceived in terms of two major constructs: warm interpersonal relationships–cold interpersonal relationships, and secure, confident people–insecure, unhappy people. Through the Rep test we gain an understanding of why Jim is so limited in his relationships to others and why he has so much difficulty in being creative. His being restricted to only two constructs hardly leaves him free to relate to people as individuals and instead forces him to perceive people and problems in steretyped or conventional ways. A world filled with so little perceived diversity can hardly be exciting, and the constant threat of insensitivity and rejection can be expected to fill Jim with a sense of gloom.

The data from the Rep test are tantalizing, much like Kelly's theory. What is there seems so clear and valuable, but one is left wondering about what is missing. Both figuratively and literally, there is the sense of the skeleton for the structure of personality, but one is left with only the bones. Jim's ways of construing himself and his environment are an important part of his personality. Assessing his constructs and his construct system helps us to understand just how he interprets events and how he is led to predict the future. But where is the flesh to go along with the bones—the sense of an individual who cannot be what he feels, the sense of an individual struggling to be warm amid feelings of hostility and struggling to relate to women although confused about his feelings toward them and confused about his own sexual identity?

Sixteen Personality Factor Inventory: Trait, Factor-Analytic Theory

Let us now move to the data from structured tests, in particular the 16 Personality Factor Inventory (16 P.F.) developed by Cattell. Jim completed both forms (A and B) of the 16 P.F. His profiles for each of these forms and for the composite of the two forms are given in Figure 10.2. First, notice that although in most cases the scores on Form A and Form B are quite close, in a number of cases they are quite different (e.g., A, B, C, N, Q_2). The following brief descriptions of Jim's personality were written by a psychologist who assessed the results of the 16 P.F. but was unaware of any of the other data on Jim.

FORM A
Jim appears as a very bright yet conflicted young man who is easily upset and quite insecure. His profile indicates he is somewhat cynical and introspective. His identity confusion is shown by the fact that he appears to be outgoing while he feels shy and restrained, and he evades responsibilities and obligations and then experiences the consequent guilt, anxiety, and depression.

FORM B
Jim presents himself as a very outgoing young man who is really quite shy, approval-seeking, dependent, and tense. Brighter than average, he is quite confused about who he is and where he is going. His profile indicates that Jim is shrewd, introspective, tends to be overly sensitive, and pays for his impulsivity with guilt and depression.

COMPOSITE FORMS A AND B
Jim presents himself as a very bright and outgoing young man although he is insecure, easily upset, and somewhat dependent. Less assertive conscientious, and venturesome than he may initially appear, Jim is confused and conflicted about who he is and where he is going, tends toward introspec-

tion, and is quite anxious. His profile suggests that he may experience periodic mood swings and may also have a history of psychosomatic complaints.

Since the 16 P.F. has been administered to college students throughout the country, we can compare Jim with the average college student. Compared to other students, Jim is higher on the following traits: outgoing, intelligent, affected by feelings–easily upset, sensitivity, depression, poor self-sentiment, anxiety.

Let us turn to the factor-analytic method in an effort to reduce the number of traits necessary to describe Jim's personality. Four second-order factors have been derived from the 16 first-order factors: Low Anxiety–High Anxiety, Introversion–Extroversion, Tenderminded Emotionality–Alert Poise, and Subduedness (group-dependent, passive)–Independence. Jim's scores are extreme on two of these factors. First, Jim is extremely high on anxiety. This suggests that he is dissatisfied with the degree to which he is able to meet the demands of life and to achieve what he desires. The high level of anxiety also suggests the possibility of physical disturbances. Second, Jim is very low on alert poise or, conversely, he is high on tenderminded emotionality. This suggests that he is not an enterprising and decisive personality. Instead, it is suggested that Jim is troubled by emotionality and often becomes discouraged and frustrated. Although sensitive to the subtleties of life, this sensitivity sometimes leads to preoccupation and to too much thought before he takes action. Jim's other two scores indicate that he is neither introverted nor extroverted and is neither excessively dependent nor independent. The outstanding characteristics are the anxiety, the sensitivity, and the emotionality.

Before we leave the 16 P.F., it should be noted that two important features came out in sharper focus on this test than on any of the other assessment devices. The first is the frequency of mood swings in Jim. In reading over the results on the 16 P.F. Jim stated that he has frequent and extreme mood swings, ranging from feeling very happy to feeling very depressed. During the latter periods, he tends to take his feelings out on others and becomes hostile to them in a sarcastic, "biting," or "cutting" way. The second feature of importance concerns psychosomatic complaints. As we mentioned previously, Jim has had considerable difficulty with an ulcer and frequently must drink milk for the condition. Notice that, although this is a serious condition that gives him considerable trouble, Jim did not mention it at all in his autobiography.

From the data on the 16 P.F. we can discern many important parts of Jim's personality. The concept of trait, expressing a broad reaction tendency and relatively permanent features of behavior, appears to be a useful one for the description of personality. We learn from the 16 P.F. that, although Jim is outgoing, he is basically shy and inhibited. Again, the characteristic of being anxious, frustrated, and conflicted comes through. But one is left wondering about whether sixteen dimensions are adequate for the description of personality, particularly when these can be reduced further to four dimensions. And one is left wondering whether a score in the middle of the scale means that the trait is not an important one for the individual or simply that he is not extreme on that characteristic. The latter appears to be the case. Yet, when one writes up a personality description

FIGURE 14.1 16 P.F. Test Profile of Jim Hersh.

16 P.F. TEST PROFILE

				Low pole description	High pole description
L	13	9	22	7	Trusting, adaptable, free of jealousy, easy to get on with (alaxia)	Suspicious, self-opinionated, hard to fool (protension)
M	16	14	30	8	Practical, careful, conventional, regulated by external realities, proper (praxernia)	Imaginative, wrapped up in inner urgencies, careless of practical matters, bohemian (autia)
N	10	14	24	7	Forthright, natural, artless, sentimental (artlessness)	Shrewd, calculating, worldly, penetrating (shrewdness)
O	14	18	32	8	Placid, self-assured, confident, serene (untroubled adequacy)	Apprehensive, worrying, depressive, troubled (guilt proneness)
Q_1	12	10	22	7	Conservative, respecting established ideas, tolerant of traditional difficulties (conservatism)	Experimenting, critical, liberal, analytical, free-thinking (radicalism)
Q_2	12	5	17	4	Group-dependent, a "joiner" and sound follower (group adherence)	Self-sufficient, prefers own decisions, resourceful (self-sufficiency)
Q_3	0	7	7	1	Undisciplined self-conflict, follows own urges, careless of protocol (low integration)	Controlled, socially-precise, following self-image (high self-concept control)
Q_4	15	19	34	8	Relaxed, tranquil, torpid, unfrustrated (low ergic tension)	Tense, frustrated, driven, overwrought (high ergic tension)

A sten of 1 2 3 4 5 6 7 8 9 10 is obtained by about 2.3% 4.4% 9.2% 15.0% 19.1% 19.1% 15.0% 9.2% 4.4% 2.3% of adults

16 PF, forms A and B, Copyright © 1956, 1957, 1961, 1962, Institute for Personality and Ability Testing. 1602-04 Coronado Drive, Champaign, Illinois, U.S.A. All property rights reserved. Printed in U.S.A.

FIGURE 10.2 16 P.F. Test Profile of Jim Hersh (16 P.F., Forms A and B, Copyright © 1956, 1957, 1961, 1962, Institute for Personality and Ability Testing. 1602–04 Coronado Drive, Champaign, Illinois, U.S.A. All property rights reserved. Printed in U.S.A.

based on the results of the 16 P.F., the major emphasis tends to fall on scales with extreme scores.

Perhaps most serious, however, is the fact that Cattell has failed to retain the virtues of the clinician in spite of his efforts to do so. The results of the 16 P.F. have the strengths and limitations of being a trait description of personality. The results are descriptive, but they are not interpretive or dynamic. Although Cattell has attempted to deal with the individual as a whole, the results of the 16 P.F. leave one with only a pattern of scores—not a whole individual. Although the theory takes into consideration the dynamic interplay among attitudes (motives), sentiments, and ergs, the results of the 16 P.F. appear unrelated to this portion of the theory. Jim is described as being anxious and frustrated, but anxious about what and why frustrated? Why is Jim outgoing and shy? Why does he find it so hard to be decisive and enterprising? The theory recognizes the importance of conflict in the functioning of the individual, but the results of the 16 P.F. tell us nothing about the nature of Jim's conflicts and how he tries to handle them. As pointed out in Chapter 9, the factor traits appear to have some degree of validity, but they also tend to be abstract and to leave out the richness of personality found in data from other assessment devices.

JIM HERSH: FIVE YEARS LATER

The material on Jim Hersh presented so far was written at approximately the time of his graduation from college. Since this book was first published and then re-published in a second edition, sufficient time had elapsed to bring discernible changes to Jim Hersh's life—to say nothing of the personality theories themselves. Here let us try to follow trends established on the basis of Jim's earlier test results and see whether current patterns of behavior follow from earlier patterns. In other words, let us attempt to assess how stable and consistent Jim had been in his personality functioning. In noting and attempting to account for significant changes, we can ask about earlier hints of potential change and about the role of changes in environmental events. We can also ask about which theories facilitated our understanding of Jim Hersh at the time of graduation and which facilitate our understanding of his functioning during the period of time since then.

Five years after graduation Jim was contacted and asked to: (1) Indicate whether there had been significant life experiences for him since graduation and, if so, to describe how they had affected him, (2) give a brief description of his personality and to describe the ways, if any, in which he had changed since graduation. His response in each of these two areas should help us answer some of the questions raised above.

LIFE EXPERIENCES—AS TOLD BY JIM HERSH

After leaving Harvard, I entered business school. I only got into one graduate school in psychology; it was not particularly prestigious, whereas I got into a number of excellent business schools, and so on that basis I chose to go to business school. I did not really enjoy business school, though it was not terribly noxious either, but it was clear to me that my interest really was in the field of psychology, so I applied to a couple of schools during the academic year, but did not get in. I had a job in a New York import–export firm over the summer, and disliked it intensely enough to once more write to graduate schools over the summer. I was accepted at two, and then went into a very difficult decision-making process. My parents explicitly wanted me to return to business school, but I eventually decided to try graduate school. My ability to make that decision in the face of parental opposition was very significant for me; it asserted my strength and independence as nothing else in my life ever had.

Going through graduate school in the Midwest in clinical psychology was extremely significant for me. I have a keen professional identification as a clinician which is quite central to my self-concept. I have a system of thinking which is well-grounded and very central to the way I deal with my environment. I am entirely pleased with the decision I made, even though I still toy with the idea of returning to business school. Even if I do it, it would be to attain an adjunct degree; it would not change the fact that my primary identification is with psychology. I also fell in love during my first year in graduate school, for the first and only time in my life. The relationship did not work out, which was devastating to me, and I've not gotten completely over it yet. Despite the pain, however, it was a life-infusing experience.

During graduate school, I took up the guitar. I play and sing fairly seriously now, and it gives me some of my happiest hours. I see it as a long-term avocation for me. I have a lot of desire to get better with it, and frequently fantasize about getting to the point where I could play at coffee houses and the like. I've gotten enough positive feedback from enough different sources to know it is within the range of possibility. It is a very important part of my life.

Last year I lived in a communal setting and it was a watershed experience for me. We worked a lot on ourselves and each other during the year, in our formal once-a-week groups and informally at any time, and it was a frequently painful, frequently joyful, and always growth-producing experience. I am convinced that I would like to live communally as my basic style of life, though I need a very special group of people to do it with and would rather live alone or with one or two other people than with just any group. Our group is thinking about getting together again in a more permanent arrangement, and I may very well decide to live with them again beginning next year. Whether or not this happens, last year's experience was very significant for me, and therapeutic in every respect.

Toward the end of last year, I began a relationship which has now become primary for me. I am living with a woman, Kathy, who is in a master's program in social work. She has been married twice. It is a sober relationship with problems involved; basically, there are some things about her that I am not comfortable with. I do not feel "in love" at this point, but there are a great many things about her that I like and appreciate, and so I am remaining in the relationship to see what develops, and how I feel about continuing to be with her. I have no plans to get married, nor much immediate interest in doing so.

The relationship does not have the passionate feeling that my other significant relationship had, and I am presently trying to work through how much of my feeling at that time was idealization and how much real, and whether my more sober feelings for Kathy indicate that she's not the right woman for me or whether I need to come to grips with the fact that no woman is going to be "perfect" for me. In any event, my relationship with Kathy also feels like a wonderful growth-producing experience, and is the most significant life experience I am currently involved in.

I think these constitute my significant life experiences since leaving Harvard.

BRIEF PERSONALITY DESCRIPTION AND CHANGES— AS TOLD BY JIM HERSH

I do not think I've changed in very basic ways since leaving college. As a result of going into psychology, I think of myself as somewhat more self-aware these days, which I think is helpful. As I remember your interpretation of the tests I took back then, you saw me as primarily depressive. At this point, however, I think of myself as being primarily obsessive. I think I am prone to depression, but on balance see myself as happier these days—less frequently depressed. I see my obsessiveness as a deeply engrained characterological pattern, and have been thinking for some time now about going into analysis to work on it (amongst other things, of course). Though I consider my thinking about this serious, I am not yet very close to actually doing it. This is at least in part because I expect to be leaving Michigan at the end of this academic year, and so entering analysis at this point obviously makes no sense. On the other hand, it's a frightening proposition requiring a serious commitment, so there is some resistance to overcome over and above the geographic issue. Nevertheless, I see it as a definite possibility for myself in the next couple of years.

Let me say a word about my history with psychotherapy as a patient. I have made a number of abortive efforts to become involved, only one of which was even moderately successful. I saw someone at college a handful of times, but as I remember it, it was very superficial in every sense. I did nothing my year at business school. During my first year in graduate school, I saw an analytically oriented psychiatrist for three "evaluative sessions," after which he recommended: (1) analysis; (2) group therapy; (3) analytically oriented individual therapy. I was not ready to either enter analysis or a group, and did not want to continue with what he considered a third alternative, so I stopped. My second year in graduate school, I saw an analytically oriented psychiatrist for between six and eight sessions, but became very frustrated with his giving me so little, so that when he recommended increasing the frequency of visits from once to twice a week, I terminated. A big issue for me was how good a therapist he was: I saw him as pretty average, and felt I wanted someone special. This is clearly a form of resistance, I know, though I still feel there was some reality to my impressions of him. During my third year in graduate school, I saw a non-traditional psychiatrist about 10 times. He used a mixed bag of techniques: cathartic, gestalt, behavioral, and generally folksy and friendly (very anti-analytic). At the end of our relationship, which I thought was somewhat useful at the time, we both felt I'd had enough therapy, and that what I needed were "therapeutic" life experiences: e.g., a relationship with a woman, some time to play, etc. Since then I have had some important therapeutic life experiences, the most significant of which was living in the house I lived in last year. As a result, I feel less immediate pressure to get help, and think of going into analysis to work through basic characterological issues (like my obsessiveness). In other words, I feel in less acute pain these days.

As I said previously, I see myself as more similar to, than different from, the way I was five years ago. I think of myself as a witty, aware, interesting and fun-loving person. I continue to be quite moody, so sometimes none of these characteristics are in evidence at all. My sexual relationship with my girl friend has put to rest my concern about my sexual adequacy (especially about premature ejaculation).

I still see myself as having an "authority" issue—i.e., being quite sensitive and vulnerable to the way in which those who have authority over me treat me. However, I see myself as having a number of important professional skills, and as being in the field I want to be in. I still have money issues—i.e., I am concerned about being paid fairly for what I do, I resent psychiatrists making more than me, I am vigilant around making sure I am not "ripped off," etc. I still have not fully come to grips with my father having money, and the fact that I will be getting some of that, but on the other hand I'm not terribly concerned about it, and it feels more like an intellectualized concern about the future than an emotional concern in the present. I am extremely compulsive, I very efficiently get done what needs to be done, and experience considerable anxiety when I am not on top of things. My life must be very well ordered for it to be possible for me to relax and enjoy myself. Unfortunately, the compulsiveness spills over into my personal life, so that my room must be orderly, my books stacked appropriately, etc., or else I experience anxiety. Again, this feels like a deeply engrained pattern which would not be easy to overcome.

PERSONALITY THEORY AND ASSESSMENT DATA: THE CASE OF JIM HERSH

By presenting the case of James Hersh we have been able to review the data gathered from a variety of assessment techniques. The attempt here has not been to learn all about any one instrument or to prove the validity of one or another instrument but to explore the personality of a single individual through the use of a variety of assessment devices and to compare the impressions gained from these devices. Our goal is further to appreciate differences in personality theories as they relate to the different kinds of data on which the theories are based.

What of the data that we have available to us? Clearly, there are important similarities but also significant differences. We began with the data from the projectives (Rorschach, TAT) and then moved to consideration of some phenomenological data (autobiography, semantic differential). How does what we have learned from one set of data compare with what we have learned from another set? The Rorschach suggested tension and anxiety behind a façade of poise. The semantic differential suggested tension and anxiety but not a façade of tact and poise. The projectives suggested considerable difficulty with women and a conflict between sexual preoccupation and hostility. The data were far less clear in the semantic differential, although we did observe what appears to be an ambivalent attitude toward the mother. There is some further suggestion of this in the autobiography, along with some defensiveness. "My relationship with my mother is superficial but mutually satisfactory. There is no depth of understanding on her part—she wants me to succeed in a very conventional way. I understand her for what she is—a loving, lovable woman. I hope this doesn't sound like I look down on her, because I respect her very much."

Although the projectives clearly suggest some confusion in sexual identity, the ratings on the semantic differential indicate that Jim perceives himself to be masculine and more identified with his father than with his mother. In his autobiography he writes. "My father and I have achieved a great deal more rapport. I have great, almost unlimited respect for him and I think he feels the same toward me. . . . I am much more like my father than my mother." Also, the semantic differential data indicate that Jim perceives himself to be weak and somewhat passive whereas the father and ideal self are perceived to be strong and active. In relation to the parents, one is tempted to ask why Jim was not able to identify with the warm, outgoing aspects of mother or with the strong, active aspects of father.

There is evidence in both the projectives and semantic differential of a lack of warmth in interpersonal relationships. However, what is clear is that percepts such as vampires and Count Dracula sucking blood do not appear on the semantic differential. These data, which have a clear primitive, oral quality to them, cannot be obtained from the semantic differential. In addition, the projectives gave far less suggestion of an individual who perceives himself as being deep, sensitive, kind, thoughtful, and basically good. Perhaps it is out of fear of expressing hostility that Jim remains inhibited. Perhaps he also confuses activity and assertiveness with hostility and thereby feels unable to be a strong man. In any case, he often is unable to *be* what he *feels*. This is something that is basic to Rogerian theory and is well expressed by Jim in the conclusion of his autobiography: "All in all, there is a great chasm between my intellectual and emotional estimates of myself, and I think this chasm must be closed before I can reach some kind of peace with myself."

The data from the semantic differential and the autobiography are not inconsistent with those from the projectives, but they are different. In both cases, there are expressions of anxiety and problems of warmth in interpersonal relationships. However, whereas in the projectives there are expressions of sadism and confusion in sexual identify, in the autobiography and semantic differential there are expressions of an individual who is not quite what he would like to be and who feels that he is not free to be himself. Thus he cannot be at peace with himself.

The data from the Kelly Rep test and from the Cattell 16 P.F. continue to tell the story of information obtained from other assessment devices that is not inconsistent with previous data and theoretical interpretations but is distinct and different from them. The trait of anxiety appears on the 16 P.F., and on the Kelly Rep test the construct insecurity was associated with the self. Similarly, both the 16 P.F. and the Rep test data suggest problems in interpersonal relationships. The projectives and semantic differential suggested a difficulty in being uninhibited with people or becoming involved. On the Rep test, Jim indicated that constructs such as Gives Love–Self-oriented, Sensitive–Insensitive, and Interested in People–Uninterested in People are important to him, in interpreting his environment. The meaning of the construct Sensitive–Insensitive may be particularly critical since, in reading over the results of the 16 P.F., Jim noted that the reference to his being overly sensitive was fundamental to understanding his personality.

The use of the term *sensitive* is ambiguous. One can be a sensitive person in terms of being sensitive to the feelings and needs of others. This kind of sensitivity would suggest an empathic and warm individual. One can also be sensitive to art and music, which may or may not be related to an interpersonal, empathic sensitivity. Finally, one can be sensitive to others in terms of being dependent on them. Thus the individual who is buoyed by compliments and depressed by criticism is sensitive to others. Or the individual who is always searching to find out whether he has hurt someone's feelings may be viewed as sensitive to others. This type of sensitivity involves a concern with others but is not expressive of warmth. This distinction is of interest in relation to Jim's high score on the Tender-minded–Emotionality factor. The score suggests that Jim is easily discouraged and frustrated, sensitive to the subtleties of life, and often thinks too much. The score suggests that Jim is sensitive to people in that he is concerned with them but not necessarily that he is a warm individual. This helps us to understand how a "sensitive" individual can show signs of rigidity and inhibition on the projectives and on the 16 P.F. and still construe himself as being warm on the semantic differential and the Rep test.

What, then, is the value of these comparisons of data from different tests of Jim Hersh? The attempt here has been to demonstrate, in an individual case, a theme that has been repeated throughout this book: Different theories of personality are based on different sets of observations and in turn lead to the investigation of different phenomena. Is Jim Hersh a Dracula, a person unable to be what he feels, a person "hung-up" on security and warmth, a person characterized by the scores on 16 factor scales, or a respondent to reinforcers in the environment? Is Jim Hersh fixated at a pregenital stage of development, limited in his efforts toward self-actualization, limited by a constricted construct system, bothered by high ergic tension, or inhibited in his responses by fears of failure and rejection by others? There is evidence that he is each of these, but also evidence that he is more than any one of them. Because of the nature of the theories and the data gained in relation to each, at various points Jim Hersh appears to be one more than the other. As Kelly (1963) has observed, the bias of the investigator influences the behavior he will look at, the observations he will be sensitive to, the questions he will ask, and how important he feels it is to report various kinds of data.

At the beginning of this chapter we asked: Are the observations obtained similar when techniques of assessment associated with the different theories are applied to the same individual? I think the answer can be that the observations obtained are different in striking and important ways, but they are not inconsistent with one another. To conclude that one knows Jim or understands his personality from just one set of observations would undoubtedly put one in the same position as the blind man who examined a small portion of the elephant and was led to a wrong conclusion on the basis of his limited observations. In part the data suggest that at times the theories talk about the same phenomena in different terms. However, the data also strongly suggest that each set of observations and each theory represents an incomplete picture of the whole individual. In a certain sense, each represents a glimpse of the total complexity of human personality.

What is needed in the future is the study of the same individuals by psychologists of different orientations. In Kelly's terms, this would permit us to assess the likeness and differences of personality theories and to determine each one's range and focus of convenience.

Picasso, Pablo. *Seated Woman*. 1927. Collection of The Museum of Modern Art.

LEARNING, BEHAVIORAL APPROACHES TO PERSONALITY

CHAPTER FOCUS: In this chapter, we study approaches to personality based on principles of learning. The chapter begins by noting that there are many different theories of learning. These theories share a focus on learned behavior and a commitment to the experimental testing of clearly defined hypotheses. Furthermore, they all attempt to identify and manipulate environmental variables that control behavior. This chapter focuses on Watson's behaviorist point of view and on three processes of learning—Pavlov's classical conditioning, Skinner's operant conditioning, and stimulus–response (S-R) theory. In Chapter 12 we consider learning, behavioral approaches to assessment and change, and then turn to an overall critical evaluation of these approaches to personality.

Psychology as the behaviorist views it is a purely objective, experimental branch of natural science. Its theoretical goal is the prediction and control of behavior. Introspection forms no essential part of its methods . . . The time seems to have come when psychology must discard all references to consciousness.

Watson, 1914, p. 31

I began to investigate the question of psychic secretion with my collaborators, Drs. Wolfson and Snarsky . . . Snarsky undertook to analyse the internal mechanism of the stimulation from the subjective point of view, i.e., he assumed that the internal world of the dog—the thoughts, feelings, and desires—is analogous to ours . . . Snarsky clung to his subjective explanation of the phenomena, but I, putting aside fantasy and seeing the scientific barrenness of such a solution, began to seek for another exit from this difficult position. After persistent deliberation, after a considerable mental conflict, I decided finally, in regard to the so-called physical stimulation, to remain in the role of a pure physiologist, i.e., of an objective external observer and experimenter, having to do exclusively with external phenomena and their relations.

Pavlov, 1928, pp. 38–39

The practice of looking inside the organism for an explanation of behavior has tended to obscure the variables which are immediately available for scientific analysis. These variables lie outside the organism, in its immediate environment and in its environmental history.

Skinner, 1953, p. 31

Science has no use for unverifiable hypotheses . . . There is reason to believe that the relative backwardness of the behavior sciences is due not so much to their inherent complexity as to the difficulty of maintaining a consistent and rigorous objectivism.

Hull, 1943, pp. 23, 28

The concern in this chapter is with approaches to personality that in many ways are radically different from the clinical point of view. And, although they share with the trait, factor-analytic approaches an emphasis on empirical investigation, they involve assumptions that lead to considerable criticism of the trait approach to personality.

In an effort to understand the learning theory approach to personality, one must be prepared to make new assumptions and to consider new strategies for research and new interpretations of old data. The learning theory approach to personality has two basic assumptions from which a number of critical points tend to follow. The first is the assumption that nearly all behavior is learned. The answer to the question of *what* psychologists should study is that they should study the processes of learning through which new behaviors are acquired. The second basic assumption is that research methodology is important—that objectivity and rigor in the testing of clearly formulated hypotheses are crucial. The answer to the question of *how* psychologists should study behavior is that they should formulate explicit hypotheses and should measure behavior in precise ways.

Notice that where Eysenck and Cattell view learning as part of the broader area of personality, the theoretical approach discussed in this chapter and the next reflects an opposite point of view: "There is no reason to assume that the study of personality offers any new or unique problems for psychology. We can consider the study of personality to be a branch of the general field of learning which investigates in particular those processes significant to human adjustment" (Lundin, 1963, p. 254). Although this may seem to be just a matter of where you cut the pie, it is of considerable importance when making decisions about where to begin the study of behavior.

Of perhaps even greater consequence, however, is the decision about methodology. The emphasis on objectivity and rigor, on testable hypotheses and the experimental control of variables, has led, for example, to an emphasis on the laboratory as the place for studying behavior. One generalizes from observations in the laboratory to real life, but only in the laboratory can one systematically study phenomena. Furthermore, the emphasis on the careful manipulation of explicitly defined variables has led to the concentration on simple, rather than complex, pieces of behavior. The assumption is that one builds toward explaining the complex through the careful study of the simple.

Although they need not have, other consequences have tended to follow from this methodological orientation. Thus, the emphasis on the careful manipulation of objectively defined variables has led to an emphasis on forces *external* to the organism as opposed to ones *internal* to it. According to the learning, or behavioral, approach, one manipulates variables in the environment and observes the consequences of these manipulations in behavior. Whereas psychodynamic theories emphasize causes of behavior that are inside the organism (for example, instincts, defenses, self-concept, constructs), learning theories emphasize causes that are in the external environment. Stimuli in the environment that can be experimentally manipulated, such as food rewards, are emphasized instead of concepts that cannot be manipulated, such as the self, the ego, and the unconscious. As Skinner argued, when we can control behavior through the manipulation of variables outside the organism, there is no need to be concerned with what goes on inside the organism.

The behavioral emphasis on external, environmental determinants has been associated with an emphasis on **situational specificity** in behavior and a de-emphasis on individual predispositions to behave in particular ways. In contrast with the emphasis in psychodynamic and trait theories on characteristics or traits that express themselves in a range of situations, behavior theory suggests that whatever consistency is found in behavior is the result of the similarity of environmental conditions that evoke these behaviors. "With the possible exception of intelligence, highly generalized behavioral consistencies have not been demonstrated, and the concept of personality traits as broad response predispositions is thus untenable" (Mischel, 1968, p. 146). In summary, the view that is presented here is that behavior is situation specific; that is, that behavior tends to change unless there is a similarity of environmental conditions.

Since behavior is situation specific and is a function of conditions in the environment, the purpose of behavioral research is to establish laws concerning behavior by relating environmental changes to changes in behavior. For example, in the **functional analysis of behavior,** one seeks to identify the conditions or *environmental stimuli* that control behavior. One is interested both in the entire range of behavior (behavioral repertoire) of the individual and in the conditions that affect the acquisition of new behaviors and the performance of previously learned behaviors. The ABC's of behavioral assessment involve an analysis of *A*ntecedent conditions (conditions that precede the behavior), *B*ehaviors exhibited (emitted) by the individual, and the *C*onsequences of these behaviors. Individual differences exist, but they are of no importance in developing behavioral laws. The same laws hold true for all individuals, and individual differences are viewed merely as blocks in the path to the discovery of these laws. As we shall see in the next chapter, the medical symptom-disease model of psychopathology is rejected. Instead there is an emphasis on the learning of maladaptive behaviors or the failure to learn adaptive behaviors. Therapy then involves the application of basic learning principles to the area of behavior change.

To use Cattell's term, the theoretical points of view that are discussed in this chapter and the next emphasize the *bivariate approach* to research. There is an emphasis on simple behaviors that lend themselves to experimental control; there is an emphasis on behavior in the laboratory as opposed to behavior in the real world; and there is the use of animals, such as rats and pigeons, as subjects for the testing of laws about behavior. Although most behavioral theorists would suggest that findings with rats need to be checked against findings with humans,

1. Empirical research is the cornerstone of theory and practice.
2. Personality theory and applied practice should be based on principles of learning.
3. Behavior is responsive to reinforcement variables in the environment and is more situation specific than suggested by other personality theories (e.g., trait, psychoanalytic).
 4. Rejection of the medical symptom–disease view of psychopathology and emphasis instead on basic principles of learning and behavior change.

FIGURE 11.1   Basic Points of Emphasis of Learning, Behavioral Approaches to Personality.

they are in general agreement that the same laws of behavior operate for members of different species. Similarly, they assume that the laws of learning that govern the behaviors of members of one age group also operate for members of another age group. As we see in Chapter 13, more recent developments in social learning theory do not necessarily make these assumptions.

Outlined here have been a number of assumptions characteristic of learning theory and the behavioral point of view. In particular, an effort has been made to begin by contrasting some of these learning theory assumptions with those made by Freud, Rogers, Kelly, and Cattell. Like the chapter on trait theory, this chapter and the next are concerned with the efforts of many individuals. There is a learning theory and behavioral point of view, but there is no one theory of learning or one behavioral theory of personality. There is a shared commitment to the importance of learning, and a shared commitment to rigorous methodology. In this chapter we first consider some of the influential figures and concentrate our attention on three major theories of learning. In studying these three approaches we see that beyond the shared commitments, there exist important differences. Before turning to these theories, however, let us consider common themes basic to the learning theory view of the person and science.

THE BEHAVIORAL VIEW OF THE PERSON

There are three broad assumptions about the nature of the person that tend to run throughout learning theory and the behavioral point of view.

1. Behavior is learned by the building up of associations.
2. People basically seek to obtain pleasure and avoid pain.
3. Behavior is basically environmentally determined.

The first characteristic suggests that complex behavior can be understood in terms of the building up and joining together of simple associative bonds between something that occurs in the environment and the organism's response to it. There is an implicit view of the brain as a huge switchboard in which incoming stimuli are connected with outgoing responses.

The second assumption, that is, that people seek to obtain pleasure and avoid pain, is most clearly evident in Thorndike's *Law of Effect.* "Any act which in a given situation produces satisfaction becomes associated with that situation, so that when the situation recurs the act is more likely than before to recur also. Conversely, any act which in a given situation produces discomfort becomes dissociated from that situation, so that when the situation recurs the act is less likely than before to recur" (1905, p. 203).

The third characteristic, an emphasis on environmental forces in determining behavior, in part follows from the first two characteristics and, as pointed out in Chapter 1, is in keeping with the American tradition. Watson, in particular, emphasized the importance of the environment over heredity. He claimed that, given a free hand in controlling the environment, he could train an infant to become any type of specialist he might select—doctor, lawyer, beggar-man, or thief. Since behavior is a function of stimulus–response connections developed mainly as a result of rewards and punishments in the environment, there is considerable room for optimism concerning the ability to shape human behavior.

THE BEHAVIORAL VIEW OF SCIENCE, THEORY, AND RESEARCH METHODS

The theory and research presented in this chapter and the next can be considered to be representative of the behavioral tradition in psychology. This means that they are opposed, on theoretical grounds, to the use of certain concepts and research methods in psychology and that they are committed to other types of concepts and methods. In the original learning position, the intent was to throw out concepts such as consciousness, will, idea, thought, and intention. The argument was that these concepts fall within the realm of private experience and, therefore, can not be subjected to public observation and empirical confirmation. Skinner (1963) suggests that we throw out concepts that attribute the visible behavior of an organism to another organism inside—to a little man or homunculus. He observes how students interpreting the learning behavior of a pigeon suggest that the pigeon *expected* reinforcement, or that it *hoped* to get food again, or that it *observed* that a certain behavior produced a particular result. Yet, according to Skinner, the behavior of the pigeon could be described without the use of any of these concepts.

The argument against the use of such concepts is not that they apply to phenomena that are inappropriate for psychologists to study. Rather, the objection is that they are defined in ways that make it impossible for them to be studied scientifically. Concepts that are not explicit, that are not open to empirical verification, are viewed as unscientific and useless. There is, then, at the heart of this criticism, a rejection of the methods used to study these concepts. Originally an attack on the method of self-observation or introspection, the view has been extended to include all observations that are not made in a public way and that can not be measured.

The view of science emphasized here attaches importance to behaviors that can be observed and to methods that involve the manipulation of phenomena. "There are, of course, other legitimate interpretations of nature and man than the scientific one and each has its own right to be pursued. The behavior scientist merely asks that he be given the same opportunity to develop a scientific account of his phenomena that his colleagues in the physical and biological fields have had" (Spence, 1948, p. 70). In general, there is a strong tendency to avoid theoretical speculation and to focus instead on empirical findings. The methodological goal is to be able to manipulate the environmental (independent) variables, to use appropriate controls so that one is observing only the effects of the particular variable under study and, then, to measure the resulting behavior (dependent variable). By establishing such cause–effect relationships, one operates within the bounds of a natural science and goes on to establish relevant laws.

As was pointed out earlier in the chapter, some of the consequences of this view of science have been an emphasis on research in the laboratory, an emphasis on behavior that can be manipulated experimentally, a tendency to minimize the importance of events going on inside of the organism, and an inclination toward the use of animals in research. Again, the following arguments are used to justify these consequences: (1) It is desirable to be able to manipulate the variables and to control the experimental conditions. (2) One can start with simple behavior and go from there to the complex. In fact, science advances from the simple to the complex. (3) The basic processes discovered in animals will likely be found to have considerable relevance to the functioning of humans.

Watson's Behaviorism

John B. Watson (1878–1958) was the founder of the approach to psychology known as **behaviorism**. He began his graduate study at the University of Chicago in philosophy, and then switched to psychology. During these years he took courses in neurology and physiology and began to do a considerable amount of animal research. Some of this research consisted of the study of the increased complexity of behavior in the rat and the associated development of the central nervous system. During the year before he received his doctorate, he had an emotional breakdown and had sleepless nights for many weeks. Watson described this period as useful in preparing him to accept a large part of Freud (Watson, 1936, p. 274). The graduate work at Chicago culminated in a dissertation on animal education and was associated with the development of an important attitude regarding the use of human subjects.

At Chicago, I first began a tentative formulation of my later point of view. I never wanted to use human subjects. I hated to serve as a subject. I didn't like the stuffy, artificial instructions given to subjects. I always was uncomfortable and acted unnaturally. With animals I was at home. I felt that, in studying them, I was keeping close to biology with my feet on the ground.

John B. Watson

More and more the thought presented itself: Can't I find out by watching their behavior everything that the other students are finding by using O's (human subjects)?

Watson, 1936, p. 276

Watson left Chicago to become a professor at Johns Hopkins University in 1908, where he served on the faculty until 1919. During his stay there, which was interrupted by a period of service during the First World War, Watson developed his views on behaviorism as an approach to psychology. These views, which emphasized the study of behavior that is observable and which excluded the study of self-observation or introspection, were presented in public lectures in 1912 and were published in 1914 in Watson's book, *Behavior*. Watson's call for the use of objective methods and the end of speculation about what goes on inside the person was greeted enthusiastically, and he was elected president of the American Psychological Association for the year 1915. His views were further developed to include the work of the Russian physiologist Pavlov, and can be found in his most significant work, *Psychology From the Standpoint of a Behaviorist* (1919).

Watson was divorced in 1919, immediately married his student Rosalie Rayner, and was forced to resign from Hopkins. The circumstances of this departure from Hopkins led him to make his livelihood in the business world. Although he had already established a considerable reputation as a psychologist, he now was forced to do studies of potential sales markets. He found, however, "that it can be just as thrilling to watch the growth of a sales curve of a new product as to watch the learning curve of animals or men" (Watson, 1936, p. 280) and became successful in business. After 1920, Watson did write some popular articles and published his book *Behaviorism* (1924), but his career as a productive theorist and experimenter closed with his departure from Hopkins. However, his hope that instructors would begin to teach objective psychology instead of what he termed "mythology" was to be realized in the years ahead.

PAVLOV'S THEORY OF CLASSICAL CONDITIONING

Ivan Petrovitch Pavlov (1949–1936) was a Russian physiologist who, in the course of his work on the digestive process, developed a procedure for studying behavior and a principle of learning that had a profound effect on the field of psychology. Around the beginning of the twentieth century Pavlov was involved in the study of gastric secretions in dogs. As part of his research he would place some food powder inside the mouth of a dog and measure the resulting amount of salivation. Coincidentally he noticed that after a number of such trials a dog would begin to salivate to certain stimuli before the food was placed in its mouth. This salivation would occur in response to cues such as the sight of the food dish or the approach of a person who generally brought the food. In other words, stimuli which previously did not lead to this response (called neutral stimuli), could now elicit the salivation response because of their association with the food powder that automatically caused the dog to salivate. To animal owners this may not seem like a startling observation. However, it led Pavlov to conduct some very significant research on the process known as **classical conditioning.**

The essential characteristic of classical conditioning is that a previously neutral stimulus becomes capable of eliciting a response because of its association with a stimulus that automatically produces the same or a similar response. In other

Ivan Petrovich Pavlov

words, the dog salivates to the first presentation of the food powder. One need not speak of a conditioning or learning process at this point. The food can be considered to be an **unconditioned stimulus** (US) and the salivation an **unconditioned response** (UR). This is because the salivation is an automatic, reflex response to the food. A neutral stimulus, such as a bell, will not lead to salivation. However, if on a number of trials the bell is sounded *just before* the presentation of the food powder, the sounding of the bell itself without the subsequent appearance of food may take on the potential for eliciting the salivation response. In this case, conditioning has occurred since the presentation of the bell alone is followed by salivation. At this point, the bell may be referred to as a **conditioned stimulus** (CS), and the salivation may be considered a **conditioned response** (CR).

In a similar way, it is possible to condition withdrawal responses to previously neutral stimuli. In the early research on conditioned withdrawal, a dog was strapped in a harness and electrodes were attached to his paw. The delivery of an electric shock (US) to the paw led to the withdrawal of the paw (UR), which was a reflex response on the part of the animal. If a bell was repeatedly presented just before the shock, eventually the bell alone (CS) would be able to elicit the withdrawal response (CR).

The experimental arrangement designed by Pavlov to study classical conditioning allowed him to investigate a number of important phenomena. For example, would the conditioned response become associated with the specific neutral stimulus alone or would it become associated with other similar stimuli? Pavlov found that the response that had become conditioned to a previously neutral stimulus would also become associated with similar stimuli, a process called **generalization**. In other words, the salivation response to the bell would generalize to other sounds. Similarly, the withdrawal response to the bell would generalize to sounds similar to the bell. What are the limits of such generalization? If repeated trials indicate that only some stimuli are followed by the unconditioned stimulus, the animal recognizes differences among stimuli, a process called **discrimination.** For example, if only certain sounds but not others are followed by shock and reflexive paw withdrawal, the dog will learn to discriminate among sounds. Thus, while the process of generalization leads to consistency of response across similar stimuli, the process of discrimination leads to increased specificity of response. Finally, if the originally neutral stimulus is presented repeatedly without at least occasionally being followed by the unconditioned stimulus, there is an undoing or progressive weakening of the conditioning or association, a process known as **extinction**. Whereas the association of the neutral stimulus with the unconditioned stimulus leads to the conditioned response, the repeated presentation of the conditioned stimulus without the unconditioned stimulus leads to extinction. For example, for the dog to continue to salivate to the bell, there must be at least occasional presentations of the food powder with the bell.

The phenomena of generalization, discrimination, and extinction are important to classical conditioning theory as well as other theories of learning. In addition to his work on these phenomena, research by Pavlov was significant in terms of a possible explanation for other phenomena such as conflict and the development of neuroses. An early demonstration of what came to be known as experimental neuroses in animals was completed in Pavlov's laboratory. A dog was conditioned to salivate to the signal of a circle. A differentiation between a circle and an ellipse was then conditioned by not reinforcing the response to the ellipse. When the ellipse was gradually changed in shape to approximate the shape of a circle, the dog first developed fine discriminations but then, as it become impossible to discriminate between the circle and the ellipse, its behavior became disorganized. Pavlov described the events as follows:

> *After three weeks of work upon this discrimination not only the discrimination fail to improve, but it became considerably worse, and finally disappeared altogether. The hitherto quiet dog began to squeal in its stand, kept wriggling about, tore off with its teeth the apparatus for mechanical stimulation of the skin, and bit through the tubes connecting the animal's room with the observer, a behavior which never happened before. On being taken into the experimental room the dog now barked violently, which was also contrary to its usual custom; in short, it presented all the symptoms of a condition of acute neurosis.*

> Pavlov, 1927, p. 291

Pavlov's work on the conditioning process clearly defined stimuli and responses and provided an objective method for the study of learning phenomena. It therefore played an influential role in the thinking of later behaviorists such as Watson. For example, shortly after the publication of *Psychology From the Standpoint of a Behaviorist* (1919), Watson reported on the conditioning of emotional reactions in an infant. The research on Albert, an eleven-month-old child, has become a classic in psychology. In this research, the experimenters, Watson and Rayner (1920), trained the infant to fear animals and objects that previously were not feared. Watson and Rayner found that striking a hammer on a suspended steel bar produced a startle and fear response in the infant Albert. They then found that if the bar was struck immediately behind Albert's head just as he began to reach for a rat, he would begin to fear the rat whereas previously he had not shown this response. After doing this a number of times the experimenters found that the instant the rat alone (without the sound) was shown to Albert, he began to cry. He had developed what is called a **conditioned emotional reaction**. Albert now feared the rat because of its emotional association with the frightening sound. Furthermore, there was evidence that Albert began to fear other objects that somewhat resembled the rat. Despite some evidence that Albert's emotional reaction was not as strong or as general as expected (B. Harris, 1979), Watson and Rayner concluded that many fears are conditioned emotional reactions. On this basis they criticized the more complex psychoanalytic interpretations.

> *The Freudians twenty years from now, unless their hypotheses change, when they come to analyze Albert's fear of a seal skin coat . . . will proba-*

bly tease from him the recital of a dream upon which their analysis will show that Albert at three years of age attempted to play with the pubic hair of the mother and was scolded violently for it . . . If the analyst has sufficiently prepared Albert to accept such a dream when found as an explanation of his avoiding tendencies, and if the analyst has the authority and personality to put it over, Albert may be fully convinced that the dream was a true revealer of the factors which brought about the fear.

Watson and Rayner, 1920, p. 14

The classical conditioning of emotional reactions is now seen by many psychologists as playing a critical role in the development of psychopathology. Particularly noteworthy here is the suggestion of Eysenck that "most if not all neurotic symptoms are produced by a process of Pavlovian conditioning" (1982, p. 30). A key element in such "symptoms" is the association of anxiety with inappropriate conditioned stimuli, just as Albert developed a conditioned emotional reaction to the rat and related stimuli. It may seem strange to find the name of Eysenck, a trait theorist, arise again here in a chapter on learning theory. However, this occurs for two reasons. First, Eysenck placed great emphasis on overt behavior and empiricism. Second, Pavlov's system provided for the importance of broad individual differences. Pavlov was a physiologist and was primarily interested in nervous system functioning. Part of his theory included an emphasis on genetic differences in nervous system activity, in particular the strength of excitatory and inhibitory processes. These differences in nervous system functioning were related by Pavlov to personality types that are similar to those later emphasized by Eysenck (Gray, 1979). Thus, Eysenck could readily tie his interest in broad individual differences or personality types to Pavlov's theory of learning and emphasis on genetic differences in nervous system activity. As we shall see in the next chapter, this view of the nature of personality and psychopathology becomes connected with a model of behavior change as well.

Most of the work on classical conditioning has focused on relatively simple reflex mechanisms that humans share with other animals. However, Pavlov also recognized the importance of speech and thought in what he called the *second signal system*. The concept of the second signal system provides for an understanding of much more complex organizations of stimuli and responses. An illustration of the importance of this concept is provided by Razran's (1939) research on *semantic conditioning*. In this research with human subjects, Razran paired the visual presentation of the words *style, urn, freeze,* and *surf* with food reinforcement, leading to the development of a salivary response to the words. He then tested whether the conditioned response would generalize to words that sounded similar (stile, earn, frieze, and serf) or to the words that sounded different but were similar in meaning (fashion, vase, chill, and wave). What would one expect to find—generalization to sound or to meaning? Razran found a significant difference in terms of the latter, suggesting that conditioning processes can be influenced by meaning or semantics. Pavlov himself did relatively little research on the second signal system, but it has continued to be a major area of investigation in

Russian psychology, including developmental studies of changes in the factors controlling conditioning processes.

The concepts of conditioned emotional responses and a second signal system provide for a considerably expanded interpretation of the importance of classical conditioning in human behavior. For example, it has been suggested that people acquire motives or goals on the basis of an association of positive and negative affect with stimuli, including symbols (Pervin, 1983; Staats & Burns, 1982). As we see in the next chapter, classical conditioning theory has played an important role in the development of procedures for behavior change. With the exception of some work in Eastern Europe (Strelau, 1983), however, relevant research has tended to focus on experimental work on learning rather than on extension of the theory as a basis for understanding personality.

SKINNER'S THEORY OF OPERANT CONDITIONING

B. F. Skinner (1904–   ) is the most influential supporter of an extreme behaviorist point of view. He is perhaps the best known American psychologist and his views about psychology and society have been the source of considerable controversy.

A View of the Theorist

The scientist, like any organism, is the product of a unique history. The practices which he finds most appropriate will depend in part upon his history . . . When we have at last an adequate empirical account of the behav-

B.F. Skinner

> *ior of Man Thinking, we shall understand all this. Until then, it may be best not to try to fit all scientists into any single mold.*

Skinner, 1959, p. 379

In this passage, Skinner takes the point of view that has been argued in each of the theory chapters in this book; that is, that psychologists' orientations and research strategies are, in part, consequences of their own life history and expressions of their own personalities.

B.F. Skinner was born in New York, the son of a lawyer who was described by his son as having been desperately hungry for praise, and a mother who had rigid standards of right and wrong. Skinner (1967) described his home during his early years as a warm and stable environment. He reported a love for school, and showed an early interest in building things. This interest in building things is particularly interesting in relation to the behavioral emphasis on laboratory equipment in the experimental setting, and because it contrasts with the absence of such an interest in the lives and research of the clinical personality theorists.

At about the time that Skinner entered college, his younger brother died. Skinner commented that he was not much moved by his brother's death and that he probably felt guilty for not being moved. Skinner went to Hamilton College and majored in English literature. At that time, his goal was to become a writer, and at one point he sent three short stories to Robert Frost, from whom he received an encouraging reply. After college, Skinner spent a year trying to write, but concluded that at that point in his life he had nothing to say. He then spent six months living in Greenwich Village in New York. During this time he read Pavlov's *Conditioned Reflexes* and came across a series of articles by Bertrand Russell on Watson's behaviorism. Although Russell thought that he had demolished Watson in these articles, they aroused Skinner's interest in behaviorism.

Although Skinner had not taken any college psychology courses, he had begun to develop an interest in the field and was accepted for graduate work in psychology at Harvard. He justified his change in goals as follows. "A writer might portray human behavior accurately, but he did not therefore understand it. I was to remain interested in human behavior, but the literary method had failed me; I would turn to the scientific" (Skinner, 1967, p. 395). Although he was not quite sure what it was about, psychology appeared to be the relevant science. Besides, he had long been interested in animal behavior (being able to recall his fascination with the complex behaviors of a troupe of performing pigeons). Furthermore, there would now be many opportunities to make use of his interest in building gadgets.

During his graduate school years at Harvard, Skinner developed his interest in animal behavior and in explaining this behavior without reference to the functioning of the nervous system. After reading Pavlov, he did not agree with him that, in explaining behavior, one could go "from the salivary reflexes to the important business of the organism in everyday life." However, Skinner believed that Pavlov had given him the key to understanding behavior. "Control your conditions (the environment) and you shall see order!'' During these and the following years, Skinner (1959) developed some of his principles of scientific methodology: (1) When you run into something interesting, drop everything else and study it. (2) Some ways of doing research are easier than others. A mechanical apparatus often makes doing research easier. (3) Some people are lucky. (4) A piece of apparatus breaks down. This presents problems, but it can also lead to (5) serendipity—the art of finding one thing while looking for something else.

After Harvard, Skinner moved first to Minnesota, then to Indiana, and then returned to Harvard in 1948. During this time he became, in a sense, a sophisticated animal trainer—he was able to make organisms engage in specific behaviors at specific times. He turned from work with rats to work with pigeons. Finding that the behavior of any single animal did not necessarily reflect the average picture of learning based on many animals, he became interested in the manipulation and control of individual animal behavior. Special theories of learning and circuitous explanations of behavior were not necessary if one could manipulate the environment so as to produce orderly change in the individual case. In the meantime, as Skinner notes, his own behavior was becoming controlled by the positive results being given to him by the animals ''under his control'' (Figure 11.2).

The basis of Skinner's operant conditioning procedure is the control of behavior through the manipulation of rewards and punishments in the environment, particularly the laboratory environment. However, his conviction concerning the importance of the laws of behavior and his interest in building things have led Skinner to take his thinking and research far beyond the confines of the laboratory environment. He built a baby box to mechanize the care of a baby, developed teaching machines that used rewards in the teaching of school subjects, and developed a procedure whereby pigeons would be used militarily to land a missile on target. He has written a novel, *Walden Two*, describing a utopia based on the control of human behavior through positive reinforcement (reward). He has committed himself to the view that a science of human behavior and the technology to be derived from it must be developed in the service of humankind.

FIGURE 11.2   ''Boy, have I got this guy conditioned! Everytime I press the bar down he drops in a piece of food.'' (Skinner, 1956)

In 1971, Skinner's *Beyond Freedom and Dignity* was published and became a national best seller. In this book, Skinner spelled out the rationale for his position that a technology of behavior in which environmental conditions are manipulated to shape human behavior offers the greatest hope for solving the problems of society. The book touched off a great deal of controversy and criticism, both of Skinner and of behaviorism. Aside from outrage at the thought of a society in which virtually all behavior was systematically controlled by external forces, Skinner's work was criticized for its neglect of essential aspects of humans—innate endowment, cognitive processes, and feelings or other states within the organism. This criticism led to Skinner's book *About Behaviorism* (1974) in which he indicated acceptance of genetic endowments and internal processes, but continued to argue the importance of controlling conditions in the external environment. "The exploration of the emotional and motivational life of the mind has been described as one of the great achievements in the history of human thought, but it is possible that it has been one of the great disasters. In its search for internal explanation, supported by the false sense of cause associated with feelings and introspective observations, mentalism has obscured the environmental antecedents which would have led to a much more effective analysis" (1974, p. 165).

Before turning to Skinner's theory as it relates to personality, it may be useful to contrast its general qualities with those of theories considered in earlier chapters. Each of the theories covered in these earlier chapters has placed considerable emphasis on structural concepts. Freud used structural concepts such as id, ego, and superego; Rogers used concepts such as self and ideal self; Kelly used the concept of constructs; and Allport, Eysenck and Cattell used the concept of traits. The concept of structure relates to relatively enduring qualities of organization and tends to be an important element in accounting for individual differences. But the behavioral approach to personality emphasizes situational specificity and minimizes the importance of broad response predispositions relative to the importance of stimuli in the external environment. Therefore, it is not surprising to find few structural concepts in learning theory. Corresponding to a lack of emphasis on structure, there is considerable emphasis on the concepts of process and, in particular, on processes that hold true for all individuals. In summary, because the theory is based on assumptions that are different from the ones of other theories, the formal properties of the theory are different from those already studied.

Skinner's Theory of Personality

Structure

The key structural unit for the behavioral approach in general, and Skinner's approach in particular, is the **response**. The nature of a response may range from a simple reflex response (for example, salivation to food, startle to a loud noise) to a complex piece of behavior (e.g., solution to a math problem, subtle forms of aggression). What is critical to the definition of a response is that it represents an external, observable piece of behavior (response) that can be related to environmental events. The learning process essentially involves the association or connection of responses to events in the environment.

In his approach to learning, Skinner distinguishes between responses elicited by known stimuli, such as an eyeblink reflex to a puff of air, and responses that cannot be associated with any stimuli. These responses are emitted by the organism and are called **operants**. Skinner's view is that stimuli in the environment do not force the organism to behave or incite it into action. The initial cause of behavior is in the organism itself. "There is no environmental eliciting stimulus for operant behavior; it simply occurs. In the terminology of operant conditioning, operants are emitted by the organism. The dog walks, runs, and romps; the bird flies; the monkey swings from tree to tree; the human infant babbles vocally. In each case, the behavior occurs without any specific eliciting stimulus . . . It is in the biological nature of organisms to emit operant behavior" (Reynolds, 1968, p. 8).

Process—Operant Conditioning

If structural units are of such minor significance to the theory, it is critical that there be considerable sophistication about the process aspects of behavior. Indeed, in the sense that a learning theory approach to personality is being considered, a process orientation is being dealt with. Before discussing some of the processes that this theory views as underlying behavior, it is important to consider the concept of reinforcer. The Skinnerians define a **reinforcer** as an event (stimulus) that follows a response and increases the probability of its occurrence. If a pigeon's pecking at a disc, which is a piece of operant behavior, is followed by a reinforcer such as food, the probability of it pecking at the disc is increased. According to this view, a reinforcer strengthens the behavior it follows and there is no need to turn to biological explanations to determine why a stimulus reinforces behavior. Skinnerians postulate that some stimuli appear to be reinforcing for all animals and appear to be innate, while other stimuli only serve as reinforcers for some animals and appear to be based on their past association with innate reinforcers, that is, stimuli that originally do not serve as reinforcers can come to do so through their association with other reinforcers. Some stimuli, such as money, become **generalized reinforcers** because they provide access to many other kinds of reinforcers.

It is important to observe here that a reinforcer is defined by its effect on behavior, an increase in the probability of a response, and is not defined in a theoretical way. Often it is difficult to know precisely what will serve as a reinforcer for behavior, as it may vary from individual to individual or from organism to organism. Finding a reinforcer may turn out to be a trial-and-error operation. One keeps trying stimuli until one finds a stimulus that can reliably increase the probability of a certain response.

The focus of the Skinnerian approach is on the qualities of responses and their relationships to rates and intervals at which they are reinforced or **schedules of reinforcements**. A simple experimental device, the Skinner box, is used to study these relationships. In this kind of box there are few stimuli, and behaviors such as a rat's pressing of a bar or a pigeon's pecking of a key are observed. It is here, according to Skinner, that one can best observe the elementary laws of behavior. These laws are discovered through the control of behavior, in this case the bar-pressing activity of the rat or the key-pecking activity of the pigeon. Behavior is understood when it can be controlled by specific changes in the environment. To understand behavior is to control it. Behavior is controlled through the choice of responses that are reinforced and the rates at which they are reinforced. Schedules of reinforcement can be based on a particular *time interval* or a particular *response interval*. In a time interval schedule, the reinforcement appears after a certain period, say every minute, regardless of the number of responses made by the organism. In response interval, or a response ratio schedule, reinforcements appear after a certain number of responses (for example, presses of a bar, pecks of a key) have been made.

Thus, reinforcements need not be given after every response, but can instead be given only sometimes. Furthermore, reinforcements can be given on a regular or a *fixed* basis, always a certain period of time or after a certain number of responses, or they can be given on a *variable* basis, sometimes after a minute and sometimes after two minutes, or sometimes after a few responses and sometimes after many responses. Each schedule of reinforcement tends to stabilize behavior in a different way.

In a sense, operant learning represents a sophisticated formulation of the principles of animal training. Complex behavior is *shaped* through a process of <u>successive approximation;</u> that is, complex behaviors are developed by reinforcing pieces of behavior that resemble the final form of behavior one wants to produce.

> *Operant conditioning shapes behavior as a sculptor shapes a lump of clay. Although at some point the sculptor seems to have produced an entirely novel object, we can always follow the process back to the original undifferentiated lump, and we can make the successive stages by which we return to this condition as small as we wish. At no point does anything emerge which is very different from what preceded it . . . An operant is not something which appears full grown in the behavior of the organism. It is the result of a continuous shaping process.*

Skinner, 1953, p. 91

The process of shaping or successive approximation is seen most clearly in the work of animal trainers. The difficult tricks performed by circus animals are not learned as complete wholes. Rather, the trainer gradually builds up sequences of learned responses through the reinforcement of particular behaviors that are then linked to or chained to one another. What started off as the learning of individual behaviors ends up as the display of a complex series of acts before a circus audience. The animal ultimately is rewarded for its behavior, but the final reward is made dependent, or contingent, upon the performance of the series of previously learned behaviors. In a similar way, complex behaviors in humans may be developed through the process of successive approximation.

While most of the emphasis in operant conditioning is on the use of positive reinforcers such as food, money, or praise, Skinnerians also emphasize the importance of negative reinforcers. A **negative reinforcer** is an unpleasant or aversive event which when removed increases the probability of occurrence of the preceding response. Just as behavior can be conditioned and shaped through the presentation of positive reinforcers such as food, so it can be shaped by the removal of a painful stimulus such as shock. In **escape learning,** a response is reinforced because it is associated with the termination of an aversive (unpleasant) stimulus. The experimenter can shape behavior by applying an aversive stimulus, such as a shock, and then allow the organism to terminate the shock by making the desired response. In **avoidance learning,** behaviors are reinforced because they allow the individual to avoid completely an aversive stimulus. Thus, in a situation similar to the classical conditioning of the withdrawal response, a tone may be sounded before the presentation of a shock. If the organism emits the desired response, the shock does not appear, and the tone may be turned off. The relevant response is reinforced because it is associated with the avoidance of the aversive shock stimulus and because it ends the aversive tone stimulus. In contrast with classical conditioning, the interest here is in the reinforcement of a response through escape or avoidance, rather than in the process by which the tone takes on aversive properties. In contrast with the situation of *positive reinforcement*, escape and avoidance behaviors are reinforced by the removal of a stimulus instead of by the presentation of stimulus.

Both escape and avoidance situations can also be contrasted with the effects of another aversive situation, namely, **punishment**. In punishment, an aversive stimulus is presented following the occurrence of an operant response. *The presentation of the aversive stimulus decreases the probability that a particular response will occur again.* However, the effect is temporary and it appears to be of little value in eliminating behavior. For this reason, Skinner has emphasized the use of positive reinforcement in the shaping of behavior.

Growth and Development

Although theories of learning have grown out of research with animals, considerable effort has been made to relate these theories to principles of human growth and development. In some ways, this is a natural development, since the socialization of the child is basically a learning process. Furthermore, it is a process in which parents attempt to use material and psychological rewards to shape the behavior of their children. The process by which children shape the behavior of their parents, through their own dispensation of rewards and punishments, has received less attention (Lewis & Rosenblum, 1974).

The Skinnerian view of growth and development continues to emphasize the importance of schedules of reinforcement in the acquisition and performance of behavior. As the child develops, responses are conditioned and remain under the control of reinforcement contingencies in the environment. The emphasis is on specific response patterns as they are influenced by specific environmental reinforcers (Gewirtz, 1968b). Children become self-reliant through the reinforcement of acts in which they take care of themselves, for instance, in eating and dressing. The child is reinforced immediately on the completion of those acts, both by material rewards such as food and by social rewards such as praise. The child becomes emotionally independent through the development of a stable rate of response (one that occurs at regular intervals) that require only occasional reinforcement. In learning to tolerate delay of gratification (reinforcement), the child may first be gratified after a brief period of delay and then gradually may be reinforced for longer periods of delay between request and gratification. After a while, delay behavior becomes stabilized, and one can say that the child has developed an ability to tolerate delays in gratification (Gewirtz, 1968a).

Skinnerians accept the view that behaviors can be imitated without being directly reinforced. However, this is true only where imitation itself has taken on the qualities of a reinforcer; that is, the positive reinforcement of a number of specific imitative responses can lead to a generalized imitative response tendency (Baer & Sherman, 1964; Baer, Peterson, & Sherman, 1967). Thus, whereas initially responses are reinforced because they match the ones of a model, ultimately the matching of responses per se becomes reinforcing. In this way, the child becomes generally imitative and learns many responses that are similar to those performed by the model.

In line with Skinnerian principles of reinforcement, Sherman (1971) has developed imitative language behavior in formerly nonimitative, speech-deficient children. Using bites of food as reinforcers for successively close approximations to what the experimenter did, Sherman was able to increase the probability of a child's imitating a new response from a very low level to nearly 100 percent. Children reinforced for doing as the experimenter did would imitate new behaviors even though the specific responses had never been trained. Furthermore, they would continue to exhibit these new behaviors in the absence of reinforcement for them—as long as other, different imitations were reinforced. Thus, from the Skinnerian point of view, new behaviors may be acquired in the course of growth and development through the process of successive approximations, or through the process of development of a generalized imitative repertoire. In either case, the behaviors are under the control of the reinforcement contingencies in the environment.

Psychopathology

The general learning theory position on psychopathology may be stated as follows: the basic principles of learning provide a completely adequate interpretation of psychopathology. Explanations in terms of symptoms with underlying causes are superfluous. According to the behavioral point of view, behavioral pathology is not a disease. Instead, it is a response pattern learned according to the same principles of behavior as are all response patterns. "The specific behavior termed abnormal is learned, maintained, and altered in the same manner as is normal behavior, and normal behavior itself may be viewed as an adjustment resulting from a particular history of reinforcement'' (Ullman & Krasner, 1969, p. 105). The authors of this quote go on to define abnormal behavior as the failure to make an appropriate response. This definition again points to the behavioral emphasis on observable behavior and specific responses. Furthermore, they suggest that definitions of adjustment must be situation specific. Again one can see the behavioral emphasis on the external environment and the minimization of factors inside the individual that may lead to consistency in behavior across situations.

The proponents of the learning theory point of view argue against any concept of the unconscious, against the concept of disease entities, and against the concept of a ''sick personality.'' Individuals are not sick, they merely do not respond appropriately to stimuli. Either they have failed to learn a response or they have learned a maladaptive response. There is no need to interpret behavior as resulting from an Oedipus complex, a self-concept, or a construct system. One need only demonstrate the ability to account for behaviors in terms of the principles of learning theory. Thus, the Skinnerian interpretation of abnormal behavior follows directly from the emphasis on reinforcement contingencies in the environment that shape and maintain response patterns. Behaviors that are labeled as pathological are learned in the same way as all other behaviors. A person may be labeled as neurotic or psychotic because of a faulty conditioning history. This faulty conditioning history may involve (1) the lack of development of a response that is normally part of a person's response repertoire (the entire range of response behavior), of (2) the development of a ''healthy'' response that is under the control of inappropriate reinforcers, or (3) the development of a response that is labeled as ''bad,'' ''sick,'' or ''neurotic'' in the society.

The first of these three pathological developments represents a case of behavioral deficit (Bandura, 1968). For example, children and adults who are socially inadequate may have had faulty reinforcement histories in which social skills were not developed. Ordinarily a variety of social skills are learned as a result of reinforcement during the socialization process. When this fails to occur, the person is left with an inadequate response repertoire with which to respond to social situations.

In the second pathological condition, a response pattern has been developed, but it is ''out of whack'' with schedules of reinforcement in the environment. People may have ''normal'' responses in their repertoires, but these responses are not being reinforced by the environment. One possible result of the withdrawal of positive reinforcement in the environment is what is ordinarily called depression. Depression represents a lessening of behavior or a lowered response rate. The depressed person is often not responsive because positive reinforcement has been withdrawn (Ferster, 1973).

The situation in which a person is out of touch with the conditions of reinforcement in the environment is viewed as basic to schizophrenia, a serious thought disorder. According to Ullman and Krasner (1975), schizophrenia is a result of the failure of the environment to reinforce certain sequences of behavior. Schizophrenics attend to unusual cues in the environment because they have not been re-inforced for attending to the social stimuli to which "normal" people respond. What is interpreted by the ordinary observer as a lack of attention is really an attention to unusual cues. What is labeled as lack of emotion and blandness is a lack of responsiveness to normal social stimuli. Related to this situation, is the development of **superstitious behavior** (Skinner, 1948). Superstitious behavior develops because of an accidental relationship between a response and reinforcement. Thus, Skinner found that if he gave pigeons small amounts of food at regular intervals regardless of what they were doing, many birds would come to associate the response that was coincidentally rewarded with systematic reinforcement. For example, if a pigeon was coincidentally rewarded while walking around in a counterclockwise direction, this response might become conditioned even though it had no cause–effect relationship with the reinforcement. The continuous performance of the behavior would result in occasional, again coincidental, reinforcement. Thus, the behavior could be maintained over long periods of time. An observer looking in on this situation might be tempted to say: "Look at that crazy pigeon."

In the third pathological condition, individuals have responses they should not have. This can be either because of a history in which these responses resulted in the avoidance of punishment or they resulted in positive reinforcement. Neurotic symptoms, such as obsessions and compulsions, are learned because they remove an aversive stimulus. What is ordinarily called masochism can have a similar basis (Sandler, 1964). According to one interpretation, masochistic individuals expose themselves to an aversive stimulus to avoid another aversive stimulus. Thus, these individuals may behave in a way that suggests that it is better to hit themselves before someone else hits them harder. Another interpretation of masochism relates to the inappropriate positive reinforcement of behaviors. According to this interpretation, masochists punish themselves because they have come to associate this response with positive reinforcement. This could happen, for example, if the reinforcement history involved self-punishment as a condition for reward, such as when a parent praises a child for having "atoned" in some way for "bad" behavior.

Other "sick" behaviors can be similarly interpreted as a result of positive reinforcement. For example, someone could develop a fetish (unusual attraction to an object) because of a history in which the desired object has been associated with reinforcement. Bandura (1968) reports two relevant cases in the literature. In one, a ten-year-old boy developed a dress fetish because his mother had paid him attention whenever he stroked her dress. In the other, a man developed an association between sexual arousal and black shiny rubber as a result of an early experience in which a group of boys seized him, tied him up, and masturbated him.

These examples illustrate how the Skinnerian avoids an emphasis on concepts such as drive, conflict, and unconscious, and instead interprets psychopathology in terms of responses and schedules of reinforcement. More generally, they illustrate the Skinnerian emphasis on personality as the organization of learned responses. Individuals have unique personalities because, in addition to inherited differences, they have unique reinforcement histories. However, the development of these idiosyncratic response organizations follows the same laws of learning.

STIMULUS-RESPONSE THEORY: HULL, DOLLARD AND MILLER

Stimulus–response (S–R) theory was being developed by people such as Hull and Dollard and Miller while Skinner was developing his operant conditioning view. However, S–R theory probably reached its peak of systematization and influence earlier than did Skinner's approach. For some time the operant and S–R approaches represented competitive points of view and considerable controversy and debate existed over their relative merits. This is not quite so true today, although differences remain and often these differences do become controversial.

A View of the Theorists

Several theorists have made significant contributions to the development of stimulus–response learning theory. Among these, however, three figures are of particular significance. The first, Clark L. Hull, made a major effort to develop a systematic, comprehensive theory of learning. The second two, John Dollard and Neal E. Miller, are particularly well-known for their efforts to bring together the remarkable accomplishments of Freud and Hull.

Clark L. Hull (1884–1952)

Hull was born in New York, but early in his life he and his family moved to a farm in Michigan. There was a considerable emphasis on religion in his family. Although at one point he had a religious conversion experience at an evangelist revival meeting, Hull began to have considerable doubt about religion and abandoned his beliefs in it.

During his early school years, Hull was very interested in mathematics and described the study of geometry as the most important event of his intellectual life. At college, he began studying math, physics, and chemistry with the goal of becoming a mining engineer. However, after two years at school, he became ill with polio and was forced to consider a new life occupation. His interest in theory and in the design of automatic equipment led him to the study of psychology. After a difficult and incomplete recovery from polio, Hull returned to college to concentrate in psychology at the University of Michigan.

After a brief stint as a teacher in Kentucky, Hull went on to graduate work in psychology at the University of Wisconsin. He first developed an interest in finding a scientific basis for aptitude testing and then systematically studied what takes place during hypnosis. During the time that he was at the University of Wisconsin, word was spreading of Watson's views of behaviorism and Hull found himself sympathetic to this new emphasis on objectivity.

Clark L. Hull

In 1929, Hull went to Yale as a professor of psychology. He had just read a translation of Pavlov's *Conditioned Reflexes* and was interested in comparisons between Pavolv's research and the experiments that were being conducted in this country. Also, he was forced to end his research on hypnosis because of an attitude of fear of hypnosis. The following years witnessed a coming together of his interests in math, geometry, theory, apparatus construction, and psychology as a natural science. In 1940, he published his *Mathematics-Deductive Theory of Rote Learning*, and, in 1943, his *Principles of Behavior*. Of particular importance was Hull's emphasis on a systematic theory of the process of instrumental learning.

Hull's emphasis on a systematic theory of learning, careful experimentation, the development of habits (stimulus–response associations) as a result of reward, and on the many facets of the instrumental learning process laid much of the groundwork for a learning theory approach to social psychology and to the study of personality. Out of Hull's framework developed attempts to understand attitude change from an instrumental learning model (Hovland & Janis, 1959), and attempts to relate the behavioral laws of learning theory to psychoanalytic phenomena (Dollard & Miller, 1950).

John Dollard (1900–1980) and Neal E. Miller (1909–   )

John Dollard was born in Wisconsin and received his undergraduate degree from the University of Wisconsin in 1922. He obtained his graduate degree (Ph.D., 1931) in sociology from the University of Chicago. Following this he taught sociology, anthropology, and psychology at Yale University. An unusual aspect of Dollard's professional development, and one that significantly influenced his later thinking, was his training in psychoanalysis at the Berlin Psychoanalytic Institute. His interest in psychoanalysis, clinical work, and the social sciences continued throughout his professional career.

Neal E. Miller also was born in Wisconsin. He received his undergraduate degree from the University of Washington and his Ph.D from Yale University in 1935. During this time he came into contact with Hull and Dollard, and also obtained training in psychoanalysis at the Vienna Institute of Psychoanalysis. He continued to spend the major part of his professional career at Yale until 1966 when he joined the faculty at Rockefeller University. During his time at Yale, Miller made many significant experimental and theoretical contributions to stimulus–response theory. These were particularly in the area of motivation and learned drives. Subsequently he has become a major figure in the area of biofeedback or the learning of voluntary control over bodily processes such as heart rate and blood pressure (N.E. Miller, 1978, 1983). In 1951 Miller was elected president of the American Psychological Association.

The collaborative work of Dollard and Miller is expressed in three major books. In the first, *Frustration and Aggression* (1939), completed with colleagues at Yale's Institute of Human Relations, there was an attempt to develop a scientific theory of aggressive behavior based on the assumption that aggression is a response to frustration. In the second, *Social Learning and Imitation* (1941), Miller and Dollard attempted to apply Hull's theory to personality and social psychology. Finally, in the third book, *Personality and Psychotherapy* (1950), Dol-

John Dollard

lard and Miller attempted to integrate the achievements of learning theory, as expressed in the works of Pavlov, Hull, and others, with the achievements of psychoanalysis, as expressed in the works of Freud, and with the achievements of other figures in the social sciences. In this book they attempted to apply the basic principles of learning to complex personality functioning, neurotic phenomena, and psychotherapy. This was significant in that it directed attention to the application of learning theory to clinical phenomena. However, in contrast with the approaches of current behavior modificationists and behavior therapists, the use of learning theory did not itself lead to the development of new therapeutic techniques.

The S–R Theory of Personality

The helpless, naked, human infant is born with primary drives such as hunger, thirst, and reactions to pain and cold. He does not have, however, many of the motives that distinguish the adult as a member of a particular tribe, nation, social class, occupation, or profession. Many extremely important drives, such as the desire for money, the ambition to become an artist or a scholar, and particular fears and guilts are learned during socialization.

Dollard and Miller, 1950, p. 62

Neal E. Miller

Structure

As in Skinner's operant theory, the key structural concept for S–R theory is the *response*. However, whereas Skinner places little importance on the stimulus that leads to and becomes associated with the response, the S–R view is that stimuli become connected to responses to form stimulus–response bonds. According to Hullian theory, an association between a stimulus and a response is called a **habit**; personality structure is largely composed of the habits, or S–R bonds, that are learned by the organism and of the relationships among these habits.

Another structural concept used by the followers of Hull is that of **drive.** A drive is broadly defined as a stimulus strong enough to activate behavior. Using the Hullian model; it is drives that make the individual respond. A distinction is made between *innate, primary drives,* and *learned, secondary drives.* The primary drives, such as pain and hunger, are generally associated with physiological conditions within the organism. "One of these is pain. Pain can reach stabbing heights of greater strength than probably any other single drive. The parching sensation of thirst, the pangs of extreme hunger, and the sore weight of fatigue are other examples of powerful innate drives. The bitter sting of cold and the insistent goading of sex are further examples" (Dollard & Miller, 1950, p. 30).

Secondary drives are drives that have been acquired on the basis of their association with the satisfaction of the primary drives. "These learned drives are acquired on the basis of the primary drives, represent elaborations of them, and serve as a façade behind which the functions of the underlying innate drives are hidden. These learned drives are exceedingly important in human behavior" (Dollard & Miller, 1950, pp. 31–32). An acquired drive of considerable importance is that of anxiety or fear. Based on the primary drive of pain, the secondary drive of anxiety is important because it can be learned quickly and become strong. Anxiety can lead the organism toward a variety of behaviors and is of particular importance in relation to abnormal behavior.

In contrast with the psychoanalytic emphasis on drives, the S–R emphasis on drives is associated with specific environmental conditions and has more to do with the question of motivation than with the differences among individuals. One studies drives in relation to the process of learning rather than in terms of the kinds of drives that characterize different individuals.

Process

According to S–R theory, learning consists of the association of stimuli with responses as a result of the reinforcement that follows these connections. In **instrumental learning** there is an emphasis on learned responses being instrumental in bringing about a desirable situation (e.g., reward, escape from pain, avoidance of pain). The Hullian model of instrumental conditioning is derived from an interest in more complex forms of learning (e.g., problem solving) than is classical or operant conditioning, and is interested also in motivation or goal-directed activity. In the Hullian model, there is an emphasis on drives that lead to internal stimuli, these stimuli then leading to responses that result in rewards. The rewards represent a reduction of the drive stimuli.

The typical experiment in instrumental learning might involve the variables affecting a rat's learning to run a maze. The experimenter changes the number of hours of food deprivation, assumes that this is related to the strength of internal drive (hunger) stimuli, and then observes the behavioral consequences of the rat's having been rewarded for making certain turns in the maze. If a hungry rat receives food for making a response or series of responses in the maze, then the probability is increased that he will make the same responses on further trials in the maze. The responses are reinforced through the reduced strength of hunger drive stimuli.

Another type of experiment is conducted in relation to instrumental escape learning. In this type of experiment (Miller, 1951), a rat is put into a box with two compartments: a white compartment with a grid as a floor, and a black compartment with a solid floor. The compartments are separated by a door. At the beginning of the experiment, the rats are given electric shocks while in the white compartment and are allowed to escape into the black compartment. Thus, a fear response is conditioned to the white compartment. A test is then made as to whether the fear of the white compartment can lead to the learning of a new response. Now, in order for the rat to escape to the black compartment, it must turn a wheel placed in the white compartment. The turning of the wheel opens the door to the black compartment and allows the rat to escape. After a number of trials, the rat begins to rotate the wheel with considerable speed. The interpretation is that the rat has acquired a fear drive in relation to the white compartment. This drive operates to activate the organism and to set the stage for reinforcement, just as the hunger drive did in the maze experiment. Escape from the white into the black compartment involves the learning of a new response—the turning of a wheel. This instrumental learning is based on the consequences of the response, escape from the white compartment, and on the associated reduction in the strength of the fear drive stimuli.

Growth and Development

In general, S–R theory interprets growth and development as consisting of the accumulation of habits, which are then related to one another in a hierarchical arrangement or order of importance. Within this general conceptualization the development of higher mental processes and imitative behavior are of particular importance.

Initially the behavior of the infant is largely a reflexive response to external stimuli and internal drives. In the course of development, however, behavior reflects the central role of thought or **higher mental processes.** Language is of particular importance in the functioning of our higher mental processes and in enabling us to go beyond simple, reflexive responses to stimuli. Language helps us to make important discriminations and generalizations. Words can be attached to drives and, through their symbolic function, themselves lead to drives being aroused. Language enables us to anticipate the future, and thus to go beyond re-inforcers in the immediate situation.

In 1941 Miller and Dollard attempted a social learning interpretation of **imita-** **tive behavior**. They suggested that there were different kinds of imitative behavior but that all such behavior could be derived from a Hullian theory of learning. Most attention was given to a process called matched-dependent behavior. The matched-dependent form of imitative behavior was assumed to occur when one person was aware of important cues in the environment while the other was not. In the socialization of children, there are many times when children are dependent on parents for the recognition of cues and, therefore, match their behavior to that of the parents. The matching of behavior then leads to rewards to the child.

The following illustrates matched-dependent behavior. Two children were playing. One child heard the father's footsteps indicating he was home from work. This child ran to the father and received some candy, which the father generally brought home for the children. The second and younger child was not aware of the footsteps as a cue for the father's return. He generally did not run when the older brother did but, on one occasion, by chance ran behind his brother. This behavior was rewarded by candy from the father and led to an increase in the running of the younger at the sight of the running of the older brother. The younger brother had been rewarded for matching the behavior of the older brother, but he was not aware of the cue for running being used by the other brother.

In an experiment to test this interpretation, Miller and Dollard rewarded one group of rats for going in the same direction in a maze as the leader and another group of rats for going in the opposite direction. Whereas the leader had been trained to make use of a cue for finding food, the other rats were without this cue. As a result, the rats reinforced for imitating the leader learned to use the response of the leader as their cue. Put in other situations, the rats continued to imitate the behavior of the leader. The rats in the other group did not show imitative behavior. In sum, the rats reinforced for following the behavior of a leader learned the response of imitating, and this learned response generalized from the original learning situation to other situations. Similar results were found in research on the learning of imitation by children.

The essential aspects of the imitative process described by Miller and Dollard are that it develops out of trial and error or random behavior and that it is based on the positive reinforcement of matching behavior. Individuals learn to imitate because they are rewarded in the course of doing so. Once such learning has occurred in relation to specific acts, it may generalize to a tendency to imitate other acts in the same person or to the imitation of other people. Thus, the child may develop a generalized tendency toward imitation.

Other efforts have been made to translate Hullian theory into principles of growth and development. Such efforts generally have emphasized the importance of rewards in parental child rearing practices. For example, in one research program the pattern of child rearing found to be most likely to result in "high conscience'' development in children was one in which the mother is generally warm and loving but also uses the threat of withdrawal of affection as a method of control (Sears, Rau, & Alpert, 1965). Later research has suggested that the concept of ''conscience'' is complex and involves many possible behaviors. Furthermore, the relationship of child-rearing practices to personality development is very complicated. As a result, there have tended to be fewer such studies relating early patterns of parental reward to the later development of broad personality characteristics.

Psychopathology

If a neurosis is functional (i.e., a product of experience rather than of organic damage or instinct), it must be learned. . .

The dynamics of conflict behavior are systematically deduced from more basic principles. Thus, a fundamental fact of neurosis—that of conflict—is tied in with general learning theory.

Dollard and Miller, 1950, pp. 8, 10

The Hullian theory of learning emphasizes the importance of drives and the reinforcement that comes from the reduction of drive stimuli. One drive that is critical in the learning of abnormal behaviors is that of anxiety. Although the details of various Hullian explanations of abnormal behavior differ, and some are supportive of psychoanalytic theory while others are not, they all state that abnormal behaviors are learned because they result in the reduction of anxiety drive stimuli.

Dollard and Miller (1950) were among the first to relate the principles of learning theory to personality phenomena, in general, and to abnormal behavior, in particular. In this effort they emphasized the concepts of drive, drive conflict, anxiety, and reinforcement through the reduction of anxiety.

According to Dollard and Miller, a neurosis represents the expression of learned conflicts that are inaccessible to verbal awareness. Neuroses are caused by conflict. In the course of development, children must learn socially accepted outlets for their drives. Particularly critical learning situations are the ones involving feeding, toilet training, and sexual and aggressive behavior. As children grow, they may wish to express certain drives but be punished for doing so by their parents. Or, children may wish to express aggression toward the parents, but be punished for this. The result of punishment is the development of an acquired fear drive in relation to certain stimuli. As we illustrated earlier in this chapter, Miller demonstrated that the response of fear could be conditioned to a previously neutral stimulus (white compartment) and then, itself, take on the properties of a drive stimulus. In some cases, the same stimulus may come to elicit both the original drive and the acquired fear drive. At this point, the individual experiences an **approach–avoidance conflict.** Thus a boy may be torn between making sexual advances toward a girl (approach) and the fear of doing so (avoidance). Another example would be of an individual who wishes to express anger (approach) but is afraid of doing so (avoidance).

Thus, the approach-avoidance conflict between two drives is the basic ingredient for the development of neurotic behavior. As a result of the conflict and the anxiety involved, the individual develops a symptom. The symptom reduces the anxiety and relieves the pressure of the conflict. For example, Dollard and Miller described the case of a twenty three-year-old married woman who had developed a number of fears, one of which was that her heart would stop beating if she did not concentrate on counting the beats. The difficulties started with her feeling faint in a store, then developed into a fear of going out alone, and then into a fear of heart trouble. Dollard and Miller interpreted the symptom as involving as sex-fear conflict. When on the streets alone, the woman was afraid of sexual temptation. She felt that someone might try to seduce her and that she would be vulnerable to the seduction. The increased sex desire accompanying the fantasied seduction touched off anxiety and guilt, leading to the sex-anxiety conflict. Going home and avoiding being alone on the streets were reinforced because they reduced the anxiety and relieved the conflict. The counting of heartbeats was similarly reinforcing because it preoccupied her and did not allow her to think of possible seductions. The counting habit was reinforced by the drop in anxiety.

The case illustrates how Dollard and Miller made use of the concepts of drive, drive conflict, anxiety, and reinforcement through drive reduction to account for the development of a neurosis. Although the details are only sketchy, the case also illustrates how Dollard and Miller attempted to use Hullian theory in a way that was consistent with psychoanalytic theory. In a similar way, they were led to interpret repression as a response inhibiting thought (i.e., a "not-thinking" response).

While most attention has been given to approach-avoidance conflicts in the development of neuroses, Dollard and Miller also emphasized the importance of approach-approach and avoidance-avoidance conflicts. In an **approach–approach conflict** the person is torn between two desirable alternatives. Should the person date one or another attractive individual, watch this great movie or the other great movie, buy this car or that car? In an **avoidance–avoidance conflict** the person is torn between undesirable, unpleasant alternatives. Should the person pay the bill now and be without money or pay a larger bill later, is divorce or living in an unpleasant situation worse, should the child tell the parent and risk punishment or stay silent and feel guilty?

There have been other efforts to use Hullian theory to explain abnormal behavior. Although they have emphasized the concepts of anxiety as a drive, and symptoms as responses that are drive reducing, they have used neither the conflict model nor psychoanalytic theory. In fact, other efforts along Hullian lines have been hostile to psychoanalytic interpretations. Whereas Dollard and Miller, in their application of learning theory to psychoanalytic concepts, continued to use a term such as symptom, current learning approaches reject such concepts. As noted earlier, they are viewed as part of a medical symptom-disease model that is rejected in favor of a behavioral-psychological model. As we see in the next chapter, S–R theory has not been as influential as classical conditioning theory and operant conditioning theory in the development of new approaches to behavior

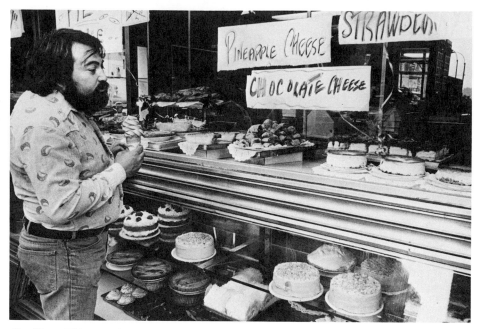

Conflict—This man is facing an approach-approach conflict in terms of what to choose to eat. If he were concerned about gaining weight, he would face an approach-avoidance conflict (i.e., the desire to enjoy the cake and the wish to avoid gaining weight).

change. In part, this is probably due to the S–R emphasis on the concept of drive, an internal variable that grew out of favor after the 1940s. In part, it also is probably due to the early efforts of Dollard and Miller to relate S–R theory to psychoanalysis rather then focusing on the application of the theory to new methods of behavior change.

MAJOR CONCEPTS AND SUMMARY

situational specificity

functional analysis

behaviorism

classical conditioning

generalization

discrimination

extinction

conditioned emotional reaction

second signal system

semantic conditioning

operant conditioning

positive and negative reinforcers

generalized reinforcers

schedules of reinforcement

shaping—successive approximation

habit

drives (primary and secondary)   imitation

ınstrumental learning   approach–avoidance conflict

higher mental processes

This chapter has focused on approaches to personality strikingly different from those previously covered. First, in contrast to the theories of Freud, Rogers, and Kelly, the learning approach comes from the laboratory rather than from the clinic. Second, in contrast to the approach of trait theorists, the learning approach emphasizes specific connections between behavior and environmental events (reinforcers), rather than broad personality dispositions. Third, in this approach, there is a much greater tendency to look for controlling conditions in the environment rather than for forces within the organism.

Watson was a significant figure who laid the foundation for the learning theory, behavioral approach to personality. Watson spelled out the rationale for a behaviorist approach to psychology. Pavlov's work on classical conditioning illustrated how a previously neutral stimulus could become capable of eliciting a response because of its association with a stimulus that automatically produced the same or similar response (e.g., the dog salivates to the bell stimulus associated with the food powder). Generalization, discrimination, and extinction represent three important processes studied by Pavlov. The classical conditioning procedure suggests that many abnormal behaviors are the result of conditioning responses to inappropriate stimuli. Watson and Rayner's case of little Albert illustrated such a conditioned emotional reaction. Eysenck has suggested that such classically conditioned reactions are the basis for all neurotic behavior and, as did Pavlov, emphasizes the importance of individual differences in nervous sytem functioning. While he primarily emphasized reflex-like behaviors shared by humans with other animals, Pavlov also emphasized the importance of speech and thought in the second signal systems. Research on semantic conditioning illustrates the importance of this system as well as the role of classical conditioning in more complex human phenomena.

In Skinner's operant conditioning, there is an interest in responses (operants) that cannot be linked with known stimuli but that are learned because they are followed by reinforcement. A reinforcer increases the probability of the responses it follows. Behavior is brought under the control of the experimenter through the manipulation of schedules of reinforcement. Complex behaviors are shaped by reinforcing successive approximations to the desired, final behavior. Imitation of behaviors occurs where the person has been reinforced for specific imitative responses and thus developed a generalized imitative response tendency. The Skinnerian interpretation of psychopathology emphasizes behavioral deficits (e.g., lack of speech, lack of social skills) and the development of maladaptive responses that are maintained by reinforcers in the environment.

In the S–R, instrumental learning approach of Hull and Dollard and Miller, habits are learned through the reinforcement of stimulus–response connections. Reinforcement consists of the reduction of drive stimuli, either of primary, innate drives, or of secondary, learned drives, such as anxiety. The emphasis in growth and development is on the development of higher mental processes and imitation. The S–R interpretation of psychopathology places major emphasis on the role of approach–avoidance conflicts and the role of anxiety drive stimuli. As with other learning approaches, the basic principles of learning are seen as adequate for an understanding of the development of abnormal behavior. Psychopathology is viewed in terms of learned maladaptive responses and adaptive responses that have not been learned adequately. In other words, a behavioral-psychological model is used rather than a medical symptom-disease model.

These three approaches to learning share certain characteristics and concepts in common. At the same time, differences remain. In particular, classical conditioning emphasizes the importance of associations among stimuli, operant conditioning ignores such associations and emphasizes response-reinforcement relationships, while S–R theory emphasizes the importance of organismic variables such as drives and higher mental processes that intervene between stimuli and responses. Within the learning literature, there is considerable controversy as to whether the three are indeed distinct learning processes or basically follow the same principles (Rescorla & Holland, 1982). In addition, there is considerable controversy concerning the role of cognition in learning. For example, whereas some psychologists would suggest that cognition is important in all forms of human learning (Brewer, 1974), others, such as Eysenck, have minimized its role in fundamental behavior processes. As we see in the next chapter, learning approaches have made significant contributions to the development of new assessment methods and new approaches to behavior change. We also see how the significance of cognitive phenomena again becomes an issue that divides behavioral psychologists.

Matisse, Henri. *Jazz*, Plate VII. 1947. Fogg Art Museum, Harvard University.

BEHAVIORAL APPROACHES TO PERSONALITY ASSESSMENT AND CHANGE

CHAPTER FOCUS: This chapter continues consideration of learning and behavioral approaches to personality. The focus here is on procedures for assessment and change. The behavioral approach to assessment emphasizes specific responses in relation to specific situations rather than global personality characteristics. Procedures for producing behavior change involve the utilization of principles from classical and operant conditioning. Here too the emphasis is on changing specific responses and their relations to environmental stimuli and reinforcers rather than on global personality change. Attention is then given to a major new development, the emphasis on cognition or internal images and self-statements. Ways in which cognitive behavioral assessment and change procedures are similar to and different from earlier procedures are considered. The chapter concludes with an overall evaluation of the strengths and limitations of learning and behavioral approaches to personality.

In contrast to the psychodynamic orientation, which focuses on the characteristics a person "has" (i.e., his "motives," "needs," "drives," "defenses," "traits," or other similar inferred traits), the behavioral approach to assessment places greater emphasis on what a person "does" in various situations. The basic unit for consideration therefore becomes the individual's response to specific aspects of his environment.

Cautela and Upper, 1976, p. 77

The major aspects of behavior modification are the focus on overt behavior and the application of concepts drawn from learning theory to attain change . . . Despite differences in approaches and techniques, we would propose that all behavior modification boils down to procedures utilizing systematic environmental contingencies to alter the subject's response to stimuli.

Ullman and Krasner, 1965, p. 29

In the previous chapter, three theories of learning were considered in conjunction with their implications for personality. A number of points of emphasis were suggested as being common to these behavioral approaches: an emphasis on empiricism, an emphasis on principles of learning, an emphasis on reinforcers and situational specificity of behavior, and a rejection of the medical symptom-disease model of psychopathology. Implicit in these four points are two additional points of emphasis: the importance of specific responses or behaviors as opposed to global personality characteristics, and the importance of current variables that maintain and control behavior as opposed to events in the past that may have contributed to the development of personality. In this chapter, we will be considering the implications of behavioral approaches for personality assessment and change. These areas represent a particular focus of convenience for these theories as they relate to personality. The amount of current work devoted to behavioral assessment and behavior therapy, as well as the gains made over the past decade, is indeed staggering. In this chapter we have a chance to consider the implications of the above points of emphasis and to contrast them with the approaches previously considered.

BEHAVIORAL ASSESSMENT

The emphasis on specific behaviors tied to defined situational characteristics forms the basis for what has come to be known as **behavioral assessment.** Heavily influenced by the thinking of Skinner, the behavioral approach to assessment emphasizes three things: (1) identification of specific behaviors, often called **target behaviors** or **target responses;** (2) identification of specific environmental factors that elicit, cue, or reinforce the target behaviors; (3) identification of specific environmental factors that can be manipulated to alter the behavior. Thus a behavioral assessment of a child's temper tantrums would include a clear, objective definition of temper tantrum behavior in the child, a complete description of the situation that sets off the tantrum behavior, a complete description of the reactions of parents and others that may be reinforcing the behavior, and an analysis of the potential for eliciting and reinforcing other nontantrum behaviors (Kanfer & Saslow, 1965; O'Leary, 1972). This **functional analysis of behavior**, involving the effort to identify the environmental conditions that control behavior, sees behavior as a function of specific events in the environment. The approach has also been called the **ABC assessment**—one assesses the *A*ntecedent conditions of the behavior, the *B*ehavior itself, and the *C*onsequences of the behavior.

Behavioral assessment generally is closely tied to treatment objectives in accordance with the pragmatic emphasis characteristic of this approach. For example, consider the task of assisting a mother who comes to a clinic because she feels helpless in dealing with her four-year-old son's temper tantrums and general disobedience (Hawkins, Peterson, Schweid, & Bijou, 1966). The psychologists involved in this case followed a fairly typical behavioral procedure to assessment and treatment. First, the mother and child were observed in the home to determine the nature of the undesirable behaviors, when they occurred, and which reinforcers seemed to maintain them. The following nine behaviors were determined to constitute the major portion of the boy's objectionable behavior: (1) biting his shirt or arm; (2) sticking out his tongue; (3) kicking or biting himself, others, or objects; (4) calling someone or something a derogatory name; (5) removing or threatening to remove his clothing; (6) saying "NO!" loudly and vigorously; (7) threatening to damage objects or persons; (8) throwing objects; (9) pushing his sister. Observation of the mother–child interaction suggested that the objectionable behavior was being maintained by attention from the mother. For example, often she would try to distract him by offering him toys or food.

The treatment program began with a behavioral analysis of the frequency with which the son expressed one of the objectionable behaviors during one-hour sessions, conducted in the home two to three times a week. Two psychologists acted as observers to ensure that there was high reliability or good agreement concerning recording of the objectionable behavior. This first phase, known as a baseline period, lasted for sixteen sessions. During this time, mother and child interacted in their usual way. Following this careful assessment of the objectionable behavior during the baseline period, the psychologists initiated their intervention or treatment program. Now the mother was instructed to tell her son to stop or to put him in his room by himself without toys each time that he emitted an objectionable behavior. In other words, there was a withdrawal of the positive reinforcer for objectionable behavior. At the same time, the mother was instructed to give her son attention and approval when he behaved in a desirable way. In other words, the positive reinforcers were made contingent on desirable behavior. During this time, known as the first experimental period, the frequency of objectionable behaviors was again counted. As can be seen in Figure 12.1, there was a marked decline in the frequency of objectionable behavior from between 18 and 113 such responses during a one-hour period (pre-experimental baseline) to between 1 and 8 such responses per session (first experimental period).

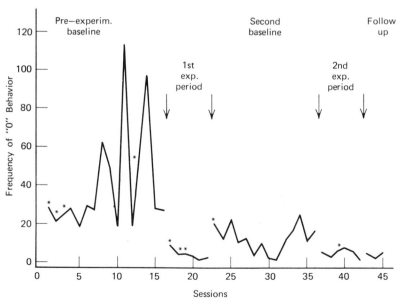

FIGURE 12.1   Number of 10-second Intervals per 1-hour Session, in which Objectionable Behavior Occurred. Asterisks Indicate Sessions in which Reliability Was Tested. (Hawkins, Peterson, Schweid, & Bijou, 1966)

Following the first experimental treatment period, the mother was instructed to return to her former behavior to determine whether it was the shift in her reinforcement behavior that was determining the change in her son's behavior. During this second baseline period, her son's objectionable behavior ranged between 2 and 24 per session (Figure 12.1). There was an increase in this behavior, though not a return to the former baseline level. However, the mother reported she had trouble responding in her previous way because she now felt more "sure of herself." Thus, even during this period she gave her son more firm commands, gave in less after denying a request, and gave more affection in response to positive behaviors in her son than was previously the case. Following this there was a return to a full emphasis on the treatment program, resulting in a decline in objectionable behavior (second experimental period). The rate of objectionable behavior was found to remain low after a 24-day interval (Follow-up period) and the mother reported a continuing positive change in the relationship.

In sum, in this case it was possible to assess the target response in the home environment as well as their reinforcers, and then to specify a treatment regimen that would result in measurable changes in the frequency of these behaviors. As well as illustrating behavioral assessment, this study illustrates an interesting variant of the experimental method—the Skinnerian **own-control** or **ABA research design** (Krasner, 1976). Basically the ABA, own-control research design involves the experimental manipulation of a specific behavior and the demonstration that changes in behavior can be attributed directly to specific changes in environmental events. One subject is used and serves as his own control relating to variations in experimental conditions. In the first or baseline phase (A) of this design, the current rate of occurrence of the behavior of interest is recorded. In the second or reinforcement phase (B), a reinforcer following the behavior of interest is introduced in an effort to increase the frequency of that behavior. Once the behavioral response has been established at the desired frequency, the reinforcer may be withdrawn (A phase) to see whether the behavior returns to the original (baseline period) rate. This is called the nonreinforcement period. Instead of comparing a subject who is reinforced with one who is not, the subject is treated differently in the various phases—he is his own control. In some research, a fourth phase is also included in which the reinforcer is reintroduced to reestablish the desired behavior (see Figure 12.1). Also, some experiments may begin with the reinforcement phase and then move to nonreinforcement and then reintroduction of reinforcement. This approach is typical when it does not make sense to begin with a baseline period, as when a new behavior is being taught.

As can be seen, in behavioral assessment there is emphasis on single variables (specific target behaviors) and the gathering of reliable and objective data. What is different about behavioral assessment in comparison to some other objective personality measures is that the behavior itself is of interest, not some theoretical construct (ego strength, extroversion) presumed to be expressed in the behavior. "Another characteristic of behavioral approaches to assessment is that their data are often direct samples of behavior in specific situations, instead of indirect and generalized indicants of behavioral predispositions'' (Kanfer & Phillips, 1970, p. 509). Perhaps an even clearer feeling for behavior assessment can be obtained by contrasting it and its associated theoretical assumptions with the theoretical assumptions and assessment devices described in the projective category. Projective test data are associated with theories that emphasize: (1) unique aspects of individuals; (2) behavior as a result of the interplay among complex internal forces (motives, drives, needs, and conflicts); (3) personality structure as involving layers of organization (as in the conscious and unconscious); (4) personality as a process through which the individual imposes organization and structure upon external stimuli in the environment; (5) a holistic understanding of behavior in terms of relationships among parts, rather than the interpretation of behavior as expressive of single parts of personality traits.

The behavioral assessment method also emphasizes behaviors specific to individuals. However, in contrast with projective tests, behavioral assessment is associated with theories having these emphases: (1) behavior as a result of external environmental forces that have eliciting and reinforcing value for the specific behaviors in question; (2) the avoidance of assumptions concerning personality dimensions (conscious, unconscious) that cannot be defined in clear behavioral terms; (3) personality as consisting of the organization of specific behavioral responses determined by environmental variables. Projective tests emphasize factors inside the individual that regulate behavior and provide for the stability of behavior across many different types of situations. Behavioral assessment emphasizes factors external to the individual that regulate behavior and provide for behavior varying according to situational characteristics.

Sign and Sample Approaches to Assessment

Mischel (1968, 1971) has contrasted these differences in terms of **sign and sample approaches to assessment**. In the *sign* approach, traits are inferred from test behavior. Test items are assumed adequate to reflect personality characteristics and interpretations are made of test behavior relative to assumed underlying traits. There is, in other words, a high level of inference from test behavior to interpretations concerning personality characteristics. In the *sample* approach, interest is in the behavior itself and how it is affected by alterations in environmental conditions. Interest is in overt behavior and it is assumed that one must understand the surrounding stimulus conditions to understand the relevant behavior. There is, in other words, a low level of inference from test behavior to other similar behaviors in the individual. The sign approach asks about motives and traits that act together to result in observed behavior; the sample approach asks about environmental variables that affect behaviors in terms of their frequency, intensity, and duration. A summary of many of these differences is give in Figure 12.2.

As noted, the main sample approach to assessment includes the analysis of specific behaviors in terms of the relevant eliciting and reinforcing environmental conditions. Often this requires a period of observation of behavior as it occurs in

	BEHAVIORAL ASSESSMENT	TRADITIONAL ASSESSMENT
Assumptions		
1 Personality concept	Behavior as a function of the environment	Behavior as a function of underlying causes
2 "Test" interpretation	Behavior as sample	Behavior as sign
3 Situations sampled	Varied and specific	Limited and ambiguous
Primary Functions	Description in behavioral-analytic terms Treatment selection Treatment evaluation	Description in psychodynamic terms Diagnostic labeling
Practical aspects		
1 Relation to treatment	Direct	Indirect
2 Time of assessment	Continuous with treatment	Prior to treatment

FIGURE 12.2   A Comparison of Traditional and Behavioral Assessment Strategies. (Cimenero, 1977)

the daily life of the individual (naturalistic observation); at other times there may be efforts to set up experimental conditions that resemble real-life situations (analogs). It would be difficult through naturalistic observation to observe an individual's fear of snakes, for example, and therefore it is necessary to observe such behavior within the context of a laboratory situation. In one of the classic efforts to use behavioral assessment within the laboratory situation, Lang and Lazovik (1963) measured changes in subjects' fears of snakes in terms of the extent of approach or avoidance behavior in relation to an actual snake. This was tested in the laboratory both before and after treatment. Although there are many categories of subject behavior in such a Behavioral Avoidance Test (BAT), basically there is an assessment of whether the subject can progress through the "Look-Touch-Hold" steps in relation to the snake. Such BATs are frequently used with the assumption that they provide clear behavioral data that are less biased than self-report ratings. Recently, however, evidence has indicated that subject behavior in such a situation may be influenced by such subtle sources of bias as instructions, subject assumptions concerning expectations of the experimenter, and a variety of contextual cues. For example, if subjects identify themselves as being afraid of snakes, they may be reluctant to fail to show their fear duing a BAT. Similarly, after treatment a subject may feel obligated to show less fear than before (Bernstein, 1973).

While observation and assessment in the natural environment are desirable, other approaches are at times necessary and may even include the use of self-report responses. For example, a questionnaire has been developed concerning specific fears that the individual may have (Fear Survey Schedule, Wolpe & Lange, 1964). Another questionnaire has been developed to determine which things in the environment are pleasurable for and therefore reinforcing to the individual (Reinforcement Survey Schedule, Cautela & Kastenbaum, 1967). Illustrative items from these tests are presented in Figure 12.3. Although these assessment devices do rely on self-report, they follow the behavioral model in terms of their emphasis on specific behaviors (fears, pleasurable things to do, responses to specific situations at college), in the attention given to environmental variables, and in the limiting of interpretations to the behaviors noted rather than interpreting these behaviors in relation to other possible personality characteristics. To the extent possible, the effort is to ask questions and make interpretations that are expressive of the sample approach to assessment. At the same time, such questionnaires elicit data that do not always agree with observations derived from other behavioral techniques. For example, responses on the Fear Survey Schedule do not always match actual behavior on a BAT. One study found that up to 64 percent of the "high-fear" subjects on the questionnaire would actually touch a snake while up to 16 percent of the "low-fear" questionnaire subjects would not (Bernstein, 1973).

To summarize this section on behavioral assessment, we have a variety of assessment techniques which (1) share certain assumptions that distinguish them from other assessment techniques, (2) tie them to personality theories that differ from theories associated with other assessment techniques and (3) result in the accumulation of different kinds of data than would be accumulated through the use of other assessment devices. Those who favor the use of these tests emphasize that they are objective and do not depend on the accuracy of self-report of the subject. Those who criticize the exclusive use of such tests suggest that they give a very restricted view of human behavior and have yet to demonstrate their predictive utility.

CHANGE   *p. 370 - 373 everything*

Despite differences among behavioral psychologists, there is a common emphasis on the importance of learning in human behavior and on the importance of a rigorous methodology in the study of this behavior. This section on change, or, as it tends to be called by learning theorists, **behavior modification** and **behavior therapy**, extends this point of view. There is no one single method of therapy that is suggested by learning theory. Different learning theorists emphasize different aspects of the learning process in their efforts to account for behavioral pathology and these explanations of behavioral pathology are associated with different treatment methods.

Before discussing the major systems of change that have been developed, it will be useful to point out the major processes of learning on which they are based. Five such processes have been suggested (Bandura, 1969; Bandura & Walters, 1963). The first is based on the process of **extinction**. Where an undesirable trait

1 FEAR SURVEY SCHEDULE (FSS-III)
J. WOLPE AND P. J. LANG

	Not at all	A little	A fair amount	Much	Very much
1 Noise of vacuum cleaners					
2 Open wounds					
3 Being alone					
10 Falling					
12 Being teased					
14 Thunder					
18 High places					
19 People with deformities					
22 Receiving injections					
48 Dogs					
72 Looking foolish					

2 REINFORCEMENT SURVEY SCHEDULE
J. R. CAUTELA AND R. KASTENBAUM
(SUBJECTS CHECK HOW MUCH PLEASURE EACH GIVES)

	Not at all	A little	A fair amount	Much	Very much
Section A.					
1 Eating					
a. ice cream					
b. candy					
c. pastry					
4 Beautiful Women					
5 Handsome Men					
11 Watching Sports					
a. football					
b. baseball					
54 Peace & Quiet					

SECTION C   SITUATIONS I WOULD LIKE TO BE IN

1 You have just led your team to victory. An old friend comes over and says, "You played a terrific game. Let me treat you to dinner and drinks."

not at all ☐   a little ☐   a fair amount ☐   much ☐   very much ☐

SECTION D
List things you do or think about more than:

5	10	15	20 times a day
_____	_____	_____	_____
_____	_____	_____	_____
_____	_____	_____	_____

FIGURE 12.3   Illustrative Items from Behavioral Assessment Questionnaire Inventories.

is being maintained by positive reinforcement, the withdrawal of this reinforcement leads to the extinction of the response. One illustration of this process is the extinction of psychotic talk about delusions through nonreinforcement (Ayllon & Michael, 1959). A decrease in psychotic talk was found when nurses did not respond to this behavior and instead reinforced, with sympathetic listening, sensible talk. A second relevant process is **discrimination learning**. As a result of discrimination learning, individuals are able to distinguish between behaviors that are being reinforced and those that are not being reinforced, or between stimuli that they need to be afraid of and stimuli that do not represent punishment. According to Dollard and Miller (1950), much of therapy consists of learning new discriminations. Through the process of discrimination learning, the individual is able to distinguish between past experiences of reinforcement and punishment and current realities.

Although extinction and discrimination learning are important processes, they have not been as critical to the development of behavior therapy as have three other processes: **counterconditioning, positive reinforcement,** and **imitation**. In counterconditioning, a desirable response that is incompatible with an undesirable response is conditioned to the same environmental stimulus. Thus, relaxation can be conditioned to a stimulus and inhibit an anxiety response (You can't be relaxed and anxious at the same time). Counterconditioning, as we shall see, is particularly relevant to procedures based on classical conditioning theory. In positive reinforcement, new behaviors are developed through the rewarding of successive approximations to the desired behavior. The use of positive reinforcement

"Leave us alone! I am a behavior therapist! I am helping my patient overcome a fear of heights!"

Behavior Therapy—**One aspect of behavior therapy involves the extinction of learned fears or phobias.** ©Sidney Harris.

is particularly relevant to the Skinnerian operant conditioning procedure. Finally, behavior can be changed through the process of imitation or modeling. New behaviors can be acquired through the observation of models, and inappropriate fears can be lost through the observation of models who are not harmed by the feared stimulus. Modeling is particularly relevant to models of change based on social learning theory, a subject we examine in the next chapter.

Behavior Change—Classical Conditioning

Behavioral therapy based on the classical conditioning model emphasizes the conditioning of new responses to stimuli that elicit undesired behaviors. An early utilization of this approach, one that followed on Watson and Rayner's (1920) study of the conditioning of the fear emotional response in Albert, was the effort of Jones (1924) to remove a fear under laboratory conditions. In this study, described as one of the earliest if not the first systematic utilization of behavior therapy, Jones attempted to treat the exaggerated fear reaction in a boy, Peter, who then was two years and ten months old. Peter was described as a generally healthy, well-adjusted child with a fear of a white rat that also extended to a rabbit, fur coat, feather, and cotton wool. Jones carefully documented the nature of the child's fear response and the conditions that elicited the greatest fear. She then set out to determine whether she could "uncondition" the fear response to one stimulus and whether such "unconditioning" would then generalize to other stimuli. Jones chose to focus on Peter's fear of the rabbit since this seemed even greater than his fear of the rat. She proceeded by bringing Peter to play at a time when the rabbit was present as well as three other children who were selected because they were fearless toward the rabbit. Gradually Peter moved from almost complete terror at the sight of the rabbit to a completely positive response. The steps noted along the way to this progress are represented in Figure 12.4.

Actually, Peter's progression through these steps was not even or unbroken, and fortunately Jones gives us a careful, explicit accounting of a fascinating chain of events. Peter had progressed through the first nine steps listed in Figure 12.4 when he was taken to the hospital with scarlet fever. After a delay of two months, Peter returned to the laboratory with his fear response at the original level. Jones describes the cause of this relapse as follows:

> *This was easily explained by the nurse who brought Peter from the hospital. As they were entering a taxi at the door of the hospital, a large dog, running past, jumped at them. Both Peter and the nurse were very much frightened . . . This seemed reason enough for this precipitate descent back to the original fear level. Being threatened by a large dog when ill, and in a strange place and being with an adult who also showed fear, was a terrifying situation against which our training could not have fortified him.*

Thus, at this point Jones began anew with "another" method of treatment, that of "direct conditioning." Here Peter was seated in a chair and given food he

1. Rabbit anywhere in the room in a cage causes fear reactions.
2. Rabbit 12 feet away in cage tolerated.
3. Rabbit 4 feet away in cage tolerated.
4. Rabbit 3 feet away in cage tolerated.
5. Rabit close in cage tolerated.
6. Rabbit free in room tolerated.
7. Rabbit touched when experimenter holds it.
8. Rabbit touched when free in room.
9. Rabbit defied by spitting at it, throwing things at it, imitating it.
10. Rabbit allowed on tray of high chair.
11. Squats in defenseless position beside rabbit.
12. Helps experimenter to carry rabbit to its cage.
13. Holds rabbit on lap.
14. Stays alone in room with rabbit.
15. Allows rabbit in play pen with him.
16. Fondles rabbit affectionately.
17. Lets rabbit nibble his fingers.

FIGURE 12.4   Steps in the "Unconditioning" of Peter's Fear of a Rabbit. (M.C. Jones, 1924)

liked as the experimenter gradually brought the rabbit in a wire cage closer to him: "Through the presence of pleasant stimulus (food) whenever the rabbit was shown, the fear was eliminated gradually in favor of a positive response." In other words, the positive feelings associated with food were counterconditioned to the previously feared rabbit. However, even in the later sessions the influence of other children who were not afraid of the rabbit seemed to be of considerable significance. And what of the other fears? Jones notes that after the "unconditioning" of Peter's fear of the rabbit, he completely lost his fear of the fur coat, feathers, and cotton wool as well. Despite the lack of any knowledge concerning the origins of Peter's fears, the "unconditioning" procedure was found to work successfully and to generalize to other stimuli as well.

Another early procedure that gained considerable attention was one developed by Mowrer and Mowrer (1928) for the treatment of bed-wetting. In general, bed-wetting in children occurs because the child does not respond to stimuli from the bladder so as to awaken and urinate in the bathroom. To deal with this condition, Mowrer and Mowrer developed a device based on the classical conditioning model. This consisted of an electrical device in the bed of the child. If the child urinated, the device activated a bell which awakened the child. Gradually stimuli from the bladder became associated with the awakening response. Eventually, the response was anticipated so that bed-wetting no longer took place.

The classical conditioning procedure also has been used in the treatment of alcoholics. For example, an aversive stimulus such as shock or a nausea-inducing agent is applied immediately after the alcoholic takes a drink. The aversive stimulus acts as an unconditioned stimulus, and the avoidance response is conditioned to the alcohol.

By far the most influential development in this area has been that of Joseph Wolpe's method of **systematic desensitization.** Interestingly, this method of therapy was developed by a psychiatrist rather than a psychologist, and by someone who originally practiced within a psychoanalytic framework. After a number of years of practice, however, Wolpe read and was impressed by the writings of Pavlov and Hull. He came to hold the view that a neurosis is a persistent, maladaptive learned response that is almost always associated with anxiety. Therapy, then, involves the inhibition of anxiety through the counterconditioning of a competing response: "If a response inhibitory to anxiety can be made to occur in the presence of anxiety-evoking stimuli so that it is accompanied by a complete or partial suppression of the anxiety response, the bond between these stimuli and the anxiety response will be weakened" (Wolpe, 1961, p. 189). In other words, therapy involves the conditioning of responses that are antagonistic to or inhibitory of anxiety. A variety of anxiety-inhibiting responses can be used for counterconditioning purposes. However, the one that has received most attention is that of deep muscle relaxation. Through a process called systematic desensitization, the patient learns to respond to certain previously anxiety-arousing stimuli with the newly conditioned response of relaxation.

The therapeutic technique of systematic desensitization involves a number of phases (Wolpe, 1968). First, there is a careful assessment of the therapeutic needs of the patient. A detailed history is taken of every symptom and of every aspect of life in which the patient experiences undue difficulty. A systematic account of

Systematic Desensitization—**Relaxation training forms a part of the behavior therapy technique called systematic desensitization. Here an early leader in the field, Dr. Arnold Lazarus, conducts a group session in relaxation training.**

the patient's life history is also obtained. After having determined that the patient's problems lend themselves to systematic desensitization, the therapist trains the patient to relax. A detailed procedure is described for helping the patient to first relax one part of the body and then all parts of the body. Whereas, at first, patients have limited success in their ability to feel free of muscle tension, by the end of about six sessions most are able to relax the entire body in seconds. The next phase of treatment involves the construction of an anxiety hierarchy. This is a difficult and complex procedure in which the therapist tries to obtain from the patient a list of stimuli that arouse anxiety. These anxiety-arousing stimuli are grouped into themes such as fear of heights, or fear of rejection. Within each group or theme, the anxiety-arousing stimuli are then ordered from the most disturbing to the least disturbing. For example, a theme of claustrophobia (fear of closed spaces) might involve placing the fear of being stuck in an elevator at the top of the list, an anxiety about being on a train in the middle of the list, and an anxiety in response to reading of miners trapped underground at the bottom of the list. A theme of death might involve being at a burial as the most anxiety-arousing stimulus, the word death as somewhat anxiety-arousing, and driving past a cemetery as only slightly anxiety-arousing. Patients can have many or few themes, and many or few items within each anxiety hierarchy.

With the construction of the anxiety hierarchies completed, the patient is ready for the desensitization procedure itself. The patient has attained the capacity to calm himself by relaxation, and the therapist has established the anxiety hierarchies. Now the therapist encourages the patient to achieve a deep state of relaxation and then to imagine the least anxiety-arousing stimulus in the anxiety hierarchy. If the patient can imagine the stimulus without anxiety, then he is encouraged to imagine the next stimulus in the hierarchy while remaining relaxed. Periods of pure relaxation are interspersed with periods of relaxation and imagination of anxiety-arousing stimuli. If the patient feels anxious while imagining a stimulus, he is encouraged to relax and return to imagining a less anxiety-arousing stimulus. Ultimately the patient is able to relax while imagining all stimuli in the anxiety hierarchies. Relaxation in relation to the imagined stimuli generalizes to relaxation in relation to these stimuli in everyday life. "It has consistently been found that at every stage a stimulus that evokes no anxiety when imagined in a state of relaxation will also evoke no anxiety when encountered in reality" (Wolpe, 1961a, p. 191).

A number of reports of clinical studies of the success of Wolpe's method have been published. The first such report by Wolpe (1958) indicated that almost 90 percent of his 210 patients were rated as cured or much improved in an average of about 30 therapeutic sessions. This is an extremely high rate of therapeutic success. Furthermore, according to Wolpe (1961), follow-up studies of these patients suggest that in most cases the therapeutic gains have been maintained. Proponents of this point of view have been led to question the psychoanalytic view that, as long as the underlying conflicts remain untouched, the patient is prone to develop a new symptom in place of the one removed (symptom substitution) (Lazarus, 1965). According to the behavior therapy point of view, there is no symptom that is caused by unconscious conflicts. There is only a maladaptive learned response, and once this response has been eliminated there is no reason to believe that another maladaptive response will be substituted for it.

Along with these uncontrolled clinical studies of the success of systematic desensitization, there have been some carefully designed laboratory investigations. One such early study was carried out by Lang and Lazovik (1963). In this study, college students who were intensely afraid of nonpoisonous snakes were randomly assigned to one of two groups. Subjects in the experimental group experienced desensitization therapy, whereas the subjects in the control group did not. Subjects in the experimental, desensitization group were found to be more able to hold or to touch a snake and reported less fear of snakes than did subjects who did not experience the desensitization therapy. Furthermore, at a six-month follow-up evaluation, subjects in the experimental group were found to hold or to increase their gains, and there was no evidence of symptom substitution.

Some important research also has been done on the comparative effectiveness of systematic desensitization and other forms of treatment. In one important study, Paul (1966) compared the effectiveness of systematic desensitization in the treatment of public-speaking situation anxiety with that of short-term, insight-oriented treatment and with a form of treatment that only emphasized therapist interest and a "fast-acting tranquilizer," which in reality was sodium bicarbonate. Subjects treated by systematic desensitization showed a significantly greater reduction in anxiety than did subjects treated by the other two forms of therapy. These gains were also significant relative to a group of subjects who had similar interpersonal performance anxieties but who received no treatment at all. In further research, Paul (Paul & Shannon, 1966) found that a group desensitization procedure also could be effective in the treatment of social-evaluative anxiety. These studies and other clinical reports suggested that the effectiveness of systematic desensitization need not be limited to the treatment of specific fears. Furthermore, a two-year follow-up of the individual and group systematic desensitization techniques indicated that the therapeutic gains had been maintained and extended. Although specifically sought, there was no evidence of relapse or symptom substitution (Paul, 1967; Paul, 1968).

To summarize, there is considerable evidence to support the effectiveness of Wolpe's counterconditioning, systematic desensitization method of treatment. The psychoanalytic suggestion that the relief from "symptoms" would be followed by a relapse or the appearance of other symptoms (symptom substitution) has been challenged, if not rejected. At the same time, some questions remain concerning the effective ingredients of systematic desensitization. Wolpe emphasized the importance of all three ingredients (i.e., graded hierarchy, muscle relaxation, imagination with relaxation). Various studies, however, have demonstrated effectiveness without one or another of these components. Thus, while some behavior therapists support the view that "the well-established efficacy of systematic desensitization is attributable to the specific components of this technique'' (Wilson, 1982, p. 516), others suggest that its effectiveness may have more to do with general expectations of therapeutic improvement set in motion by the procedure (Kazdin & Wilcoxon, 1976).

Behavior Change—Operant Conditioning

Although not a clinician, Skinner's approach to the control of behavior has had a considerable impact on therapeutic efforts. This has been particularly true beginning with the 1960s and with psychotic as opposed to neurotic difficulties. The Skinnerian approach to behavior change or **behavior modification** does not involve the use of a therapist. Instead, it involves the use of an expert in operant conditioning who can serve as a behavioral technician or behavioral engineer. It is the task of this technician to specify the target behaviors, to define the desired new behaviors, to determine the rewards to which the patient will respond, and to determine the schedules of reinforcement that must be used to shape the desired behaviors. As in all operant conditioning, the emphasis is on the use of reinforcement to shape the desired behaviors through a series of successive approximations.

Some of the details of the operant conditioning approach to behavior modification are indicated in the following report of the successful treatment of a case of hysterical blindness (blindness without physical cause) (Brady & Lind, 1961). The patient was a forty-year-old man who had been blind for two years. The patient suddenly became blind in both eyes while he was shopping with his wife and mother-in-law. Medical examinations clearly indicated that there was no physical cause for the blindness and this was a case of hysteria. Psychiatric and drug treatments were tried but were unsuccessful. Finally, a program of operant conditioning was begun. As analysis of the patient's behavior suggested that he had a need for approval and was sensitive to criticism. Therefore, praise and approval were used as the behavior-shaping reinforcers. The patient was put in a situation where he was reinforced for responding every 18 to 21 seconds. A correctly spaced button-pressing response (18 to 21 seconds since the previous one) was reinforced with praise and approval, whereas an incorrectly spaced response resulted in disapproval and criticism. This system of reinforcement was sometimes supplemented by special privileges and trips for good performance and withdrawal of these rewards for poor performance.

In the first six sessions a stable response was developed. Then a light bulb was put in the room where it could not be seen directly by the patient. The light went on after 18 seconds and off after 21 seconds. Thus, the patient could improve his performance by using this visual cue. For the next ten sessions the patient appeared to avoid the light and his performance fell. The light was then put at full intensity in clear view. The patient was told that the light would help him to know when to respond properly. Performance improved, but the patient suggested he was able to use the heat from the bulb as a cue. Performance continued to improve as the intensity of the light was decreased. Finally, the patient exclaimed that he could see and use his eyesight to distinguish among a number of different cues in the testing situation. At the time of the report, the patient had regained his sight for more than one year and was functioning well in a variety of situations.

The operant approach to behavior change was illustrated in the section on behavioral assessment where the frequency of a boy's objectionable behavior was modified through changes in the mother's reinforcement behavior (Figure 12.1). While in some cases the goal is modification of an isolated behavior or target responses, in other cases there is an effort to modify other responses as well. For example, we can consider the case of Joey, an eight-year-old boy who refused to go to school and was very dependent on his mother (Wahler & Pollio, 1968). Many of his difficulties, such as the refusal to go to school and his fears concerning his parents' safety, were characteristic of a school phobia. The investigators assumed that the parents were maintaining the dependent behavior and decided to use them as the major therapeutic agents in a program of behavior modification. The therapeutic sessions were twenty minutes long and were held twice weekly in a playroom. During a ten-minute segment of each session, Joey spent time alone with the professional behavior therapist. The therapist was used to facilitate change and to train the parents in the use of reinforcements to change behavior.

The first four sessions were used to observe Joey's behavior and to develop categories of behavior that could be used in tests of whether significant changes did occur. Five response classes were obtained: Smiling, Spontaneous Nonverbal Behavior, Spontaneous Verbal Behavior, Aggressive Behavior, and Cooperative Behavior. Cooperative behavior included following suggestions or commands from others and was expressive of Joey's dependence on others. Parent and therapist responses to these behaviors were defined as social attention stimuli. They presumably were the events that were affecting the rate of each of Joey's behaviors.

Following these sessions, there were five sessions in which observers recorded whether each of the above types of responses occurred within a ten-second interval. Twelve reinforcement sessions followed the baseline observations. In these sessions, the social attention reinforcements provided by the therapist and the parents were made contingent on specific responses. Now all responses other than the ones classified as cooperative (dependent) were to be reinforced. The parents were told that they were not to offer their attention and approval for dependent behavior and that they should offer it following the other responses from Joey. During the first ten-minute segments the parents observed the therapist attempt to shape Joey's behavior through this schedule of reinforcements. The observers continued to record the frequency of the response classes. At this point, the therapist undertook two reversal sessions in which he only reinforced the dependent behavior. These two sessions involved an effort to determine whether a change in the reinforcement contingencies would lead to a return to Joey's original behavior. The parents did not change their behavior during this period because they did not want to return to their old habits. Finally, there were five reinforcement sessions in which the professional therapist returned to a schedule of reinforcement for nondependent behavior. The parents continued with their schedule of reinforcements.

In sum, there were five baseline observation sessions, twelve reinforcement sessions, two reversal (professional therapist) sessions, and five final reinforcements sessions. The frequency of Joey's responses in each of the five response classes was reliably recorded at ten-second intervals. The impact of the professional therapist's reinforcement schedules on Joey's behavior is shown in Figure 12.5. Note that the category Cooperative Behavior related to dependent behaviors that they were trying to decrease. The data indicate clear evidence of a change in Joey's behavior in accordance with the schedule of reinforcements followed by the therapist. The charts of frequency counts of responses with his mother and with his father showed a very similar pattern except for the lack of significant change during the two reversal periods. This is understandable since they did not alter their behavior during these sessions. The change in response rate during the fourth session appears to have been because of an incident during the session in which Joey objected to being left alone after the meeting; Joey cried and the therapist and father felt "compelled" to offer suggestions during the session.

The frequency counts of Joey's behavior give clear evidence of change produced by changes in the reinforcement schedules followed by the therapist and

FIGURE 12.5 Frequency counts of Joey's response classes over all therapy periods with the professional therapist. (Wahler & Pollio, 1968)

parents. Furthermore, Joey's attendance at school began to increase during the second reinforcement series of sessions. This record of improvement in attendance continued for the five-month period during which follow-up data were gathered. The parents also reported considerable improvement as a result of the behavior therapy program. Joey played more frequently with his peers and worried less about his own welfare or that of his parents. However, information obtained from measures of Joey's self-concept indicated lesser change in this area.

The authors' conclusion concerning the data on the frequency counts of responses are stated as follows. "The data presented indicate much progress: progress which takes Joey from a depressed, possibly even suicidal, child at the beginning of therapy to a much less constricted and more effective child at the conclusion of twenty-four twenty-minute reinforcement sessions" (Wahler & Pollio, 1968, p. 56).

As has been noted, much of the therapeutic work with operant conditioning is done with psychotic patients. An important development in this area was the work of Ayllon in the analysis of the ward behavior of patients (Ayllon & Michael, 1959). This analysis clearly suggested that the nurses and other staff personnel were often reinforcing the behaviors they wished to abolish. This led to the suggestion that the nurse might be used as a behavioral engineer; that is, the nurses could make sure that they were only reinforcing the desired behaviors. In a further development of this strategy, Ayllon (Ayllon & Michael, 1962) attempted to deal with feeding problems through the use of operant conditioning techniques. An analysis of patient behavior suggested that social reinforcements in the form of coaxing and attention were shaping the behavior of patients so that they would eat only with assistance. A new schedule of reinforcements was then instituted. Refusals to eat were no longer followed by social reinforcement and access to the dining room was made contingent upon the performance of a series of responses. After a while it became possible in many cases to use food or entrance into the dining room as a reinforcer for many desired behaviors. Whereas previously patients were being shaped by their social environment into rejecting food, now food became a sufficient reinforcer to control the normal eating behavior of the psychotic patients.

The logical extension of the work of Ayllon has been the development of what is called a **token economy** (Ayllon & Azrin, 1965). Under a token economy, the behavioral technician rewards, with tokens, the various patient behaviors that are considered desirable. The tokens in turn can be exchanged by the patient for desirable products, such as candy and cigarettes. Thus, for example, patients could be reinforced for activities such as serving meals or cleaning floors. In a tightly controlled environmental setting, possibly in a state hospital for long-term psychiatric patients, it is feasible to make almost anything that a patient wants contingent on the desired behaviors.

A similar token economy was set up by Atthowe and Krasner (1968). Again, attainment of the "good things in life" was made contingent on the patient's performing the desired behaviors. Here it was found that the tokens themselves became valuable to the patients and hoarding and theft started to occur. A complex system of banking and identification of tokens had to be established. In any case, we are told that the results in terms of patient behavior were quite favorable. Although "cures" did not occur, there was a definite increase in patient responsibility and activity. Figure 12.6 demonstrates, for example, how group activity level increased and decreased as a function of reward level. Also, 21 patients left the hospital, almost double the number who left in the previous year. Finally, staff morale increased, working on the token ward became a sign of prestige and two additional wards adopted similar token economies because of the usefulness of the technique for modifying patient behavior. Similar principles have been used in a patient rehabilitation program existing outside the hospital in the natural environment (Atthowe, 1973).

According to a 1970 report, there are over 100 token economies in existence in over 50 different institutions (Krasner, 1970). By now these numbers may well have doubled. There is evidence in support of the effectiveness of token economies with severely disturbed patients and with mentally retarded individuals in increasing such behaviors as social interaction, self-care, and job performance. Token economies also have been used effectively to decrease aggressive behavior in children and to decrease marital discord (Kazdin, 1977).

In sum, the Skinnerian behavioral technician seeks a straightforward application of the operant conditioning method to the problem of behavior change. Target behaviors are selected, and reinforcement is made contingent on performance of the desired responses. We have here, then, a view that emphasizes how the environment acts upon people, as opposed to how people act upon the environment. This view has resulted in a group of social engineers who are committed to acting on the environment. Watson suggested that through control of the environment he could train an infant to become any type of specialist he might select. Skinnerian social engineers take this principle one step further. As seen in the development of token economies, as well as in the development of communes based on Skinnerian principles, there is an interest in the design of environments that will control broad aspects of human behavior.

COGNITIVE BEHAVIOR MODIFICATION

No current discussion of behavioral approaches to personality can be complete without inclusion of developments in cognitive behavior modification (Franks & Wilson, 1980). While this approach remains true to the basic principles of behavioral learning, in other ways it represents a radical new departure. Within a relatively short period of time, perhaps a decade or so, it has become one of the dominant themes among psychologists using behavioral approaches to personality and behavior change.

What is this new development about and how can we account for the rapid increase in interest? The defining characteristic of *cognitive behavior modification* is an interest in what people think and say to themselves. While at first this may not seem like a major point, recall Watson's rejection of speculation concerning

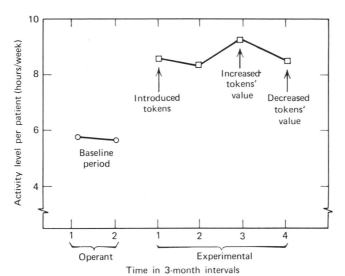

FIGURE 12.6   Group activity level as a function of tokens given for the activity. (Ullmann & Krasner, 1969; redrawn from Atthowe & Krasner, 1968)

what goes on inside the person and Skinner's criticism of mentalism and the attribution of causes to internal processes. While behaviorism mainly emphasized objectivity in description and measurement, radical behaviorism led to the rejection of concern with internal processes such as thinking and feeling and to the exclusive concern with overt behavior. Thus, for behavioral psychologists to show any interest in thoughts and images is indeed an important departure; it is also one that has come under increasing attack by more conservative behaviorists.

At this point there is no one theory of cognitive behavior and no one method of assessment or technique for producing change. As indicated, what is common to the relevant approaches is an emphasis on thought and imagery. In addition, a number of characteristics define them as behavioral and distinguish them from cognitive psychology generally and other cognitive approaches such as that of Kelly's personal construct theory. First, cognitive behavioral psychologists emphasize specific responses rather than overall cognitive structure or organization. Cognitions are viewed as behaviors, similar to other (nonverbal) behaviors, and subject to the same laws of learning (Meichenbaum, 1976, p. 145). Second, there is an emphasis on the importance of the situation in defining the cognitions that may be useful and relevant or dysfunctional and inappropriate. Thus, cognitive behavioral psychologists emphasize the role of people's cognitions (e.g., what they say to themselves) in their problems, particularly as they relate to the demands of specific tasks. Third, there is an emphasis on present cognition rather than on the developmental roots of current cognitions. Finally, there is an emphasis on conscious processes and their measurement rather than on unconscious processes that may only be inferred and are impossible to verify. In these ways, then, these cognitive approaches remain committed to a behavioral tradition.

The causes of the development of interest in cognitive behavior modification have to do with events both inside and outside of behavior therapy (Mahoney & Arnkoff, 1978). Outside of behavior therapy, there has been a cognitive revolution in psychology generally. Spurred by developments in computers and theory, cognitive processes have been emphasized increasingly in personality theory and research. (We discuss this trend in the two chapters that follow.) Inside of behavior therapy, a number of developments have proved significant. First, systematic desensitization, which involves imagery, is now recognized as a cognitive process. Second, the effects of behavior therapy are neither so generalized nor so durable as might be desired. This has led to an interest in procedures, such as those involving self-reinforcement and self-control, that may be less dependent on environmental contingencies. Third, some of these self-control procedures involve internal processes. In one such procedure, *covert conditioning* or covert sensitization (Cautela, 1967), an image is used in the conditioning process. For example, the treatment of an obese patient might involve imagining feeling nauseous following eating while the treatment of an exhibitionist might involve imagining exposing himself and then being apprehended by the police, events involving considerable shame and embarrassment (Barlow & Wincze, 1980). These developments within behavior therapy, as well as those in psychology more generally, have contributed to an almost explosive interest in procedures for cognitive assessment and change. It is to these procedures that we now turn.

Cognitive Behavioral Assessment

Following in the tradition of behavioral assessment generally, *cognitive behavioral assessment* involves the functional analysis of relevant cognitions and task demands. Here the concern is with the cognitive skills that are necessary to perform a task and with a person's cognitive processes that are associated with a performance deficit. In particular, there is an interest in irrational beliefs, irrational expectancies, and negative self-statements that are specific to a person, to a situation, and to a disorder (Kendall, 1982). For example, some irrational beliefs and self-statements may be assessed as being involved in depression. To take one illustration, the Automatic Thoughts Questionnaire (ATQ) has been developed to measure the frequency of occurrence of automatic negative thoughts (negative self-statements) that are associated with depression (Hollon & Kendall, 1980). It is based on cognitions reported to be associated with dysphoric experiences and scores on it have been found to be associated, clinically, with depression. Typical items are presented in Figure 12.7.

Self-statements have been found to be of considerable import in social behavior. An early and influential study in this area involved analysis of the components of assertive behavior (Schwartz & Gottman, 1976). One question considered was whether low-assertive individuals are deficient in their knowledge of assertive behaviors. In other words, are people generally not assertive because they do not know about assertive behavior? This was not found to be the case. Rather, low-assertive subjects were found to report more negative and fewer positive self-statements compared to subjects high in assertive behavior. Utilized in this research was the Assertiveness Self-Statement Test (ASST), which is a questionnaire involving self-statements that make it easier and harder to refuse a request. Illustrative positive and negative self-statements are presented in Figure 12.7. Positive and negative self-statements have also been found to play a role in the ease with which males will engage in heterosocial behavior (Mandel & Shrauger, 1980). In sum, we see here an emphasis in cognitive behavioral assessment on self-statements that facilitate or interfere with performance on a specific task or in a special situation.

Self-report in cognitive behavioral assessment has been used not only on behaviors that can be verified but on internal processes that cannot. These data represent exactly those eschewed by behaviorists. Indeed, self-report questionnaires are often the target of attack by behavioral psychologists. Yet, "aided by the surge of cognitivism in behavior therapy, self-reports are now acceptable" (Franks & Wilson, 1980, p, 209). While behavioral psychologists still generally prefer direct measurement of responses, many now subscribe to the view that "people can be excellent sources of information about themselves" (Mischel, 1981, p. 482). Supporters of this view suggest that self-reports represent behaviors in themselves, regardless of their validity or accuracy, and that self-reports have not been shown to be any more unreliable or invalid than other types of measurement, particularly where relatively straightforward information is involved (Cautela & Upper, 1976).

Illustrative Items From the Automatic Thoughts Questionnaire (ATQ)

1. I feel like I'm up against the world.
2. I wish I were a better person.
3. My life is a mess.
4. My future is bleak.
5. I can't finish anything.

Illustrative Items From the Assertiveness Self-Statement Test (ASST)

Illustrative Problematic Situation: You have been standing in line at the movie theater for about 20 minutes. Just as you are getting close to the box office three people who you know only slightly from your dorm come up to you and ask if you would let them cut in front of you.

Positive (Refuse Request) Self-Statements: I was thinking that I am perfectly free to say no; I was thinking that this request was an unreasonable one.

Negative (Not-Refuse Request) Self-Statements: I was thinking that the other person might be hurt or insulted if I refused; I was worried about what other people might think about me if I refused.

FIGURE 12.7 Cognitive Behavioral Assessment. (Hollon & Kendall, 1980; Schwartz & Gottman, 1976)

Cognitive Behavior Change

Cognitive behavior therapists continue to be behavioral in their use of performance-based procedures and in their commitment to behavioral change, but they are cognitive in the sense that they believe cognitive change to be an important mechanism that accounts for the effectiveness of behavioral procedures.

Davison and Neale, 1982, p. 616

Many who survey the field are being led to the conclusion that behavior therapy is becoming wholly cognitive, as is psychology generally (Meichenbaum & Cameron, 1982). The arguments made in defense of this development are that all learning involves cognitive processes (Brewer, 1974) and that to utilize cognitive self-control procedures is to increase the effectiveness of behavior therapists. Cognitive behavior therapy or *cognitive behavior modification* is a general classification that includes many therapeutic techniques based on a variety of theoretical models. The common denominator to these approaches is an interest in the nature and modification of client cognitions. However, as one considers the approaches included in this category, "the differences across approaches are at least as striking as the similarities" (Meichenbaum & Cameron, 1982, p. 312). The result is that all behavior therapists do not agree that every procedure of cognitive therapy is representative of cognitive *behavior* therapy; some even go so far as to suggest that cognitive procedures as a group do not represent behavior therapy at all. Let us here consider three approaches to illustrate the range of theory and technique currently being emphasized.

Some time ago Albert Ellis, a former psychoanalyst, developed a system of change known as *Rational-Emotive Therapy* or RET (Ellis & Harper, 1975). According to Ellis the causes of psychological difficulties are irrational beliefs or irrational statements we make to ourselves—that we *must* do something, that we *have to* feel some way, that we *should* be some kind of person. Illustrative irrational beliefs are presented in Figure 12.8. In terms of research, a relationship has been found between such irrational beliefs and interpersonal, examination, and public-speaking anxieties as well as other common psychological difficulties (Goldfried & Sobocinski, 1975). Therapy then involves efforts to assess and change the particular irrational beliefs that are creating the difficulties. This may be done through logic, argument, persuasion, ridicule, or humor. Whatever the method, the point is for the client to remove the mystique and power of the belief. Although Ellis' approach was neglected by behavior therapists during the phase of their exclusive concern with overt motor behavior, it has now elicited greater interest.

A second approach, one that is much more in the mainstream of cognitive behavior modification, is Meichenbaum's (1977) work on *self-instructional training* and stress inoculation. This procedure involves helping clients to cope with stress through the development of more adaptive self-statements. Basically, training involves three stages. First, clients are made aware of how various images and self-

1. *Need for Approval.* I must have love or approval from all of the people I find significant.
2. *Perfectionism and Fear of Failure.* I must prove that I am thoroughly competent, adequate, and achieving. I must have great competence or talent in some important area.
3. *Blame.* When people act obnoxiously and unfairly, I should blame and damn them, and see them as bad, wicked, or rotten individuals.
4. *Frustration = Catastrophe.* I have to view things as awful, terrible, horrible, and catastrophic when I get seriously frustrated, treated unfairly or rejected.
5. *Helplessness.* Emotional misery comes from external pressures, and I have little ability to control or change my feelings.
6. *Preoccupation.* If something seems dangerous or fearsome, I must preoccupy myself with it and make myself anxious about it.
7. *Avoidance.* I can more easily avoid facing many life difficulties and self-responsibilities than undertake more rewarding forms of self-discipline.
8. *Victim of the Past.* My past remains all-important and because something once strongly influenced my life it must keep determining my feelings and behavior today.
9. *Chasing Nirvana.* People and things should turn out better than they do and I must view it as awful and horrible if I don't find good solutions to life's grim realities.
10. *Passivity and Boredom—Avoiding Risks.* I can achieve maximum human happiness by inertia and inaction or by passively and uncommittedly enjoying myself.

FIGURE 12.8   Illustrative Irrational Beliefs. (Ellis & Harper, 1975)

statements can be adaptive or maladaptive. Next, clients are taught to monitor their own ''internal dialogue'' and to consider replacing maladaptive thoughts and self-statements with more adaptive cognitions. For example, a student might find that during exams he has interfering thoughts concerning other matters or mainly focuses on how little time he has left or how poor a student he is. A better coping strategy is to focus on the task at hand, to tell himself to ''slow down,'' and to reassure himself that he will do all right if he uses the skills and resources available to him. Finally, clients actually practice these self-statements and cognitive coping strategies in situations that approximate those often found to be stressful.

Meichenbaum's approach is illustrated in some research he did with students high on test anxiety. Meichenbaum (1972) found that test-anxious college students attend to aspects of the situation that are irrelevant to the task, have irrelevant thoughts that intrude into consciousness, and experience high emotional arousal that interferes with performance. The question was whether these thoughts and self-verbalizations can be modified through a cognitive modification treatment program. Students found to be high in test anxiety were exposed to anxiety-arousing conditions to establish a baseline performance level. These conditions consisted of being given a test that they were told is a measure of general intelligence and can be used to predict college grades. These ego-involving, stress-inducing instructions were followed by two self-report measures of anxiety and two measures of performance found to be affected by anxiety. The students were then divided into three groups: the first underwent cognitive modification procedures; the second, systematic desensitization treatment; and the third was a waiting-list control group. The two treatment groups each received eight therapy sessions. In these eight sessions the cognitive modification group was made aware of how anxiety-provoking thoughts and self-statements interfere with performance. They were trained to make task relevant self-statements ("I can do well on this exam. I am competent."), to use imagery of coping and mastery behaviors (such as imagining themselves studying for an exam or performing well on an exam) in otherwise anxiety-arousing situations, and to practice other adaptive relaxation behaviors. In its eight therapy sessions, the systematic desensitization group followed the traditional use of progressive relaxation training described earlier in the chapter.

Following this period, the members of all three groups were readministered the previous tests to measure the effectiveness of the treatments—the two self-report measures of anxiety, the two performance tests found to be affected by anxiety, and a measure of test-taking anxiety used in the original screening procedure. In addition, academic performance was measured at the end of the semester and, a month after the completion of treatment (or waiting) the subjects again completed the questionnaire on test-taking anxiety. The results indicated that the cognitive modification procedure was most effective in reducing test anxiety as assessed by test performance in analogous test situations, self-report, and grade point average (Figure 12.9). The members of the cognitive modification group also showed significant improvement on the test-taking anxiety questionnaire. This research demonstrates how both the cognitive modification approach and the *clinical analogue* approach to research work. In clinical analogue research there is an attempt to demonstrate the effectiveness of a change procedure under conditions that approximate, but that are not identical to, those occurring naturally or without experimental control. Thus, while the conditions of performance and treatment are not identical to ordinary clinical and test situations, the research is useful in demonstrating the utility of cognitive modification treatment under conditions of controlled treatment and objective measurement.

Finally, note may be made of *problem-solving therapy*. Attention here is focused on tasks that must be managed in a situation and the requisite problem-solving skills. For example, Mahoney and Mahoney (1976) have attempted to use this approach in the treatment of obesity. Personal problems are likened to those of the research scientist, an apprenticeship format is established, and a SCIENCE program is undertaken:

S   Specify general problem
C   Collect information
I   Identify causes or patterns
E   Examine options
N   Narrow options and experiment

C   Compare data
E   Extend, revise, or replace

For the obese client–apprentice, the program might include collecting data on eating and exercise patterns, identifying problem areas, considering various procedures for change, experimenting with alternative procedures and discarding those that are ineffective while expanding upon those that are helpful. Some success with this procedure has been reported.

As noted, the procedures utilized in cognitive behavior therapy are diverse. In some cases they may resemble procedures utilized by other approaches. For example, the SCIENCE program would appear to be similar to Kelly's fixed-role therapy. However, while there is a common emphasis on behavior and cognition, the cognitive modification approaches are much more pragmatic, specific, and circumscribed in their change efforts. In addition, there is greater effort to tie treatment to systematic, objective research.

CRITICAL EVALUATION

We have now covered considerable ground, including a variety of theoretical and applied approaches. It is time to take stock of learning, behavioral approaches to

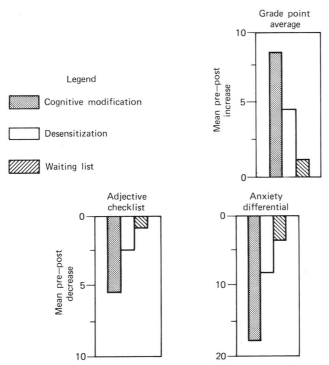

FIGURE 12.9   Mean Reduction and Increase in Manifestations of Test Anxiety from Pretreatment to Posttreatment. (Meichenbaum, 1972)

CURRENT APPLICATIONS AND IMPLICATIONS

If You Can Image It, Perhaps You Can Do It

What is the relation of imagery, an internal cognitive process, to action? Can you do something you can't imagine and, alternatively, does it help to first imagine something you want to do?

Psychologists have begun to be interested in the uses to which imagery processes, both natural and directed, can be put. For example, patients are encouraged by therapists to imagine various scenes, both to determine the nature of their fears as well as to develop positive courses of action. One of the most interesting applications of such efforts is in the world of sports. Take, for example, the efforts of Dan Smith, assistant coach of the University of Illinois basketball team and doctoral candidate in sports psychology. Finding a not terribly bright out-

look for the team, Smith undertook a psychological training program that involved relaxation and imagery training: "We went ahead to create vivid, controlled images in the mind's eye. We taught each player to see himself taking a good shot, making it and then feeling a sense of reward, a positive emotion, for doing it. They applied the technique to other things such as playing defense and ball handling." The results? Both players and coaches report striking benefits from utilization of the program.

What are the limits of such programs? Clearly there are physical-talent limits. Beyond this, however, we have just begun to explore the potential role of imagery in facilitating performance as well as how we experience action.

SOURCE: *New York Times*, March 7, 1983, C2.

---

personality. In considering their strengths and limitations, we must keep in mind that we are not considering a unified approach. Perhaps to an even greater extent than any of the approaches considered previously, there is here diversity of view and even hostility among alternative behavioral camps. As we shall see, this in itself may be both a strength and a weakness of the approach.

Strengths of Learning, Behavioral Approaches

Three major contributions may be noted in relation to learning, behavioral approaches: a commitment to systematic research and theory development; a recognition and exploration of the role of situational, environmental variables in influencing behavior; a pragmatic approach to treatment leading to important new developments.

***Behavior Therapy*—Behavior therapists focus on specific problems and take an active approach toward the goal of behavioral change.** ©1983 by The New York Times Company. Cartoon by Gil Eisner.

Behavioral psychologists share a commitment to empiricism or systematic research. Whatever the differences in theory, the various approaches tend to be characterized by a respect for scientific methodology and a respect for evidence in support for a new point of view. In contrast with the development of psychoanalysis, and to a certain extent with that of phenomenology and humanistic approaches, behavioral psychology has been largely tied to academic departments. There the emphasis is on clarity in defining constructs and on replicability in verifying data. While at times these constraints may impose limitations on what is studied and how phenomena are conceptualized, they also set some useful boundaries on armchair speculation and quasi-religious debate. Thus, to a greater extent than most other approaches considered to this point, the behavioral approach emphasizes laboratory research or clinical analogue research, both of which lead to the establishing of causal relationships.

Because behavioral psychologists have emphasized research and because they have been based in academic departments, there has been an openness to new developments in more narrow as well as in more general areas of psychology (Bower, 1982). This is not to say that theoretical biases are given up easily, but rather that there is a commitment to discovery as opposed to dogma. Thus, not only are experiments designed to test competing theories but new data can provide the basis for theoretical development. To a certain extent we see evidence of this in the development of cognitive behavior modification. To an even greater extent, we see evidence of this in the development of social learning theory (Chapter 13). The general point, however, is that learning theory is not a static entity. Research efforts continue to be active on a wide variety of fronts as more variables are explored, in greater depth, over a greater variety of subjects, and in more diverse situations. As one studies the relevant literature, there is at least some sense of a cumulative expansion of what is studied and how phenomena are conceptualized.

The second contribution and strength of learning, behavioral theory is a recognition of the role of environmental and situational variables in behavior. Most behavioral approaches emphasize the importance of regulating or maintaining conditions in the environment; all emphasize the importance of situational analysis. For some time traditional personality theory and assessment gave minimal attention to such variables. The importance of the situation or environment was noted by psychoanalytic and trait theorists, but there was not active exploration or conceptual development. In many ways, it has been unfortunate that the emphasis on situational variables and situation-specific aspects of performance became associated with the person-situation controversy. As most personality psychologists now recognize, both personality and situational variables enter into behavior and our effort must be to understand how they relate to one another. The particular contribution of the behavioral approach has been to call attention to the variability and flexibility that is characteristic of much of human behavior and to call attention to the diversity of skills that are relevant to specific tasks.

Related to the above has been a pragmatism characteristic of behavior therapists, a pragmatism that has led to the development of many important procedures for behavior change. In contrast with the focus of many traditional treatment programs on young, attractive, verbal, intelligent, and successful patients, many behavior modification programs started by treating individuals on whom almost everyone else gave up—the chronic schizophrenic, the autistic child, the retarded, the addicted, and so on. Traditional therapy programs were not working and new approaches were required. Behavior therapists filled the void, in particular with the application of Skinnerian principles in behavior modification programs. These programs have raised moral and ethical issues concerning the control of human behavior, but on the whole significant gains have been made in assisting people who otherwise would have been left untouched.

While work with these populations continues, there has been a movement toward treating a broader range of patients. In addition, there has been an effort to increase the generality and durability of results. As noted, these goals have been particularly relevant to the development of cognitive, self-control procedures. At this time behavior therapy includes a wide range of techniques based on classical conditioning, operant conditioning, and cognitive principles. These techniques are being applied to clients of all age groups, in a variety of settings, and with a wide range of difficulties. At this point the challenge often faced by the behavior therapist is which technique to use among the many available and others being developed.

Limitations of Learning, Behavioral Approaches

If the strengths outlined above seem significant, the limitations to be detailed are no less noteworthy. In some cases they speak to the very same issues already covered, suggesting that the reality is not always as pretty as the picture presented. For example, with its concern for objectivity and rigor there has been an oversimplification of personality and the neglect of important phenomena. Human behavior is complex. Measurement of one response or one component of the personality system may give a very incomplete picture of what is occurring, and an exclusive emphasis on one mechanism of change may give a very inaccurate representation of the multiple processes leading to multiple effects (Schwartz, 1982). Human personality involves structure and organization as well as discrete responses, and it involves motivation and emotion as well as overt behavior.

There are many components to the criticism that learning theorists oversimplify behavior. One component is the claim that the principles of learning used are derived from research on rats and other subhuman animals, and there is a question as to whether the same principles are involved in human learning. In other words, can rat laws be applied to human behavior? A second component of this criticism is the claim that the behaviors studied by the learning theorists are superficial. In their effort to gain experimental rigor and control over relevant variables, learning theorists have limited themselves to simple, specific responses and have avoided complex behaviors. We may recall here Cattell's argument that the bivariate method limits investigators to the study of a few variables, and this means that they must ignore behaviors that cannot be produced in the laboratory.

A third and critical component of the criticism regarding oversimplification is concerned with cognitive behavior. Cognitive behavior involves the way in which the individual receives, organizes, and transmits information. The work of many psychologists gives clear evidence of the importance of an understanding of cognitive behavior. Yet, for a long time behaviorists avoided considering these phenomena. Whether because of a reluctance to look at internal processes or because of a reluctance to consider complex processes, learning theorists stuck fast in their attempts to understand all behavior in terms of stimulus–response bonds or in terms of operants and successive approximation.

We have seen that some behavioral psychologists have attempted to emphasize cognitive variables and integrate them into their theoretical and applied systems. While clearly an influential development, it also is one that has met with considerable resistance and attack. As Meichenbaum (1979) notes, a sign that cognitive behavior modification has come of age is that it has been vehemently and vituperatively attacked—not only from without behavior therapy, but from within. Thus, this development has been characterized as "a step in the wrong direction" (Ledwidge, 1978) and proponents of it characterized as "malcontents" (Wolpe, 1976). One review concludes "Cognitive behavior modification: Who needs it?" (Greenspoon & Lamal, 1978) and Eysenck (1982) contends that there is no need to invoke cognitive mechanisms in the explanation of neurotic disorders and therapeutic change. According to Eysenck and others, the results of all behavior therapies with neurotics can be accounted for in terms of typical Pavlovian extinction. Thus, while we have suggested that a strength of behavioral approaches to personality is an openness to theoretical development, clearly there are limitations in this regard in at least some quarters.

In his criticism of cognitive approaches, Eysenck (1982) suggests that there is no cognitive learning theory. This brings us to our second criticism, that there is a gap generally between theory and practice. First, there is no agreed upon theory of learning that stands as the foundation for behavioral psychology. While Eysenck and Skinnerians are critical of cognitive theory, others suggest that conditioning theory is dead and that all learning is cognitive (Erwin, 1978; Meichenbaum & Cameron, 1982). The problem becomes even more compounded when one considers the relation between theory and practice; that is, to what extent do the techniques actually follow from theory? Though systematic desensitization presumably follows from Hullian and Pavlovian theory, there is question concerning the extent of the relationship and, in any case, considerable question concerning the effective processes involved (Kazdin & Wilson, 1978; Levis & Malloy, 1982). Things are not much better in relation to cognitive behavior modification, where there is agreement that the current enthusiasm far outstrips the theoretical and empirical base (Meichenbaum & Cameron, 1982). Sometime ago a supporter of behavior therapy suggested that it is a group of techniques rather than a theory-based scientific procedure: "When you eliminate the polemics and politics and gratuities, however, what remains of the theory to define the field and to tell you what it is about? Not a whole lot" (London, 1972, p. 916). Are things any better with more recent developments? Consider the following statement, also by supporters: "The contemporary cognitive learning therapist might be said to be engaging in the art of applying a science which does not yet exist" (Mahoney & Arnkoff, 1978, p. 710).

Finally, let us consider the effectiveness of behavioral approaches to treatment. There is a need for evidence concerning the effectiveness of most behavioral treatment procedures, particularly where they are used with actual clinical populations and in relation to significant effects that are maintained over time. Initially, there was a burst of enthusiasm for the successes of behavior therapy, as is often the case with a new development. Following this, some sobering questions were raised, including the following: To what extent is there, in behavior therapy, successful generalization from one situation to another and from one response to another? To what extent are the results durable or stable over time? Are the originally published success rates accurate and are behavioral techniques equally successful with all patients?

Historically, a problem with behavior therapy has been that often the results do not generalize and/or they do not remain stable over time. Questions have been raised, for example, as to whether results obtained in the laboratory or clinic are maintained in the natural environment (Bandura, 1972; Kazdin & Bootzin, 1972). In addition, some studies suggest that in many patients gains are eventually lost (Eysenck & Beech, 1971). Finally, techniques found to be useful with mild prob-

FIGURE 12.10   **SUMMARY OF STRENGTHS AND LIMITATIONS OF LEARNING, BEHAVIORAL APPROACHES**

STRENGTHS	LIMITATIONS
1. Committed to systematic research and theory development.	1. Oversimplifies personality and neglects important phenomena.
2. Recognizes the role of situational and environmental variables in influencing behavior.	2. Lacks a single, unified theory; gap between theory and practice.
3. Takes a pragmatic approach to treatment which can lead to important new developments.	3. Requires further evidence to support claims of treatment's effectiveness.

lems in the laboratory may be found to be of far lesser significance when applied to clients with more serious difficulties. While there are many reports of success, a recent review of the literature concluded that "research in which the effectiveness of behavior therapy has been compared to other treatment approaches has failed to provide convincing support for the superiority of behavior therapy" (Turkat & Forehand, 1980, p. 17).

Summary Evaluation

It is, of course, hard to evaluate in an overall way approaches that often are so diverse. However, the strengths and limitations noted do have general relevance. It should be noted that the criticism of learning, behavioral approaches to personality have not gone unchallenged. To the charge of oversimplification, the suggestion is that one must start somewhere and that it makes sense to start with simple events. Similarly, it is suggested that as understanding progresses, there is movement from the simple to the complex. To questions concerning theory, the suggestion is that many learning processes may exist and that the development of techniques of behavior change can themselves facilitate the further development of theory. In other words, not only does treatment success not always depend on theoretical understanding but in some cases it can lead to such understanding. Finally, to questions concerning effectiveness the suggestion is made that there is sufficient empirical basis for encouragement. Generally, behavior therapists receive enough intermittent reinforcement to maintain them in the belief that they are on the right track and that further success lies ahead.

In sum, the qualities of rigor, objectivity, and measurability of concepts have appeal for those who have accepted the values of the scientist, and work in academic settings. In addition, successes in applied efforts have buoyed hopes and created a sense of optimism about the future. While considerable controversy and soul searching goes on, generally there is the hope that eventually there will evolve a single, integrated framework that retains the values of scientific objectivity and provides for an understanding of complex behavior.

MAJOR CONCEPTS AND SUMMARY

and Read summary

target behaviors, responses
functional analysis of behavior
ABC assessment
own-control, ABA design
sign and sample approaches to assessment
behavior modification
behavior therapy
extinction
discrimination learning
counterconditioning

positive reinforcement
imitation
systematic desensitization
token economy

Read

cognitive behavior modification
covert conditioning
cognitive behavioral assessment
rational-emotive therapy (RET)
self-instructional learning
clinical analogue research

In this chapter we have continued with our consideration of learning, behavioral approaches to personality by focusing on procedures for assessment and change. Behavioral assessment procedures follow from the basic assumptions of learning, behavioral theory. Thus, there is an emphasis on target behaviors or target responses and their relation to stimuli and reinforcers in specific situations. A functional analysis of behavior includes an analysis of the *A*ntecedent conditions of the behavior of interest, the *B*ehavior itself, and the *C*onsequences of the behavior—the ABCs of behavioral assessment. A distinction has been drawn between sign and sample approaches to assessment. Whereas in sign approaches personality and behavior are inferred from test responses, in sample approaches interest is in the behavior itself and how it is affected by environmental conditions. Those who emphasize behavioral assessment support the utility of sample approaches and are critical of sign approaches to personality assessment. When questionnaires rather than direct observation of behavior are used, test items generally relate to specific behaviors or reinforcers rather than to traits or general personality characteristics.

While there is no single method of behavior therapy or behavior modification, the procedures included in this category emphasize principles of learning theory including extinction, discrimination learning, counterconditioning, positive reinforcement, and imitation. The application of principles of classical conditioning is seen in the classic case of Peter's fear of a white rabbit, in the treatment of bedwetting in children, and in Wolpe's method of systematic desensitization. In systematic desensitization, the relaxation response is counterconditioned to a graded, imagined hierarchy of stimuli that formerly were associated with anxiety. In behavior modification involving the use of Skinnerian principles of operant conditioning, desired behaviors are shaped through stages of successive approximation. The ABA or own-control design can be used to demonstrate that the reinforcers being manipulated are indeed the causal agents in the change process. The application of these principles to the regulation of behavior in an institutional setting is seen in a token economy. Under such circumstances, desired behaviors are rewarded with tokens that can then be exchanged for desired articles.

Recently, some behavior psychologists have become interested in internal processes such as thoughts and images. These cognitive behavioral psychologists remain behavioral in their emphasis on objective research, learning, and specific responses rather than on global personality characteristics. However, they depart from the earlier behavioral tradition in their emphasis on cognitive processes. This development stems in part from the broader cognitive revolution in psychology and in part from an interest in self-control procedures that may produce more generalized and durable therapeutic effects. Also, cognitive processes were already seen as part of therapeutic procedures such as systematic desensitization (imagined scenes or situations) and covert conditioning. In cognitive behavioral assessment, there is an interest in thoughts and self-statements associated with specific people, situations, or problems. A cognitive functional analysis involves assessment of the cognitive skills necessary for effective performance of specific tasks and the presence or absence of such skills in an individual, as well as the presence of interfering thoughts and self-statements. Such an assessment provides the basis for efforts at training the development of necessary skills, the relevant procedures falling under the general rubric of cognitive behavior modification. The diversity involved in such procedures is seen in the illustrated approaches of rational-emotive therapy, self-instructional training, and problem-solving therapy. Some such efforts involve clinical analogues, or controlled therapeutic procedures approaching those found in actual clinical practice.

Because there is considerable diversity to learning, behavioral approaches, any overall evaluation will be more relevant to some approaches than to others; however, some strengths and limitations would generally appear to apply to all such approaches. Behavioral psychologists share a positive commitment to research and generally are open to theoretical developments that better account for empirical data. Also, the pragmatic approach to treatment has encouraged innovation and the development of important procedures of behavior change. Often the application of these treatment procedures has involved populations previously neglected by psychotherapists. Finally, the emphasis on situational and environmental variables that influence behavior has been a useful correction to procedures of assessment and change that tended toward exclusive emphasis on global personality characteristics. At the same time, behavioral theory and behavior psychologists would appear to be limited in their oversimplification of personality and neglect of important phenomena. People are complex, with many factors, including motivational and emotional variables, entering into behavior. Cognitive behavioral psychologists have attempted to include exploration of internal thought processes. However, their efforts are not universally accepted by behavioral psychologists and as yet there is no cognitive behavioral theory of personality. This brings us to the second limitation—the lack of a unified, systematic theory of learning and a clear connection between theory and therapeutic procedures. As it is now, there are competing theories and often at best a vague relation between a therapeutic technique and a theory of learning. Finally, despite the admirable respect for research and the commitment to experimental investigation of therapeutic procedures, there is a need for demonstration of the effectiveness of behavioral treatment procedures on a wide range of cases, in a wide range of settings, and in the hands of diverse practitioners. Efforts that are successful in analogue studies with a select group of clients are not always found to be equally successful under the more demanding conditions of general practice.

In concluding consideration of learning, behavioral approaches to personality, we have paved the way for consideration of social learning theory. Social learning theory represents a very recent effort at systematic conceptualization that attempts to build on the strengths of past theories of learning while, at the same time, avoiding their pitfalls. It is to this approach to personality that we now turn.

Picasso, Pablo. *Man with a Hat*. 1912. Collection of The Museum of Modern Art, New York. Purchase.

SOCIAL LEARNING THEORY: BANDURA AND MISCHEL

CHAPTER FOCUS: In this chapter we consider a personality theory that shares many features with earlier learning approaches, but remains distinctive. Social learning theory focuses attention on the conditions that affect the acquisition, performance, and maintenance of behavior. Particular attention is given to observational learning or modeling, in which people acquire complex patterns of behavior even without being rewarded. Also examined are cognitive processes as they affect learning, self-control, and the perception of self-efficacy or the perceived ability to cope with situations in the environment.

This conception of human functioning then neither casts people into the role of powerless objects controlled by environmental forces nor free agents who can become whatever they choose. Both people and their environments are reciprocal determinants of each other.

Bandura, 1977a, p. vii

I would conceptualize observational learning as essentially a cognitive process, and our theories of learning are moving in a more cognitive direction.

Bandura, 1976, p. 245

Behavior is generated by the person, not by a self, ego or other agent distinct from the individual. And "self-control" refers to the powers of the person to regulate or control his own actions, thus overcoming the power of "stimulus [situational] control."

Mischel, 1977, p. 50

In the social learning view, psychological changes, regardless of the method used to achieve them, derive from a common mechanism. . . .Psychological procedures, whatever their form, alter expectations of personal efficacy.

Bandura, 1977a, p. 79

Social learning theory has for some time been presented as part of learning theory, but it now warrants separate consideration. In the academic community social learning theory is probably the most popular personality theory, and it is gaining increasing numbers of adherents in the clinical community as well. The theory has been most clearly represented in the works of two psychologists, Albert Bandura and Walter Mischel.

Social learning theory is distinct from the other theories we have studied in a number of ways. First, in contrast to most, if not all, of the other theories, it is questionable whether a specific social learning theory exists. Many would argue that social learning theory is a point of view based on some general principles rather than a fully developed theory. A theory has nevertheless been evolving and there has been a recent attempt by Bandura (1977a) to systematize it. Second, as it has evolved, social learning theory has attempted to integrate and go beyond some of the earlier points of view. It has attempted to go beyond such divisions in the field as the relative importance of internal and external determinants of behavior and a behavioral "as opposed to" humanistic view of the person. As will be seen, according to social learning theory there is always a process of interaction between the organism and its environment, a process Bandura calls **reciprocal determinism.** Through the development of cognitive structures and mechanisms of self-control, the person influences the environment as well as being influenced by it. Finally, social learning theory is distinct from other theories in that it is currently advancing the most and receiving the most attention.

Given this state of evolution of theory and current popularity, how can it be differentiated further from the theories previously considered? As noted in Chapter 9, Mischel has been critical of traditional trait and psychoanalytic theory. His influential book *Personality and Assessment* (1968) took such views to task for their emphasis on internal dispositions that presumably lead to consistency in behavior across situations. Instead, Mischel presented a social learning view that emphasized the significant influence of varying contingencies of reinforcement in the environment. Thus, in contrast to trait and psychoanalytic positions, social learning theory places less emphasis on structure (dispositions) and greater emphasis on the organism's ability to respond to a changing environment.

Such a view might fit neatly within traditional learning theory (see Chapters 11 and 12). However, while social learning theory developed out of earlier learning points of view, its suggestion that learning occurs in the absence of rewards represented the beginnings of a major break with tradition. Whereas both Hullian and Skinnerian theories of learning emphasize reward, Bandura suggests that rewards are far more important in the *performance* of learned behaviors than in their acquisition. Indeed, Bandura's emphasis on learning in the absence of reinforcement continues to be a major point of contention between him and Skinnerians.

Finally, in its most recent forms social learning theory is distinctive in its emphasis on cognition within the framework of learning theory. Cognitive processes were emphasized by Kelly in his personal construct theory (Chapters 7 and 8), but he threw out many traditional concepts in psychology generally and in studies of learning in particular. In contrast, social learning theory emphasizes the role of cognitive operations within the person in the context of general principles of learning and cognition.

This chapter considers a theory that is still evolving and growing in popularity and influence. It is different from traditional trait and psychoanalytic views in its emphasis on the variability of behavior in response to changing circumstances in the environment. It is different from traditional Hullian and Skinnerian learning theory in its emphasis on learning independent of reinforcement and in its emphasis on cognitive processes.

A VIEW OF THE THEORISTS

Albert Bandura (1925–   )

Little is known about the early life of Bandura other than that he grew up in northern Alberta, Canada. He went to college at the University of British Columbia. On graduation he chose to do graduate work in clinical psychology at the University of Iowa because it was known for the excellence of its research on learning processes. Even then Bandura was interested in the applications of learning theory to clinical phenomena. In an interview Bandura indicated that he "had a strong interest in conceptualizing clinical phenomena in ways that would make them amenable to experimental test, with the view that as practitioners we have a responsibility for assessing the efficacy of a procedure, so that people are not subjected to treatments before we know their effects" (quoted in Evans, 1976, p. 243). At Iowa he was influenced by Spence, a follower of Hull, and by the general emphasis on careful conceptual analysis and rigorous experimental investigation. During that time he was also influenced by the writings of Miller and Dollard.

After obtaining his Ph.D. at Iowa in 1952, Bandura went to Stanford and began to work on interactive processes in psychotherapy and on family patterns that lead to aggressiveness in children. The work on familial causes of aggression, with Richard Walters, his first graduate student, gave rise to the emphasis on the central role of modeling influences (learning through observation of others) in personality development. These findings and consequent laboratory investigations of modeling processes resulted in the books *Adolescent Aggression* (1959)

Albert Bandura.

and *Social Learning and Personality Development* (1963). Since then he continued with research on aggression, modeling and observational learning, and the processes of behavior change. Bandura describes himself as conducting a multifaceted research program aimed at clarifying aspects of human capability that should be emphasized in a comprehensive theory of human behavior. The emphasis on human capabilities is an important aspect of Bandura's recent thinking and research. It is related to his interest in processes of development and therapeutic change and is associated with what some perceive as a humanist emphasis in his work. Professor Bandura has received a number of distinguished scientific achievement awards. In 1974 he was elected president of the American Psychological Association and in 1980 he received the Association's Distinguished Scientific Contribution Award "for masterful modeling as researcher, teacher, and theoretician."

Walter Mischel (1930–   )

Mischel's early life and roots in psychology, like Bandura's, are known only sketchily. Mischel was born in Vienna and lived his first nine years "in easy playing distance of Freud's house." He describes the possible influence of this period as follows:

> When I began to read psychology Freud fascinated me most. As a student at City College (in New York, where my family settled after the Hitler-caused forced exodus from Europe in 1939), psychoanalysis seemed to provide a comprehensive view of man. But my excitement fizzled when I tried to apply ideas as a social worker with "juvenile delinquents" in New York's Lower East Side: somehow trying to give those youngsters "insight" didn't help either them or me. The concepts did not fit what I saw, and I went looking for more useful ones.

> Mischel, 1978, personal communication

The experience with "juvenile delinquents" is of particular interest for two reasons. First, it probably relates to Mischel's long-standing interest in the psychological mechanisms underlying delay of gratification and self-control. Second, there is a similarity to Bandura in that both did their early clinical work with aggressive youngsters.

Mischel did his graduate work at Ohio State University where he came under the influence of two significant figures: "George Kelly and Julian Rotter were my dual mentors and each has enduringly influenced my thinking" (Mischel, 1978, personal communication). The work of George Kelly has already been discussed. The thinking of Julian Rotter (1954) has only lately become popular in the field of personality, primarily because of his concept of internal–external locus of control (Chapter 2). However, Rotter's views were developed much earlier and had a

Walter Mischel.

number of distinguishing elements. First, Rotter emphasized learning theory in relation to important human social (interpersonal) phenomena; second, he emphasized the importance of situational factors as well as person factors in behavior. Rotter was critical of personality theories and measurement devices that ignored the contribution of situational factors to the variability in any person's behavior. Third, Rotter emphasized the importance of cognitive processes in learning as opposed to mechanical stimulus–response connections. In particular, he emphasized the importance of individual *expectancies* concerning reinforcements for various behaviors in particular situations. These concepts, together with those emphasized by Kelly, have increasingly played a major role in Mischel's thinking in particular and social learning theory in general. Mischel describes his work in relation to that of his dual mentors as follows: "I see my own work both with cognition and with social learning as clearly rooted in their contributions, a focus on the person both as construer and actor, interacting with the vicissitudes of the environment, and trying to make life coherent even in the face of all its inconsistencies" (Mischel, 1978, personal communication).

After completing his graduate work at Ohio State, Mischel spent a number of years at Harvard University and then joined Bandura at Stanford. His current work focuses on how people categorize events and on how they can and do overcome "stimulus control" through cognitive self-control. An example of the latter is his work on how people use thought to delay gratification more easily by refocusing their attention or by changing their interpretation of the situation altogether. In 1978 he received the Distinguished Scientist Award from the Clinical Psychology Division of the American Psychological Association.

VIEW OF THE PERSON

Both Bandura and Mischel recognize the relationship of a general view of the person to a theory of personality and have attempted to be explicit concerning this view. In a statement very much in tune with a point made throughout this book, Bandura notes that "views about human nature influence which aspects of psychological functioning are studied most thoroughly and which remain unexamined. Theoretical conceptions similarly determine the paradigms used to collect evidence which, in turn, shape the particular theory" (1977, p. vi). In other words, there is a back-and-forth or reciprocal relationship between a view of the person, a program of research, and a theory of personality.

Current social learning theory emphasizes a view of the person as active, using symbolic (cognitive) processes to represent events and communicate with others, and capable of choice and self-regulation. Social learning theory rejects the view that the person is either a passive victim of unconscious impulses and past history or a passive respondent to environmental events. Theories of personality that emphasize internal factors to the exclusion of environmental events are rejected because of their disregard for the individual's responsiveness to varying situations. At the same time, theories that emphasize external factors to the exclusion of internal factors also are rejected because of their failure to consider the role of cognitive functioning and self-regulation in behavior. "Theories that explain human behavior as solely the product of external rewards and punishments present a truncated image of people because they possess self-reactive capacities that enable them to exercise some control over their own feelings, thoughts, and actions" (Bandura, 1977a, p. 129).

Rejecting both the view that people are driven by inner forces and that they are buffeted by environmental stimuli, social learning theory suggests that behavior can be explained in terms of a reciprocal interaction between personal and environmental determinants. People are influenced by environmental forces but they also choose how to behave. The person is both responsive to situations and actively constructs and influences situations. Through the use of thought and symbols people can go beyond immediate experience and anticipate the future. However, such cognitive processes themselves are largely determined by experience. Furthermore, plans for the future generally are, to some extent, influenced by expectations concerning rewards and punishments. In a view that recalls Kelly, social learning theory suggests that the person is both free and determined: "Within the process of reciprocal determinism lies the opportunity for people to influence their destiny as well as the limits of self-direction" (Bandura, 1977a, p. vii).

Basically, social learning theory sees the person, when functioning properly, as a well-tuned organism capable of adapting to changing conditions in the environment. The ongoing process of reciprocal determinism involves valuing certain environmental events (outcomes), discriminating among situations in terms of their potential to result in these valued outcomes, judging one's ability to cope, deciding which situations to enter into and how to behave in them, and using feedback information concerning the results of these decisions. The feedback information concerning behavioral outcomes is then used to form further discriminations, expectancies, and decisions. In a sense, the person is a problem-solving organism seeking to behave in ways that will maximize both rewards in the environment and internal rewards in the form of self-praise. Mischel describes the emerging image of the human being as follows:

> *The image is one of the human being as an active, aware problem-solver, capable of profiting from an enormous range of experiences and cognitive capacities, possessing great potential for good or ill, actively constructing his or her psychological world, and influencing the environment but also being influenced by it in lawful ways—even if the laws are difficult to discover and hard to generalize. . . . It is an image that has moved a long way from the instinctual drive-reduction models, the static global traits, and the automatic stimulus-response bonds of traditional personality theories. It is an image that highlights the shortcoming of all simplistic theories that view behavior as the exclusive result of any narrow set of determinants, whether these are habits, traits, drives, reinforcers, constructs, instincts, or genes and whether they are exclusively inside or outside the person. It will be exciting to watch this image change as new research and theorizing alter our understanding of what it is to be a human being.*
>
> Mischel, 1977, p. 253

This current view of the person suggests a shift from what earlier appeared to be a more passive view of the organism. While a social learning view of the person was not spelled out in earlier papers, there certainly was much more of an emphasis on how contingencies in the environment regulate, influence, guide, and direct behavior. The emphasis on cognitive control and self-regulation is a later development in social learning theory. One can only speculate why this should have occurred. Probably there were both scientific and personal reasons. In terms of the former, Bandura and Mischel recognized that the same situation could lead to very different behaviors in people. Furthermore, a variety of experiments were suggesting the importance of cognitive factors in learning. In terms of the latter, the Skinnerian view of an organism shaped by environmental events probably did not sit well with their own personal beliefs. Thus, the view of a reciprocal relationship between person and environment allowed for the integration of earlier work on the importance of reinforcement with later work on cognitive control and with personal beliefs and values.

VIEW OF SCIENCE, THEORY, AND RESEARCH METHODS

Both Bandura and Mischel are committed to the use of theory and empirical research. There is a strong commitment to concepts that are clear and based on systematic observations. Theories that emphasize motivational forces in the form of needs, drives, and impulses are criticized for being vague and inferred from the behavior they supposedly caused. In other words, too often it is said that a person has an aggressive impulse or trait because they behave aggressively and that they behave aggressively because of their instinct or motive for aggression.

Whereas extreme behaviorism rejects the study of cognitive processes because of a distrust for introspective data, Bandura and Mischel feel that such inner processes must be studied and that the use of some types of self-report is both legitimate and desirable. They suggest that self-reports which are general, based on long-term recall, and involve anxiety that can lead to defensiveness are *not* likely sources of reliable information. However, self-reports that are specific, given as events occur and under conditions that do not arouse evaluative apprehensions, can be valuable aids in understanding cognitive processes. In defense of the use of verbal self-reports, Bandura notes that "vast numbers of people are outfitted by ophthalmologists with suitable corrective eyeglasses on the basis of verbalized discriminations of printed and pictorial stimuli. They can be easily outfitted with defective eyeglasses by reporting that the blurred stimuli are the clearer ones. However, this would hardly constitute justification for renouncing the optometric enterprise. Rather than decrying the limitations of verbal probes of thought, we should be improving the tools for measuring it" (Bandura, 1978a, p. 15).

In sum, social learning theory is concerned with both a broad variety of aspects of human behavior and with scientific rigor. There is a concern both with conceptual clarity and with theoretical formulation, with important inner processes and with systematic observations. In all likelihood it is this blend of concern with important human events and scientific respectability that most accounts for the theory's current popularity.

SOCIAL LEARNING THEORY OF PERSONALITY

The stage has been set for considering the details of the social learning theory of personality. In tune with the learning theories presented earlier, there is an emphasis on responses and learning processes and much less emphasis on structures or organization. In addition, there is an emphasis on situational specificity. Indeed, as noted earlier, Mischel has been at the forefront of the attack on trait theory and the associated suggestion of cross-situational consistency in behavior (Mischel & Peake, 1982, 1983). Instead, social learning theorists suggest that responses are learned and maintained in relation to specific situation characteristics, and that people generally make careful discriminations among situations. This, in turn, leads to a lack of consistency or stability in behavior across situations. The consistency question has become one of the central issues in current personality theory and research and, unfortunately, at times social learning theorists have been portrayed as denying individual differences or the existence of personality. As we shall presently see, neither is the case. What is the case is that there is an interest in different kinds of phenomena and different personality variables.

Structure

Personality structures, to the extent that social learning theory emphasizes them, can be seen as based on cognitive and self-regulatory processes. In his cognitive social learning reconceptualization of personality, Mischel (1973) rejected global personality characterizations in favor of personality variables that emphasize the uniqueness of the person and the variability of behavior. Thus, for example, how the person construes and organizes the surrounding world, how situations are categorized as well as how reinforcers are valued are seen as important personality variables. Through the employment of cognitive categories and expectancies the person is able to discriminate among situations and respond adaptively. In addition, two concepts are noteworthy. First is the concept of **goals** or **plans**. This concept accounts for behavior that is maintained for extended periods of time in the absence of (sometimes in spite of) external consequences (Mischel, 1973). The concept of goals or plans also suggests an organization to personality processes that would not otherwise be present. In other words, our goals or plans guide us in establishing priorities among rewards and in selecting among actions that might otherwise seem of equal value. Goals–plans enable us to go beyond momentary influences and to organize our behavior over extended periods of time.

The second concept worthy of note is that of the **self**. The self is not a structure per se but a concept used to explain cognitive processes such as self-conceptions, self-praise, self-criticism, and self-control (Bandura, 1977b; Mischel, 1977). People's self-conceptions and self-regulatory mechanisms are critical for understanding what goes on between environmental inputs and behavior. As the organism develops, it increasingly uses the processes of self-control and self-regulation to direct behavior. However, it should be clear that this concept of self is not identical to other concepts of the self. For example, the social learning concept of self does not suggest "an extra causal agent that dwells in the person and somehow generates or causes behavior in ways that are separable from the organism in which 'it' resides" (Mischel, 1977, pp. 49–50). The social learning concept of self refers to processes that are part of the person's psychological functioning. In a sense, the person does not have a structure called "the self," but rather self-processes that are part of the person. In addition, earlier concepts of the self are criticized for being too global. Rather than having a self-concept, social learning theory suggests that a person has self-conceptions and self-control processes which may vary from time to time and from situation to situation.

A particular aspect of the perception of self has become central to Bandura's thinking, that concerning **self-efficacy** or the perceived ability to cope with specific situations. The concept of self-efficacy relates to judgments people make concerning their ability to perform behaviors relevant to a specific task or situation. According to Bandura, the influence of self-percepts of efficacy is widespread, including the following: (1) *which activities* people engage in ("People avoid activities that they believe exceed their coping capabilities, but they undertake and perform assuredly those that they judge themselves capable of managing." 1982, p. 123); (2) *how much effort* will be expended in a situation; (3) *how* *long* people will persist in the face of obstacles; (4) *thought patterns* while engaged in a task; and (5) *emotional reactions* while anticipating a situation or while involved in it. Clearly, we think, feel, and behave differently in situations in which we feel confident of our ability than in situations in which we are insecure or feel incompetent. In sum, self-percepts of efficacy influence thought patterns, motivation, performance, and emotional arousal.

These influences of self-efficacy are spelled out further throughout this chapter. For now, however, it is important to consider how Bandura assesses self-efficacy and how he distinguishes it from what might appear to be related concepts. In terms of assessment, Bandura emphasizes what he calls a **microanalytic research strategy.** According to this strategy, detailed measures of perceived self-efficacy are taken before performance of behaviors in specific situations. Thus, subjects are asked to designate in a specific situation those tasks they can do and their degree of certainty about doing them successfully. This strategy reflects the view that self-efficacy judgments are situation specific and do not represent global dispositions that can be measured by comprehensive personality inventories. As noted before, a global self-concept is criticized because it "does not do justice to the complexity of efficacy self-perceptions, which vary across different activities, different levels of the same activity, and different situational circumstances" (Bandura, 1981, p. 225). Finally, the concept is distinguished from Rotter's concept of locus of control and Selgiman's concept of learned helplessness. Self-efficacy judgments relate to perceptions of one's ability to perform certain activities and not to one's ability to control outcomes or reinforcers. Generally, there is a relationship between task requirements and outcomes. However, this is not always the case in that sometimes one may be able to perform certain critical tasks but reinforcement for performance may be beyond one's control. What is important here is Bandura's suggestion that it is self-efficacy judgments that operate as the critical cognitive mediators of action.

Process

It can be seen that the emphasis on cognitive processes and the interplay between external and internal sources of influence is critical to the understanding of social learning theory. It is these processes that increasingly have been emphasized by social learning theory and increasingly have set it apart from other theories of learning.

Social learning theory emphasizes two processes distinct from other learning theories of personality—observational learning and self-regulation. Observational learning involves the ability to learn complex behaviors by watching others. "Because people can learn from example what to do, at least in approximate form, before performing any behavior, they are spared needless errors" (Bandura, 1977b, p. 22). Self-regulation involves the ability of individuals to exercise influence over their own behavior rather than reacting mechanically to external influences. Both observational learning and self-regulation involve considerable use of thought (cognitive) processes. Both are influenced by rewards and punishments, but they are not determined by them.

Observational Learning

The theory of **observational learning** suggests that people can learn merely by observing the behaviors of others. The person being observed is called a model. There is evidence to suggest that an individual can learn behaviors by observing a model perform these behaviors. Thus, for example, the child may learn language by observing parents and other people speaking, a process called **modeling**. The type of behaviors under consideration are often included under the terms *imitation* and *identification*. However, imitation has the very narrow connotation of response mimicry and, at the other extreme, identification implies an incorporation of entire patterns of behavior. Modeling involves something broader than imitation but less diffuse than identification. In addition, these terms are rejected because they have been associated with stimulus–response reinforcement theories and with psychoanalytic theory. These theories are considered inadequate in accounting for the observed data.

The theories of Hull and Skinner are viewed as inadequate in the following ways: (1) They do not account for the appearance of new, or novel behaviors. (2) In particular, they do not account for the appearance of new, large segments of behavior in their entirety; that is, they do not account for the fact that, with a model, full patterns of behavior can be acquired that would be difficult to account for in terms of a slow, gradual conditioning process. (3) The acquisition of these response patterns appears to occur independent of reinforcement variables. (4) The first appearance of the behaviors learned may not occur for days, weeks, or months after the model has been observed. The importance of the process of observational learning is well described by Bandura:

> *The provision of social models is also an indispensable means of transmitting and modifying behavior in situations where errors are likely to produce costly or fatal consequences. Indeed, if social learning proceeded exclusively on the basis of rewarding and punishing consequences, most people would never survive the socialization process. . . . In fact, it would be difficult to imagine a socialization process in which language, mores, vocational and avocational patterns, the familial customs of a culture, and its educational, social, and political practices were shaped in each new member by selective reinforcement without the response guidance of models who exhibit the accumulated cultural repertoires in their own behavior.*
>
> Bandura, 1969a, p. 213

Observational learning, then, accounts for the learning of new, complex patterns of behavior independent of reinforcements.

An important part of the theory of modeling is the distinction made between **acquisition** and **performance**. The early research suggested that children who ob-

Modeling—**Social learning theorists emphasize the importance of observing others in the acquisition of behavior.** Drawing by Opie; © 1978 The New Yorker Magazine, Inc.

served a model rewarded for aggressive behavior would reproduce these behaviors, and those who observed the model punished would not. Since learning is expressed in performance, this might suggest that reinforcements to the model are critical for the learning process. However, many of the children who did not reproduce the model's aggressive behavior in the test situation were able to describe it with considerable accuracy. This led to an experiment in which children observed a model express aggressive behavior with either rewarding consequences, punishing consequences, or no consequences. Although in the initial test situation (No Incentive), the children who observed the punished model performed fewer imitative acts than the children observing other models, this difference could be wiped out by offering the children attractive incentives for reproducing the model's behavior (Positive Incentive, See Figure 13.1) (Bandura, Ross, & Ross, 1963). In other words, the consequences to the model for the aggressive acts had an effect on the children's performance of these acts but not on the learning of the aggressive behaviors.

A number of other studies have since demonstrated that the observation of consequences to a model affects performance but not acquisition. The difference between acquisition and performance suggests, however, that in some way the children were being affected by what happened to the model; that is, either on a cognitive basis or on an emotional basis, or both, the children were responding to the consequences to the model. The suggestion here is that the children learned certain emotional responses by sympathizing with the model; that is, vicariously by observing the model. Not only can behavior be learned through observation,

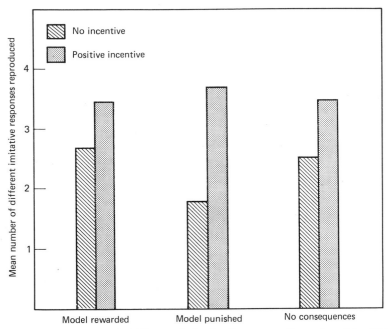

FIGURE 13.1   Mean Number of Different Imitative Responses Reproduced by Children as a Function of Response Consequences to the Model and Positive Incentives. (Bandura, 1965)

subject will infers what will happen

but emotional reactions (fear responses) can also be conditioned on a vicarious basis. The effects of **vicarious conditioning** were demonstrated in an experiment by Berger (1962) in which subjects who observed a model being shocked after the signal of a buzzer developed, vicariously, conditioned emotional reactions to the buzzer. The process of vicarious conditioning was demonstrated further in a study by Bandura and Rosenthal (1966). Here again it was found that emotional reactions would be conditioned to a previously neutral stimulus if the subjects observed a model who appeared to be shocked after the appearance of the stimulus.

The discussion above has indicated that behavioral responses and emotional reactions can be acquired through the process of observational learning. In addition to specific responses, rules or general plans for action can be learned through observation. For example, by observing models people may acquire rules concerning language and grammar as well as standards for evaluating their own behavior and that of others. In other words, modeling involves the acquisition of abstract principles as well as the acquisition of discrete responses.

Although at first glance observational learning may appear a simple process, in reality it is not. Not all observers appear to acquire the model's behavior patterns. Apparently this has something to do with the characteristics of the model (e.g., prestige) and characteristics of the observer (e.g., dependence on others). What is important to recognize is that according to the theory the individual is actively thinking about and expanding on external stimuli. ''In social learning theory observers function as active agents who transform, classify, and organize modeling stimuli into easily remembered schemes rather than as quiescent cameras or tape recorders that simply store isomorphic representations of modeled events'' (Bandura, 1971a, p. 20). Performance of observed behaviors may, initially, only roughly approximate these behaviors. Skills are developed as the person progressively matches overt behavior against the conception of the desired behavior. It is the symbol or generalized conception that guides corrective adjustments in the process of continuous skill refinement.

✝*Self-regulation*

Bandura distinguishes between the acquisition of responses and the maintenance, regulation, or performance of responses. Learning, response acquisition, occurs through observation and through the positive and negative effects that actions produce (response consequences). Among the responses learned are **standards** for expecting reinforcement from others and standards for reinforcing oneself. We learn to set appropriate goals for ourselves and to reward ourselves with self-praise or punish ourselves with self-criticism by observing models engaged in such behavior and by being reinforced directly for such behavior. If responses are thus acquired through observation and direct reinforcement, how are they maintained or regulated? According to Bandura, "Behavior is, in fact, extensively regulated by its consequences. Responses that result in unrewarding or punishing effects tend to be discarded, whereas those that produce rewarding outcomes are retained. Human behavior, therefore, cannot be fully understood without considering the regulatory influence of response consequences'' (1977a, p. 96).

That statement would appear to put social learning theory in agreement with other reinforcement theories as far as performance is concerned—reinforcement contingencies determine whether behavior appears. However, this is not the case. First, social learning theory does not view reinforcers as establishing stimulus–response connections. Rather, what is being established are certain expectations concerning the results of various actions and the development of general rules of action. Rather than an automatic, mechanical connection between behavior and reinforcement there is a complex cognitive process. Rather than being maintained by its immediate consequences, behavior is maintained by **expectancies** or anticipated consequences. In addition, rather than behavior being regulated exclusively by external reinforcers there is the process of **self-reinforcement** through which individuals reward themselves for attaining standards they set for themselves. These performance standards serve as motivators for behavior. It is the anticipation of satisfactions for desired accomplishments and dissatisfactions with insufficient accomplishments that provides the incentive for our efforts. Performance standards and anticipated consequences thus explain goal-directed behavior.

The emphasis on the development of standards for self-reinforcement and on cognitive processes are of critical importance for social learning theory. Through them the emphasis is shifted from a purely external, environmental locus of control to an emphasis on both internal and external factors. In other words, it is true that behavior is affected by its consequences. However, since the consequences result in expectancies in the person and since many consequences or reinforcements are self-generated (self-reward or self-punishment), one cannot say that behavior is maintained by the environment alone. People experience consequences directly, they experience consequences vicariously through the observation of others, and they experience consequences that they create for themselves. All three kinds of consequences affect behavior. The person integrates information from these sources over a period of time and thereby is led to certain general conclusions and rules of action. Thus, behavior is not maintained by the person or by the situation but by the back-and-forth reciprocal relationship between the two: "To the oft-repeated dictum, 'change contingencies and you change behavior,' should be added the reciprocal side, 'change behavior and you change the contingencies'" (1977a, p. 203). Through the development of such cognitive mechanisms people not only are able to exercise some control over their lives but also are able to establish plans or goals for the future. In other words, people can change the environmental contingencies that eventually will affect their behavior. The capacities to anticipate the future, to set standards, and to experience self-satisfaction and self-criticism are critical in permitting us to engage in endeavors over long periods of time. Human behavior is regulated by cognitive processes that integrate information coming from external and from self-generated consequences. Expectancies of reward from external and internal sources serve as incentives and guides for action.

Self-efficacy and Performance

As previously noted, Bandura increasingly has emphasized the importance of self-perceptions of efficacy as cognitive mediators of action. While considering action and once engaged in it, people make judgments concerning their ability to perform various task requirements. These self-efficacy judgments influence thought ("This is what I need to do and I can make it." versus "I'll never manage this. What will people think of me?"), emotion (excitement, joy versus anxiety, depression), and action (greater commitment versus inhibition, immobilization). A person sets standards and goals, both distant (long-term) and proximal (immediate), and makes judgments concerning the ability to perform the tasks necessary for goal achievement. While influenced by situations, people are active in terms of establishing goals, making self-efficacy judgments, and making self-evaluative judgments.

An earlier edition of this text criticized social learning theory for its relative lack of concern with human motivation. More recently this has been an important area of concern and Bandura (1982a) has increasingly emphasized a purposive view of human action. In a relevant piece of research, Bandura and Cervone (1984) studied the effects of goals and performance feedback on motivation. The hypothesis tested was that performance motivation reflects both the presence of goals and the awareness of how one is doing relative to standards: "Simply adopting goals, whether easy or personally challenging ones, without knowing how one is doing seems to have no appreciable motivational effects" (1984,

p. 123). The assumption was that greater discrepancies between standards and performance would generally lead to greater self-dissatisfaction and efforts to improve performance. However, a critical ingredient of such efforts is self-efficacy judgments, and thus the research tested the hypothesis that self-efficacy judgments, as well as self-evaluative judgments, mediate between goals and goal-directed effort.

In this research, subjects performed a strenuous activity under one of four conditions: goals with feedback on their performance, goals alone, feedback alone, an absence of goals and feedback. Following this activity, described as part of a project to plan and evaluate exercise programs for postcoronary rehabilitation, subjects rated how self-satisfied or self-dissatisfied they would be with the same level of performance in a following session. In addition, they recorded their perceived self-efficacy for various possible performance levels. Their effortful performance was then again measured. In accord with the hypothesis, the condition combining both goals and performance feedback had a strong motivational impact, whereas neither goals alone nor feedback alone was of comparable motivational significance (Figure 13.2, Part A). Also, subsequent effort was most intense when subjects were both dissatisfied with substandard performance and were high on self-efficacy judgments for good attainment. Neither dissatisfaction alone nor positive self-efficacy judgments alone had a comparable effect. And, often there was a reduction in effort where there was both low dissatisfaction with performance and low perceived self-efficacy (Figure 13.2, Part B). The authors concluded that there was clear evidence in support of the theory that goals have motivating power through self-evaluative and self-efficacy judgments.

Growth and Development   Skip 417-424

The social learning theory of growth and development follows from the principles already established. A behavioral repertoire and skills in processing information, or **cognitive competencies,** are developed through observational learning and direct experience. In addition, the development of expectancies, plans, and self-regulatory functions are important. These developing competencies are greatly influenced by experience, but biological factors do enter in. Bandura describes the interplay between experiential and biological factors as follows:

> *Human competencies are not fashioned solely through experience. Biological factors, of course, set constraints on behavioral development, and evolved biological systems predispose organisms to perceive and to learn critical features of their immediate environment. . . . The specific forms that behavior takes, the frequency with which it is expressed, and the situations in which it is displayed are largely determined by social learning factors. Because of the limited inborn programming of action patterns, human nature is characterized as a vast potentiality that can be fashioned by direct and vicarious experiences into a variety of forms with biological limits.*

> Bandura, 1979

Part A. Relation of Performance to Goals and Feedback

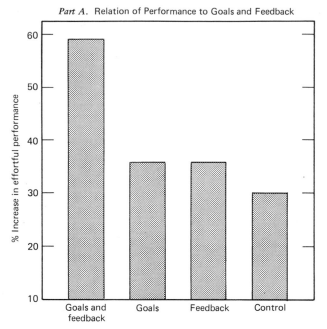

FIGURE 13.2   Self-Evaluative and Self-Efficacy Mechanisms in Motivation.
A. Mean percent increase in effortful performance under conditions varying in goals and performance feedback. (see above)
B. Mean change in effortful performance, between the first and final minute of the session, by subjects in the goals and feedback condition as a function of differential combinations of levels of self-dissatisfaction (S-DIS) and perceived self-efficacy (S-EFF) for goal attainment. (Bandura & Cervone, 1984) (see page 419)

While social learning theory recognizes the importance of biological factors, it does not emphasize maturational factors in the way that is done by stage theorists such as Piaget and Freud. Stage theorists assume that a structure emerges in the course of maturation and that the acquisition of cognitive skills and rules at one stage is dependent upon the person having passed through previous stages. Social learning theory emphasizes social influence variables and suggests that individuals need not learn various skills in a fixed, sequential fashion. Furthermore, the suggestion is made that the person's cognitive functioning is not uniform at a particular level but may vary from issue to issue and from situation to situation (Rosenthal & Zimmerman, 1978). Bandura suggests that a major problem with stage theories is that it is hard to find people who fit them well. Most people exhibit a mixture of thought patterns that span several "stages." Rather than viewing people in terms of stages or categories, it is suggested that we view them in terms of the individuality of their thought and action.

Finally, the suggestion is made that stage doctrines underestimate human capabilities and accept as unchangeable certain limitations which otherwise might be modified. In contrast, social learning theory suggests that earnest teaching efforts

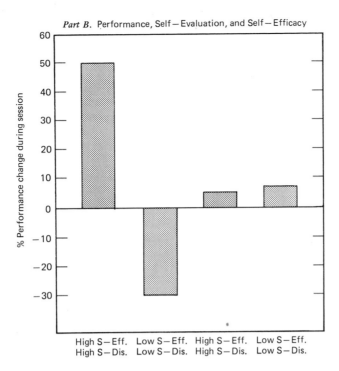

Part B. Performance, Self—Evaluation, and Self—Efficacy

y-axis: % Performance change during session

x-axis labels:
High S—Eff.   Low S—Eff.   High S—Eff.   Low S—Eff.
High S—Dis.   Low S—Dis.   High S—Dis.   Low S—Dis.

may eradicate deficiencies formerly attributed to shortcomings in children: "Greater progress can be achieved in identifying the developmental determinants of complex abilities, by analyzing the prior competencies needed to master them, than by categorizing people into ill-fitting types" (Bandura, 1977a, p. 47).

In terms of the development of capabilities and competences, Bandura (1981) places particular emphasis on the development of self-efficacy. One's sense of self-efficacy comes from many sources—actual accomplishments, vicarious experiences through observing others, verbal persuasion, and emotional arousal. Direct personal experiences of accomplishment in relation to specific goals is of importance generally and specifically in relation to the development of intrinsic interest. For example, in some relevant research, it was demonstrated that children who set attainable goals that were then mastered heightened their perceived self-efficacy and their interest in activities that initially held little attraction for them (Bandura & Schunk, 1981). Children who feel highly efficacious in relation to an activity can develop a level of intrinsic interest in it that is not possible for children filled with self-doubt and anxiety. These results fit with other research which suggests that external rewards are not critical for the development of interest and, in fact, may interfere with the development of intrinsic interest (Deci, 1975; Lepper & Greene, 1978).

The social learning theory view of growth and development can be illustrated further by consideration of three areas: aggression, moral judgments, and delay of gratification. In terms of the development of aggressive behavior, a distinction is made among the acquisition of aggressive responses, the events that instigate these behaviors, and the processes that regulate and maintain aggression (Bandura, 1977a). In other words, social learning theory seeks to explain how aggressive patterns are developed, what provokes people to behave aggressively, and what sustains such actions once they have begun.

In general, aggression is learned through observation of aggressive models and learning by direct experience. Aggressive styles of behavior are learned from observation of family models ("Familial violence breeds violent styles of conduct."), from observation of peer behavior ("The highest incidence of aggression is found in communities in which aggressive models abound."), and from observation of models through mass media such as television ("Both children and adults today have unlimited opportunities to learn the whole gamut of violent conduct from televised modeling within the comfort of their homes.").

In terms of the activation of aggression, social learning theory emphasizes how aggressive behaviors can be provoked by painful stimulation, by expectations of reward for such behavior, or by both. What is emphasized is that when a person is aroused by painful or aversive events it may or may not lead to an aggressive response. Whether or not the person responds aggressively depends both on the interpretation of the conditions of arousal and the expectations of consequences for aggressive behavior. Such a view is distinct from an instinct view, which focuses on an automatic buildup of aggressive energy, and from other learning theories that view aggressive behavior as a response to frustration (Figure 13.3). According to social learning theory, frustration may or may not lead to aggression, and aggression can occur in the absence of frustration. Thus, whether or not frustration leads to aggression depends on how the person interprets the arousal, the alternative modes available for response, and the expectations of consequences for these various responses given the particular situation.

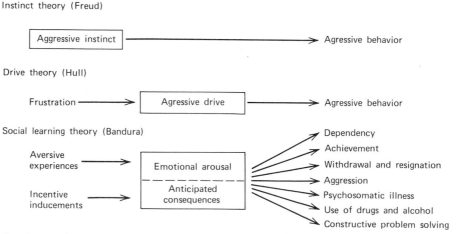

FIGURE 13.3   Comparison of Social Learning Theory of Aggression with Instinct and Drive Theories of Aggression.

Finally, aggressive behavior is sustained or ended, depending on its consequences. As with other behaviors, aggressive behavior is regulated by its consequences, which can come from three sources—**direct external consequences, vicarious experiencing of consequences to others,** and **self-produced consequences.** The first two are social consequences while the third are personal consequences. Aggressive behavior may be stopped through threats of external punishment or through expectations of self-condemnation, otherwise known as control through fear and guilt, respectively. Guilt involves the learning of ethical and moral standards of behavior. But these standards may be dropped or used in a way to justify aggressive behavior. Thus, through such processes a "reprehensible," aggressive act can be considered "honorable": "Over the years much destructive and reprehensible conduct has been perpetrated by decent, moral people in the name of religious principles and righteous ideologies. Acting on moral or ideological imperative reflects not an unconscious defense mechanism, but a conscious offense mechanism" (Bandura, 1977a, p. 43).

The observation of models and the development of standards and self-control mechanisms are important not only in aggression but in moral judgments and in toleration of delays in gratification as well. Social learning theory views moral judgments as complex, multidetermined social decisions (Rosenthal & Zimmerman, 1978). General rules are formed from a wide range of experience. At the same time, considerable **discrimination** may be involved in invoking different moral judgments in different circumstances. Since people vary their judgments depending on circumstances, it is hard to fit them into moral judgment types. And, because many more factors begin to be considered in moral judgments and greater discrimination is used in the application of various moral criteria to specific situations, moral judgment processes do become more complex with age. In addition, as children mature there is a shift from external to internal control. Initially, parents use punishment and the threat of punishment to discourage certain behaviors. In successful socialization, however, there is a "gradual substitution of symbolic and internal controls for external sanctions and demands. After moral standards of conduct are established by instruction and modeling, self-evaluative consequences serve as deterrents to transgressive acts" (Bandura, 1977a, p. 43). Obviously, both the development of more complex rules of moral judgment and the increased use of internal controls depend on the development of increasingly complex cognitive skills and abilities.

Considerable research has been done on the effects of models in the acquisition of moral standards and rules for moral judgments. For example, it has been demonstrated that children can be influenced in the kinds of judgments they make by exposure to different models. Thus, children who judge behavior in terms of the intent of the act (whether harm or injury was intended), and who are exposed to models judging behavior in terms of consequences (whether harm or injury actually occurred), come to modify their behavior toward making the latter kinds of moral judgment. The opposite kind of shift in moral judgment is made by children who judge behavior in terms of consequences and then are exposed to models who judge behavior in terms of intentions (Bandura & McDonald, 1963).

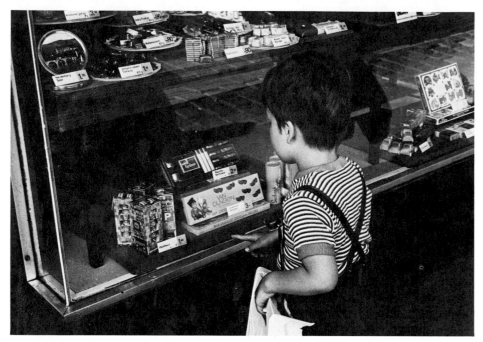

Delay of Gratification—**Children must learn to postpone pleasure until the proper time. Here a child considers how much he will have to save to get a desired toy.**

Research also has demonstrated the importance of modeling and observational learning in the development of performance standards for success and reward that may then serve as the basis for **delays in gratification**. Children exposed to models setting high standards of performance for self-reward tend to limit their own self-rewards to exceptional performance to a greater degree than do children who have been exposed to models setting lower standards or to no models at all (Bandura & Kupers, 1964). Children will model standards even if they result in self-denial of available rewards (Bandura, Grusec, & Menlove, 1967) and will also impose learned standards on other children (Mischel & Liebert, 1966). Children can be made to tolerate greater delays in receiving gratification if they are exposed to models exhibiting such delay behavior.

The effects of a model on delay behavior in children is well illustrated in research by Bandura and Mischel (1965). Children found to be high and low in delay of gratification were exposed to models of the opposite behavior. In a live-model condition, each child individually observed a testing situation in which an adult model was asked to choose between an immediate reward and a more valued object at a later date. The high-delay children observed a model who selected the immediately available reward and commented on its benefits whereas the low-delay children observed a model who selected the delayed reward and commented on the virtues of delay. In a symbolic-model condition, children read verbal accounts of these behaviors, the verbal account again being the opposite of the child's pattern of response. Finally, in a no-model condition children were just appraised of the choices given the adults. Following exposure to one of these three procedures, the children were again given a choice between an immediate reward and a more valuable reward. The results were that the high-delay children in all three conditions significantly altered their delay-of-reward behavior in favor of immediate gratification. The live-model condition produced the greatest effect (Figure 13.4). The low-delay children exposed to a delay model significantly altered their behavior in terms of greater delay, but there was no significant difference between the effects of live and symbolic models. Finally, for both groups of children, the effects were found to be stable when the tests were readministered four to five weeks later.

As was mentioned previously, the performance of observed behaviors clearly is influenced by the observed consequences to the model. For example, children who watch a film in which a child is not punished for playing with toys that were prohibited by the mother are more likely to play with prohibited toys than are children who see no film or see a film in which the child is punished (Walters & Parke, 1964). The old saying "Monkey see, monkey do" is not completely true.

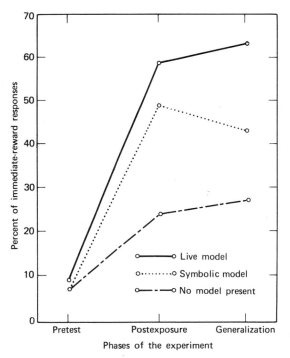

FIGURE 13.4 Mean Percentage of Immediate-reward Responses by High-delay Children on Each of Three Test Periods for Each of Three Experimental Conditions. (Bandura & Mischel, 1965)

It would be more appropriate to say "Monkey sees rewarded or not punished, monkey does." After all, the monkey is no fool.

The ability to delay gratification involves the development of **cognitive and behavioral competencies**. Relevant behaviors are acquired through the observation of others and through direct experience. The ability to delay gratification is determined by the outcomes expected, as influenced by past direct personal experience, observation of consequences to models such as parents and peers, and self-reactions. Delay decisions are influenced by context and circumstances. Thus, people who exhibit control in some circumstances may act impulsively in others. Gratification may not be delayed because the person lacks the necessary skills for delay or because the rewards expected for delay do not outweigh those expected for nondelay. The discriminations people make among situations and the variability found in their behavior are such as to reject stage theories as well as trait and psychoanalytic theories of conscience or superego: "Rather than acquiring a homogeneous conscience that determines uniformly all aspects of their self-control, people develop subtler discriminations that depend on many moderating variables and involve complex interactions" (Mischel, 1977, p. 39).

CLINICAL APPLICATIONS

Psychopathology

To a certain extent the social learning view of psychopathology is in accord with the view presented in Chapter 12. For example, the earlier views and social learning theory share these points of emphasis: (1) Rejection of the medical symptom-disease model in favor of a model emphasizing the learning of maladaptive behaviors. (2) An emphasis on the present as opposed to the past: "Instead of asking 'why did he become this kind of person?,' behavioral approaches ask 'what is *now* causing him to behave as he does?'" (Mischel, 1976, p. 252). (3) An emphasis on overt behavior rather than underlying dynamics. (4) An emphasis on therapy as the learning of new patterns of thinking and behaving rather than therapy as cure to some underlying cause. What differentiates social learning theory from the Hullian and Skinnerian views is the emphasis on cognitive variables, particularly as they enter into self-evaluative processes and judgments concerning self-efficacy.

According to social learning theory, maladaptive behavior is the result of dysfunctional learning. As with all learning, maladaptive responses can be learned as a result of direct experience or as the result of exposure to inadequate or "sick" models. Thus, Bandura (1968) suggests that the degree to which parents themselves model forms of aberrant behavior is often a significant causal factor in the development of psychopathology. Again, there is no need to look for traumatic incidents in the early history of the individual or for the underlying conflicts. Nor is there necessarily the need to find a history of reinforcement for the initial acquisition of the pathological behavior. On the other hand, once the behaviors have been learned through observational learning, it is quite likely that they have become manifest and that they have been maintained because of direct and vicarious reinforcement.

While the learning of specific overt behaviors is important in psychopathology, increasingly social learning theory has come to emphasize the role of **dysfunctional expectancies** and **self-conceptions**. People may erroneously expect painful events to follow some events or pain to be associated with specific situations. They then may act so as to avoid certain situations or in a way that creates the very situation they were trying to avoid. An example would be the person who fears that closeness will bring pain and then acts in a hostile way, resulting in rejection by others and presumed confirmation of the expectancy that closeness leads to disappointment and rejection. Cognitive processes not only enter into such dysfunctional expectancies but also into **dysfunctional self-evaluations**. One example would be the person who fails to develop standards for self-reward and thus experiences boredom or almost complete dependence on momentary, external pleasures. Even more common are the problems associated with the development of overly severe standards. Such developments lead to excessive self-punishment and depression: ''In more extreme forms, harsh standards for self-evaluation give rise to depressive reactions, chronic discouragement, feelings of worthlessness, and lack of purposefulness. Excessive self-disparagement, in fact, is one of the defining characteristics of depression'' (Bandura, 1977a, p. 141).

In addition to emphasizing the role of stringent internal standards of self-evaluation in depression, Bandura (1982) suggests that feelings of inefficacy play a major role. That is, the preceived inability to influence events relevant to one's life can lead to feelings of futility and despondency. A distinction is drawn between two perceived sources of futility: ''People can give up trying because they seriously doubt that they can do what is required. Or they may be assured of their capabilities but give up trying because they expect their efforts to produce no results due to the unresponsiveness, negative bias, or punitiveness of the environment'' (Bandura, 1982, p. 140). These two sources of futility are seen as distinct and associated with different behavioral outcomes and affective reactions. The behavioral and affective responses associated with self-efficacy judgments and outcome expectances are presented in Figure 13.5. Bandura's view here is similar to a part of the attribution interpretation of depression (Chapter 2), that which emphasizes the attribution of failure to personal deficiences of a generalized and enduring nature. It is such attributions that constitute a profound sense of personal inefficacy.

The social learning view of psychopathology may be contrasted with the psychoanalytic and other views of anxiety and defense. According to Bandura, the social learning view differs on two counts. First, there is a different view of anxiety. In social learning theory, anxiety results from **perceived inefficacy** in coping with potentially aversive events rather than from the threat of unconscious impulses. Whereas in depression, perceived inefficacy is related to gaining desired outcomes; in anxiety, perceived inefficacy is related to potentially injurious events. Second, anxiety is not seen as leading to **defensive** (avoidance) **behaviors**.

FIGURE 13.5   Interactive Effects of Self-percepts of Efficacy and Response Outcome Expectations on Behavior and Affective Reactions. (Bandura, 1982) (Copyright 1982 by the American Psychological Association. Reprinted by permission.)

Rather, anxiety *and* defensive, avoidance behavior both are seen as resulting from expectancies of injury. It is this expectation and the perceived inability to cope that leads to both anxiety and defensive behaviors.

Defensive behaviors, as responses to threat or the signal of the potential for a painful outcome, are difficult to unlearn because they remove the person from the circumstances. This is a phenomenon that in the past has been called the "neurotic paradox" and which Bandura describes as the problem of "subjective confirmation" of the utility of defensive behavior.

> *Avoidance prevents the organism from learning that the real circumstances have changed. The failure of anticipated hazards to materialize reinforces the expectation that the defensive maneuvers forestalled them. This process of subjective confirmation is captured in the apocryphal case of a compulsive who, when asked by his therapist why he snapped his fingers ritualistically, replied that it kept ferocious lions away. When informed that obviously there were no lions in the vacinity to ward off, the compulsive replied 'See, it works!'*

Bandura, 1977a, p. 62

The social learning theory of psychopathology emphasizes the acquisition of maladaptive, dysfunctional behaviors and expectancies as the result of direct experience and observational learning. Such behaviors and expectancies are then maintained by their consequences, either external or internal. Particularly important is the role of learned expectancies of harm or injury and the sense of inefficacy or inability to cope with a perceived threat. Such expectancies and self-evaluations lead to defensive behaviors that are difficult to unlearn because their value is subjectively confirmed when harm does not occur. The social learning theory view of therapy consequently emphasizes the importance of changes in the sense of inefficacy and in the exposure to situations previously feared and avoided. Throughout, the emphasis is on specific learned expectancies and behaviors rather than on "underlying dynamics" or generalized defensive styles.

Change

Therapeutic work within the social learning framework is relatively recent, though it has become an important area of theory and research. Bandura's efforts increasingly have been directed toward developing methods of therapeutic change and toward working out a unifying theory of behavioral change (Bandura, 1976; 1977a). In many ways the emphasis given to developments in this area is quite remarkable. Indeed, Bandura goes so far as to suggest that "the worth of a theory is ultimately judged by the power of the change procedures it produces" (1976, p. 253). While emphasizing the importance of the development of such procedures, Bandura is extremely cautious in his approach. He suggests that therapeutic procedures should be applied clinically only after there is understanding of the basic mechanisms by which change is effected and there has been adequate testing of the effects of preliminary methods.

According to Bandura, the change process involves not only the acquisition of new patterns of thought and behavior, but also their generalization and maintenance. The treatment approach emphasized is the acquisition of cognitive and behavioral competencies through **modeling** and **guided participation**. In the former, desired activities are demonstrated by various models who experience positive consequences or at least no adverse consequences. Generally, the complex patterns of behavior that are to be learned are broken down into subskills and increasingly difficult subtasks so as to ensure optimal progress. In guided participation the individual is assisted in performing the modeled behaviors.

Much of the research on therapeutic modeling and guided participation has been carried out in the laboratory using severe snake phobias and children's avoidance of dogs as targets of behavior change. In one early study the modeling technique was compared with systematic desensitization and with a no-treatment control condition (Bandura, Blanchard, & Ritter, 1967). The subjects were people who answered a newspaper advertisement offering help to people with a snake phobia. Subjects were tested for how much contact they could stand to have with a snake both before and after they participated in one of the following four conditions: (1) *live modeling with participation* (a model demonstrated the desired behavior and then assisted the subject to learn increasingly more difficult responses); (2) *symbolic modeling* (subjects observed a film that showed children and adults engaged in progressively more threatening interactions with a large king snake. Subjects were also trained to relax while watching the film); (3) *systematic desensitization;* (4) control—no treatment. The results were that the control subjects remained unchanged in their avoidance behavior, the symbolic modeling and systematic desensitization subjects showed substantial reductions in phobic behavior, and the live modeling combined with guided participation subjects showed the most substantial improvement. Live modeling with guided participation proved to be a superior and unusually powerful treatment that eliminated the snake phobia in virtually all of the subjects. As an illustration, all of the subjects in this group progressed to the point where they were able to sit in a chair with a snake in their laps for 30 seconds.

A study of nursery school children who were afraid of dogs found that observation of another child playing with a dog helped to remove much of the fear and avoidance behavior (Bandura, Grusec, & Menlove, 1967). Of particular importance is the fact that these gains were maintained at a follow-up test one month later. In another study, Bandura and Menlove (1968) demonstrated that watching films of models playing with dogs could be helpful in reducing children's avoidance behavior. A particularly interesting finding was the possibility that the real-life models themselves were afraid of dogs. Whereas only one parent in a group of bold children reported any fear of dogs, in the group of avoidant children many of the parents were found to have such a fear.

These studies relate to the reduction of fear and avoidance behavior through the observation of models. What is the process that underlies such changes? Bandura's most recent explanation of the change process is a marked shift from his earlier views but is in accordance with his current emphasis on cognitive pro-

Guided Participation—**Bandura emphasizes the role of modeling and guided participation in behavior change. Here a woman who is afraid of snakes is being helped to overcome her fear by a woman who models the desired behavior.**

cesses. In his earlier interpretations of psychotherapy as a learning process, Bandura (1961) emphasized such therapeutic processes as extinction, discrimination learning, counterconditioning, and reinforcement. However, his most recent statement suggests that psychological procedures, whatever their form, alter the level and strength of **self-efficacy** or the perceived ability to cope with specific situations (Bandura, 1982). Cognitive processes are part of psychopathology in that these processes involve dysfunctional expectancies and perceptions of self-inefficacy. Such expectancies and self-perceptions lead to anxiety and the defensive avoidance of threatening situations. Therefore, it makes sense that an effective therapeutic procedure would alter such expectancies and self-perceptions. Procedures such as modeling and guided participation help to effect such changes and thereby enable the person to reduce anticipatory fears and avoidance behaviors. At the root of such procedures, as well as other diverse therapeutic procedures, is a cognitive process involving changed expectations of personal efficacy.

Is there evidence to support this theory of psychological change? A number of studies have been conducted in which individuals with phobias have received treatment while their efficacy expectations and behaviors were measured (Bandura & Adams, 1977; Bandura, Adams, & Beyer, 1977; Bandura, Reese, and Adams, 1982). As predicted, subject statements of self-efficacy consistently predicted performance on tasks of varying levels of difficulty or threat. In other words, as therapeutic procedures led to improvement in perceived self-efficacy, individuals were increasingly able to confront previously feared objects.

For example, in one such illustrative research effort, subjects who suffered from chronic snake phobia were assigned to one of three conditions: *participant modeling* (therapist models the threatening activities and subjects gradually perform the tasks along with therapist assistance until they can be performed alone); *modeling* (subjects observe the therapist perform the tasks but do not engage in them); *control condition* (Bandura, Adams, & Beyer, 1977). Both before and after these conditions, the subjects were tested on a Behavioral Avoidance Test (BAT), consisting of twenty-nine performance tasks requiring increasingly more threatening interactions with a red-tailed boa constrictor. The final task involved letting the snake crawl in their lap while their hands were held passively at their sides. To test the generality of change, subjects were also tested after treatment with a dissimilar threat—a corn snake. In addition, efficacy expectations were obtained before treatment, after treatment but before the second administration of the BAT, following the second administration of the BAT, and again one month following the completion of treatment. The results indicated that participant modeling and modeling produced significant increases in approach behavior toward both the similar threat and the dissimilar threat as well as significant increases in self-efficacy judgments (Figure 13.6). These gains clearly surpassed those made by subjects in the control condition. In addition, self-efficacy judgments (before the second BAT) were uniformly accurate predictors of performance; that is, strong self-efficacy judgments were associated with higher probabilities of successful task performance. These efficacy expectations in fact had superior predictive power over past performance! Follow-up data indicated that

FIGURE 13.6   Level of Self-efficacy and Approach Behavior Displayed by Subjects toward Different Threats after Receiving Vicarious (Modeling) or Performance-based Participant Modeling Treatments or No Treatment. (In the posttest phase, level of self-efficacy was measured prior to and after the behavioral avoidance tests with the two subjects.) (Bandura, Adams, & Beyer, 1977; Copyright 1977 by the American Psychological Association. Reprinted by permission.)

the subjects not only maintained their gains in self-efficacy and approach behavior but achieved some further improvements. In sum, the data supported the utility of guided participation and the social learning view that treatments improve performance because they raise expectations of personal efficacy.

A variety of criticisms have been made of Bandura's work and theory of change, especially by behaviorists who take the view that cognitions cannot be causes of behavior. His responses give further clarification of his thinking:

Criticism 1
Therapy consists of the acquisition of skills, not changes in self-efficacy.

Bandura Response
People with equal skills perform differently depending on the level and intensity of their self-efficacy perceptions. People who have been desensitized to the same extent show varying levels of behavioral performance when confronting feared objects. Whereas desensitization level may be a weak predictor of performance, self-efficacy judgments are excellent predictors.

CURRENT APPLICATIONS AND IMPLICATIONS

Giving Up Addictions and Avoiding Relapse

An incredible number of people suffer from compulsive patterns of behavior that have an addictive quality to them—smoking, overeating, gambling, drinking, drugs. Often they give up the troublesome pattern of behavior for a period of time, only to find that it returns. What is it that accounts for relapse and how can its risks be minimized?

While many people claim a physiological basis for addictive behavior, two points are noteworthy: (1) In some of these compulsive patterns it is clear that no true physiological addiction exists. Yet, a psychological craving remains. Generally, periods of intense craving are associated with feelings of threat and inability to cope with events. (2) Many people are able to go through an extended period of abstinence only to experience a relapse—overeating after weight loss, habitual smoking after abstinence, and so on. Researchers in this area have identified a common element in the relapse process. Those who are able to maintain abstinence perceive themselves as more able to cope with and affect events than do those who relapse. They have better self-efficacy judgments. Many people show occa-

Self-efficacy—**Bandura suggests that feelings of self-efficacy are key in the responses of alcoholics and drug addicts to relapse.**

sional lapses from total abstinence. Those who relapse, however, treat the event as a statement about themselves and their efficacy. Thus, they make statements such as "I'm a failure," or "I just can't do it," or "I have no will-power." Already feeling vulnerable in relation to the task at hand, they treat occasional lapses in a way that only serves to damage further their beliefs in themselves.

In treating addictions and compulsive patterns of behavior, getting people to abstain is only part of the job. In many cases this turns out to be easier than helping them to remain abstinent. Evidently changing the way they interpret occasional lapses and enhancing their feelings of self-efficacy concerning abstinence are an important part of the work that needs to be done.

SOURCE: G.A. Marlatt and J.R. Gordon, 1980; *New York Times,* February 23, 1983, Cl.

Criticism 2
Therapy consists of the reduction of anxiety.

Bandura Response
Defensive behavior can occur with or without anxiety and, whereas anxiety levels may show little relationship to behavioral change, personal self-efficacy statements show a strong relationship. In the social learning analysis, anxiety is reduced by enhancing perceived ability to cope (self-efficacy).

Criticism 3
Verbal self-reports of efficacy affect behavior and are unreliable.

Bandura Response
There is no evidence of this and the argument against self-reports has more to do with conceptual orthodoxy than with their usefulness in prediction.

Criticism 4
The clinical work is limited to snake phobias treated in the laboratory and cannot be generalized to clinic situations and broader difficulties.

Bandura Response
Laboratory investigations of behavioral change do not involve artificially created situations. The behavioral dysfunctions and processes of change are identical to the clinical situation. Furthermore, the results of the treatment for snake phobias have profound consequences for the people involved: "To contend that because phobics completely avoid a threatening object it has no impact on their daily living is to miss the point that it is the avoidance maneuvers that constrict and impair the phobic's life. . . . The treatments being

analyzed in these laboratory investigations enable people burdened with such phobias to master their fears and to engage in activities they formerly avoided, and it eliminates their ruminative thoughts and nightmares'' (1978, pp. 9394). Furthermore, modeling procedures now are being applied widely to diverse psychological conditions (Rosenthal & Bandura, 1978).

A CASE EXAMPLE

It is interesting and perhaps significant that few, if any, in-depth individual cases have been reported by proponents of social learning theory. One extended case illustration of a behavior therapy approach to treatment illustrates that such therapy is not simple and straightforward. In this case the treatment of a depressed and anxious woman involved *51* sessions over a period of *two* years (Goldfried & Davison, 1976). It is related to social learning theory in its emphasis on modeling, self-monitoring, and feelings of self-adequacy. However, many other therapeutic techniques were used as well, and it cannot be seen strictly as illustrative of social learning theory.

Mischel (1968, 1976) has taken a case previously reported in the literature and interpreted it from a social learning standpoint. Originally reported by two psychiatrists–psychoanalysts in a book on the psychological trauma experienced by servicemen during the Second World War (Grinker & Spiegel, 1945), the case involved a bombardier who, during one of his missions, experienced psychological and physical trauma. His plane was damaged by flak and although it began to dive, was pulled out of the dive just before crashing. However, the bombardier was hurled against the bombsight. Upon return to flight duty, he found that he would become faint whenever the plane reached an altitude of about 10,000 feet. This, of course, interfered with his continuation on active duty.

Mischel notes that the analysts concluded that the bombardier's fainting was related to deep, underlying anxieties rooted in his childhood experiences. Instead of such a dynamic explanation Mischel suggests a social behavior analysis according to which the emotional trauma probably was conditioned to the altitude the plane reached at about the time of the mishap. When he went on a flight and reached that altitude he would reexperience the cues connected with the accident and become emotionally helpless. Therefore, the causes of the problem lie in the current conditions rather than in early childhood antecedents. Rather than needing insight therapy Mischel suggests that ''the treatment implications seem clear for social behavior theory: render the traumatic cues neutral by desensitizing him to them through slow, graded exposure under conditions that prevent arousal and that, instead, insure incompatible responses such as relaxation'' (1968, p. 267). Mischel is critical of the approach that emphasizes events in childhood, defenses against feelings, dynamic explanations, and the value of insight. Instead, he argues for an emphasis on the conditions precipitating the difficulty, the situational factors maintaining the problem, and the kinds of structured tasks or situations that will facilitate new kinds of learning.

GENERAL VIEW   Psychological procedures, whatever their format, serve as ways of creating and strengthening expectations of personal effectiveness. Social learning therapy emphasizes the acquisition of cognitive and behavioral competencies through modeling and guided participation.

ATTRIBUTES OF GOOD MODELS: RELEVANCE AND CREDIBILITY   Models who compel attention, who instill trust, who appear to be realistic figures for self-comparison, and whose standards seem reasonable to the learner will be good sources for therapeutic modeling effects. These attributes may be summarized in terms of the positive functions of relevance and credibility.

SOME ILLUSTRATIVE RULES FOR INDUCING AND MAINTAINING DESIRED CHANGES

1. Structure the tasks to be learned in an orderly, stepwise sequence.
2. Explain and demonstrate general rules or principles. Check client's understanding and provide opportunities for clarification.
3. Provide guided simulated practice with feedback concerning success and error.
4. Once the desired behavior is established, increase opportunities for self-directed accomplishment.
5. Test newly acquired skills in the natural environment under conditions likely to produce favorable results.
6. Test skills in increasingly more demanding situations until a satisfactory level of competence and self-efficacy has been obtained.

FIGURE 13.7   Summary of Social Learning Therapy.

CRITICAL EVALUATION

Strengths of the Theory

Social learning theory is probably the current favorite among academic personality psychologists, and a good number of clinicians would also label themselves social learning psychologists. The term *social learning* has been in use at least since 1941 and, as noted, in 1954 Rotter suggested a social learning position that emphasized expectancies, the subjective value of reinforcers, and the situational variability of behavior. Yet, it is only during the past decade that a social learning theory has evolved and achieved widespread popularity and influence. How can we account for this growth in popularity and influence? Probably the major factors have been the attention given to experimentation and evidence and a parallel consideration of important human phenomena. Beyond this there is an impressive openness to change and development as well as a continuing concern with other points of view and more general social issues. These strengths of social learning theory will be considered in greater detail.

7. Provide opportunity for therapist consultation and feedback during periods of increased independent mastery.

THERAPEUTIC EFFECTS OF MODELING

1. *Development of New Skills.* Through observing models and through guided participation people acquire new patterns of behavior and new coping strategies. For example, submissive clients learn to model assertive behavior.

2. *Changes in Inhibitions About Self-expression.* As a result of modeling, responses already available to the person may be weakened or strengthened. For example, inhibitory effects can occur as a result of observing models receive negative consequences for certain behaviors. Disinhibitory effects, which are more common in therapy, result from observing models perform behaviors without adverse consequences or with positive consequences. Fears may be overcome in this way.

3. *Facilitation of Pre-existing Patterns of Behavior.* Behaviors already available to the person and which are not associated with anxiety may occur more often as a result of modeling influences. For example, learners may be aided to become more skillful conversationalists.

4. *Adoption of More Realistic Standards for Judging One's Own Performance.* Observing models reward themselves for varying levels of performance can affect the learner's self-standards. For example, rigid self-demands characteristic of depressed people can be relaxed as a result of modeling.

CONCLUSION   "A burgeoning literature confirms the value of modeling treatments for redressing deficits in social and cognitive skills, and for helping to remove defensive avoidance behavior" (Rosenthal and Bandura, 1978, p. 622).

FIGURE 13.7   (Continued)

Concern with Experimentation and Evidence

Developments in social learning theory have been grounded in careful experimental research. Bandura and Mischel, as well as other social learning theorists, have been concerned with defining concepts in ways that leave them open to empirical verification and have always conducted active research programs. The record of phenomena investigated and the ways in which they have been investigated is impressive. For example, the research on modeling indicates that the observation of models can lead to the acquisition of new responses and to changes in the frequency of occurrence of behaviors already learned. The range of behaviors investigated includes aggression, moral judgments, setting of standards, vicarious conditioning of fears, delay of gratification, and helping behavior. Children and adults have been found to be influenced by a wide range of models—live humans, filmed humans, verbally presented models of behavior, and cartoons. The process of modeling has been studied in terms of the influences of model characteristics, observer characteristics, and observed consequences to the model of the demonstrated behavior—an impressive record of research.

Importance of Phenomena Considered

Most social learning research has been conducted with the social behaviors of humans. Thus, in considering the evidence, we are not asked to make large extrapolations from animal research to humans and from simple behaviors to complex human processes. Social learning theory investigates and attempts to account for the very phenomena that are of interest to most people—aggression, the effects of parents and mass media on children, the change of dysfunctional behaviors, the development of self-regulatory capacities, and the increase of control over one's life.

A Theory Open to Change

Social learning theory has changed and evolved over the years. A comparison of *Social Learning and Personality Development* (1963) by Bandura and Walters with Bandura's *Social Learning Theory* (1977a) gives ample testimony to the changes that have come about. The emphasis on behavior, observational learning, and the importance of maintaining behavior has been continued. However, with time there has been an increased emphasis on cognitive processes and self-regulation. Not only are external events emphasized, but internal ones are emphasized as well. In the process of reciprocal determinism we not only have environmental contingencies shaping people but also people shaping environmental contingencies. Not only is there an emphasis on behavior but one on cognition and emotion as well. Furthermore, there is an emphasis on the relationships among thought, feeling, and overt behavior. Social learning theorists have tried to remain informed about developments in other areas of psychology and to adjust their position so that it remains consistent with these developments. Beyond this, social learning theory itself has influenced and contributed to other parts of psychology. While social learning theory draws on advances in fields such as cognition and development, it also contributes to these advances.

Focus of Attention on Important Issues

Social learning theorists have played a valuable role in criticizing other theoretical positions (psychoanalytic, trait, Skinnerian) and in bringing critical issues to the forefront, among them the role of reinforcement in the acquisition and performance of behavior. Mischel, in particular, has been influential in drawing attention to the problems associated with views that overemphasize trait factors. The person-situation controversy has led in some wasteful directions, such as examining whether persons *or* situations are more important in determining behavior. Generally, however, it has led to a more realistic assessment of the complex, interacting causes of behavior.

View of the Person and Social Concern

Social learning theory offers a view of the person that is more reasonable than a robot or telephone switchboard and suggests possible solutions to problems of genuine social concern. Social learning approaches are used to help people with common problems of life. Yet they are also considered in relation to larger problems of social change. Bandura (1977a) considers the soundness of a legal system of deterrence, the potential for creating environments conducive to learning and intellectual development, and the interplay between personal freedom and limits on conduct that must exist in every society. Interestingly enough, he concludes his book: "As a science concerned with the social consequences of its applications, psychology must promote public understanding of psychological issues that bear on social policies to ensure that its findings are used in the service of human betterment" (p. 213).

Limitations of the Theory

Given these significant strengths, what are the limitations of social learning theory? Some of these are associated with new developments and the fact that many of the approaches are recent. Social learning theory has shown a constructive openness to change but has not followed a path that has led to a carefully integrated network of theoretical assumptions. Many of the concepts, findings, and therapeutic procedures have been challenged by proponents of alternative points of view. Finally, social learning theory would appear to continue to ignore phenomena of importance that are recognized by other approaches. Again, these points will be considered in greater detail:

Social Learning Theory Is Not a Systematic, Unified Theory

Social learning theory is not a theory in the sense of a network of assumptions tied together in a systematic way leading to specific predictions. More recent efforts at systematic formulation have been made. However, occasionally diverse concepts are merely lumped together and sometimes opposing findings would appear to fit equally well into the theory. An example of the former would be the concepts emphasized by Mischel (1973) in his cognitive social learning reconceptualization of personality. In this paper Mischel emphasizes the importance of such personality variables as competencies, personal constructs, expectancies, and plans. These variables appear to be important but how they relate to one another in a consistent, organized, integrated way is unclear.

New Problems Have Arisen with New Developments

Perhaps not unexpectedly, each new development in social learning theory creates new criticism and new difficulties. Social learning theory's emphasis on the learning of complex acts in the absence of reinforcement has been attacked consistently by Skinnerians, who suggest, for example, that observational learning may, in fact, illustrate a generalized imitative response that is sometimes, but not always, reinforced (Gewirtz, 1971). Skinnerians suggest that while the individual may learn, without being reinforced, a response performed by a model, this does not mean that reinforcement was not a necessary part of the overall learning process; one cannot determine this without knowing the reinforcement history of the individual. Other psychologists, working within a strict behaviorist framework are critical of the recent emphasis on internal variables and verbal self-report. Developments here have occurred with an eye toward past pitfalls of research on the self and the use of verbal reports. It is strange, perhaps welcome, to see social learning psychologists emphasizing what people have to report about themselves. However, it remains to be seen whether detailed verbal report procedures and supportive reporting conditions can take care of the fact that people often are unaware of processes in themselves. Years of research on the concept of self have left us with a host of major unresolved problems (Wylie, 1974). Can social learning theory find a way to overcome them?

Social Learning Theory Neglects or Gives Minimal Emphasis to Some Important Areas

It undoubtedly is impossible for a theory of personality to be truly encompassing at this time. Accepting such qualifications, it would still appear that social learning theorists ignore or give minimal emphasis to significant aspects of human functioning. Without accepting all of the viewpoint of stage theorists, maturational factors would appear to be important in the feelings people experience and in the way that they process information. Sexual feelings do become increasingly important at particular times in the life cycle and the thinking of a child is fundamentally different from that of an adult in a variety of ways. Beyond this, while social learning theory recognizes the importance of motivational factors and conflict, it gives relatively little attention to these processes. Recently the concept of incentives has been used, and the concepts of standards and plans do have motivational properties, but this remains an area in need of further development. For example, how are goals acquired and activated? What is the role of emotion in this process (Pervin, 1983)? Conflict, which would seem to be such an important part of our lives, particularly the part that distresses us, does not even appear as a separate heading in the subject index of Bandura's most recent work. Finally, there remains in social learning theory a lack of concern with the system aspects of human personality functioning. The human functions as both a biological and a psychological system. The parts of the system are important not only for themselves but also in terms of their implications for other parts of the system. It is one thing to say that behavior is situationally variable. It is another thing to ignore relationships among different aspects of personality functioning. Whether one speaks in terms of concepts such as wholeness, organization, Gestalt qualities, or other concepts, it would appear to be important for a theory to recognize the links that occur among different processes and the implications they have for one another.

Many Developments Are Recent and Findings Should be Regarded as Preliminary Rather than Conclusive

Throughout its history, psychology generally, and the field of psychotherapy in particular, has been beset with fads. Therefore one must be cautious in distinguishing between actual progress and overzealous commitment to a new idea.

Whereas at one time theories that emphasized cognitive processes were viewed with skepticism, later such theories were adopted readily: "1976 could well be designated the year of cognition for both theoretician and practitioner. Like the activities of Superman and the Scarlet Pimpernel, cognition is in the air, it is here, there, and everywhere" (Franks & Wilson, 1977, p. vii). Without minimizing their importance in human behavior, we should be careful about prematurely accepting cognitive processes as our basic explanatory concepts.

While the results of guided participation and modeling are significant, these therapeutic processes remain to be tested by other therapists, with different patients and with different problems. Bandura has answered critics who suggest that his results are of limited generalizability. However, the history of psychotherapy is filled with methods that were introduced as solving the problems of those in psychological distress. Most recently, evaluation of efforts in the area of behavior modification and behavior therapy should make us aware of the complexities of the problem and the work that remains to be done.

In sum, there are good grounds both for enthusiasm about social learning theory and for caution and even skepticism. Social learning theory represents a major development. It is still evolving, and its further efforts are worthy of careful attention.

FIGURE 13.8 **SUMMARY OF STRENGTHS AND LIMITATIONS OF SOCIAL LEARNING THEORY**

STRENGTHS	LIMITATIONS
1. Has impressive research record.	1. Is not a systematic, unified theory.
2. Considers important phenomena.	2. Contains potential problems associated with the utilization of verbal self-report.
3. Shows consistent development and elaboration as a theory.	3. Requires more exploration and development in certain areas (e.g., motivation, affect, system properties of personality organization).
4. Focuses attention on important theoretical issues.	4. Provides findings concerning therapy that are tentative rather than conclusive.

MAJOR CONCEPTS AND SUMMARY

reciprocal determinism

goals–plans

self

self-efficacy

microanalytic research

observational learning

modeling

acquisition, performance, and
    maintenance of behaviors

vicarious conditioning

internal standards

self-regulation

expectancies

direct, vicarious, and self-produced
    consequences

discrimination among situations

delay of gratification

cognitive and behavioral
    competencies

dysfunctional expectancies

self-conceptions

dysfunctional self-evaluation

self-efficacy and inefficacy

defensive behaviors

guided participation

self-efficacy expectations

Social learning theory is an evolving, influential, and popular theory of personality. It shares with the Hullian and Skinnerian positions an emphasis on the central importance of learned patterns of behavior. However, its emphasis on learning independent of reinforcement and the importance of cognitive processes results in a different view of the human organism. The human organism is one that affects the environment as well as is affected by it, one that responds to information from the environment in an organized and selective way rather than in a mechanical way, and one that is capable of responding to self-reward and self-punishment as well to external forms of reinforcement. Instead of emphasizing internal (person) factors *or* external (environment) factors, social learning theory stresses the process of reciprocal determinism between person and environment.

Social learning theory distinguishes between response acquisition and response performance. As is evident in observational learning, reinforcement is not necessary for response acquisition; people can learn complex behaviors through the observation of others performing such behaviors. Emotional reactions as well can be conditioned vicariously through the observation of others. Such learning processes have functional, adaptive value since we are thereby spared the inefficiency and hazards of trial-and-error learning. Learning from observing others, modeling, involves something broader than imitation but less diffuse and global than identification. Considerable attention has been directed to the factors that influence the modeling process (for example, consequences to the model) and to the components of this process.

While reinforcement is not critical for the acquisition of responses, it is critical for the performance and maintenance or regulation of behavior. According to social learning theory, behavior is regulated by its consequences—which can come from the person (self-praise and self-criticism) as well as from the environment. Among the responses an individual learns are standards of goal attainment and standards for self-reinforcement. These standards permit the person to continue working toward a goal in the absence of outside reward or despite outside interference and punishment. They form the basis for self-regulation and self-control. While behavior is regulated by internal and external consequences, it is the expectation of these consequences that is important rather than the mechanical linking of behavior with reinforcement. Here, too, there is an emphasis on cognitive processes and reinforcement as representing information from the environment.

Although the main focus remains on processes explaining the acquisition and maintenance of behavior, social learning theory has recently also emphasized structural concepts such as goals–plans and the self. Goals–plans are derived from learned standards for reinforcement and help to establish priorities among alternative patterns of behavior, particularly over long periods of time. The concept of self does not represent a little person inside the organism controlling behavior but rather a set of cognitive processes involved in self-conception, self-reinforcement, and self-regulation. Self-concepts and self-control processes are viewed as relatively specific and as varying from situation to situation and from time to time.

Particularly important here is the concept of self-efficacy or the person's judgment of his or her ability to perform the tasks relevant to a particular situation. Self-efficacy judgments are viewed as cognitive mediators of action, functioning together with self-evaluative judgments to mediate between goals and actual performance. In other words, goals and external reinforcement expectancies are important in behavior, but feedback information that is utilized to make self-efficacy and self-evaluative judgments also is crucial. Self-efficacy judgments influence thought patterns, motivation, performance, and emotional arousal. In tune with the general social learning rejection of broad dispositional personality characteristics, such as traits, self-efficacy judgments are viewed as changing and relatively situation specific, and as best assessed through a microanalytic research strategy.

Social learning theory views growth and development as resulting from the interplay of biological and experiential factors. It is critical of stage theories that suggest a fixed order of development and a single level for a person's cognitive processes. Instead, social learning theory emphasizes the potential for cognitive development and the processes through which cognitive functioning varies from issue to issue and situation to situation. As noted, this is true of developing self-efficacy judgments that are based on direct experience (performance accomplishments), vicarious experience, communications from significant others, and emotional arousal. Considerable research attention has been directed toward an understanding of the development of aggressive behavior, moral judgments, and tolerance for delay of gratification. Similar principles are stressed throughout.

For example, a distinction is made between the factors that determine the acquisition of responses, those that instigate these responses, and those that regulate and maintain the responses. Behavioral responses are acquired through observational learning or direct experience. Behavior is activated by internal or external stimuli and/or expectations of reward. Behavior is then sustained or terminated, depending on its consequences. Expectancies concerning consequences arise from three sources—direct external consequences, vicarious experiencing of consequences to others, and self-produced consequences. Information from these three sources is combined to lead both to discriminations among situations in terms of their potential for various consequences and to the formation of general rules of behavior.

Social learning theory rejects the medical symptoms–disease model of psychopathology and sees abnormal behavior as being on a continuum with normal behavior. According to social learning theory, behavior that is maladaptive or pathological represents the result of dysfunctional learning of behaviors, expectancies, and standards for self-reward. Such maladaptive responses are learned, as are other behaviors, either directly or through the observation of inadequate models. A central role in the interpretation of psychopathology is given to the feeling of inefficacy. This is experienced when the person perceives the self as unable to cope with a threat or a situation expected to lead to pain or injury and leads to defensive behaviors. Anxiety, in this view, does not lead to defensive behaviors. Anxiety and defensive behaviors both are seen as resulting from perceived inefficacy in coping with potentially aversive events rather than as causing one another.

Whereas anxiety involves judgments of inefficacy in relation to potentially threatening events, depression involves judgments of inefficacy in relation to gaining desired outcomes. Overly stringent self-evaluative standards are also viewed as playing a role in depression. Feelings of futility may arise either because the person perceives the self as unable to do what is required (self-inefficacy) or because the environment is viewed as punitive or unresponsive. However, the implications for emotion and action are different in the two cases.

Defensive behaviors are difficult to unlearn because they remove the person from the threatening circumstances and prevent one from revising one's expectancies. The task in psychotherapy, then, is to increase the sense of self-efficacy so that previously avoided situations may be confronted and new expectancies learned. According to social learning theory, all psychological procedures, whatever their form, alter the level and strength of self-efficacy or the perceived ability to cope with specific situations. Modeling and guided participation have been used in therapeutic efforts. Recent research has suggested that self-efficacy expectations are excellent predictors of performance and are superior in this regard to past performance itself.

Interest in and support for social learning theory is probably largely influenced by its dual emphasis on experimentation and important personality and social phenomena. In addition, proponents of the theory have shown a striking willingness to revise the theory as new evidence emerges. At the same time, it has been criticized for not being a truly systematic theory and for ignoring or giving minimal attention to important areas such as maturation, motivation, conflict, and the holistic (system) properties of the organism. In addition, although the recent developments in social learning theory are noteworthy, they have created new conceptual and methodological difficulties. It is too early to evaluate fully the potential of therapeutic efforts based on social learning theory. The theory represents a significant effort and has already been associated with noteworthy research accomplishments. How much it can be extended and systematized in the future remains to be seen.

Scott, Patrick. *Woman Carrying Grasses*. 1958. Collection The Museum of Modern Art, New York. Elizabeth Bliss Parkinson Fund.

omit

14

A COGNITIVE, INFORMATION-PROCESSING APPROACH TO PERSONALITY

CHAPTER FOCUS: The world about us and within us is filled with many events and a vast array of information. From all that we can observe, what is it that we do observe? From all the ways that we can view people, ourselves, and events, how do we end up selecting certain representations and explanations? Living in a complex and changing world in which it is important to make decisions, how do we go about organizing information in order to make our lives reasonably stable and productive? These are the kinds of questions that are of interest to cognitive personality psychologists and the kinds of questions that concern us in this chapter. Here we turn to a different model of human functioning than we considered previously—the computer. Here we also consider an approach more firmly tied to experimental psychology than to clinical work, an approach more narrowly attuned to concepts and research procedures than to a comprehensive theory of personality. Notwithstanding these facts, this approach is perhaps at present the main exploratory thrust in the field of personality theory.

In a normal revolution, and in any biological model, the central energy is information. And in the new process of production, information is the central energy . . . That's a major industrial revolution of which we're at the very beginning.

Drucker, Interview, 1982

The information processing view of the person takes the computer as its guiding metaphor.

Bower, 1978, p. 123

Theories of personality tend to be associated with models of human nature. To take two illustrations already noted: in psychoanalytic theory, there is the model of the person as a hydraulic energy system; in personal construct theory, there is the model of the person as a scientist. Since the 1960s, we have witnessed in psychology a revolution—the cognitive revolution. This revolution in psychology has matched the technological revolution in industry. The technological revolution is that of the computer and information processing. The cognitive revolution's model of the person is that of a complex, sophisticated—though error-prone—processor of information.

Like all such models, this one cannot be taken completely literally. No psychologist would suggest that people are the same as computers or that computers can, as yet, perform all the thinking operations of humans. However, such models are viewed as useful in conceptualizing how people think and in defining which issues are particularly important to investigate. Thus, many psychologists have begun to probe ways in which people do function like computers. Computers are information-processing devices in which information is received or encoded, stored or remembered, and retrieved when needed. The key terms here are encoding, memory, and retrieval, and the question of import becomes how people encode, store and retrieve information.

Given this model, which aspects of human information processing appear to be of particular importance to investigate? And, accepting it only as a model, are there any uniquely human qualities of thought and information processing that need to be kept in mind? As we live our daily lives, we are exposed to a great deal of information concerning ourselves, others, and social behavior. How do we organize and utilize this information to make sense out of the world? How do we go about developing representations of the world about us and of ourselves, and how do we develop causal explanations for events? What categories do we use to classify people, situations, and events? What rules do we follow in interpreting events and do these rules sometimes lead us into trouble? These are some of the questions of interest to the cognitive personality psychologist and represent the kinds of questions that we address in this chapter.

Before turning to these questions, let us consider the history of this approach and place it in its proper context relative to other theories already considered. In relation to the former, cognitive personality psychologists have borrowed heavily from the concepts and research procedures of experimental cognitive psychologists. Whereas the cognitive revolution in experimental psychology dates back to the 1960s, the current wave of interest in personality dates back to the late 1970s and early 1980s. In relation to the latter, we can consider three significant ways in which cognitive personality psychology departs from the views presented earlier in the text. First, until now we have considered theories of personality. In the present case, there is no cognitive or information-processing theory of personality. Rather, there is research that will lead, one hopes, to an understanding of cognitive functioning and thereby eventually to a comprehensive theory of personality. Second, most theories presented in this text take clinical case material as their point of departure. This is seen most clearly in the theories of Freud, Rogers, and Kelly. In other cases, as in trait theory, the focus is on individual differences. In the work to be discussed, the point of departure is experimental cognitive psychology rather than clinical work. The effort is to tie personality psychology to experimental work in cognitive psychology. Third, following from the point just made, the work of cognitive personality psychologists focuses more on general aspects of information processing rather than it does on individual differences. There are, of course, potential gains and losses associated with these efforts and changes in direction. We will come back to this issue at the end of the chapter. For now, however, let us try to understand the context within which a cognitive information-processing model is applied to personality theory and research.

REPRESENTATION OF THE WORLD ABOUT US

Starting from birth, we are bombarded with information concerning people and events in the world. How do we go about organizing this information? In this section, we will consider research in three relevant areas—the organization of information relevant to *people* in the world, the organization of information relevant to *situations*, and the organization of information relevant to *events*.

Organizing Information Relevant to People

When asked to describe people we know, which terms do we use? In thinking about friends, we find that we use particular terms to describe them and that sometimes we group people into types—we say that a friend has these characteristics or is this type of person. In meeting new people, we also find that we tend to be sensitive to particular characteristics and to perceive them in particular terms. In some cases, these perceived characteristics are more or less neutral; in other cases they are heavily value laden. Thus, for example, one may describe someone in physical terms (e.g., tall, ruddy, angular) that may not express value preferences or in trait terms (e.g., honest, kind, hostile) that are generally associated with considerable emotion. People differ in the terms they use to describe people and in the ways they organize these terms or categories, but everyone seeks to organize the information they have relative to others. Given the diversity of people we encounter, each of whom also behaves somewhat differently according to the situation, such organization is necessary for us to make sense out of and provide stability to the world we encounter. If we were more equipped with innate or programmed responses, such cognitive constructions would not be necessary. In the absence of such responses, however, we must so organize and structure our experiences that we avoid being overwhelmed with information and detail. What kinds of categories do we form to simplify things? What kinds of perceived regularities enable us to make some predictions about what we can expect in our interactions with others?

Such questions are addressed in the area known as person perception or **implicit personality theory.** The term implicit personality theory relates to the suggestion that each of us has a theory of personality, defined in terms of the traits we believe go together in people. Such theories are considered implicit in that most people cannot make explicit their trait categories or organize them as part of a formal theory of personality. Research in this area dates back at least to the 1950s. Early research focused on the tendency of people to perceive a person as having one characteristic and to then assume that she or he possesses a related characteristic. For example, if a person is perceived to be intelligent, what is the likelihood that that person will also be perceived as warm, generous, or feminine? Research also focused on the general dimensions people use to perceive others, with three dimensions found to be fairly general: *evaluation* (to what extent are people good or bad?), *activity* (to what extent are people active or passive?), and *potency* (to what extent are people strong or weak?).

A problem with this research was that it required everyone to use the same trait terms and often required subjects to rate abstract people rather than people they actually knew. These problems were solved by Rosenberg (1977; Rosenberg & Sedlak, 1972) in a method that allowed subjects to describe, in their own words, people they knew—including themselves. In addition, they could describe the feelings they associated with each of these people. This resulted in a list of people known to the subject and a list of traits and feelings associated with them. The subject then rated each person on the list in terms of the relevance of each trait and feeling. From this, Rosenberg could determine the traits and feelings that people tend to link with one another in the perception of self and others.

What general categories might one expect to emerge? In Kelly's terms, what constructs do people generally use to perceive and experience the human world? First, Rosenberg found an *evaluative* (good–bad) dimension in the categorization of people. In other words, apparently a major component in our perception of self and others is a like–dislike judgment and a decision about whether or not we feel good about the person being perceived. Rosenberg also found that this evaluative judgment seemed to involve two major concerns—a social concern (being accepted by or intimate with others) and a competence concern (being successful or competent in some area). Some illustrative traits and feelings associated with these categories are presented in Figure 14.1.

While clearly of general interest, such lists of trait categories fail to do justice to the uniqueness of each individual's implicit theory of personality. Can such a method be utilized to capture a person's unique representation of others in the surrounding world? A demonstration of how this could be done was provided in an analysis of the author Theodore Dreiser's portrayal of women in his book *A Gallery of Women* (Rosenberg & Jones, 1972). In this book, Dreiser (1929) provided sketches of fifteen women. In the course of describing these women, he applied one hundred trait terms to 241 different characters. It was thereby possible to assess the trait categories and personality dimensions that were the basis for Dreiser's perception of people, at least as expressed in this book. Three dimen-

Positive Social	Negative Social	Positive Competence	Negative Competence
friendly	unfriendly	intelligent	unintelligent
warm	cold	reliable	unreliable
witty	dull	skillful	clumsy
humorous	humorless	determined	frivolous
popular	unpopular	cautious	impulsive
happy	unhappy	artistic	unimaginative
generous	unsympathetic	serious	superficial

FIGURE 14.1   Illustrative Trait and Feeling Categories Used in the Perception of Self and Others. (Rosenberg, 1977)

sions were found to be of particular significance and each was associated with specific characteristics: *male* (handsome, great, erratic, sincere)–*female* (attractive, sensual, lovely, understanding); *conform* (serious, nice, ambitious, shrewd)–*does not conform* (fighter, free, lonely, sad); *hard* (critical, indifferent, cold)–*soft* (sensual, kind, sympathetic). In other words, the suggestion was that Dreiser used these three dimensions, and the associated traits, to judge and categorize people.

What was of particular interest in this analysis was that these dimensions could be related to themes in Dreiser's life. For example, a salient feature of Dreiser's life was his involvement with women. His sexual involvement with women is expressed in certain traits he clearly associated with them—attractive, sensual, alluring. While some traits he associated with women are perhaps part of a more general stereotype of women, it is interesting that Dreiser did not characterize women as more conforming than men. He also associated such traits as defiant, intelligent, and cold with women, which is of interest since in his personal life he was drawn to women who were unconventional and intellectually strong. The second dimension noted, conform–does not conform, was also of interest because it could be related to the theme of conflict with the forces of convention, which was a part of Dreiser's life. Indeed, one biographer formulated "Dreiser's Law" as follows: "Beliefs held by the multitude, the bourgeois and their leaders, are likely to be wrong per se. Beliefs held by unconventionalists which fly in the face of orthodoxy are in all probablility right" (Swanberg, 1965, p. 181).

Rosenberg's research considers the trait categories and dimensions people use to perceive others. However, it does not address the question of how people go about forming categories. Also, it does not indicate how new people or objects are assigned to categories once they have been established. For example, how do I go about establishing a category of competence, and how do I decide whether to associate someone with that category? Or, to take another example, how do I form the categories of dogs and cats and then assign animals accordingly? Furthermore, is there some overall organization to these categories, or are they all of equal importance? These are questions addressed by cognitive psychologists. For example, a group of cognitive psychologists studied such questions by asking subjects to list characteristics they associate with various objects (Rosch, 1978). Illustrative objects were car, eagle, city bus, and bird. Then another group of subjects judged the truth or accuracy of these characteristics to see if there was agreement concerning these characteristics. Additional subjects then were asked to organize the objects into categories, with some categories being more inclusive than others. These and related studies led to the following conclusions:

1. Subjects can reach high levels of agreement concerning characteristics associated with specific categories. For example, subjects agree about characteristics defining a car or dog.

2. Whether or not an object is assigned to membership in a category depends on its sharing characteristics with other members of that category.

3. No one characteristic may be critical or sufficient to define membership in that category. Thus, for example, no one characteristic may be necessary or

sufficient to describe a car as a sports car. Rather, membership is defined by a pattern of characteristics. Sports cars can vary considerably in terms of specific details but share a general pattern of characteristics.

4. Different categories possess different patterns of characteristics though there may be some overlap between categories. Thus, for example, sedans and sports cars have different patterns of characteristics though the two car categories also share certain characteristics in common. Animals and furniture represent different object categories with different patterns of characteristics, though both some animals and some pieces of furniture have four legs.

5. While no member of a category is likely to have all of the characteristics included as descriptive of membership in that category, some members best exemplify the category. For example, a Porsche might best exemplify a sports car. Such an object is called a **prototype.**

6. At the other extreme, because of overlapping characteristics between categories, some objects are difficult to classify. There is a fuzziness or ambiguity at the boundaries. For example, is a hatchback a sedan or a sports car? We designate some such cases as hybrids or crosses between categories (Figure 14.2).

7. Good agreement can be found concerning a taxonomy or hierarchical arrangement of categories. Two such hierarchical arrangements are illustrated in Figure 14.3.

FIGURE 14.2   The Ambivan Planned by Chrysler Motors. A Hybrid or Cross Between the Car Categories of Van and Station Wagon. (*New York Times*, November 15, 1982)
Hybrids and Fuzzy Boundaries—**Hybrids represent objects that are difficult to classify because they have characteristics of more than one category. For example, is this new car by Chrysler a sedan or a station wagon?**

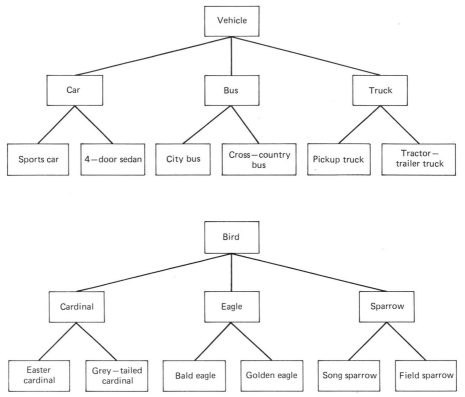

FIGURE 14.3   Illustrative Taxonomies or Hierarchical Category Structures. (Adapted from Rosch, Mervis, Gray, Johnson, & Boyes-Braem, 1976)

8. Categories at different levels in the hierarchy are useful for different purposes. Categories at the lowest level are rich in defining characteristics while categories at the top are the most distinctive from one another. Middle-level categories such as car and eagle are particularly valuable because they are sufficiently specific and concrete to be useful in differentiating objects from one another while still being sufficiently general to be economical to use.

9. These middle-level categories tend to be the first ones used in perceiving the environment and the earliest categories named by children.

What are the implications of such research in cognitive psychology for personality? Do we form categories in perceiving people along lines similar to those developed in perceiving nonhuman objects and, if so, what are the implications for personality functioning? Before turning to some relevant research, you might think about the categories you use in perceiving others. Are they similar to those used by Dreiser or otherwise suggested in the Rosenberg research (Figure 14.1)? Can they be hierarchically arranged? What are the personality and physical characteristics that define membership in a category? Let us turn now to a series of studies by Cantor and Mischel (1979; Cantor, Mischel, & Schwartz, 1982) in which the following questions were addressed: (1) Given a list of objects (titles of persons), will people sort them into similar categories? For example, how might the persons listed in Figure 14.4 be categorized? (2) Can the categories formed be arranged hierarchically with good agreement? For example, if one were to form three levels of categories from the above list, as was done in Figure 14.3, what would they look like? (3) Will the objects or titles in each category be clearly identifiable in terms of the characteristics they share with one another? (4) Are there special features and advantages associated with categories at one or another level? That is, does it make a difference whether we use a more or less inclusive category in perceiving others in the world about us?

As in the earlier research, a group of subjects was asked to sort cards containing the titles listed in Figure 14.4 into categories. To start, the subjects were given four titles as high-level categories (emotionally unstable person, person committed to a cause, cultured person, extroverted person) and then asked to sort under them the remaining thirty-two titles into middle- and low-level categories. The resulting hierarchical structures showed good agreement with one another along the lines represented in Figure 14.5.

Having found good agreement concerning the hierarchical categorization of person titles, Cantor and Mischel had additional subjects list the attributes they associated with each title and rate the likelihood that a category member would have each characteristic. This resulted in a picture of which characteristics seemed particularly descriptive and critical for the inclusion of a person in a particular category. In sum, each person or title could be defined in terms of the number and quality of descriptive characteristics associated with it.

These data have two important implications. The first implication of the Cantor and Mischel data concerns how we go about assigning people to categories. The suggestion here is that for each category there are characteristics which are

Phobic	Campaign manager	Claustrophobic	Criminal
Social activist	Antiwar protestor	Hasidic Jew	madman
Gourmet	Cultured person	(orthodox)	Committed (to
Extrovert	Religious devotee	Press agent for	belief/cause)
Circus clown	Supporter of	the President	person
Strangler	community	Practical joker	Sophisticated
Acrophobic	orchestra	in a fraternity	person
Nun	Torturer	Fighter against	Emotionally
Patron of the arts	Buddhist monk	child abuse	unstable
Comic joker	Couturier	"P.R. type"	person
World traveler	Television	Hydrophobic	Donator to
Donator to	comedian	Save-the-whale	museum
repertory theater	Salesman	campaigner	Rapist

FIGURE 14.4   List of Person Titles To Be Categorized. (Based on Cantor & Mischel, 1979)

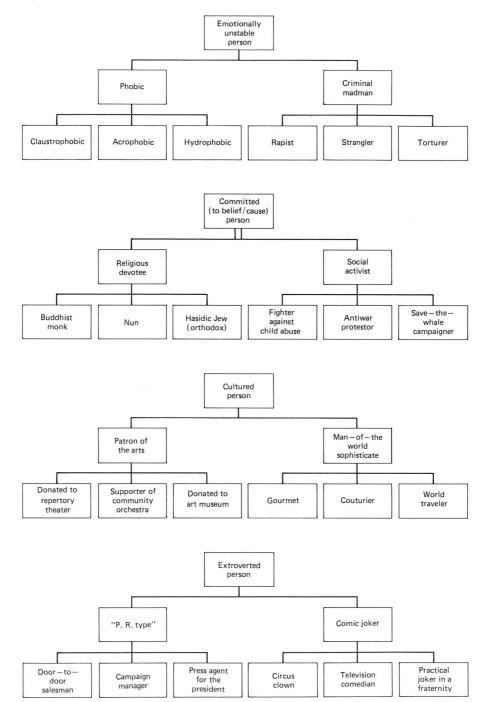

FIGURE 14.5 Four Illustrative Person Taxonomies. (Cantor & Mischel, 1979)

taken to most exemplify or be most illustrative of a person in a given category. Generally, no one characteristic is necessary or sufficient to define category membership, but rather it is a pattern of characteristics. It is this pattern of characteristics, which exemplifies membership in the category, that represents a *prototype*. In other words, when asked to describe an extroverted person we think in terms of a prototype or image of someone who best combines the characteristics of extroverted people. No one extrovert may possess all these characteristics, but each may possess some; and that is enough for them to be included in the category. The prototype is thus a kind of ideal type, and members of the category need not each possess either all of the characteristics or any single characteristic of the ideal type in order to be included in the category. As we meet people we tend to match them against prototypes of categories and then assign them membership in a particular category accordingly.

In some cases the boundaries of the categories we use are clear-cut, as in the difference between male and female. In other cases, the boundaries between categories may be fuzzy, as when we classify someone as a child or an adolescent, as an adolescent or a young adult (Lewis, 1982). Also, some objects are more clear-cut in category assignment than are others. We can easily say about some things that they are a car or a truck, or about some people that they are an introvert or an extrovert. On the other hand, in some cases we may find it hard to assign a vehicle to membership in a car or truck category (e.g., VW camper) or to say that a person is an introvert or an extrovert. Presumably, what we do here is go along weighing the evidence, seeing the extent to which a person expresses the characteristics associated with one prototype and does not express those associated with a different prototype, and make our judgments accordingly. Apparently, however, there is some push toward making a judgment since assigning someone to a category facilitates prediction of behavior and memory for details about them (Cantor & Mischel, 1979). While clearly advantageous in these ways, we must also appreciate that assigning someone to a category can make us overlook inconsistencies in behavior or, on the other hand, exaggerate an inconsistency because it departs from a prototype.

The second implication of the data concerns the advantages and disadvantages of using categories at each of the levels illustrated in Figure 14.5. For example, it was found that middle-level and low-level categories are particularly rich in the number of attributes associated with them. Being able to assign people to one of these categories allows one to be more specific about their characteristics than if they are assigned to a high-level category. On the other hand, high-level categories are more differentiated from one another in that they share fewer characteristics. In other words, categories at low levels have lots of characteristics associated with them, but some or many of these might be shared by members of more than one category. Categories at the highest level are less rich in detail but also hold few characteristics in common with one another. Overall, categories at the middle level have the benefits of being relatively rich and distinctive. This is of particular interest since it suggests that overall we may be better off using middle-level categories to perceive people, though for some purposes categories at either higher or lower level may be more appropriate. We may think here of Eysenck's (Chapter 9) hierarchical organization of personality in terms of types, traits, and responses. The suggestion would be that we naturally are drawn to the trait or middle level in perceiving others, since overall such terms provide for the best combination of richness of detail, differentiation among people, and economy of thought. At other times, however, we are drawn to a higher level of describing people in terms of types or to the lower level of organization in describing people in terms of habits or behaviors.

Before turning to further illustrations of the information-processing approach to personality, we may pause here to consider some of the implications of the above work for personality theory and our understanding of people. First, we have some insight into how we perceive and organize information concerning the interpersonal world about us. For example, we may think of how we organize information in terms of categories with shared patterns of characteristics and assign people we meet to membership in a category according to the match of their characteristics with those defining a specific category. Second, we have some insight into the advantages and disadvantages of categories at varying levels of inclusion and abstraction. In particular, we can appreciate why traits are attractive categories for both lay people and psychologists—that is, they are both descriptive and economical to use. Third, we can also appreciate the utility of an approach to personality that is tied to research procedures and findings in cognitive psychology. Finally, we can see in this work certain similarities with the work of George A. Kelly and, at the same time, some distinct differences. In relation to the latter, we can contrast Cantor and Mischel's emphasis on experimental research and processes through which people organize information, as opposed to Kelly's emphasis on more clinical procedures and the structure of a construct system. We shall return to these and related issues again at the end of the chapter. At that time we will also more fully consider the strengths and limitations of the information-processing approach to personality.

Organizing Information Relevant to Situations

Personality psychologists have always recognized that situations play a vital role in how people behave. As was indicated earlier in this text, even trait theorists recognize that situations are important in influencing which traits would come into play at any one time. However, the situationist attack on trait theory and "traditional personality theory" focuses attention on the need for understanding how situations influence behavior. As it turns out, this is not an easy question, in particular since often it is difficult to specify just what the situation is (Pervin, 1978). One of the most difficult issues has been whether to define a situation objectively or in terms of how it is perceived by a person. Some psychologists would suggest that situations have objective properties regulating behavior and that it is to these properties we must attend. For example, driving on a highway is regulated by lanes and speed limits. Skinner's work in the control of behavior through manipulation of situational reinforcers represents such a view. On the other hand, other psychologists suggest that it is the meaning of situations that influences behavior. This being the case, we must understand how people perceive and interpret situations before we can predict the effects of situations on behavior.

If behavior is influenced by the perceived environment, then we must be interested in how people organize information concerning situations and how they go about classifying them. In many ways the issues are similar to those discussed in relation to the perception of people. Which aspects of situations do people attend to? Are they formal characteristics (e.g., home, school, work, recreation, small, large, public, private), or do they have to do with perceived qualities such as reinforcers? Are there situational terms that are comparable to the trait terms used for people? Do people perceive situations in terms of dimensions that are similar to those used for people (e.g., good–bad, interesting–dull, conforming–nonconforming)? Do people categorize situations in a hierarchical fashion similar to the ways in which they categorize people?

Psychologists have almost always been intrigued with the idea of reinforcers as critical elements of situations. There is for us an intuitive appeal to the idea that we behave in situations according to what we expect will follow various behaviors. In other words, without necessarily going through a conscious decision-making process we process information concerning potential reinforcers in the situation and act accordingly. Thus, for example, the social learning theorist Rotter (1955) suggests that people perceive situations in terms of reinforcers associated with specific behaviors. Each reinforcement has a value for the person and a perceived probability of following that behavior in the situation. A person might expect love or affection to follow as a likely consequence of their being kind and to value love and affection highly. Alternatively, they might expect rejection to follow as an unavoidable result of hostility on their part and to seek to avoid rejection at all costs. Such values and expectancies associated with behaviors can be specific to certain situations or be part of a person's generalized expectancies concerning their relationships with others. In either case, the point is that attention is focused on the reinforcers in the situation and their connections to alternative behaviors. Situations can be viewed, then, in terms of perceived behavior—outcome relationships.

More recently, the social learning theorists Bandura (1977) and Mischel (1977a) have extended this view to suggest that people behave similarly in situations perceived to be similar in their reinforcement contingencies. Again, the suggestion is that people attend to reinforcement information in a situation, act in terms of this information, and categorize situations accordingly. I have often been struck with how much sense such a suggestion makes to me and others. Yet, evidence in support of it is lacking, and there is instead evidence that while reinforcers are important, other factors also influence our behavior and that we process many other kinds of information concerning what is going on in a situation. What are some of the other aspects of situations to which we attend? The British social psychologist Argyle (1981) suggests that people attend to features of situations such as the goals of the participants and the rules of behavior. The goals and rules associated with a cocktail party are different than those for a lecture, and those for soccer or rugby are different than those for cricket. Although one could argue that reinforcers may still be involved, a third alternative takes us even further away from such a view. Here the suggestion is that we perceive situations in terms of the same three dimensions that we use to perceive people—*evaluation* (good–bad), *activity* (fast–slow), and *potency* (strong–weak). In addition, perception of situations in these ways leads us to associate certain feelings with them (Mehrabian & Russell, 1974).

Is one of these necessarily more accurate than the others? Are other constructions and ways of organizing situation information possible? The interesting thing is that one could argue that people do not perceive and classify situations in any fixed way. Rather they are capable of attending first to some aspects of a situation and then to other aspects, and of categorizing a situation first in one way and then in a different way. In other words, people may have multiple ways of construing situations and be capable of shifting among them depending on their own goals and characteristics of the situation itself. One may at one point construe a situation as a social occasion and then rapidly reconstrue it as a business situation. One may think of a situation in terms of its potential reinforcers but then respond to it in terms of feelings associated with it.

Let us consider here two illustrative research efforts in this area. The two are similar in considering how subjects perceive situations but are quite different in the analyses made of these perceptions. The first approach follows from the above analysis of person categories and person prototypes (Cantor, 1981; Cantor, Mischel, & Schwartz, 1982). In this case subjects were asked to sort thirty-six situations into a hierarchical category structure. Two illustrative situation hierarchies are presented in Figure 14.6. Subjects were then asked to describe characteristics common to situations in each category. From this a consensual list of situation characteristics was derived leading to the development of a *situational consensual prototype.* For example, "Being at a Revival Meeting" was associated with characteristics such as the following: preacher, togetherness, chanting, singing, bibles, emotion, loud shouting. Generally each situation prototype consisted of a combination of physical characteristics of the situation, characteristics (traits) of people in the situation, feelings associated with the situation, and behaviors associated with the situation. The conclusions drawn from the research were similar to those with which we are familiar: (1) People can readily form and agree upon a hierarchical taxonomy of situations; (2) People can readily describe and agree upon characteristics associated with situations; (3) Situation prototypes generally include physical characteristics of the situation, personality and feeling characteristics of the participants, and expected behaviors; (4) Middle-level situation categories (e.g., Being at a Demonstration, Being at a Party) are particularly rich in detail and well differentiated from characteristics associated with other categories. In sum, once more there is evidence of the utility of people using a categorical approach and forming behavioral expectations on the basis of these categories. Apparently in entering into a situation, we attend to and encode certain information that leads us to say "This is X kind of situation." On the basis of

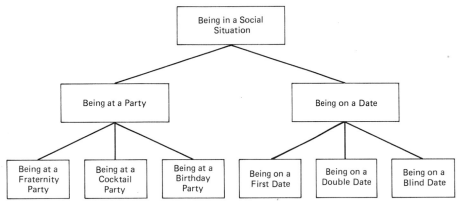

FIGURE 14.6   Two Illustrative Situation Taxonomies. (Cantor, Mischel, & Schwartz, 1982)

this categorization, we generate a range of additional feelings and behavioral expectations—both for ourselves and for those with whom we will be interacting.

The second approach to the analysis of situations places greater emphasis on individual perceptions of situations and perceived feelings and behaviors associated with these situations (Pervin, 1976, 1977). In this approach the situations considered are unique to the life of the individual rather than abstract generalizations established by the experimenter. In addition, the situation categories and situation–behavior relationships are established for each individual rather than being analyzed across subjects. Consider for yourself the task presented to the subjects. First, they are asked to form a list of situations in their current life or recent past. The subjects review their daily lives and list representative situations in terms of who is there, what is going on, where it takes place, and when it occurs. For example, a subject might list a specific situation of presenting an idea before a class, being on a date, or being alone with a good friend. The subjects then describe each situation as well as their feelings and behaviors in the situation. This generates a list of situation characteristics, feelings, and behaviors. The subjects then rate the applicability or relevance of each situation characteristic, feeling, and behavior to each of the original situations that had been listed. In this way it is possible to study each subject's categorizations of situations and perceptions of feelings and behaviors associated with these categories.

How might one categorize the situation in one's own life? And, what kinds of patterns of feelings and behaviors might be associated with these situation categories? Let us consider the answers to these questions for two subjects. The data for each subject were factor analyzed to determine which situation characteristics, feelings, and behaviors seemed to go together. The results for two subjects are presented in the tables that follow (Figures 14.7 and 14.8). Considering Figure 14.7, we can see that Jennifer groups some situations into a category titled "Home-Volatile." These situations are emotional; in them she feels angry and insecure and behaves in a caring, concerned fashion—at least in terms of her perceptions. She also perceives a group of situations with friends that, though again emotional, are now associated with caring and concerned feelings. Interestingly enough, she associates some of the same behaviors with these situations that she does with the home-volatile situations where the feelings are quite different. Considering Figure 14.8 we can see that Ben also has a category of situations associated with friends but the illustrative situations, situation characteristics, feelings, and behaviors associated with this category are different from those reported by Jennifer. One may similarly consider Ben's family category of situations and contrast it with the characteristics Jennifer associates with this category.

While the specific situations studied through this research procedure are unique to each individual, generally subjects list situations that fall into such categories as home, school, work, recreation with peers. The situations can also be characterized as falling within such categories as positive social, negative social, and competence–self-esteem. The dimensions of situations that appear to be most significant for the subjects are: friendly–unfriendly, tense–calm, interesting–dull, and constrained–free. What is interesting about these situation dimensions is that they are similar to dimensions often used to categorize people and that they heavily emphasize the emotion-eliciting qualities of situations. These qualities tend to be common to the categorizations of most subjects. However, the situations listed under each category and the patterns of feelings and behaviors associated with each category are unique to the individual. Thus, as noted, both Jennifer and Ben have a category for home–family and one for friends, but the nature of the situations listed in them and the associated situation characteristics, feelings, and behaviors differ considerably. Some categories may also be unique to the individual as in Jennifer's "Uncertain" category and Ben's "Band-Conflict" category. Finally, each subject has a reported pattern of feeling and behavior that in some ways is constant across all situations, in some ways is generally present except for some situations, and in some ways is never present except perhaps for a few situations. For example, according to her reports Jennifer is almost always sensitive,

Situation Categories	Illustrative Situations	Situation Traits	Feelings	Behaviors
Home—Volatile	mother blows up at me honest with parents about leaving mother refuses gift someone else comes home upset	emotional, angry, volatile, excitable	angry, pressured, involved, insecure, unhappy	sensitive, concerned, caring, suppressed, confused, not compulsive
School, Work—Pressure to Perform	have to participate in class have to perform at work do the job wrong at work in a strange place	demanding, threatening, pressuring, awkward, challenging, embarrassing, unconcerned	self-conscious, challenged, vulnerable, awkward, pressured, anxious	self-conscious, controlled, ambitious, determined, compulsive, cool, responsible, diligent, nonrebellious
Friends, Alone	with friend—no problem with friend—problem alone	emotional, gentle, friendly, generous	caring, concerned, comfortable, melancholy, sad	concerned, caring, emotional, involved, insightful, responsive
Uncertain	come home from Philadelphia in a crowd taking the bus to class want to leave to go to Philadelphia in a strange place	ambiguous, nondefined uncertain, unconcerned, ignoring	bottled-up, melancholy, sad, lonely, frustrated, confused	preoccupied, detached, quiet, self-conscious, controlled, cool, introverted

FIGURE 14.7 Illustrative Situation Categories—Jennifer. (Pervin, 1976) (Copyright 1976 by the American Psychological Association. Reprinted by Permission.)

Situation Categories	Illustrative Situations	Situation Traits	Feelings	Behaviors
Social-Friends	drinking with Joe talking with Paul harmony in the band with girl friend	uninhibited, comfortable, open, flexible, receptive, masculine, talkative, not demanding	humorous, participating, not guilty, happy	uninhibited, receptive, friendly, masculine, humorous, tolerant, attentive
Work-Nonstimulating Situations	in a nonstimulating classroom living with group in Edison loading cartons at work at a boring party	boring, unstimulating, masculine, independent, traditional, affected by mood	eager to leave, aloof, bored, withdrawn	loner, aloof, masculine, intolerant, adamant
Family	visit my parents talk with my mother visit sister and her family	affectionate, loving, traditional, caring	emotional, affectionate, guilty, not free, not relaxed	affectionate, loving, emotional, masculine, bright, sensitive, loyal, not uninhibited, compromising
Army	working at Army headquarters in Army drills short timer in Army	humorous, authoritarian, new, serious, tense, militaristic, traditional, structured	nervous, powerless, scared, learning	nervous, learning, growing, masculine, eager, not uninhibited, sleepy
Band-Conflict	conflict in the band new band performance	challenging, demanding, musically tight, exclusive, frustrating	together, interested, participating, not calm, not secure	responsible, contributing, serious, decisive, demanding, intolerant, controlling, loyal

FIGURE 14.8 Illustrative Situation Categories—Ben. (Pervin, 1976) (Copyright 1976 by the American Psychological Association. Reprinted by permission.)

vulnerable, and insightful. She also is friendly, warm, and accepting most of the time except when she is in some volatile home situations, at which times she is uniquely irritable, angry, upset, depressed, uncontrolled, and rebellious. She also tends to be involved and caring, except when she is detached, preoccupied, introverted, controlled, and cool. While some individuals may be introverted in all situations and some individuals extroverted in all situations, many individuals are introverted in some situations and extroverted in others. Individuals may differ, then, in the behaviors on which they are stable or varying or in the kinds of situations in relation to which their behavior varies. To summarize this research, we may suggest the following:

1. People appear to form categories of situations and situation–feeling–behavior relationships as well as forming categories of people.
2. There appear to be some common dimensions to the categorization of situations, these dimensions being related to dimensions used in the categorization of people.
3. Each person appears to perceive a unique pattern of stability and change in feelings and behaviors in relation to different categories of situations.

In considering the organization of information concerning situations and situation–behavior relationships, it is important to recognize differences among situations and people. In relation to situations we may consider, for example, the extent to which they are highly structured, constraining, or scripted. The concept of

Scripts—**Some situations, such as eating in a restaurant, require following a clearly defined series of behaviors.**

script has been used by some proponents of a computer model to define a series or pattern of behaviors considered to be appropriate for that situation (Schank & Abelson, 1977). For example, behavior in a restaurant generally is highly scripted. Not only are specific behaviors well defined but the order or sequence of behaviors is clearly set forth. Generally we act out roles in such situations and our behavior is regulated by norms or sanctions for behaving in an inappropriate way. Violating the script in a restaurant may sometimes be funny, but more often it leads to errors in the meal being served or in being asked to leave, particularly if the restaurant is busy or is formal in atmosphere. Functioning in such cases requires us to recognize that we are in a scripted situation and to call forth images of the required scripts. A breakdown in either cognitive skill, or in the skill in performing the requisite behaviors, leads to difficulties. On the other hand, other situations are less structured or scripted. For example, an informal meeting among friends generally is associated with fewer prescriptions or well-defined scripts. Under such circumstances often people feel less inhibited or "more able to be themselves."

Just as some situations call for more careful monitoring of what is going on and what is prescribed, so too there are individual differences in the extent to which people monitor or regulate their behavior according to situational cues. Snyder (1974, 1979) has developed a scale to measure such individual differences (Figure 14.9). The *high* **self-monitoring** *individual* is one who is highly sensitive to cues of situational appropriateness and regulates his or her behavior accordingly. In a moderate form, such a person shows competence in handling a great variety of situations; in an extreme form, such a person can be a chameleon, always changing to meet the situation and never being sure of who they are. On the other hand, the *low self-monitoring individual* is less attentive to social information and generally behaves more in accord with internal feelings and attitudes. In a moderate form, such a person can demonstrate independence and fortitude; in an extreme form, such an individual can show an insensitivity to the feelings and wishes of others. A variety of differences have been found to be associated with high self-monitoring (HSM) and low self-monitoring (LSM) scores. Some of these are described by Snyder as follows:

1. HSMs are better able to intentionally express and communicate emotions and expressive behavior than are LSMs.

2. HSMs are better able to deceive others in face-to-face interviews than are LSMs.

3. HSMs are better able to correctly infer the emotional state of others than are LSMs.

4. HSMs are more discriminating about situations and more variable in their behavior across situations than are LSMs.

5. HSMs generally appear to other people to be more friendly, outgoing, extroverted and less worried, anxious, or nervous than LSMs.

6. HSMs are less influenced in their self-presentations by changes in mood states than are LSMs.

My behavior is usually an expression of my true inner feelings. (F)

At parties and social gatherings, I do not attempt to do or say things that others will like. (F)

When I am uncertain how to act in a social situation, I look to the behavior of others for cues. (T)

I sometimes appear to others to be experiencing deeper emotions than I actually am. (T)

I laugh more when I watch a comedy with others than when alone. (T)

In different situations and with different people, I often act like very different persons. (T)

T = True, F = False

FIGURE 14.9 Illustrative Items and Scoring for the Self-Monitoring Scale. (Snyder, 1974)

7. HSMs remember more information about other people and make more inferences concerning the traits of others than do LSMs.

To summarize this section, we have considered the ways in which people organize information concerning situations and situation–behavior scenarios. To a certain extent discussion here has paralleled that concerning the organization of person-relevant information. There is evidence that people categorize situations so as to make manageable relevant information and to make predictable the social world. There also is evidence that such categories are organized into a hierarchical structure with categories higher in the structure being more differentiating and categories lower in the structure being richer in detail. There is evidence of some common categories and dimensions of categories among people but there also is evidence of diversity in classification and uniqueness of categorization of specific situations. Each person appears to perceive a unique pattern of stability and change in his or her behavior in relation to categories of situations and, in all likelihood, also perceives distinctive patterns in the behavior of others. Finally, situations differ in how constraining or scripted they may be and individuals differ in how attentive they are to situational cues concerning appropriate behavior.

Organizing Information Relevant to Events

In the past two sections we have been concerned with how people organize information relevant to people and situations. In this section we are concerned with how people organize information relevant to events, in particular with how they go about attributing causes to events. We see someone hit or yell at another and we infer some reason for the action. Is the person generally hostile? Was something malicious done to them? We see someone act in a strange way. Were they not feeling well? Was our previous picture of them inaccurate and now we have to view them in a new way? These are the kinds of inferences and attributions we are constantly making in our daily lives, and it is these processes that have been of considerable interest to social psychologists since the 1960s. For example, it has been found that we tend to attribute the causes of behavior in other people to their traits or personality characteristics whereas we tend to attribute the causes of our own behavior to situations (Jones & Nisbett, 1971). One reason for this difference may be that we observe others in a limited range of situations and see them acting consistently whereas we observe our own behavior over a much wider range of situations and see it varying accordingly. The interesting point here, aside from the general issue of how we go about attributing causes, is that social psychologists have suggested that trait or personality-characteristic attributions represent a bias based on limited information. Furthermore, they suggest that trait personality psychologists may be similarly biased in their observations and thereby exaggerate the importance of personality consistency and neglect the role of situational determinants of behavior.

We already are familiar with the fact that individuals may maintain beliefs about their ability to influence or control events in their lives (e.g., learned helplessness and locus of control, Chapter 2). A related area of research has concerned people's explanations for success or failure. Weiner (1979) has suggested that there are three dimensions relevant to causal explanations. The first dimension, related to the work of Rotter on locus of control, concerns whether causes are perceived as coming from within (internal) or from outside (external) the person. This dimension has been named **locus of causality**. A second dimension of causality concerns whether the cause is stable and relatively fixed as opposed to being unstable or variable. The implications for causal attributions from combining these two dimensions can be seen in Figure 14.10. Accordingly, we can attribute success or failure to *ability* ("I am bright."), *effort* ("I tried hard."), *task difficulty* ("The test was easy."), or *chance or luck* ("I was lucky in guessing right.").

Additional dimensions have been suggested, but the point here is that people make causal attributions and that such attributions have important psychological implications. For example, such attributions have important implications for motivation. A person is more likely to persist at a task if it is viewed as one involving effort than if success or failure is viewed as being due to chance. Similarly, a person will behave differently if they believe health or illness is due to internal or external causes ("I am a sickly person." vs. "The flu bug got me.") and whether they believe in the efficacy of self-care ("Basic health principles prevent illness."

CAUSE	Internal	External
Stable	Ability	Task difficulty
Variable	Effort	Chance or luck

FIGURE 14.10   Possible Causal Attributions for Success and Failure. (Weiner, 1974)

vs. "One can do little to prevent illness.") (Lau, 1982). Some fascinating and extremely important insights into how women seek to understand and explain the trauma of breast cancer are presented in Figure 14.11 (Taylor, 1982).

Casual attributions also are important aspects of stereotypes. For example, success in males and failure in females tend to be attributed to ability whereas failure in men and success in women tend to be attributed to effort or luck (Deaux, 1976). Finally, differences in casual attribution have important implications for emotion. As noted in relation to learned helplessness, depression is seen as resulting from an internal, stable, global attribution. Other illustrations of emotional consequences of causal attributions would be to feel proud following success and a causal attribution to ability and to feel guilty following failure and a causal attribution to effort (Weiner, 1979). It should be clear that what is being suggested here is that attributions cause certain emotions, beliefs, and motivations to follow. However, some research suggests that pleasant and unpleasant events themselves account for emotion and motivation, with attributions only part of the cause of what follows or may themselves be part of that response (Covington & Omelich, 1979; Smith & Kluegel, 1982; Stephan & Gollwitzer, 1981). Basically, the question is that of the relation of attributions to emotion and motivation—causes of them, correlates of them, or even responses to them. It may be recalled here that similar questions were raised in Chapter 2 concerning the relation between attributions for helplessness and depression. This remains an area of continuing investigation.

---

1. An event that is clearly followed by another event may be seen as causing that event (e.g., belief that breast cancer was caused by a recent auto accident).

2. An event that is located close to (spatial proximity) another event may be seen as having been caused by it (e.g., belief that continued pressure to an area near the breast caused breast cancer).

3. Causes resemble effects and big effects are produced by big causes whereas small effects are produced by small causes (e.g., cancer is a large effect and must have been produced by a large cause rather than an accumulation of small events).

4. Unknown causes are associated with similar or representative known causes (e.g., a malignant lump is attributed to a blow to the breast since lumps are usually caused by blows).

5. Frequent co-occurrences of events are seen as having a causal relationship (e.g., a woman attributed a causal quality to her golf club since four of her acquaintances here had also developed breast cancer).

6. Attributions are made to single causes rather than multiple causes (e.g., cancer is caused by stress, a virus, heredity, OR an environmental carcinogen rather than by an interaction among many of these).

FIGURE 14.11 Illustrations of Errors of Causal Attribution in Patients with Breast Cancer. (S. E. Taylor, 1982)

Theory and research in relation to causal attributions views the person as an **intuitive social scientist**, trying to gather and organize data that will be useful in predicting and controlling events (Nisbett & Ross, 1980; Ross, 1981). The emphasis here is on people as seeking information and understanding rather than on people seeking instinctual gratification or self-esteem. Explanations of findings are in the form of information-processing strategies rather than in terms of motivation. When errors in judgment and inference are observed they are explained in terms of shortcomings in information-processing strategies rather than in terms of motivation. Thus, for example, internal or external attributions for success and failure are viewed as results of the data available to the person rather than as serving self-protective functions. In the illustrations provided of causal attributions for breast cancer, the emphasis was on information-processing errors rather than on the anxiety generated by uncertainty, the terror of believing there is an internal process of growth that has gradually gone out of control, or the guilt associated with the idea that something was done to cause the illness or not done that could have prevented the illness. Similarly, superstitions are seen as coming from observation of chance relationships among events rather than from underlying wishes and fears. The fact that people maintain certain beliefs despite nonsupportive evidence is explained in terms of a tendency to weight confirming evidence more heavily than disconfirming evidence rather than in terms of a motivation for being right. In sum, the argument is made "that many phenomena generally regarded as motivational. . .can be understood better as products of relatively passionless information-processing errors than of deep-seated motivational forces" (Nisbett & Ross, 1980, p. 12). The point here is that all of us necessarily utilize strategies to organize information concerning events and to make inferences concerning the future. However, inherent in our ordinary information-processing activity are cases of incorrect information, memory, and inference.

REPRESENTATION OF THE SELF

Until now, attention has focused on people's efforts to organize information concerning the world around them—people, situations, events. Additional information to be acquired, organized, processed, stored, and retrieved relates to the self. As has been seen in earlier chapters, the concept of self has been significant in many theories of personality. What is the unique contribution offered by a cognitive, information-processing approach to the self?

An important impetus for work in this area was the research by Markus (1977). She suggested that people form cognitive structures about the self just as they do about other phenomena. Such cognitive structures are called **self-schemata**: "Self-schemata are cognitive generalizations about the self, derived from past experience, that organize and guide the processing of the self-related information contained in an individual's social experiences" (p. 63). As is true with other schemata or concepts, self-schemata influence whether information is attended to, how it is structured, and the ease with which it can be remembered. For exam-

1. **Observational Bias.**   Our pre-existing theories bias what we see and lead us to see in others what we expect. (Seen in stereotypes about individuals and groups.)

2. **Discounting Error.**   We ignore events that do not confirm our beliefs or discount their significance by considering them as exceptions to the rule. (Seen in stereotypes about individuals or groups.)

3. **Categorizing Error.**   We may judge things to be similar or people to be alike (i.e., belonging to the same category) on the basis of superficial similarities and ignore fundamental but subtle differences. (Seen in stereotypes about individuals and groups.)

4. **Causal Interpretation Error.**   We may view events that follow one another in time to be causally related when they are unrelated or both are caused by something else. (Seen in superstitious behavior.)

5. **Prediction Error.**   We may make inaccurate predictions because we follow incorrect principles or overweight evidence that is vivid and salient. (Seen, for example, in people who are sensitive to rejection and who vividly recall each instance of slight or rejection.)

SUM.   In ordinary life people look at the wrong data, weight the data improperly, and make incorrect inferences. The errors of the intuitive, lay, or naive scientist are best understood as cognitive failings rather than as motivational.

FIGURE 14.12   Cognitive Errors in Everyday Life. (Based on Nisbett & Ross, 1980)

ple, Markus suggested that people with particular self-schemata should be able to process relevant information with ease, retrieve relevant behavioral evidence, and resist evidence counter to the self-schemata. In research investigating these hypotheses, she had subjects rate themselves on several scales relevant to the independent–dependent personality dimension. On the basis of their responses, she formed three groups of subjects: *Independents* (or subjects who tended to rate themselves as independent on the scales); *Dependents* (or individuals who tended to rate themselves as dependent on the scales); and *Aschematics* (or individuals who did not show any clear tendency to rate themselves as independent or dependent). The latter individuals were assumed to lack a self-schema for the independent–dependent personality dimension.

Having formed these three groups, Markus compared their behavior on four tasks. In the first task, subjects observed words being flashed on a screen and responded by indicating whether or not the word was self-descriptive. Some of the words were independent adjectives (e.g., individualistic, adventurous, self-confident), some were dependent adjectives (e.g., conforming, submissive, dependent), and some were unrelated to either. Independents were found to judge more of the independent words as self-descriptive than did Dependents, while the reverse was true for dependent words. Aschematics were midway between for both sets of words. In addition, Independents were faster at making *me* or self-descriptive judgments for independent adjectives than for dependent adjectives, while the reverse was true for Dependents. Aschematics did not differ in response speed to the two sets of adjectives.

In the second task subjects were given some of the words from the independent and dependent word lists and asked to give evidence from their past behavior of the relevance of each trait or characteristic. The data here supported the hypothesis that since a schema reflects past behavior, schematic subjects should be able to provide relevant behavioral evidence. Independent subjects wrote more behavioral descriptions for independent words than did subjects in the other groups. Dependent subjects wrote more behavioral illustrations for dependent words than did members of the other two groups. In the third task, subjects rated the likelihood of their behaving in various ways. The behaviors rated had previously been determined to be expressive of independent or dependent personalities. In accord with the hypothesis, Independent subjects rated the independent behaviors as more likely to be expressed by them than the dependent behaviors, while the reverse was true for the Dependents. Aschematics did not differ in their probability ratings for the two sets of behaviors. In responses to a final task, Markus found evidence that Independents and Dependents resisted information contrary to the ways in which they thought of themselves. In both cases subjects showed evidence of rejecting the accuracy of test information that was incongruent with their self-schemata. In sum, data from the four tasks supported the utility of the concept of self-schemata or cognitive generalizations about the self that organize, summarize, and explain behavior.

More recently Markus and her colleagues have followed a similar strategy in the investigation of self-schemata related to gender. All people are aware of sex differences. Individuals differ, however, in the meanings they associate with sex differences and in the extent to which they represent themselves as masculine, feminine, and androgynous (possessing both masculine and feminine attributes). Do people who have masculine self-schemata (give themselves high self-ratings on traits such as aggressive, dominant, acting as leader), feminine self-schemata (high self-ratings on traits such as gentle, emotional, sensitive), and androgynous self-schemata (high self-ratings on both sets of traits) differ from one another as well as from gender aschematics (people who rate themselves low on both masculine and feminine sets of traits) in their processing of gender-related information? Evidently this is, indeed, the case. Consistent with earlier studies, it was found that people for whom masculine schemata are an important part of their identity remember more masculine than feminine attributes, require shorter processing time for "me" judgments to these attributes, are more confident of these judgments, and are able to provide more examples of past masculine behavior than feminine behavior. Individuals with feminine self-schemata demonstrate the reverse pattern of information processing. On the other hand, subjects identified as high on androgyny are able to process masculine and feminine information with equal efficiency. Finally, individuals who rate themselves as low on both masculine and feminine characteristics give low confidence ratings for gender-related self-judgments and are relatively poor in supplying behavioral evidence in support of gender-related self-descriptions (Markus, Crane, Bernstein, & Siladi, 1982). In sum, people differ in the extent to which they incorporate masculine and feminine concepts into their self-concepts. The extent to which people define themselves as masculine, feminine, or androgynous then plays a significant role in how they process gender-relevant information in the world about them. What makes this of particular significance is that these schemata are not only used in relation to the self, but are used in relation to the perception of others as well (Fong & Markus, 1982).

Markus' research involved already formed schemata. Additional research has involved investigation of the development of self-schemata, research on how self-schemata affect attention and memory, and how self-schemata are maintained in social interaction. In relation to the development of the concept of self, one question asked is: What leads people to infer that they have particular traits (Locksley & Lenauer, 1981)? Research suggests that people infer they have a trait or personality characteristic when they observe themselves behaving in a particular way. In other words, just as we infer personality characteristics from the behavior of others, so we observe our own behavior and accordingly infer our own personality characteristics. Associated with this will be typical errors in concept formation. Thus, in forming a self-schema we may exaggerate the stability of certain behaviors relative to situational influences and occurrences of other behaviors. Similarly, we may see superficially similar behaviors as related while in fact they are different. Since people generally have a bias for confirming evidence over disconfirming evidence, they may observe and recall confirming evidence more readily. What is particularly interesting about such an accounting of the development and maintenance of self-schemata is that it again emphasizes ''informational gains'' over ''motivational or emotional gains''; that is, the emphasis is on everyday problems of inference error and bias rather than on ego-enhancing or self-esteem biases. In this way, cognitive processes relevant to the concept of self are seen as following the same rules as cognitive processes relevant to other concepts rather than following a process of their own.

Evidence has been accumulating that once we establish self-schemata these cognitive structures influence what we attend to. For example, the evidence suggests that attention to the self greatly restricts our ability to attend to information that is not self-relevant (Bargh, 1982). Also, because people experience events with themselves as the central focus, self-relevant information is more easily and quickly accessed than other information. Again, the emphasis is on the *informational relevance* of self-schemata rather than on their *emotional significance*. Extending this role of self-schemata, the suggestion has been made that such schemata or cognitive generalizations about the self form the basis for *all* of our perceptions of others: ''All incoming stimuli are evaluated according to the relevance to the self'' (Markus & Smith, 1981, p. 245). Does this mean that we evaluate others in the same way that we evaluate ourselves? Not necessarily. While similar categories and category characteristics may be used, it also is possible for us to use different categories or category criteria in our self-judgment than in our judgment of others. The self provides a framework against which we can judge others, highlighting their similarities to us or their differences from us, but we are not totally bound by the framework.

Research also suggests the power of self-schemata in recall. Attending to words in terms of whether they are self-relevant increases our ability to remember them. This supports our intuitive sense that often we learn material better when we can see how it relates to us (Rogers, Kuiper, & Kirker, 1977). We can return here to the concept of prototype. Do we have a prototype concept of ourselves and, if so, what are the memory implications of such a prototype? If the self is a cognitive category like other categories, we should have a prototypical self-concept ("This is what I am *really* like.") and we should most easily remember material relevant to this concept. A recent study indeed found that people best remember photographs of themselves which are rated as most exemplary of their "real self" (Yarmey & Johnson, 1982). Note that the prototype concept of real self is different from the concept of ideal self. The concept of what one is really like or most like is different from the prototype concept of what one would most want to be like, and the two prototypes can be very similar to or very different from one another.

Finally, we can consider how self-schemata are confirmed and may prove to be resistant to change. One relevant component has already been suggested above in terms of our bias toward confirming evidence over disconfirming evidence. There is clear evidence that people prefer self-confirmatory social feedback over self-disconfirmatory feedback (Swann & Read, 1981).There also is evidence to suggest that people solicit self-confirming evidence from others and present themselves in ways that will elicit confirming evidence from others (Baumeister, 1982; Swann & Hill 1982). In other words, people not only extrapolate supportive evidence from an unfolding reality but actively manage and maintain that reality. As described by Snyder (1981), high self-monitors choose to live in worlds that allow them to bring out their various selves whereas low self-monitors choose worlds that allow them to "be themselves." Of course, people often are unaware of the extent to which they maintain certain patterns of social interaction. Processes such as these may help to appreciate why changes in the self-concept are so often difficult to produce. Also, this may explain the beneficial effects of therapies that encourage people to behave differently to elicit different responses from others.

Summarizing this section on the representation of the self we may say that from a cognitive, information-processing point of view the self is an important cognitive structure that influences the encoding, organization, and memory of a great deal of information. Treatment of the self as a cognitive category allows one to study it in the same way as other cognitive categories and to understand its functioning in terms of cognitive processes followed by all conceptual categories. The self is an important conceptual category but it is not some internal homunculus or controlling agent. We may associate specific aspects with the self and may even tie certain motives to the self-concept, but we should not ignore the role of "everyday cognitive processes" in accounting for how we treat self-relevant information. In other words, while concepts such as ego-enhancement and self-esteem may have some utility, we should be aware that more straightforward information-processing interpretations may account for the phenomena equally well and in a more parsimonious way.

THE RELATION OF INFORMATION-PROCESSING THEORY TO TRADITIONAL PERSONALITY THEORY

Having had the opportunity to consider the cognitive, information-processing approach to personality, what can be said about it relative to approaches previously considered? Clearly, certain concepts sound familiar. On the other hand, many aspects are distinctive.

The cognitive emphasis in this chapter reminds one of the work of George Kelly. Kelly emphasized the person as a scientist and the importance of constructs and the construct system in psychological functioning. Kelly suggested that constructs are organized in a hierarchical fashion and that people can be quite flexible in utilizing their constructs—people have constructs but their constructs need not have them. Indeed, Mischel states that "Kelly suggested, long before others, that the same orientation and principles ought to be used in talking about our 'subjects' as about ourselves. He thus foreshadowed much in contemporary psychology and his wisdom has not yet been fully recognized" (1981, p. 16).

In addition, one may be reminded of the work of Carl Rogers in the cognitive emphasis on the concept of self and in the emphasis on how people give meaning to the world about them. Here too Mischel (1981), in reviewing work in the area of personality and cognition, recognizes that Rogers anticipated current developments in emphasizing the importance of the phenomenal world and the concept of self. Finally, one can see parallels between social learning theory and personality information-processing theory. Here we can point to Bandura's emphasis on cognitive processes in modeling and self-efficacy judgments as well as Mischel's emphasis on cognitive processes in self-regulation and in discriminating among situations. Indeed, to the extent that social learning theory has become *cognitive* social learning theory and to the extent that students of Bandura and Mischel are at the forefront of efforts to relate cognition and personality, one can question whether the two even form separate categories from one another. If personality research has gone cognitive and gone social, so too has personality learning theory.

While noting these similarities, one can at the same time observe critical differences between personality information-processing theory and the works of Kelly and Rogers. The works of Rogers and Kelly emanated from clinical experience whereas the work in information processing derives from the experimental laboratory. Rogers and Kelly were attempting to develop a theory of personality whereas the work presented in this chapter might better be construed as an *approach to* personality rather than a *theory of* personality. Both Rogers and Kelly were interested in the study and understanding of individuals while cognitive personality psychologists have yet to demonstrate the utility of their approach for the understanding of an individual or the utility of studying the individual for learning about people generally. While emphasizing process and change, Rogers and Kelly both emphasized the importance of structure and the continuity of personality as well. While recognizing structure and consistency, cognitive personality psychologists tend to give greater emphasis to process and variability in personality functioning. Finally, both Rogers and Kelly emphasized the importance of phenomena such as conflict and emotion, in particular the affect of anxiety. In contrast, cognitive personality psychologists tend to be more interested in individual competencies and normal information-processing errors than they are in people's responses to threat and the development of pathology.

If such differences between cognitive personality theory and the theories of Rogers and Kelly are noteworthy, differences between the former and traditional personality theory (psychoanalytic and trait theory) are even more apparent and noteworthy (Figure 14.13). At the heart of this difference lies the emphasis of traditional personality theory on structure and consistency–stability in personality functioning. In contrast with this lies the cognitive personality psychologist's emphasis on processes and the flexibility inherent in people's ability to discriminate among situations and manage their behavior accordingly. In addition, traditional personality theory places much greater emphasis on human motivation than is true for cognitive personality psychologists. As has been noted previously, the latter see people as *information seeking* rather than *pleasure seeking*. Finally,

Traditional Personality Theory	Cognitive, Information-Processing Theory
1. Stability and consistency of personality	1. Discriminativeness and flexibility of behavior
2. Generalized predictions of person's behavior	2. Predictions specific to situations
3. Emphasis on structure-stability	3. Emphasis on process–fluidity
4. Dispositions, traits, needs	4. Category structures, belief systems, inferential strategies
5. Motivation and dynamics	5. Cognitive economics and everyday cognitive processes
6. Needs and defenses	6. Cognitive competencies
7. Self as unitary concept	7. Self as composed of multiple schema
8. Self as causal agent	8. Self as schema or generalized cognitive construction
9. Importance of unconscious processes	9. Importance of automatic information processing

FIGURE 14.13   Prototypic Characteristics of Two Personality Theories.

CURRENT APPLICATIONS AND IMPLICATIONS

Computer Personalities?

If we can use computers as a model for personality, can we also use computers to model personality? Many psychologists in the area of artificial intelligence think so, as they go about the task of trying to simulate human thought and behavior on the computer. At this point not only can you play chess with the computer, but you can interact with nine different computer personalities in a variety of social situations.

"THAT DAMN COMPUTER THINKS IT KNOWS IT ALL!"

A recent article in the *Wall Street Journal* asks: Can the computer learn how to be a football coach? Football fans undoubtedly are familiar with the picture of a coach on the sidelines with a list of plays and formations that are believed to work in various situations. Can a computer incorporate the information used by a coach to call plays in a dynamic way? Can it produce a winning coach? Can it help to reduce stress and burnout? Can it enlighten us about how human information processing works? These are some of the questions being asked by Roger Schank at the Yale University Artificial Intelligence Laboratory. And, according to the article, Professor Schank also believes that a properly programmed computer might even make a good president some day.

Another creative and challenging effort along these lines has been Kenneth Mark Colby's computer modeling of a paranoid mind. Starting from a theory that suggests that paranoia expresses a strategy of blaming others as a protective defense against the painful affect of shame-humiliation ("I am being wronged, harassed, etc." versus "I am inadequate and to blame"), a computer has been programmed to respond to a psychiatric interview as a paranoid person might. Can psychiatrists interacting with a patient or a computer at the other end

Computers and Personality—**Cognitive psychologists use the computer as a model for personality and try to model human behavior on computers.** ©Robert Schochet.

of a teletype machine tell which is which—paranoid computer or paranoid person? Evidently not. The responses from the "paranoid mind" of the computer seem indistinguishable from those of the paranoid mind of the person.

Can a computer be programmed to "think" and "feel" like a person?

Evidently so. Can such computer simulations of human personality enlighten us about how people really function? That remains for the future to tell. Can computers eventually "really" think, feel, and have personalities? That, perhaps, is for philosophers to debate.

SOURCES: K.M. Colby, 1981; *Wall Street Journal*, March 30, 1983, p.1.

cognitive personality psychologists emphasize the importance of experimental observation of behavior and of relating concepts of internal processes to behaviors that can be measured. In contrast, traditional personality theory puts greater faith in clinical observation (psychoanalytic theory) and in responses to questionnaires (trait theory). Personality questionnaires in particular are discounted by cognitive personality psychologists because they are viewed as getting at a person's *construction* of personality rather than at a person's *actual* personality (Shweder, 1982). According to cognitive personality psychologists, we should be studying people's category structures and inference processes rather than their needs and dispositions, we should be studying behavior and cognitive representations of behavior rather than responses to questionnaires or projective techniques, and we should ally ourselves with other parts of psychology such as cognitive and social psychology rather than pursuing an entirely independent course of action.

EVALUATING THE STRENGTHS AND LIMITATIONS OF A COGNITIVE, INFORMATION-PROCESSING APPROACH TO PERSONALITY

Earlier in this chapter, the question was asked as to whether the cognitive, information-processing approach has any distinctive contribution to make to personality. Having considered some of the relevant theory and research, what can be suggested?

It would appear that there are two main contributions and strengths of this approach. First, it is tied to an experimental foundation in cognitive psychology and continues with that tradition while investigating issues in personality. Many personality theories have suffered from the problem of vague concepts and difficulty in suggesting relevant experimental efforts. To a certain extent, this has been true of psychoanalysis; to a greater extent, it has been true of humanistic and human growth potential theories. Also, most theories of personality have arisen independently of other ongoing efforts in psychology. Where commonalities with other parts of psychology could be observed this had more to do with a common influence than with the results of one having an impact upon the results of another. Thus, when one considers the various theories covered in this book, one often finds it hard to say what aspects that are fundamental to the theory have been learned from other areas of psychology. This is particularly true for the more clinical theories presented earlier in the text and somewhat less true for the theories of learning presented later. With the cognitive, information-processing approach, however, we encounter a radical departure from this tradition. In going social and cognitive, personality psychologists following this approach have attempted to take from social psychology and cognitive psychology concepts and experimental procedures that might be useful in exploring personality. Not only was this done initially but there remains a continuous fertilization, at times even blurring of the boundaries of social, cognitive, and personality psychology. While back in the 1950s there was a "new look" in relating perception and personality to one another, this movement did not seem to have the foundation or the momentum expressed in current pursuits.

The second strength of the cognitive, information-processing approach to personality lies in the phenomena investigated. While emphasizing an experimental tradition, important aspects of human personality functioning have not altogether been neglected. Consider here the issues covered in this chapter—how individuals organize their representations of people, situations, events, and themselves. These indeed are topics that strike one as the kinds of issues that should be of concern to personality psychologists. Thus, when parallels are noted between issues explored by cognitive personality psychologists and earlier theories of personality, this may be taken as a strength. The approach is not neglecting long-standing issues that remain of concern to us. Whereas for some time experimental psychologists ignored questions of the self and questions of consciousness and thought, these psychologists are prepared to tackle them. While remaining committed to the laboratory, for the most part they remain aware of and concerned about phenomena observed in daily living.

And what of the limitations of the approach? Here we may again consider two relevant points. First, we can examine the underlying model critically. Second, we can consider whether in following in the footsteps of cognitive psychology major aspects of personality functioning have been neglected. Turning to the first point, how useful is the computer, information-processing model that underlies this approach to personality? We must recall that a model need not be an accurate reflection of human behavior for it to be useful in the study of that behavior. Thus, when it comes down to it, the question is not whether humans function like computers but whether studying people *as if* they function like computers assists us in understanding their behavior. Relevant to this is the question of whether the model misleads us into thinking about phenomena in ways that are not useful.

To a certain extent, the jury is still out deliberating on this question. We do know that in many ways people do not think like computers, let alone behave like them. George A. Miller was one of the early leaders in the development of computer models of human thinking. Today he suggests that "how computers work seems to have no real relevance to how the mind works any more than a wheel shows how people walk" (1982, p. C8). Computers are becoming faster and capable of handling increasing amounts of information. We are becoming increasingly sophisticated in writing programs to make the computer think like humans. However, many people believe that the nature of human thinking is fundamentally different from machine thinking. Not only does a machine inevitably require a person to select the information to be stored and write the program for organizing information, two critical processes in information processing, but machines do not make the many economies and irrational connections that are part of human thought. In addition, people make judgments such as attributing intent to the action of others. While it is possible to make a computer think in an analogous way (Colby, 1982), there remains a considerable gap between the two. Furthermore, it is possible that thinking about social phenomena in a social context is fundamentally different from the isolated processing of neutral information.

This last point brings us to the second criticism of this approach. This is that in going cognitive, psychology has neglected such important human phenomena as affect and motivation. In following in the footsteps of cognitive psychology, personality psychologists may be in danger of committing the same errors without breaking new ground. In gaining our head, we may be in danger of losing our soul. A short time ago there was a symposium of outstanding social and personality psychologists presenting papers on "social knowing." Consider the following commentary on these papers by Ulric Neisser (1980), one of the founding fathers of the cognitive revolution in psychology:

> . . . information processing concepts are overused in social psychology just as I think they are in cognitive psychology. (p. 601)
>
> I am disturbed by the extraordinarily narrow perspective from which scholars in this field approach their work. . . . The symposium is about "social knowing," a process which has something to do with assessing motives. . . . Freud's observations and insights on such matters . . . have affected every institution in western culture, but they receive no recognition here. (p. 602)
>
> The study of "social knowing" is not the first branch of psychology to be based on a rather passive conception of human nature. Most modern cognitive theories make the same assumption: the perceiver simply takes in information, without attempting to change the situation or even explore it in any active way. (p. 604)

During the 1920s and 1930s behaviorism was particularly strong in this country and the study of cognitive processes was not popular. The learning theorist Tolman was an exception in this regard, emphasizing the importance of cognition and criticizing the popular telephone switchboard model (stimulus–response) of human behavior. One psychologist who was critical of Tolman suggested that he left animals buried in thought and did not consider why they made the choices they did (Guthrie, 1952). Similarly, today a leading cognitive psychologist suggests that "just as cognitive psychology presents the danger of leaving the human subject lost in thought without being able to act, so does the current approach [to cognition and personality] leave unsolved the problem of how action occurs" (Posner, 1981, p. 340).

Sometime ago the distinction was made between "cold cognition" and "hot cognition." Psychologists, including both cognitive psychologists and cognitive personality psychologists, have tended to study cold cognition. While studying important phenomena, they have tended to study the more emotionally neutral aspects of these phenomena in the relatively cool setting of the laboratory. But true social cognition in important life situations may be fundamentally different from the cool, detached processes that have typically been the focus of investigation. In reviewing the results of research following the information processing model, a leading cognitive psychologist suggested that there was "sterility overall, for the organism we are analyzing is conceived as pure intellect. . . . Alas, that description does not fit actual behavior. . . . I conclude that there is more to human intelligence than the pure cognitive system, and that a science of Cognition cannot afford to ignore these other aspects" (Norman, 1980, p. 4). Prominent among these other aspects were emotion and motivation. And, here too attention was drawn to Freud's efforts to understand the linkages between emotions or motivation and thought.

FIGURE 14.14 **SUMMARY OF STRENGTHS AND LIMITATIONS OF A COGNITIVE, INFORMATION PROCESSING APPROACH TO PERSONALITY**

STRENGTHS	LIMITATIONS
1. Ties its approach to work in experimental cognitive psychology.	1. Has yet to achieve an integrated theory of personality.
2. Defines concepts clearly and makes them accessible to experimental investigation.	2. Neglects affect and motivation as important correlates and determinants of cognition.
3. Considers some important aspects of human personality functioning (e.g., how people represent other people, situations, events, and themselves).	3. Neglects individual differences and the organization of cognitive processes.

The cognitive, information-processing approach to personality is still early in its development. There are clear signs that psychologists working in this area are becoming concerned about the relation of emotions and motivation to thinking. However, how far they will be able to come to grips with these issues while retaining this model remains to be seen. In the meantime, we can recognize the contributions of this approach to the field while remaining guarded in our optimism concerning its future success.

MAJOR CONCEPTS AND SUMMARY

implicit personality theory	locus of causality
prototype	intuitive social scientist
script	self-schemata
self-monitoring	

In this chapter we considered material from the information-processing revolution in psychology. The analogy has been made to a computer that takes in (encodes), stores, organizes, and retrieves information. By using the concepts and research methods of experimental cognitive psychologists, personality psychologists have attempted to explore how people organize and utilize information concerning their own experiences and behaviors. Three things in particular distinguish this approach to personality from others we have considered. (1) The theory uses a model based on computer functioning; (2) it is not truly a theory of personality but rather an approach to conceptualization and research; (3) it is more clearly tied to other parts of psychology (cognitive and social) than is true for the more clinical theories of personality presented earlier in the text.

Given the diversity of people and behavior about us we are required to organize the relevant information to provide some structure and stability to our interpersonal world. The organization of this information is called our implicit theory of personality or conceptualization of the personality characteristics that people have and how these characteristics are organized. Research in the area of person perception and implicit personality theory has considered the kinds of categories people use in perceiving others, how these categories are formed, and the utility of these categories generally as well as the utility of categories at differing levels of abstraction. In general, it has been found that we organize information concerning both physical objects and people in terms of categories with shared patterns of characteristics and assign people we meet to membership in a category according to the match of their characteristics with those defining a specific category. This assignment process may be facilitated by some representation of a prototype for that category. Difficulties arise because of the fuzziness of boundary categories so that we may meet people who are hybrids or do not easily fit into one or another category. The categories we use are arranged in a hierarchical fashion similar in some ways to the type, trait, and behavior hierarchy suggested by trait theorists. Categories at varying levels have different strengths and limitations with middle-level categories striking a balance between being economical yet rich in detail.

Discussion of how we organize information relevant to situations followed a similar theme. There is evidence that people categorize situations in a hierarchical fashion so as to make information manageable and to make the world predictable. People differ in the situation categories they form, in the organization of these categories, and in the characteristics they use to define the categories. Each person appears to perceive a unique pattern of stability and change in behavior in relation to different categories of situations. Situations differ in how constraining or scripted they are; individuals differ in how attentive they are to situational cues concerning appropriate behavior. People who are very attentive to such situation cues are called high self-monitors and contrasted with low self-monitors who rely more upon internal cues and who tend to be consistent in their behavior from situation to situation.

The third area considered was that of the organization of information concerning events, in particular how we go about attributing causes to events. Here the person is viewed as an intuitive social scientist trying to gather and organize data that will be useful in making comprehensible and predictable events in the world about them. People appear to be concerned with whether events are caused from within or from without (locus of causality) and whether causes are stable or unstable. Thus, people distinguish between events due to ability, effort, task difficulty, and chance or luck. Such causal attributions are important for understanding a wide range of phenomena including motivation, stereotypes, and superstitions. While necessary and useful for daily living, these cognitive organizations and inference processes sometimes lead us to erroneous conclusions. It is suggested that many such phenomena otherwise attributed to motivational forces can better be understood as products of information-processing errors.

Finally, we have considered how people organize information concerning the self and the implications of these organizations. Cognitive structures concerning the self have been called self-schemata. There is evidence that people develop such categories or concepts, probably partly through the observation of their own behavior, and that once developed they have a powerful influence on what is observed or encoded and what is remembered. People are particularly sensitive to self-relevant information and memory is facilitated when information is associated with self-schemata. In addition, there appears to be a bias toward accepting information confirmatory of existent self-schemata as opposed to disconfirmatory information. It is again suggested that many errors people make in relation to self-relevant information are better understood in terms of everyday cognitive processes rather than in terms of motivational principles such as the need for self-esteem.

The content and concepts emphasized by cognitive personality psychologists are similar in some ways to that emphasized by Kelly and Rogers. However, the latter were more influenced by clinical work and were more concerned with the study of individual differences. In contrast, cognitive personality psychologists have borrowed more from the work of cognitive and social psychologists and focused more on general principles of cognitive functioning established primarily through laboratory research. Such a focus results in certain gains and strengths for the cognitive, information processing approach to personality. It allows psychologists who follow this approach to investigate important phenomena (i.e., how we organize the world about us and within us) in a systematic fashion that is related to the work being done by psychologists in other fields. It also calls attention to the enormous capacity people have for differentiating among events and for organizing information in varying ways. However, this approach has been criticized for using a model, that of the computer, that is not only limiting but misleading and for neglecting the importance of such critical human phenomena as affect and motivation.

©Alice Brickner.

AN OVERVIEW OF PERSONALITY THEORY, ASSESSMENT, AND RESEARCH

CHAPTER FOCUS: In this chapter we return to some of the major points covered in this book and consider the different theories of personality in relation to them. Our goal is a deeper understanding of the issues and, through the process of contrast and comparison, a greater appreciation of the theories. First, there is a return to some of the issues that divide personality theorists. Second, there is an overview of the concepts emphasized by each theory as it attempts to explain the what, how, and why of human behavior. Finally, attention is again drawn to relationships among theory, assessment, and research. Throughout the emphasis is on recognizing the distinctive contributions each approach can make toward a more complete understanding of human behavior.

Views about human nature influence which aspects of psychological functioning are studied most thoroughly and which remain unexamined. Theoretical conceptions similarly determine the paradigms used to collect evidence which, in turn, shape the particular theory. Limiting the scope of scientific inquiry to certain psychological processes to the neglect of other important ones can reinforce a truncated image of the human potential.

Bandura, 1977a, p. vi

This book has been an adventure into a greater understanding of why people behave as they do and how we may, in the future, proceed toward a clearer understanding of this behavior. The major focus has been on how different theories of personality conceptualize human behavior. There has been, as well, discussion of alternative approaches to assessment and research. Finally, we have considered relationships among types of theories, assessment techniques, and styles of conducting research; in other words, how different theories of personality may lead to the study of different aspects of personality functioning and the use of different means for gathering data. In this final chapter, let us take stock of some of the ground that has been covered and consider some of the issues that remain open.

A RETURN TO SOME ISSUES THAT DIVIDE PERSONALITY THEORISTS

In the first chapter we considered some issues that divide personality theorists. It was suggested that personality theorists repeatedly have confronted certain basic issues. Their solutions to these issues in part reflected their own life experiences as well as social and scientific trends current at the time of their work. Beyond this, it was suggested that theoretical positions on these issues affected which aspects of human functioning were chosen for investigation and how these aspects of human functioning were investigated. Let us briefly return to these issues in the light of previous study of the major theoretical orientations current today.

Philosophical View of the Person

We have seen that implicit in most theories of personality is a general, philosophical view of human nature. Periodically an article or book appears in the literature that addresses this issue in clear and forthright terms. For example, one distinguished psychologist recently called for an increased emphasis on a view of humans as active, selecting, choosing organisms as opposed to a view of humans as passive organisms responding in a mechanical way to stimuli: "Individuals create themselves . . . it is development we must study, but it is the development of the shaper rather than the shaped" (Tyler, 1978, pp. 233–234).

The theorists covered in this text present a diversity of views: Freud's view of the person as an energy system; Rogers' view of the person as a self-actualizing organism; Kelly's view of the person as a scientist; the Skinnerian view of the person as responding to environmental reinforcement contingencies; the cognitive, social learning view of the person as a problem-solving organism; the computer model of the person as a complex information processor. Of course, other views are possible—and within any singie orientation, such as trait theory, different views can emerge. Furthermore, such lables or capsule descriptions fail to do justice to the complexity inherent in each view. At the same time, these capsule descriptions capture a distinctive element in each theoretical perspective and help to make us aware of the differing views that do exist. Of particular interest here is the emphasis on cognition found in so many recent theoretical developments (psychoanalytic ego psychology, cognitive behavior modification, cognitive social learning theory, and cognitive information processing personality theory).

Each view of the organism opens up certain avenues of thought, research, and analysis. Each also potentially closes off other important lines of emphasis and investigation. The early S–R view of the person inhibited recognition of the importance of higher-order cognitive functions. The current cognitive emphasis may serve to correct this imbalance, but it may also lead us to ignore other important areas of experience such as motivation and emotion. The point here is not that one view is right or wrong but that such views exist and that it is important to be aware of them in understanding each theory as well as in assessing its strengths and limitations.

Internal and External Causes of Behavior

A second, related issue, is whether the causes of behavior are inside the person or in the environment. In Chapter 1 Freud and Skinner were contrasted as representing extreme positions on this issue. There was also discussion of how in recent years attention was first directed to *whether* behavior is caused by the "person" or the "situation," then to *how much* behavior was caused by person and situation factors, and finally to *how* person and situation factors interact with one another to determine behavior.

In the theories covered, this issue came out most clearly in relation to trait theory and social learning theory. At one extreme, trait theory has been characterized as suggesting that people are consistent or stable in their behavior over time and across situations. Psychoanalytic theory, with its similar emphasis on personality structure, has been seen as emphasizing internal causes of behavior and general stability in personality functioning. At the other extreme, learning theory has been characterized as emphasizing environmental determinants of behavior and the variability or situational specificity of behavior. Such characterizations are to some extent accurate and useful in highlighting important theoretical differences. At the same time, it should be clear that none of these theories emphasizes only one set of causes. To a certain extent, they are all interactionist in their emphasis; they all emphasize the interaction between individual and environment, or person and situation, in determining behavior. Trait theory, for example, does recognize the importance of situational factors in affecting which traits are activated as well as affecting the moods of the individual. It is inconceivable that a trait theorist or a psychoanalytic theorist would expect a person to behave the same way in all situations. On the other hand, social learning theory recognizes the importance of person factors in terms of concepts such as plans–goals, cognitive and behavioral competencies, self-efficacy, and self-regulation. Indeed, most recently the concept of reciprocal determinism or the mutually causal relationship between person and situation has become a cornerstone of social learning theory.

As with other issues in the field, emphasis often shifts in one direction or another—in this case in terms of relative emphasis on internal, person factors or on external, environmental factors. At one point considerable evidence was presented to suggest that human behavior is quite variable over time and across situations. Such evidence was used to challenge traditional trait and psychodynamic views of personality structure and personality dispositions (Mischel, 1968). More recently, evidence has been presented to suggest that human behavior is more consistent, both over time and across situations, than had been suggested previously (Epstein, 1979, 1983; Olweus, 1980). Such consistency does not seem to be be explained by unchanged environmental circumstances. Indeed, we often are impressed with how resistant some behavior is to change despite dramatic changes in environmental circumstances. Thus, whereas at one point situational determinants were emphasized, many psychologists are again emphasizing "dispositions or reaction tendencies within the individuals, however conceptualized" (Olweus, 1979, p. 14).

While important differences remain in the relative emphasis on internal (person) and external (situation) causes, all theories of personality recognize that both are important in understanding behavior. Perhaps we can now expect to find theorists who increasingly will address questions in terms of both sets of causes rather than with an almost exclusive emphasis on one or another set of causes. All personality theorists recognize that there is both consistency and variability to individual behavior. The task, then, is to account for the pattern of stability and change that characterizes people (Pervin, 1983).

The Unity of Behavior and the Concept of the Self

There is movement in human organisms, as living systems, toward integrated functioning and the reduction of conflict. Personality theories differ in the extent to which they emphasize the patterned, unified, system aspects of human functioning and efforts toward the reduction of conflict. An emphasis on the unity of behavior may be seen to be greatest in the clinical theories of Freud, Rogers, and Kelly. With the exception of Allport, it is much less present in trait theories and learning theories. Why should this be? Undoubtedly the reasons are complex and varied, but a number of points can be considered. First, clinical theories are based on observations of many behaviors of a single individual. The theories of Freud, Rogers, and Kelly evolved out of these clinical observations. Their efforts were directed toward understanding relationships among thoughts, behaviors, and feelings. Almost of necessity, they were struck with the issues of conflict and threats to the coherence of the system as reported to them by their patients. While clinical approaches based on learning theory exist and are important, they evolved out of theories rather than initially serving as the basis for them. In fact, it is probably true that as clinical approaches based on learning theory have developed they have increasingly emphasized the complexity and system aspects of human functioning.

A second point to be considered is the emphasis in trait theories, at least those based on factor analysis, and in learning theories on the systematic exploration of particular variables. The belief here is that an understanding of human behavior can come through the systematic study of particular variables or processes and then consideration of complex relationships among variables and processes. The strategy is to study phenomena systematically and to build from the simple to the complex. Pattern and organization become important when one has a clear enough grasp of the parts that constitute the pattern or organization.

The concept of self traditionally has been used to give expression to the patterned, organized aspects of personality functioning. In psychoanalytic theory, the concept of ego gives expression to the person's self-experiencing as well as to the "executive" or integrative aspects of system functioning. While sometimes portrayed as a person or homunculus inside the individual ("The ego seeks to reduce conflict"), it really is descriptive of processes going on within the person. For both Rogers and Kelly the concept of self played an important integrative function. For Rogers, the person seeks self-actualization and to make the self and experience congruent with one another. For Kelly, the constructs associated with the self and how they are organized play a central role in the person's functioning. The emphasis on the concept of self as an organizing entity is perhaps most clearly expressed in the view of Allport. The concept of self, or proprium as he called it, gave testimony to the complex, organized aspects of the mature human system.

In their efforts to avoid the vague, romantic, and fanciful, learning theorists traditionally have avoided the concept of self. In particular, the self as a homunculus within the person that determines action has been criticized. Still, as we have witnessed, recent developments in social learning theory place heavy emphasis on the concept of self. This is a somewhat different concept of self, however, involving standards for self-praise and self-criticism as well as other self-regulatory functions. Nevertheless, it is a self concept. The concept of efficacy, or ability to perform the behavior necessary for certain outcomes, an increasingly important part of Bandura's theory, involves cognitions or beliefs about the self. It is seen as a broadly integrative concept that can account for diverse findings. Thus, at this point cognitive social learning theory also has come to emphasize both the organized aspects of the human personality and the importance of the self concept in such organization. Finally, the organizing and directing functions of self-schemata are clearly articulated in the cognitive information-processing view. Just as any complex system may have higher-order control units, so the self may be viewed as consisting of schemata or constructs that organize and integrate the functioning of other parts of the system.

While the utility and necessity of the concept of self continues to be debated, theories of personality appear to be drawn to it continuously. Interpretations of it clearly differ from theory to theory, and theories differ in their emphasis on it. At the same time, in one form or another, the concept of self enters into most theories and attests to the important ways in which we experience ourselves, to the myriad ways in which we understand ourselves, and to the organized aspects of our functioning.

Varying States of Awareness and the Concept of the Unconscious

Interest in varying states of awareness and altered states of consciousness has been increasing in psychology. This probably is due in part to interest in "mind-expanding" drugs during the 1960s and to the broader interest in brain functioning. Such phenomena are fascinating, yet they represent complex problems for theory, assessment, and research.

As noted at the outset, many theorists are uncomfortable with the concept of the unconscious as formulated by Freud. The notion of things "buried in the unconscious" or of "unconscious forces striving for expression" is too metaphorical for most systematic thinkers. Yet, if we accept the view that we are not always aware of factors affecting our behavior, how are we to conceptualize such phenomena? Is it merely that we do not attend to them and that focusing of our attention "brings them into awareness?" Is it the case, as some learning theorists suggest, that what others view as unconscious processes actually consist of rehearsed behaviors that flow automatically, that they consist of overlearned inhibited responses (Mischel, 1976, p. 434)? In other words, is there no need to consider special processes and label them as unconscious; rather, we can say that we do not think of certain things because there are stronger responses inhibiting such thoughts?

As we have seen, both Rogers and Kelly avoided the concept of the unconscious. Instead, they emphasized concepts that involve aspects of the person's functioning which are not available to awareness. Rogers stated the view that experiences incongruent with the self concept may be distorted and/or denied. Threatening feelings may be unavailable to awareness but experienced through the process of subception. Kelly suggested that one or both poles of a construct may be submerged and unavailable to awareness. Each of these theories describes a defensive process resulting in important aspects of personality functioning being unavailable to awareness. Though learning theorists such as Dollard and Miller accepted such processes and attempted to interpret them within the framework of Hullian theory, other learning theorists reject such concepts as vague and unnecessary. Although initially expressing little interest in unconscious processes, cognitive theorists have recently been concerned with them—albeit not necessarily in the terms suggested by psychoanalytic theorists.

The problem of evaluating the importance of such phenomena and conceptualizing them continues to be with us. If much of our behavior is governed by reinforcements, both from within ourselves as well as from others, are we always aware of what these reinforcers are? If not, why not? Is it because some of them were learned in infancy, prior to the development of verbal labels? Is it because some are so much a part of our daily lives that we no longer attend to them? Or is it because often we "choose" not to be aware of things that make us anxious and uncomfortable? How much attention is paid to these phenomena and how they are interpreted continue to be important issues upon which theories of personality differ.

Relationships among Cognition, Affect, and Overt Behavior

As we have seen, personality theories differ in the attention given to cognitive, affective, and behavioral processes. Understanding the intricate relations among them remains a significant task. Although Freud emphasized cognitive and drive processes, he assigned a central role to affects in his conceptualization of human behavior. This is seen most clearly in relation to the affect of anxiety, but he and his followers also were concerned with other affects such as anger, depression, guilt, shame, jealousy, and so on. There is interest in overt behavior but only as an expression or manifestation of the workings of thought and drive processes. Rogers and Kelly both emphasized the person as an active construer of events, but for Rogers the "felt experience" was central whereas for Kelly emotions followed from cognitive interpretations. The latter emphasis also is found in current attribution and other cognitive theories. In these theories cognitive properties are central and primary to feelings and overt behavior. Radical behaviorism, of course, focused exclusively on overt behavior. However, behavior therapists increasingly have become concerned with cognitive processes and, even more recently, with the influences of affective processes.

Historically, many issues in psychology initially get framed in either–or terms. Is it heredity or environment? Person or situation? Then there is debate about which is more important. Finally, there is recognition that the issues are more complex than "either–or", "more important than" solutions. There is recognition that multiple factors enter into complex functioning, the individual factors contributing to a greater or lesser amount at different times and in different situations. The critical question then becomes one of understanding relationships among variables rather than choosing among them. Thus, the question becomes how heredity and environment interact and how person and situation variables mutually affect one another. In a similar vein, we are coming to understand that people are always thinking, feeling, and behaving and what remains to be understood is how these processes interact in the ongoing stream of human functioning.

Influences of the Past, Present, and Future on Behavior

When we think of Freud, we almost automatically think of behavior being governed by the past. When we think of Kelly, we think of the person as striving to anticipate the future. Prediction becomes the key to understanding behavior. Skinner's emphasis on past reinforcement contingencies can be contrasted with social learning theory's emphasis on expectancies. Is behavior regulated by the past or by our expectations of the future? Is there a difference between the two?

This is yet another issue that divides personality theorists. Often the differences among theorists are subtle but important in their implications. For example, Bandura's suggestion that past reinforcements are important for what has been *learned* but that expectancies about future reinforcement are important for what is *performed* is a subtle but important distinction. It involves not only the important distinction between the acquisition and the performance of behavior but also an important emphasis on cognitive functioning. In fact, there appears to be a close relationship between an emphasis on the future and an emphasis on cognitive processes. This is not surprising, since the development of higher mental processes and the capacity for language are necessary for an organism to be able to construct a future world.

In reality, of course, past events and our anticipation of future events affect one another as well as our experiences in the present. How we anticipate the future is inevitably linked to our past. However, it is probably also the case that how we view the future influences our construction of the past. For example, if we are depressed about the future we may feel bound by our past, whereas if we are optimistic about the future we may perceive the past as having been liberating. Our views of the past, present, and future are all parts of our experience. An understanding of the relationships among these views, then, becomes the task of each theory of personality.

PERSONALITY THEORY AS AN ANSWER TO THE QUESTIONS OF WHAT, HOW, AND WHY

In Chapter 1 it was stated that a theory of personality should answer the questions of *what, how*, and *why*. In the chapters on Freud, Rogers, Kelly, trait theory, learning theory, and social learning theory, the concepts and principles used to account for human personality were considered. A summary of some of the major concepts relevant to each theory is given in Figure 15.1. At this point, let us review some of these concepts, consider the similarities among the theories, and raise some remaining questions.

Personality Structure

Each theory that has been studied here suggests concepts relevant to the structure of personality; each theory presents conceptual units that can be used to describe individuals. The theories differ not only in the content of these units but also in their level of abstraction and in the complexity of the structural organization. Freud's structural units are at a very high level of abstraction. One cannot observe an id, ego, or superego, or a conscious, preconscious, or unconscious. Somewhat less abstract are the structural units used by Rogers and Kelly. Many problems remain in current definitions of the self, but the definitions offered by Rogers do suggest some methods of systematic investigation. Similarly, although the defining properties of constructs need to be clarified further, a technique for assessing the construct system of an individual is available to us.

The structural units of Cattell vary in their level of abstraction, with source traits being more abstract than surface traits. At the lowest level of abstraction is the major structural unit used by learning theorists to describe behavior—the response. Whether it refers to a simple reflex or a complex behavior, the response is always external and observable. It is defined by the behavior. In this case, one does not go from the specific act to an abstract structural unit. The act itself is the structural unit. Instead of being internal to the organism and only indirectly observable, the response is part of the observable behavior of the organism.

Social learning theory started with a similar emphasis on the overt, behavioral response. The units of the person were concrete, clearly defined, and objectively measured. Variations in response were tied to equally clearly defined and objectively measured variations in the environment. With the development of an emphasis on cognitive activities and self-regulatory behavior, however, there was a shift toward emphasis on more abstract structural units. Concepts such as standards, self-efficacy judgments, and goals or plans tend to be more abstract than the concept of a response. Furthermore, they require different tools of measurement and this has resulted in a defense of the use of verbal reports on the part of social learning theorists. At the same time, it should be clear that this movement toward an emphasis on different kinds of units has not lessened the concern for rigor, objectivity, and measurement. Social learning theorists continue to emphasize concepts that are clear in their meaning and specific in the appropriate

FIGURE 15.1 SUMMARY OF MAJOR THEORETICAL CONCEPTS

THEORIST OR THEORY	STRUCTURE	PROCESS	GROWTH AND DEVELOPMENT
FREUD	Id, ego, superego; unconscious, preconscious, conscious.	Life and death instincts; cathexes and anticathexes; anxiety and the mechanisms of defense.	Erogenous zones; oral, anal, phallic stages of development; Oedipus complex.
ROGERS	Self; ideal self	Self-actualization; congruence of self and experience; incongruence and defensive distortion and denial.	Congruence and self-actualization versus incongruence and defensiveness.
KELLY	Constructs	Processes channelized by anticipation of events.	Increased complexity and definition to construct system.
CATTEL	Traits	Attitudes; motives; ergs; sentiments.	Multiple abstract variance analysis (MAVA); age trends.
LEARNING THEORY	Response	Classical conditioning; instrumental conditioning; operant conditioning.	Imitation; schedules of reinforcement and successive approximations.
SOCIAL LEARNING THEORY	Expectancies; standards; goals–plans; self-efficacy	Observational learning; vicarious conditioning; symbolic processes, self-evaluative and self-regulatory processes.	Social learning through observation and direct experience; development of self-efficacy judgments and standards for self-regulation.

PATHOLOGY	CHANGE	ILLUSTRATIVE CASE
Infantile sexuality; fixation and regression; conflict; symptoms.	Transference; conflict resolution; ''Where id was, ego shall be.''	Little Hans
Defensive maintenance of self; incongruence.	Therapeutic atmosphere: congruence, unconditional positive regard, empathic understanding.	Mrs. Oak
Disordered functioning of construct system.	Psychological reconstruction of life; invitational mood; fixed-role therapy.	Ronald Barrett
Heredity and environment; conflict; anxiety.	Change in trait structure.	Jim Hersh
Maladaptive learned response patterns.	Extinction; discrimination learning; counter-conditioning; positive reinforcement; imitation; systematic desensitization; behavior modification.	Peter; Joey
Learned response patterns; excessive self-standards; problems in self-efficacy.	Modeling; guided participation; increased self-efficacy.	Reinterpretation of bombardier case.

method of measurement. This is equally true for psychologists emphasizing cognitive, information-processing approaches. These psychologists, often associated with social learning theorists, emphasize concepts such as attributions and schemata that are measured in systematic ways.

In addition to differences in their level of abstraction, theories also differ in the complexity of structural organization. This complexity may be considered in terms of the number of units involved and whether they are formed in some kind of *hierarchial arrangement* in relation to one another. Cattell's theory clearly involves a complex structural organization of personality. Not only are there many units but here is also a hierarchical arrangement of these units into surface traits, source traits, and second-order factors (types). Similarly, Eysenck emphasizes a hierarchical organization of structural units, starting with responses at the lowest level and progressing on up to habits, traits, and types. Kelly's system allows for a complex system of constructs—one in which there are many constructs, some superordinate and others subordinate. However, the complexity of organization is viewed as varying considerably with the individual personality. The psychoanalytic framework includes many structural units and almost unlimited possibilities for interrelationships among the units. Although no clear hierarchical structure is set forth, the concept of personality types clearly indicate layers of organization beyond that of specific behaviors.

In contrast to such a complexity of personality structure is the fairly simple structure described by most learning theorists. There are few categories of responses, no suggestion that behavior generally involves the expression of many units at the same time, and a definite bias against the concept of personality types, which implies a stable organization of many different responses. Indeed, it may again be noted that the social learning theorist Mischel was particularly critical of trait and psychoanalytic theories for their emphasis on a hierarchical organization of personality. Cognitive theory, particularly in its emphasis on category formation and prototypes, should provide for a hierarchical view of the organization of personality. However, this has not been the case since cognitive psychologists typically have been interested in information processing rather than in the structural organization of personality.

These differences in levels of abstraction and complexity of structural organization can be related to differences in the general importance attached to structure in behavior. The concept of structure generally is used to account for the more stable aspects of personality and for the consistency of individual behavior over time and over situations. To consider two extremes: psychoanalytic theory places great emphasis on the stability of behavior over time, whereas learning theory does not; psychoanalytic theory places great emphasis on the consistency of behavior across situations, whereas learning theory does not; psychoanalytic theory places great emphasis on individual differences, whereas learning theory does not. At one extreme, psychoanalytic theory involves abstract units and a complex structural organization. At the other extreme, learning theory involves concrete units and little emphasis on the organization of these units. In other words, there appears to be a relationship between the importance attributed to structure by a theory and the theory's emphasis on stability and consistency in human behavior.

Process

In our review of theories of personality, the major conceptions in psychology concerning the "why" of behavior have been identified. As indicated in Chapter 1, many theories of motivation emphasize the efforts on the part of the individual to *reduce tension*. The push toward tension reduction is clearly indicated in psychoanalytic theory, in Cattell's theory, and in Hull's approach to learning theory. For Freud, the individual's efforts are directed toward expressing the sexual and aggressive instincts and, thereby, toward the reduction of the tension associated with these instincts. For Cattell, the individual is directed toward the expression of attitudes, at the basis of which are the ergs and the energy associated with them. For Hull, and for Dollard and Miller, reinforcement is associated with the satisfaction of primary or secondary drives and, thereby, with the reduction of drive-induced tension.

Rogers' theory gives expression to the motivational model suggesting that individuals often *seek tension*. Rogers suggests that individuals seek self-actualization, that they want to grow and to realize their inner potentials even at the cost of increased tension. However, Rogers also places emphasis on a third motivational force—*consistency*. The particular kind of consistency emphasized by Rogers is a congruence between self and experience. For Kelly, who also emphasizes consistency, the relevant variables are different. According to Kelly, it is important that the individual's constructs be consistent with one another, so that the predictions from one do not cancel out the predictions from another. It is also important that predictions be consistent with experiences, or, in other words, that events confirm and validate the construct system.

Although operant learning theory and social learning theory both emphasize the importance of reinforcement, they do not do so in terms of drive reduction as happens in Hullian stimulus–response theory. For Skinner reinforcements affect the probability of a response, but there is no use of an internal concept of drive or tension. In social learning theory the emphasis is on cognitive processes and the development of expectancies. Reinforcers are critical for performance but not for the acquisition of behavior. Expectancies concerning reinforcement guide and direct behavior. In this way they serve a motivational function. In a sense, the person is oriented toward accurate prediction, in Kelly's terms, but it is specifically the fulfillment of expectancies concerning positive reinforcement. In a related way, information-processing theorists suggest that many aspects of human performance attributed to motivational factors may, in fact, be better understood as the consequence of using particular cognitive strategies or heuristics.

Notice that these motivational models are only in conflict with one another if we assume that all behavior must follow the same motivational principles. In relation to structure, we need not assume that the individual only has drives, that one only has a concept of the self, or that one only has personal constructs. In the same way, we need not assume that the individual is always reducing tension, or always striving toward actualization, or always seeking consistency. It may be that all three models of motivation have something to say about human behavior. An individual may at some points be functioning so as to reduce tension, at other times so as to actualize the self, and at other times to achieve cognitive consistency. Another possibility is that, at one time, two kinds of motivation are operating, but they are in conflict with one another. For example, the individual may seek to relieve aggressive urges through hitting someone but also have fond feelings for the person involved and view this behavior as "out of character." A third possibility is that two kinds of motivation may combine to operate in support of one another. Thus, to make love to someone can represent the reduction of tension from sexual urges, an actualizing expression of the self, and an act consistent with the self-concept and with predictions from one's construct system. If room is left for more than one process model, it becomes the task of psychologists to define the conditions under which each type of motivation will occur and the ways in which the different types of motivation can combine to determine behavior. At the same time, we must be careful not to feel compelled to account for all behavior in terms of motivation. Certain processes are best understood in terms of their own characteristics, without necessarily bringing other explanatory principles into play.

Growth and Development

In Chapter 1 we considered the causes of personality—cultural, social class, familial, and genetic. None of the theories studied really gives adequate attention to the variety of factors that determine growth and development. Cattell has done important work on the influences of heredity and environment, and on age trends in personality development. Psychoanalytic theory gives attention to the role of biological and environmental factors in personality development, but in most cases this remains speculative. It is disappointing that Rogers and Kelly have so little to say in this area. Finally, although the learning theorists have done a great deal to interpret the processes through which cultural, social class, and familial influences are transmitted, there has been a serious neglect of biological factors. Also, until recently learning theorists tended to give insufficient attention to the important area of cognitive growth and development. Important contributions are, however, now being made by social learning theorists. For example, Bandura has been doing research on the development of memory codes or symbols in observational learning and Mischel has been researching how children develop methods for tolerating increased delays in reinforcement. As personality psychologists increasingly emphasize cognitive variables, they are able to incorporate into their work the considerable body of research and theory devoted to cognitive development.

In considering the theorists covered in the text, differences concerning two questions about development become apparent. The first concerns the utility of the concept of stages of development and the second concerns the importance of early experiences for later personality development. Psychoanalytic theory attaches great importance to the concept of stages of development, and Cattell's work on age trends suggests that certain periods are critical for the formation of different traits. It is also true that psychoanalytic theory places the greatest emphasis on the early years of growth and development. There is impressive evidence that the early years are important for many personality characteristics. More specifically, the research suggests that the effects of the environment are greatest at the time of rapid change in a personality characteristic (Bloom, 1964; Scott, 1968). Since change and development are most rapid for many personality characteristics during the early years, it is during these years that environmental forces exert their greatest impact. This is not to say that the early years are critical for every characteristic. Different characteristics have different developmental curves, and for some the period of most rapid development may be during the teens or even later in life. Nor is this to suggest that the effects of early experiences are permanent. However, generally, the early environment is of critical importance. This is true because often it is a period of rapid growth and because what is learned during these years sets the stage for later learning.

An understanding of the critical ages for different developments in personality is essential for theoretical progress and for progress in our efforts to correct various arrests in growth. Since, generally, it is not possible to make resources available to children over the course of many years, it would be extremely valuable to know at which ages the commitment of human resources would most make a difference. For example, if we are interested in the development of certain cognitive skills that develop most rapidly in prepuberty, the commitment of human resources to preschool children may be wasteful. On the other hand, if we know that the initial period for the development of an ability is between the ages of six and eight, the commitment of resources to children of a later age will nct represent the most effective use of these resources.

Psychopathology

The forces producing psychopathology are interpreted differently by the theorists. However, the concept of conflict is essential to a number of them. This is most clearly the case in psychoanalytic theory. According to Freud, psychopathology occurs when the instinctive urges of the id come into conflict with the functioning of the ego. Cattell holds a similar view, emphasizing the importance of conflict between a drive that has been stimulated and some force that is blocking it. It already has been observed that, although Rogers does not emphasize the importance of conflict, one can interpret the problem of incongruence in terms of a conflict between experience and the self-concept. Although learning theory offers a number of explanations for psychopathology, at least one of these explanations emphasizes the importance of approach–avoidance conflicts.

The concept of conflict makes sense as a relevant variable in psychopathology. However, there is a need for a greater distinction between frustration and conflict. A drive being blocked does not represent conflict, though this may lead to a conflict situation. A state of conflict exists where two or more incompatible forces are striving for expression at the same time. The parts of a system are in conflict if the gratification of one part is achieved at the cost of frustration of another part of the system. In contrast, in an integrated system the parts are either functioning independently of each other or are in harmony with one another. In the latter case, the achievement of a goal leads to a variety of kinds of gratification.

Many complex questions concerning psychopathology remain unanswered. For example, we know that cultures vary in the incidence of various forms of psychopathology. Depression is rare in Africa, but is common in the United States. Why? Conversion symptoms, such as hysterical paralysis of the arm or leg, were quite common in Freud's time but are observed much less frequently today. Why? Are there important differences in the problems that people in different cultures face? Or do they face the same problems but cope with them differently? Or is it just that some problems are more likely to be reported than others and that this varies with the individual culture? If people today are more concerned with problems of identity than with problems of guilt, if they are more concerned with the problem of finding meaning than of relieving sexual urges, what are the implications for psychoanalysis and the other theories of personality? Although each of the theories of personality can offer some explanation for suicide, do all seem equally plausible? Can any of the theories account for the fact that the suicide rate for college students is higher than that for individuals of comparable age who are not in college and higher than the one for any other age group?

We are at a point at which the whole question of the nature of psychopathology is under reexamination. Questions are being raised concerning the disease model of mental illness, the responsibilities of the person who is ill, and illness in society as opposed to illness in the individual. Whereas psychoanalytic theory suggests that someone is ill with a "sick personality," learning theory suggests that the individual has learned a maladaptive response. But how, within the scope of either of these theories, do we account for the prevalence of psychological disorders in current society? And how, within the scope of either of these theories, do we account for the situation wherein some seemingly maladaptive responses have, in reality, adaptive qualities? Thus, for example, in their book *Black Rage*, Grier and Cobbs (1968) describe how the mistrustful, almost paranoid behavior of many blacks is based on reality and has adaptive qualities. The answers to questions like these go beyond the theories of personality we have considered, but they are relevant to them.

Change

An analysis of the change concepts of the theorists suggests that, in some cases, the point of focus for one is different from that for another. For example, the following questions concerning change are given varying amounts of attention by each theorist: What is changed? What are the conditions for change? What is the process in change?

Psychoanalytic theory, in its emphasis on changes in the relationship between the unconscious and the conscious and between the ego and the id, is particularly concerned with structural change. Kelly, in his analysis of psychotherapy as the psychological reconstruction of life, is also concerned with structural change. In contrast, Rogers is most concerned with the conditions that make change possible. Although in his research he has attended to structural change (for example, changes in self–ideal-self discrepancy), this has been for the purpose of having a criterion against which he could measure the effectiveness of different variables (for example, congruence, unconditional positive regard, empathic understanding). Kelly pointed out the importance of an atmosphere of experimentation and invitational mood, but there is little research to suggest the variables critical in establishing this atmosphere or mood. Psychoanalysts have been quite concerned with the quality of the transference relationship as it affects change, but this has been, for the most part, from a practical standpoint and has had little impact on the theory as a whole.

The process of change is a particular focus of convenience for learning theory. The following learning processes are used to account for a wide range of changes related to a variety of forms of psychotherapy: extinction, discrimination learning, counterconditioning, positive reinforcement, imitation. Whereas, initially, learning concepts were used to explain treatment effects associated with other theories, more recently these concepts have been used in the development of learning-based treatment methods. This development of technique out of a theory of the process of change is healthy. A clear illustration of therapeutic technique as an outgrowth of theory is Bandura's work on modeling and guided participation. It is also interesting to note here that while therapy or psychological change has not been a major aspect of social learning theory, it is becoming an increasingly important part of it. In fact, Bandura suggests that developments in this area may well serve as a test of the theory generally. In contrast, many aspects of psychoanalysis and Rogerian therapy are based on earlier developments in these theories and do not represent direct outgrowths from them. For example, the basic structure of psychoanalysis and emphasis on free association and dream interpretation remained the same despite major changes in the theory itself.

There are, of course, basic and important differences in the theories concerning the potential for change. At one extreme would be psychoanalytic theory, which suggests that fundamental personality change is quite difficult. This view is related to the psychoanalytic emphasis on structure and the importance of early experiences. If structure is important and is developed early in life, it follows that basic change later in life is difficult. Many of the early learning theorists (e.g., Hull, Dollard, Miller), particularly those who attempted to relate learning theory to psychoanalytic theory, were similarly pessimistic about the potential for change. However, the more recent developments in operant conditioning, social learning theory, and cognitive behavior therapy have led to much greater optimism for change. These theorists place little emphasis on structure and great emphasis on the potential to change behavior. With faith in their ability to shape behavior through the manipulation of external rewards, the behavior modificationists are at the other extreme from psychoanalysts.

Change, of course, is not limited to psychotherapy—it occurs at all levels and to varying degrees. Consider, for example, the following description of changes in a professional hockey player whose fortunes have risen and declined:

> *As Gilbert stayed at home earlier this season, with little to do but consider his future, he saw that his entire personality was changing. "I didn't have any patience at all," Gilbert said. "I realized not a long time ago I was reacting like it was not me. I'm always the type of guy who will laugh all the time. I don't worry about nothing."*
>
> *"I was acting like I was always angry," he said. "It seemed like everything was bothering me. I was thinking too much about retiring. I love to play with my kids. I would sit at the table and say, 'Don't do that. Don't do this.' It was bad. I think I'm a great father, but all of a sudden I changed, day and night. My wife said, 'If you keep going that way, what will they think? You've changed so much.'"*

New York Times, December 4, 1982, p. 10

In considering the question of how people change, we again recognize the extent to which theories of personality emphasize different processes of change, different conditions for change, and change in different aspects of personality functioning. Some of these differences may well represent competing and conflicting points of view; others, various terms for similar processes. Finally, some differences may result from attending to different aspects of the person. Sorting these out represents a task for both students and professionals in the field.

RELATIONSHIPS AMONG THEORY, ASSESSMENT, AND RESEARCH

At various times in this book, theory, assessment, and research have been considered separately. However, throughout, the attempt has been made to keep in mind the intimate relationships among the three. Indeed, this has been a major theme throughout the book.

In Chapter 1, theory as an attempt to fit together and explain a wide variety of facts with a few assumptions was considered. In Chapter 2 the tools that personality psychologists use to observe and measure behavior in a systematic way were discussed. It is clear that research involves the use of assessment techniques to develop and test theory. What of the relationships among theory, assessment, and research? Here we can note a relationship between the assumptions basic to theories and the techniques of assessment generally associated with these theories. For example, a psychodynamic theory such as psychoanalysis is associated with the Rorschach, a phenomenological theory such as that of Rogers with the interview and measures of the self-concept, a factor analytic theory such as that of Cattell with psychometric tests, and a learning theory approach with objective tests. Do different theories of personality tend to lead to different techniques of assessment and to different kinds of observations about individuals? Are such differences in theory and assessment then also related to strategies for research, leading to clinical and experimental attitudes? To what extent are these theories associated with a greater or lesser emphasis on naturalistic observation, questionnaire research, or laboratory experimentation?

The clinical approach emphasizes dynamics, individual differences, the entire personality, the history of the individual, flexibility in observation, prediction from an understanding of the individual, and theory that postulates internal processes and allows for concepts that cannot be verified directly. "Theoretical issues require the retention of some variables that cannot be quantified with any elegance whatsoever. Similarly, if we in psychology turn away from the attempt to measure unconscious motives, for example, because of the fact that this can't be done today with demonstrable reliability or validity, this vitally important area of personality will be neglected" (Holt, 1962a, p. 274). The experimental approach emphasizes consistency across individuals, changes in one or two responses under various experimental conditions rather than the pattern of many responses, tends to be ahistorical, emphasizes rigor in experimental design and theoretical conceptualization, and allows for the use of animals as subjects. "We cannot attribute a principle learned from the study of rats to human conduct until we have also observed it operating in the human species. However, once we have done so, our rat experiment may have given us a more precise understanding of the principle involved because of the more adequate controls imposed" (Lundin, 1961, p. 47).

Do differences such as these exist among psychologists generally? In a study of the psychological value systems of psychologists, Thorndike (1954) obtained ratings from 200 psychologists on the contributions made by a number of outstanding people to psychology. An analysis of these ratings suggested two major dimensions along which the psychologists made their judgments. The first factor was labeled laboratory versus clinic, and indicated that some psychologists valued laboratory research, while others valued the clinical study of the individual. The second factor located by Thorndike was labeled psychometric versus verbal approach and distinguished between psychologists who value analytic study with psychometric (statistical) techniques and psychologists who value a global and typological approach to the study of behavior.

If indeed such a theme runs throughout the study of personality, to what can it be attributed? In his review of the history of psychology, Boring (1950) noted that over time the experimentalists became more technical and electronically oriented, while the clinicians did not. He went on to suggest that clinicians usually liked other people, whereas "the experimentalists often did not, preferring rats for subjects as being less embarrassing socially or at any rate more pliant, convenient and exploitable than human subjects" (Boring, 1950, p. 578). Boring concluded that the split may be a result of personality differences between members of the two orientations.

Clearly the emphasis here is not on whether one or another approach to theory, assessment, and research is right or wrong. Rather it is on the strengths and limitations of each and the relationships among the three. Is it not possible that different aspects of one's personality may be studied with greater or lesser accuracy with different assessment devices? Is it not possible that some phenomena can be observed quite easily in the laboratory while others cannot? Is it not possible that each assessment device and research approach has its own potential sources of error or bias? Should we not be aware that limiting ourselves to one approach to assessment and research may restrict our observations to phenomena directly relevant to a specific theoretical position? In such circumstances we may be led to confuse accuracy in a few predictions with more general aspects concerning the quality of a theory. It may be useful to be aware of restrictive relationships among theory, assessment, and research and also appreciative of the contributions that different theories, assessment devices, and research procedures can make to our understanding of human behavior.

A FINAL SUMMING UP

In a certain sense, every person is a psychologist. Every person develops a view of human nature and a strategy for predicting events. The theory and research presented in this book represent the efforts of psychologists to systematize what is known about human personality and to suggest areas for future exploration. The attempt has been to focus on similarities in what these psychologists have been trying to do and on differences in what they view as being the best mode of operation. Although psychologists as a group are more explicit about their view of the person than is the average layperson, and although they are more systematic in their efforts to understand and predict human behavior, there are individual differences among them. In this book the theories of many psychologists have been considered in detail. They represent major theories in the field today although not the only theories, and they are representative of the diversity of approach that can be considered reasonable and useful.

An effort has been made in this text to demonstrate that theory, assessment, and research are related to one another. In most cases some consistency can be found in the nature of theory proposed, the types of tests used to obtain data, and the problems suggested for investigation. A distinction was drawn between the psychologists who emphasize individual differences and those who emphasize general principles, between the correlational approach and the experimental approach, between the psychologists who use projective tests and those who use objective tests, between those who emphasize stability and consistency in behavior and those who emphasize change and situational specificity, and between those who emphasize individuals and those who emphasize environments. Finally, we proposed that the theories of personality covered need not be considered mutually exclusive. In a very real sense, each represents a glimpse of the total picture. Human behavior is like a very complex jig-saw puzzle. The theories of personality considered have offered us many possible pieces for solution of the puzzle. Although some pieces may have to be discarded as not fitting the puzzle at all, and many remain outstanding, undoubtedly many of the pieces offered will be there when the final picture is put together.

GLOSSARY

ABA Research. A Skinnerian variant of the experimental method consisting of one subject exposed to three experimental phases: (A) a baseline period, (B) introduction of reinforcers to change the frequency of specific behaviors, and (A) withdrawal of reinforcement and observation of whether the behaviors return to their earlier frequency (baseline period).

ABC Approach. In behavioral assessment, an emphasis on the identification of antecedent (A) events and the consequences (C) of behavior (B); a functional analysis of behavior involving indentification of the environmental conditions that regulate specific behaviors.

Acquiescence. A kind of response style or bias in which there is a tendency to agree with test items regardless of their content.

Acquisition. The learning of new behaviors, viewed by Bandura as independent of reward and contrasted with performance—which is seen as dependent on reward.

Aggression (Kelly). In Kelly's personal construct theory, the active expansion of the person's construct system.

Aggressive Instincts. Freud's concept for those drives directed toward harm, injury, or destruction.

Anal Character. Freud's concept for a personality type that expresses a fixation at the anal stage of development and relates to the world in terms of the wish for control or power.

Anal Stage. Freud's concept for that period of life during which the major center of bodily excitation or tension is the anus.

Anxiety. An emotion expressing a sense of impending threat or danger. In Kelly's personal construct theory anxiety occurs when the person recognizes that his or her construct system does not apply to the events being perceived.

Approach–Avoidance Conflict. In S–R theory, the simultaneous presence of opposing drives to move toward an object and away from it.

Attitude. In Cattell's theory, a strength of interest in following a particular course of action; a readiness to act in a certain direction in a given situation.

Attributional Style Questionnaire. A questionnaire designed to measure attributions concerning learned helplessness along three dimensions: internal (personal)–external (universal), specific–global, stable–unstable.

Behavior Modification. The approach to therapeutic treatment (behavior change) based on Skinner's operant conditioning theory.

Behavior Therapy. An approach to therapeutic treatment (behavior change) based on learning theory and focusing on specific behavioral difficulties.

Behavioral Aftereffects. Behavioral effects that are a result of environmental conditions that do not show up during exposure to a condition but at some later point (e.g., Glass and Singer's conclusions regarding the consequences of adaptation to stress).

Behavioral Assessment. The emphasis in assessment on specific behaviors that are tied to defined situational characteristics (e.g., ABC approach).

Behavioral Competencies. Abilities to behave in particular ways, particularly emphasized in social learning theory in relation to performance, as in delay of gratification.

Behaviorism. An approach within psychology, developed by Watson, that restricts investigation to overt, observable behavior.

Bivariate Method. Cattell's description of the method of personality study that follows the classical experimental design of manipulating an independent variable and observing the effects on a dependent variable.

Cardinal Trait. Allport's concept for a disposition that is so pervasive and outstanding in a person's life that virtually every act is traceable to its influence.

Castration Anxiety. Freud's concept for the boy's fear, experienced during the phallic stage, that the father will cut off the son's penis because of their sexual rivalry for the mother.

Causal Attribution. In the revised theory of learned helplessness and depression, attributions made on three dimensions: internal (personal)–external (universal), specific–global, and stable–unstable.

Central Trait. Allport's concept for a disposition to behave in a particular way in a range of situations.

Classical Conditioning. A process, emphasized by Pavlov, in which a previously neutral stimulus becomes capable of eliciting a response because of its association with a stimulus that automatically produces the same or a similar response.

Client-Centered Therapy. Rogers' term for his earlier approach to therapy in which the counselor's attitude is one of interest in the ways in which the client experiences the self and the world.

Clinical Analogue. An approach to research in which there is an attempt to demonstrate a change in the behavior of interest under conditions that approximate, but are not identical to, conditions found in the natural environment (e.g., efforts to duplicate aspects of a regular therapeutic treatment program while still maintaining control over the relevant variables).

Clinical Method. Cattell's description of the method of personality study in which there is an interest in complex patterns of behavior as they occur in life but variables are not assessed in a systematic way.

Cognition. The person's thought processes, including perception, memory, and language. The term is used to refer to the ways in which the organism processes information concerning the environment and the self.

Cognitive Behavior Assessment. An approach to assessment, associated with cognitive behavior therapy, that emphasizes the measurement of specific thoughts and self-statements made by the person, particularly in problematic situations.

Cognitive Behavior Modification. An approach to therapeutic treatment (behavior change) in which there is an emphasis on change in specific aspects of the person's thinking processes.

Cognitive Competencies. Abilities to think in a variety of ways, particularly emphasized in social learning theory in relation to the ability to delay gratification.

Cognitive Complexity–Simplicity. An aspect of a person's cognitive functioning which at one end is defined by the use of many constructs with many relationships to one another (complexity) and at the other end by the use of few constructs with limited relationships to one another (simplicity).

Competence Motivation. White's concept for motivation that emphasizes behavior directed toward dealing competently or effectively with the environment, even if this involves an increase in tension.

Conditioned Emotional Reaction. Watson and Rayner's term for the development of an emotional reaction to a previously neutral stimulus, as in Little Albert's fear of rats.

Congruence. Rogers' concept expressing an absence of conflict between the perceived self and experience. Also one of three therapist conditions suggested as essential for growth and therapeutic progress. (*See also* **Empathic Understanding** and **Unconditional Positive Regard.**)

Conscious. Those thoughts, experiences, and feelings of which we are aware.

Constriction. In Kelly's personal construct theory, the narrowing of the construct system so as to minimize incompatibilities.

Construct. In Kelly's theory, a way of perceiving, construing, or interpreting events.

Construct System. In Kelly's theory, the hierarchical arrangement of constructs.

Contrast Pole. In Kelly's personal construct theory, the contrast pole of a construct is defined by the way in which a third element is perceived as different from two other elements that are used to form a similarity pole.

Core Construct. In Kelly's personal construct theory, a construct that is basic to the person's construct system and cannot be altered without serious consequences for the rest of the system.

Correlational Research. An approach to research, described by Cronbach, in which existing individual indifferences are measured and related to one another, in contrast with the experimental approach to research.

Counterconditioning. The conditioning or learning of responses that interfere with previously learned responses to stimuli, as in the counterconditioning of a pleasurable response to a previously fear-provoking stimulus.

Covert Conditioning. A method of behavior change associated with classical conditioning in which scenes are paired in imagination with reinforcing consequences.

Death Instinct. Freud's concept for drives or sources of energy that are directed toward death or a return to an inorganic state.

Defense Mechanisms. Freud's concept for those devices used by the person to reduce anxiety that result in the exclusion from awareness of some thought, wish, or feeling.

Defensive Behaviors. Efforts on the part of the person, emphasized both by Freud and Rogers, to ward off anxiety.

Delay of Gratification. The postponement of pleasure until the optimum or proper time, a concept particularly emphasized in social learning theory in relation to self-regulation.

Demand Characteristics. Cues that are implicit (hidden) in the experimental setting and influence the subject's behavior.

Denial. A defense mechanism, emphasized both by Freud and Rogers, in which threatening feelings are not allowed into awareness.

Dilation. In Kelly's personal construct theory, the broadening of a construct system so that it will be more comprehensive.

Direct Consequences. In social learning theory, the external events that follow behavior and influence future performance, contrasted with vicarious consequences and self-produced consequences.

Discrimination. In conditioning, the differential response to stimuli depending on whether they have been associated with pleasure, pain, or neutral events.

Disguised Tests. Tests in which the subject is unaware of the purpose of the test and the ways in which responses will be interpreted.

Distortion. According to Rogers, a defensive process in which experience is changed so as to be brought into awareness in a form that is consistent with the self.

Dream Interpretation. In psychoanalysis, the use of dreams to understand the person's unconscious wishes and fears.

Drive, Primary. In Hull's theory, an innate internal stimulus that activates behavior (e.g., hunger drive).

Drive, Secondary. In Hull's theory, a learned internal stimulus, acquired through association with the satisfaction of primary drives, that activates behavior (e.g., anxiety).

Dysfunctional Expectancies. In social learning theory, maladaptive expectations concerning the consequences of specific behaviors.

Dysfunctional Self-evaluation. In social learning theory, maladaptive standards for self-reward that have important implications for psychopathology.

Ego. Freud's structural concept for the part of personality that attempts to satisfy drives (instincts) in accordance with reality and the person's moral values.

Emitted Behaviors. In Skinner's theory, behaviors or responses that cannot be associate with known preceding stimuli.

Empathic Understanding. Rogers' term for the ability to perceive experiences and feelings and their meanings from the standpoint of another person. One of three therapist conditions essential for therapeutic progress. (*See also* **Congruence** and **Unconditional Positive Regard**.)

Energy System. Freud's view of personality as involving the interplay among various forces (e.g., drives, instincts) or sources of energy.

Erg. Cattell's concept for innate biological drives that provide the basic motivating power for behavior.

Erogenous Zones. According to Freud, those parts of the body that are the sources of tension or excitation.

Existentialism. An approach to understanding people and conducting therapy, associated with the human potential movement, that emphasizes phenomenology and concerns inherent in existing as a person. Derived from a more general movement in philosophy.

Expectancies. In social learning theory, what the individual anticipates or predicts will occur as the result of specific behaviors in specific situations (anticipated consequences).

Experimental Research. An approach to research, described by Cronbach, in which the experimenter manipulates the variable and is interested in general laws, in contrast with the correlational approach to research.

Experimenter Expectancy Effects. Unintended experimenter effects involving behaviors that lead subjects to respond in accordance with the experimenter's hypothesis.

Extinction. In conditioning, the progressive weakening of the association between a stimulus and a response; in classical conditioning because the conditioned stimulus is no longer followed by the unconditioned stimulus;

and in operant conditioning because the response is no longer followed by reinforcement.

Extroversion. In Eysenck's theory, one end of the introversion–extroversion dimension of personality characterized by a disposition to be sociable, friendly, impulsive and risktaking.

Factor Analysis. A statistical method for determining those variables or test responses that increase and decrease together. Used in the development of personality tests and of some trait theories (e.g., Cattell, Eysenck).

Fear (Kelly). In Kelly's personal construct theory, fear occurs when a new construct is about to enter the person's construct system.

Fixation. Freud's concept expressing a developmental arrest or stoppage at some point in the person's psychosexual development.

Fixed Role Therapy. Kelly's therapeutic technique that makes use of scripts or roles for people to try out, thereby encouraging people to behave in new ways and to perceive themselves in new ways.

Focus of Convenience. In Kelly's personal construct theory, those events or phenomena that are best covered by a construct or by the construct system.

Free Association. In psychoanalysis, the patient's reporting to the analyst of every thought that comes to mind.

Functional Analysis. In behavioral approaches, particularly Skinnerian, the indentification of the environmental stimuli that control behavior.

Functional Autonomy. Allport's concept that a motive may become independent of its origins; in particular, motives in adults may become independent of their earlier basis in tension reduction.

Generalization. In conditioning, the association of a response with stimuli similar to the stimulus to which the response was originally conditioned or attached.

Generalized Reinforcer. In Skinner's operant conditioning theory, a reinforcer that provides access to many other reinforcers (e.g., money).

Genuineness. Rogers' term for the ability of a person to be himself or herself and honest in relation to another person. One of three therapist conditions necessary for therapeutic progress.

Goals–Plans. In social learning theory, desired future events that motivate the person over extended periods of time and enable the person to go beyond momentary influences.

Guided Participation. A treatment approach emphasized in social learning theory in which a person is assisted in performing modeled behaviors.

Habit. In Hull's theory, an association between a stimulus and a response.

Hierarchy. The organization of things in a graded order or according to rank (e.g., Eysenck's conceptualization of personality and Kelly's view of the personal construct system).

Higher Mental Processes. In S–R theory, the central role of thought in behavior that allows organisms to go beyond reflexive responses to stimuli.

Hostility (Kelly). In Kelly's personal construct theory, making others behave in an expected way to validate one's own construct system.

Human Potential Movement. A group of psychologists, represented by Rogers and Maslow, who emphasize the actualization or fulfillment of individual potential, including an openness to experience.

Id. Freud's structural concept for the source of the instincts or all of the drive energy in people.

Ideal Self. The self-concept the individual would most like to possess. A key concept in Rogers' theory.

Identification. The acquisition, as characteristics of the self, of personality characteristics perceived to be part of others (e.g., parents).

Idiographic Approach. An approach emphasized by Allport in which particular attention is given to the intensive study of individuals and the organization of personality variables in each person.

Imitation. Behavior that is acquired through the observation of others. In S–R theory, the result of the process called matched-dependent behavior in which, for example, children match their behavior to that of their parents and this is followed by reward.

Impermeable Construct. In Kelly's personal construct theory, a construct that does not allow new elements into it.

Implicit Personality Theory. The lay person's beliefs concerning the characteristics or traits of people that go together, implicit in that they are not made explicit and are not part of a formal theory of personality.

Incongruence. Rogers' concept for the existence of a discrepancy or conflict between the perceived self and experience.

Inefficacy. In social learning theory, the inability to cope with a perceived threat or other important situation.

Instrumental Learning. In S–R theory, the learning of responses that are instrumental in bringing about a desirable situation.

Interactionism. The view within psychology that behavior can be understood in terms of relationships between variables that affect one another, as in person and situation variables, or interact to determine behavior.

Internal–External (I–E) Scale. The personality scale developed by Rotter to measure the extent to which the person has developed a generalized expectancy that he or she has the ability to control life's events (i.e., internal locus of control) as opposed to the generalized expectancy that life's events are the result of external factors such as chance, luck, or fate (i.e., external locus of control).

Internal Standards. A concept in social learning theory emphasizing how behavior may be regulated and maintained by learned standards for reinforcement (e.g., pride, shame) which are now part of the individual.

Introversion. In Eysenck's theory, one end of the introversion–extroversion dimension of personality characterized by a disposition to be quiet, reserved, reflective, and risk avoiding.

Intuitive Social Scientist. A view of ordinary people as trying to gather and organize information in the course of which certain rules or heuristics are used and errors made. The emphasis is on cognitive rather than motivational influences in personality functioning.

Jenkins Activity Survey. A personality questionnaire designed to measure Type A behavior patterns associated with increased risk of heart disease.

Laboratory Research. Research conducted in the laboratory which typically emphasizes experimenter control over the variables of interest and the investigation of cause–effect relationships among a few variables. (*See* **Experimental Research**)

L-Data. In Cattell's theory, life-record data relating to behavior in everyday-life situations or to ratings of such behavior.

Learned Helplessness. Seligman's concept expressing an animal's or person's learning that outcomes are not affected by his or her behavior.

Libido. Freud's concept for the energy of the life instincts directed toward sexual gratification and pleasure.

Life Instinct. Freud's concept for drives or sources of energy (libido) directed toward the preservation of life and sexual gratification.

Locus of Causality. In Weiner's scheme of causal attributions, a dimension that relates to whether the person perceives causes of events as coming from within (internal) or from outside (external).

Locus of Control. Rotter's concept expressing a generalized expectancy or belief concerning the determinants of rewards and punishments. (*See* **Internal–External Scale**)

Loosening. In Kelly's personal construct theory, the use of the same construct to make varied predictions.

Maintenance. Bandura's concept for the conditions that regulate behavior once it has been initiated.

MAVA Method (Multiple Abstract Variance Analysis). Cattell's method for determining the relative influence of heredity and environment in the development of specific personality traits.

Mechanisms of Defense. (See Defense Mechanisms)

Microanalytic Research. Bandura's suggested research strategy concerning the concept of self-efficacy where specific rather than global self-efficacy judgments are recorded.

Modeling. Bandura's concept for the process of reproducing behaviors learned through the observation of others.

Multivariate Method. Cattell's description of the method of personality study, favored by him, in which there is study of the interrelationships among many variables at once.

Naturalistic Observation. An approach to research that involves the study of phenomena as they occur naturally (in their own environment) and without efforts toward experimental manipulation and control.

Need for Positive Regard. (See Positive Regard)

Negative Reinforcer. In Skinner's operant conditioning theory, the removal of an unpleasant or aversive stimulus that results in an increase in the probability of occurrence of the preceding response.

Neuroticism. In Eysenck's theory, a dimension of personality defined by stability and low anxiety at one end as opposed to instability and high anxiety at the other end.

Objective Tests. Tests in which the subject is asked to give a correct response.

Observational Learning. Bandura's concept for the process through which people learn merely by observing the behavior of others, called models.

Oedipus Complex. Freud's concept expressing the boy's sexual attraction to the mother and fear of castration by the father who is seen as a rival.

Operant Conditioning. Skinner's term for the process through which the characteristics of a response are determined by its consequences.

Operants. in Skinner's theory, behaviors that appear (are emitted) without being specifically associated with any prior (eliciting) stimuli and are studied in relation to the reinforcing events that follow them.

Oral Character. Freud's concept for a personality type that expresses a fixation at the oral stage of development and who relates to the world in terms of the wish to be fed or to swallow.

Oral Stage. Freud's concept for that period of life during which the major center of bodily excitation or tension is the mouth.

OT-Data. In Cattell's theory, objective test data or information about personality obtained from observing behavior in miniature situations.

Own-Control Design. A Skinnerian variant of the experimental method in which one subject is used and serves as his own control while experimental conditions are varied. **(See ABA Design)**

Paradigm. Kuhn's concept for a model that is commonly accepted by scientists in a field and that defines the field of observations and the methods to be used in research.

Performance. The production of

learned behaviors, viewed by Bandura as dependent on rewards, in contrast to the acquisition of new behaviors, which is seen as independent of reward.

Peripheral Construct. In Kelly's personal construct theory, a construct that is not basic to the construct system and can be altered without serious consequences for the rest of the system.

Permeable Construct. In Kelly's personal construct system, a construct that allows new elements into it.

Person–Situation Controversy. A controversy between those psychologists who emphasize the importance of personal (internal) variables in determining behavior and those who emphasize the importance of situational (external) influences.

Personality. Those characteristics of the person, or of people generally, that account for consistent patterns of response to situations.

Phallic Character. Freud's concept for a personality type that expresses a fixation at the phallic stage of development and who strives for success in competition with others.

Phallic Stage. Freud's concept for that period of life during which excitation or tension begins to be centered in the genitals and during which there is an attraction to the parent of the opposite sex.

Phenomenology. An approach within psychology that focuses on how the person perceives and experiences the self and the world.

Pleasure Principle. According to Freud, psychological functioning based on the pursuit of pleasure and the avoidance of pain.

Positive Regard, need for. Rogers' concept expressing the need for warmth, liking, respect, and acceptance from others.

Positive Reinforcer. In Skinner's operant conditioning theory, a stimulus that results in an increase in the probability of occurrence of the response that preceded it.

Preconscious. Freud's concept for those thoughts, experiences, and feelings of which we are momentarily unaware but can readily bring into awareness.

Preverbal Construct. In Kelly's personal construct theory, a construct that is used but cannot be expressed in words.

Process. In personality theory, the concept of process refers to the motivational aspects of personality.

Projective Test. A test that generally involves vague, ambiguous stimuli and allows subjects to reveal their personalities in terms of their distinctive responses (e.g., Rorschach, TAT).

Prototype. The pattern of characteristics that best illustrates or exemplifies membership in a category. The prototype represents an ideal type with members of the category not necessarily possessing all of the characteristics of the propotype.

Psychoticism. In Eysenck's theory, a dimension of personality defined by a tendency to be solitary and insensitive at one end as opposed to accepting social custom and being caring about others at the other end.

Q-Data. In Cattell's theory, personality data obtained from questionnaires.

Q-Sort. An assessment device in

which the subject sorts statements into categories following a normal distribution. Used by Rogers as a measure of statements regarding the self and ideal self.

Range of Convenience. In Kelly's personal construct theory, those events or phenomena that are covered by a construct or by the construct system.

Rational Emotive Therapy. A therapeutic approach, developed by Albert Ellis, that emphasizes change in irrational beliefs that have destructive emotional and behavioral consequences.

Reality Principle. According to Freud, psychological functioning based on reality in which pleasure is delayed until an optimum time.

Reciprocal Determinism. The mutual effects of variables on one another (e.g., Bandura's emphasis on personal and environmental factors continuously affecting one another).

Regression. Freud's concept expressing a person's return to ways of relating to the world and self that were part of an earlier stage of development.

Reliability. In test construction, a measure of the consistency of scores derived from the test; a measure of the freedom from chance error of the obtained scores.

Rep Test (Role Construct Repertory Test). Kelly's test to determine the constructs used by a person, the relationships among constructs, and how the constructs are applied to specific people.

Response Style. The tendency of some subjects to respond to test items in a consistent, patterned way that has to do with the form of the questions and/or answers rather than with their content.

Role. Behavior considered to be appropriate for a person's place or status in society. Emphasized by Cattell as one of a number of variables that limit the influence of personality variables on behavior relative to situational variables.

Sample Approach. Mischel's description of assessment approaches in which there is an interest in the behavior itself and its relation to environmental conditions, in contrast to sign approaches that infer personality from test behavior.

Schedule of Reinforcement. In Skinner's operant conditioning theory, the rate and interval of reinforcement of responses (e.g., response ratio schedule and time intervals).

Script. A series or pattern of behaviors considered to be appropriate for a situation.

Second Signal System. Pavlov's concept emphasizing the importance of speech and thought in human classical conditioning.

Secondary Disposition. Allport's concept for a disposition to behave in a particular way that is relevant to few situations.

Self. A concept many psychologists use to express pattern, organization, and consistency in personality functioning; in social learning theory, cognitive processes (schemata) associated by the person with the I or Me.

Self-actualization. The fundamental tendency on the part of the organism to actualize, maintain, and enhance itself. A concept emphasized by Rogers and other members of the human potential movement.

Self-concept. The perceptions and meaning associated with the self, Me, or I.

Self-conceptions. In social learning theory, cognitive evaluations of the self. Dysfunctional self-evaluations, for example, are viewed as being important in psychopathology.

Self-consistency. Rogers' concept expressing an absence of conflict among perceptions of the self.

Self-efficacy. In social learning theory, the perceived ability to cope with specific situations.

Self-efficacy Expectations. In social learning theory, the expectations on the part of the person concerning his or her ability to perform specific behaviors in a situation.

Self-esteem. The person's evaluative regard for the self or personal judgment of worthiness.

Self-experience Discrepancy. Rogers' emphasis on the potential for conflict between the concept of self and experience—the basis for psychopathology.

Self-instructional Learning. A procedure for behavior change, emphasized by Meichenbaum and others, that emphasizes the acquisition of adaptive self-statements.

Self-monitoring. Snyder's concept defining the extent to which people monitor or regulate their behavior according to situational cues. High self-monitoring individuals are sensitive to cues of situational appropriateness and regulate their behavior accordingly while low self-monitoring individuals behave more in accord with internal feelings and attitudes.

Self-produced Consequences. In social learning theory, the consequences to behavior that are produced person-

ally (internally) by the individual and that play a vital role in self-regulation and self-control.

Self-regulation. Bandura's concept for the process through which the person regulates his or her own behavior.

Self-schemata. Cognitive generalizations about the self, derived from past experience, that organize and guide the processing of self-related information.

Semantic Conditioning. The classical conditioning of responses to the meaning of words. Associated with Pavlov's emphasis on the second signal system.

Sentiment. Cattell's concept for environmentally determined patterns of behavior that are expressed in attitudes (i.e., readiness to act in a certain direction) and are linked to underlying ergs (i.e., innate biological drives).

Sexual Instincts. Freud's concept for those drives directed toward sexual gratification or pleasure.

Shaping. In Skinner's operant conditioning theory, the modification of behavior in a specific direction through the reinforcement of specific responses.

Sign Approach. Mischel's description of assessment approaches that infer personality from test behavior, in contrast with a sample approach to assessment.

Similarity Pole. In Kelly's personal construct theory, the similarity pole of a construct is defined by the way in which two elements are perceived to be similar.

Situational Specificity. The emphasis on behavior as varying according to the situation in opposition to the emphasis by trait theorists on consistency in behavior across situations.

Sixteen Personality Factor Inventory (16 P.F.). Cattell's personality questionnaire, derived from the use of factor analysis, measuring personality on sixteen dimensions.

Social Desirability. The perceived social value of a response to a test item that may lead to a subject responding in terms of the perceived acceptability (desirability) of a response rather than in terms of its actual relevance to the self.

Source Trait. In Cattell's theory, behaviors that vary together to form an independent dimension of personality, which is discovered through the use of factor analysis.

State. Emotional and mood changes (e.g., anxiety, depression, fatigue) which Cattell suggested may influence the behavior of a person at a given time. The assessment of both traits and states is suggested to predict behavior.

State Anxiety. In Cattell's theory, a temporary state of anxiety, distinguished from trait anxiety.

Structure. In personality theory, the concept of structure refers to the more enduring and stable aspects of personality.

Subception. A process emphasized by Rogers in which a stimulus is experienced without being brought into awareness.

Submerged Construct. In Kelly's personal construct theory, a construct that once could be expressed in words but now either one or both poles of the construct cannot be verbalized.

Subordinate Construct. In Kelly's personal construct theory, a construct that is lower in the construct system and is thereby included in the context of another (superordinate) construct.

Successive Approximation. In Skinner's operant conditioning theory, the development of complex behaviors through the reinforcement of behaviors that increasingly resemble the final form of behavior to be produced.

Superego. Freud's structural concept for the part of personality that expresses our ideals and moral values.

Superordinate Construct. In Kelly's personal contruct theory, a construct that is higher in the construct system and thereby includes other constructs within its context.

Surface Trait. In Cattell's theory, behaviors that appear to be linked to one another but do not in fact increase and decrease together.

Symptom. In psychopathology, the expression of psychological conflict or disordered psychological functioning. For Freud, a disguised expression of a repressed impulse.

Systematic Desensitization. A technique in behavior therapy in which a competing response (relaxation) is conditioned to stimuli that previously aroused anxiety.

Target Behaviors. In behavioral assessment, the identification of specific behaviors to be observed and measured in relation to changes in environmental events.

Tension-Reduction Model. A view of motivation which suggests that behavior is directed toward the reduction of tensions associated with drives or needs.

Theory. A set of assumptions and concepts used to explain existing empirical findings and suggest findings that are expected in the future.

Threat (Kelly). In Kelly's personal construct theory, threat occurs when the person is aware of an imminent, comprehensive change in his or her construct system.

Tightening. In Kelly's personal construct theory, the use of constructs to make the same predictions regardless of circumstances.

Token Economy. Following Skinner's operant conditioning theory, an environment in which individuals are rewarded with tokens for desirable behaviors.

Trait. A disposition to behave in a particular way as expressed in a person's behavior over a range of situations.

Trait Anxiety. In Cattell's theory, a generalized tendency to have a high anxiety level, distinguished from state anxiety.

Transference. In psychoanalysis, the patient's development toward the analyst of attitudes and feelings rooted in past experiences with parental figures.

Type. The classification of people into a few groups, each of which has its own defining characteristics (e.g., introverts and extroverts).

Type A Behavior Pattern. A pattern of personality characteristics or behaviors such as competitiveness, quick action, hostility, and a pressured way of life that are associated with increased risk of heart disease.

Unconditional Positive Regard. Rogers' term for the acceptance of a person in a total, unconditional way. One of three therapist conditions, suggested as essential for growth and therapeutic progress. (*See also* **Congruence** and **Empathic Understanding**)

Unconscious. Those thoughts, experiences, and feelings of which we are unaware. According to Freud this unawareness is the result of repression.

Validity. In test construction and evaluation, the extent to which a test measures what it claims to measure.

Verbal Construct. In Kelly's personal construct theory, a construct that can be expressed in words.

Vicarious Conditioning. Bandura's concept for the process through which emotional responses are learned through the observation of emotional responses in others.

Vicarious Consequences. In social learning theory, the observed consequences to the behavior of others that influence future performance.

Zeitgeist. The prevailing mood or spirit within a field at a particular time.

BIBLIOGRAPHY

Abernethy, E. M. The effect of sorority pressures on the results of a self-inventory. *Journal of Social Psychology*, 1954, **40**, 177–183.

Abraham, K. A short study of the development of the libido, viewed in the light of mental disorders. 1924, in *On character and libido development: Six essays by Karl Abraham*. New York: Norton, 1966.

Abramson, L. Y., Garber, J., & Seligman, M. E. P. Learned helplessness in humans: An attributional analysis. In J. Garber & M. E. P. Seligman (Eds.), *Human helplessness*. New York: Academic, 1980.

Abramson, L. Y., Seligman, M. E. P., & Teasdale, J. D. Learned helplessness in humans: Critique and reformulation. *Journal of Abnormal Psychology*, 1978, **87**, 49–74.

Achenbach, T., & Zigler, E. Social competence and self-image disparity in psychiatric and nonpsychiatric patients. *Journal of Abnormal and Social Psychology*, 1963, **67**, 197–205.

Adams-Webber, J. R. Actual structure and potential chaos: Relational aspects of progressive variations within a personal construct system. In D. Bannister (Ed.), *Perspectives in personal construct theory*. New York: Academic Press, 1970. Pp. 31–46.

Adams-Webber, J. R. *Personal construct theory: Concepts and applications*. New York: Wiley, 1979.

Adams-Webber, J. R. Assimilation and contrast in personal judgment: The dichotomy corollary. In J. C. Mancuso & J. R. Adams-Webber (Eds.), *The construing person*. New York: Praeger, 1982.

Adorno, T. W., Frenkel-Brunswik, E., Levinson, D. J., & Sanford, R. N. *The authoritarian personality*. New York: Harper, 1950.

Akeret, R. U. Interrelationships among various dimensions of the self concept. *Journal of Counseling Psychology,* 1959, **6**, 199–201.

Alexander, F., & French, T. M. *Psychoanalytic therapy*. New York: Ronald, 1946.

Alker, H. A. Is personality situationally specific or intrapsychically consistent? *Journal of Personality,* 1972, **40**, 1–16.

Allport, F. H. & Allport, G. W. Personality traits: Their classification and measurement. *Journal of Abnormal & Social Psychology,* 1921, 16, 1–40.

Allport, G. W. *Personality*: A psychological interpretation. New York: Holt, Rinehart and Winston, 1937.

Allport, G. W. The trend in motivational theory. *American Journal of Orthopsychiatry,* 1953, **23**, 107–119.

Allport, G. W. *Becoming.* New Haven, Conn.: Yale University Press, 1955.

Allport, G. W. European and American theories of personality. In H. P. David & H. von Bracken (Eds.), *Perspectives in personality theory,* New York: Basic Books, 1957. Pp. 3–26.

Allport, G. W. What units shall we employ? In G. Lindzey (Ed.), *Assessment of human motives.* New York: Holt, Rinehart and Winston. 1958. Pp. 239–260.

Allport, G. W. *Pattern and growth in personality.* New York: Holt, Rinehart and Winston, 1961.

Allport, G. W. The general and the unique in psychological science. *Journal of Personality,* 1962, **30**, 405–421.

Allport, G. W. Autobiography. In E. G. Boring & G. Lindzey (Eds.), *A history of psychology in autobiography.* New York: Appleton-Century-Crofts, 1967.

APA Ethical Principles of Psychologists. *American Psychologist,* 1981, **36**, 633–638.

APA Monitor. The spreading case of fraud. 1982, **13**, p. 1.

Argyle, M. The experimental study of the basic features of situations. In D. Magnusson (Ed.), *Toward a psychology of situations.* Hillsdale, N.J.: Erlbaum, 1981.

Aronson, E., & Carlsmith, J. M. Performance expectancy as a determinant of actual performance. *Journal of Abnormal and Social Psychology,* 1962, **65**, 178–182.

Aronson, E. & Mettee, D. R. Dishonest behavior as a function of differential levels of induced self-esteem. *Journal of Personality and Social Psychology,* 1968, **9**, 121–127.

Atthowe, J. M., Jr. Behavior innovation and persistence. *American Psychologist,* 1973, **28**, 34–41.

Atthowe, J. M., Jr., & Krasner, L. A. A preliminary report of the application of contingent reinforcement procedures and token economy on a "chronic" psychiatric ward. *Journal of Abnormal Psychology,* 1968, **73**, 37–43.

Ayllon, T., & Azrin, H. H. The measurement and reinforcement of behavior of psychotics. *Journal of the Experimental Analysis of Behavior,* 1965, **8**, 357–383.

Ayllon, T., & Michael, J. The psychiatric nurse as a behavioral engineer. *Journal of the Experimental Analysis of Behavior,* 1959, **2**, 323–334.

Baer, D. M., Peterson, R. F., & Sherman, J. A. The development of imitation by reinforcing similarity to a model. *Journal of the Experimental Analysis of Behavior,* 1967, **10**, 405–416.

Baer, D. M. & Sherman, J. A. Reinforcement control of generalized imitation in young children. *Journal of Experimental Child Psychology,* 1964, **1**, 37–49.

Baldwin, A. L. The effect of home environment on nursery school behavior. *Child Development,* 1949, **20**, 49–61.

Baldwin, A. L. *Theories of child development.* New York: Wiley, 1968.

Bandura, A. The Rorschach white space response and "oppositional" behavior. *Journal of Consulting Psychology,* 1954, **18**, 17–21.(a)

Bandura, A. The Rorschach white space response and perceptual reversal. *Journal of Experimental Psychology,* 1954, **48**, 113–117.(b)

Bandura, A. Psychotherapy as a learning process. *Psychological Bulletin,* 1961, **58**, 143–159.

Bandura, A. Social learning through imitation. In M. R. Jones (Ed.), *Nebraska symposium on motivation.* Lincoln: University of Nebraska Press, 1962. Pp. 211–215.

Bandura, A. Influence of models' reinforcement contingencies on the acquisition of imitative responses. *Journal of Personality and Social Psychology,* 1965, **1**, 589–595.

Bandura, A. A social learning interpretation of psychological dysfunctions. In P. London & D. Rosenhan (Eds.), *Founda-*

tions of abnormal psychology. New York: Holt, Rinehart and Winston, 1968. Pp. 293–344.

Bandura, A. Social-learning theory of identificatory processes. In D. A. Goslin (Ed.), *Handbook of socialization theory and research.* Chicago: Rand McNally, 1969. Pp. 213–262.(a)

Bandura, A. *Principles of behavior modification.* New York: Holt, Rinehart and Winston, 1969.(b)

Bandura, A. Analysis of modeling processes. In A. Bandura (Ed.), *Psychological modeling.* Chicago: Aldine-Atherton, 1971. Pp. 1–62.(a)

Bandura, A. Psychotherapy based upon modeling principles. In A. E. Bergin & S. Garfield (Eds.), *Handbook of psychotherapy and behavior change.* New York: Wiley, 1971. Pp. 653–708.(b)

Bandura, A. The process and practice of participant modeling treatment. Paper presented at the Conference on the Behavioral Basis of Mental Health, Ireland, 1972.

Bandura, A. Social learning perspective on behavior change. In A. Burton (Ed.), *What makes behavior change?* New York: Brunner/Mazel, 1976. Pp. 34–57.

Bandura, A. *Social learning theory.* Englewood Cliffs, N.J.: Prentice-Hall, 1977.(a)

Bandura, A. Self-efficacy: Toward a unified theory of behavioral change. *Psychological Review,* 1977, **84**, 191–215.(b)

Bandura, A. On paradigms and recycled ideologies. *Cognitive Therapy and Research,* 1978, **2**, 79–103.(a)

Bandura, A. The self system in reciprocal determinism. *American Psychologist,* 1978, **33**, 344–358.(b)

Bandura, A. Psychological mechanisms of aggression. In M. Von Cranach, K. Foppa, W. LePenies, & D. Ploog (Eds.), *Human ethology: Claims and limits of a new discipline.* Cambridge: Cambridge University Press, 1979.

Bandura, A. Self-referent thought: A developmental analysis of self-efficacy. In J. Flavell & L. Ross (Eds.), *Social cognitive development.* Cambridge: Cambridge University Press, 1981.

Bandura, A. Self-efficacy mechanism in human agency. *American Psychologist,* 1982, **37**, 122–147.

Bandura, A., & Adams, N. E. Analysis of self-efficacy theory of behavioral change. *Cognitive Therapy and Research,* 1977, **1**, 287–310.

Bandura, A., Adams, N. E., & Beyer, J. Cognitive processes mediating behavioral change. *Journal of Personality and Social Psychology,* 1977, **35**, 125–139. (Copyright 1977 by the American Psychological Association. Reprinted by permission.)

Bandura, A., & Barab, P. G. Conditions governing nonreinforced imitation. *Developmental Psychology,* 1971, **5**, 244–255.

Bandura, A., Blanchard, E. B., & Ritter, B. J. The relative efficacy of modeling therapeutic approaches for producing behavioral, attitudinal and affective changes. Unpublished manuscript, Stanford University, 1967.

Bandura, A., & Cervone, D. Self-evaluative and self-efficacy mechanisms governing the motivational effect of goal systems. *Journal of Personality and Social Psychology,* 1984, in press.

Bandura, A., Grusec, J. E., & Menlove, F. L. Some social determinants of self-monitoring reinforcement systems. *Journal of Personality and Social Psychology,* 1967, **5**, 449–455.

Bandura, A., & Kupers, C. J. Transmission of patterns of self-reinforcement through modeling. *Journal of Abnormal and Social Psychology,* 1964, **69**, 1–9.

Bandura, A. & McDonald, F. J. Influence of social reinforcement and the behavior of models in shaping children's moral judgments. *Journal of Abnormal and Social Psychology,* 1963, **67**, 274–281.

Bandura, A., & Menlove, F. L. Factors determining vicarious extinction of avoidance behavior through symbolic modeling. *Journal of Personality and Social Psychology,* 1968, **8**, 99–108.

Bandura, A., & Mischel, W. Modification of self-imposed delay of reward through exposure to live and symbolic models. *Journal of Personality and Social Psychology,* 1965, **2**, 698–705.

Bandura, A., Reese, L., & Adams, N. E. Microanalysis of action and fear arousal as a function of differential levels of perceived self-efficacy. *Journal of Personality and Social Psychology,* 1982, **43**, 5–21.

Bandura, A., & Rosenthal, T. L. Vicarious classical conditioning as a function of arousal level. *Journal of Personality and Social Psychology,* 1966, **3**, 54–62.

Bandura, A., Ross, D., & Ross, S. Imitation of film-mediated aggressive models. *Journal of Abnormal and Social Psychology,* 1963, **66**, 3–11.(a)

Bandura, A., Ross, D., & Ross, S. Vicarious reinforcement and imitative learning. *Journal of Abnormal and Social Psychology,* 1963, **67**, 601–607.(b)

Bandura, A., & Schunk, D. H. Cultivating competence, self-efficacy, and intrinsic interest. *Journal of Personality and Social Psychology,* 1981, **41**, 586–598.

Bandura, A., & Walters, R. H. *Adolescent aggression.* New York: Ronald, 1959.

Bandura, A., & Walters, R. H. *Social learning and personality development.* New York: Holt, Rinehart and Winston, 1963.

Bannister, D. The nature and measurement of schizophrenic thought disorder. *Journal of Mental Science,* 1962, **108**, 825–842.

Bannister, D. (Ed.), *New perspectives in personal construct theory.* New York: Academic Press, 1977.

Bannister, D., & Agnew, J. The child's construing of self. *Nebraska symposium on motivation,* 1977, **24**, 99–126.

Bannister, D., & Fransella, F. A grid test of schizophrenic thought disorder. *British Journal of Social and Clinical Psychology,* 1966, **5**, 95–102.

Bannister, D., & Fransella, F. *Inquiring man: The theory of personal constructs.* Baltimore: Penguin, 1971.

Bannister, D., & Fransella, F. *A manual for repertory grid technique.* New York: Academic Press, 1977.

Barber, T. X. *Pitfalls in human research.* New York: Pergamon, 1976.

Barbu, Z. Studies in children's honesty. *Quarterly Bulletin of the British Psychological Society,* 1951, **2**, 53–57.

Bargh, J. A. Attention and automaticity in the processing of self-relevant information. *Journal of Personality and Social Psychology,* 1982, **43**, 425–436.

Barlow, D. H., & Wincze, J. P. Treatment of sexual deviations. In S. Leiblum & L. A. Pervin (Eds.), *Principles and practice of sex therapy.* New York: Guilford, 1980.

Barratt, B. The development of peer perception: A content analysis with children from 8 to 14 years. Unpublished manuscript, Harvard University, 1977.

Bateson, G. A., Jackson, D. D., Haley, J., & Weakland, J., Jr. Toward a theory of schizophrenia. *Behavioral Science,* 1965, **1**, 251–264.

Baumeister, R. F. A self-presentational view of social phenomena. *Psychological Bulletin,* 1982, **91**, 3–26.

Beck, A. T. *Cognitive therapy and the emotional disorders.* New York: International Universities Press, 1976.

Becker, W. C. Consequences of different kinds of parental discipline. In M. L. Hoffman & L. W. Hoffman (Eds.), *Review of Child Development Research,* Vol. 1. New York: Russell Sage Foundation, 1964, 169–208.

Bem, D. J., & Allen, A. On predicting some of the people some of the time: The search for cross-situational consistencies in behavior. *Psychological Review,* 1974, **81**, 506–520.

Bender, M. P. Does construing people as

similar involve similar behavior towards them? A subjective and objective replication. *British Journal of Social and Clinical Psychology,* 1976, **15**, 93–95.

Berger, S. M. Conditioning through vicarious investigation. *Psychological Review,* 1962, **69**, 450–466.

Bergin, A. E., & Strupp, H. H. *Changing frontiers in the science of psychotherapy.* New York: Aldine-Atherton, 1972.

Bergmann, G., & Spence, K. W. Operationism and theory in psychology. *Psychological Review,* 1941, **48**, 1–14.

Berkowitz, L., & Donnerstein, E. External validity is more than skin deep. *American Psychologist,* 1982, **37**, 245–257.

Bernstein, D. A. Situational factors in behavioral fear assessment: A progress report. *Behavior Therapy,* 1973, **4**, 41–48.

Bibring, E. The mechanism of depression. In P. Greenacre (Ed.), *Affective disorders.* New York: International Universities Press, 1953.

Bieri, J. Changes in interpersonal perceptions following social interaction. *Journal of Abnormal and Social Psychology,* 1953, **48**, 61–66.

Bieri, J. Cognitive complexity—simplicity and predictive behavior. *Journal of Abnormal and Social Psychology,* 1955, **51**, 263–268.

Bieri, J. Complexity—simplicity as a personality variable in cognitive and preferential behavior. In D. W. Fiske & S. R. Maddi (Eds.), *Functions of varied experience.* Homewood, Ill.: Dorsey, 1961. Pp. 355–379.

Bieri, J., Atkins, A., Briar, S., Leaman, R. L., Miller, H., & Tripoldi, T. *Clinical and social judgment.* New York: Wiley, 1966.

Bijou, S. W. Experimental studies of child behavior, normal and deviant. In L. Krasner & L. P. Ullmann (Eds.), *Research in behavior modification.* New York: Holt, Rinehart and Winston, 1965. Pp. 56–81.

Bijou, S. W. *Child development: The basic stage of early childhood.* Englewood Cliffs, N.J.: Prentice-Hall, 1976.

Bindra, D., & Scheier, I. H. The relation between psychometric and experimental research in psychology. *American Psychologist,* 1954, **9**, 69–71.

Block, J. Advancing the psychology of personality: Paradigmatic shift or improving the quality of research? In D. Magmusson & N. Endler (Eds.), *Personality at the crossroads.* Hillsdale, N.J.: Erlbaum, 1977.

Bloom, B. S. *Stability and change in human characteristics.* New York: Wiley, 1964.

Blum, G., & Miller, D. R. Exploring the psychoanalytic theory of the "oral character." *Journal of Personality,* 1952, **20**, 287–304.

Bonarius, H. Research in the personal construct theory of George A. Kelly: Role construct repertory test and basic theory. In B. A. Maher (Ed.), *Progress in experimental personality research.* New York: Academic Press, 1965. Pp. 1–46.

Bonarius, H. The interaction model of communication: Through experimental research toward existential relevance. In A. W. Landfield (Ed.), *Nebraska Symposium on Motivation.* Lincoln: University of Nebraska Press, 1977, Pp. 291–343.

Bonarius, H., Holland, R., & Rosenberg, S. (Eds.) *Personal construct psychology. Recent advances in theory & practice.* London: Macmillan, 1981.

Boring, E. G. *A history of experimental psychology.* New York: Appleton-Century-Crofts, 1950.

Bower, G. H. Contacts of cognitive psychology with social learning theory. *Cognitive Therapy and Research,* 1978, **2**, 123–146.

Bower, G. H. Mood and memory. *American Psychologist,* 1981, **36**, 129–148. Copyright 1981 by the American Psychological Association. Reprinted by permission.

Brady, J. P., & Lind, D. L. Experimental

analysis of hysterical blindness. *American Medical Association Archives of General Psychiatry,* 1961, **4**, 331–339.

Bramel, D. Some determinants of defensive projection. Unpublished doctoral dissertation, Stanford University, 1960.

Bramel, D., & Friend, R. Hawthorne, the myth of the docile worker, and the class bias in psychology. *American Psychologist,* 1981, **36**, 867–878.

Brewer, W. F. There is no convincing evidence for operant or classical conditioning in adult humans. In W. B. Weimer & D. S. Palermo (Eds.), *Cognition and the symbolic processes.* Hillsdale, N.J.: Erlbaum, 1974.

Brierly, D. W. The use of personality constructs by children of three different ages. Unpublished Ph.D. thesis, London University, 1967.

Brim, O. G., & Kagan, J. (Eds.) *Continuity and change in human development.* Cambridge, Mass.: Harvard University Press, 1980.

Brown, I. B., Jr., & Inouye, D. K. Learned helplessness through modeling: The role of perceived similarity in competence. *Journal of Personality and Social Psychology,* 1978, **36**, 900–908.

Brown, N. O. *Life against death.* New York: Random House, 1959.

Bruner, J. S. You are your constructs. *Contemporary Psychology,* 1956, **1**, 355–356.

Burton, R. V. Generality of honesty revisited. *Psychological Review,* 1963, **70**, 481–499.

Burton, R. V. Validity of retrospective reports assessed by the multitrait-multimethod analysis. *Developmental Psychology Monographs,* 1970, **3**, No. 3, Part 2.

Buss, D. M. Paradigm for personality? *Contemporary Psychology,* 1982, **27**, 341–342.

Butler, J. M. The use of a psychological model in personality testing. *Educational & Psychological Measurements,* 1954, **14**, 77–89.

Butler, J. M., & Haigh, G. V. Changes in the relation between self-concepts and ideal concepts consequent upon client centered counseling. In C. R. Rogers & R. F. Dymond (Eds.), *Psychotherapy and personality change.* Chicago: University of Chicago Press, 1954. Pp. 55–75.

Campbell, J. B., & Hawley, C. W. Study habits and Eysenck's theory of extroversion-introversion. *Journal of Research in Personality,* 1982, **16**, 139–146.

Cantor, N. A cognitive-social approach to personality. In N. Cantor & J. F. Kihlstrom (Eds.), *Personality, cognition, and social interaction.* Hillsdale, N.J.: Erlbaum, 1981.

Cantor, N., & Mischel, W. Prototypes in person perception. *Advances in Experimental Social Psychology,* 1979, **12**, 3–52.

Cantor, N., Mischel, W., & Schwartz, J. C. A prototype analysis of psychological situations. *Cognitive Psychology,* 1982, **14**, 45–77.

Carlson, E. R., & Carlson, R. Male and female subjects in personality research. *Journal of Abnormal and Social Psychology,* 1960, **61**, 482–483.

Carlson, R. Where is the person in personality research? *Psychological Bulletin,* 1971, **75**, 203–219.

Carr, A. C. An evaluation of nine nondirective psychotherapy cases by means of the Rorschach. *Journal of Consulting Psychology,* 1949, **13**, 196–205.

Cartwright, D. S. Self-consistency as a factor affecting immediate recall. *Journal of Abnormal and Social Psychology,* 1956, **52**, 212–218.

Cartwright, D. S., Kirtner, W. L., & Fiske, D. W. Method factors in changes associated with psychotherapy. *Journal of Abnormal and Social Psychology,* 1963, **66**, 164–175.

Cattell, R. B. The main personality factors in questionnaire, self-estimated material. *Journal of Social Psychology,* 1950, **31**, 3–38.

Cattell, R. B. Personality and motivation theory based on structural measurement. In J. L. McCary (Ed.), *Psychology of per-*

sonality. New York: Logos, 1956. Pp. 63–120.(a)

Cattell, R. B. Validation and interpretation of the 16 P.F. questionnaire. *Journal of Clinical Psychology,* 1956, **12,** 205–214.(b)

Cattell, R. B. The dynamic calculus: Concepts and crucial experiments. In M. R. Jones (Ed.), *Nebraska symposium on motivation.* Lincoln: University of Nebraska Press, 1959. Pp. 84–134.(a)

Cattell, R. B. Personality theory growing from multivariate quantitative research. In S. Koch (Ed.), *Psychology: The study of a science.* New York: McGraw-Hill, 1959. Pp. 257–327.(b)

Cattell, R. B. Foundations of personality measurement theory in multivariate expressions. In B. M. Bass & I. A. Berg (Eds.), *Objective approaches to personality assessment.* Princeton, N.J.: Van Nostrand, 1959. Pp. 42–65.(c)

Cattell, R. B. Personality measurement functionally related to source trait structure. In S. Messick & J. Ross (Eds.), *Measurement in personality and cognition.* New York: Wiley, 1962. Pp. 249–267.

Cattell, R. B. Personality, role, mood, and situation perception: A unifying theory of modulators. *Psychological Review,* 1963, **70,** 1–18.(a)

Cattell, R. B. The nature and measurement of anxiety. *Scientific American,* 1963, **208,** 96–104.(b)

Cattell, R. B. *The scientific analysis of personality.* Baltimore: Penquin, 1965.(a)

Cattell, R. B. Methodological and conceptual advances in the evaluation of hereditary and environmental influences and their interaction. In S. G. Vandenberg (Ed.), *Methods and goals in human behavior genetics.* New York: Academic Press, 1965. Pp. 95–130.(b)

Cattell, R. B. Psychological theory and scientific method. In R. B. Cattell (Ed.), *Handbook of multivariate experimental psychology.* Chicago: Rand McNally, 1966. Pp. 1–18.

Cattell, R. B. The principles of experimental design and analysis in relation to theory building. In R. B. Cattell (Ed.), *Handbook of multivariate experimental psychology.* Chicago: Rand McNally, 1966. Pp. 19–66.

Cattell, R. B. A more sophisticated look at structure: Perturbation, sampling, role, and observer trait-view theories. In R. B. Cattell, & R. M. Dreger (Eds.), *Handbook of modern personality theory.* Washington: Hemisphere, 1977. Pp. 166–220.

Cattell, R. B. *Personality and learning theory.* New York: Springer, 1979.

Cattell, R. B. *Personality and learning theory. Vol. 2: A systems theory of maturation and structured learning.* New York: Springer, 1980.

Cattell, R. B. *Structured personality learning theory.* New York: Praeger, 1983.

Cattell, R. B., & Baggaley, A. R. The objective measurement of motivation. I. Development and evaluation of principles and devices. *Journal of Personality,* 1956, **24,** 401–423.

Cattell, R. B., Blewett, D., & Beloff, J. The inheritance of personality: A multiple variance analysis of nature–nurture ratios for personality factors in Q-data. *American Journal of Human Genetics,* 1955, **7,** 122–146.

Cattell, R. B., & Child, D. *Motivation and dynamic structure.* New York: Wiley 1975.

Cattell, R. B., & Cross, P. Comparison of the ergic and self-sentiment structures found in dynamic traits by R- and P-techniques. *Journal of Personality,* 1952, **21,** 250–270.

Cattell, R. B., & Delhees, K. H. Seven missing normal personality factors in the questionnaire primaries. *Multivariate Behavioral Research,* 1973, **8,** 173–194.

Cattell, R. B., & Dreger, R. M. (Eds.) *Handbook of modern personality theory.* Washington: Hemisphere, 1977.

Cattell, R. B., & Eber, H. W. *Handbook for the Sixteen Personality Factor Ques-*

tionnaire: The 16 PF Test. Champaign, Ill.: Institute for Personality and Ability Testing. 1957, 1962.

Cattell, R. B., Eber, H. W., & Tatsuoka, M. M. *Handbook for the 16 PF Questionnaire.* Champaign, Ill.: IPAT, 1970.

Cattell, R. B., & Nichols, K. E. An improved definition, from 10 researchers, of second order personality factors in Q-data (with cross-cultural checks). *Journal of Social Psychology,* 1972, **86,** 187–203.

Cattell, R. B., Radcliffe, J. A., & Sweeney, A. B. The nature and measurement of components of motivation. *Genetic Psychology Monographs,* 1963, **68,** 49–211.

Cattell, R. B., Radcliffe, J. A., & Sweeney, A. B. Components in motivation strength in children compared with those in adults. *Journal of Genetic Psychology,* 1964, **70,** 65–1112.

Cattell, R. B., & Rickels, K. Diagnostic power of IPAT objective anxiety neuroticism tests. *Archives of General Psychiatry,* 1964, **11,** 459–465.

Cattell, R. B., Rickels, K., Weise, C., Gray, B., & Yee, R. The effects of psychotherapy upon measured anxiety and regression. *American Journal of Psychotherapy,* 1966, **20,** 261–269.

Cattell, R. B., & Scheier, I. H. *The meaning and measurement of neuroticism and anxiety.* New York: Ronald, 1961.

Cattell, R. B., & Stice, G. F. *Handbook for the sixteen personality factor questionnaire.* Champaign, Ill.: Institute for Personality and Ability Testing, 1962.

Cattell, R. B., & Tatro, D. F. The personality factors, objectively measured, which distinguish psychotics from normals. *Behavior Research and Therapy,* 1966, **4,** 39–51.

Cattell, R. B., & Warburton, F. W. A cross-cultural comparison of patterns of extraversion and anxiety. *British Journal of Psychology,* 1961, **52,** 375.

Cautela, J. R., & Kastenbaum, R. A. A reinforcement survey schedule for use in therapy, training and research. *Psychological Reports,* 1967, **20,** 1115–1130.

Cautela, J. R., & Upper, D. The Behavioral Inventory Battery: The use of self-report measures in behavioral analysis and therapy. In M. Hersen & A. Bellack (Eds.), *Behavioral assessment: A practical handbook.* New York: Pergamon, 1976.

Champagne, B., & Pervin, L. A. The relation of perceived situation similarity to perceived behavior similarity: Implications for social learning theory. Unpublished manuscript, 1983.

Chodorkoff, B. Self perception, perceptual defense, and adjustment. *Journal of Abnormal and Social Psychology,* 1954, **49,** 508–512.

Ciminero, A. R. Behavioral assessment: An overview. In A. R. Ciminero, K. S. Calhoun, & H. E. Adams (Eds.), *Handbook of behavioral assessment.* New York: Wiley, 1977. Pp. 3–14.

Ciminero, A. R., Calhoun, K. S., & Adams, H. E. (Eds.) *Handbook of behavioral assessment.* New York: Wiley, 1977.

Cleaver, E. *Soul on ice.* New York: Dell, 1968.

Coan, R. W. Child personality and developmental psychology, In R. B. Cattell (Ed.), *Handbook of multivariate experimental psychology.* Chicago: Rand McNally, 1966. Pp. 732–752.

Coan, R. W. Dimensions of psychological theory. *American Psychologist,* 1968, **23,** 715–722.

Colby, K. M. Modeling a paranoid mind. *Behavioral & Brain Sciences,* 1981, **4,** 515–560.

Cole, J. K., Landfield, A. W. (Eds.) *Personal construct psychology. Nebraska symposium on motivation.* Lincoln: Univ. of Nebraska Press, 1976.

Combs, A. W., & Super, D. W. The self, its derivative terms, and research. *Journal of Individual Psychology,* 1957, **13,** 134–145.

Condon, T. J., & Allen, G. J. The role of psychoanalytic merging fantasies in systematic desensitization: A rigorous methodological examination. *Journal of Abnormal Psycholoy,* 1980, **89,** 437–443.

Coopersmith, S. *The antecedents of self-*

esteem. San Francisco: W. H. Freeman, 1967.

Covington, M. V., & Omelich, C. L. Are the causal attributions causal? A path analysis of the cognitive model of achievement motivation. *Journal of Personality and Social Psychology,* 1979, **37,** 1487–1504.

Crockett, W. H. Cognitive complexity and impression formation. In B. A. Maher (Ed.), *Progress in experimental personality research.* New York: Academic Press, 1965. Pp. 47–90.

Crockett, W. H. The organization of construct systems: The organization corollary. In J. C. Mancuso & J. R. Adams-Webber (Eds.), *The construing person.* New York: Praeger, 1982.

Cronbach, L. J. The two disciplines of scientific psychology. *American Psychologist,* 1957, **12,** 671–684.

Cronbach, L. J. *Essentials of psychological testing.* New York: Harper, 1960.

Cronbach, L. J., & Meehl, P. E. Construct validity in psychological tests. *Psychological Bulletin,* 1955, **52,** 281–302.

Crowne, D. P. Review of R. B. Cattell, the scientific life, analysis of personality. *Contemporary Psychology,* 1967, **12,** 40–41.

Crowne, D. P., & Marlowe, D. *The approval motive: Studies in evaluative dependence.* New York: Wiley, 1964.

Crowne, D. P., & Stephens, M. W. Critique of self-concept methodology. *Psychological Bullein,* 1961, **58,** 104–121.

Damarin, F. L., & Cattell, R. B. Personality factors in early childhood and their relation to intelligence. *Monographs of the Society for Research in Child Development,* 1968, **33,** 1–95.

Danker-Brown, P., & Baucom, D. H. Cognitive influences on the development of learned helplessness. *Journal of Personality and Social Psychology,* 1982, **43,** 793–801.

Dashiell, J. F. Some rapproachments in contemporary psychology. *Psychological Bulletin,* 1939, **36,** 1–24.

Davids, A., & Pildner, H., Jr. Comparison of direct and projective methods of personality assessment under differing conditions of motivation. *Psychological Monographs,* 1958, **72** (11, Whole No. 464).

Davison, G. C. Systematic desensitization as a counterconditioning process. *Journal of Abnormal Psychology,* 1968, **73,** 91–99.

Davison, G. C., & Neale, J. M. *Abnormal psychology: An experimental clinical approach.* New York: Wiley, 1982.

Davison, G. C., & Wilson, T. Critique of desensitization: Social and cognitive factors underlying the effectiveness of Wolpe's procedure. *Psychological Bulletin,* 1972, **78,** 28–31.

Davison, G. C., & Wilson, G. T. Processes of fear-reduction in systematic desensitization: Cognitive and social reinforcement factors in humans. *Behavior Therapy,* 1973, **4,** 1–21.

Deci, E. L. *Intrinsic motivation.* New York: Plenum, 1975.

Deutsch, M., & Krauss, R. M. *Theories in social psychology.* New York: Basic Books, 1965.

De Vellis, R. F., DeVellis, B. M., & McCauley, C. Vicarious acquisition of learned helplessness. *Journal of Personality and Social Psychology,* 1978, **36,** 894–899.

Diggory, J. C. *Self-evaluation.* New York: Wiley, 1966.

Diven, K. Certain determinants in the conditioning of anxiety reactions. *Journal of Psychology,* 1937, **3,** 291–308.

Dixon, N. F. *Preconscious processing.* Chichester, England: Wiley, 1981.

Dollard, J., Doob, L. W., Miller, N. E., Mowrer, O. H., & Sears, R. R. *Frustration and aggression.* New Haven, Conn.: Yale University Press, 1939.

Dollard, J., & Miller, N. E. *Personality and psychotherapy.* New York: McGraw-Hill, 1950.

Dreiser, T. *A gallery of women.* New York: Liveright, 1929.

Duck, S. Two individuals in search of agreement: The commonality corollary.

In J. C. Mancuso & J. R. Adams-Webber (Eds.), *The construing person.* New York: Praeger, 1982.

Dudek, S. Z. In search of a comedic syndrome. *Contemporary Psychology,* 1982, **27**, 867–869.

Dymond, R. F. Adjustment changes over therapy from self-sorts In C. R. Rogers & R. F. Dymond (Eds.), *Psychotherapy and personality change.* Chicago: University of Chicago Press, 1954. Pp. 76–84.(a)

Dymond, R. F. Adjustment changes over therapy from thematic apperception test ratings. In C. R. Rogers & R. F. Dymond (Eds.), *Psychotherapy and personality change.* Chicago: University of Chicago Press, 1954. Pp. 109–120.(b)

Eagle, M., Wolitzky, D. L., & Klein, G. S. Imagery: Effect of a concealed figure in a stimulus. *Science,* 1966, **18**, 837–839.

Educational and Industrial Testing Service. 1967 catalog of tests, books, and guidance materials. San Diego, Calif., 1967.

Edwards, A. L. The relationship between the judged desirability of a trait and the probability that the trait will be endorsed. *Journal of Applied Psychology,* 1953, **37**, 90–93.

Edwards, A. L. Social desirability and personality test construction. In B. M. Bass & I. A. Berg (Eds.), *Objective approaches to personality.* Princeton, N.J.: Van Nostrand, 1959. Pp. 101–116.

Ellis, A., & Harper, R. A. *A new guide to rational living.* North Hollywood, Calif.: Wilshire, 1975.

Endler, N. S., Hunt, J. McV., & Rosenstein, A. J. An S–R inventory of anxiousness. *Psychological Monographs, 1962,* **76**, (17, Whole No. 536).

Endler, N. S., & Magnusson, D. (Eds.) *Interactional psychology and personality.* Washington, D.C.: Hemisphere (Halsted-Wiley), 1976.

Engel, M. The stability of the self-concept in adolescence, *Journal of Abnormal and Social Psychology,* 1959, **38**, 211–215.

Epstein, S. The stability of behavior: I. On predicting most of the people most of the time. *Journal of Personality and Social Psychology,* 1979, **37**, 1097–1126.

Epstein, S. A research paradigm for the study of personality and emotions. In M. M. Page (Ed.), *Personality: Current theory and research.* Lincoln, Nebr.: Universtiy of Nebraska Press, 1983.

Epting, F. R. An appraisal of personal construct psychotherapy. In H. Bonarius, R. Holland, & S. Rosenberg (Eds.), *Personal construct psychology: Recent advances in theory and practice.* London: Macmillan, 1981.

Erdelyi, M. H. Not now: Comment on Loftus and Loftus. *American Psychologist,* 1981, **36**, 527–528.

Erdelyi, M. H., & Goldberg, B. Let's not sweep repression under the rug: Toward a cognitive psychology of repression. In J. F. Kihlstrom & F. J. Evans (Eds.), *Functional disorders of memory.* Hillsdale, N.J.: Erlbaum, 1979.

Ericsson, K. A., & Simon, H. A. Verbal reports as data. *Psychological Review,* 1980, **87**, 215–251.

Erikson, E. *Childhood and society.* New York: Norton, 1950.

Erwin, E. *Behavior therapy: Scientific, philosophical, and moral foundations.* New York: Cambridge University Press, 1978.

Evans, R. I. *The making of psychology.* New York: Knopf, 1976.

Eysenck, H. J. *Dimensions of personality,* London: Routledge & Kegan Paul, 1947. (Reprinted by permission.)

Eysenck, H. J. The organization of personality. *Journal of Personality,* 1951, **20**, 101–117.

Eysenck, H. J. *The scientific study of personality.* London: Routledge & Kegan Paul, 1952.

Eysenck, H. J. A dynamic theory of anxiety and hysteria. *Journal of Mental Science,* 1955, **101**, 28–51.

Eysenck, H. J. The inheritance of extraversion-introversion. *Acta Psychologica,* 1956, **12**, 429–432.

Eysenck, H. *Sense and nonsense in psychology.* Baltimore: Penguin, 1957.

Eysenck, H. J. Learning theory and behavior therapy. *Journal of Mental Science,* 1959, **105**, 61–75.

Eysenck, H. J. (Ed.) *Handbook of abnormal psychology.* New York: Basic Books, 1961.

Eysenck, H. J. *The structure of human personality.* London: Methuen, 1970. (Reprinted by permission.)

Eysenck, H. J. *Eysenck on extraversion.* London: Crosby, Lockwood, Staples, 1973.

Eysenck, H. J. *The inequality of man.* San Diego, Calif.: Edits Publishers, 1975.

Eysenck, H. J. Personality and factor analysis: A reply to Guilford. *Psychological Bulletin,* 1977, **84**, 405–411.

Eysenck, H. J. The conditioning model of neurosis. *Behavioral and Brain Sciences,* 1979, **2**, 155–199.

Eysenck, H. J. *Personality genetics and behavior.* New York: Praeger, 1982.

Eysenck, H. J., & Beech, H. R. Counter conditioning and related methods. In A. E. Bergin & S. Garfield (Eds.), *Handbook of psychotherapy and behavior change.* New York: Wiley, 1971. Pp. 543–611.

Eysenck, H. J., & Rachman, S. *The causes and cures of neurosis.* San Diego, Calif.: Knapp, 1965.

Eysenck, H. J., & Wilson, G. D. *The experimental study of Freudian theories.* London: Methuen, 1973.

Farberow, N. L., & Shneidman, E. S. (Eds.) *The cry for help.* New York: McGraw-Hill, 1961.

Ferster, C. B. Classification of behavioral pathology. In L. Krasner & L. P. Ullman (Eds.), *Research in behavior modification.* New York: Holt, Rinehart and Winston, 1965. Pp. 6–26.

Ferster, C. B. A functional analysis of depression. *American Psychologist,* 1973, **28**, 857–870.

Feshbach, S. The stimulating effects of a vicarious aggressive activity. *Journal of Abnormal and Social Psychology,* 1961, **63**, 381–385.

Festinger, L. *A theory of cognitive dissonance.* Evanston, Ill.: Row, Peterson, 1957.

Festinger, L., & Bramel, D. The reactions of humans to cognitive dissonance. In A. J. Bachrach (Ed.), *Experimental foundations of clinical psychology.* New York: Basic Books, 1962. Pp. 254–279.

Fiedler, F. E. A comparison of therapeutic relationships in psychoanalytic, nondirective, and Adlerian therapy. *Journal of Consulting Psychology,* 1950, **14**, 436–445.

Fiedler, F. E. Engineer the job to fit the manager. *Harvard Business Review,* 1965, **43**, 115–122.

Fisher, A. E. Unpublished doctoral dissertation. Pennsylvania State University, 1955.

Fisher, S., & Fisher, R. L. *Pretend the world is funny and forever: A psychological analysis of comedians, clowns, and actors.* Hillsdale, N.J.: Erlbaum, 1981.

Fisher, S., & Greenberg, R. P. *The scientific credibility of Freud's theories and therapy.* New York: Basic Books, 1977.

Fiske, D. W. *Strategies for personality research.* San Francisco: Jossey-Bass, 1978.

Fiske, D. W., & Goodman, G. The post therapy period. *Journal of Abnormal Psychology,* 1965, **70**, 169–179.

Fong, G. T., & Markus, H. Self-schemas and judgments about others. *Social Cognition,* 1982, **1**, 191–204.

Ford, D. H., & Urban, H. B. *Systems of psychotherapy.* New York: Wiley, 1963.

Frank, L. K. Projective methods for the study of personality. *Journal of Psychology,* 1939, **8**, 389–413.

Frankl, V. E. *The doctor and the soul.* New York: Knopf, 1955.

Frankl, V. E. On logotherapy and existential analysis. *American Journal of Psychoanalysis,* 1958, **18**, 28–37.

Franks, C. M., & Wilson, G. T. (Eds.)

Annual review of behavior therapy, theory, and practice. New York: Brunner/Mazel, 1978.

Franks, C. M., & Wilson, G. T. (Eds.) *Annual review of behavior therapy: Theory and practice.* New York: Brunner/Mazel, 1980.

Franks, C. M., Wilson, G. T., Kendall, P. C., & Brownell, K. D. *Annual review of behavior therapy: Theory and practice.* New York: Guilford, 1982.

Freud, S. *Three essays on sexuality.* London: Hogarth, 1953. Original edition, 1905.

Freud, S. The interpretation of dreams. In *Standard edition.* Vols. 4 & 5. London: Hogarth Press, 1953. (First German edition 1900.)

Freud, S. Analysis of a phobia in a five-year-old boy. In *Standard edition.* Vol. 10. London: Hogarth Press, 1959. (First German edition 1909.)

Freud, S. Instincts and their vicissitudes. In *Standard edition.* Vol. 14. London: Hogarth Press, 1957. (First German edition 1915.)

Freud, S. Beyond the pleasure principle. In *Standard edition.* Vol. 18. London: Hogarth Press, 1955. (First German edition 1920.)

Freud, S. Psycho-analytic notes upon an autobiographical account of a case of paranoia (dementia paranoides). In *Collected Papers,* Vol. III. New York: Basic Books, 1959. Originally published in 1911.

Freud, S. *A general introduction to psychoanalysis.* New York: Permabooks, 1953. Boni & Liveright edition, 1924.

Freud, S. *Civilization and its discontents.* London: Hogarth, 1949. Original edition, 1930.

Freud, S. *New introductory lectures on psychoanalysis.* New York: Norton, 1933.

Freud, S. An outline of psychoanalysis. *International Journal of Psychoanalysis,* 1940, **21**, 27–84.

Fromm, E. *Sigmund Freud's mission.* New York: Harper, 1959.

Funder, D. C., & Ozer, D. J. Behavior as a function of the situation. *Journal of Personality and Social Psychology,* 1983, **44**, 107–112.

Gaensbauer, T. J. The differentiation of discrete affects. *Psychoanalytic Study of the Child,* 1982, **37**, 29–66.

Gage, N. L. Paradigms for research on teaching. In N. L. Gage (Ed.), *Handbook of research on teaching.* Chicago, Ill.: Rand McNally, 1963.

Gallup, G. G. Toward a comparative psychology of mind. In R. L. Mellgren (Ed.), *Animal cognition and behavior.* New York: Elsevier/North-Holland, in press.

Gardner, R. W., Jackson, D. N., & Messick, S. J. Personality organization in cognitive controls and intellectual abilities. *Psychological Issues,* 1960, Monograph No. 8.

Garfield, S. L., & Bergin, A. E. *Handbook of psychotherapy and behavior change,* 2d ed. New York: Wiley, 1978.

Geer, J. H., & Turteltaub, A. Fear reduction following observation of a model. *Journal of Personality and Social Psychology,* 1967, **6**, 327–331.

Gendlin, E. T. Client-centered developments and work with schizophrenics. *Journal of Counseling Psychology,* 1962, **9**, 205–211.

Gewirtz, J. L. The role of stimulation in models for child development. In L. L. Dittmann (Ed.), *Early child care: The new perspectives.* New York: Atherton, 1968. Pp. 139–168.(a)

Gerwitz, J. L. On designing the functional environment of the child to facilitate behavioral development. In L. L. Dittmann (Ed.), *Early child care: The new perspectives.* New York: Atherton, 1968, Pp. 169–213.(b)

Gewirtz, J. L. Conditional responding as a paradigm for observational, imitative learning and vicarious imitative learning and vicarious reinforcement. In H. W. Reese (Ed.), *Advances in child development and behavior.* New York: Academic Press, 1971. Pp. 274–304.

Gilmore, J. Toward an understanding of imitation. In E. C. Simmerl, R. A. Hoppe, & G. A. Milton (Eds.), *Social facilitation and imitative behavior.* Boston: Allyn and Bacon, 1968. Pp. 217–238.

Glass, D. C. *Behavior patterns, stress, and coronary disease.* Hillsdale, N.J.: Lawrence Erlbaum, 1977.

Glass, D. C., & Carver, C. S. Helplessness and the coronary-prone personality. In J. Garber & M. E. P. Seligman (Eds.), *Human helplessness.* New York: Academic Press, 1980.

Glass, D. C., & Singer, J. E. *Urban stress.* New York: Academic Press, 1972.

Glucksberg, S. General discussion of issues: Relationships between cognitive psychology and the psychology of personality. In N. Cantor and J. Kihlstrom (Eds.), *Personality, cognition, and social interaction.* Hillsdale, N.J.: Erlbaum, 1981.

Glucksberg, S., & King, L. J. Motivated forgetting mediated by implicit verbal chaining: A laboratory analog of repression. *Science,* October 27, 1967, 517–519.

Goffman, E. *The presentation of self in everyday life.* Garden City, N.Y.: Doubleday, 1959.

Goldfried, M. R., & Davison, G. C. *Clinical behavior therapy.* New York: Holt, Rinehart and Winston, 1976.

Goldstein, K. *The organism.* New York: American Book, 1939.

Gordon, J. E. Review of R. B. Cattell's *Personality and social psychology. Contemporary Psychology,* 1966, **11**, 236–238.

Gottesman, I. I. Heritability of personality: A demonstration. *Psychological Monographs,* 1963, **77** (9, Whole No. 572).

Gottesman, I. I., & Shields, J. Schizophrenia in twins: 16 years' consecutive admissions to a psychiatric clinic. *British Journal of Psychiatry,* 1966, **112**, 809–818.

Gray, J. A. *Pavlov.* London: Fontana, 1979.

Gray, J. A. A critique of Eysenck's theory of personality. In H. J. Eysenck (Ed.), *A model for personality.* Berlin: Springer-Verlag, 1981.

Greene, M. A. Client perception of the relationship as a function of worker-client cognitive styles. Unpublished doctoral dissertation, Columbia University School of Social Work, 1972.

Greenspan, S. I. A consideration of some learning variables in the context of psychoanalytic learning perspective. *Psychological Issues,* 1975, **9**, Monograph No. 33.

Greenspoon, J. The reinforcing effects of two spoken sounds on the frequency of two responses. *American Journal of Psychology,* 1955, **68**, 409–416.

Greenspoon, J. Verbal conditioning and clinical psychology. In A. J. Bachrach (Ed.), *Experimental foundations of clinical psychology.* New York: Basic Books, 1962.

Greenspoon, J., & Lamal, P. A. Cognitive behavior modification—who needs it? *Psychological Record,* 1978, **28**, 323–335.

Grier, W. H., & Cobbs, P. M. *Black rage.* New York: Bantam, 1968.

Grinker, R. R., & Spiegel, J. P. *Men under stress.* Philadelphia: Blakiston, 1945.

Groddeck, G. *The book of the it.* New York: Vintage, 1961. Original edition 1923.

Grummon, D. L., & John, Eve S. Changes over client-centered therapy evaluated on psychoanalytically based TAT scales. In C. R. Rogers & R. F. Dymond (Eds.), *Psychotherapy and Personality Change.* Chicago: University of Chicago Press, 1954. Pp. 121–144.

Guilford, J. P. Factors and factors of personality. *Psychological Bulletin,* 1975, **82**, 802–814.

Gump, P. V. A statistical investigation of one psychoanalytic approach and a comparison of it with nondirective therapy. Unpublished M.A. thesis, Ohio State University, 1944.

Gur, R. C., & Sackeim, H. A. Self-deception: A concept in search of a phenomenon. *Journal of Personality and Social Psychology,* 1979, **37,** 147–169.

Haigh, G. Defensive behavior in client-centered therapy. *Journal of Consulting Psychology,* 1949, **13,** 181–189.

Haimowitz, N. R. An investigation into some personality changes occurring in individuals undergoing client-centered therapy. Unpublished Ph.D. dissertation, University of Chicago, 1948.

Halkides, G. An experimental study of four conditions necessary for therapeutic change. Unpublished doctoral dissertation, University of Chicago, 1958.

Hall, C. S. *A primer of Freudian psychology.* New York: Mentor, 1954.

Hall, C. S., & Lindzey, G. *Theories of personality.* New York: Wiley, 1957.

Halpern, J. Projection: A test of the psychoanalytic hypothesis. *Journal of Abnormal Psychology,* 1977, **86,** 536–542.

Harris, B. Whatever happened to Little Albert? *American Psychologist,* 1979, **34,** 151–160.

Harris, J. G., Jr. Validity: The search for a constant in a universe of variables. In M. A. Rickers-Ovsiankina (Ed.), *Rorschach psychology.* New York: Wiley, 1960. Pp. 380–439.

Harrison, R. Cognitive change and participation in a sensitivity-training laboratory. *Journal of Consulting Psychology,* 1966, **30,** 517–520.

Hartshorne, H., & May, M. A. *Studies in the nature of character: Studies in deceit.* New York: Macmillan, 1928.

Haughton, E., & Ayllon, T. Production and elimination of symptomatic behavior. In L. P. Ullmann & L. Krasner (Eds.), *Case studies in behavior modification.* New York: Holt, Rinehart and Winston, 1965, Pp. 94–98.

Havener, P. H., & Izard, C. E. Unrealistic self-enhancement in paranoid schizophrenics. *Journal of Consulting Psychology,* 1962, **26,** 65–68.

Havens, L. Review of D. Wyss, Psychoanalytic schools from the beginning to the present. *Psychotherapy and the Social Science Review,* July 13, 1973.

Hawkins, R. P., Peterson, R. F., Schweid, E., & Bijou, S. W. Behavior therapy in the home: Amelioration of problem parent–child relations with the parent in a therapeutic role. *Journal of Experimental Child Psychology,* 1966, **4,** 99–107.

Hayden, B. C. Experience—A case for possible change: The modulation corollary. In J. C. Mancuso & J. R. Adams-Webber (Eds.), *The construing person.* New York: Praeger, 1982.

Hebb, D. O. The role of neurological ideas in psychology. *Journal of Personality,* 1951, **20,** 39–55.

Heilbrun, K. Silverman's subliminal psychodynamic activation: A failure to replicate. *Journal of Abnormal Psychology,* 1980, **89,** 560–566.

Heine, R. W. An investigation of the relationship between change in personality from psychotherapy as reported by patients and the factors seen by patients as producing change. Unpublished doctoral dissertation, University of Chicago, 1950.

Helper, M. M. Parental evaluations of children and children's self-evaluations. *Journal of Abnormal and Social Psychology,* 1958, **56,** 190–194.

Hendrick, I. *Facts and theories of psychoanalysis.* New York: Knopf, 1934.

Hendrick, I. The discussion of the "instinct to master." *Psychoanalytic Quarterly,* 1943, **12,** 561–565.

Herrnstein, R. J. The evolution of behaviorism. *American Psychologist,* 1977, **32,** 593–602.

Hesse, H. *Siddhartha.* New York: New Directions, 1951.

Hesse, H. *Demian.* New York: Harper, 1965. Originally published in 1925.

Hilgard, E. R. Human motives and the concept of self. *American Psychologist,* 1949, **4,** 374–382.

Hill, W. F. Learning theory and the acquisition of values. *Psychological Review,* 1960, **67,** 317–331.

Hinkle, D. N. The change of personal constructs from the viewpoint of a theory of implications. Unpublished doctoral dissertation, Ohio State University, 1965.

Hiroto, D. S. Locus of control and learned helplessness. *Journal of Experimental Psychology,* 1974, **102**, 187–193. (Copyright 1974 by the American Psychological Association. Reprinted by permission.)

Hiroto, D. S., & Seligman, M. E. P. Generality of learned helplessness in man. *Journal of Personality and Social Psychology,* 1975, **31**, 311–327.

Hitt, W. D. Two models of man. *American Psychologist,* 1969, **24**, 651–658.

Hobbs, N., & Robinson, S. Adolescent development and public policy. *American Psychologist,* 1982, **37**, 212–223.

Hoffman, A. E. A study of reported behavior changes in counseling. *Journal of Consulting Psychology,* 1949, **13**, 190–195.

Hogan, R. On adding apples and oranges in personality psychology. *Contemporary Psychology,* 1982, **27**, 851–852.

Holdstock, T. L., & Rogers, C. R. Person-centered theory. In R. J. Corsini (Ed.), *Current personality theories.* Itasca, Ill.: Peacock, 1977, Pp. 125–152.

Hollingshead, A. B., & Redlich, F. C. *Social class and mental illness.* New York: Wiley, 1958.

Hollon, S. D., & Kendall, P. C. Cognitive self-statements in depression: Development of an Automatic Thoughts Questionnaire. *Cognitive Therapy and Research,* 1980, **4**, 383–395.

Holmes, D. S. Existence of classical projection and the stress-reducing function of attribution projection: A reply to Sherwood. *Psychological Bulletin,* 1981, **90**, 460–466.

Holt, R. R. A clinical-experimental strategy for research in personality. In S. Messick & J. Ross (Eds.), *Measurement in personality and cognition.* New York: Wiley, 1962. Pp. 269–283.(a)

Holt, R. R. Individuality and generalization in the psychology of personality: An evaluation. *Journal of Personality,* 1962, **30**, 377–402.(b)

Holt, R. R. *Methods in clinical psychology.* New York: Plenum, 1978.

Holtzman, W. H. Methodological issues in P technique. *Psychological Bulletin,* 1962, **59**, 248–256.

Honess, T. Children's implicit theories of their peers: A developmental analysis. *British Journal of Psychology,* 1979, **70**, 417–424.

Honess, T. Self-reference in children's descriptions of peers: Egocentricity or collaboration? *Child Development,* 1980, **51**, 476–480.

Horn, J. L. Motivation and the dynamic calculus concepts from multivariate experiment. In R. B. Cattell (Ed.), *Handbook of multivariate experimental psychology.* Chicago: Rand McNally, 1966. Pp. 611–641.

Horney, K. *The neurotic personality of our time.* New York: Norton, 1937.

Horney, K. *Feminine psychology.* New York: Norton, 1973.

Horney, K. *Our inner conflicts.* New York: Norton, 1945.

Howarth, E. A. A factor analysis of selected markers for objective personality factors. *Multivariate Behavioral Research,* 1972, **7**, 451–476.

Howe, M. J. A. Biographical evidence and the development of outstanding individuals. *American Psychologist,* 1982, **37**, 1071–1081.

Hull, C. L. *Mathematico-deductive theory of rote learning.* New Haven, Conn.: Yale University Press, 1940.

Hull, C. L. *Principles of behavior.* New York: Appleton, 1943.

Hull, C. L. Autobiography in E. G. Boring, H. S. Langfeld, H. Werner, & R. M. Yerkes (Eds.), *A history of psychology in autobiography.* Worcester, Mass.: Clark University Press, 1952, Pp. 143–162.

Hundleby, J. D., Pawlik, K., & Cattell, R. B. *Personality factors in objective test devices: A critical integration of a quarter* *of a century's research.* San Diego, Calif.: Knapp, 1965.

Hunt, J. McV. Effects of infant feeding-frustration upon adult hoarding in the Albino rat. *Journal of Abnormal and Social Psychology,* 1941, **36**, 338–360.

Hunt, J. McV. Traditional personality theory in the light of recent evidence. *American Scientist,* 1965, **53**, 80–96.

Hunt, J. McV. Psychological development: Early experience. *Annual Review of Psychology,* 1979, **30**, 103–144.

Huntley, C. W. Judgments of self based upon records of expressive behavior. *Journal of Abnormal and Social Psychology,* 1940, **35**, 398–427.

Ichheiser, G. Misinterpretation of personality in everyday life and the psychologist's frame of reference. *Character and Personality,* 1943, **12**, 145–152.

Inkeles, A. Sociology and psychology. In S. Koch (Ed.), *Psychology: A study of a science.* New York: McGraw-Hill, 1963.

Jackson, D. N., & Messick, S. Content and style in personality assessment. *Psychological Bulletin,* 1958, **55**, 243–252.

Janis, I. L. Psychodynamic aspects of stress tolerance. In S. Z. Klausner (Ed.), *The quest for self-control.* New York: Free Press, 1965, Pp. 215–247.

Jaspars, J. M. F. Individual cognitive structures. *Proceedings of the seventeenth international congress of psychology.* Amsterdam: North-Holland, 1964.

Jenkins, C. D. The coronary-prone personality. In W. D. Gentry & R. B. Williams (Eds.), *Psychological aspects of myocardial infarction and coronary disease.* St. Louis: Mosby, 1979.

Jenkins, C. D., Roseman, R. H., & Zymanski, S. J. *The Jenkins Activity Survey for Health Prediction* (Form B). Boston: Authors, 1972.

Jensen, A. R. Personality. *Annual Review of Psychology,* 1958, **9**, 295–322.

Jensen, A. R. Review of the Maudsley Personality Inventory, In O. K. Buros (Ed.), *Sixth mental measurements yearbook.* Highland Park, N.J.: Gryphon Press, 1965. Pp. 288–291.

Jones, E. *The life and work of Sigmund Freud,* Vol. 1. New York: Basic Books, 1953; Vol. 2, 1955; Vol. 3, 1957.

Jones, E. E., & Nisbett, R. E. The actor and the observer: Divergent perceptions of the causes of behavior. In E. E. Jones, D. E. Kanouse, H. H. Kelley, R. E. Nisbett, S. Valins, & B. Weiner (Eds.), *Attribution: Perceiving the causes of behavior.* Morristown, N.J.: General Learning Press, 1971.

Jones, M. C. A laboratory study of fear. The case of Peter. *Pedagogical Seminar,* 1924, **31**, 308–315.

Jonietz, A. K. A study of the phenomenological changes in perception after psychotherapy as exhibited in the content of Rorschach percepts. Unpublished Ph.D. dissertation, University of Chicago, 1950.

Jourard, S. M., & Remy, R. M. Perceived parental attitudes, the self, and security. *Journal of Consulting Psychology,* 1955, **19**, 364–366.

Jung, C. G. *The integration of the personality.* New York: Farrar & Rinehart, 1939.

Kagan, J. Personality development. In P. London and D. Rosenhan (Eds.), *Foundations of abnormal psychology.* New York: Holt, Rinehart and Winston, 1968. Pp. 117–173.

Kagan, J. Emergent themes in human development. *American Scientist,* 1976, **64**, 186–196.

Kahn, M. W. Clinical and statistical prediction revisited. *Journal of Clinical Psychology,* 1960, **26**, 115–118.

Kahn, M., and Baker, B. Desensitization with minimal therapist contact, *Journal of Abnormal Psychology,* 1968, **73**, 198–200.

Kalish, H. I. Behavior therapy, In B. B. Wolman (Ed.), *Handbook of clinical psychology.* New York: McGraw-Hill, 1965.

Kallmann, F. J. The genetic theory of schizophrenia. *American Journal of Psychiatry,* 1946, **103**, 309–322.

Kamin, L. J. *The science and politics of I. Q.* Hillsdale, N.J.: Erlbaum, 1974.

Kanfer, F. H., & Karoly, P. Self-control: A behavioristic excursion into the lion's den. *Behavior Therapy,* 1972, **3**, 398–416.

Kanfer, F. H., & Phillips, J. S. *Learning foundations of behavior therapy.* New York: Wiley, 1970.

Kanfer, F. H., & Saslow, G. Behavioral analysis: An alternative to diagnostic classification. *Archives of General Psychiatry,* 1965, **12**, 519–538.

Katahn, M., & Koplin, J. H. Paradigm clash. *Psychological Bulletin,* 1968, **69**, 147–148.

Katz, P., & Zigler, E. Self-image disparity: a developmental approach. *Journal of Personality and Social Psychology*, 1967, **5**, 186–195.

Kazdin, A. E. *The token economy: A review and evaluation.* New York: Plenum, 1977.

Kazdin, A. E., & Bootzin, R. R. The token economy:An evaluative review. *Journal of Applied Behavior Analysis,* 1972 **5**, 343–372.

Kazdin, A. E. & Rogers, T. On paradigms and recycled ideologies: Analogue research revisited. *Cognitive Therapy and Research,* 1978, **2**, 105–117.

Kazdin, A. E. & Wilcoxon, L. A. Systematic desensitization and nonspecific treatment effects: A methodological evaluation. *Psychological Bulletin,* 1976, **83**, 729–758.

Kazdin, A. E. & Wilson, G. T. *Evaluation of behavior theory: Issues, evidence, and research strategies.* Cambridge, Mass.: Ballinger, 1978.

Kelly, E. L. Consistency of the adult personality. *American Psychologist,* 1955, **10**, 659–681.

Kelly, G. A. *The psychology of personal constructs.* New York: Norton, 1955.

Kelly, G. A. Man's construction of his alternatives. In G. Lindzey (Ed.), *Assessment of human motives.* New York: Holt, Rinehart and Winston, 1958. Pp. 33–64. (a)

Kelly, G. The theory and technique of assessment. *Annual Review of Psychology,* 1958, **9**, 323–352.(b)

Kelly, G. A. Suicide: The personal construct point of view. In N. L. Faberow & E. S. Schneidman (Eds.), *The cry for help.* New York: McGraw-Hill, 1961. Pp. 255–280.

Kelly, G. A. Non-parametric factor analysis of personality theories. *Journal of Individual Psychology,* 1963, **19**, 115–147.

Kelly, G. A. The language of hypothesis: Man's psychological instrument. *Journal of Individual Psychology,* 1964, **20**, 137–152.

Kendall, P. C. Behavioral assessment and methodology. In C. M. Franks, G. T. Wilson, P. C. Kendall, & K. D. Brownell (Eds.), *Annual Review of behavior therapy: Theory and practice.* New York: Guilford, 1982.

Kessler, C. Semantics and non-directive counseling. Unpublished M. A. thesis, University of Chicago, 1949.

Keniston, K. *The uncommitted.* New York: Harcourt, Brace, & World, 1965.

Kirschenbaum, H. *On becoming Carl Rogers.* New York: Delacorte, 1979.

Klein, G. S. The personal world through perception. In R. R. Blake & G. V. Ramsey (Eds.), *Perception: An approach to personality.* New York: Ronald, 1951. Pp. 328–355.

Klein, G. S. Need and regulation. In M. R. Jones (Ed.), *Nebraska symposium on motivation.* Lincoln: Nebraska University Press, 1954. Pp. 224–274.

Klein, G. S. *Perception, motives and personality.* New York: Knopf, 1970.

Klein, G. S. *Psychoanalytic theory: An exploration of essentials.* New York: International Universities Press, 1976.

Klein, G. S., Barr, Harriet L., & Wolitzky, D. L. Personality. *Annual Review of Psychology,* 1967, **18**, 467–560.

Klein, G. S., & Krech, D. The problem of personality and its theory. Journal of Personality, 1951, **20**, 2–23.

Kleinmuntz, B. *Personality measurement.* Homewood, Ill.: Dorsey, 1967.

Kline, P. *Fact and fantasy in Freudian theory* (2nd edition). London: Methuen, 1981.

Kluckhohn, C. *Mirror for Man*. New York: McGraw-Hill, 1949.

Kluckhohn, C. Culture and behavior. In G. Lindzey (Ed.), *Handbook of social psychology*. Cambridge, Mass.: Addison-Wesley, 1954. Pp. 921–976.

Kluckhohn, C., & Morgan, W. Some notes on Navaho dreams. In G. B. Wilbur & W. Muensterberger (Eds.), *Psychoanalysis and culture*. New York: International Universities Press, 1951. Pp. 120–131.

Kohut, H. *The analysis of the self*. New York: International Universities Press, 1971.

Kohut, H. *The restoration of the self*. New York: International Universities Press, 1977.

Krasner, L. The behavioral scientist and social responsibility: No place to hide. *Journal of Social Issues*, 1965, **21**, 9–30.

Krasner, L. Token economy as an illustration of operant conditioning procedures with the aged, with youth, and with society. In D. J. Levis (Ed.), *Learning approaches to therapeutic behavior change*. Chicago: Aldine, 1970. Pp. 74–101.

Krasner, L. Behavior therapy. *Annual Review of Psychology*. Palo Alto, Calif.: Annual Reviews, 1971, Pp. 483–532. (a)

Krasner, L. The operant approach in behavior therapy. In A. E. Bergin & S. L. Garfield (Eds.), *Handbook of psychotherapy and behavior change*. New York: Wiley, 1971. Pp. 612–652. (b)

Krasner, L., & Ullmann, L.P. *Behavior influence and personality*. New York: Holt, Rinehart and Winston, 1973.

Krech, D., & Crutchfield, R. S. *Elements of psychology*. New York: Knopf, 1958.

Kris, E. Danger and morale. *American Journal of Orthopsychiatry*, 1944, **14**, 147–155.

Kuhn, T. S. *The structure of scientific revolutions*, 2d ed. Chicago: University of Chicago Press, 1970.

Lacey, J. I. The evaluation of autonomic responses: Toward a general solution. *Annals of the New York Academy of Science*, 1956, **67**, 123–164.

Laing, R. D. *The divided self*. London Tavistock, 1959.

Laing, R. D. *The politics of experience*. New York: Ballantine, 1967.

Lambert, M. J., DeJulio, S. S., & Stein, D. M. Therapist interpersonal skills: Process, outcome, methodological considerations and recommendations for future research. *Psychological Bulletin*, 1978, **85**, 467–489.

Landfield, A. W. *Personal construct systems in psychotherapy*. Chicago: Rand McNally, 1971.

Landfield, A. W.(Ed.) *1976 Nebraska symposium on motivation*. Lincoln: University of Nebraska Press, 1977.

Landfield, A. W. A construction of fragmentation and unity. In J. C. Mancuso & J. R. Adams-Webber (Eds.), *The construing person*. New York: Praeger, 1982.

Landfield, A. W., & Leitner, L. M.(Eds.) *Personal construct psychology: Psychotherapy and personality*. New York: Wiley-Interscience, 1980.

Langer, E. J., Janis, I. L., & Wolfer, J. A. Reduction of psychological stress in surgical patients. *Journal of Experimental Social Psychology*, 1975, **11**, 155–165.

Langer, E. J., & Rodin, J. The effects of choice and enhanced personal responsibility for the aged: A field experiment in an institutional setting. *Journal of Personality and Social Psychology*, 1978, **34**, 191–198.

Lang, P. J. Stimulus control, response control, and the desensitization of fear. In D. J. Levis (Ed.), *Learning approaches to therapeutic behavior change*. Chicago: Aldine, 1970. Pp. 148–173.

Lang, P. J. The application of psychophysiological methods to the study of psychotherapy and behavior modification. In A. E. Bergin & S. Garfield (Eds.), *Handbook of psychotherapy and behavior change*. New York: Wiley, 1971, Pp. 75–125.

Lang, P. J., & Lazovik, A. D. Experimental desensitization of a phobic. *Jour-*

nal of Abnormal and Social Psychology, 1963, **66**, 519–525.

Langner, T. S., & Michael, S. T. *Life stress and mental health.* New York: Free Press, 1963.

Lau, R. R. Origins of health locus of control beliefs. *Journal of Personality and Social Psychology*, 1982, **42**, 322–324.

Lazarus, A. A. Behavior therapy, incomplete treatment and symptom substitution. *Journal of Nervous and Mental Disease*, 1965, **140**, 80–86.

Lazarus, A. A. Learning theory and the treatment of depression. *Behavior Research and Therapy*, 1968, **6**, 83–89.

Lazarus, A. A., & Davison, G. C. Clinical innovation in research and practice. In A. E. Bergin & S. L. Garfield (Eds.), *Handbook of psychotherapy and behavior change.* New York: Wiley, 1971, Pp. 196–213.

Lazarus, R. S. The costs and benefits of denial. In S. Breznitz (Ed.), *Denial of stress.* New York: International Universities Press, 1983.

Lecky, P. *Self-consistency: A theory of personality.* New York: Island, 1945.

Ledwidge, B. Cognitive behavior modification: A step in the wrong direction? *Psychological Bulletin*, 1978, **85**, 353–375.

Lepper, M. R., & Greene, D.(Eds.) *The hidden costs of reward: New perspectives on the psychology of human motivation.* Hillsdale, N.J.: Erlbaum, 1978.

Levine, R. A. *Culture, behavior, and personality.* Chicago: Aldine, 1973.

Levis, D. J., & Malloy, P. F. Research in infrahuman and human conditioning. In G. T. Wilson & C. M. Franks (Eds.), *Contemporary behavior therapy: Conceptual and empirical foundations.* New York: Guilford, 1982.

Lewinsohn, P. M., Steinmetiz, J. L., Larson, D. W., & Franklin, J. Depression-related cognitions: Antecedent or consequence. *Journal of Abnormal Psychology*, 1981, **90**, 213–219.

Lewis, M. Newton, Einstein, Piaget and the concept of self: The role of the self in the process of knowing. In L. S. Liben (Ed.), *Piaget and the foundation of knowledge.* Hillsdale, N.J.: Erlbaum, 1982.

Lewis, M., & Brooks-Gunn, J. *Social cognition and the acquisition of self.* New York: Plenum, 1979.

Lewis, M., Feiring, C., McGuffog, C., & Jaskir, J. Predicting psychopathology in six year olds from early social relations. *Child Development*, 1984, in press.

Lewis, M., & Rosenblum, L. A. (Eds.) *The effect of the infant on its caregiver.* New York: Wiley, 1974.

Lewis, M., Young, G., Brooks, J., & Michalson, L. The beginning of friendship. In M. Lewis & L. A. Rosenblum (Eds.), *Friendship and peer relations.* New York: Plenum, 1975. Pp. 27-66.

Liddell, H. S. Conditioned reflex method and experimental neurosis. In J. McV. Hunt (Ed.), *Personality and the behavior disorders.* New York: Ronald, 1944. Pp. 389–412.

Lieberman, D. A. Behaviorism and the mind. *American Psychologist*, 1979, **34**, 319–333.

Lifton, R. J. *Thought reform and the psychology of totalism.* New York: Norton, 1963.

Locksley, A., & Lenauer, M. Considerations for a theory of self-influence processes. In N. Cantor & J. F. Kihlstrom (Eds.), *Personality, cognition, and social interaction.* Hillsdale, N.J.: Erlbaum, 1981.

Loehlin, J. C. Rhapsody in G. *Contemporary Psychology*, 1982, **27**, 623.

Loevinger, J., & Knoll, E. Personality: Stages, traits, and the self. *Annual Review of Psychology*, 1983, **34**, 195–222.

Lord, C. G. Predicting behavioral consistency from an individual's perception of situational similarities. *Journal of Personality and Social Psychology*, 1982, **42**, 1076–1088.

Lovaas, O. I., Koegel, R., Simmons, J. Q., & Long, G. S. Some generalization and follow-up measures on autistic children in behavior therapy. *Journal of Applied Behavior Analysis*, 1973, **6**, 131–166.

Lundin, R. W. *Personality: an experimental approach*. New York: Macmillan, 1961.

Lykken, D. T. Multiple factor analysis and personality research. *Journal of Experimental Research in Personality*, 1971, **5**, 161–170.

Lykken, D. T. Research with twins: The concept of emergenesis. *Psychophysiology*, 1982, **19**, 361–373.

Mackinnon, D. W. & Dukes, W. Repression. In L. Postman (Ed.), *Psychology in the making*. New York: Knopf, 1962. Pp. 662–744.

Macleod, R. B. The place of phenomenological analysis in social psychological theory. In J. H. Rohrer & M. Sherif (Eds.), *Social psychology at the crossroads*, New York: Harper, 1951. Pp. 215–241.

Macleod, R. B. Phenomenology: A challenge to experimental psychology. In T. W. Wann (Ed.), *Behaviorism and phenomenology*. Chicago: University of Chicago Press, 1964. Pp. 47–73.

Madison, P. *Freud's concept of repression and defence: Its theoretical and observational language*. Minneapolis: University of Minnesota Press, 1961.

Magnusson, D. Learned helplessness—welfare for good or bad. *Skandina Viska Enskilda Barsken Quarterly Review*, 1980, **3-4**, 67–74.

Magnusson, D., & Endler, N. S. (Eds.), *Personality at the crossroads: Current issues in interactional psychology*. Hillsdale, N.J.: Erlbaum, 1977.

Maher, B. *Principles of psychopathology*. New York: McGraw-Hill, 1966.

Maher, B. *Clinical psychology and personality: The selected papers of George Kelly*. New York: Wiley, 1969.

Mahoney, M. J. *Cognition and behavior modification*. Cambridge, Mass.: Ballinger, 1974.

Mahoney, M.J. Publication prejudices: An experimental study of confirmatory bias in the peer review system. *Cognitive Therapy and Research*, 1977, **1**, 161–175.

Mahoney, M. J., & Arnkoff, D. Cognitive and self-control therapies. In S. Garfield & A. E. Bergin (Eds.), *Handbook of psychotherapy and behavior change*. New York: Wiley, 1978.

Mahoney, M. J. & Bandura, A. Self-reinforcement in pigeons. *Learning and motivation*, 1972, **3**, 293–303.

Mahoney, M. J., Kazdin, A. E., & Kenigsberg, M. Getting published. *Cognitive Therapy and Research*, 1978, **2**, 69–70.

Mahoney, M. J., & Mahoney, K. *Permanent weight control*. New York: Norton, 1976.

Maier, N. R. F. *Frustration: The study of behavior without a goal*. New York: McGraw-Hill, 1949.

Maier, N. R. F. Maier's Law. *American Psychologist, 1960*, **15**, 208–212.

Mancuso, J. C., & Adams-Webber, J. R. (Eds.), *The construing person*. New York: Praeger, 1982.

Mandel, N. M., & Shrauger, J. S. The effects of self-evaluative statements on heterosocial approach in shy and nonshy males. *Cognitive Therapy and Research*, 1980, **4**, 369–381.

Marcia, J. E., Rubin, B. M. & Efran J. S. Systematic desensitization: Expectancy change or counterconditioning? *Journal of Abnormal Psychology*, 1969, **74**, 382–387.

Marks, J., Sonoda, B. & Schalock, R. Reinforcement versus relationship therapy for schizophrenics. *Journal of Abnormal Psychology, 1968*, **73**, 397–402.

Markus, H. Self-schemata and processing information about the self. *Journal of Personality and Social Psychology*, 1977, **35**, 63–78.

Markus, H., Crane, M., Bernstein, S., & Siladi, M. Self-schemas and gender. *Journal of Personality and Social Psychology*, 1982, **42**, 38–50.

Markus, H., & Smith, J. The influence of self-schemata on the perception of others. In N. Cantor & J. F. Kihlstrom (Eds.), *Personality, cognition, and social interaction*. Hillsdale, N.J.: Erlbaum, 1981.

Marlatt, G. A., & Gordon, J. R. Determinants of relapse: Implications for the maintenance of behavior change. In P. O. Davidson & S. M. Davidson (Eds.), *Behavioral medicine: Changing health lifestyles*. New York: Brunner/Mazel, 1980.

Maslow, A. H. *Motivation and personality*. New York: Harper, 1954.

Maslow, A. H. *Toward a psychology of being*. Princeton, N.J.: Van Nostrand, 1968.

Maslow, A. H. *The farther reaches of human nature*. New York: Viking, 1971.

Matthews, K. A. Psychological perspectives on the Type A behavior pattern. *Psychological Bulletin*, 1982, **91**, 293–323.

May, M. A. Foreword. In J. W. Dollard, L. W. Doob, N. E. Miller, O. H. Mowrer, & R. R. Sears, *Frustration and aggression*. New Haven, Conn.: Yale University Press, 1939.

May, R. *The meaning of anxiety*. New York: Ronald, 1950.

Mayo, C. W., & Crockett, W. H. Cognitive complexity and primacy; recency effects in impression formation. *Journal of Abnormal and Social Psychology*, 1964, **68**, 335–338.

McArthur, C., Waldron, E., & Dickinson, J. The psychology of smoking. *Journal of Abnormal and Social Psychology*, 1958, **56**, 267–275.

McCleary, R.A., & Lazarus, R. S. Autonomic discrimination without awareness. *Journal of Personality, 1949,* **18**, 171–179.

McClelland, D. C. *The achieving society*. Princeton, N.J.: Van Nostrand, 1961.

McCoy, M. M. Positive and negative emotion: A personal construct theory interpretation. In H. Bonarius, R. Holland, & S. Rosenberg (Eds.), *Personal construct psychology: Recent advances in theory and practice*. London: Macmillan, 1981.

McGinnies, E. Emotionality and perceptual defense. *Psychological Review*, 1949, **56**, 244–251.

McGuire, W. J. Some impending reorientations in social psychology: Some thoughts provoked by Kenneth Ring. *Journal of Experimental Social Psychology*, 1967, **3**, 124–139.

McNemar, Q. At random: Sense and nonsense. *American Psychologist*, 1960, **15**, 295–300.

Medinnus, G. R. & Curtis, F. J. The relation between maternal self-acceptance and child acceptance. *Journal of Consulting Psychology*, 1963, **27**, 542–544.

Mednick, S. A. A learning theory approach to research in schizophrenia. *Psychological Bulletin*, 1958, **55**, 316–327.

Meehl, P. E. The dynamics of "structured" personality tests. *Journal of Clinical Psychology*, 1945, **1**, 296–303.

Mehrabian, A., & Russell, J. A. *An approach to environmental psychology*. Cambridge, Mass.: MIT Press, 1974.

Meichenbaum, D. Cognitive modification of test anxious college students. *Journal of Consulting and Clinical Psychology*, 1972, **39**, 370–380. (Copyright 1972 by the American Psychological Association. Reprinted by permission.)

Meichenbaum, D. Cognitive factors in behavior modification: Modifying what clients say to themselves. In C. M. Franks & G. T. Wilson (Eds.), *Annual review of behavior therapy*. New York: Brunner/Mazel, 1973. Pp. 416–431.

Meichenbaum, D. *Cognitive-behavior modification: An integrative approach*. New York: Plenum, 1977.

Meichenbaum, D. Cognitive behavior modification: The need for a fairer assessment. *Cognitive Therapy & Research*, 1979, **3**, 127–132.

Meichenbaum, D., & Cameron, R. Cognitive behavior therapy. In G. T. Wilson & C. M. Franks (Eds.), *Contemporary behavior therapy: Conceptual and empirical foundations*. New York: Guilford, 1982.

Meichenbaum, D., Turk, D., & Burstein, S. The nature of coping with stress. In

I. G. Sarason & C. D. Spielberger (Eds.), *Stress and anxiety*. Washington, D.C.: Hemisphere, 1975. Pp. 337–360.

Melges, F. T., & Weisz, A. E. The personal future and suicidal ideation. *Journal of Nervous and Mental Disease*, 1971, **153**, 244–250.

Messick, S. Personality Structure. *Annual Review of Psychology*. Palo Alto, Calif.: Annual Reviews, 1961. Pp. 93-128.

Migler, B., & Wolpe, J. Automated self-desensitization: A case report. *Behavior Research and Therapy*, 1967, **5**, 133–135.

Milgram, N. A., & Helper, M. M. The social desirability set in individual and grouped self-ratings. *Journal of Consulting Psychology*, 1961, **25**, 91.

Milgram, S. Some conditions of obedience and disobedience to authority. *Human Relations*, 1965, **18**, 57–76.

Miller, G. Quoted in the *New York Times*, November 12, 1982, page C1.

Miller, N. E. Theory and experiment relating psychoanalytic displacement to stimulus-response generalization. *Journal of Abnormal and Social Psychology*, 1948, **43**, 155–178.

Miller, N. E. Comments on theoretical models: Illustrated by the development of a theory of conflict behavior. *Journal of Personality*, 1951, **20**, 82–100.

Miller, N. E. Biofeedback and visceral learning. *Annual review of psychology*, 1978, **29**, 373–404.

Miller, N. E. Behavioral medicine: Symbiosis between laboratory and clinic. *Annual Review of Psychology*, 1983, **34**, 1–31.

Miller, N. E., & Dollard, J. *Social learning and imitation*. New Haven, Conn.: Yale, 1941.

Miller, S., & Mangan, C. E. Interacting effects of information and coping style in adapting to gynecologic stress: Should the doctor tell all? *Journal of Personality and Social Psychology*, 1983, **45**, 223–236.

Mischel, W. Delay of gratification, need for achievement, and acquiesence in another culture. *Journal of Abnormal and Social Psychology*, 1961, **62**, 543–552.

Mischel, W. *Personality assessment*. New York: Wiley, 1968.

Mischel, W. *Introduction to personality*. New York: Holt, Rinehart and Winston, 1971.

Mischel, W. Toward a cognitive social learning reconceptualization of personality. *Psychological Review*, 1973, **80**, 252–283.

Mischel, W. *Introduction to personality*. New York: Holt, Rinehart and Winston, 1976.

Mischel, W. Self-control and the self. In T. Mischel (Ed.), *The self: Psychological and philosophical issues*. Totowa, N.J.: Rowman & Littlefield, 1977. Pp. 31–64.

Mischel, W. Personality and cognition: Something borrowed, something new? In N. Cantor & J. F. Kihlstrom (Eds.), *Personality, cognition, and social interaction*. Hillsdale, N.J.: Erlbaum, 1981.

Mischel, W. A cognitive-social learning approach to assessment. In T. V. Merluzzi, C. R. Glass, & M. Genest (Eds.), *Cognitive assessment*. New York: Guilford, 1982.

Mischel, W., & Peake, P. K. Beyond déjà vu in the search for cross-situational consistency. *Psychological Review*, 1982, **89**, 730–755.

Mischel, W., & Peake, P. K. Analyzing the construction of consistency in personality. In M. M. Page (Ed.), *Personality: Current theory and research*. Lincoln: University of Nebraska Press, 1983.

Mischel, W., & Grusec, J. Determinants of the rehearsal and transmission of neutral and aversive behaviors. *Journal of Personality and Social Psychology*, 1966, **3**, 197–205.

Mischel, W., & Liebert, R. M. Effects of discrepancies between observed and imposed reward criteria on their acquisition and transmission. *Journal of Personality and Social Psychology*, 1966, **3**, 45–53.

Mischel, W., & Liebert, R. M. The role of power in the adoption of self-reward patterns. *Child Development*, 1967, **38**, 673–683.

Monson, T. C., Hesley, J. W., &

Chernick, L. Specifying when personality traits can and cannot predict behavior: An alternative to abandoning the attempt to predict single-act criteria. *Journal of Personality and Social Psychology*, 1982, **43**, 385–399.

Morgan, C. D., & Murray, H. A. A method for investigating fantasies. *Archives of Neurology and Psychiatry*, 1935, **34**, 289–306.

Morgan, W. G. Non-necessary conditions or useful procedures in desensitization: A reply to Wilkins. *Psychological Bulletin*, 1973, **79**, 373–375.

Morin, S. F. Heterosexual bias in psychological research on lesbianism and male homosexuality. *American Psychologist*, 1977, **32**, 629–637.

Morrison, J. K., & Cometa, M. C. Variations in developing construct systems: The experience corollary. In J. C. Mancusco & J. R. Adams-Webber (Eds.), *The construing person*. New York: Praeger, 1982.

Moss, P. D., & McEvedy, C. P. An epidemic of over-breathing among schoolgirls. *British Medical Journal* Nov. 26, 1966, 1295–1300.

Mowrer, O. H., & Mowrer, W. A. Enuresis: A method for its study and treatment. *American Journal of Orthopsychiatry*, 1928, **8**, 436–447.

Muench, G. A. An evaluation of non-directive psychotherapy by means of the Rorschach and other tests. *Applied Psychology Monographs*, 1947 (13), 1–103.

Munroe, R. L. *Schools of psychoanalytic thought*. New York: Dryden, 1955.

Murray, E. J. A case study in a behavioral analysis of psychotherapy. *Journal of Abnormal and Social Psychology*, 1954, **49**, 305–310.

Murray, E. J., & Berkun, M. M. Displacement as a function of conflict. *Journal of Abnormal and Social Psychology*, 1955, **51**, 47–50.

Murray, E. J., & Jacobson, L. I. The nature of learning in traditional and behavioral psychotherapy. In A. E. Bergin & S. Garfield (Eds.), *Handbook of psychotherapy and behavior change*. New York; Wiley, 1971. Pp. 709–747.

Murray, H. A. *Explorations in personality*. New York: Oxford University Press, 1938.

Murray, H. A., & Kluckhohn, L. A conception of personality. In C. Kluckhohn, H. Murray, & D. M. Schneider (Eds.), *Personality in nature, society, and culture*. New York: Knopf, 1956. Pp. 3–49.

Neimeyer, R. A. The structure and meaningfulness of tacit construing. In H. Bonarius, R. Holland, & S. Rosenberg (Eds.), *Personal construct psychology: Recent advances in theory and practice*. London: Macmillan, 1981.

Neisser, U. *Cognitive psychology*. New York: Appleton-Century-Crofts, 1967.

Neisser, U. On "social knowing." *Personality and Social Psychology Bulletin*, 1980, **6**, 601–605.

Nesselroade, J. R., & Bartsch, T. W. Multivariate perspectives in the construct validity of the trait-state distinction. In R. B. Cattell & R. M. Dreger (Eds.), *Handbook of modern personality theory*. Washington, D.C.: Hemisphere, 1977. Pp. 221–238.

Nesselroade, J. R., & Delhees, K. H. Methods and findings in experimentally based personality theory. In R. B. Cattell (Ed.), *Handbook of multivariate experimental psychology*. Chicago: Rand McNally, 1966. Pp. 563–610.

Newcomb, T. M., Koening, K. E., Flachs R., & Warwick, D. P. *Persistence and change*. New York: Wiley, 1967.

Nisbett, R., & Ross, L. *Human inference: Strategies and shortcomings of social judgment*. Englewood Cliffs, N.J.: Prentice-Hall, 1980.

Nisbett, R. E., & Wilson, T. D. Telling more than we know: Verbal reports on mental processes. *Psychological Review*, 1977, **84**, 231–279.

Norman, D. A. Twelve issues for cognitive science. *Cognitive Science*, 1980, **4**, 1–32.

Olds, J. Self-stimulation of the brain. *Science*, 1958, **127**, 315–324.

O'Leary, K. D. The assessment of psychopathology in children. In H. C. Quay & J. S. Werry (Eds.), *Psychopathological disorders of childhood*. New York: Wiley, 1972 Pp. 234–272.

Olweus, D. The consistency issue in personality psychology revisited. *British Journal of Social and Clinical Psychology*, 1980, **19**, 377–390.

Olweus, D. Continuity in aggressive and withdrawn, inhibited behavior patterns. *Psychiatry and Social Science*, 1981, **1**, 141–159.

Opler, M. K., & Singer, J. L. Ethnic differences in behavior and psychopathology. *International Journal of Social Psychiatry*, 1956, **2**, 11–23.

Orne, M. T. On the social psychology of the psychological experiment: With particular reference to demand characteristics and their implications. American Psychologist, 1962, **17**, 776–783.

Orne, M. T., & Schreibe, K. E. The contribution of nondeprivation factors in the production of sensory deprivation effects: The psychology of the "panic button." *Journal of Abnormal and Social Psychology*, 1964, **68**, 3–13.

Osgood, C. E., & Luria, Z. A blind analysis of a case of multiple personality using the semantic differential. *Journal of Abnormal & Social Psychology*, 1954, **49**, 579–591.

Osgood, C. E., Suci, G. J., & Tannenbaum, P. H. *The measurement of meaning*. Urbana, Ill.: University of Illinois Press, 1957.

Patterson, G. R. Behavioral intervention procedures in the classroom and in the home. In A. E. Bergin & S. L. Garfield (Eds.), *Handbook of psychotherapy and behavior change*. New York: Wiley, 1971. Pp. 751–775.

Paul, G. L. *Insight vs desensitization in psychotherapy*. Stanford, Calif.: Stanford University Press, 1966.

Paul, G. L. Insight versus desensitization in psychotherapy two years after termination. *Journal of Consulting Psychology*, 1967, **31**, 109–118.

Paul, G. L. Two year follow-up of systematic desensitization in therapy groups. *Journal of Abnormal Psychology*, 1968, **73**, 119–130.

Paul, G. L., & Shannon, D. T. Treatment of anxiety through systematic desensitization in therapy groups. *Journal of Abnormal Psychology*, 1966, **71**, 124–135.

Pavlov, I.P. *Conditioned Reflexes*. London: Oxford University Press, 1927.

Pavlov, I. P. *Lectures on conditioned reflexes*. Vol. 2. London: Oxford University Press, 1928.

Pervin, L. A. Rigidity in neurosis and general personality functioning. *Journal of Abnormal and Social Psychology*, 1960, **61**, 389–395.

Pervin, L.A. Existentialism, psychotherapy, and psychology. *American Psychologist*, 1960, **15**, 305–309.

Pervin, L. A. Predictive strategies and the need to confirm them: Some notes on pathological types of decisions. *Psychological Reports*, 1964, **15**, 99–105.

Pervin, L. A. A twenty-college study of Student x College interaction using TAPE (Transactional Analysis of Personality and Environment): Rationale, reliability, and validity. *Journal of Educational Psychology*, 1967, **58**, 290–302.(a)

Pervin, L. A. Satisfaction and perceived self-environment similarity: A semantic differential study of student-college interaction. *Journal of Personality*, 1967, **35**, 623–634. (b)

Pervin, L. A. Performance and satisfaction as a function of individual-environment fit. *Psychological Bulletin*, 1968, **69**, 56–68.

Pervin, L. A. A free-response description approach to the analysis of person-situation interaction. *Journal of Personality and Social Psychology*, 1976, **34**, 465–474.

Pervin, L. A. The representative design of person-situation research. In D. Magnusson & N. S. Endler (Eds.), *Personality at the crossroads: Current issues in interactional psychology*. Hillsdale, N.J.: Erlbaum, 1977.

Pervin, L.A. Definitions, measurements,

and classifications of stimuli, situations, and environments. *Human Ecology*, 1978, **6**, 71–105.

Pervin, L. A. *Current controversies and issues in personality.* New York: Wiley, 1978. (Second Edition, 1984)

Pervin, L. A. Idiographic approaches to personality. In J. McV Hunt & N. Endler (Eds.), *Personality and the behavior disorders.* New York: Wiley, 1983.

Pervin, L. A., & Lewis, M. (Eds.) *Perspectives in interactional psychology.* New York: Plenum, 1978.

Pervin, L. A., & Lilly, R. S. Social desirability and self–ideal self on the semantic differential. *Educational and Psychological Measurement,* 1967, **27**, 845–853.

Pervin, L. A., & Rubin, D. B. Student dissatisfaction with college and the college dropout: A transactional approach. *Journal of Social Psychology,* 1967, **72**, 285–295.

Peskin, H. Unity of science begins at home: A study of regional factionalism in clinical psychology. *American Psychologist,* 1963, **18**, 96–100.

Peterson, C., Schwartz, S. M., & Seligman, M. E. P. Self-blame and depressive symptoms. *Journal of Personality and Social Psychology,* 1981, **41**, 253–259.

Peterson, C., Semmel, A., von Baeyer, C., Abramson, L. Y., Metalsky, G. I., & Seligman, M. E. P. The Attributional Style Questionnaire. *Cognitive Therapy and Research,* 1982, **6**, 287–300.

Pfungst, O. *Clever Hans: A contribution to experimental, animal, and human psychology.* New York: Holt, Rinehart and Winston, 1911.

Phares, E. J. Locus of control. In H. London & J. E. Exner, Jr. (Eds.), *Dimensions of personality.* New York: Wiley, 1978. Pp. 263–304.

Poch, S. M. A study of changes in personal constructs as related to interpersonal prediction and its outcomes. Unpublished doctoral dissertation, Ohio State University, 1952.

Pohl, R. L., & Pervin, L. A. Academic performance as a function of task requirements and cognitive style. *Psychological Reports,* 1968, **22**, 1017–1020.

Pollack, J. M. Obsessive-compulsive personality: A review. *Psychological Bulletin,* 1979, **86**, 225–241.

Posner, M. Cognition and personality. In N. Cantor & J. F. Kihlstron (Eds.), *Personality, cognition, and social interaction.* Hillsdale, N.J.: Erlbaum, 1981.

Raimy, V. C. Self-reference in counseling interviews. *Journal of Consulting Psychology,* 1948, **12**, 153–163.

Rapaport, D. A critique of Dollard and Miller's "Personality and Psychotherapy." *American Journal of Orthopsychiatry,* 1953, **23**, 204–208.

Raskin, N. J. Analysis of six parallel studies of the therapeutic process. *Journal of Consulting Psychology,* 1949, **13**, 206–220.

Razran, G. A quantitative study of meaning by a conditioned salivary technique. *Science,* 1939, **90**, 89–91.

Rescorla, R. A., & Holland, P. C. Behavioral studies of associative learning in animals. *Annual Review of Psychology,* 1982, **33**, 265–308.

Reynolds, G. S. *A primer of operant conditioning.* Glenview, Ill.: Scott, Foresman, 1968.

Rickels, K., & Cattell, R. B. The clinical factor validity and trueness of the IPAT verbal and objective batteries for anxiety and repression. *Journal of Clinical Psychology,* 1965, **21**, 257–264.

Riesman, D. *The lonely crowd.* Garden City, N.Y.: Doubleday, 1950.

Ring, K. Experimental social psychology: Some sober questions about some frivolous values. *Journal of Experimental-Social Psychology,* 1967, **3**, 113–123.

Rodin, J., & Langer, E. Long-term effects of a control-relevant intervention with institutionalized aged. *Journal of Personality and Social Psychology,* 1977, **35**, 897–902.

Rogers, C. R. *Clinical treatment of the problem child.* Boston: Houghton Mifflin, 1939.

Rogers, C. R. The process of psychotherapy. *Journal of Consulting Psychology,* 1940, **4**, 161–164.

Rogers, C. R. *Counseling and psychotherapy.* Boston: Houghton Mifflin, 1942.

Rogers, C. R. Significant aspects of client-centered therapy. In H. M. Ruitenbeek (Ed.), *Varieties of personality theory.* New York: Dutton, 1964. Pp. 168–183. Originally presented in 1946.

Rogers, C. R. Some observations on the organization of personality *American Psychologist,* 1947, **2**, 358–368.

Rogers, C. R. Client-centered therapy. Boston: Houghton Mifflin, 1951.

Rogers, C. R. Some directions and end points in therapy. In O. H. Mowrer (Ed.), *Psychotherapy: Theory and research.* New York: Ronald, 1953. Pp. 44–68.

Rogers, C. R. The case of Mrs. Oak: A research analysis. In C. R. Rogers & R. F. Dymond (Eds.), *Psychotherapy and personality change.* Chicago: University of Chicago Press, 1954. Pp. 259–348.

Rogers, C. R. Some issues concerning the control of human behavior. *Science,* 1956, **124**, 1057–1066.

Rogers, C. R. A process conception of psychotherapy. *American Psychologist,* 1958, **13**, 142–149.

Rogers, C. R. A theory of therapy, personality, and interpersonal relationships as developed in the client-centered framework. In S. Koch (Ed.), *Psychology: A study of science.* New York: McGraw-Hill, 1959. Pp. 184–256.

Rogers, C. R. *On Becoming a person.* Boston: Houghton Mifflin, 1961.(a)

Rogers, C. R. A tentative scale for the measurement of process in psychotherapies. In M. P. Stein (Ed.), *Contemporary Psychotherapies.* New York: Free Press, 1961, Pp. 113–127.(b)

Rogers, C. R. The process equation in psychotherapy. *American Journal of Psychotherapy,* 1961, **15**, 27–45.(c)

Rogers, C. R. The actualizing tendency in relation to "motives" and to consciousness. In M. R. Jones (Ed.), *Nebraska symposium on motivation.* Lincoln: University of Nebraska, 1963. Pp. 1–24.

Rogers, C. R. Toward a science of the person. In T. W. Wann (Ed.), *Behaviorism and phenomenology.* Chicago: University of Chicago Press, 1964. Pp. 109–133.

Rogers, C. R. Client-centered therapy. In S. Arieti (Ed.), *American Handbook of Psychiatry.* New York: Basic Books, 1966. Pp. 183–200.

Rogers, C. R. (Ed.) *The therapeutic relationship and its impact: A study of psychotherapy with schizophrenics.* Madison, Wisc.: University of Wisconsin Press, 1967.

Rogers, C. R. *On encounter groups.* New York: Harper, 1970.

Rogers, C. R. *Becoming partners: Marriage and its alternatives.* New York: Delacorte, 1972(a)

Rogers, C. R. My personal growth. In A. Burton (Ed.), *Twelve therapists.* San Francisco: Jossey-Bass, 1972. Pp. 28–77.(b)

Rogers, C. R. In retrospect: Forty-six years. Distinguished professional contribution award address. American Psychological Association Convention, Montreal, August 1973.

Rogers, C. R. *Carl Rogers on personal power.* New York: Delacorte, 1977.

Rogers, C. R. *A way of being.* Boston: Houghton Mifflin, 1980.

Rogers, C. R., & Dymond, R. F. (Eds.) *Psychotherapy and personality change.* Chicago: University of Chicago Press, 1954.

Rogers, C. R., Gendlin, E. T., Kiesler, D. J., & Truax, C. B. *The therapeutic relationship and its impact: A study of the psychotherapy of schizophrenics.* Madison: University of Wisconsin Press, 1967.

Rogers, C. R., & Skinner, B. F. Some issues concerning the control of human behavior: A symposium. *Science,* 1956, **124**, 1057–1066.

Rogers, T. B., Kuiper, N. A., & Kirker,

W. S. Self-reference and the encoding of personal information. *Journal of Personality and Social Psychology,* 1977, **35,** 677–688.

Rorschach, H. *Psychodiagnostics.* Bern: Huber, 1921.

Rosch, E. Principles of categorization. In E. Rosch & B. B. Lloyd (Eds.), *Cognition and categorization.* Hillsdale, N.J.: Erlbaum, 1978.

Rosch, E., Mervis, C., Gray, W., Johnson, D., & Boyes-Braem, P. Basic objects in natural categories. *Cognitive Psychology,* 1976, **8,** 382–439.

Rosen, E. Differences between volunteers and non-volunteers for psychological studies. *Journal of Applied Psychology,* 1951, **35,** 185–193.

Rosenberg, S. Personal constructs in person perception. *Nebraska Symposium on Motivation,* 1977, **24,** 179–242.

Rosenberg, S. A theory in search of its zeitgeist. *Contemporary Psychology,* 1980, **25,** 898–900.

Rosenberg, S., & Jones, R. A. A method of investigating and representing a person's implicit theory of personality: Theodore Dreiser's view of people. *Journal of Personality and Social Psychology,* 1972, **22,** 372–386.

Rosenberg, S., & Sedlak, A. Structural representations of implicit personality theory. *Advances in Experimental Social Psychology,* 1972, **6,** 235–297.

Rosenblatt, A. D., & Thickstun, G. T. Modern psychoanalytic concepts in a general psychology. *Psychological Issues,* 1977, **11,** Monograph No. 42–43.

Rosenhan, D. Some origins of concern for others. M. P. Mussen (Ed.), *New directions in child psychology.* New York: Holt, Rinehart and Winston, 1969. Pp. 134–154.

Rosenthal, R. The effect of the experimenter on the results of psychological research. In B. A. Maher (Ed.), *Progress in experimental personality research,* Vol. 1 New York: Academic Press, 1964. Pp. 80–114.

Rosenthal, R., & Jacobson, L. *Pygmalion in the classroom.* New York: Holt, Rinehart and Winston, 1968.

Rosenthal, R., & Rosnow, R. L. (Eds.) *Artifact in behavioral research.* New York: Academic Press, 1969.

Rosenthal, R., & Rubin, D. Interpersonal expectancy effects: The first 345 studies. *Behavioral & Brain Sciences,* 1978, **3,** 377–415.

Rosenthal, T., & Bandura, A. Psychological modeling: Theory and practice. In S. L. Garfield & A. E. Bergin (Eds.), *Handbook of psychotherapy and behavior change.* New York: Wiley, 1978. Pp. 621–658.

Rosenthal, T. L., & Zimmerman, B. J. *Social learning and cognition.* New York: Academic Press, 1978.

Rosenzweig, S. Need-persistive and ego-defensive reactions to frustration as demonstrated by an experiment on repression. *Psychological Review,* 1941, **48,** 347–349.

Ross, L. The "intuitive scientist" formulation and its developmental implications. In J. H. Flavell & L. Ross (Eds.), *Social cognitive development.* Cambridge: Cambridge University Press, 1981.

Rotter, J. B. *Social learning and clinical psychology.* Englewood Cliffs, N.J.: Prentice-Hall, 1954.

Rotter, J. B. The role of the psychological situation in determining the direction of human behavior. In M. R. Jones (Ed.), *Nebraska Symposium on Motivation.* Lincoln: University of Nebraska Press, 1955.

Rotter, J. B. Generalized expectancies for internal versus external control of reinforcement. *Psychological Monographs,* 1966, 80, (Whole No. 609).

Rotter, J. B. *The development and application of social learning theory.* New York: Praeger, 1982.

Rubinstein, E. A. Warning: The surgeon general's research program may be dangerous to preconceived notions. *Journal of Social Issues,* 1976, **32,** 18–34.

Rudin, S. A. & Stagner, R. Figure-ground

pheonomena in the perception of physical and social stimuli. *Journal of Psychology* 1958, **45**, 213–225.

Runyan, W. M. Why did Van Gogh cut off his ear? The problem of alternative explanations in psychobiography. *Journal of Personality and Social Psychology,* 1981, **40**, 1070–1077.

Runyan, W. M. In defense of the case study method. *American Journal of Orthopsychiatry,* 1982, **52**, 440–446.

Sackeim, H. A., & Gur, R. C. Self-deception, other-deception, and self-reported psychopathology. *Journal of Consulting and Clinical Psychology,* 1979, **47**, 213–215.

Salmon, P. A psychology of personal growth in D. Bannister (Ed.), *Perspectives in personal construct theory.* New York: Academic Press, 1970. Pp. 197–221.

Sandler, J. Masochism: An empirical analysis. *Psychological Bulletin,* 1964, **62**, 197–204.

Sanford, N. Personality: Its place in psychology. In S. Koch (Ed.), *Psychology: A study of a science.* New York: McGraw-Hill, 1963, Pp. 488–592.

Sarason, I. G. *Personality: An objective approach.* New York: Wiley, 1966.

Schachter, S. The interaction of cognitive and physiological determinants of emotional state. In L. Berkowitz (Ed.), *Advances in experimental social psychology.* New York: Academic Press, 1964. Pp. 49–80.

Schachter, S., & Singer, J. Cognitive, social, and physiological determinants of emotional state. *Psychological Review,* 1962, **69**, 379–399.

Schafer, R. *Psychoanalytic interpretation in Rorschach testing.* New York: Grune & Stratton, 1954.

Schafer, R. *A new language for psychoanalysis.* New Haven, Conn.: Yale, 1976.

Schafer, R. *Language and insight.* New Haven, Conn.: Yale University Press, 1978.

Schank, R., & Abelson, R. *Scripts, plans, goals, and understanding.* Hillsdale, N.J.: Erlbaum, 1977.

Schneider, D. J. Personal construct psychology: An international menu. *Contemporary Psychology,* 1982, **27**, 712–713.

Schneider, J. M. College students' belief in personal control. *Journal of Individual Psychology,* 1971, **27**, 188.

Schwartz, G. E. Integrating psychobiology and behavior therapy: A systems perspective. In G. T. Wilson & C. M. Franks (Eds.), *Contemporary behavior therapy: Conceptual and empirical foundations.* New York: Guilford, 1982.

Schwartz, R. M., & Gottman, J. M. Toward a task analysis of assertive behavior. *Journal of Consulting and Clinical Psychology,* 1976, **44**, 910–920.

Scott, J. P. *Early experience and the organization of behavior.* Belmont, Calif.: Wadsworth, 1968.

Sears, R. R. Experimental studies of projection. I. Attribution of traits. *Journal of Social Psychology,* 1936, **7**, 151–163.

Sears, R. R. Relation of fantasy aggression to interpersonal aggression. *Child Development,* 1950, **21**, 5–6.

Sears, R. R., Rau, L., & Alpert, R. *Identification and child-rearing.* Standford, Calif.: Stanford University Press, 1965.

Sechrest, L. The psychology of personal constructs. In J. M. Wepman & R. W. Heine (Eds.), *Concepts of personality.* Chicago: Aldine, 1963. Pp. 206–233.

Sechrest, L. J. Personal constructs theory. In R. J. Corsini (Ed.), *Current personality theories.* Itasca, Ill.: Peacock, 1977. Pp. 203–241.

Sechrest, L. A passion for theory. *Contemporary Psychology,* 1979, **24**, 19–20.

Sechrest, L., & Jackson, D. N. Social intelligence and accuracy of interpersonal predictions. *Journal of Personality,* 1961, **29**, 167–182.

Seeman, J. Perspectives in client-centered therapy. In B. B. Wolman (Ed.), *Handbook of Clinical Psychology.* New York:

McGraw-Hill, 1965. Pp. 1215–1229.

Seligman, M. E. P. *Helplessness.* San Francisco: Freeman, 1975.

Sheerer, E. T. An analysis of the relationship between acceptance of and respect for others in ten counseling cases. *Journal of Consulting Psychology,* 1949, **13,** 169–175.

Sherman, J. A. Imitation and language development. In H. W. Reese (Ed.), *Advances in child development and behavior.* New York: Academic Press, 1971. Pp. 239–272.

Sherwood, G. G. Self-serving biases in person-perception: An examination of projection as a mechanism of defense. *Psychological Bulletin,* 1981, **90,** 445–459.

Sherwood, G. G. Consciousness and stress reduction in defensive projection: A reply to Holmes. *Psychological Bulletin,* 1982, **91,** 372–375.

Shevrin, H., & Dickman, S. The psychological unconscious: A necessary assumption for all psychological theory? *American Psychologist,* 1980, **35,** 421–434.

Shields, J. Heredity and environment. In H. J. Eysenck & G. D. Wilson (Eds.), *A textbook of human psychology.* Baltimore: University Park Press, 1976.

Shields, S. Functionalism, Darwinism, and the psychology of women: A study in social myth. *American Psychologist,* 1975, **30,** 739–754.

Shontz, F. C. *Research methods in personality.* Englewood Cliffs, N.J.: Prentice-Hall, Inc., 1965.

Shotwell, A. M., Hurley, J. R., & Cattell, R. B. Motivational structure of a hospitalized mental defective. *Journal of Personality,* 1961, **62,** 422–426.

Shweder, R. A. Fact and artifact in trait perception: The systematic distortion hypothesis. *Progress in Experimental Personality Research,* 1982, **11,** 65–100.

Sigel, I. E. Social experience in the development of representational thought: Distancing theory. In I. E. Sigel, D. Brodzinsky, & R. Golinkoff (Eds.), *New directions in Piagetian theory and practice.* Hillsdale, N.J.: Erlbaum, 1981.

Signell, K. A. Cognitive complexity in person perception and nation perception: A developmental approach. *Journal of Personality,* 1966, **34,** 517–537.

Silverman, L. H. Psychoanalytic theory: The reports of its death are greatly exaggerated. *American Psychologist,* 1976, **31,** 621–637.

Silverman, L. H. A comment on two subliminal psychodynamic activation studies. *Journal of Abnormal Psychology,* 1982, **91,** 126–130.

Silverman, L. H., Ross, D. L., Adler, J. M., & Lustig, D. A. Simple research paradigm for demonstrating subliminal psychodynamic activation: Effects of oedipal stimuli on dart-throwing accuracy in college men. *Journal of Abnormal Psychology,* 1978, **87,** 341–357. (Copyright 1978 by the American Psychological Association. Adapted by permission.)

Sixteen Personality Factor Inventory. Champaign Ill. Institute for Personality and Ability Testing, 1962.

Skinner, B. F. *Walden two.* New York: Macmillan, 1948.

Skinner, B. F. Are theories of learning necessary? *Psychological Review,* 1950, **57,** 193–216.

Skinner, B. F. *Science and human behavior.* New York: Macmillan, 1953.

Skinner, B. F. A case history in the scientific method. *American Psychologist,* 1956, **11,** 221–233.

Skinner, B. F. *Cumulative record.* New York: Appleton-Century-Crofts, 1959.

Skinner, B. F. Behaviorism at fifty. *Science,* 1963, **140,** 951–958.

Skinner, B. F. Autobiography. In E. G. Boring & G. Lindzey (Eds.), *A history of psychology in autobiography.* New York: Appleton-Century-Crofts, 1967. Pp. 385–414.

Skinner, B. F. *Beyond freedom and dignity.* New York: Knopf, 1971.

Skinner, B. F. I have been misunderstood. *The Center Magazine,* 1972, March—April, 63–65.

Skinner, B. F. *About behaviorism.* New York: Knopf, 1974.

Skinner, B. F., & Rogers, C. R. Some issues concerning the control of human behavior: A symposium. *Science,* 1965, **124,** 1057–1066.

Skolnick, A. Motivational imagery and behavior over twenty years. *Journal of Consulting Psychology,* 1966, **30,** 463–478.

Smith, E. R., & Kluegel, J. R. Cognitive and social bases of emotional experience: Outcome, attribution, and affect. *Journal of Personality and Social Psychology,* 1982, **43,** 1129–1141.

Smith, M. B. The phenomenological approach in personality theory: Some critical remarks. *Journal of Abnormal and Social Psychology,* 1950, **45,** 516–522.

Snyder, M. Self-monitoring of expressive behavior. *Journal of Personality and Social Psychology,* 1974, **30,** 526–537.

Snyder, M. Self-monitoring processes. *Advances in Experimental Social Psychology,* 1979, **12,** 85–128.

Snyder, M. On the influence of individuals on situations. In N. Cantor & J. F. Kihlstrom (Eds.), *Personality, cognition, and social interaction.* Hillsdale, N.J.: Erlbaum, 1981.

Snyder, W. U. An investigation of the nature of non-directive psychotherapy. *Journal of General Psychology,* 1945, **33,** 193–223.

Solyom, L., & Miller, S. A. Differential conditioning procedure as the initial phase of the behavior therapy of homosexuality. *Behavior Research Therapy,* 1965, **3,** 147–160.

Spence, K. W. The postulates and methods of behaviorism. *Psychological Review,* 1948, **55,** 67–78.

Spence, K. W. A theory of emotionally based drive (D) and its relation to performance in simple, learning situations. *American Psychologist,* 1958, **13,** 131–141.

Staats, A. Q., & Burns, G. L. Emotional personality repertoire as cause of behavior: Specification of personality and interaction principles. *Journal of Personality and Social Psychology,* 1982, **43,** 873–886.

Steiner, J. F. *Treblinka.* New York: Simon & Schuster, 1966.

Stephan, W. G., & Gollwitzer, P. M. Affect as a mediator of attributional egotism. *Journal of Experimental Social Psychology,* 1981, **17,** 443–458.

Stephenson, W. *The study of behavior.* Chicago: University of Chicago Press, 1953.

Stevens, S. S. The operational definition of psychological concepts. *Psychological Review,* 1935, **42,** 517–527.

Stock, D. An investigation into the interrelations between the self concept and feelings directed towards other persons and groups. *Journal of Consulting Psychology,* 1949, **13,** 176–180.

Strelau, J. *Temperament, personality, activity.* London: Academic Press, 1983.

Suinn, R. M., Osborne, D., & Winfree, P. The self concept and accuracy of recall of inconsistent self-related information. *Journal of Clinical Psychology,* 1962, **18,** 473–474.

Sullivan, H. S. *The interpersonal theory of psychiatry.* New York: Norton, 1953.

Sulloway, F. J. *Freud: Biologist of the mind.* New York: Basic Books, 1979.

Surwit, R. S., Williams, R. B., & Shapiro, D. *Behavioral approaches to cardiovascular disease.* New York: Academic, 1982.

Swanberg, W. A. *Dreiser.* New York: Scribner, 1965.

Swann, W. B., & Hill, C. A. When our identities are mistaken: Reaffirming self-conceptions through social interaction. *Journal of Personality and Social Psychology,* 1982, **43,** 59–66.

Swann, W. B., & Read, S. J. Acquiring self-knowledge: The search for feedback that fits. *Journal of Personality and Social Psychology,* 1981, **41**, 1119–1128.

Szasz, T. S. *The myth of mental illness.* New York: Harper, 1961.

Tagiuri, R. Person perception. In G. Lindzey & E. Aronson (Eds.), *Handbook of social psychology.* Reading, Mass.: Addison-Wesley, 1969.

Taylor, J. A. Drive theory and manifest anxiety. *Psychological Bulletin,* 1956, **53**, 303–320.

Taylor, S. E. Social cognition and health. *Personality and Social Psychology Bulletin,* 1982, **8**, 549–562.

Tharp, R. G., & Wetzel, R. J. *Behavior modification in the natural environment.* New York: Academic, 1969.

Theorell, T., & Rahe, R. H. Life change events, ballistocardiography, and coronary death. *Journal of Human Stress,* 1975, **1**, 18–24.

Thetford, W. N. An objective measurement of frustration tolerance in evaluating psychotherapy. In W. Wolff & J. A. Precker (Eds.), *Success in psychotherapy.* New York: Grune & Stratton, 1952. Chapter 2.

Thorndike, E. L. *The elements of psychology.* New York: A G. Seiler, 1905.

Thorndike, R. L. The psychological value systems of psychologists. *American Psychologist,* 1954, **9**, 787–790.

Tomkins, S. S. Commentary. The ideology of research strategies. In S. Messick & J. Ross (Eds.), *Measurement in Personality and Cognition.* New York: Wiley, 1962. Pp. 285–294.

Tripoldi, T., & Bieri, J. Cognitive complexity as a function of own and provided constructs. *Psychological Reports,* 1963, **13**, 26.

Truax, C. B. Reinforcement and nonreinforcement in Rogerian psychotherapy. *Journal of Abnormal Psychology,* 1966, **71**, 1–9.

Turner, R. H., & Vanderlippe, R. H. Self-ideal consequence as an index of adjustment. *Journal of Abnormal and Social Psychology,* 1958, **57**, 202–206.

Turkat, I. D., & Forehand, R. The future of behavior therapy. *Progress in Behavior Modification,* 1980, **9**, 1–47.

Tversky, A., & Kahneman, D. Judgment under uncertainty: Heuristics and biases. *Science,* 1974, **185**, 1124–1131.

Tyler, L. E. *The psychology of human differences.* New York: Appleton-Century-Crofts, 1965.

Tyler, L. E. *Individuality.* San Francisco: Jossey-Bass, 1978.

Tyrer, P., Lewis, P., & Lee, I. Effects of subliminal and supraliminal stress on symptoms on anxiety. *Journal of Nervous and Mental Disease,* 1978, **166**, 88–95.

Ullmann, L. P., & Krasner, L. (Eds.) *Case studies in behavior modification.* New York: Holt, Rinehart and Winston, 1965.

Ullmann, L. P., & Krasner, L. *A psychological approach to abnormal behavior.* Englewood Cliffs, N.J.: Prentice-Hall, 1969.

Ulmann, L. P., & Krasner, L. *A psychological approach to abnormal behavior.* Englewood Cliffs, N.J.: Prentice-Hall, 1975.

Valins, S., & Ray, A. A. Effects of cognitive desensitization on avoidance behavior. *Journal of Personality and Social Psychology,* 1967, **7**, 345–350.

Vandenberg, S. G. The hereditary abilities study: Hereditary components in a psychological test battery. *American Journal of Human Genetics,* 1962, **14**, 220–237.

Van Kaam, A. *Existential foundations of psychology.* Pittsburgh: Duquesne University Press, 1966.

Vargas, M. J. Changes in self-awareness during client-centered therapy. In C. R. Rogers & R. F. Dymond (Eds.), *Psychotherapy and personality change.* Chicago: University of Chicago Press, 1954. Pp. 145–166.

Vernon, P. E. *Personality assessment.* New York: Wiley, 1963.

Wachtel, P. L. Psychodynamics, behavior therapy, and the implacable experimenter: An inquiry into the consistency of personality. *Journal of Abnormal Psychology,* 1973, **82,** 324-334.

Wahler, R. G., & Pollio, H. R. Behavior and insight: A case study in behavior therapy. *Journal of Experimental Research in Personality,* 1968, **3,** 45-56.

Walker, A. M., Rablen, R. A., & Rogers, C. R. Development of a scale to measure process changes in psycho-therapy. *Journal of Clinical Psychology,* 1960, **16,** 79-85.

Walters, R. H. Some conditions facilitating the occurrence of imitative behavior. In E. C. Simmel, R. A. Hoppe, & G. A. Milton (Eds.), *Social facilitation and imitative behavior.* Boston: Allyn and Bacon, 1968. Pp. 7-30.

Walters, R. H., & Parke, R. D. Influence of the response consequences to a social model on resistance to deviation. *Journal of Experimental Child Psychology,* 1964, **1,** 269-280.

Watson, J. B. *Behavior.* New York: Holt, Rinehart and Winston, 1914.

Watson, J. B. *Psychology from the standpoint of a behaviorist.* Philadelphia: Lippincott, 1919.

Watson, J. B. *Behaviorism.* New York: People's Institute Publishing Co., 1924.

Watson, J. B., & Rayner, R. Conditioned emotional reactions. *Journal of Experimental Psychology,* 1920, **3,** 1-14.

Watson, J. B. Autobiography. In C. Murchison (Ed.), *A history of psychology in autobiography.* Worcester, Mass.: Clark University Press, 1936. Pp. 271-282.

Watson, J. D. *The double helix.* New York: Atheneum, 1968.

Webb, W. B. The choice of the problem. *American Psychologist,* 1961, **16,** 223-227.

Weber, S. J., & Cook, T. D. Subject effects in laboratory research: An examination of subject roles, demand characteristics, and valid inference. *Psychological Bulletin,* 1972, **77,** 273-295.

Weiner, B. A theory of motivation for some classroom experiences. *Journal of Educational Psychology,* 1979, **71,** 3-25.

Weiner, B., & Litman-Adizes, T. An attributional, expectancy-value analysis of learned helplessness and depression. In J. Garber & M. E. P. Seligman (Eds.), *Human helplessness.* New York: Academic, 1980.

Weiss, J. M. Effects of coping response on stress. *Journal of Comparative and Physiological Psychology,* 1968, **65,** 251-260.

Weiss, J. M. Somatic effects of predictable and unpredictable shock. *Psychosomatic Medicine,* 1970, **32,** 397-409.

Weitz, J. Criteria for criteria. *American Psychologist,* 1961, **16,** 228-231.

Weissman, A. E., & Ricks, D. F. *Mood and personality.* New York: Holt, Rinehart and Winston, 1966.

White, B. J. The relation of self-concept and parental identification to women's vocational interests. *Journal of Counseling Psychology,* 1959, **6,** 202-206.

White, P. Limitations of verbal reports of internal events: A refutation of Nisbett and Wilson and of Bem. *Psychological Review,* 1980, **87,** 105-112.

White, R. W. Motivation reconsidered: The concept of competence. *Psychological Review,* 1959, **66,** 297-333.

White, R. W. Competence and the psychosexual stages of development. In M. R. Jones (Ed.), *Nebraska Symposium on Motivation.* Lincoln: University of Nebraska Press, 1960.

Wiggins, J. S. *Personality and prediction: Principles of personality assessment.* New York: Addison-Wesley, 1973.

Wilkins, W. Desensitization: Social and cognitive factors underlying the effectiveness of Wolpe's procedure. *Psychological Bulletin,* 1971, **76,** 311-317.

Williams, J. *The psychology of women.* New York: Norton, 1976.

Williams, J. R. A test of the validity of the P-technique in the measurement of internal conflict. *Journal of Personality,* 1959, **27,** 418-437.

Wilson, G. Introversion/Extroversion. In H. London & J. E. Exner (Eds.), *Dimensions of personality*. New York: Wiley, 1978. Pp. 217–261.

Wilson, G. T. Adult disorders. In G. T. Wilson & C. M. Franks (Eds.), *Contemporary behavior therapy: Conceptual and empirical foundations*. New York: Guilford, 1982.

Wilson, G. T., & Franks, C. M. (Eds.) *Contemporary behavior therapy: Conceptual and empirical foundations*. New York: Guilford, 1982.

Wilson, T. D., Hull, J. G., & Johnson, J. Awareness and self-perception: Verbal reports on internal states. *Journal of Personality and Social Psychology,* 1981, **40**, 53–71.

Winett, R. A., & Winkler, R. C. Current behavior modification in the classroom: Be still, be quiet, be docile. *Journal of Applied Behavior Analysis,* 1972, **5**, 499–504.

Wing, C. W., Jr. Measurement of personality. In D. K. Whitla (Ed.), *Handbook of measurement and assessment in behavioral sciences*. Reading, Mass.: Addison-Wesley, 1968. Pp. 315–347.

Wolf, S. "Irrationality" in a psychoanalytic psychology of the self. In T. Mischel (Ed.), *The self: Psychological and philosophical issues*. Totowa, N.J.: Rowman & Littlefield, 1977. Pp. 203–223.

Wolpe, J. The systematic desensitization treatment of neuroses. *Journal of Nervous and Mental Disorders,* 1961, **132**, 189–203.

Wolpe, J. *The practice of behavior therapy*. New York: Pergamon, 1969.

Wolpe, J., & Lang, P. J. A fear survey schedule for use in behavior therapy. *Behavior research and therapy,* 1964, **2**, 27–30.

Wolpe, J., & Lazarus, A. A. *Behavior therapy techniques: A guide to the treatment of neuroses*. New York: Pergamon, 1966.

Wolpe, J., & Rachman, S. Psychoanalytic "evidence". A critique based on Freud's case of Little Hans. *Journal of Nervous and Mental Disease,* 1960, **130**, 135–148.

Wylie, R. C. *The self-concept*. Lincoln: University of Nebraska Press, 1961.

Wylie, R. C. The present status of self theory. In E. F. Borgatta & W. W. Lambert (Eds.), *Handbook of personality theory and research*. Chicago: Rand McNally, 1968, Pp. 728–787.

Wylie, R. C. *The self-concept,* rev. ed. Lincoln: University of Nebraska Press, 1974.

Yarmey, A. D., & Johnson, J. Evidence for the self as an imaginal prototype. *Journal of Research in Personality,* 1982, **16**, 238–246.

Zimbardo, P. G. On the ethics of intervention in human psychological research: With special reference to the Stanford prison experiment. *Cognition,* 1973, **2**, 243–256.

PHOTO CREDITS

Chapter 1   Page 8: Anestis Diakopoulos/Picture Group. Page 11: W. del Turo Newsday, Inc.

Chapter 2   Page 42: United Press International. Page 45: Marcia Weinstein. Page 46: The Bettman Archive.

Chapter 3   Page 64: Max Halberstadt. Page 77: Drawing by Handelsman; © The New Yorker Magazine, Inc. 1972. Page 83: Joel Gordon. Page 88: Alan Carey/The Image Works. Page 93: Jon Erikson.

Chapter 4   Page 106: Courtesy Dr. Henri Ellenberger. Page 108: Drawing by Ross; © 1974 The New Yorker Magazine, Inc. Page 109: Reprinted by permission of Hans Huber, Publishers. Page 110: Courtesy Harvard University News Office. Page 112: United Press International. Page 119: Plate 53 from ''Bergasse 19,'' Sigmund Freud's Home and Offices, Vienna 1938, the Photographs of Edmund Engleman, Basic Books, Inc. Publishers, N.Y. Page 127: Courtesy Alfred Adler Consultation Center. Page 128: NASA. Page 129: Karsh, Ottawa/Woodfin Camp. Page 131: Courtesy Karen Horney Clinic, Inc. New York City. Page 132: Frank Siteman/Picture Cube. Page 133 (top) Catherine Ursillo/Photo Researchers. Page 133 (bottom) Frank Siteman/Stock Boston. Page 134: Courtesy William Alanson White Psychiatric Foundation. Page 135: Alan Carey/The Image Works.

Chapter 5   Page 153: Courtesy Charles Schneider. Page 159: Elizabeth Crews. Page 166: Jaye R. Phillips/Picture Cube. Page 167: Drawing by H. Martin; © 1971 The New Yorker Magazine, Inc. Page 170: James R. Holland/Stock Boston.

Chapter 6   Page 181: Mark Antman/The Image Works. Page 194: Courtesy Kurt Goldstein. Page 196: Courtesy Brandeis University. Page 197: United Press International.

Chapter 7   Page 216: Courtesy Ralph Norman. Page 224: Sabine Weiss/Photo Researchers. Page 233: Marc & Evelyne Bernheim/Woodfin Camp. Page 235: Michael Weisbrot/Stock Boston.

Chapter 8   Page 246: Drawing by Lippman; © 1972 The New Yorker Magazine, Inc.

Chapter 9   Page 268: Courtesy Harvard University News Office. Page 273 (top) Fredrik D. Bodin/Picture Group. Page 273 (bottom): Frank Sitmen/Stock Boston. Page 279: Courtesy University of Illinois. Page 285: United Press International.

Chapter 11   Page 334: The Bettmann Archive. Page 335: The Bettmann Archive. Page 339: Kathy Bendo. Page 352: Courtesy Rockefeller University. Page 358: Joel Gordon.

Chapter 12   Page 372: © Sidney Harris. Page 375: Van Bucher/Photo Researchers. Page 391: © 1983 by The New York Times Company. Cartoon by Gil Eisner.

Chapter 13   Page 404: Courtesy Stanford University. Page 406: Charlyce Jones. Page 413: Drawing by Opie; © 1978 The New Yorker Magazine, Inc. Page 422: Owen Franken/Stock Boston. Page 428: Susan Rosenberg/Photo Researchers. Page 431: M. M. Mammano/Photo Researchers.

Chapter 14   Page 451: Courtesy Dodge/Chrysler Corp. Page 463: Hazel Hanken. Page 475: © Robert Schochet.

INDEX